■ REVISION CHECKLIST–Considering You...

Using the FACT acronym, ask yourself these questi...

☑ Does my essay FIT together, presenting a centra[...] Does my thesis statement accurately reflect the content of my essay, or have I included material that has no bearing on the main point?

☑ Have I included all the material my reader will need to grasp my meaning, or do I need to ADD information or examples?

☑ Have I included material that fits the thesis but needs to be CUT because it is uninteresting, uninformative, or repetitious?

☑ Does a TEST of my organization show that the writing flows smoothly, with clear transitions between the various ideas?

Responding to Your Peers' Drafts – *Chapter 3*

If you'll be evaluating your peers' drafts, ask yourself these questions:

☑ What is the main point of this essay?

☑ What is the biggest problem?

☑ What is the greatest strength?

☑ What material doesn't seem to fit the main point or the audience?

☑ What questions has the author not answered?

☑ Where should more details and examples be added? Why?

☑ At what point does the paper fail to hold my interest? Why?

☑ Where is the organization confusing?

☑ Where is the writing unclear or vague?

Strengthening Paragraph Structure and Development – *Chapter 14*

☑ Does each paragraph have only one central idea?

☑ Is the idea stated in a topic sentence or clearly implied?

☑ Does the topic sentence help to develop the thesis statement?

☑ Do the sentences within each paragraph advance the topic sentence?

☑ Does each paragraph contain enough supporting detail?

☑ Is each paragraph appropriately organized?

☑ Is the relationship between successive sentences clear?

☑ Is each paragraph clearly and smoothly related to those that precede and follow it?

☑ Does the introduction arouse interest and set the appropriate tone?

☑ Does the conclusion reflect the content of the essay and provide a sense of completeness?

Sharpening Sentences and Word – *Chapters 15 and 16*

☑ Are my sentences clearly and effectively constructed?

☑ Have I varied the pattern and length of my sentences?

☑ Do I know the meanings of the words I use?

☑ Do I explain meanings my reader may not know?

☑ Have I used the appropriate tone and level of diction?

☑ Does/would figurative language enhance my style?

☑ Have I avoided wordiness, euphemisms, clichés, mixed metaphors, and sexist language?

Editing the Draft – Handbook

☑ Have I inspected my writing for the types of errors listed in the editing symbols on the back endpapers?

Second Edition

Strategies for Successful Writing

A Rhetoric, Reader, and Handbook

James A. Reinking
Andrew W. Hart
with Robert von der Osten
All of Ferris State University

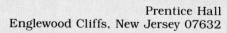
Prentice Hall
Englewood Cliffs, New Jersey 07632

Library of Congress Cataloging-in-Publication Data

REINKING, JAMES A.
   Strategies for successful writing : a rhetoric, reader, and
handbook : annotated instructor's edition / James A. Reinking,
Andrew W. Hart, Robert von der Osten.—2nd ed.
      p. cm.

   Includes index.
   ISBN 0-13-852054-2
   1. English language—Rhetoric.   2. English language—
Grammar   3. College readers.   I. Hart, Andrew W.
II. Osten, Robert von der.   III. Title.
PE1408.R426   1991c
808'.0427—dc20
                                    90-49996
                                    CIP

Interior design: *Anne T. Bonanno*
Editorial/production supervision: *WordCrafters Editorial Services, Inc.*
Cover design: *Bruce Kenselaar*
Manufacturing buyer: *Herb Klein, David Dickey*
Cover photo: *Reginald Wickham*

© 1991, 1988 by Prentice-Hall, Inc.
A Division of Simon & Schuster
Englewood Cliffs, New Jersey 07632

Printed in the United States of America
10   9   8   7   6   5   4   3   2   1

ISBN 0-13-852054-2

ACKNOWLEDGMENTS

R. T. Allen, "The Porcupine," from *Children, Wives, and Other Wildlife* by Robert Thomas Allen.
   Copyright © 1970 by Robert Thomas Allen (N.Y.: Doubleday, 1970).
Bonnie Angelo, "Those Good Ole Boys," *Time*, Sept. 27, 1976, p. 47.
Maya Angelou, "Momma's Encounter," from *I Know Why the Caged Bird Sings*. Copyright © 1969 by
   Maya Angelou. Reprinted by permission of Random House, Inc.
"Antigen," *Encyclopaedia Britannica*, 1974, I, 417.

(Acknowledgments continue on page 678, which constitutes an extension of the copyright page.)

Prentice-Hall International (UK) Limited, *London*
Prentice-Hall of Australia Pty. Limited, *Sydney*
Prentice-Hall Canada Inc., *Toronto*
Prentice-Hall Hispanoamericana, S.A., *Mexico*
Prentice-Hall of India Private Limited, *New Delhi*
Prentice-Hall of Japan, Inc., *Tokyo*
Simon & Schuster Asia Pte. Ltd., *Singapore*
Editora Prentice-Hall do Brasil, Ltda., *Rio de Janeiro*

For Scott

Brief Contents

RHETORIC

READER

HANDBOOK

Contents

■ **Chapter 16**
Diction, Tone, Style   233

Toward Clear Diction 233
Toward Rhetorical Effect 239
Special Stylistic Techniques 249
Eliminating Flawed Diction 253

■ **Chapter 17**
The Essay Examination   258

Studying for the Examination 258
Types of Test Questions 259
Preparing to Write 259
Writing the Examination Answer 260

■ **Chapter 18**
Writing About Literature   267

The Elements of Literature 267
Writing a Paper on Literature 288
Example Student Essay on Literature: "Scratchy Wilson: No Cardboard
   Character" by Wendell Stone 291

■ **Chapter 19**
The Library Research Paper   295

Learning About Your Library 295
Choosing a Topic 296
Assembling a Working Bibliography 300
Taking Notes 310
Organizing and Outlining 319
Writing Your Research Paper 322
Acknowledging and Handling Your Sources Properly
   (MLA and APA Formats) 324
Example Student Research Paper: "Robots in Industry: A Boon for
   Everyone" by Christine Harding 344

HANDBOOK

Preface

The second edition of *Strategies for Successful Writing: A Rhetoric, Reader, and Handbook* is a comprehensive textbook that offers ample material for a full year of freshman composition. Instructors teaching a one-term course can make selections from Chapters 1–16, from whatever types of specialized writing suit the needs of their students, and from appropriate essays in the Reader.

Because we strongly believe that an effective composition textbook should address the student directly, we have aimed for a style that is conversational yet clear and concise. We believe that our style invites students into the book, lessens their apprehensions about writing, and provides a model for their own prose.

CHANGES IN THE SECOND EDITION

The enthusiastic response to the first edition by both teachers and students has been most gratifying. The second edition retains the many popular features of the first and incorporates a number of improvements, suggested by users and reviewers, that should considerably enhance the utility of the text. Among these changes the following are especially significant.

- The approach has been broadened so that it integrates coverage of both the writing process and the written product. We examine both the characteristics of the completed essay and the procedure involved in creating it—in short, the end as well as the means.
- The discussion of the writing process now spans Chapters 2 and 3. Chapter 2 contains new sections on keeping a journal and composing with a word processor. Chapter 3 features a notably expanded treatment of revising and editing that shows students how to apply the FACT (Fit, Add, Cut, Test) acronym to their writing, revise with a word processor, and evaluate their peers' drafts.
- The writing strategies have been rearranged to follow a general progression from least to most complex. In addition, a separate chapter is now devoted to each strategy. Discussions in each case detail specific planning, drafting, and revising guidelines and also pose practical heuristic questions.
- A new chapter (Chapter 13) on mixing the writing strategies explains why and how most essays combine several strategies.
- The chapter on writing about literature now offers more detailed writing guidelines and explanations of literary terms, carefully selected heuristic questions,

PRINT SUPPLEMENTS FOR INSTRUCTORS

Annotated Instructor's Edition (85205-3)

The *Annotated Instructor's Edition* consists of the entire student edition as well as strong instructional support. The material in the margins of the text consists of background information on particular aspects of writing; key insights into how students view writing projects and why they experience difficulties; assorted ethical issues that should spark lively class discussions; answers to all discussion questions and to appropriate exercises in the text; supplementary exercises; as well as suggested teaching strategies, classroom activities, and instructor readings. Some of our suggestions begin with "you might"; others, to avoid potentially annoying repetition, do not. All suggestions have worked well for us over the years. Taken together, these resources should simplify the planning and enhance the classroom performance of instructors charting their course or refining their direction. Seasoned instructors may also wish to examine the many suggestions and sample those that seem intriguing.

We cordially invite instructors to participate in the next edition of the *Annotated Instructor's Edition*. Please share your teaching resources or comments with us by sending them to James Reinking, c/o College English Editor, Prentice Hall, Englewood Cliffs, NJ 07632. Items published will be acknowledged.

Strategies for Teaching Composition and Supplementary Exercises (85204-6)

This supplement offers various suggestions for teaching freshman composition, sample syllabi for a sequence of three ten-week trimesters and two fifteen-week semesters, numerous guidelines for responding to student writing, and a detailed set of grading standards. In addition, it contains an extra set of twenty-item exercises that parallel those in the Handbook section of *Strategies*. These exercises can be used either in the classroom or as assignments.

PRINT SUPPLEMENTS FOR STUDENTS

The Research Organizer (72182-9)

This convenient new tool is designed to help students assemble their research paper notes and drafts in an organized and efficient manner. It offers guidance on the research process and provides space for students to record their search strategy, notes, citations, outlines, and drafts. This supplement will make preparing for a research paper easier and more efficient by allowing students to categorize the majority of their materials.

Model Research Papers for Writers (58797-2)

This collection of 11 reproducible student research papers, in fields ranging from biology and political science to art history and English literature, provides clear examples of documentation, stylistic conventions, and formal requirements for various disciplines.

Contemporary View Program

This 32 page collection of articles from *The New York Times* provides students with timely reading selections that serve as both writing models and springboards for discussion.

and greater coverage of the planning–organizing–writing process that culminates in the student paper.

▌ The chapter on the library research paper features several improvements that make it even more informative and accessible. A sample pacing schedule not only encourages students to plan their work and meet appropriate deadlines but also enables them to track their progress. The discussion of plagiarism has been expanded, and documentation formats for additional sources students are likely to use have been added, as has a section on data bases. The documentation section has been repositioned at the end of the chapter to avoid interrupting the discussion of planning, researching, organizing, and writing the paper. Finally, we now provide complete coverage of the APA documentation system.

▌ Over 30 percent of the selections in the Reader are new to this edition. The first essay in each section of the Reader has been annotated in the margin to show which features of the strategy are included. These annotations not only facilitate student understanding but also help link the Rhetoric and Reader into an organic whole. The argument section includes paired essays that propose different solutions to the drug problem, thus demonstrating the controversial nature of argument and allowing students to weigh the evidence and engage in debate.

▌ All professional essays have been grouped in the Reader, and all student essays, over 20 percent of which are new to this edition, accompany the strategy chapters.

▌ We have improved the Handbook by adding sets of connected discourse exercises to the "Sentence Errors" and "Punctuation and Mechanics" sections. These exercises feature unfolding narratives that engage and retain student interest, and therefore facilitate learning. Numerous additions make the glossary of word usage one of the most comprehensive available in any text. Finally, tab indexing has been added to each page in order to provide easy access to the desired section.

THE RHETORIC

In addition to these improvements, the text offers many other noteworthy features. The Rhetoric consists of twenty chapters, grouped into four parts. The first part includes three chapters. Chapter 1 introduces students to the purposes of writing, the qualities of good writing, and the need for audience awareness. Chapter 2 looks at the planning and drafting stages of the composing process. Chapter 3 takes students through the various stages of the revision process, starting with a systematic procedure for revising the whole essay and then moving to pointers for revising its component parts. Sets of revision checklists pose key questions for students to consider. Chapters 2 and 3 are unified by an unfolding case history that includes the first draft of a student paper, the initial revision marked with changes, and the final version. Notes in the margin highlight key features of the finished paper.

The ten chapters in the second part (Chapters 4–13) feature the various writing strategies, or modes, used to develop papers. These strategies are presented as natural ways of thinking, as problem-solving strategies, and therefore as effective ways of organizing writing. This part concludes with a chapter on mixing the writing strategies which explains and shows that writers frequently mix these patterns in assorted combinations for various purposes.

Except for Chapter 13, the discussion in each chapter follows a similar approach, first explaining the key elements of the strategy and then providing detailed planning, drafting, and revising guidelines. A complete student essay, accompanied by questions, follows the discussion section. These essays represent realistic, achievable goals and spur student confidence, while the questions reinforce the general principles of good writing and underscore the points we make in our discussions. Each chapter ends with fifteen carefully chosen writing suggestions.

In the third part, we shift from full-length essays to the elements that make them up. Chapter 14 first discusses paragraph unity; it then takes up the topic sentence, adequate development, organization, and coherence, and finally introductory, transitional and concluding paragraphs. Throughout this chapter, as elsewhere, carefully selected examples and exercises form an integral part of the instruction.

Chapter 15 focuses on various strategies for creating effective sentences. Such strategies as coordinating and subordinating ideas and using parallelism help students to increase the versatility of their writing. The concluding section offers practical advice on crafting and arranging sentences so that they work together harmoniously.

Chapter 16, designed to help students improve their writing style, deals with words and their effects. We distinguish between abstract and concrete words as well as between specific and general terms, and we also discuss the dictionary and thesaurus. Levels of diction—formal, informal, and technical—and how to use them are explained, as are tone, various types of figurative language, and irony. The chapter concludes by pointing out how to recognize and avoid wordiness, euphemisms, clichés, mixed metaphors, and—new to this edition—sexist language.

The fourth and final part of the Rhetoric concentrates on four specialized types of college and on-the-job writing. Chapter 17 offers practical advice on studying for exams, assessing test questions, and writing essay answers. To facilitate student comprehension, we analyze both good and poor answers to the same exam question and provide exercises that require students to perform similar analyses.

Chapter 18 uses Stephen Crane's "The Bride Comes to Yellow Sky" as a springboard for its discussion. The chapter focuses on plot, point of view, character, setting, symbols, irony, and theme—the elements students will most likely be asked to write about. For each element, we first present basic features and then offer writing guidelines. The chapter ends with a section that details the development of a student paper.

Chapter 19 is a thorough and practical guide to research writing. In response to reviewer suggestions, we have given special emphasis to avoiding plagiarism and documenting source material. The latest versions of both the MLA and APA documentation formats are included. As in Chapters 2 and 3, a progressive case history gradually evolves from the first draft into the final version of a student paper. The two versions are positioned on facing pages for easy compari-

Supplementary Essays for Writers (70705-9)

This collection of 31 essays by well-known professional writers is available at a nominal price to students using *Strategies for Successful Writing*. Each essay is accompanied by questions for discussion and writing, and each rhetorical section ends with several writing suggestions. Instructors adopting *Strategies* receive a free copy of *Supplementary Essays for Writers* and may reproduce individual essays for their students.

Webster's New World Dictionary, Third College Edition (94978-4)

This authoritative, hardcover dictionary contains more than 6,500 American words and phrases and more than 176,000 entries. Instructors may provide their students with this outstanding resource at a substantially discounted price when it is ordered with *Strategies for Successful Writing*.

SOFTWARE

Blue Pencil

This acclaimed interactive editing program allows students to practice their writing skills by making revisions in paragraph-length passages on the computer screen. The program is organized around skills that students use most often in their writing. A counter at the bottom of the screen keeps track of the remaining corrections, and feedback is given for each response that students enter. If students encounter difficulty with a particular topic or concept, they can receive additional instruction from the program. Blue Pencil includes a final review in which all skill categories are presented together. A site license can be provided for computer labs. Available for both IBM® and Macintosh®.

Blue Pencil Authoring System

This program allows instructors to modify existing Blue Pencil exercises or to create entirely new ones customized for the needs of their students. It includes two Blue Pencil exercise disks totaling 80 passages, 40 on each disk, representing many skill areas. Instructors may customize the existing passages by adding or deleting errors to be corrected and/or modifying the feedback and hints available to students. On-line directions and a helpful manual are included. Available for IBM® as a sale item to instructors only.

Webster's New World Writer

The student edition of this easy-to-learn and easy-to-use commercial word-processing package includes an extensive spelling checker. Ideal for student writers, the program won *PC Magazine's* Literary Choice Award. Students may purchase the documentation book and either 5¼" or 3½" disks as a complete package. As a special promotion, adopters of *Strategies for Successful Writing* can obtain a site license free, and students may purchase the documentation booklet at a special low price. Available for IBM®.

Book/disk package 5¼" disk (94983-4)
Book/disk package 3½" disk (94727-5)
Book only (94982-6)

Write Now™ (97109-3)

The student edition of this full-featured word-processing program includes such features as a 50,000 word dictionary, automatic and immediate repagination, and autonumbering footnotes. *Write Now* is the winner of *MacUser* magazine's Best New Word Processor Award. A book/disk package is available to students at a substantially discounted price with the purchase of *Strategies for Successful Writing*. Available for Macintosh®.

son, and the final draft features notes in the margin that indicate changes made during revision. Our detailed treatment should make supplemental handouts or a separate research paper guide unnecessary.

Chapter 20 speaks to a practical reality by reminding students that the value of writing extends beyond the English classroom. Example letters address a variety of practical situations—for example, applying for a summer job.

THE READER

The Reader expands the utility of the text by providing a collection of forty-one carefully selected professional models that illustrate the various writing strategies and display a wide variety of styles, tones, and subject matter. These essays, together with the nine student models that accompany the various strategy chapters, should make a separate reader unnecessary.

Each of the essays clearly illustrates the designated pattern, each has been thoroughly class tested for student interest, and each provides a springboard for a stimulating discussion. In making our selections we have aimed for balance and variety:

1. Some are popular classics by acknowledged prose masters; some, anthologized for the first time, are by fresh, new writers.
2. Some are straightforward and simple, some challenging and complex.
3. Some adopt a humorous, lighthearted approach, some a serious, thoughtful one.
4. Some take a liberal stance, some a conservative one, and some address feminist and minority concerns.
5. A few are rather lengthy; most are relatively brief.

In addition, we have aimed for a balance within the group of essays representing each writing strategy. For example, three of the narratives feature an unstated point and one an indirectly stated point. Two of the cause-and-effect essays highlight causes, one deals with effects, and one explores both. The argument essays display various types of appeals and evidence.

For each writing strategy, the essays are generally arranged from simple to more complex. A brief biographical note about the author precedes each selection, and stimulating questions designed to enhance student understanding of structure and strategy follow it, along with a writing assignment suggested by the essay's subject matter.

THE HANDBOOK

The comprehensive Handbook consists of six parts: "Sentence Elements," "Editing to Correct Sentence Errors," "Editing to Correct Faulty Punctuation and Mechanics," "Spelling," "Glossary of Word Usage," and "Glossary of Grammatical Terms." Explanations skirt unneeded grammatical terminology and are reinforced by exercises in the first three parts. A separate booklet containing an extra set of 20-item exercises that parallel those in the Handbook is available upon request to instructors who adopt the book. The spelling unit presents four useful spelling rules and an extensive list of commonly misspelled words. The glossary of word usage offers similarly comprehensive coverage of troublesome usages. The glossary of grammatical terms includes brief definitions of terms discussed in detail earlier in the Handbook, together with page numbers directing users to the expanded discussions. Instructors can use the handbook either as a reference guide or as a basis for class discussion.

ACKNOWLEDGMENTS

Like all textbook writers, we are indebted to many people. Our colleagues at Ferris State University and elsewhere have assisted us in numerous ways: critiquing the manuscript; testing approaches, essays, and exercises in their classrooms; and suggesting writing models for the text. They include Joe Dugas, Belden Durtschi, Hugh Griffith, Doug Haneline, Don Hanzek, Walt Hoeksema, and Fred Howting. Special thanks are due Ada Lou Carson and Paul Devlin, whose eyes for fine detail prevented numerous oversights on our part. Our greatest debt is to Robert von der Osten, whose keen judgment and classroom expertise significantly influenced the direction and content of this edition. We are also grateful to our reviewers, whose many suggestions greatly improved our text: Ellen Bourland, Wallace College; Walter J. Dudek, Fullerton College; Ellen Dugan-Barrette, Brescia College; Betty Hart, Fairmont State College; John Martin, Moraine Valley Community College; Virginia Oram, Richland College; Catherine Rahmes, Cincinnati Technical College.

Many thanks are also due to the outstanding team at Prentice Hall, whose editorial expertise, genial guidance, and promotional efforts have been vital to this project: Phil Miller, Editor in Chief for Humanities, who first saw the potential in our approach, proposed the Annotated Instructor's Edition, and suggested and supported many other improvements; Kate Morgan, Senior Development Editor for English, who helped plan this edition and kept us on track; Linda Zuk, who is the ideal Production Editor: knowledgeable, efficient, understanding of and responsive to authors' concerns; Frances Andersen, who copyedited our manuscript with keen judgment and remarkable precision; Colette Conboy, who helped us solve crucial problems at critical junctures; and Tracy Augustine and Gina Sluss, whose marketing expertise will help our book find its way. Finally, we'd like to thank Paul Hart for the material he contributed on word processing and Norma Reinking for her meticulous proofreading of the entire text.

J.A.R.
A.W.H.

Prentice Hall/Simon & Schuster Transparencies for Writers (70320-7)

This set of 100 two- and four-color transparencies features exercises, examples, and suggestions for student writing that focus on aspects of the writing process—from generating ideas and shaping an outline, to preparing a draft and revising and editing the final paper, to effectively using research sources. These transparencies also cover grammar, punctuation, and mechanics through overlays that show how sentence and paragraph errors can be corrected most effectively.

The Prentice Hall Critical Thinking Audio Study Cassette

This 60 minute cassette helps students develop their critical thinking skills—from asking the right questions to helpful tips on how to become a more effective learner.

Rhetoric

■ Chapter 1

Writing: A First Look

Why write? Hasn't the tempest of technology swept all of us into a brave, new electronic world? Aren't its telephones, portable cassette recorders, and computer networks—all the magical devices of our new electronic estate—fast dooming ordinary writing? Not long ago, some people thought and said so, but events haven't supported those predictions. Although electronic devices have made some writing unnecessary, the written word flourishes both on campus and in the world of work. Furthermore, there's every evidence that writing will become even more important in the future.

Writing offers very real advantages to both writers and readers:

1. It provides a permanent record of thoughts, actions, and decisions.
2. It makes communication more precise and effective.
3. It saves the reader's time; we absorb information more swiftly when we read it than when we hear it.

Many people will expect you to write for them. College instructors ask you to write reports, research papers, and essay exams. Job hunting usually requires you to write application letters. And once you're hired, writing will probably figure in your duties. You might be asked to discuss the capabilities of new computer equipment, report on a conference you attended, or explain the advantages of new safety procedures to supervisors or staff. Perhaps you'll propose that your organization install a new security system, conduct a market survey, or develop an alternate traffic flow pattern. The ability to write will help you earn better grades, land the job you want, and advance afterwards in your career.

Furthermore, writing ability yields personal benefits. You might need to defend a medical reimbursement claim that you filed with your health insurer, request clarification of an inadequate or ambiguous set of directions, or document a demand for replacement of a faulty product. Skill in writing will help you handle these situations.

THE PURPOSES OF WRITING

Whenever you write, you need some clear purpose to guide you. If you don't know why you're writing, neither will your reader. Fulfilling an assignment doesn't qualify as a real writing purpose, although it may well be what sends you to your desk. Faced with a close deadline for a research paper or report, you may tell yourself, "I'm doing this because I have to." An authentic purpose, however, requires you to answer this question: What do I want this piece of writing to do for both my reader and myself?

Purpose, as you might expect, grows out of the writing occasion—some situation that prompts you to put your thoughts on paper. You explore the consequences of the greenhouse effect in a report for your science instructor. You write an editorial for the college newspaper to air your frustration over inadequate campus parking. You propose that your organization replace an outdated piece of equipment with a state-of-the-art model. Clearly, your purpose stems from the writing occasion.

Here are four common *general writing purposes*, two or more of which often join forces in a single piece:

To inform.   Presenting information is one of the most common writing purposes. The boating enthusiast who tells landlubber classmates how to handle a skiff plays the role of teacher, as does the researcher who summarizes the results of an investigation for co-workers. Some professional writers carve careers out of writing articles and books that fill gaps in the public's knowledge of timely topics. Instructors often ask you to write exams and papers so that they can gauge how well you have mastered the course material.

To persuade.   You probably have strong views on many issues, and these feelings may sometimes impel you to try swaying your reader. In a letter to the editor, you might attack a proposal to establish a nearby chemical waste dump. Or, alarmed by a sharp jump in state unemployment, you might write to your state senator and argue for a new job-training program.

To express yourself.   Creative writing includes personal essays, fiction, plays, and poetry, as well as journals and diaries. But self-expression has a place in other kinds of writing, too. Almost everything you write offers you a chance to display your mastery of words and to enliven your prose with vivid images and fresh turns of phrase.

To entertain.   Some writing merely entertains; some writing couples entertainment with a more serious purpose. A light-hearted approach can help your reader absorb dull or difficult material. Satire lets you expose the shortcomings of individuals, ideas, and institutions by poking fun at them. An intention to entertain can add savor to many kinds of writing.

Besides having one or more *general purposes*, each writing project has its

CLASSROOM ACTIVITIES

1.   Pair students and have them orally exchange a brief personal history. Next time the class meets, have students write down what they remember of their partner's history. They will quickly see the importance of an accurate, written record.
2.   Bring in copies or overheads of a week's worth of interoffice memos to demonstrate the variety of situations that require writing.
3.   Have each student identify some personal situations (beyond those listed in the text) that require writing. This type of activity, along with the previous two, helps set the stage for a writing course.

TEACHING STRATEGY

Students often overgeneralize their purpose for writing; they merely state, for instance, that they want to inform the reader. To help students crystallize their thoughts for an essay, require that they precisely state their purpose, the writing occasion, and how these variables influence their plans. You might have them complete a pre-writing sheet, which you either respond to before they write or examine when you read the final copy. Or you could supply the purpose and occasion and refer to them as you respond to drafts. Either approach reinforces the notion that purpose is *not* merely fulfilling an assignment.

own *specific purpose*. For instance, you may argue the advantages of owning a solar home, explain why some people join religious cults, express your feelings about conformity, or satirize a presidential candidate's views.

Having a specific purpose assists you at every stage of the writing process. It helps you define your audience, select the details, language, and approach that best suit their needs, and avoid going off in directions that won't interest them. The following example from the newspaper *USA Today* has a clear and specific purpose.

We'll Trash *USA Today*, Too

J. Winston Porter

1 What will you do with *USA Today* after you finish reading it? If you're like most of us, you'll put the paper out with the garbage and it'll end up buried in a landfill. Over 80% of all household and commercial garbage ends up this way, and this is a problem.

2 The USA is relentlessly producing more and more trash, and we are rapidly running out of landfill space. At the same time, new landfills and incinerators are encountering local opposition. Before we are truly wallowing in waste, we need to declare a war on garbage.

3 The first battle we need to win is for public acceptance of a strategy that includes reducing the amount of waste generated and increasing the amount recycled. EPA is pushing a national goal of recycling 25% of all garbage within the next four years. But waste reduction and recycling aren't enough to stem the tide of trash that threatens to engulf us. We will continue to need safe landfilling of some garbage and incineration, preferably with energy recovery, as another option. EPA and the states are working to strengthen environmental controls on these facilities. The appropriate mix of waste reduction and recycling, landfilling and incineration should be "custom designed" by states and localities.

4 How can we all do our part? To begin with, we must recognize that we all contribute to the garbage problem. Next, we should cooperate in efforts to reduce the amount of trash requiring disposal. Finally, we must adopt new attitudes about disposal, because there will always be trash to be handled. This means that instead of simply opposing any new disposal facilities, citizens should assist in choosing the best options.

5 Recycling is the cornerstone of a sound waste-management strategy. We all have special responsibilities to make recycling work. Individuals must be willing to participate in local programs. Local governments should plan programs and operate required facilities. States should do statewide planning and enforce their own laws and regulations. Industry should step up its recycling efforts. The federal government should provide national leadership, research and information-sharing as well as develop certain underlying regulations.

6 No one segment of society can, alone, lead us to victory in the war on garbage. Instead, we need a coordinated national effort to confront the solid-waste issue head-on.

From *USA Today*, July 11, 1988, page 8A.

Porter hints at his purpose in the first paragraph by noting that the disposal of garbage in landfills poses a problem. The last sentence of paragraph 2 states the purpose clearly. The remaining paragraphs name the strategies that he recommends to wage war on garbage and explain how individuals, government, and industry can all contribute. Everything Porter has written relates to his purpose.

Now examine the next paragraph, which does *not* have a firmly fixed specific purpose.

> Community is a sea in which people swim unconsciously, like
>
> fish. We fail to recognize our neighbors as fellow humans,
>
> and they show the same lack of fellow-feelings for us. A
>
> complete lack of concern for one another is evident in
>
> today's complex society. What is community? Is it a plant? A
>
> building? A place? A state of being? Knowing what it is, we
>
> can see if such a place exists. To know community, one must
>
> realize who he or she is. Identity of a person is the first
>
> step in establishing a community.

This student writer can't decide what aspect of community to tackle. The opening sentence attempts a definition, but the next two veer onto the shortcomings of the modern community. Notice how aimlessly the thoughts drift. The vague leadoff sentence asserts "Community is a sea . . . ," but the later question "What is community?" contradicts this opening. Also, if community is a plant, a building, or a place, why must we realize who we are in order to know it? This contradictory and illogical paragraph reveals a writer groping for a purpose.

The paragraph, however, isn't a wasted effort. These musings offer several possibilities. By developing the first sentence, the writer might show some interesting similarities between community and a sea. By pursuing the idea in the second and third sentences, he might show the callous nature of modern society. The last two sentences might lead to a statement on the relationship between individual and community. A specific purpose can sometimes emerge from preliminary jottings.

PERSPECTIVE

Good writing, of course, depends on the writer's grasp of purpose and audience. No one would expect a letter to a friend to approximate a magazine article. You can help students understand that good writing is a function of context. Students and instructors often have a different sense of what makes for good writing. What we see as well developed and significant they might see as tedious and pompous. Good writing instruction helps students to understand that our sense of good writing is not arbitrary but stems from how readers receive writing.

THE QUALITIES OF GOOD WRITING

Three qualities—fresh thinking, a sense of style, and effective organization—help to ensure that a piece of prose will meet your reader's expectations.

Fresh thinking. You don't have to astound your readers with something never before discussed in print. Genuinely unique ideas and information are scarce commodities. You can, however, freshen your writing by exploring personal insights and perceptions. Using your own special slant, you might show a connection between seemingly unrelated items, as Kathy Roth does when she likens office "paper pushers" to different kinds of animals (pages 414–416). Keep the expression of your ideas credible, however; farfetched notions spawn skepticism.

Sense of style.   Readers don't expect you to display the stylistic flair of Erma Bombeck or Art Buchwald. Indeed, such writing would impair the neutral tone needed in certain kinds of writing, such as technical reports and legal documents. Readers *do*, however, expect you to write in a clear style. And if you strengthen it with vivid, forceful words, readers will absorb your points with even greater interest. The chapters ahead show you how to use language in ways that project your own views and personality. Chapters 15 and 16, in particular, will help you develop a sense of style, as will the many readings throughout the book.

Effective organization.   A paper should have a beginning, a middle, and an end; that is, an introduction, a body, and a conclusion. The introduction sparks interest and acquaints the reader with what is to come. The body delivers the main message and exhibits a clear connection between ideas so that the reader can easily follow your thoughts. The conclusion ends the discussion so the reader feels satisfied rather than suddenly cut off. Organizational patterns, or strategies of development, are the subject of Chapters 4–13. Pages 208–214 discuss introductions and conclusions.

Freshness, style, and organization are weighted differently in different kinds of writing. A writer who drafts a proposal to pave a city's streets will probably attach less importance to fresh thinking than to clear writing and careful organization. On the other hand, fresh thinking can be very important in a description of an autumn forest scene. You will learn more about these qualities throughout this book.

THE AUDIENCE FOR YOUR WRITING

Everything you write is aimed at some audience—a person or group you want to reach. The ultimate purpose of all writing is to have an effect on a reader (even if that reader is you), and therefore purpose and audience are closely linked. Our earlier discussion makes this point clear by noting that your purpose can be to inform *someone* of something, to persuade *someone* to believe or do something, to express feelings or insights to *someone*, or to entertain *someone*. Any of these objectives requires that you *know* that someone, the audience for your writing.

Writing operates on a delayed-action fuse, detonating its ideas in the readers' minds at a later time and place. Sometimes problems follow. In face-to-face conversations, you can observe your listeners' reactions, and whenever you note signs of hostility, boredom, or puzzlement, you can alter your tone, offer some examples, or ask a question. You can also use gestures and facial expressions to emphasize what you're saying. When you write, however, the words on the page

CLASSROOM ACTIVITIES

1. Bring in a newspaper article, magazine article, and professional essay on the same topic. Have students identify textual differences, account for them, and identify what is common to the texts. Suggest that the common qualities are features of good writing; also suggest the qualities that are specific to particular writing situations.
2. Have students rank three different versions of the same paper or memo. One version might be vague and general, another ineffectively organized, and the third a clear example of good writing. Compare student rankings and discuss the reasons for their decisions.

SUGGESTED INSTRUCTOR READINGS

Booth, W. C. "The Rhetorical Stance." College Composition and Communication 14 (1963): 139–145. Defines the quality of writing as a balance among subject, object, and the writer's persona.
Dillon, G. L. Constructing Texts. Bloomington: Indiana UP, 1981. Insists that good writing reflects social conventions and should be taught accordingly.
Hirsch, E. D. The Philosophy of Composition. Chicago: U of Chicago P, 1977. Attempts to deduce a definition of good writing based on how we supposedly read texts.

PERSPECTIVE

Audience is a difficult concept for students since they are most familiar with writing that is aimed exclusively at their instructor. The classroom situation often ties them to that assumption. You might attempt therefore to broaden their sense of audience. Students should understand that assorted readers with a variety of characteristics will receive and react to their writing and that reader response must be anticipated.

carry your message. Once written work has left your hands, it's on its own. You can't call it back to clear up a misunderstanding or satisfy a disgruntled reader.

Establishing rapport with your audience is easy when you're writing for your friends or someone else you know a great deal about. You can then judge the likely response to what you say. Often, though, you'll be writing for people you know only casually or not at all: employers, customers, fellow townsfolk, and the like. In such situations, you'll need to assess your audience before starting to write.

A good way to size up your readers is to develop an audience profile. This profile will emerge gradually as you answer the following questions:

1. What are the educational level, age, social class, and economic status of the audience I want to reach?
2. Why will this audience read my writing? To gain information? Learn my views on a controversial issue? Enjoy my creative flair? Be entertained?
3. What attitudes, needs, and expectations do they have?
4. How are they likely to respond to what I say? Can I expect them to be neutral? Opposed? Friendly?
5. How much do they know about my topic? (Your answer here will help you gauge whether you're saying too little or too much.)
6. What kind of language will communicate with them most effectively? (See "Level of Diction" section in Chapter 16.)

College writing assignments sometimes ask you to envision a reader who is intelligent but lacking specialized knowledge, receptive but unwilling to put up with boring or trite material. Or perhaps you'll be assigned, or choose, to write for a certain age group or one with particular interests. At other times, you'll be asked to write for a specialized audience—one with some expertise in your topic. This difference will affect what you say to each audience and how you say it.

Let's see how audience can shape a paper. Suppose you are explaining how to take a certain type of X-ray. If your audience is a group of lay readers who have never had an X-ray, you might note at the outset that taking one is much like taking an ordinary photograph. Then you might explain the basic process, including the positioning of the patient and the equipment, comment on the safety and reliability of the procedure, and note how much time it takes. You probably would use few technical terms. If, however, you were writing for radiology students, you might emphasize exposure factors, film size, and required views. This audience would understand technical terms and want a detailed explanation of the procedure. You could speak to these readers as colleagues who appreciate precise information.

Audience shapes all types of writing in similar fashion, even your personal writing. Assume you've recently become engaged, and to share your news you write two letters: one to your clergyman, the other to your best friend back home. You can imagine the differences in details, language, and general tone of each letter. Further, think how inappropriate it would be if you accidentally sent the letter intended for one to the other. Without doubt, different readers call for different approaches.

EXERCISE ■   The three excerpts below deal with the same subject—antigens—but each explanation is geared to a different audience. Read the passages carefully; then answer the following questions:

1. What audience does each author address? How do you know?
2. Identify ways in which each author appeals to a specific audience.

1.
  The human body is quick to recognize foreign chemicals that enter it. "Foes" must be attacked or otherwise got rid of. The most common of these foes are chemical materials from viruses, bacteria, and other microscopic organisms. Such chemicals, when recognized by the body, are called *antigens*. To combat them, the body produces its own chemicals, protein molecules called *antibodies*. Each kind of antigen causes the production of a specific kind of antibody. Antibodies appear in the body fluids such as blood and lymph and in the body's cells.

L. D. Hamilton, "Antibodies and Antigens,"
The New Book of Knowledge

2.
  [An] *Antigen* [is a] foreign substance that, when introduced into the body, is capable of inducing the formation of antibodies and of reacting specifically in a detectable manner with the induced antibodies. For each antigen there is a specific antibody, the physical and chemical structure of which is produced in response to the physical and chemical structure of the antigen. Antigens comprise virtually all proteins that are foreign to the host, including those contained in bacteria, viruses, protozoa, helminths, foods, snake venoms, egg white, serum components, red blood cells, and other cells and tissues of various species, including man. Polysaccharides and lipids may also act as antigens when coupled to proteins.

"Antigen," *Encyclopaedia Britannica*

3.
  The substance with stimulates the body to produce antibodies is designated *antigen* (antibody stimulator). . . .
  Most complete antigens are protein molecules containing aromatic amino acids, and are large in molecular weight and size. However, it has been demonstrated that other macromolecules, such as pure polysaccharides, polynucleotides, and lipids, may serve as complete antigens.
  However, certain other materials, incapable of stimulating antibody formation by themselves can, in association with a protein or other carrier, stimulate antibody formation and are the antigenic determinants. These determinants are referred to as *incomplete antigens* or *haptens* and they are able to react with antibodies which were produced by the determinant-protein complex.
  However, before an antigen can stimulate the production of antibodies, it must be soluble in the body fluids, must reach certain tissues in an unaltered form, and must be, in general, foreign to the body tissues. Protein taken by mouth loses its specific foreign-protein characteristics when digested in the alimentary tract. It reaches the tissues of the body as amino acids or other altered digested products of protein. Consequently, it no longer meets the requirements for antigenic behavior.

Orville Wyss and Curtis Eklund,
Microorganisms and Man

Flowers, L. "Writer-Based Prose: A Cognitive Basis for Problems in Writing." College English 41 (1979): 19–37. Shows how students can go from writer-oriented prose to reader-oriented prose and supplies excellent examples.

Gibson, W. "Authors, Speakers, Readers, and Mock Readers." College English 11 (1950): 254–69. Distinguishes the different roles an audience can assume in reading a work.

Maimon, E. P. "Talking to Strangers." College Composition and Communication 30 (1979): 364–69. Indicates how important it is for students to recognize that they are addressing strangers who will not necessarily share their experiences or their present context.

EXERCISE ANSWERS

Passage 1 is aimed at a broad, general audience, including young people. To reach this audience, Hamilton has used short sentences and everyday words and, to help his readers understand the term being discussed, has likened antigens to "foes." Passage 2 is aimed at an audience of educated adults. Its sentences are longer and more intricate than those in passage 1, and it uses a number of technical terms—helminths, polysaccharides, lipids—that would puzzle most readers in a general audience. Passage 3 is aimed at students in the field of immunology. Because these readers will become specialists, the authors use more technical terms and provide a more detailed explanation than do the first two writers. Wyss and Eklund assume that the reader understands the basics of antigens and concentrate on presenting specialized information concerning them.

Just as you would not dial a telephone number at random and then expect to carry on a meaningful conversation, so you should not expect to communicate effectively without a specific audience in mind.

Several times in this chapter we've referred to your audience, the final target of your writing. But it's also important that your writing please you, too—that it satisfy your sense of what good writing is and what the writing task requires. You are, after all, your own first reader.

■ Chapter 2

Planning and Drafting Your Paper

Many students believe that good essays are dashed off in a burst of inspiration by born writers. Students themselves often boast that they cranked out their topnotch papers in an hour or so of spare time. Perhaps. But for most of us, writing is primarily a skill we can learn and a process we can master, though natural ability and even inspiration may sometimes help.

Although successful writers can often describe how they go about their work, writing is a flexible process. No one order guarantees success, and no one approach works for every writer. Some writers establish their purpose and draft a plan for carrying it out at the start of every project. Others begin with a tentative purpose or plan and discover their final direction as they write. As a project proceeds, the writer is likely to leapfrog backward and forward one or more times rather than to proceed in an orderly, straightforward sequence. Part way through a first draft, for instance, a writer may think of a new point to present, then pause and jot down the details needed to develop it. Similarly, part of the conclusion may come to mind as the writer is gathering the details for supporting a key idea.

Regardless of how it unfolds, the writing process consists of the following stages. Advancing through each stage will guide you if you have no plan or if you've run into snags with your approach. Once you're familiar with these stages, you can combine or rearrange them as needed.

Understanding the assignment
Zeroing in on a topic
Gathering information
Organizing the information
Developing a thesis statement
Writing the first draft
Planning and drafting with a word processor

UNDERSTANDING THE ASSIGNMENT

Instructors differ in making writing assignments. Some specify the topic, some give you several topics to choose from, and still others offer you a free choice. Likewise, some instructors dictate the length and format of the essay, whereas others don't. Whatever the case, be sure you understand the assignment before you go any further.

Think of it this way: if your boss asked you to report on ways of improving the working conditions in your office and you turned in a report on improving worker benefits, would you expect the boss's approval? Following directions is crucial, so if you have any questions about the assignment, ask your instructor to clear them up right then. Don't be timid; it's much better to ask for directions than to receive a low grade for failing to follow them.

ZEROING IN ON A TOPIC

A subject is a broad discussion area: sports, college life, culture, and the like. A topic is one small segment of a subject; for example, testing athletes for drug use, Nirvana College's academic probation policy, the videocassette phenomenon. If you choose your own topic, pick one narrow enough so that you can develop it properly within any length limitation. Avoid sprawling, slippery issues that lead to a string of trite generalities.

In addition, choose a familiar topic or one you can learn enough about in the time available. Avoid overworked topics such as arguments about open visitation in dormitories or the use of marijuana, which generally repeat the same old points. For example, nearly every case for legalizing marijuana contends that it is no more harmful than alcohol, quotes an expert who maintains that it's not addictive, and argues that blocking legalization doesn't prevent use. Such familiar arguments won't arouse reader interest.

Strategies for Finding a Topic

Whenever your instructor assigns a general subject, you'll need to stake out a limited topic suitable for your paper. If you're lucky, the right one will come to mind immediately. More often, though, you'll need to resort to some special strategy. Here are six proven strategies that many writers use. Not all of them will work for everyone, so experiment to find those that produce a topic for you.

Tapping your personal resources.   Personal experience furnishes a rich storehouse of writing material. Over the years, you've packed your mind with memories of family gatherings, school activities, movies, concerts, plays, parties, TV programs, dates, discussions, arguments, and so on. All these experiences can provide suitable topics. Suppose you've been asked to write about some aspect of education. Recalling the difficulties you had last term at registration, you might argue for better registration procedures. Or if you're a hopeless TV addict who must write on some advertising topic, why not analyze video advertising techniques?

Anything you've read in magazines or journals, newspapers, novels, short stories, or textbooks can also trigger a topic. O. Henry's short story "The Last Leaf," in which a character almost dies of pneumonia, might suggest a paper on some miracle drug or a bout of illness you had. An article reviewing the career of a well-known politician might stir thoughts of a friend's experience in running for the student council. Possibilities crowd our lives, waiting for us to recognize and seize them.

EXERCISE ■   **Select five of the subjects listed below. Tapping your personal resources, name one topic suggested by each. For each topic, list three questions that you might answer in a paper.**

Life on a city street	A best-selling book
A particular field of work	Some aspect of nature
Some branch of the federal bureaucracy	Marriage
Concern for some aspect of the environment	Contemporary forms of dancing
Parents	Youth gangs
Saving money	Fashions in clothing
Home ownership	Trendiness
Schools in your town	Human rights
Leisure activities	Public transportation
The two-income family	Childhood fears
	A new scientific discovery
	A religious experience

Keeping a journal.   Many writers, not comfortable relying on their memories, record their experiences in a journal—a private gathering of entries accumulated over a period of time. Journal keeping provides an abundance of possible writing topics as well as valuable writing practice.

The hallmark of the journal entry is the freedom to explore thoughts, feelings, responses, attitudes, and beliefs. In your own private domain you can express your views without reservation, without concern for "doing it right." *You* control the content and length of the entry without being held to a specified topic or number of words.

A few simple guidelines ensure effective journal entries:

1. Write in any kind of notebook that appeals to you; the content, not the package, is the important thing.
2. Write on a regular basis—at least five times a week if possible. In any event don't write by fits and starts, cramming two weeks' entries into one sitting.
3. Write for ten to twenty minutes, longer if you have more to say. Don't aim for

PERSPECTIVE

Students often mistakenly believe that they have no personal resources to tap or that their own experiences are invalid for a paper. To overcome this perception, have each student brainstorm or freewrite about some personal experience and then present the results to the class. The ensuing discussion can help students see that they may indeed have legitimate things to say about a variety of experiences, even though some research might be necessary.

TEACHING STRATEGIES

1. At the beginning of the term, you might have students fill out a personal interest inventory, indicating favorite activities, movies seen, books read, and the like. Then use these inventories to formulate in-class examples for discussion and to help students who are having trouble finding topics.
2. To help students convert personal experiences into topics, have them write about some concern, such as problems they have had in school, and then formulate a series of topics related to the problems. Possibilities include registration difficulties, coping with on- or off-campus life, studying effectively, and overcoming homesickness.

PERSPECTIVE

Unless students understand just what their journals are meant to accomplish, they aren't likely to use them properly. Several kinds of journals are possible. *Personal response:* allows students to record stray thoughts and ideas as well as interesting experiences. Beyond having students write a certain amount each day, instructors impose no restrictions. *Focused response:* features a collection of responses to topics set by the instructor and is tailored toward future writing assignments or specific skills being introduced. Thus students who will write comparison and description essays may be asked to write a page or two contrasting two family members or describing a fellow student. *Reading log:* allows students to summarize reading assignments, possibly connect readings to their own experience, compare different readings, or record their thoughts while reading. Such a log helps prepare for a paper based on readings.

TEACHING STRATEGIES

1. Students are likely to confuse journals with diaries and jot down diary-type entries. To counter this tendency, show them examples of what you'll expect and specify the purpose of journal assignments. Focused responses avoid this problem.
2. Many students are likely to write as little as possible and dash off all their entries at the last minute. It is therefore a good idea to review journals frequently.

CLASSROOM ACTIVITIES

1. To use journal entries in class, set up small groups and have students share their focused responses to a reading assignment or a specific question. A discussion aimed at developing a topic for a paper could follow.
2. Ask students to examine recent journal entries, circle possible topics, write them on the board, and discuss their topic potential. Point out how personal matters can generate reader interest. While no one else in the class may ever encounter one particular student's obnoxious uncle, almost everyone will deal with a difficult relative.

uniform entry length; for example, three paragraphs or a page and a half. Simply explore your reactions to the happenings in your life or to what you have read, heard in class, or seen on television. The length will take care of itself.

Let's examine a typical journal entry by Sam, a freshman composition student.

Last week went back to my hometown for the first time since my family moved away and while there dropped by the street where I spent my first twelve years. Visit left me feeling very depressed. Family home still there, but its paint peeling and front porch sagging. Sign next to the porch said house now occupied by Acme Realtors. While we lived there, front yard lush green and bordered by beds of irises. Now an oil-spattered parking lot. All the other houses on our side of the street gone, replaced by a row of dumpy buildings housing dry cleaner, bowling alley, hamburger joint, shoe repair shop, laundromat. All of them dingy and rundown looking, even though only a few years old.

Other side of street in no better shape. Directly across from our house a used-car dealership with rows of junky looking cars. No trace left of the Little League park that used to be there. Had lots of fun playing baseball and learned meaning of sportsmanship. To left of the dealership my old grade school, now boarded and abandoned. Wonder about my fifth-grade teacher Mrs. Wyrick. Is she still teaching? Still able to make learning a game, not a chore? Other side of dealership the worst sight of all. Grimy looking plant of some sort pouring foul smelling smoke into the air from a discolored stack. Smoke made me cough.

Don't think I'll revisit my old street again.

This journal entry could spawn several essays. Sam might explore the causes of residential deterioration, define sportsmanship, explain how Mrs. Wyrick made learning a game, or argue for stricter pollution control laws.

EXERCISE ■   Write journal entries over the next week or two for some of the following items that interest you. If you have trouble finding a suitable topic for a paper, review the entries for possibilities.

Pleasant or unpleasant conversations   Cultural or sporting events
Developing relationships   College life: myth vs. reality
Single or married life   Public figures—politicians; movie,
Parents   rock, or sports stars
Financial or occupational   World trouble spots
considerations   Courses you are taking
Ideas gained through reading

Sorting out a subject.   All of us sort things. We do it whenever we tackle the laundry, clear away a sinkful of dishes, or tidy up a basement or garage. Let's see how we might handle a cluttered basement. To start off, we'd probably sort the contents according to type: books in one spot, clothing in a second, toys in a third. That done, chances are we'd do still more sorting, separating children's books from adults' and stuffed animals from games. As we looked over and handled the different items, long-buried, bittersweet memories might start flooding from our subconscious. Memories of an uncle, now dead, who sent this old adventure novel . . . of our parents' pride when they saw their child had learned to ride that now battered bicycle . . . of the dance that marked the debut of the evening gown over there.

Sorting out a subject follows a similar scenario. First, we break our broad subject into categories and subcategories, then allow our minds to roam over the different items and see what topics we can turn up. The chart on page 16 shows what one student found when she explored the general topic of public transportation.

As you'll discover for yourself, some subjects yield more topics than others; some, no topics at all.

PERSPECTIVE

The sorting approach can not only turn up specific topics but also lead students to cut across categories. Instead of focusing on the hazards of the subway system, a student may compare the safety of two or more types of public transportation.

CLASSROOM ACTIVITY

Students often find it helpful to sort a topic as a class. Pooling brainpower generates more potential topics and also demonstrates the approach.

EXERCISE ■   Select two of the following subjects; then subdivide those two into five topics.

Advertising   Movies   The space program
Dwellings   Occupations   Sports
Fashions   Popular music   Television programs
Magazines   Social classes Vacations

Results of Sorting out the Subject Public Transportation

Land			Water		Air	
Buses	Taxis	Trains	Sea-going	Lake, River	Airplanes	Helicopters
County bus service for the handicapped	Rights of passengers	The Orient Express, the Twentieth Century Limited	The Titanic		Airline deregulation	Air taxis
Bus tours	Preventing crimes against drivers	Monorails	Luxury liners		Overbooking flights	Cargo
Jitney buses		Preventing subway crimes	Theme cruises		Making air travel safer	
Problem of smoking on buses		Guardian Angels	Modern sea pirates		Coping with hijacking	
Improving bus terminals		Amtrak	Traveling by freighter		Causes and prevention of jet lag	
Designing buses to accommodate the handicapped		Japan's high speed trains	The impact of overseas flights on ship travel		Development of the Stealth bomber	
		Deterioration of railroad tracks			Noise pollution around airports	

Asking questions. Often, working your way through these basic questions will lead you to a manageable topic.

1. Can I define my subject?
2. Does it break into categories?
3. If so, what comparisons can I make among these categories?
4. If my subject is divided into parts, how do they work together?
5. Does my subject have uses? What are they?
6. What are some examples of my subject?
7. What are the causes or origins of my subject?
8. What impact has my subject had?

Let's convert these general questions into specific questions about telescopes, a broad general subject:

1. What is a telescope?
2. What are the different kinds of telescopes?
3. How are they alike? How do they differ?
4. What are the parts of each kind of telescope, and how do they work together?
5. What are telescopes used for?
6. What are some well-known telescopes?
7. Who invented the telescope?
8. What impact have telescopes had on human life and knowledge?

Each of these questions offers a starting point for a suitably focused essay. Question 3 might launch a paper comparing reflecting and refracting telescopes; question 6 might be answered in a paper about the planning and construction of the 200-inch reflecting telescope at California's Mount Palomar observatory.

PERSPECTIVE

Students find it easier to write about questions than topics. Questions require us to generate ideas; topics can be tombstones to thought. It often helps to have students translate topics into questions and then develop a set of related questions.

EXERCISE ■ **Convert the general questions into specific questions about two of the following subjects; then suggest two essay topics for each of your two subjects.**

Astrology	Games	Shopping malls
Books	Microorganisms	Stars
Colleges	Plays	Television
Emotions	Religion	Warships

Freewriting. The freewriting strategy snares thoughts as they race through your mind, yielding a set of sentences that you then look over for writing ideas. To begin, turn your pen loose and write for about five minutes on your general subject. Put down everything that comes into your head, without worrying about grammar, spelling, or punctuation. What you produce is for your eyes alone. If the thought flow becomes blocked, write "I'm stuck, I'm stuck . . ." until you break the mental logjam. When your writing time is up, go through your sentences one by one and extract potential topic material. If you draw a blank, write for another five minutes and look again.

PERSPECTIVE

Freewriting was heralded by Peter Elbow, who initially used it as a strategy to help MIT engineers whose writing anxiety blocked their writing. A useful way to unlock the mind and bring up interesting and new associations, it can be used at any point in the writing process to help students develop new approaches to papers in progress. Don't expect splendid results every time: students who think trite thoughts produce trite freewriting. And like any activity, freewriting becomes more effective with repeated use. It can be unfocused, with students writing whatever comes into their heads, or focused on some subject or topic.

The following example shows the product of one freewriting session. Jim's instructor had assigned a two- or three-page paper on some sports-related topic, and since Jim had been a member of his high school tennis team, his thoughts naturally turned toward this sport.

> Sports. If that's my subject, I'd better do something on tennis. I've played enough of it. But what can I say that would be interesting? It's very popular, lots of people watch it on TV. Maybe I could write about the major tennis tournaments. I'm stuck. I'm stuck. Maybe court surfaces. That sounds dull. I'm stuck. Well, what about tennis equipment, clothing, scoring? Maybe my reader is thinking about taking up the game. What do I like about tennis? The strategy, playing the net, when to use a topspin or a backspin stroke, different serves. I'm stuck. I'm stuck. Maybe I could suggest how to play a better game of singles. I used to be number one. I can still remember Coach harping on those three Cs, conditioning, concentration, consistency. I'm stuck. I'm stuck. Then there's the matter of special shots like lobs, volleys, and overheads. But that stuff is for the pros.

This example suggests at least three papers. For the beginning player, Jim could focus on equipment and scoring. For the intermediate player, he might write on conditioning, concentration, and consistency; for the advanced player, on special shots.

Brainstorming.   Brainstorming, a close cousin of freewriting, captures fleeting ideas in words, fragments, and sometimes sentences, rather than in a series of sentences. Brainstorming garners ideas faster than the other strategies do. But unless you move immediately to the next stage of writing, you may lose track of what some of your fragmentary jottings mean.

To compare the results of freewriting and brainstorming a topic, we've converted our freewriting example into this list, which typifies the results of brainstorming.

Popularity of tennis	Equipment
Major tournaments	Clothing
Court surfaces	Scoring

Doubles strategy   Conditioning

Singles strategy   Concentration

Playing the net   Consistency

Topspin   Special shots—lobs, drop

Backspin   volleys, overheads

Different serves

EXERCISE ■   **Return to the five subjects you selected for the exercise on page 13. Freewrite or brainstorm for five minutes on each one; then choose a topic suitable for a two- or three-page essay. State your topic, intended audience, and purpose.**

Narrowing a familiar subject may yield not only a topic but also the main divisions for a paper on it. Jim's freewriting session uncovered several possible tennis topics as well as a way of approaching each: by focusing on lobs, drop volleys, and overheads when writing about special shots, for example. Ordinarily, though, the main divisions will emerge only after you have gathered material to develop your topic.

Now that you're familiar with some narrowing strategies, let's examine the first segment of a case history that shows how one student handles a writing assignment. This segment illustrates the use of a narrowing strategy to find a topic. Later segments focus on the remaining stages of the writing process.

TEACHING STRATEGIES
1. Brainstorming and free-writing can be combined. A student can brainstorm, select an item from the resulting list, free-write about it, and then brainstorm an item from the free-writing list.
2. Following the practice of business, have the class brainstorm a subject as a group, write their responses on the board, weed out ideas inappropriate for papers, then brainstorm some more.
3. Some students claim to be stuck after listing just two or three ideas. Nudge them into jotting down *any* ideas, no matter how absurd they seem. They can always be deleted later.

CASE HISTORY ■

George's writing class has been talking and reading about the importance people attach to their recreation and the many forms it can take. His instructor asks the class to write a three- or four-page paper on some aspect of recreation. To begin, George uses the sorting strategy and comes up with two major categories of topics: those based primarily on reading and those based on personal experience. Under the first category, he includes legalized casino gambling, vacationing in national parks, and collecting baseball cards; under the second he lists his hobby of coin collecting, his interest in playing bridge, and the recreational possibilities of his hometown, Mt. Pleasant. Because he has only marginal interest in the topics in the first category, he rules all of them out. After weighing the possibilities of the items in the second category, he concludes that Mt. Pleasant

offers the most potential and elects to pursue that topic for a high
school audience.

This case history continues on page 22.

GATHERING INFORMATION

Once you have a topic, you'll need things to say about it. This supporting
material can include facts, ideas, examples, observations, sensory impressions,
memories, and the like. Without the proper backup, papers lack force, vividness,
and interest and may confuse or mislead readers.

Strategies for Gathering Information

If you are writing on a familiar topic, much of your supporting material may
come from your own head. Brainstorming is the best way to retrieve it. With
unfamiliar topics, brainstorming won't work. Instead, you'll have to do some
background reading. Whatever the topic, familiar or unfamiliar, talking with
friends, parents, neighbors, or people knowledgeable about the topic can also
produce useful ideas.

Brainstorming.   Brainstorming a topic, like brainstorming a subject, yields a
set of words, fragments, and occasionally sentences that will furnish ideas for the
paper. Assume that Jim, the student who explored the subject of tennis, wants to
show how conditioning, concentration, and consistent play can improve one's
game. His brainstorming list might look like this:

keeping ball in play	temper distractions
don't try foolish shots	don't continually drive
placing ball so opponent	ball with power
runs	two-on-one drill
staying in good condition	lobbing ball over
yourself	opponent's head
running	returning a down-the-line
jogging	passing shot
skipping rope	don't try spectacular
keeps you on your toes	overheads
keeping your mind only on	chance for opponent to make
the game	mistake
personal distractions	game of percentages
courtside distractions	games are lost, not won

You can see how some thoughts have led to others. For example, the first jotting, "keeping ball in play," leads naturally to the next one, "don't try foolish shots." "Placing ball so opponent runs" leads to "staying in good condition yourself," which in turn leads to ways of staying in condition and so forth.

Branching is a helpful and convenient extension of brainstorming that allows you to add details to any item in your list. Here's how you might use this technique to approach "courtside distractions."

Don't worry if your brainstorming notes look chaotic and if some seem irrelevant. Sometimes the most unlikely material turns out to be the freshest and most interesting. As you organize and write your paper, you'll probably combine, modify, and omit some of the notes, as well as add others.

EXERCISE ■ **Prepare a brainstorming sheet of supporting details for one of the topics you developed for the exercise on page 19.**

Reading. When you have to grapple with an unfamiliar topic, look in the library for material to develop it. Before going there, however, turn to Chapter 19, The Library Research Paper, and read what we say under the headings "The Card Catalog," "Computerized Card Catalogs," and "Periodical Indexes." These sections tell you how to unearth promising references to investigate. Once you have a list of references, start searching for the books or articles. Look through each one you find and jot down any information that looks useful, either as direct quotations or in your own words.

Whenever you use a direct quotation or rephrased material in your paper, you must give proper credit to the source. If you don't, you are guilty of plagiarism, a serious offense that can result in a failing grade for the course or even expulsion from college. Unless you're doing a library research paper, your instructor will probably require only that you name the speaker or writer and the publication in which the material appeared. (See "Handling Quotations" and "Avoiding Plagiarism," Chapter 19.)

Talking with others. You can expand the pool of ideas gained through brainstorming or reading by talking with some of the people around you. Imagine you're writing a paper about a taxpayers' revolt in your state. After checking the leading state newspapers at the library, you find that most of the discontent centers on property taxes. You then decide to supplement what you've read by asking questions about the tax situation in your town.

Your parents and neighbors tell you that property taxes have jumped 50 percent in the last two years. The local tax assessor tells you that assessed valuations have risen sharply and that state law requires property taxes to keep pace. She also notes that this situation is causing some people on fixed incomes to lose their homes. A city council member explains that part of the added revenue is being used to repair city streets, build a new library wing, and buy more fire-fighting equipment. The rest is going to the schools. School officials tell you they're using their extra funds to offer more vocational courses and to expand the program for learning-disabled students. As you can see, asking questions can broaden your perspective and provide information that will help you to write a more worthwhile paper.

CASE HISTORY ■   *(Continued from page 20)*

After choosing to write about the recreational possibilities of his hometown, George brainstorms to gather appropriate material. The result is a twenty-item list. After checking it over, George decides that three items—the local chamber-music orchestra, little theater, and barbershop quartet—would hold little interest for his teenage audience, and he drops them. The remaining items are as follows:

End-of-World parties	crazy activities of party-
crowded streets	goers
Cold Water Lake	Mt. Pleasant Mall
Lake Isabella Dam	Embers restaurant
Island Park activities	Holiday Inn
live bands	Nelson Park Zoo
baseball games	Mt. Pleasant Speedway
small gatherings	mall parking
Mt. Pleasant Meadows	Boomer's Nightclub

This case history continues on pages 25–26.

ORGANIZING THE INFORMATION

If you have ever listened to a rambling speaker spill out ideas in no particular order, you probably found it hard to pay attention to the speech, let alone make sense of it. So, too, with disorganized writing. A garbled listing of ideas serves no one; an orderly presentation highlights your ideas and helps communication succeed.

Your topic determines the approach you take. In narrating a personal experience, such as a mishap-riddled vacation, you'd probably trace the events in the order they occurred. In describing a process, say caulking a bathtub, you'd take the reader step by step through the procedure. To describe a hillside view near your home, you might work from left to right. Or you could first paint a word picture of some striking central feature and then fan out in either direction. Other topics dictate other patterns, such as comparison and contrast, cause and effect, and illustration. Chapters 4–12 describe the basic patterns in detail.

You can best organize long pieces of writing, such as library research papers, by following a formal outline. (See Chapter 19, "Organizing and Outlining.") For shorter papers, however, a simple, informal system of *flexible notes* will do nicely.

The Flexible Notes System

To create a set of flexible notes, write each of your key points at the top of a separate sheet of paper. If you have a thesis statement, refer to it for your key points. Next, list under each heading the supporting details that go with that heading. Drop any details that don't fit and expand any points that need more support. When your sheets are finished, arrange them in the order you expect to follow in your essay. The notes for the tennis paper might look like this:

Conditioning

staying in good condition   two-on-one drill
   yourself   lobbing ball over
running   opponent's head
jogging   returning a down-the-line
skipping rope   passing shot
keeps you on your toes

Concentration

keeping your mind only on the game
overcome distractions: personal, courtside, temper

Consistency

keeping ball in play
don't try foolish shots

placing ball so opponent runs

don't continually drive ball with power

don't try spectacular overheads

chance for opponent to make mistake

game of percentages

games are lost, not won

Since conditioning, concentration, and consistency are simultaneous concerns, this listing arranges them according to their probable importance—starting with the least important.

Now you're ready to draft a plan showing how many paragraphs you'll have in each part of the essay and what each paragraph will cover. Sometimes the number of details will suggest one paragraph; other times you'll need a paragraph block—two or more paragraphs. Here's a plan for the tennis essay.

Conditioning

staying in good condition yourself

running

jogging   Off-the-court

skipping rope   conditioning

keeps you on your toes

two-on-one drill

lobbing ball over opponent's head
                                                 On-the-court
returning a down-the-line passing   conditioning
  shot

Concentration

keeping your mind only on the game

overcome distractions: personal, courtside, temper

Consistency

keeping ball in play

don't try foolish shots

placing ball so opponent runs   Placing shots

don't continually drive ball with power

don't try spectacular overheads

chance for opponent to make mistake

game of percentages

games are lost, not won

} Playing percentages

These groupings suggest two paragraphs about conditioning, one about concentration, and two about consistency.

EXERCISE ■   **Organize into flexible notes the supporting details that you prepared for the exercise on page 21. Arrange your note pages in a logical sequence and draft a plan showing the number and content of the paragraphs in each section.**

CASE HISTORY ■   *(Continued from page 22)*

A careful look at his brainstorming list shows George that its items fall into six categories: parties, swimming, parks, shopping, racing, and dining. After sorting the items into these categories, he draws up the following paragraph-by-paragraph plan:

Parties

End-of-World parties	One
crowded streets	paragraph
crazy antics of party-goers	on partying

Swimming

Cold Water Lake	One paragraph
Lake Isabella Dam	on each
	swimming spot

Parks

Island Park activities	One paragraph
live bands	on each park
baseball games	
small gatherings	
Nelson Park Zoo	

Shopping

Mt. Pleasant Mall   One paragraph

plenty of parking   on shopping

Racing

Mt. Pleasant Meadows   One paragraph on

Mt. Pleasant Speedway   each racing spot

Dining

Embers restaurant   One paragraph

Holiday Inn   on each dining

Boomer's Nightclub   spot

This case history continues on pages 28—29.

DEVELOPING A THESIS STATEMENT

A thesis statement presents the main idea of a piece of writing, usually in one sentence. The thesis statement points you in a specific direction, helping you to stay on track and out of tempting byways. In addition, it tells your reader what to expect.

Thesis statements can emerge at several points in the writing process. If an instructor assigns a controversial topic on which you hold strong views, the statement may pop into your head right away. At other times it may develop as you narrow a subject to a topic. Occasionally, you even have to write a preliminary draft to determine your main idea. Usually, though, the thesis statement emerges after you've gathered and examined your supporting information.

As you examine your information, search for the central point and the key points that back it up; then use these to develop your thesis statement. Converting the topic to a question may help you to uncover backup ideas and write a thesis statement. For example:

Topic: The uncertain future of robots in American industry.

Question: What are some of the drawbacks of using robots in American industry?

Thesis statement: The expense of producing robots, the lack of qualified personnel to service them, and the moral problems of replacing workers with them—all cloud the future of robots in American industry.

The thesis statement stems from the specifics the student unearthed while answering the question.

Requirements of a Good Thesis Statement

Unless intended for a lengthy paper, a thesis statement *focuses on just one central point or issue*. Suppose you prepare the following thesis statement for a two- or three-page paper:

```
Centerville College should reexamine its policies on aid to

students, open admissions, and vocational programs.
```

This sprawling statement would commit you to grapple with three separate issues. At best, you could make only a few general remarks about each one.

To correct matters, consider each issue carefully in light of how much it interests you and how much you know about it. Then make your choice and draft a narrower statement. The following thesis statement would do nicely for a brief paper. It shows clearly that the writer will focus on *just one issue*.

```
Because of the rising demand among high school graduates for

job-related training, Centerville College should expand

its vocational offerings.
```

A good thesis statement also *tailors the scope of the issue to the length of the paper*. No writer could deal adequately with "Many incoming college freshmen face crucial adjustment problems" in two or three pages. The idea is too broad to yield more than a smattering of poorly supported general statements. Paring it down to "Free time is a responsibility that challenges many college freshmen," however, results in an idea that could probably be developed adequately.

A good thesis statement further provides *an accurate forecast of what's to come*. If you plan to discuss the effects of overeating, don't say that "Overeating stems from deep-seated psychological factors and the easy availability of convenience foods." Such a statement, incorrectly suggesting that the paper will focus on causes, would only mislead and confuse your reader. On the other hand, "Overeating leads to obesity, which can cause or complicate several serious health problems" accurately represents what's to follow.

Finally, a good thesis statement is *precise, often previewing the organization of the paper*. Assertions built on fuzzy, catchall words like *fascinating, bad, meaningful*, or *interesting*, or statements like "My paper is about . . . " tell neither writer nor reader what's going on. To illustrate:

```
New York is a fascinating city.

My paper is about no-fault divorce.
```

These examples raise a host of questions. Why does the writer find New York fascinating? Because of its skyscrapers? Its night life? Its theaters? Its restaurants? Its museums? Its shops? Its inhabitants? And what about no-fault divorce? Will

3. Some students can become fixated on the thesis statement, constantly reworking it as though it were a replacement for the draft. Others will never get beyond the most general restatement of a topic. In both cases, encourage students to write a preliminary draft before formulating a thesis statement.
4. Other students resist modifications in their thesis because changes require additional effort. You might show them how one of your thesis statements evolved as new information surfaced or ideas developed.

CLASSROOM ACTIVITIES
1. Have the class brainstorm a topic, formulate several possible thesis statements, evaluate them against the requirements of a good thesis statement, and select the best one.
2. Have students review one another's thesis statements, write down any questions about their scope and adequacy, then return the responses to their authors. This exercise can help students redefine and redirect their efforts.

the writer attack it, defend it, trace its history, suggest ways of improving it? To find out, we must journey through the paper, hoping to find our way without a road-map sentence.

Now look at the rewritten versions of those faulty thesis statements:

I love New York because of its many theaters and museums.

Compared to traditional divorce, no-fault divorce is less expensive, promotes fairer settlements, and reflects a more realistic view of the causes of marital breakdown.

These statements tell the reader not only what points the writer will make but also the order they will follow.

Omission of Thesis Statement

Not all papers have explicit thesis statements. Narratives and descriptions, for example, often merely support some point that is unstated but nevertheless clear, and professional writers sometimes imply their thesis rather than state it openly. Nonetheless, a core idea underlies and controls all effective writing.

Changing Your Thesis Statement

Unlike diamonds, thesis statements aren't necessarily forever. Before your paper is in final form, you may need to change your thesis statement several times. If you draft the thesis statement during the narrowing stage, you might change it to reflect what you uncovered while gathering information. Or you might amend it after writing the first draft so that it reflects your additions and deletions.

Tentative or final, formulated early or late, the thesis statement serves as a beacon that spotlights your purpose.

EXERCISE ANSWERS

1. This statement is not precise. It could mean that the writer will discuss (a) the causes of absenteeism; (b) the effects of absenteeism; (c) the efforts industry is making to reduce absenteeism. Any attempt to discuss these aspects adequately would require far more than two or three pages.

2. This thesis statement is satisfactory. Its topic is narrow enough to be covered adequately in two or three pages, and it signals the organization of the paper.

3. This thesis statement offers no clue to why Acme College is not well run. Does the writer

CASE HISTORY ■ *(Continued from page 26)*

His paragraph-by-paragraph plan competed, George now drafts a thesis statement that names all categories.

Mt. Pleasant offers parties, great swimming spots, pleasant parks, race tracks, fine dining, and excellent shopping.

After carefully examining this initial effort, he realizes that three of the categories could be lumped together under the umbrella category "recreation spots." He alters the statement to read as follows.

Mt. Pleasant offers parties, great recreation
spots, fine dining, and excellent shopping.

This case history continues on pages 30–33.

EXERCISE ▪

A. **Write a thesis statement for the sheet of supporting details that you developed for the exercise on page 25.**

B. **Reread "Requirements of a Good Thesis Statement"; then explain why each of the following does or does not qualify as an effective thesis statement for a two- or three-page essay.**

1. My paper discusses the problem of employee absenteeism in American industry.
2. Living on a small island offers three advantages: isolation from city problems, the opportunity to know your neighbors, and the chance to go fishing whenever you want.
3. Although I don't know much about running a college, I know that Acme College is not run well.
4. Expanding our nation's armaments increases the chance of nuclear war and imposes an unneeded tax burden on the American taxpayer.
5. Many people, motivated by the desire to begin a new and more virtuous life, have abandoned the established modes of life and set up communities based on utopian ideals.
6. Vacationing in Britain is a nice way to spend a summer.
7. Extending Middletown's intracity transit system will save consumers money, reduce pollution, and increase city revenues.
8. Most cable TV companies provide subscribers with several specialized-program channels.

WRITING THE FIRST DRAFT

Now on to the first draft of your essay. The writing should go rather quickly. After all, you have a topic you're qualified to write about, a thesis statement that indicates your purpose, enough information to develop it, and a written plan to follow.

But sometimes when you sit down to write, the words won't come, and all you can do is doodle or stare at the blank page. Perhaps the introduction is the problem. Many writers are terrified by the thought of the opening paragraph. They want to get off to a good start but can't figure out how to begin. If this

mean that (a) The administrators are doing a poor job? (b) The faculty is underpaid and poorly motivated? (c) The course offerings are inadequate? (d) The school doesn't provide adequate recreational facilities? Furthermore, by saying "Although I don't know much about running a college," the student undermines his or her credibility.

4. This thesis statement fails on two counts. First, it makes two separate assertions—about war and taxes. Second, each assertion is too complex to be discussed adequately in a short paper.

5. This is a good thesis statement. It could be explained in two or three pages, and the phrase "motivated by the desire to begin a new and more virtuous life" signals the approach that the writer will take.

6. This thesis statement, like 3, is far too imprecise. Vacationing in Britain might be nice for several reasons, including the opportunity to (a) meet and mingle with the British people; (b) enjoy London's theaters and nightlife; (c) tour the nation's historic cities and shrines; (d) enroll for a summer program at Oxford or Cambridge. A better thesis statement might be, "Vacationing in Britain offers the traveler a chance to visit the birthplaces of some of the world's foremost literary figures."

7. This thesis statement commits the writer to deal with three separate issues, any one of which would require two or three pages. The discussion needs narrowing to just one issue.

8. Another good thesis statement, this one restricts the writer to a topic that suits the length limitations. The paper might include paragraphs about channels devoted to sports, religion, movies, and children's programs.

PERSPECTIVE

Reiterate that a first draft is not a final draft, might not be anything like a final draft, can be subject to massive change, might be thrown out entirely, is an experiment. Despite these caveats, many students will attempt to get it right on the first try in order to save time. You might jokingly label this version the zero draft, fertilizer draft, or overhaul draft. Students approach drafting differently. Some use notes and plans to build a more organized draft; others merely refer to notes and then experiment with getting ideas on paper, well aware that the draft will probably need reorganization and more information.

TEACHING STRATEGIES

1. If you have basic students, you might show them how *you* write a draft, perhaps using an overhead. Students are amazed to discover that even teachers write in a series of fits and starts and change direction.
2. Have basic writers prepare a draft in class. If you see them repeatedly making corrections at the sentence and word level, encourage them to move on with their ideas and reassure them that they can work on mechanics later.
3. If students get stuck, have them write about what they want to say in the paper, then use the results along with their written plan to develop a draft. Many who are stuck need to consider whether they have enough information.

SUGGESTED INSTRUCTOR READINGS

Perl, S. "The Composing Processes of Unskilled College Writers." Research in the Teaching of English 13 (1978): 317–36. A good case study of why and how students have trouble developing drafts.

happens to you, skip the introduction for the time being. Once you have drafted the body of the paper, an effective opening often comes more easily.

Here are some general suggestions for writing a first draft.

1. Stack your thesis statement, flexible notes, and written plan in front of you. They will start you thinking.
2. Skip every other line (double-space) and leave wide margins. Then you'll have room to revise later.
3. Write quickly; capture the drift of your thoughts. Concentrate on content and organization. Get your main points and supporting details on paper in the right sequence. *Don't* spend time correcting grammatical or punctuation errors, improving your language, or making the writing flow smoothly. You might lose your train of thought and end up doodling or staring again.
4. Take breaks at logical dividing points, for example, when you finish discussing a key point. Before you start to write again, scan what you've written.

Now for some specific suggestions that will help you with the actual writing:

1. Rewrite your thesis statement at the top of your first page to break the ice and build momentum.
2. Write your first paragraph, introducing your essay and stating your thesis. If you get stuck here, move on to the rest of the paper.
3. Follow your plan as you write. Begin with your first main point and work on each section in turn.
4. Look over the supporting details listed under the first heading in your flexible notes. Write a topic sentence stating the central idea of the paragraph.
5. Turn the details into sentences; use one or more sentences to explain each one. Add other related details, facts, or examples if they occur to you.
6. When you move from one paragraph to the next, try to provide a transitional word or sentence that connects the two.
7. Write your last paragraph, ending your essay in an appropriate fashion. If you get stuck, set your conclusion aside and return to it later.

EXERCISE ■ **Using the plan you prepared for the exercise on page 21, write the first draft of an essay.**

CASE HISTORY ■ *(Continued from page 29)*

George now uses his thesis statement and paragraph-by-paragraph plan to write the following draft. Notice the slight changes in the thesis statement wording and in paragraphing, a common occurrence at this writing stage. Without question this draft needs extensive revision. We'll return to it early in the next chapter to discuss the necessary changes.

Pianko, S. "Reflection: A Critical Component of the Composing Process." <u>College Composition and Communication</u> 30 (1979): 275–78. Discusses how students need to reflect when writing and how instructors can encourage such reflection.

Mt. Pleasant

Welcome to Mt. Pleasant, the home of Central Michigan University and the oil capital of this state. You have chosen the right town to visit because there are so many things for a high school student here. There are parties, great recreation spots, fine places to dine, and even excellent shopping.

I am sure you have all heard of Mt. Pleasant's famous "End-of-the-World Parties," which have been featured in nationwide news stories. These parties are a riot, both literally and figuratively. At the end of the school year, all the CMU students gather on fraternity row to celebrate the start of summer. For blocks and blocks, the streets are filled to overflowing with people pushing their way along with drinks in their hands to yet another bash. It is probably one of the rowdiest parties you could attend. People do all kinds of crazy things including climbing on rooftops and burning couches in the street. There was even one party-goer who stripped naked. That's what I call rowdy.

If you are not into partying, maybe a mellow day on the beach would do you some good. There is a beautiful lake called Cold Water Lake that has crystal clear water and a scenic beach. This beach is the "hit spot" on a sunny day, so you will want to be there.

If you're out for some wet-n-wild swimming fun, then Lake Isabella Dam is the place for you. It is a huge slippery slide about a hundred yards long pitched

at a 160-degree angle. One could spend all day there and
not get bored of sliding away.

After swimming, you could go to Island Park in
the center of town. This park is unique because it is
surrounded by a river that flows around it; it is Mt.
Pleasant's own Island of Paradise. There are many
activities at the park including live bands, small
gatherings, and baseball games. This park is the main
hangout for teens in Mt. Pleasant. For the children,
there is also Nelson Park which has a small zoo with
bear, deer, badger, and many other kinds of North
American wildlife.

If you are a person who likes to shop, then you
will want to visit the Mt. Pleasant Mall at the edge of
town. It has all the convenience stores necessary for a
fulfilling day of shopping. There is always plenty of
parking.

Mt. Pleasant also has places for those of you who
like to gamble. Mt. Pleasant Meadows has fun-filled,
action-packed horse races all weekend long. There is
also a concession stand and a bar. The Meadows is just
waiting for you to bet and win big.

If you like horse racing, then you might also
enjoy the car racing at Mt. Pleasant Speedway. On
Fridays there is a high-speed stock car race all night
long. So come see the fast cars, bright lights, and the
excitement of racing waiting for you.

Let's not forget about the fine dining Mt.
Pleasant has to offer. There is an elegant restaurant
called The Embers that matches all the fine cuisine in
the world. There is also a Holiday Inn which hosts a

PERSPECTIVE

Several kinds of computer programs—including those that focus on interactive planning, outlining, and mechanics—are available to help students. The word-processing program, however, is the most useful because it makes planning, drafting, and revising so much easier. Various programs that differ in power and complexity are available. If your class is scheduled for a word-processing lab, review the literature and available programs with the lab director and select the one that best suits the needs of your class.

TEACHING STRATEGIES

1. Rather than relying only on the manual to teach students how to use the word processor, develop simple handouts that build computer skills step by step. It helps if you are in the lab while students learn the program and draft a brief practice paper. Students need to become familiar with the functions of the computer before being assigned a longer paper.

2. If students plan and draft using their own word processor, ask them to print out the different stages of their work so that you can review them and offer pointers. Often students view a computer as an electronic hot rod and speed prematurely into a draft.

```
class A restaurant and nightclub. The club is called

Boomers and presents well-known comedians to entertain

you throughout the night.

     Mt. Pleasant has much to offer you: fine dining,

excitement, and relaxation. Why not come and see for

yourself.
```

This essay will be revised in the next chapter.

PLANNING AND DRAFTING WITH A WORD PROCESSOR

Because of the advantages that they offer at every writing stage, word processors, which couple a keyboard with a computer, video screen, and printer, gain converts daily. When using one of these units, you can save what you write, insert new material into your copy, delete unwanted sections, move sections around, and when you are ready, print out copies.

If your college provides word processors for student use, read the manual for your unit to discover its capabilities and commands before attempting to compose with it. Frustration results when you simultaneously try to write a paper and get the word processor to do your bidding.

Although they are most useful for revision, word processors can also help you plan and draft your essay. As you search for a topic, you can brainstorm or freewrite, entering into your word processor whatever words, phrases, or ideas come to mind. For best results, do this for about ten minutes; then stop, print out a copy of your entries, and comb through them for bits and pieces that seem promising. Enter these items in the word processor and use them to further brainstorm or freewrite until you arrive at a suitable topic.

If you approach a topic through the set of questions on page 17, enter them into the word processor, convert them into specific questions related to your broad subject area, and then enter your answers. Scour these answers for leads that you can develop through brainstorming, freewriting, or library research.

When you outline on a word processor, you can experiment with different arrangements of your material and add or delete freely. As the writing progresses and new ideas surface, revamp the outline accordingly. Keep a printout copy of each outline version so you can backtrack and retrieve any one that later suits your needs.

As you move to the drafting stage, don't hesitate to experiment with your ideas; changes are very easy to make on a word processor. If your writing stalls, simply note the spot with an asterisk or other marker. Then, when you finish the draft, return to that spot for further work by using the keyboard's automatic "find" function. Always remember to keep a copy of each version of your draft. You may decide that an early effort is better than your later ones.

TEACHING STRATEGIES

1. Because changes can be made so easily, some students become compulsive about re-working words and sentences and therefore lose any sense of the overall paper. Encourage them to push forward.

2. Other students, seeing their ideas first on screen and then in print, prematurely conclude that their work is finished. Remind them that typed doesn't necessarily mean finished.

3. Still other students find that words and ideas flow so readily that they forget to edit or limit their work. Remind these students to make choices.

4. Dogs may not have eaten student homework, but far too often computers do. Students need frequent reminders to save. It's helpful if they keep a print copy, the saved original, and a backup of major work.

SUGGESTED INSTRUCTOR READINGS

Daiute, Writing and Computers. Reading, MA: Addison-Wesley, 1985. Includes a section on using computers in the composition classroom.

Schwartz, H. J., and L. S. Bridwell-Bowles. "A Selected Bibliography on Computers in Composition: An Update." College Composition and Communication 38 (1987): 453–57. A helpful annotated bibliography of computer programs for the composition classroom.

Zinsser, W. Writing with a Word Processor. New York: Harper, 1973. Provides a detailed account of how to approach writing with a word processor and describes how the word processor affects the composing process.

TEACHING STRATEGIES

1. Because students often blur the distinction between revision and proofreading/editing, try to maintain a clear difference between the two in your syllabus, class discussions, and responses to their drafts.
2. Students benefit greatly when you *show* them how to revise. You might use an overhead to make and explain revision decisions or to present several drafts of a paper, identifying the changes that were made. The best drafts are those closest to the types of writing students will actually do.

CLASSROOM ACTIVITY

You might give students useful metaphors for the writing process. Writing could be described as working with clay, where one shapes and reshapes a figure; as gardening, where constant weeding, watering, and waiting are required; as a relationship, where people meet, slowly get to know each other, and kiss only after they are comfortable. The more plastic the metaphor, the better. Ask students to jot down their metaphors for writing (often very punitive) and discuss their features, making it clear that writing is not a straight line from first idea to final draft.

■ Chapter 3

Revising and Editing Your Paper

All of us at one time or another have said something careless to a friend or date and then spent the rest of the night regretting our words. In contrast, when we write we can make sure we say exactly what we mean. Good writers don't express themselves perfectly on the first try, but they do work hard at revising their initial efforts.

Just what is revision? Don't confuse it with proofreading or editing, the final stage of the writing process, where you carefully inspect your word choice, spelling, grammar, and punctuation. Revision is much more drastic, often involving an upheaval of your draft as you change its content and organization in order to communicate more effectively.

Most of what you read, including this book, has been considerably altered and improved as the writers progressed through early drafts. This fact shouldn't surprise you. After all, a rough copy is merely a first attempt to jot down some ideas in essay form. No matter how well you gather and organize your material, you can't predict the outcome until you've prepared a draft. Sometimes only touch-up changes are required. More often though, despite your efforts, this version will be incomplete, unclear in places, possibly disorganized. You might even discover an entirely different idea, focus, or approach buried within it. During revision you keep changing things—your focus, approach to the topic, supporting material, and thesis statement—until the results satisfy you.

Inexperienced writers often mistakenly view initial drafts as nearly finished products rather than as experiments to alter, or even scrap, if need be. As a result, they often approach revision with the wrong attitude. To revise successfully, you need to control your ego and your fear and become your own first critical reader. Set aside natural feelings of accomplishment ("After all, I've put a great deal of thought into this") and dread ("Actually, I'm afraid of what I'll find if I look too closely"). Instead, recognize that revision offers an opportunity to upgrade your strong features and strengthen your weak ones.

PREPARING TO REVISE

To distance yourself from your writing and sharpen your critical eye, set your first draft aside for at least a half day, longer if time permits. When you return to it, gear up for revision by jotting down your intended purpose and audience before you read your paper. These notations will help keep your changes on track. In addition, note any further ideas that have occurred to you.

The right attitude is vital to effective revision. Far too many students hastily skim their essays to reassure themselves that "Everything sounds O.K." Avoid such a quick-fix approach. If your draft appears fine on first reading, probe it again with a more critical eye. Try putting yourself in your reader's place. Will your description of a favorite getaway spot be clear to someone who has never seen it? Will your letter home asking for money really convince parents who might think they've already given you too much? Remember: If you aren't critical now, anticipating confusion and objections, your reader certainly will be later.

Reading your draft aloud will force you to slow down, and you will often hear yourself stumble over problem sections. You'll be more likely to uncover errors such as missing words, excessive repetition, clumsy sentences, and sentence fragments. Be honest in your evaluation; don't read in virtues that aren't there or that exaggerate the writing quality.

Read your essay at least three times, once for each of these reasons:

To improve the development of the essay as a whole
To strengthen paragraph structure and development
To sharpen sentences and words

When you finish reading your paper for content, make a final meticulous sweep to search for errors and problems that mar your writing. Use the Personal Revision Checklist on the inside back cover of this book to note your own special weaknesses, perhaps some problem with punctuation or a failure to provide specific support. Later chapters discuss paragraphs, sentences, and words in detail. Check these chapters for more information about the points introduced here.

TEACHING STRATEGIES

1. Suggest that students who have problems with revision write an entirely new draft without reference to the old one. Then ask them to take the best elements of each and combine them in a third draft. This approach helps students loosen their commitment to any one draft.

2. Before they begin revising, have students write down their purpose and audience so they gain perspective on the project. Then ask them to read their drafts from beginning to end and note possible changes that would improve the paper. Alternatively, ask how they might like to change their purpose and audience, given their experience of writing the draft.

3. Role playing can help introduce revision. Ask students to assume the role of their audience and read their drafts, then write the probable responses of the audience.

4. To encourage revision, have students write a draft from a different perspective. To illustrate, for a narrative, they could attempt a retelling from the point of view of a different participant.

CONSIDERING THE WHOLE ESSAY

If you only inspect your draft sentence by sentence, you can easily overlook how its parts work together. A better approach is to step back and view the overall essay rather than its separate parts, asking questions such as "Does the beginning mesh with the end?" "Does the essay wander?" "Has anything been left out?" In this way you can gauge how part relates to part and to the whole. Use the acronym *FACT* to guide this stage of your revision.

F. Ask yourself first whether the whole essay *FITS* together, presenting a central point for a specific audience. Have you delivered what the thesis statement

TEACHING STRATEGIES

1. You may wish to hand out evaluation sheets with specific revision questions, geared to the assignment, for students to answer. (Evaluation questions are included in later chapters of the text.) Or ask students to fill out a FACT sheet indicating the needed changes in their drafts. In any case, encourage the class

not to merely respond "yes" or "no" to questions, but to identify precisely what is causing problems and why. You could collect these sheets with the final drafts.
2. Students often identify problems and then do nothing about them. Require your students to suggest, and then carry out, a plan for making changes in their drafts.
3. Students find it easy to learn from acronyms. The editors of *Fortune,* noted for quality reporting and superb prose, encourage their writers to think about DARK (Don't Assume the Reader Knows) and AGO (Acute Grasp of the Obvious) when preparing an article. These acronyms can also alert students to the common problems of inadequate support and trite information.
4. Generally it is best to strike a balance between supplying the responses students need in order to develop, on the one hand, and increasing their responsibility over their own work, on the other. To achieve this goal, you could have students revise a draft before they receive any feedback.

CLASSROOM ACTIVITIES

1. You might take the lead and show students how to mark up a draft while revising.
2. Before students revise their own drafts, have the class apply revision guidelines to sample drafts similar to the ones students will write.

CLASSROOM ACTIVITIES

1. Before students begin to read the FACT analysis of this essay, you might have them complete their own FACT sheet. Then have the class (perhaps in small groups) compare their analyses to the text analysis.
2. Have students candidly state their feelings about all the changes this draft is undergoing. Many will be discouraged by all the work, but they should recognize that if this draft can be salvaged, almost anyone's writing can be improved (one of the reasons we use this realistic example).

promises? First drafts often include paragraphs, or even large sections, that have little bearing on the main point. Some drafts contain the kernels of several different essays. Furthermore, one section of a draft might be geared to one audience (parents, for example) and another section to an entirely different audience (students, perhaps). As you read each part, verify its connection to your purpose and audience. Don't hesitate to chop out sections that don't fit, redo stray parts so they accord with your central idea, or alter your thesis statement to reflect better your supporting material. Occasionally, you might even expand one small, fertile section of your draft into an entirely new essay.

A. Whenever we write first drafts, we unwittingly leave out essential material. As we revise, we need to identify and fill these gaps. Ask yourself: "Where will the reader need more information or examples to understand my message?" Then *ADD* the appropriate sentences, paragraphs, or even pages.

C. First drafts often contain material that fits the thesis but doesn't contribute to the essay. Writing quickly, we tend to repeat ourselves, include uninteresting or uninformative examples, and crank out whole paragraphs when one clear sentence would suffice. As you revise, *CUT* away this clutter with a free hand. Such paring can be painful, especially if you're left with a skimpy text, but your message will emerge with much greater clarity. As you've probably guessed, revising a draft often requires both adding and cutting.

T. Carefully *TEST* the organization of your essay. The text should flow smoothly from point to points with clear transitions between the various ideas. Test the organization by outlining your major and minor points, then checking the results for logic and completeness. Alternatively, read the draft and note its progression. Look for spots where you can clarify connections between words and thus help your readers.

Chapters 4–12 explain nine different writing strategies, each concluding with revision questions geared specifically to that strategy. Use these questions, together with the *FACT* of revision, to help you revise more effectively.

CASE HISTORY ■   *(Continued from page 33)*

   Now let's apply the *FACT* approach to the first draft of George's Mt. Pleasant essay, which you read on pages 31–33. As we indicated there, the draft needs extensive work.

   FIT. Much of George's draft doesn't fit his high school audience. Most of these students won't care about Mt. Pleasant being the oil capital of Michigan, won't be able to attend "End-of-the-World Parties" (which some will find distasteful), and won't have money for fine dining or nightclubs, even assuming they would be admitted. How then to proceed? George has two choices: target his intended audience more accurately or change it entirely. Either decision requires drastic revisions.

   ADD. Assuming George keeps his high school audience, he needs to expand the essay at several points. As things stand, he offers only skimpy details about the water activities and never indicates where the different attractions are located or why the mall is appealing. These shortcomings must be corrected and other attractions introduced and discussed—for example, affordable places for teens to eat. Another audience would of course require different additions.

CUT. With cutting as with adding, audience determines what parts of the essay go and what parts stay. For high schoolers, George should drop any mention of Mt. Pleasant's oil status, "End-of-the-World Parties," and nightclubs. Similarly, fine dining has no place in the essay except perhaps as something reserved for special occasions. For a different audience, some of the sections mentioned under ADD might be deleted.

TEST. The introduction suggests that the essay will first discuss parties, then recreation spots and places to dine, and finally places to shop. However, the body reverses the order of the last two, and the conclusion summarizes these features in a different order. Such false signals only confuse a reader. George also errs in opening with "End-of-the-World Parties," which could cause some readers to react negatively. The essay does flow well from point to point although too many paragraphs begin with "If you."

Without question, George's essay requires considerable work, whatever audience he chooses. After weighing his choices, he elects to stay with teenagers and zero in on Mt. Pleasant as a summer fun spot.

TEACHING STRATEGY

You may encounter a few students who become so involved in revising that they fail to complete a final draft. Probably they are confused about the nature of revision or subconsciously fear having their draft evaluated. Show them this gravestone and caption, which we saw many years ago and never forgot.

As you read your own essay, note on a separate sheet of paper problems to solve, ideas to add, and changes to try. When you mark the actual essay, make your job easier by using these simple techniques.

1. To delete something, cross it out lightly; you may decide to resurrect it later.
2. To add a section of text, place a letter (A, B, C, D) at the appropriate spot and write the new material on a separate sheet, keyed to the letter. Make changes within sections by crossing out what you don't want and writing the replacement above it or nearby.
3. To rearrange the organization, draw arrows showing where you want things to go, or cut up your draft and rearrange the sections by taping them on new sheets of paper. Use whatever method works best for you.

CASE HISTORY ■ *(Continued from page 36)*

After setting his draft aside for a couple of days, George revises it carefully. The original draft, showing deleted material, some added information, and a series of letters that mark where other new material should go, appears on pages 38 and 40. The other new material, keyed to the letters on the draft, appears on facing pages.

Mt. Pleasant

Welcome to Mt Pleasant, the home of Central
Michigan University and the oil capital of this state.
You have chosen the right town to visit because there are
so many things for a high school student here. There are
parties, great recreation spots, fine places to dine, and
excellent shopping.

(A)

I am sure you have all heard of Mt. Pleasant's
famous "End-of-the-World Parties," which have been
featured in nationwide news stories. These parties are a
riot, both literally and figuratively. At the end of the
school year, all the CMU students gather on fraternity
row to celebrate the start of summer. For blocks and
blocks, the streets are filled to overflowing with people
pushing their way along with drinks in their hands to yet
another bash. It is probably one of the rowdiest parties
you could attend. People do all kinds of crazy things
including climbing on rooftops and burning couches in the
street. There was even one party-goer who stripped naked.
That's what I call rowdy.

If you ~~are not into partying, maybe a mellow day on~~ like to swim or just lie on the beach, just a few miles west of
Mt. Pleasant off Beal City Road
~~the beach would do you some good. There~~ is beautiful ~~lake~~
~~called~~ Cold Water Lake ~~that has~~ with its crystal clear water and a
surrounded by hills and woods.
scenic beach, This beach is the "hit spot" on a sunny day. You
can always find a volleyball game to join; or you can simply throw around a
~~so~~ you will want to be there. frisbee, do some boy or girl watching, or
just bask in the sun. The swimming, of course,
is great.
If you're out for some wet-n-wild swimming fun,
just down the road from Cold Water Lake,
then Lake Isabella Dam, is the place for you. The ~~is~~ a huge dam forms

slippery slide about a hundred yards long pitched at a
You can a whole
160-degree angle. ~~One could~~ spend ~~all~~ day there and not

get bored of sliding away.
If you want to stay closer to town,
~~After swimming,~~ you ~~could~~ can go to Island Park in the
off Main Street.
center of town, This park is unique because it is

38

A.   If you get tired of driving out to the same old Lake
        Michigan beach this summer, you might think about giving
        Mt. Pleasant a try for something different. The Mt.
        Pleasant area offers swimming, canoeing, and hiking; a
        chance to get together with other teens; horse and auto
        racing; a college campus to wander around; movies,
        museums, video games, and shopping for rainy days; and
        lots of places to eat. What more can you ask for?

B.   Canoeing can be great fun. Near the Mt. Pleasant
        area there are a number of scenic rivers that are a
        delight to canoe. There is the Chippewa River, the Cold
        Water River, the north and south branches of the Salt
        River, and further to the west the exciting white-water
        Pine River. Near or on each river are places that rent
        canoes at a reasonable rate and even provide you with
        transportation from your destination back to your cars.

        For those of you who like to hike, Deerfield Park, a
        few miles west of town on M-20, provides 25 miles of
        nature trails. These secluded trails that meander
        through a natural forest and gentle, rolling hills can be
        a great place to take someone special for a quiet stroll.
        You will be sure to spot a variety of birds as well as
        squirrels, raccoons, and chipmunks. If you are really
        lucky, you might even spot a deer or two. Closer to town,
        on Harris Street, Mission Creek Woodland Park offers 60
        acres of forest trails, a creek, and picnicking area.

C.   For those of you who will be going to college in a
        few years, you might want to take the time to wander
        around the Central Michigan University campus and try
        college on for size. Its ivy-covered brick buildings and
        tree-lined walkways give you the feel of real college
        life. When summer semester is in session, you might also

surrounded by a river that flows around it; it is Mt.

Pleasant's own Island of Paradise. There are many

activities at the park including live bands, small

gatherings, and baseball games. This park is the main

hangout for teens in Mt. Pleasant, *so you will always find something to do. If you want a break, nearby* ~~For the children, there~~ is also Nelson Park which has a small zoo with bear,

deer, badger, and many other kinds of North American

Wildlife.

If you are a person who likes to shop, then you will

want to visit the Mt. Pleasant Mall at the edge of twon.

It has all the convenience stores necessary for a

fulfilling day of shoping. There is always plenty of

parking. (C)

If you are looking for something different, on Mission Road ~~Mt. Pleasant also has places for those of you who~~ *north of M-20,* ~~like to gamble.~~ Mt. Pleasant Meadows has fun-filled, *For only $2.00, you can enjoy the suspense of cheering your favorite to victory.*

action-packed horse races all weekend long. There is also

a concession stand, ~~and a bar. The Meadows is just waiting for you to bet and win big.~~

~~If you like horse racing, then~~ You might also enjoy

the car racing at Mt. Pleasant Speedway. On Fridays there

are ~~is~~ high-speed stock car race*s* all night long. So come see

the fast cars, bright lights, and the excitement of

racing waiting for you. ← (D)

Let's not forget about the fine dining Mt. Pleasant

has to offer. There is an elegant restaurant called The

Embers that matches all the fine cuisine in the world.

There is also a Holiday Inn which hosts a class A (E)

restaurant and nightclub. The club is called Boomers and

presents well-known comedians to entertain you

throughout the night.

Mt. Pleasant has much to offer you: ~~fine dining,~~ *swimming, hiking, parks, racing. It is a fun alternative to whatever you are doing this summer.* ~~excitement, and relaxation,~~ Why not come and see for

yourself.

want to stroll through a few buildings, look around the library, and visit the bookstore. If you stop to watch students bustle to class, you could be watching your own future.

D.   On rainy days, there is still a lot to do in Mt. Pleasant. There are several multi-screened movie theaters that give you a choice of the most recent releases. You can also engage in a little time travel at the Center for Cultural and Natural History in Rowe Hall on the CMU campus. This museum includes lumbering tools, Civil War artifacts, a variety of household items from different historical periods, and an exhibit of wildlife, including the remains of a mastodon. You can play video games at the Royal Oasis Family Amusement Center in the campus mall on Mission Street. Or you can spend some time shopping.

E.   Because Mt. Pleasant is a college town, there are a number of great cheap places to eat. The McDonald's on Mission Street is the wildest place to get a Big Mac you will ever see. With fancy chrome palm trees and glossy plastic cutouts of people having a great time, it is like an Art Deco scene. You have to see it to believe it. There are, of course, all the great fast-food places and pizza shops. If you are interested in taking a date to some place special and don't mind spending a little money in the process, you might try The Embers, a restaurant rated as "one of Michigan's finest." When you are looking for a place to eat in Mt. Pleasant, you have many great choices.

Case history continues on page 47.

Although this draft is not perfect, George's revisions have considerably improved the paper. He does, however, have more to do. (The final, polished version of the essay appears on pages 48–51.) Never stop revising your work until you are completely satisfied with the results.

"NOW THAT WE'VE BOILED YOUR PAPER DOWN TO THE RELEVANT MATERIAL, I THINK YOU'RE READY TO RE-WRITE."

Reprinted by permission of Richard N. Bibler.

EXERCISE ■   List George's other options for revising this draft; then indicate the necessary changes if he had decided to write for readers between the ages of thirty-five and forty-five.

EXERCISE ■ Use the FACT acronym to revise the draft you prepared for the exercise on page 30.

STRENGTHENING PARAGRAPH STRUCTURE AND DEVELOPMENT

Once you finish considering the essay as a whole, examine your paragraphs one by one, applying the *FACT* approach that you used for the whole paper. Make sure each paragraph *FITS* the paper's major focus and develops a single central idea. If a paragraph needs more support or examples, *ADD* whatever is necessary. If a paragraph contains ineffective or unhelpful material, *CUT* it. *TEST* the flow of ideas from paragraph to paragraph and clarify connections, both between and within paragraphs, as necessary. Ask the basic questions in the checklist that follows about each paragraph, and make any needed revisions.

REVISION CHECKLIST FOR PARAGRAPHS ■

■ Does the paragraph have one, and only one, central idea?
■ Does the central idea help to develop the thesis statement?
■ Does each statement within the paragraph help to develop the central idea?
■ Does the paragraph need additional explanations, examples, or supporting details?
■ Would cutting some material make the paragraph stronger?
■ Would reorganization make the ideas easier to follow?
■ Can the connections between successive sentences be improved?
■ Is each paragraph clearly and smoothly related to those that precede and follow it?

Don't expect to escape making any changes; some readjustments will undoubtedly be needed. Certain paragraphs may be stripped down or deleted, others beefed up, still others reorganized or repositioned. Chapter 14 contains more information on writing effective paragraphs.

EXERCISE ■ Here are three sample student paragraphs. Evaluate each according to the Revision Checklist for Paragraphs and suggest any necessary changes.

1.   I can remember so many times when my father had said
    that he was coming to pick me up for a day or two. I was
    excited as a young boy could be at the thought of seeing my
    father. With all the excitement and anticipation raging

2. This paragraph, touching briefly on several different ideas, is in reality the skeleton of a short paper that needs fleshing out with more details. The writer should explain the reasons for her indecision, tell what she had to gain by joining the team, add a more descriptive account of the tryouts and selection process, and redo the conclusion. What did she do when her name was finally read? What did she feel? "More than happy" doesn't say much. What would being selected have meant to her?

3. This paragraph seems to have one basic idea (the hikers making a dash for "it"), but the sentences are not clearly connected. For example, "Earlier in the day it had been a perfectly clear day" is out of logical order. Furthermore, additional information about the rainstorm, which is implied but never discussed, is obviously needed.

Possible Revision

For hours we had been waiting under the overhang of an abandoned hut while the rain poured down. Earlier in the day it had been perfectly clear, so none of us had brought ponchos on our short hike through the woods. The downpour had caught us unprepared. We had thought it would let up as sudden storms usually do, but no relief was in sight. Worse, it would soon be dark. None of us wanted to stand there all night, so we didn't have much choice. Even if we were going to get thoroughly soaked, we had to make a dash for the car.

PERSPECTIVE

Many students think sentences and words are revised only to correct errors. They should understand that their sentence structure and word choice can

inside of me, I would wait on the front porch. Minutes would seem like hours as I would wait impatiently.

2.   Going to high school for the first time, I couldn't decide if I should try out for the team or wait for the next year. Since I had time and I had been on other squads, I decided ''why not.'' I had nothing to lose but a lot to gain. Tryouts were not as hard as I thought, but I just knew I had to be on the squad. The tryout consisted of learning the routine they made up, making up your own routine, doing splits, and making a chant. Yet although these things were not that hard, I still was not sure whether I would make the team or not. The time came for the judges to make their decisions on who made the squad. Totaling the votes, they handed the results to the coach. She gave her speech that all coaches give. We were all good, but only a few could be picked for the team. As she started to read the names, I got hot. When she called my name, I was more than happy.

3.   For hours we had been waiting under the overhang of an abandoned hut. None of us had thought to bring ponchos on our short hike through the woods. Soon it would be dark. Earlier in the day it had been a perfectly clear day. We all agreed that we didn't want to stand here all night in the dark, so we decided to make a dash for it.

SHARPENING SENTENCES AND WORDS

Next, turn your attention to sentences and words. You can improve your writing considerably by finding and correcting sentences that convey the wrong meaning or are stylistically deficient in some way. Consider, for example, the following sentences.

Just Mary was picked to write the report.
Mary was just picked to write the report.
Mary was picked to write just the report.

The first sentence says that no one except Mary will write the report, the second says that she was recently picked for the job, and the third says that she will write nothing else. Clearly, each of these sentences expresses a different meaning.

Now let's look at a second set of sentences.

> Personally, I am of the opinion that the results of our membership drive will prove to be pleasing to all of us.
>
> I believe the results of our membership drive will please all of us.

The wordiness of the first sentence slows the reader's pace and makes it harder to grasp the writer's meaning. The second sentence, by contrast, is much easier to grasp.

Like your sentences, your words should also convey your thoughts precisely and clearly. Words are, after all, your chief means of communicating with your reader. Examine the first draft and revised version of the following paragraph, which describe the early morning actions of the writer's roommate. The italicized words identify points of revision.

■ **First Draft**

> Coffee cup in hand, she _moves_ toward the bathroom. The coffee spills _noisily_ on the tile floor as she _reaches_ for the light switch and _turns_ it on. After _looking_ briefly at the face in the mirror, she _walks_ toward the bathtub.

■ **Revised Version**

> Coffee cup in hand, she _stumbles_ toward the bathroom. The coffee she spills on the tile floor makes _a slapping sound_ as she _gropes_ for the light switch and _flips_ it on. After _squinting_ briefly at the face in the mirror, she _shuffles_ toward the bathtub.

Note that the words in the first draft are general and imprecise. Exactly how does she move? With a limp? With a strut? With a spring in her step? And what does "noisily" mean? A thud? A roar? A sharp crack? The reader has no way of knowing. Recognizing this fact, the student revised her paragraph, substituting vivid, specific words. As a result, the reader can visualize the actions more sharply.

Don't confuse vivid, specific words with "jawbreaker words"—those that are complex and pretentious. (Most likely all of the words in the revised version are in your vocabulary.) Words should promote communication, not block it.

usually be improved so as to have greater impact on readers. On the other hand, students must keep this level of revision in its place—as a type of polish applied after the body work of major revision has been completed.

TEACHING STRATEGIES

1. If you take up the different sentence strategies discussed in Chapter 15, you might have students select several sentences from their text and rewrite them using the different strategies.

2. Because students have different abilities, some teachers prefer to identify each one's problems on his or her draft rather than addressing such matters in the classroom.

CLASSROOM ACTIVITIES

1. Have students exchange papers and circle sentences that seem ineffective. The writer could then prepare several improved versions of each.

2. Have students circle vague or ineffective words in their own drafts or those of others and then develop a list of possible substitutes.

3. Use examples from your own writing to demonstrate how you might revise a sentence. Put the changes on the board and explain why each was made.

4. Provide students with several versions of the same sentence. Have them rank the sentences according to effectiveness and explain their decisions.

REVISION CHECKLIST FOR SENTENCES ▪

▌ What sentences are not clearly expressed or logically constructed?
▌ What sentences seem awkward, excessively convoluted, or lacking in punch?
▌ What words require explanation or substitution because the reader may not know them?
▌ Where does my writing become wordy or use vague terms?
▌ Where have I carelessly omitted words or mistakenly used the wrong word?

EXERCISE ANSWER
See the suggested rewrite, answer 1, page 43.

Chapters 15 and 16 discuss sentences and words in detail.

**SUGGESTED
INSTRUCTOR READING**

Christensen, F., ed. The Sentence and the Paragraph. Urbana, IL: NCTE, 1963. Includes not only an account of the generative sentence and paragraph but provides excellent examples of revised paragraphs and sentences.

EXERCISE ▪   Reread exercise paragraph 1 on pages 43—44 and revise the sentence structure and word choice to create a more effective paragraph.

PROOFREADING YOUR DRAFT

TEACHING STRATEGIES
1. It usually pays dividends if you allow five to ten minutes of class time for one final proofreading, perhaps to look for sentence errors. Make it clear that you expect the other proofreading to be done outside class.
2. Make sure students know that errors will be penalized and just how severe the penalty will be.
3. Encourage students to use the Personal Revision Checklist on the inside back cover of the text to record any errors they discover.

After revising your draft, proofread or edit it to correct errors in grammar, punctuation, and spelling. Since we often overlook our own errors simply because we know what we meant, proofreading can be difficult. Inch through your draft deliberately, moving your finger along slowly under every word. Repeat this procedure several times, looking first for errors in grammar, then for sentence errors and problems in punctuation and mechanics, and finally for mistakes in spelling. Be especially alert for problems that have plagued your writing in the past.

When you finish proofreading your draft, you might want to team up with one or more classmates and read one another's work critically. The fresh eye you bring to the task can uncover shortcomings that would otherwise go unnoticed. Pages 52–61 discuss peer editing in detail.

Effective proofreading calls for you to assume a detective role and probe for errors that weaken your writing. If you accept the challenge, you will certainly improve the quality of your finished work.

WRITING THE INTRODUCTION AND CONCLUSION

If you've put off writing your introduction, do it now. Generally, short papers begin with a single paragraph that includes the previously drafted thesis statement, which sometimes needs to be rephrased so that it meshes smoothly with the rest of the paragraph. The introduction acquaints the reader with your topic; it should clearly signal your intention as well as spark the reader's interest. Pages 208–210 discuss and illustrate effective introductions.

The conclusion wraps up your discussion. Generally a single paragraph in short papers, a good ending summarizes or supports the paper's main idea. Pages 211–214 discuss and illustrate effective conclusions.

SELECTING A TITLE

All essays require titles. Unless a good title unexpectedly surfaces while you are writing, wait until you finish the paper before choosing one. Since the reader must see the connection between what the title promises and what the essay delivers, a good title must be both accurate and specific.

Titling the Mt. Pleasant essay "Shopping in Mt. Pleasant" would mislead the reader, as shopping is mentioned only briefly. A specific title suggests the essay's focus rather than just its topic. For example, "Teenage Fun in Mt. Pleasant" is clearer and more precise than simply "Mt. Pleasant." The essay is geared to teenage activities, not a description of the city as a whole.

To engage your reader's interest, you might try your hand at a clever or catchy title, but don't get so carried away with creativity that you forget to relate the title to the paper's content. Here are some examples of common and clever titles:

Common	"Handling a Hangover"
Clever	"The Mourning After"
Common	"Buying Your Home with Other People's Money"
Clever	"Home Free"

Use a clever title only if its wit or humor doesn't clash with the overall purpose and tone of the paper.

CASE HISTORY ■ *(Concluded)*

After carefully proofreading and fine tuning the second draft of his Mt. Pleasant essay, George prepares the final version, which follows. Margin notes highlight key changes. Compare the revised and final versions to see how these changes have improved the essay.

General title made specific

Slightly rearranged listing
reflects organization of
essay

First sentence rephrased
and divided into two to
avoid repeated "if you"
paragraph openings and
lessen awkwardness

Last sentence reworded to
lessen awkwardness

Paragraph rewritten to
liven and add variety to
phrasing

Teenage Fun in Mt. Pleasant

If you get tired of driving out to the same old
Lake Michigan beach this summer, you might think about
trying Mt. Pleasant for something different. The Mt.
Pleasant area offers swimming, canoeing, and hiking; a
city park where you can socialize with other teens; a
college campus to wander around; horse and auto racing;
movies, a museum, video games, and shopping for a rainy
day; and many places to eat. What more can you ask?

For swimming or merely lying on the beach, you
can't beat Cold Water Lake, just a few miles west of Mt.
Pleasant off Beal City Road. This lake boasts crystal
clear water and a scenic beach surrounded by hills and
woods. Here you can always find a volleyball game to
join, throw a frisbee around, do some boy or girl
watching, or bask in the sun. The swimming, of course,
is great.

If you prefer some wet-and-wild swimming fun,
then Lake Isabella Dam, a short drive down the road from
Cold Water Lake, is the place for you. The dam forms a
slippery slide about 100 yards long which is pitched at
a 160-degree angle. You can spend a whole day there and
not get bored with sliding.

Canoeing can be wonderful fun, and the Mt.
Pleasant area offers a number of rivers that will
delight anyone who likes this activity. If you prefer
calm-water canoeing, you can try the Chippewa River,
the Cold Water River, or the north or south branches of
the Salt River. If your taste runs to the exciting

white-water variety, you will find the Pine River made
to order. Near or on each river are places that rent
canoes at reasonable rates and even provide you with
transportation from your destination back to your car.

For anyone who likes to hike, Deerfield Park, a
few miles west of town on M-20, provides 25 miles of
nature trails. These secluded trails that meander
through a natural forest and gentle, rolling hills can
be a fine place to take someone special for a quiet
stroll. You will no doubt see a variety of birds as well
as squirrels, raccoons, and chipmunks. If you're
really lucky, you might spot a deer or two. Closer to
town, on Harris Street, Mission Creek Woodland Park
offers 60 acres of forest trails, a creek, and a
picnicking area.

> "fine place" substituted because "great" overused in essay. "see" substituted to avoid using "spot" twice

Island Park, located in the Pine River just off
Main Street, offers you a chance to meet other
teenagers without going out of town. Here you can
listen to live bands, play or watch baseball games,
have picnics, or just get together and talk. This park
is the main hangout for Mt. Pleasant teens, so you
should have no trouble making new friends. Nearby is
Nelson Park, which has a small zoo where you can see
deer, bear, badger, and many other kinds of local
wildlife.

> Paragraph rewritten to avoid "if you" opening, liven and tighten phrasing. Opportunity to make friends added.

Planning to attend college? If you are, then you
might want to spend some time wandering around the
Central Michigan University campus and giving it a
close look. Strolling past ivy-covered buildings and
along tree-lined walkways will give you the feel of

> Opening reworded to eliminate cliché and liven phrasing

real college life. When summer semester is in session, you might also want to walk through a few buildings, look around the library, and visit the bookstore. If you stop to watch students bustle to class, you could be watching your own future.

To sample something different, pay a visit to Mt. Pleasant Meadows on Mission Road north of M-20 some weekend and enjoy the fun-filled, action-packed horse races you'll find there. For just two dollars, you can enjoy the thrill of cheering your favorite to victory. The Mt. Pleasant Speedway offers you the chance to sample a second kind of racing. Each Friday the speedway puts on a night-long program of high-speed stock car races. Fast horses or fast cars—either ensures you an evening of high excitement.

On rainy days, you can still find much to do in Mt. Pleasant. Several multi-screen movie theaters give you a choice of the most recent releases. You can also do a little time traveling at the Center for Cultural and Natural History in Rowe Hall on the college campus. This museum includes lumbering tools, Civil War artifacts, a variety of household items from different historical periods, and an exhibit of wildlife, including the remains of a mastodon. You can play video games at the Royal Oasis Family Amusement Center in the campus mall on Mission Street. Or you can spend some time shopping for clothing, books, records, or gifts in the many mall stores.

Mt. Pleasant has a wide range of great eating

First two sentences reworded and combined to avoid "if you" opening and tighten phrasing

Third sentence made smoother

Final sentence replaced to strengthen ending

First two sentences rewritten to liven phrasing

Final sentence: types of shopping added

places. The McDonald's on Mission Street is the most

striking place to get a Big Mac that you will probably

ever see. With fancy chrome palm trees and glossy

plastic cutouts of people having a good time, it

resembles an Art Deco movie set. There are, of course,

many other fast-food places such as Arby's, Burger

King, Taco Bell, Kentucky Fried Chicken, and Little

Caesar's. If you are interested in taking a date to some

place special and don't mind spending the money to do

it, you might try The Embers, a restaurant rated as

''one of Michigan's finest.'' There you'll find cloth

napkins and tablecloths, soft lights, and a menu

offering an outstanding selection of meat and seafood.

Your date will be sure to like it.

    Mt. Pleasant offers enough recreational choices

to satisfy any teenager. Why not come and investigate

for yourself?

> Word "cheap" omitted; Embers restaurant expensive. "wildest" replaced with "most striking" for more accuracy

> Other fast-food restaurants named

> Details about Embers added

> Weak ending sentence replaced with stronger one

> Conclusion changed to reiterate audience

It is crucial that you view revision not as a hasty "touch up" job or as a quick sweep through your draft just prior to handing it in. Instead, revision should be an ongoing process that often involves an upheaval of major sections as you see your draft through your reader's eyes and strive to write as well as you can. Only when you reach that summit have you finished revising.

REVISING WITH A WORD PROCESSOR

Many writers prefer the advantages of revising on a word processor. All word-processing programs allow you to write over unwanted sections of your draft, add new information, delete useless material, and move parts of the text around. Learn all the commands of your particular program and experiment to see exactly what your options are. The following practical tips will improve your efficiency.

1. Always keep a backup copy of everything. Accidentally erasing a file or losing your work to an electrical power surge is not uncommon. In addition, save

PERSPECTIVE

Word processors make revising easier. Research demonstrates that students who use them are more likely to revise. The changes, however, may not always be wise. Students entranced with the block-move command often move chunks of text without integrating them into the body of the draft, thus creating a very disjointed essay. Other students add or delete material without adjusting the surrounding material. Some students keep back-spacing and reworking sentences until those sentences become incoherent. Sometimes previous sections are integrated with revised sections or notes are left in the draft. In some cases it is evident that the scope of the revision equals the amount of material that fills the screen at any given time.

TEACHING STRATEGIES

1. Ask students to perform at least the final revision on a printout.
2. If your school has a computer lab, show students how to use the word-processing program for revision. Many students have limited knowledge of this operation. Direct them to open a new file for one of their paragraphs, draft several versions, and then reinsert the best one into their draft.
3. In the lab you can enter your comments directly onto the student's disk. Some programs allow you to create a margin for your comments. With others, you simply insert the comments into the text. These practices make your comments rather difficult to ignore.
4. If you collect drafts with the final paper, insist in advance that students using a word processor print out copies of early drafts. Otherwise, early drafts will vanish as students make their changes.

PERSPECTIVE

Peer groups can accomplish several important things. First, providing readers other than the instructor helps students understand that what they produce are public documents—not private

copies of your earlier drafts, either as printouts or on disk; selected parts may prove useful later, and new papers sometimes sprout from old drafts. You can either save each draft under variations of your file name—"COPY A, COPY B, COPY C"—or keep deleted sections in specially labeled files.

2. Jot down helpful ideas or comments in your text as you revise. Enclose them with a special symbol, such as < >, and either save them in a separate file or delete them later if they serve no purpose.

3. If you struggle with a section of the text, write two or three versions and then pick your favorite. You might even open a new file, experiment freely, and then use the best version in your draft.

4. Don't allow the program to control how you revise. The easy-to-use, gentle-touch keyboards can lull you into a lapse of judgment and cause you to forget whether your words are worth writing. Pages of worthless material could pile up. Furthermore, don't be tempted to do what the commands make easiest: fiddle endlessly with sentences and words, never develop the essay as a whole, and move blocks of writing around indiscriminately. Avoid being electronically bewitched and make only those additions and changes that improve your writing.

5. Always revise using a printout. If you use just the computer, you are limited to only one screen at a time. A printed page has a different look. In addition, a printout allows you to compare several pages at once: you can see, for example, how the second paragraph might be more effective if repositioned on page 4.

6. When you finish revising, check the coherence of your draft. The writing must flow smoothly at the points where you have added, deleted, or moved sections of text. In addition, altered sentences must be clearly written and logically constructed. You can best check the essay's flow with a printout.

7. Proofreading with a word processor poses certain dangers. For example, a spelling check function can't judge whether you used the wrong word (*form* instead of *from*) or confused identical sounding but differently spelled words (their, there, they're). Furthermore, the unit will sometimes flag words that are not misspelled but are simply not in the computer's list. In addition, there are few good programs to check grammar or punctuation. *You* are still the ultimate proofreader.

PEER EVALUATION OF DRAFTS

At various points in the writing process, your instructor may ask you and your classmates to read and respond to one another's papers. Peer response often proves useful because even the best writers cannot always predict how their readers will react to their writing. For example, magazine articles designed to reduce the fear of AIDS have, in some cases, increased anxiety about the disease. Furthermore, we often have difficulty seeing the problems with our own drafts because so much hard work has gone into them. What seems clear and effective to us can be confusing or boring to our readers. Comments from our peers can frequently launch a more effective essay.

Just as the responses of others help you, so will your responses help them. You don't have the close, involved relationship with your peers' writing that you do with your own. Therefore, you can gauge their drafts objectively. This type of critical evaluation will eventually heighten your awareness of your own writing strengths and weaknesses. And knowing how to read your own work critically is one of the most important writing skills you can develop.

Responding to Your Peer's Drafts

Responding to someone else's writing is easier than you might imagine. It's not your job to spell out ways to make the draft more effective, how to organize it, what to include, and the type of language to use. The writer must make these decisions. Your job is to *identify* problems, *not solve* them. You can do that best by responding honestly to the draft.

Some responses are more helpful than others. You don't help the writer by casually observing that the draft "looks O.K." Such a response doesn't point to problem areas; rather it suggests that you didn't read the paper carefully and critically. Wouldn't you inform a friend who was wearing clothes that looked terrible *why* they looked terrible? The same attitude should prevail about the writing of others, something that makes a statement just as clothes do. Nor is a vague comment such as "the introduction is uninteresting" helpful. Point out *why* it is uninteresting. For instance, you might note that "The introduction doesn't interest me in the paper because it is very technical, and I get lost. I ask myself why I should read on." Below are two more examples of ineffective responses and their more effective counterparts.

Ineffective

The paper was confusing.

Effective

Paragraphs 2, 3, and 4 confused me. You jumped around too much. First you wrote about your experience on the first day of college, then you went on to how much you enjoyed junior high school, and finally you wrote about what you want to do for a career. I don't see how these ideas relate or why they are in the order that they are.

letters to their instructors. Furthermore, it is gratifying for students to learn that they can communicate. When peers identify problems, writers see that such matters are not simply instructor concerns but actually affect communication. For those acting as peer readers, a critical response to another person's paper helps develop the kind of eye they can eventually apply to their own writing. Often students detect a problem in someone else's paper and then recognize that they have the same problem. Peer groups can be a helpful teaching tool, but they won't work brilliantly on the first attempt. It will take several papers for students to acclimate. Peer groups can be used throughout the revision process. In the first stages of drafting, they can provide sympathetic readers for writers trying to figure out what they want to say and also help writers chart their course. Once a rough draft is finished, peer groups can identify its strengths and problems.

TEACHING STRATEGIES

1. For peer groups to work, students must know how to evaluate papers. You might first demonstrate on a sample draft, focusing on how a reader would honestly respond. Next, ask students to respond individually to a sample draft and then discuss their comments. Finally, have peer groups judge samples and discuss these judgments in class. **2.** You can set up peer groups in different ways. If students form their own groups, those of like ability might join together, as might friends, who could be reluctant to respond critically to each other's papers. Alternatively, you could organize the groups so that different levels of ability are represented, making sure that every strong writer is matched with another strong writer who can provide effective responses. Groups of three to five participants are best.

3. You can direct groups to respond in different ways. Some instructors prefer to have the writer read the paper aloud and "readers" respond orally. Oral responses, however, often cause student minds to wander, and most writers forget the comments. Another alternative is to have students exchange papers and respond in writing. This procedure reinforces the importance of written communication, allows students more time to reflect on their response, provides more responses, and establishes a written record of the responses.

4. Just as you can guide students to respond generally to a draft, you can also guide peer responses by posing a set of specific questions, similar to the revision questions in each chapter, which are keyed to particular features of the assignment.

5. To prevent students from ignoring peer responses, have all writers review the comments they receive, prepare a written plan that incorporates them, and turn in peer responses along with their revised draft.

6. You may have to speak to students who are not making an effort to provide quality peer responses.

**SUGGESTED
INSTRUCTOR READINGS**

Bruffee, K. "Peer Tutoring and the 'Conversation of Mankind.'" Writing Center. Ed. Gary Olsen. Urbana, IL: NCTE, 1984. 3–15. Argues that peer tutors can, in some cases, be more effective than the instructor.
Using Student Writing Response Groups in the Classroom. Curriculum Publication no. 12. Berkeley: Bay Area Writing Project, U of California P, 1980.

Ineffective

More examples would help.

Effective

When you indicate that college can be a scary place, I get no real idea of why or how. What are the things that you think make college scary? I would like some examples.

Here are some steps to follow when responding to someone else's draft. First, read the essay from beginning to end without interruption. On a separate sheet of paper, indicate what you consider the main idea. The writer can then see whether the intended message has come through. Next, identify the biggest problem and the biggest strength. Writers need both negative and positive comments. Finally, reread the paper and write either specific responses to each paragraph or your responses to general questions such as the ones that follow. In either case, don't comment on spelling or grammar unless it really inhibits your reading.

PEER RESPONSE CHECKLIST ■

- What is the main point of this essay?
- What is the biggest problem?
- What is the biggest strength?
- What material doesn't seem to fit the main point or the audience?
- What questions has the author not answered?
- Where should more details or examples be added? Why?
- At what point does the paper fail to hold my interest? Why?
- Where is organization confusing?
- Where is the writing unclear or vague?

As you learn the various strategies for successful writing, new concerns will arise. Questions geared to these concerns appear in the revision section that concludes the discussion of each strategy.

An Example of Peer Response

The following is the first draft of a student essay and a partial peer response to it. The response features three of the nine general questions and also comments on one paragraph. Before you read the response, try evaluating this essay yourself and then compare your reactions to those of the other student.

Captive Breeding in Zoos

This paper is about captive breeding. Today,   1
humans hinder nature's species right to survive. Man is
making it hard for over one hundred species of animals
to continue to exist. But captive breeding in the
worlds zoos may be just what the doctor ordered. This
rescue attempt is a complex and difficult undertaking.
Captive breeding of endangered species is complicated
by the special social and physical requirements of
individual species.

There are many social problems that have to be   2
solved for the successful reproduction of endangered
species in zoos. Mating is one of the most important of
these problems. One propagation "must" for many
felines, pandas, and pygmy hippopotami is the complete
separation of sexes until they're "ready." Leland
Stowe says that cheetahs almost never get together
unless they can't see or smell each other ahead of time.
When females exhibit a certain behavior, they bring on
the male.

Male—female compatibility is a social problem.   3
Great apes seem to be as particular as people in
choosing mates. Stowe tells about an orangutan that
turned a cold shoulder on the females in the National
Zoo located in Washington, D.C. Then they shipped him
to a zoo in Colorado. There, he took up with one of the
females. The curator of the zoo, William Zanten, says
he's "been siring offspring ever since."

Social factors hurt care of infant primates.   4

Sheldon Campbell talks about this in <u>Smithsonian</u>
magazine. He writes about the problems of breeding
golden marmosets. These are monkeys that live in
Brazil. The scientists found that captive-born parents
neglected their young. Sometimes they even killed
them. The problem was due to the fact that the marmosets
had no experience living in a family situation. They
didn't know what to do. Emily Hahn writes about
gorillas in <u>The New Yorker</u>. She says that those raised
by humans make poor mothers. Those raised by dutiful
mothers make good parents.

    The second important stumbling block to   5
successful captive breeding is physical problems.
Ignorance of dietary needs can be bad. Stowe talks
about the captive breeding of gorillas and says that
when this breeding was first getting started, infants
exhibited a very high mortality rate. Then the babies
were given iron and meat protein, the latter rich in
Vitamin B-12. They were sprinkled on bananas, and the
bananas were fed to the babies. The survival rate
markedly improved.

    Animals can be bred more easily if they are in an   6
environment that duplicates that animal's natural
habitat. Hooved and horned animals are an easy job
because of the similarity in terrain and climate of
their natural habitats to zoo habitats. Polar bears are
a lot tougher. Mothers want to be let alone until their
cubs are up and about. Because of this fact, the bears
often kill their babies. Stowe says they solved this
problem by building replicas of arctic ice caves. The

mothers and cubs are left alone until they emerge from
the cave. John Perry, Director of the National Zoo,
said this:

> The world is our zoo--a zoo that must be well-
> managed, its resources carefully husbanded, for
> these are the only resources it can ever have. We
> have appointed ourselves the keepers of this zoo, but
> we cannot live outside its gates. We are of it. Our
> lives are inextricably intertwined with the lives of
> all that live within. Their fate will be ours.

Our endangered species can survive only by nature's
implacable test--sustained births by second and third
generations. It will take decades to reach such a
verdict of success. Thus we can see that captive
breeding is beset by many problems.

What is the main point of this essay?

*I think this paper is saying that the only chance for
endangered species is that they reproduce in zoos
but that it is hard to get them to breed in captivity.*

What is the biggest problem?

*I can't see how each paragraph connects to the main point of
the paper or to each other. They seem disconnected. What
does "Male-Female compatibility is a social problem"
have to do with the problem of reproduction or with
the previous paragraph on mating? Also, there are a number
of very unclear statements that leave me with many
questions. How is man making it hard for over a
hundred species to exist? What do you mean when you
say "almost never get together," "bring on the male," "took
up with," and "an easy job?"*

What is the biggest strength?

I hadn't thought much about this question, so it was something new for me. I liked the examples about specific animals and the problems that they have in captivity. I especially liked the fact that the writer gave me several problems that occur when animals are bred in captivity. The writer didn't oversimplify.

Response to paragraph 4

Do social factors always hurt the care of infant primates? Your statement seems too general. Shouldn't you combine some of your sentences? The first six sentences seem to abruptly jump from one point to the next; the writing is not smooth. How did you get from marmosets to gorillas? The jump confuses me. Also, were the "dutiful mothers" humans or gorillas?

Acting upon Your Peer's Response

Sometimes you need strong nerves to act upon a peer response. You can easily become defensive or discount your reader's comments as foolish. Remember, however, that as a writer you are trying to communicate with your readers, and that means taking seriously the problems they identify. Of course, you decide which responses are appropriate, but even an inappropriate criticism sometimes sets off a train of thought that leads to good ideas for revision.

Examine the revised version of the captive breeding essay which follows and note how some of the peer responses have been taken into account. Clear transition sentences link paragraphs to the thesis statement and to each other. Vague statements identified in the earlier draft have been clarified. In the fourth paragraph the writer connects the discussion of the marmosets to that of the gorillas by changing the order of the two sentences that precede the final one and combining them, thereby identifying poor parenting as the key problem with both kinds of primates. Finally, she indicates what she means by "dutiful mother."

As you read this revised version, carefully examine the margin notes, which highlight key features of the essay.

Captive Breeding: Difficult But Necessary

Today, as in the past, humans encroach upon the
basic right of nature's species to survive. Through
ignorance, oversight, and technological developments,
we are threatening the survival of over one hundred
animal species. Until their environments can be
safeguarded against harmful human intrusion, the last
chance for the threatened species may be captive
breeding in zoos. But this rescue attempt is a complex
and difficult undertaking. In particular, each species
presents social and physical problems that must be
solved if breeding is to succeed.

Among the social problems that complicate
successful reproduction, mating problems loom
especially large. For instance, the male and female of
many feline species must be kept completely separated
until both animals are ready to mate. Leland Stowe,
writing in National Wildlife magazine, notes that
cheetahs almost never mate unless kept where the one
cannot see or smell the other. Once the female shows
signs of receptivity, a male is placed in her cage, and
mating then occurs. Pandas and pygmy hippopotami show
the same behavior.

A related social problem with certain species is
male-female compatibility. Great apes, for instance,
seem to be as particular as human beings in choosing
mates. Stowe relates an amusing case of a male

1

Title: specific and accurate

Introduction: arresting
statement

Thesis statement and
statement of organization

2

Topic sentence with link
to thesis statement

Specific details: problems
with cheetahs

Mention of other species
with mating problems

3

Topic sentence, with link
to preceding paragraph.
Linking device

Specific example: problem with particular orangutan	orangutan that totally spurned the females in the Washington, D.C. National Zoo. Shipped to a zoo in Colorado, he succumbed to the charms of a new face and has, according to curator William Zanten, ''been siring offspring ever since.''

Topic sentence, with link to preceding paragraph

Specific details: problems with marmosets

    Social factors can also imperil proper care of infant primates. In a Smithsonian magazine article, Sheldon Campbell talks about the problems scientists encountered in trying to breed golden marmosets, a species of Brazilian monkey. Early attempts failed because the captive–born parents neglected and sometimes accidentally killed their babies. Observation showed that the problem occurred because the marmosets had no experience living in a family situation——they simply didn't know how to handle their offspring. Gorillas reared by humans may also make poor mothers, reports Emily Hahn in The New Yorker. On the other hand, those reared by dutiful mothers, whether human or gorilla, are usually good parents themselves.

4

Mention of other species with rearing problems

Linking device

Transition sentence: signals switch to discussing physical problems

Topic sentence, with link to transition sentence

Specific details: problems with gorillas

Linking device

    Physical problems rival social problems as stumbling blocks to successful captive breeding. Ignorance of a species' dietary needs, for instance, can have disastrous consequences. Early in the captive breeding of gorillas, infants exhibited a very high mortality rate, Stowe notes. Then meat protein and iron, the former rich in Vitamin B–12, were sprinkled on bananas and fed to the babies. As a result, the survival rate markedly improved.

5

An environment that duplicates a species' natural habitat favors easy propagation. Hooved and horned animals present few breeding problems because the zoo habitats are similar in terrain and climate to their natural habitats. Polar bears, on the other hand, present difficult problems. Unless the mothers have complete privacy until the cubs can get around, they often kill the babies. To prevent this from happening, Stowe says, zoos now construct replicas of arctic ice caves and leave mothers and cubs completely alone until the new family emerges from the cave.

6   Topic sentence

   Linking device

In his book The World's a Zoo John Perry, director of the National Zoo, has spoken of the need to save our endangered species.

7   Conclusion: quotation plus statement reinforcing idea that captive breeding presents difficulties

> The world is our zoo—a zoo that must be well-managed, its resources carefully husbanded, for these are the only resources it can ever have. We have appointed ourselves the keepers of this zoo, but we cannot live outside its gates. We are of it. Our lives are inextricably intertwined with the lives of all that live within. Their fate will be ours.

The difficulty, unfortunately, is as great as the urgency of this problem. Only sustained births by second- and third-generation captive animals can ensure the survival of our endangered species. And it will take decades to achieve the necessary success.

Narratives play an important role in many writing courses for two reasons. First, they offer a convenient launch point since many students find it relatively easy to tell stories about their lives. Second, many occupations require narrative writing. For example, a social worker may prepare a client's case history, a police officer write up a shooting incident, a business manager detail a series of problems with a staff member, a scientist trace the development of a research project.

TEACHING STRATEGIES

1. Have each student bring to class an example of a narrative.
2. You might generate a class discussion that attempts to answer exactly what we gain when we exchange stories about ourselves with others. Some possible answers: (a) the story helps us pull our life into a pattern; (b) hearing about someone else's life gives us perspective on our own; (c) narratives help us understand how other people live; (d) swapping narratives binds us together as a community.
3. To prepare students for writing a narrative, ask them to freewrite in their journals about memorable events in their lives. Emphasize that they include as much detail as possible. These journal entries can become background material for the narrative assignment.
4. You could progress from narratives to types of expository writing. For example, students could write a narrative about what it means to grow up. Then they might write a process essay on the stages of adolescence or a cause-and-effect essay on the problems of growing up.
5. Some students have trouble writing personal narratives because they feel uncomfortable writing about themselves. A number of alternative narrative assignments can work well for such students. They can interview and report on the life of someone else, investigate and trace the development of some professional's career, or narrate a campus or community event.

■ **Chapter 4**

Narration: Relating Events

Clicking off the evening news and padding toward bed, Heloise suddenly glimpsed, out of the corner of her eye, a shadow stretching across the living room floor from under the drawn curtains.

"Wh—who's there?"

No response.

Edging backward toward the phone, her eyes riveted on the shadow, she stammered, "I—I don't have any money."

Still no answer.

Reaching the phone, she gripped the receiver and started to lift it from its cradle. Just then. . . .

Just now you've glimpsed the start of a *narrative*. A narrative relates a series of events. The events may be real—as in histories, biographies, or news stories—or imaginary, as in short stories and novels. The narrative urge stirs in all of us, and like everyone else, you have responded almost from the time you began to talk. As a child, you probably swapped many stories with your friends, recounting an exciting visit to a circus or amusement park or an unusually funny experience with your pet. Today you may tell a friend about the odd happening in your biology laboratory or on the job.

PURPOSE

A narrative, like any other kind of writing, makes a point or has a purpose. The point can either be stated or left unstated, but it always shapes the writing.

Some narratives simply tell what happened or establish an interesting or useful fact. The reporter who writes about a heated city council meeting or a lively congressional committee hearing usually wants only to set facts before the public.

Most narratives, however, go beyond merely reciting events. Writers of history and biography delve into the motives underlying the events and lives they portray, while narratives of personal experience offer lessons and insights. In the following conclusion to a narrative about an encounter with a would-be mugger, the writer offers an observation on self-respect.

> I kept my self-respect, even at the cost of dirtying my fists with violence, and I feel that I understand the Irish and the Cypriots, the Israelis and the Palestinians, all those who seem to us to fight senseless wars for senseless reasons, better than before. For what respect does one keep for oneself if one isn't in the last resort ready to fight and say, "You punk!"?

> Harry Fairlie, "A Victim Fights Back"

ACTION

Action plays a central role in any narrative. Other writing often only suggests action, leaving readers to imagine it for themselves:

> A hundred thousand people were killed by the atomic bomb, and these six were among the survivors. They still wonder why they lived when so many others died. Each of them counts many small items of chance or volition—a step taken in time, a decision to go indoors, catching one streetcar instead of the next—that spared him. And now each knows that in the act of survival he lived a dozen lives and saw more death than he ever thought he would see. At the time, none of them knew anything.

> John Hersey, *Hiroshima*

This passage suggests a great deal of action—the flash of an exploding bomb, the collapse of buildings, screaming people fleeing the scorching devastation—but *it does not present the action*. Narration, however, re-creates action:

> When I pulled the trigger I did not hear the bang or feel the kick—one never does when a shot goes home—but I heard the devilish roar of glee that went up from the crowd. In that instant, in too short a time, one would have thought, even for the bullet to get there, a mysterious, terrible change had come over the elephant. He neither stirred nor fell, but every line of his body had altered. He looked suddenly stricken, shrunken, immensely old, as though the frightful impact of the bullet had paralyzed him without knocking him down. At last, after what seemed a long time—it might have been five seconds, I dare say—he sagged flabbily to his knees. His mouth slobbered. An enormous senility seemed to have settled upon him. One could have imagined him thousands of years old. I fired again into the same spot. At the second shot he did not collapse but climbed with desperate slowness to his feet and stood weakly upright, with legs sagging and head drooping. I fired a third time. That was the shot that did for him. You could see the agony of it jolt his whole body and knock the last remnant of strength from his legs. But in falling he seemed for a moment to rise, for as his hind legs collapsed beneath him he seemed to tower upward like a huge rock toppling, his trunk reaching skywards like a tree. He

TEACHING STRATEGIES

1. Have students keep a weekend log of actions that could be part of a narrative; then discuss how these events might function in a narrative.
2. Examine sample narratives to see how the basic action of the plot fits together. Students are often surprised at how little plot action many professional narratives contain.

CLASSROOM ACTIVITY

Take this simple action: "John finally kissed her. He waited on the step. Mary turned to watch him leave." Have students, working in small groups or individually, see how they might detail the action to show what happened. Discuss the alternate versions produced.

trumpeted, for the first and only time. And then down he came, his belly towards me, with a crash that seemed to shake the ground even where I lay.

George Orwell, "Shooting an Elephant"

Orwell's account offers a stark, vivid replay of the slaying, leaving nothing significant for the reader to infer.

A few words of caution are in order here. Action entails not only exotic events such as the theft of mass-destruction weapons. A wide variety of more normal events also qualify as action: a long, patient wait that comes to nothing, an unexpected kiss after some friendly assistance, a disappointing gift that signals a failed relationship. Furthermore, the narrative action must all relate to the main point—not merely chronicle a series of events.

CONFLICT

Conflict and its resolution, if any, is crucial to a narrative since it motivates and often structures the action. Some conflicts pit one individual against another or against a group, such as a union, company, or religious body. In others, the conflict may involve either an individual and nature or two clashing impulses in one person's head. Read the following student paragraph and note how common sense and fear struggle within the writer, who has experienced a sharp, stabbing pain in his side.

Common sense and fear waged war in my mind. The first argued that a pain so intense was nothing to fool with, that it might indicate a serious or even life-threatening condition. Dr. Montz would be able to identify the problem and deal with it before it worsened. But what if it was already serious? What if I needed emergency surgery? I didn't want anyone cutting into me. "Now wait a minute," I thought. "It's probably nothing serious. Most aches and pains aren't. I'll see the doctor, maybe get some pills, and the problem will clear up overnight. But what if he finds something major, and I have to spend the night in the hospital getting ready for surgery or recovering from it? I think I'll just ignore the pain."

Luis Rodriguez

POINT OF VIEW

A narrative writer may adopt either a first-person or third-person point of view. In first-person narration, one of the cast of characters tells what happened, whereas a third-person narrator stays completely out of the story. Personal narratives and autobiographies use the first-person, biographies and histories use the third person, and fiction embraces both points of view.

In first-person narration, pronouns such as *I, me, mine, we,* and *ours* identify the storyteller. With the third person, the narrator remains unmentioned, and the characters are identified by nouns and such pronouns as *he, she, him,* and *her*. These two paragraphs illustrate the difference.

PERSPECTIVE
Point of view can be a complex matter to discuss. The first-person narrator, of course, need not be the author, or even the main character, of a narrative. Third-person narrators can possess various degrees of omniscience. With a capable class you might examine different points of view and their effects on a narrative.

First-Person Narration

We would go to the well and wash in the ice-cold, clear water, grease our legs with equally cold stiff Vaseline, then tiptoe into the house. We wiped the dust from our toes and settled down for schoolwork, cornbread, clabbered milk, prayers and bed, always in that order. Momma was famous for pulling the quilts off after we had fallen asleep to examine our feet. If they weren't clean enough for her, she took the switch . . . and woke up the offender with a few aptly placed burning reminders.

Maya Angelou, "Momma's Encounter"

As this example shows, first-person narrators may refer to other characters in the narrative by using nouns and third-person pronouns.

Third-Person Narration

In the depths of the city walk the assorted human creatures who do not suspect the fate that hangs over them. A young woman sweeps happily from store to store, pushing a baby carriage along. Businessmen stride purposefully into their office buildings. A young black sulks down the sidewalks of his tenement, and an old woman tugs her shopping basket across a busy thoroughfare. The old woman is not happy; she has seen better days. Days of parks and fountains, of roses and grass, still stir in her memory. Reaching the other side, she stops and strains her neck upward, past the doorways, past the rows and rows of mirror glass, until her eyes rest on the brilliant blue sky so far away. She looks intently at the sky for a few minutes, noting every cloud that rolls past. And the jet plane. She follows the plane with her deep-socketed eyes and for some unexplainable reason suspects danger. She brings her gaze back to earth and walks away as the jet releases a large cloud of brownish-yellow gas. The gas hangs ominously in the air for a while, as if wanting to give humankind just a few more seconds. Then the cloud slowly descends to the surface, dissipating as it goes. By the time it reaches the glittering megalopolis, it is a colorless, odorless blanket of death.

Richard Latta

EXERCISE ▪ Identify the point of view in each of the following excerpts.

1.   The bus screeched to a stop, and Pat stepped out of it and onto the sidewalk. Night enveloped the city, and a slight drizzle fell around her as she made her way to Al's office. Turning the corner, she stepped into the dark entryway. The receptionist had gone home, so she proceeded directly to the office. She knocked on the door and entered. Al, standing behind his desk and looking out the window, turned toward her with a startled look on his face.

Jennifer Webber

2.   It had really begun back in the Charlestown Prison, when Bimbi first made me feel envy of his store of knowledge. Bimbi had always taken charge of any conversation he was in, and I had tried to emulate him. But every book I picked up had few sentences which didn't contain anywhere from one to nearly all of the words that

might as well have been in Chinese. When I just skipped those words, of course, I really ended up with little idea of what the book said. So I had come to the Norfolk Prison Colony still going through only book-reading motions. Pretty soon, I would have quit even these motions, unless I had received the motivation that I did.

Malcolm X, *The Autobiography of Malcolm X*

KEY EVENTS

Any narrative includes many separate events, enough to swamp your narrative boat if you try to pack them all in. Suppose you wish to write about your recent attack of appendicitis in order to make a point about heeding early warnings of an oncoming illness. Your list of events might look like this:

Awakened	Greeted fellow	Returned to work
Showered	employees	Began afternoon's
Experienced acute	Began morning's	work
but passing	work	Collapsed at work
pain in abdomen	Felt nauseated	station
Dressed	Met with boss	Was rushed to
Ate breakfast	Took coffee break	hospital
Opened garage	Visited bathroom	Underwent
door	Experienced more	diagnostic
Started car	prolonged pain	tests
Drove to work	in abdomen	Had emergency
Parked in	Walked to	operation
employee lot	cafeteria	
Entered building	Ate lunch	

A narrative that included all, or even most, of these events would be bloated and ineffective. To avoid this outcome, identify and build your narrative around its key events—those that bear directly on your purpose. Include just enough secondary events to keep the narrative flowing smoothly, but treat them in sketchy fashion. The pain and nausea certainly qualify as key events. Here's how you might present the first attack of pain.

> My first sign of trouble came shortly after I stepped out of the shower. I had just finished toweling when a sharp pain in my lower right side sent me staggering into the bedroom, where I collapsed onto an easy chair in the corner. Biting my lip to hide my groans, I sat twisting in agony as the pain gradually ebbed, leaving me gray faced, sweat drenched, and shaken. What, I asked myself, had been the trouble? Was it ulcers? Was it a gallbladder attack? Did I have stomach cancer?

This passage *convinces*, not just tells, the reader that an attack has occurred. Its details vividly convey the nature of the attack as well as the reactions of the victim. As in any good narrative, the reader shares the experience of the writer, and the two communicate.

DIALOGUE

Dialogue, or conversation, animates many narratives, livening the action and helping draw the reader into the story. Written conversation, however, doesn't duplicate real talk. In speaking with friends, we repeat ourselves, throw in irrelevant comments, use slang, lose our train of thought, and overuse expressions like "you know," "uh," and "well." Dialogue that reproduced real talk would weaken any narrative.

Good dialogue resembles real conversation without copying it. It features simple words and short sentences while avoiding the over-repetition of phrases like "he said" and "she replied." If the conversation unfolds smoothly, the speaker's identity will be clear. To heighten the sense of reality, the writer may use an occasional sentence fragment, slang expression, pause, and the like, as in this passage.

> Mom was waiting for me when I entered the house.
>
> "Your friends. They've been talking to you again. Trying to persuade you to change your mind about going into baseball. Honey, I wish you'd listen to them. You're a terrific ballplayer. Just look at all the trophies and awards you've. . . . " She paused. "Joe's mother called me this morning and asked if you were playing in the game on

Saturday. Davey, I wish you would. You haven't played for

two weeks. Please. I want you to. For me. It would be so good

for you to go and--and do what you've always. . . . "

"O.K., Mom, I'll play. But remember, just for you."

Diane Pickett

Note the mother's use of the slang expression "terrific" and of sentence fragments like "your friends" and "for me" as well as the shift in her train of thought and the repetition of "and." All of this lends an air of reality to the mother's talk.

WRITING A NARRATIVE

Planning and Drafting the Narrative

Most of the narratives you write for your composition class will relate a personal experience and therefore use the first person. On occasion, though, you may write about someone else and therefore use the third person. In either case make sure the experience you pick illustrates some point. A paper that indicates only how you violated a friend's confidence may meander along to little purpose. But if that paper is shaped by some point you wish to make—for instance, that you gained insight into the obligations of friendship—the topic can be worthwhile. To get started, do some guided brainstorming, asking yourself these questions.

What experience in my life or that of someone I know would be worth narrating?
What point does this experience illustrate? (Try to state the point in one or two sentences.)
What people were involved and what parts did they play?

When you have pinpointed a topic, use further brainstorming to garner supporting material. Here are some helpful questions:

What background information is necessary to understand the events?
What action should I include?
What is the nature of the conflict? Was it resolved? If so, how?
Which events play key roles, which are secondary, and which should go unmentioned?
Is any dialogue necessary?

Before you start to write, develop a plot outline showing the significant events in your narrative. For each one, jot down what you saw, heard, or did, and what you thought or felt.

PERSPECTIVE

While writing a narrative seems like a straightforward activity, the process can be difficult for some students. They don't feel that there is anything in their lives worth writing about, and they find it hard to link their events to a purpose.

TEACHING STRATEGY

To prepare students for writing a narrative, you might focus class discussion, and even journal writing, around a common theme such as "What does it really take to be a friend?" Such preparation often convinces students that they have something to say and provides a purpose for their papers.

ETHICAL ISSUES

How responsible is a writer for the content of a narrative? Is it acceptable to extol the virtues of, for instance, a destructive rampage, racist activities, or the joys of substance abuse? To explore this matter, have students role play, some representing the writer, some potential readers, some actual readers whose lives were influenced by the narrative.

On the other hand, is it deceptive to present a fictional narrative as though it were factual? Take, for instance, the fictional biographies and endorsements common in advertising. What responsibility does the company have to accurately indicate the basis of the ad? Again, have students role play and represent the various positions.

Use the opening of your paper to set the stage for what follows. You might tell when and where the action occurred, provide helpful background information, note the incident that activated the chain of events, or identify the problem from which the action grew. If you state your main point directly, do it here or in the conclusion.

The body of the narrative should move the action forward until a turning point is about to be reached. Build the body around your key events. To avoid stranding your reader, use time signals whenever the development of the action might be unclear. Words, phrases, and clauses like *now*, *next*, *finally*, *after an hour*, and *when I returned* help the reader understand the sequence of events. Don't get carried away, though; a paper loaded with time signals makes the sequence seem more important than the events themselves. Finally, think about how you can best use conflict and dialogue to heighten narrative interest.

The conclusion should tie up any loose ends, settle any unresolved conflicts, and lend an air of completion to the narrative. Effective strategies to think about include introducing a surprise twist, offering a reflective summary of the events, noting your reaction to them, or discussing the aftermath of the affair.

Revising the Narrative

As you revise, follow the guidelines in Chapter 3, and in addition ask yourself these questions:

Have I made the point, stated or unstated, that I intended?
Does all of the action relate to the main point?
Is the conflict handled appropriately?
Have I included all of the key events that relate to my purpose? Given each the right emphasis? Used time indicators where needed?
Is my point of view appropriate?
Does my dialogue ring true?

EXAMPLE STUDENT ESSAY OF NARRATION

The Beach Bum

Gail Bartlett

Pete Miller was his name. I met him that summer on   1
the beach of Sanford Lake. I was lying on my extra-large
towel, letting the hot sun soak the water droplets off

my body, when some clumsy fool flopped by and flipped
sand all over me. Jerking up, an angry glare on my face,
I was ready to scream at the clod when my mouth opened
wide in surprise. This fox was tall with jet-black hair
and sky-blue eyes. The summer sun had tanned his body to
a golden brown which made me envious as I compared it to
my own vague coloring. It was clearly evident that he
had spent most of his summer on this beach. Immediately
my anger evaporated, and a smile came to my face. In a
flirting tone I joked, "Hey, Bud, watch where you're
kicking that sand."

He grinned back and said, "Come on out in the   2
water, and I'll help you wash it off, unless, of course,
you want it left on. I can see you've already discovered
it helps for a deep tan. Ha!"

I decided I had nothing to lose and hopped off my   3
towel. As we raced to the water, I could sense him
glancing at me, and I knew at once that he had
intentionally tripped in the sand only to get my
attention. This pleased me but made me even more self-
conscious than usual. Not many guys noticed me, and I
never was quite sure how to act.

For the rest of the afternoon, we swam in the warm   4
water. Never before would I have wasted a good tanning
sun like that day's to play in the water, but for some
reason I felt this day was different. He must have been
all alone, for I didn't meet any of his friends. It was
only the two of us, and I was very grateful, for I knew I
would not be so much at ease if there were others
around. To my amazement, he asked me out for the next
night to go to a bonfire he and his buddies were having

farther down the beach. I accepted hesitantly, as I had dated only a few times before.

With great pains I tried to decide what I should wear. Wanting to impress him, I didn't wear my usual jeans and grubby sweatshirt. Instead I chose my new plaid slacks and halter top, which were not at all comfortable. While nervously waiting for him, I dabbed on a little extra perfume and a few extra swishes of blusher. The doorbell rang, and instantaneously I was on my feet and at the door. The introduction to my parents wasn't exactly what I would describe as smooth, and I certainly was not at ease.

We arrived at the fire about 9:00 P.M., and already twenty of his friends had gathered. They were just beginning to pass the beer, and when he handed me one I accepted for fear of disappointing him if I said no. It was not normal for me to drink, and I didn't feel myself at all. I became afraid of what his friends would think of me. They were laughing and telling jokes, but, not wanting to say something that would embarrass him, I sat silent. When asked a question by his closest friend, I could only shake my head in answer. The first hour went by quickly, for my date stayed by my side and tried in vain to include me in the conversation. I could not force myself to act normally. It was as though I were being rated, and I wanted a high score so badly I would not allow my true personality to show through for fear of not fitting in and being rejected. I felt as if I were going to suffocate. It was hard for me to hold back my laughter as the jokes grew increasingly funny. Only a timid giggle would I let escape my lips. My date

became discouraged--I now can see why--but at that time
the reason puzzled me. He left me to talk to a girl on
the other side of the fire who was casually telling a
joke. She spoke freely and with the confidence I wished
I had. He enjoyed her easy manner, and so did many of
the others. I could tell this by the way they were
attracted to her side of the fire. Everyone was having a
jolly time, and there I sat, suppressing myself in
fear. Finally the guy I had wanted so much to impress
returned and asked in a cold tone, "Are you about ready
to go?"

    I answered with disappointment, "I am, if you   7
are."

    We slowly trudged to the car, making trite   8
comments along the way. On the way home I wanted so
badly to tell him that I was not usually so quiet and
shy. I wanted to tell him how much fun I really could be
and that I had acted as I had only because I was afraid
he or his friends would think me odd or different in
some way. But instead of saying all this, I only sat in
a quiet closet, drawing myself farther into the corner
with every mile.

    As I climbed into bed, I was angry with myself and   9
vowed that I would never be that way again. I would
force myself to be natural, no matter what anyone
thought. It seemed certain that I would never be given
another chance with this fox. Two weeks passed without
my seeing or hearing a word from him. Every day I sat
and daydreamed of what could have happened that night
had I been myself and a little more at ease. Things
could have worked out so nicely for me.

Two weeks later, after I had given up all hope, I   10
answered the ringing phone one night with a bored
hello. Lo and behold, it was the beach bum! My nerves
shook and my eyes watered as I told him I would be happy
to go to a skating party with him that weekend. Hanging
up the phone, I released an exultant scream and ran to
my room to think in quiet. This time I was not going to
wear anything but my usual jeans, and I would act the
way I felt.

Through my upstairs bedroom window, I watched   11
him slowly advance to the door, and I could feel that
this was going to be the night I wanted so badly. We
left the house, and I glanced quickly over at him with a
confident smile as we strolled down the sidewalk. The
skating rink was crowded, and I recognized most of the
people there as his friends whom I had met before. I was
surprised at how much friendlier they were to me than at
our previous meeting. It was all because I wore a smile
and not only listened to them talk but also offered a
few quips of my own. When one of the guys skated up
beside me and put his arm around me, I didn't look at
the floor and shy away as I had done before but returned
his warmness by putting my arm around him. My date
seemed to enjoy my company and stayed near me the whole
evening, glancing at me every now and then in disbelief
that I could be the girl he had taken out two weeks
before. We laughed and joked the night away, and things
went much more smoothly than the last time.

While returning to my home he said, "I had a   12
wonderful time tonight and would like to see you again

sometime. You're really a lot more fun than I thought
you were. Why were you so quiet at the bonfire?"

       Slyly I answered, "Oh, was I quiet that night?"   13
With a grin and a look from the corner of his eye, he
squeezed my hand. To myself I thought, "How much better
it is to be yourself and act the way you feel rather
than to try to please others." It had seemed such a hard
ordeal to get the others to like and accept me in the
beginning, but now I realized that it hadn't been their
fault at all—only mine.

DISCUSSION QUESTIONS ■

1. Identify the point of view of the narrative.
2. List the words, phrases, and clauses that serve as time signals. What has the writer accomplished by using them?
3. This narrative spans about two weeks. At what points has the writer omitted events? Why?
4. What sentence states the point of the narrative? Why is it positioned where it is?

SUGGESTIONS FOR WRITING ■

1. **Write a personal narrative about an experience that:**

   a. altered either your opinion of a friend or acquaintance or your views about some important matter
   b. taught you a lesson or something about human nature
   c. caused you great sorrow or joy
   d. exposed you to the danger of serious injury or death
   e. acquainted you with some previously unrecognized facet of your character or personality
   f. brought about a significant change in your way of life

Keep in mind all the key narrative elements: purpose, action, conflict, point of view, key events, and dialogue.

DISCUSSION QUESTIONS

1. The writer adopts the first-person point of view, as shown by her use of "I," "me," and "my." At times she makes judgments concerning her date's attitude and feelings, but these are always based on his actions, tone of voice, or the like. At no time does she adopt an omniscient stance and enter her date's mind.

2. The writer uses time indicators frequently—for example, in the fourth and next-to-the-last sentences of paragraph 1, the second sentence of paragraph 3, the first sentence of paragraph 4, the fourth sentence of paragraph 5, the first sentences of paragraphs 6, 9, and 10, as well as in a number of other places. These indicators tell the reader precisely when each event occurs.

3. The writer says nothing about the events that occurred between the time she accepted the first date and the time she selected the clothing to wear on it. Similarly, she says nothing about the automobile ride to the bonfire, what she did between the time her date left her and she climbed into bed, or the two weeks between her first and second dates. These events were omitted because they would do nothing to move the narrative forward.

4. The next-to-the-last sentence states the point of the narrative. As positioned, it is effective because it draws a lesson from the events that have occurred, providing a climax to the narrative.

SUGGESTED INSTRUCTOR READINGS

Beach, R. "Differences in Autobiographical Narratives of English Teachers, College Freshmen, and Seventh Graders." College Composition and Communication 38 (1987): 56–69. Discusses the differences in the three groups' self-concepts and knowledge of literary conventions.

Bret, C. "Remedial Writers and Fictive Techniques." College Composition and Communication 39 (1988): 27–30. Shows less experienced writers how to use such techniques as plot, characterization, and dialogue to develop a personal narrative.

Campbell, J. "Stepping Through a Mirror: The Historical Narrative Assignment." College Composition and Communication 38 (1987): 95–97. Historical narratives in which students present the events through the persona of historical figures can provide a research-oriented alternative to the personal narrative.

Crew, L. "Rhetorical Beginnings: Professional and Amateur," College Composition and Communication 38 (1967): 346–49. Reviews the opening paragraphs of a number of essays and concludes that professional writers often begin their essays with narrative while students frequently begin with rhetorical questions.

2. **A maxim is a concise statement of a generally recognized truth. Noting the key elements above, write a personal narrative that illustrates one of the following maxims or another that your instructor approves.**

    a. A little learning is a dangerous thing.
    b. The more things change, the more they stay the same.
    c. It's an ill wind that blows no good.
    d. Don't judge a book by its cover.
    e. The road to hell is paved with good intentions.
    f. Pride goeth before a fall.

■ Chapter 5

Description: Presenting Impressions

TEACHING STRATEGY

To show students how the writer's perspective affects observation and description, you might have several students, or the entire class, describe one campus feature. Then have students read the descriptions out loud and discuss why the descriptions varied.

SUGGESTED INSTRUCTOR READING

Berthoff, A. Forming, Thinking, Writing: The Composing Imagination. Rochelle Park, NJ: Hayden, 1978. Explores relationships among observing, thinking and writing and provides several interesting activities to help students become self-conscious observers and thinkers.

PERSPECTIVE

Students should recognize that purpose dictates how we observe and describe. While an advertising copywriter might search for dramatic embellishments, a scientist writing a lab report will try to remain objective. Students often have difficulty with description because they lose sight of their purpose.

TEACHING STRATEGIES

1. Ask students to review their reading material for a week, note where description is used, why, and how that purpose shaped the description.
2. Ask students to select an advertising description and rewrite it as if they were objective observers, or do the reverse. Then discuss the changes they made and why.

CLASSROOM ACTIVITY

Have students select a class partner and then describe him or her for (1) identification at a crowded airport; (2) a police bulletin; (3) an ad in a dating magazine. Then have students compare descriptions, note the changes, and point out how purpose influenced them.

> The sound of sizzling hot dogs, cooking on a grease-spattered grill, gave way to the whirling buzz of a cotton-candy machine. Fascinated, we watched as the white cardboard cone was slowly transformed into a pink, fluffy cloud. Despite its Fiberglas appearance, the sticky puffs melted on my tongue into sweet sugar. Soon our faces and hands were gummed with goo.

You are there. Seeing, hearing, touching, tasting. This is one student writer's *description* of a small segment of a county fair. Effective description creates sharply etched word pictures of objects, persons, scenes, events, or situations. Sensory impressions—reflecting sight, sound, taste, smell, and touch—form the backbone of descriptive writing. Often, they build toward one dominant impression that the writer wants to evoke.

The human mind is not merely a logical thinking machine. Because of our emotional makeup, we react with shock to a photo of a battered victim of child abuse. We feel stirrings of nostalgia upon hearing a song from our past. We smile with satisfaction when quenching our summer thirst with tart sips from a tall, frosted drink. Responses like these, as much as the ability to think rationally, help define the human makeup.

PURPOSE

Description rarely occurs in pure form but often enriches other kinds of writing. It appears in histories and biographies, fiction and poetry, journalism and advertising, and occasionally even in technical writing. Some descriptions merely create images and mood, as when a writer paints a word picture of a boggy, fog-shrouded moor. But description can also stimulate understanding or lead to action. A historian may juxtapose the splendor of French court life with the wretchedness of a Paris slum to help explain the French Revolution. And everyone knows the persuasive power of advertising's descriptive enticements.

Description will provide effective backup for the writing you do in your composition classes, helping you to drive home your points with force and vividness.

SENSORY IMPRESSIONS

Precise sensory impressions begin with close physical or mental observation. If you can reexamine your subject, do it. If not, recall it to mind; then capture its features with appropriate words. When you can't find the right words, try a comparison. Ask yourself what your subject (or part of it) might be likened to. Does it smell like a rotten egg? A ripe cantaloupe? Burning rubber? Does it sound like a high sigh? A soft rustle? To come across, the comparison must be accurate and familiar. If the reader has never smelled a rotten egg, the point is lost.

Here is a passage marked by particularly vivid sight impressions.

> After our meal we went for a stroll across the plateau. The day was already drawing to a close as we sat down upon a ledge of rock near the lip of the western precipice. From where we sat, as though perched high upon a cloud, we looked out into a gigantic void. Far below, the stream we had crossed that afternoon was a pencil-thin trickle of silver barely visible in the gloaming. Across it, on the other side, the red hills rose one upon another in gentle folds, fading into the distance where the purple thumblike mountains of Adua and Yeha stretched against the sky like a twisting serpent. As we sat, the sun sank fast, and the heavens in the western sky began to glow. It was a coppery fire at first, the orange streaked with aquamarine; but rapidly the firmament expanded into an explosion of red and orange that burst across the sky sending tongues of flame through the feathery clouds to the very limits of the heavens. When the flames had reached their zenith, a great quantity of storks came flying from the south. They circled above us once, their slender bodies sleek and black against the orange sky. Then, gathering together, they flew off into the setting sun, leaving us alone in peace to contemplate. One of the monks who sat with us, hushed by the intensity of the moment, muttered a prayer. The sun died beyond the hills; and the fire withdrew.
>
> Robert Dick-Read, *Sanamu: Adventures in Search of African Art*

At first, the western sky glows with a "coppery fire," which then expands into "an explosion of red and orange" that sends "tongues of flame" heavenward and then withdraws as the sun disappears. Comparisons strengthen the visual impression: the "pencil-thin" stream, the "thumblike" mountains stretching across the sky "like a twisting serpent." The familiar pencil, thumb, and serpent help us to visualize the unfamiliar landscape.

The next passage focuses on taste:

> My own special chef's salad is a taste bud's delight. The cool moistness of fresh lettuce, the plump cherry tomatoes that squirt their tart juices against the palate, the hard-boiled egg slices garnished with paprika, and the bland, buttery avocados offer a soothing contrast to the fiery Mexican peppers that burn their way down the throat, the mouth-puckering saltiness of anchovies, and the intense bitterness of black Greek olives. Assorted garnishes add their own special zest: sugar-cured ham slivers, crisp, smoke-flavored bacon bits, pungent garlic salt, and crunchy herbed croutons. Sharp blue cheese dressing tops everything, adding its final piquancy to the assorted taste sensations.

> Rick Price

As we read this passage, we can almost taste the tart tomatoes, fiery peppers, bitter olives, and sharply piquant dressing.

Most descriptions blend several sense impressions rather than focusing on just one. In the following excerpt, Mark Twain, reminiscing about his uncle's farm, includes all five. As you read it, note which impressions are most effective.

> As I have said, I spent some part of every year at the farm until I was twelve or thirteen years old. The life which I led there with my cousins was full of charm, and so is the memory of it yet. I can call back the solemn twilight and mystery of the deep woods, the earthy smells, the faint odors of the wild flowers, the sheen of rain-washed foliage, the rattling clatter of drops when the wind shook the trees, the far-off hammering of woodpeckers and the muffled drumming of wood pheasants in the remoteness of the forest, the snapshot glimpses of disturbed wild creatures scurrying through the grass—I can call it all back and make it as real as it ever was, and as blessed. I can call back the prairie, and its loneliness and peace, and a vast hawk hanging motionless in the sky, with his wings spread wide and the blue of the vault showing through the fringe of their end feathers. I can see the woods in their autumn dress, the oaks purple, the hickories washed with gold, the maples and the sumachs luminous with crimson fires, and I can hear the rustle made by the fallen leaves as we plowed through them. I can see the blue clusters of wild grapes hanging among the foliage of the saplings, and I remember the taste of them and the smell. I know how the wild blackberries looked, and how they tasted, and the same with the

pawpaws, the hazelnuts, and the persimmons; and I can feel the thumping rain, upon my head, of hickory nuts and walnuts when we were out in the frosty dawn to scramble for them with the pigs, and the gusts of wind loosed them and sent them down. I know the stain of blackberries, and how pretty it is, and I know the stain of walnut hulls, and how little it minds soap and water, also what grudged experience it had of either of them. I know the taste of maple sap, and when to gather it, and how to arrange the troughs and the delivery tubes, and how to boil down the juice, and how to hook the sugar after it is made, also how much better hooked sugar tastes than any that is honestly come by, let bigots say what they will.

Mark Twain, *Autobiography*

EXERCISE ANSWER

Explain to students that the rationale for this exercise is to sharpen perception and word choice. Point out that some of their observations might be useful in a paper, depending on the purpose.

ALTERNATE EXERCISE

Provide students with pictures of scientific objects—a chemical solution, the back of the eye, a particular rock, a galaxy formation—and have them describe as objectively as possible what they observe. To make the exercise more challenging, bring in paired pictures of very similar objects, such as two types of viruses, and have students describe them accurately enough so the reader can match the description with the appropriate object.

EXERCISE ■ **Spend some time in an environment such as one of the following. Concentrate on one sense at a time. Begin by observing what you see; then jot down the precise impressions you receive. Now do the same for impressions of touch, taste, smell, and sound.**

1. The woods in the early morning
2. A city intersection
3. A restaurant or cafeteria
4. A scenic spot under a full moon
5. A storm
6. A pool or other recreation area
7. A crowded classroom or hallway
8. A grocery store
9. A park or playground
10. A holiday gathering

DOMINANT IMPRESSION

Skillful writers select and express sensory perceptions in order to create a *dominant impression*—an overall mood or feeling such as joy, anger, terror, or distaste. This impression may be identified or left unnamed for the reader to deduce. Whatever the choice, a verbal picture of a storm about to strike, for example, might be crafted to evoke feelings of fear by describing sinister masses of slaty clouds, cannon salvos of thunder, blinding lightning flashes, and viciously swirling wind-caught dust.

The following paragraph establishes a sense of security as the dominant impression:

A marvellous stillness pervaded the world, and the stars together with the serenity of their rays seemed to shed upon the earth the assurance of everlasting security. The young moon recurved, and shining low in the west, was like a slender shaving thrown up from a bar of gold, and the Arabian Sea, smooth and cool to the eye like a sheet of ice, extended its perfect level to the perfect circle of a dark horizon.

The propeller turned without a check, as though its beat had been part of the scheme of a safe universe; and on each side of the *Patna* two folds of water, permanent and sombre on the unwrinkled shimmer, enclosed within their straight and diverging ridges a few white swirls of foam bursting in a low hiss, a few wavelets, a few ripples, a few undulations that, left behind, agitated the surface of the sea for an instant after the passage of the ship, subsided splashing gently, calmed down at last into the circular stillness of water and sky with the black speck of the moving hull remaining everlastingly in its centre.

Joseph Conrad, *Lord Jim*

The first sentence directly identifies the impression, "security," to which the "stillness" and the "serenity" contribute. Other details also do their part: the "smooth" sea, the "perfect circle" of the horizon, the "safe universe," the quick calming of the water, and the moving hull "everlastingly" in the center of water and sky.

EXERCISE ■   **Select one of the following topics and write a paragraph that evokes a particular dominant impression. Omit any details that run counter to your aim.**

1. A multi-alarm fire
2. A repair facility (automobile, appliance, and so on)
3. A laboratory
4. Some aspect of summer in a particular place
5. A religious service
6. A doctor's or dentist's office
7. A dark street
8. A parade or other celebration
9. Some landmark on your college campus
10. A municipal night court or small-claims court

TEACHING STRATEGY

To help students complete the exercise in this section, encourage them to list all their observations, then select the relevant details, and finally write the paragraph. Students could draw on the material from the previous exercise for this assignment.

VANTAGE POINT

You may write a description from either a fixed or a moving vantage point. A fixed observer remains in one place and reports only what can be perceived from there. Here is how Marilyn Kluger describes the Thanksgiving morning sounds she remembers hearing from her bed as a child.

TEACHING STRATEGY

Using the essays in the Reader, have students identify the vantage points assumed by different writers, how they signal these vantage points, and how they indicate changes in location.

On the last Thursday in November, I could stay in bed only until the night chill left the house, hearing first the clash of the heavy grates in the huge black iron range, with its flowery scrolls and nickled decorations, as Mother shook down the ashes. Then, in their proper sequence, came the sounds of the fire being made—the rustle of newspaper, the snap of kindling, the rush of smoke up the chimney when Mother opened the damper, slid the regulator wide open, and struck a match to the kerosene-soaked corncobs that started a quick hot fire. I listened for the bang of the cast-iron lid dropping back into place and for the tick of the stovepipes as fierce flames sent up their heat, then the sound of the lid being lifted again as Mother fed more dry wood and lumps of coal to the greedy new fire. The duties of the kitchen on Thanksgiving were a thousandfold, and I could tell that Mother was bustling about with a quicker step than usual.

Marilyn Kluger, "A Time of Plenty"

A moving observer views things from a number of positions, signaling changes in location with phrases such as "moving through the turnstile" and "as I walked around the corner." Below, H. L. Mencken takes us with him as he observes from a moving express train.

On a Winter day some years ago, coming out of Pittsburgh on one of the expresses of the Pennsylvania Railroad, I rolled eastward for an hour through the coal and steel towns of Westmoreland county. It was familiar ground; boy and man, I had been through it often before. But somehow I had never quite sensed its appalling desolation. Here was the very heart of industrial America, the center of its most lucrative and characteristic activity, the boast and pride of the richest and grandest nation ever seen on earth—and here was a scene so dreadfully hideous, so intolerably bleak and forlorn that it reduced the whole aspiration of man to a macabre and depressing joke. Here was wealth beyond computation, almost beyond imagination—and here were human habitations so abominable that they would have disgraced a race of alley cats.

I am not speaking of mere filth. One expects steel towns to be dirty. What I allude to is the unbroken and agonizing ugliness, the sheer revolting monstrousness, of every house in sight. From East Liberty to Greensburg, a distance of twenty-five miles, there was not one in sight from the train that did not insult and lacerate the eye. Some were so bad, and they were among the most pretentious—churches, stores, warehouses, and the like—that they were downright startling; one blinked before them as one blinks before a man with his face shot away. A few linger in memory, horrible even there: a crazy little church just west of Jeannette, set like a dormer-window on the side of a bare, leprous hill; the headquarters of the Veterans of Foreign Wars at another forlorn town, a steel stadium like a huge rat-trap somewhere further down the line. But most of all I recall the general effect—of hideousness without a break. There was not a single decent house within eyerange from the Pittsburgh suburbs to the Greensburg yards. There was not one that was not mis-shapen, and there was not one that was not shabby.

H. L. Mencken, "The Libido for the Ugly"

The phrase "on one of the expresses of the Pennsylvania Railroad" signals that Mencken will be a moving observer, and "From East Liberty to Greensburg" pinpoints the extent of his journey. "West of Jeannette," "another forlorn town," and "somewhere further down the line" specify the positions from which he views the church, the headquarters of the veterans' organization, and the stadium.

Whatever your vantage point, fixed or moving, report only what would be apparent to someone on the scene. If you describe how a distant mountain looks from a balcony, don't suddenly leap to a description of a mountain flower: you couldn't see it from your vantage point.

EXERCISE ■

1. **Writing as a fixed observer, describe in a paragraph your impressions of one of the following. Be sure to indicate your vantage point.**

    a. A post office lobby two weeks before Christmas
    b. The scene following a traffic accident
    c. A classroom when the bell rings
    d. A campus lounge
    e. An office
    f. The entrance to some building

2. **Writing as a moving observer, describe in a paragraph or two your impressions as you do one of the following things. Clearly signal your movements to the reader.**

    a. Walk from one class to another
    b. Shop in a grocery store
    c. Walk from your home to the corner
    d. Cross a long bridge
    e. Water-ski
    f. Go through a ticket line and enter a theater, auditorium, or sports arena

ALTERNATE EXERCISE

Have students describe the same object or scene from several different vantage points and then write a brief account of the differences and the impact on the description.

SELECTION OF DETAILS

Effective description depends as much on exclusion as on inclusion. Don't try to pack every possible detail into your paper by providing an inventory of, for example, a room's contents or a natural setting's elements. Such an approach shows only that you can see, not write. Instead, select details that deliberately point toward the mood or feeling you intend to create. Read the following student description of nighttime skiing.

> The glowing orb of the moon, shedding its pale, silvery radiance on the ski slope, seemed to cast a spell. Crystal iridescence of powdered snow twinkled in the night. Shadows cast by the skiers appeared as mysterious silhouettes darting in and out among snow—covered trees. The gentle breeze combing through the branches created a lulling musical chant which drifted into my head, taking control. Delicate snowflakes danced by, kissed me on the face, and seemed to beckon me up the hill.

> Sue Mutch

This writer evokes a sense of enchantment by noting the "pale, silvery radiance" of the moon, the "crystal iridescence" of the snow, the "mysterious silhouettes" of the skiers, and the "lulling musical chant" of the wind. She ignores such details as the boisterous snatches of conversation among the skiers, the crunch of ski poles digging into the snow, and the creaking towline moving to the top of the slope. Mentioning these things would detract from the desired mood.

ARRANGEMENT OF DETAILS

Description, like any other writing, must have a clear pattern of organization to guide the reader and help you fulfill your purpose. Often some spatial arrangement works nicely. You might, for example, move systematically from top to bottom, left to right, front to back, nearby to far away, or the reverse of these patterns. To describe Saturday afternoon at the football game, you might start with the crowded parking lot, move into the bustling stadium, and finally zoom in on the sights, sounds, and smells of the playing field. Or if you wanted to highlight the surroundings rather than the central event, the order could be reversed. Going another route, you might start with some striking central feature and then branch out to the things around it. To capture the center of a mall, you might first describe its ornate fountain illuminated with flashing, multicolored lights, shift to the reflection of the lights on the skylight above, and end by portraying the surrounding store fronts.

Sometimes a description follows a time sequence. A writer might, for example, portray the changes in a woodland setting as winter gives way to spring and spring, in turn, yields to summer.

TEACHING STRATEGIES
1. You might provide both a purpose and an audience in your assignment. You could ask students to describe their favorite vacation spot for the Sunday supplement of a local newspaper in order to help readers decide whether they'd like to visit it. The class can then observe and discuss how other writers have solved a similar writing problem. Or you might give a more technically oriented assignment: for example, to describe a dangerous intersection as part of a report to the local road commission.
2. Encourage students to develop extensive lists of sensory details. Such lists provide excellent raw materials for essays.

WRITING A DESCRIPTION

Planning and Drafting the Description

If you're choosing your own topic, always select one that is familiar. Don't describe the inside of a restaurant kitchen or Old Faithful geyser in Yellowstone National Park if you've never seen either one. Instead, opt for some place where you've actually worked or a locale you've recently visited. If you keep a journal, thumb through it for possible leads.

For each potential topic that surfaces, ask yourself the following questions. They will direct your attention to matters you'll need to address.

What do I want to accomplish by writing this description? Create one or more
   impressions? Help the reader understand something? Persuade the reader to act?
Who is my audience and why would this topic interest them?
What dominant impression will I develop?

To help gather and organize support for your topic, pose these additional questions.

> What details should I include?
> What sensory impressions are associated with each detail? (Jot down any words that you feel will best convey the impressions.)
> How does each detail contribute to the dominant impression?
> What sequence should I follow in presenting my impressions? (Map out the sequence, setting up a 1-2-3 listing or possibly a paragraph-by-paragraph plan.)

Begin your paper with an introduction that eases the reader into your topic. You might, for example, provide a historical overview, ask a provocative question, or snare the reader's attention with an arresting statement.

Develop each major feature in one or more paragraphs. Present each feature in the order you've mapped out. To ensure that the reader follows your thoughts, clearly signal any shifts in vantage point or time. As you write, aim for vivid, original language. We've all encountered writers who tell us that raindrops "pitter-patter," clouds are "fleecy white," and the sun is "a ball of fire." Such stale, worn out language does nothing to sharpen our vision of the rain, the clouds, or the sun. In contrast, read how one student describes the sounds in her kitchen at breakfast time:

> Sure signs of a new day are the sounds in the kitchen as breakfast is prepared. The high sigh of the gas just before it whooshes into flame and settles into a whispering hum blends with the gurgling of the water for the morning coffee. Soon the gloop, gloop, gloop of the coffee sets up a perky beat. Then in mingles the crackle of creamy butter on a hot skillet and the shush of an egg as it meets this fiery foe. Ribbons of bacon start to sizzle in the spitting grease. The soft rustle of plastic as bread is removed from its wrapper floats on the air and seems to form part of the atmosphere. The can opener whirs, and the orange juice concentrate drops with a splat into the blender, which whizzes together the orange cylinder and splashed—in water. For minutes after the blender stops, tiny effervescing bubbles fizz.
>
> Kim Burson Swiger

CLASSROOM ACTIVITY

To prepare for this assignment, choose a site that every student knows and have the class brainstorm and plan. Then show students how they can progress from notes to draft.

You are there in the kitchen, hearing the carefully selected and freshly described sounds.

A word of caution about making your writing vivid. Some students are tempted to enhance their descriptions by stringing together a chain of adjectives without considering the effect on a reader. Wouldn't you react with dismay upon being told that

"A dented, cylindrical, silver-gray, foul-smelling, overloaded trash can sat in the alley"?

As you can see, more than the garbage can is overloaded here. Resist the temptation to inject similar sentences into your description. Carefully examine your adjectives and eliminate those that don't advance your purpose.

End your paper by pulling your material together in some way. If you've created an impression or mood, you might offer your reaction to it. If you want your reader to understand something, you might spell your message out. If you wish to persuade, you might urge some action.

Revising the Description

As you revise, apply the guidelines in Chapter 3 and ask the following questions.

Have I written with a clear sense of purpose and audience in mind?

Have I conveyed how my topic looks, sounds, feels, tastes, or smells? Would comparisons or more precise descriptive terms help convey my perceptions?

Have I evoked one dominant impression? Can I strengthen this impression by adding certain selected details? By eliminating details that detract from the impression?

Have I used an appropriate vantage point? If the observer is moving, have I signaled changes in location? Have I included only details that would be visible to the observer?

Have I arranged my details in an order appropriate to the topic?

TEACHING STRATEGIES

1. Since students usually under-write descriptions, you might have them freewrite additional sensory details for key parts of their papers and then incorporate the best material into their draft.
2. Peer responses can reveal under-written or misplaced description, especially if peers are asked to write down their questions and identify vague passages.
3. Have students circle their key descriptive terms and brainstorm possible substitutes.

ETHICAL ISSUES

How responsible is a writer for accurate, nondistorted description? Is it acceptable to exaggerate the merits of a place in order to encourage tourism or sell real estate? How much can the writer omit and still be fair to the reader? Have students role play a situation where some represent the tourist bureau, others the ad writer, and still others the disappointed tourists who spent money only to discover a place that fails to match the description.

EXAMPLE STUDENT ESSAY OF DESCRIPTION

The Big One

Rebecca Mutch

With a final crack of a bat and a lofting fly   1

ball, baseball ended for the year. The last swirl of

water gurgling down the drain of the community pool marked the end of its season. These closings marked the beginning of another event, the county fair. This season I was elected to take my little brother on a ride—"the big one," in his words.

2

Once again I found myself in the familiar grass lot bordering the fairground. The fair itself was completely surrounded by a fence. No one could see what was inside. The only clues were carried in the wind. Muffled echoes of carnies hawking their games, excited squeals of children, and blaring carnival tunes, frequently punctuated by sharp, crackling static, blended with the tantalizing fragrance of popcorn, the spicy aroma of pizza, and the sweet molasses smell of caramel corn.

3

As we entered the main gate and handed our tickets to the men whose baskets already overflowed with torn stubs, my eyes immediately confirmed what my ears and nose had already reported. In one step we had gone from a semiquiet and relaxed world into an ever-revolving one. Dazzling lights, blinking out of control, seemed to flirt with anyone and everyone. Children, their white T-shirts covered with splotches of chocolate and mustard, dashed ahead of their parents and returned shortly, screaming about the giant bear that waited ahead. The distant, shuffling crowds appeared as moving shadows, their features blurred.

4

The little tug on my sleeve reminded me of that big ride that waited ahead. The path up the midway, packed with a cushion of sawdust, was strewn with empty popcorn boxes, scraps of papers, and crumpled cigarette packages.

DISCUSSION QUESTIONS

1. The writer's movements are indicated in paragraph 2 (". . .I found myself in the familiar grass lot bordering the fairground."), paragraph 3 ("As we entered the main gate. . ."), paragraph 4 ("The path up the midway. . ."), paragraph 5 ("The sound of sizzling hot dogs. . .gave way to the whirling buzz. . ."), paragraph 6 ("We scuffled along with the rhythm of the crowd and before long arrived at. . .the rides."), paragraph 7 (". . .we made our way dizzily to the car.")

2. Like most descriptions, this one relies primarily on impressions of sight. Particularly vivid sight details occur in paragraph 3 ("Dazzling lights, blinking out of control. . ." and ". . .white T-shirts covered with splotches of chocolate and mustard. . ."), paragraph 4 ("The path. . .was strewn with empty popcorn boxes. . ."), paragraph 5 ("The enormous purple teddy bear which smiled down mockingly. . ." and ". . .the white cardboard cone was slowly transformed into a pink fluffy cloud."), paragraph 6 ("Sparks shot out" and "Swirling and whirling, these pieces caught the reflection of the neon lights, and. . .produced a world of spectrum colors."), and paragraph 7 ("The fairground was soon a kaleidoscope of fantastic images and colors.").

Vivid sound impressions occur in paragraph 1 (". . .a final crack of a bat" and "The last swirl of water gurgling down the drain"), paragraph 2 ("Muffled echoes of carnies," "excited squeals of children," "blaring carnival tunes," and "sharp, crackling static"), paragraph 3 ("children. . .screaming about the giant bear. . ." and "shuffling crowds"), paragraph 5 ("pennants whipping and snapping," "BBs clinked," "A backboard thudded and a hoop clanked," "The sound of sizzling hot dogs," and "the whirling buzz of a cotton-candy machine"), paragraph 6 ("The sounds of metal

Game booths and food huts, their pennants   5
whipping and snapping in the wind, dotted the path on
both sides and formed two long serpent-like strings of
pleasure. BB's clinked against tin objects in the
shooting gallery. Hawkers with greased hands and pudgy
fingers tried to lure suckers toward their gaudy
booths. A backboard thudded and a hoop clanked as still
another young man tried to win the enormous purple
teddy bear which smiled down mockingly from its perch
above. The sound of sizzling hot dogs, cooking on a
grease-spattered grill, gave way to the whirling buzz
of a cotton-candy machine. Fascinated, we watched as
the white cardboard cone was slowly transformed into a
pink, fluffy cloud. Despite its Fiberglas appearance,
the sticky puffs melted on my tongue into sweet sugar.
Soon our faces and hands were gummed with goo.

We scuffled along with the rhythm of the crowd   6
and before long arrived at those metallic contraptions
of nuts and bolts——the rides. The sounds of metal
clanging and banging filled the air. Sparks shot out
from where the metal pieces slapped together. Swirling
and whirling, these pieces caught the reflection of the
neon lights and, together with the sparks, produced a
world of spectrum colors.

This was it. The Ferris wheel stood towering   7
before us. As the seat gently swayed, we waited for the
ride to begin. The motor belched and then slowly
started to turn; goose bumps formed on my brother's
bare arms, and his eyes grew larger as the ride picked
up speed. The fairground was soon a kaleidoscope of
fantastic images and colors. The wind whipped through
my hair and snapped it back, stinging my face at times.

Both of us were screaming uncontrollably. Suddenly, with no apparent slowdown, the ride was over, and we made our way dizzily to the car.

My brother talked about the big one for weeks.   8
For me it brought back many fond memories and let me, just for an evening, be a child again.

DISCUSSION QUESTIONS ▪

1. This description features a moving observer. Where are the writer's movements indicated?
2. Point out details that appeal to each of the five senses.
3. Reread paragraph 7. Identify perceptive observations used to describe the Ferris wheel ride.
4. How is the essay organized? For its purpose, is this pattern appropriate?

SUGGESTIONS FOR WRITING ▪   Choose one of the following topics or another that your instructor approves for an essay of description. Create a dominant impression by using carefully chosen, well-organized details observed from an appropriate vantage point. Try to write so that the reader actually experiences your description.

1. Holiday shopping
2. A rock concert
3. An exercise class
4. A graduation audience
5. A shopping center
6. A pet store or zoo
7. A busy city intersection
8. The view from your bedroom window
9. Getting caught in a storm
10. A fast-food restaurant
11. Your house after a party
12. An outdoor place of special importance to you
13. A run-down part of town
14. An automobile
15. An arcade

clanging and banging" and "the metal pieces slapped together"), and paragraph 7 ("The motor belched.").

Vivid impressions of smell and taste occur in paragraph 2 ("the tantalizing fragrance of popcorn, the spicy aroma of pizza, and the sweet molasses smell of caramel corn.") and paragraph 5 ("the sticky puffs melted on my tongue into sweet sugar.").

Finally, impressions of touch appear in paragraph 4 ("The little tug on my sleeve. . ."), paragraph 5 ("Soon our faces and hands were gummed with goo."), paragraph 7 ("As the seat gently swayed," "goose bumps formed on my brother's bare arms," and "The wind whipped through my hair. . .stinging my 1face at times.").

3. Perceptive observations in paragraph 7 include the bulk of the towering Ferris wheel, the swaying of its seat, the belching of the motor as the huge contraption slowly starts to turn, the kaleidoscopic view from its top, and the whipping of the wind through the writer's hair. The observations help recreate, in the reader's mind, the experience of riding on a Ferris wheel.

4. The organization takes the reader inside the fairgrounds, down the midway and finally to the rides—an appropriate pattern since the climactic event of the essay is the ride on the Ferris wheel.

SUGGESTED INSTRUCTOR READINGS

Brand J. "Descriptive Experiment," School Arts 12 (1979): 44–45. Provides a provocative and imaginative assignment that uses description.

Taylor, M. "Draw: A Heuristic for Expressive Writing." Journal of Teaching Writing 4 (1985): 210–14. Demonstrates how a form of creative description can help students to develop ideas for expressive writing.

Chapter 6

Process Analysis: Explaining How

"Hey Bill, I'd like you to take a look at Mr. Gorgerise's car. He's really fuming. Says the engine's burning too much oil, running rough, and getting poor mileage. Check it out and see what you can find."

Bill begins by removing the spark plugs, hooking a remote-control starter to the starter in the car, and grounding the ignition to prevent the car's starting accidentally. Next, he fits a compression pressure gauge into the sparkplug hole by cylinder number one, starts the engine, and reads and records the pressure; then he does the same for each of the other cylinders. Finally, he compares the readings with one another and the auto maker's engine specs. The verdict? An excessively worn engine that needs rebuilding. Bill has carried out a *process*, just one among many that fill his workdays.

As we pursue our affairs, we perform processes almost constantly, ranging from such daily rituals as brewing a pot of coffee and flossing our teeth to taking a picture, taping a compact disc, preparing for a date, or replacing a light switch. Often we share our special technique for doing something—for example, making chicken cacciatore—by passing it on to a friend.

Many popular publications feature process analyses which help readers to sew zippers in garments, build catamarans, live within their means, and improve their wok technique. Process analysis also frequently helps you meet the writing demands of your courses. A political science instructor may ask you to explain how George Bush won the presidential nomination in 1988, or a biology instructor may want an explanation of how bees find their way back to the hive. Another instructor may call for directions relating to some process in your field—for example, analyzing a chemical compound, taking fingerprints, or obtaining a blood sample. Later, depending on your job, your employer may require directions for assembling a device or developing a new computer system.

As these examples show, a process can be nontechnical, historical, scientific, natural, or technical.

KINDS OF PROCESS ANALYSIS PAPERS

Some process analysis papers offer directions for readers who will carry out the procedure. These readers may be technical or professional personnel who need the information to perform a work-related task. Other papers detail procedures for audiences that won't perform them.

A how-to-do-it paper must include everything the reader needs to know in order to ensure a successful outcome. Its directions take the form of polite commands, often addressing readers directly as "you." This approach helps involve readers in the explanation and emphasizes that the directions must, not merely should, be followed. Here is an illustration.

TEACHING STRATEGIES
1. Ask students to evaluate the two kinds of process writing in the Reader. "How to Adopt a Stray" and "How to Give a Speech" offer directions; "The Spider and the Wasp" and "Behind the Undertaker's Door" tell how processes are carried out. Have students identify the different purposes of these essays and how they influence the form of address, material included, and organization.
2. Students might consider the changes needed if "How to Give a Speech" explained how a process was performed.
3. In some high school English classes, students have been warned endlessly not to use "you" in their writing. You might reassure them that "you" can be appropriate, identify works they have read that follow the "you approach," but also establish where "you" is not appropriate.

> To prepare a bacterial smear for staining, first use an inoculating loop to place a drop of distilled water on a clean glass microscope slide. Next, pass the loop and the opening of the tube containing the bacterial culture to be examined through a Bunsen burner flame to sterilize them. From the tube, remove a small bit of culture with the loop, and rub the loop in the drop of water on the slide until the water covers an area one and one-half inches long and approximately the width of the slide. Next, reflame the opening of the culture tube to prevent contamination of the culture, and then plug it shut. Allow the smear to air dry, and then pass the slide, smear side up, through the flame of the burner until it is warm to the touch. The dried smear should have a cloudy, milky-white appearance.
>
> Darryl Williams

A process analysis paper directed at nondoers tells how a process is or was performed or took place. These papers can serve a wide range of purposes—for example, to satisfy popular curiosity; to point up the importance, difficulty, or danger of a process; or to cast a process in a favorable or unfavorable light. Such papers, though often quite detailed, do not provide enough information for the reader to perform the task successfully.

Papers of this sort do not issue polite commands or address the reader as "you." Instead, the writer uses the first person (*I*, *we*), the third person (*he*, *she*, *it*, or some noun), or the passive voice, in which the subject of the sentence receives, rather than performs, the action, and the doer is unnamed ("Two samples were used for testing"). Three examples follow.

First Person, Active Voice

Thus, when I now approach a stack of three two-inch cinder blocks to attempt a breaking feat, I do not set myself to "try hard," or to summon up all my strength. Instead I relax, sinking my awareness into my belly and legs, feeling my connection with the ground. I breathe deeply, mentally directing the breath through my torso, legs, and arms. I imagine a line of force coming up from the ground through my legs, down one arm, and out through the stone slabs, and down again into the ground, penetrating to the center of the earth. I do not focus any attention on the objects to be broken. Although when I am lifting or holding them in a normal state of consciousness the blocks seem tremendously dense, heavy, and hard, in the course of my one- or two-minute preparation their reality seems to change, as indeed the reality of the whole situation changes. . . . When I make my final approach to the bricks, if I regard them at all they seem light, airy, and friendly; they do not have the insistent inner drive in them that I do.

Don Ethan Miller, "A State of Grace:
Understanding the Martial Arts"

Third Person, Active Voice

To define a word . . . the dictionary editor places before him the stack of cards illustrating that word; each of the cards represents the use of the word by a writer of some literary or historical importance. He reads the cards carefully, discards some, re-reads the rest, and divides up the stack according to what he thinks are the several senses of the word. Finally, he writes his definition, following the hard-and-fast rule that each definition must be based on what the quotations in front of him reveal about the meaning of the word.

S. I. Hayakawa, *Language in Thought and Action*

Third Person, Passive Voice

The analyzer was adjusted so the scale read zero and was connected to the short sampling tube which had previously been inserted into the smoke stack. The sample was taken by depressing the bulb the requisite number of times, and the results were then read and recorded. The procedure was repeated, this time using the long sampling

tube and sampling through the fire door.

Charles Finnie

EXERCISE ■   Examine your favorite newspaper or magazine for examples of process analysis. Bring them to class for group discussion of which kind each represents and the writer's purpose.

WRITING A PROCESS ANALYSIS

Planning and Drafting the Process Analysis

As always, when the choice is yours, select a familiar topic. If you're not the outdoor type and prefer a Holiday Inn to the north woods, don't try to explain how to plan a campout. Muddled, inaccurate, and inadequate information will result. On the other hand, if you've pitched many a tent, you might want to share your technique with your readers.

Finding a suitable topic should be easy. But if you do hit a snag, turn to the strategies on pages 12–19. In any event, answer the following questions for each potential choice:

Will the reader find this process useful or interesting?
Should I provide directions for the reader to follow or simply explain how others perform the process?
Can I explain the process adequately within any assigned length?

To help accumulate the necessary details for the body of your paper, ponder this second set of questions.

What separate actions make up the process? (Be especially careful not to omit any action that is obvious to you but wouldn't be to your reader. Such an oversight can ruin your reader's chances of success.)
What is the reason for each action?
If I'm providing directions, what warnings will the reader need in order to perform the process properly and safely?

When you have your answers, record them in a chart similar to this one.

Action	*Reason for Action*	*Warning*
First action	First reason	First warning
Second action	Second reason	Second warning

PERSPECTIVE

When writing process papers, students often assume the reader is somewhat familiar with the process. When explaining how to prepare for skin diving, they might take for granted that the reader has had diving instruction. Thus they are tempted to omit information that "the reader will already know." Tell students that most process papers are written for novices who will need all the help they can get.

TEACHING STRATEGIES

1. Ask students to examine some of the essays in the Reader and list their apparent assumptions about an audience. Or bring to class some instructions that don't assume the reader's limited background knowledge, perhaps instructions for installing or operating electronic equipment or computers.
2. To help students see how a process is developed, break down a finished essay, such as "How to Give a Speech," into a chart similar to the one on page 93.
3. To help students understand process writing, you could have them break down a complex process from one of their textbooks into its component parts. Alternatively, ask them to become knowledgeable about some procedure, such as how to use a library tool, change majors, or gain certification in some occupation. They might conduct interviews as part of the assignment.
4. To demonstrate the consequences of imprecise instructions, point out that the official review of the Three Mile Island incident cited ambiguity in the operating manual as one of the causes of the disaster.

CLASSROOM ACTIVITIES

1. Have students brainstorm (in small groups or as the entire class) instructions for an activity that they all know. List the results on the board and check them as a group for completeness, accuracy, and organization.

2. To demonstrate the importance of writing exact instructions, hand out a simple diagram to the class. Have students write instructions for drawing it, exchange just the instructions, and then follow them *exactly* as they attempt to reproduce the diagram. If the instructions don't call for pen or pencil and paper, for example, the reader would not proceed. Once students finish drawing their shapes, have them compare their results with the original to determine the differences.

3. No law decrees that process must be serious. Perhaps have students try brainstorming humorous instructions for avoiding muggers, staying up late, cramming for an exam, or the like.

ETHICAL ISSUE

Who is responsible if a writer produces unclear or inaccurate instructions for a company's product and a reader, following those instructions, is injured? Have students role play this scenario, with some representing the writer, others the company, and still others the injured party. Have the class establish criteria for when a writer is, and is not, responsible.

DISCUSSION QUESTION

The writer notes that grilling hamburgers is "a simple process that almost anyone can master" and that the grilled patties are "a treat that almost everyone will enjoy."

Sometimes a reason will be so obvious no mention is necessary, and many actions won't require warnings. When you've completed the chart, review it carefully and supply any missing information. If necessary, make a revised chart.

EXERCISE ■

1. **Develop a complete list of the actions involved in one of the following processes; then arrange them in an appropriate order.**

    a. Baking bread
    b. Assembling or repairing some common household device
    c. Carrying out a process related to sports
    d. Breaking a bad habit
    e. Building a fire in a fireplace

2. **Examine your favorite newspaper or magazine for examples of process analysis. Bring them to class for group discussion of how they illustrate step-by-step directions.**

Start your paper by identifying the process and arousing your reader's interest. You might, for instance, note the usefulness of the process or the ease of carrying it out. If the reader will perform the process, list any items needed to do the work and note any special conditions required for a successful outcome. A paper explaining how to grill hamburgers might begin as follows.

> Grilling hamburgers on an outdoor charcoal grill is a simple process that almost anyone can master. Before starting, you will need a clean grill, charcoal briquets, charcoal lighter fluid and matches, hamburger meat, a plate, a spatula, and some water to put out any flames caused by fat drippings. The sizzling, tasty patties you will have when you finish are a treat that almost everyone will enjoy.

DISCUSSION QUESTION ■   How does the writer try to induce the reader to perform the process?

Use the body of the paper to discuss the procedure in detail. Before starting to write, however, scrutinize your list of actions and group related ones together to form steps, the major subdivisions of the procedure. The following actions constitute the first step—getting the fire going—of the hamburger-grilling paper.

remove grill rack	light briquets
stack charcoal briquets	spread briquets out

Present each step in one or more paragraphs so each is distinct and easily grasped.

Develop each step in appropriate detail. For information-only papers, merely provide a good general idea of what the process entails and, where it would be helpful, the reason for an action. Papers providing directions to follow are another matter. If you've ever muttered under your breath as you struggled to assemble something that came with fuzzy or inadequate directions, you know the importance of presenting steps clearly, accurately, and fully. Therefore, think hard about what the reader needs to know. Note the reason for any action unless the reason is obvious. Flag each difficult or dangerous step with a cautionary warning. If two steps must be performed simultaneously, tell the reader at the start of the first one. In some places you may want to tell readers what to expect if they have completed the instructions properly. Feedback lets readers know they are on track or that they need to redo something.

Let's see how the first step of the hamburger-grilling paper might unfold.

> The first step is to get the fire going. Remove the grill rack and stack about twenty charcoal briquets in a pyramid shape in the center of the grill. Stacking allows the briquets to burn off one another and thus produces a hotter fire. Next, squirt charcoal lighter fluid over the briquets. Wait about five minutes so that the fluid has time to soak into the charcoal. Then toss in a lighted match. The flame will burn for a few minutes before it goes out. When this happens, allow the briquets to sit for another fifteen minutes so that the charcoal can start to burn. Once the burning starts, do not squirt on any more lighter fluid. A flame could quickly follow the stream back into the can, causing it to explode. As the briquets begin to turn from pitch black to ash white, spread them out with a stick so that they barely touch one another. Air can then circulate and produce a hot, even fire, the type that makes grilling a success.

DISCUSSION QUESTIONS ■

1. At what points has the writer provided reasons for doing things?
2. Where has he included a warning?

Some processes can unfold in *only one order*. When you shoot a free throw in basketball, for example, you step up to the line and receive the ball before lining up the shot, and you line up the shot before releasing the ball. Other processes can be carried out in an *order of choice*. When you grill hamburgers, you can make the patties either before or after you light the charcoal. If you have an option, use the order that has worked best for you.

End your paper with a few brief remarks that provide some perspective on the process. A summary of the steps often works best for longer, multi-step processes. Other popular choices include evaluating the results of the process or discussing its importance. The paper on hamburger grilling ends the latter way.

```
Once the patties are cooked the way you like them, remove

them from the grill and place them on buns. Now you are ready

to enjoy a mouthwatering treat that you will long remember.

                                                    E. M. Pryzblyo
```

Revising the Process Analysis

TEACHING STRATEGIES
1. Students should know that they can revise their process papers effectively by following the instructions and seeing if everything works.
2. If the assignment allows it, have students exchange essays and then attempt to follow each other's instructions, reporting on any failures. If this exchange isn't possible, peer response works especially well with process papers since the peer is more likely than the writer to identify omissions and point out other problems.

To revise, follow the guidelines in Chapter 3 and pose these questions.

Have I written consistently for someone who will perform the process or someone who will merely follow it?
Have I included every necessary action? Explained any purpose that is unclear?
Have I warned about any steps that are dangerous or might be performed improperly?
Are my steps presented in an appropriate order? Developed in sufficient detail?

EXAMPLE STUDENT ESSAY OF PROCESS ANALYSIS

```
                        The ABC's of CPR


                        Kathy Petroski
```

TEACHING STRATEGY
You might have students identify the warnings and feedback that accompany the actual steps. Suggest that they reread the directions, omit these elements, and note the effectiveness of the essay with and without the omissions.

```
        A heart attack, drowning, choking, or an              1

electric shock--any of these can stop a person's

breathing. The victim, however, need not always die.

Many lives that would otherwise be lost can be saved
```

simply by applying the ABC's of CPR--cardiopulmonary resuscitation. CPR requires no special equipment. However, no one should attempt it without first receiving qualified instruction on a mannequin. Here's how it is performed. When you are certain that the victim's breathing and pulse have stopped, start CPR immediately. If breathing and circulation aren't restored within five minutes, irreversible brain damage occurs.

<u>A</u> stands for opening the airway. Lay the victim   2
in a supine (face up) position on a firm surface. Once the victim is correctly positioned, quickly tilt the head as far back as possible by placing one hand beneath the neck and gently lifting upward. In an unconscious person, the tongue falls to the back of the throat and blocks the air passages. Hyperextending the head in this fashion pulls the tongue from that position, thus allowing air to pass. At the same time tilt the forehead back with the other hand until the chin points straight upward. The relaxed jaw muscles will then tighten, opening the air passage to the lungs. Remove your hand from the forehead and, using your first two fingers, check the mouth for food, dentures, vomitus, or a foreign object. Remove any obstruction with a sweeping motion. These measures may cause the patient to start breathing spontaneously. If they do not, mouth-to-mouth resuscitation must be started.

<u>B</u> stands for breathing. While maintaining your   3
grasp behind the neck, pinch the victim's nostrils shut with the index finger and thumb of your other hand. Open your mouth, and place it over the victim's mouth so that

a tight seal is formed. Such contact allows air to reach
and expand the lungs. If the seal is incomplete, you
will hear your own breath escaping. Deliver four quick,
full breaths without allowing the victim's lungs to
deflate completely between breaths; then remove your
mouth and allow him to exhale passively. At this point,
check the carotid pulse to determine whether the heart
is beating. To do so, place the tips of your index and
middle fingers laterally into the groove between the
trachea (windpipe) and the muscles at the side of the
neck. If no pulse is evident, artificial circulation
must be started.

C means circulation. Locate the lower end of the   4
sternum (breastbone), and move upward approximately
the width of two fingers. At this point, firmly apply
the heel of one hand, positioning the fingers at right
angles to the length of the body and keeping them
slanted upward. If the hand is positioned any higher or
lower on the sternum, serious internal injuries in the
abdomen or chest are possible. Now place the heel of
your second hand on top of your first. The fingers may
be interlaced or interlocked, but they must not touch
the chest, or the force of your compressions may
fracture ribs.

Keeping your elbows straight and pushing down   5
from the shoulders, apply firm, heavy pressure until
the sternum is depressed approximately one and one-
half to two inches. Rock forward and backward in a
rhythmic fashion, exerting pressure with the weight of
your body. This action squeezes the heart against the
immobile spine with enough pressure to pump blood from
the left ventricle of the heart into general

circulation. Compress the chest, and then immediately release the pressure, fifteen times. Do not, at any point in the cycle, remove your hands from the chest wall. Counting the compressions aloud will help develop a systematic cycle, which is essential for success. When the fifteen have been completed, pinch the nose as described above, seal the victim's mouth with your own, and deliver a quick breath of air. As the victim exhales, inhale another breath and deliver it, and then compress the chest an additional fifteen times. Alternate respiration and compression steps, timing yourself so as to deliver approximately eighty compressions per minute.

At various intervals, quickly check the   6
effectiveness of your CPR technique. Lift the eyelids and notice if the pupils are constricted—a key sign that the brain is receiving enough oxygen. In addition, if the bluish color of the victim is decreasing and spontaneous breathing and movement are increasing, the victim has responded favorably.

To maximize the chances for survival, do not   7
interrupt this technique for more than five or ten seconds. Continue the ABC's of CPR until competent medical help or life-support equipment arrives.

DISCUSSION QUESTIONS ■

1. How does the writer use the letters *A*, *B*, and *C* from the CPR technique in this paper?
2. How does the opening paragraph prepare the reader for what follows?
3. Where does the essay indicate the purposes of actions?
4. What order has the writer used? Explain why this order is a good choice.
5. Is the writer merely explaining how the process is carried out, or does she intend for the reader to follow the directions? Defend your answer.

DISCUSSION QUESTIONS

1. The letters *A*, *B*, and *C* in the title suggest the step-by-step procedure that the paper develops. Furthermore, *A*, *B*, and *C* are linked to "airway," "breathing," and "circulation."
2. The introduction points out that the process requires no special equipment, just "presence of mind." In addition, the opening paragraph clarifies why the process is useful—a life could be saved—and why action must occur within a five-minute span: to prevent brain damage.
3. The essay indicates the purposes of actions in sentences five and seven of paragraph 2, sentence four of paragraph 3, sentences four and six of paragraph 4, sentences three and six of paragraph 5, and sentence two of paragraph 6.
4. The writer used fixed order because the process must follow one particular sequence.
5. This essay explains a procedure for the reader to follow. It addresses the reader as "you" and presents directions in the form of polite commands.

**SUGGESTED
INSTRUCTOR READINGS**

Berman, N. "Language, Process, and Tinkertoys." College Composition and Communication 26 (1975): 390–92. To help students develop language skills, Berman suggests that they construct something with tinkertoys and then write instructions so others can duplicate their product.

Kroll, B. "Explaining How to Play a Game: The Development of Informative Writing Skills." Written Communication 3: 195–218. To show how students develop as writers, Kroll uses an assignment in which they are taught to play a game and then asked to write instructions for it.

SUGGESTIONS FOR WRITING ■ Write a process analysis on one of the topics below or one approved by your instructor. The paper may provide instructions for the reader to follow or tell how a process is performed. Prepare a complete list of steps, arrange them in an appropriate order, and follow them as you write the body of your essay.

1. Succeeding at pinball or your favorite video game
2. Programming a computer
3. Making a good impression on a first date
4. Breaking a bad habit
5. Dealing with a bite of a poisonous snake
6. Training a dog or another pet
7. Preparing for a two-week vacation
8. Growing a particular type of fruit or vegetable in a home garden
9. Carrying out a process related to your hobby
10. Preparing your favorite meal
11. Studying for an examination
12. Performing a process required by your job
13. Achieving some important goal
14. Building the body beautiful
15. Being the life of a party

■ Chapter 7

Illustration: Making Yourself Clear

PERSPECTIVE

Illustration isn't merely a writing strategy. Often we understand a general assertion only when we connect it to one or more specific examples. Illustration is therefore the cornerstone of all writing that deals with ideas and of all the writing strategies discussed in this book. Students should understand the importance of connecting general ideas to specific examples and the pivotal role that illustration will play in much of their college and on-the-job writing.

TEACHING STRATEGIES

1. Have students review their textbooks and lecture notes to determine where illustration is used effectively to clarify and where it is either missing or badly used. Ask students to evaluate communication effectiveness with and without illustration.
2. To strengthen their illustrations, writers often use narration or description as support. If you've already covered these strategies, you might ask students to examine the illustration essays in the Reader, point out any instances where narration and description are used, and explain why.
3. Have students list communication situations in their lives, other classes, or careers where illustration would be either helpful or essential.

"It doesn't pay to fight City Hall. For example, my friend Josie. . . ."

"Many intelligent people lack common sense. Take Dr. Brandon. . . ."

"Topnotch women tennis players are among the biggest moneymakers in sports. Last year, for instance, Steffi Graff. . . ."

"Predicting the weather is far from an exact science. Two winters ago, a surprise snowstorm. . . ."

Have you ever noticed how often people use *illustrations* (examples) to clarify general statements?

Ordinary conversations teem with "for example . . ." and "for instance . . . ," often in response to a furrowed brow or puzzled look. Hank Cassidy serves as the perfect example of a good ole boy, or Chicago's Watertower Plaza illustrates a vertical shopping mall. But illustration is not limited to concrete items. Teachers, researchers, and writers often present an abstract principle or natural law, then supply concrete examples that bring it down to earth. An economics instructor might illustrate compound interest by an example showing how much $100 earning 5 percent interest would appreciate in ten years. Examples can also persuade, as when advertisers trot out typical satisfied users of their products to induce us to buy.

The old saw that a picture is worth a thousand words best explains the popularity of illustration. The concrete is always easier to grasp than the abstract, and examples add savor to what might otherwise be flat and vague.

SELECTING APPROPRIATE EXAMPLES

CLASSROOM ACTIVITY

Ask students to bring in different examples of illustration and then either in small or large groups compare them to determine the different types, their purposes, their relative effectiveness, and any problems.

TEACHING STRATEGY

You might have students examine the essays in the Reader and then evaluate the appropriateness, number, and organization of the examples.

Make sure that your examples stay on target, that is, actually support your general statement and do not veer off into an intriguing side issue. For instance, if you're making the point that the lyrics in a rock group's latest album are not in good taste, don't inject comments on the fast life-style of one of its members. Instead, provide examples of lyrics that support your claim, chosen from different songs in the album to head off objections that your examples aren't representative.

Furthermore, see that your examples display all the chief features of whatever you're illustrating. Don't offer Hank Cassidy as an example of a typical good ole boy unless he fits the general mold by being a fun-loving, easy-going beer guzzler who likes to hang out with other men. Alternatively, consider this example of a hacker, a compulsive computer programmer.

> Bob Shaw, a 15-year-old high-school student, is a case in point. Bob was temporarily pulled off the computers at school when he began failing his other courses. But instead of hitting the books, he continues to sulk outside the computer center, peering longingly through the glass door at the consoles within.
>
> Pale and drawn, his brown hair unkempt, Bob speaks only in monosyllables, avoiding eye contact. In answer to questions about friends, hobbies, school, he merely shrugs or mumbles a few words aimed at his sneakered feet. But when the conversation turns to the subject of computers, he brightens—and blurts out a few full sentences about the computer he's building and the projects he plans.
>
> Dina Ingber, "Computer Addicts"

Clearly, Shaw fits the general description of hackers, programmers who have "a drive so consuming it overshadows nearly every other part of their lives and forms the focal point of their existence."

NUMBER OF EXAMPLES

How many examples will you need? One long one, several fairly brief ones, or a large number of very short ones? Look to your topic for the answer. To illustrate the point that a good nurse must be compassionate, conscientious, and competent, your best bet would probably be one example, since one person must possess all these traits.

When dealing with trends, however, you'll need several examples. To show that parents have been rearing children more and more permissively over the last half century, at least three examples are called for: one family from around 1940, a second from about 1965, and a third from the present time. Sometimes topics that do not involve trends require more than one example, as when you demonstrate the sharp differences between Japanese and American attitudes toward work.

Finally, some topics require a whole series of examples. If you're contending that many everyday expressions have their origins in the world of gambling, you'd need many examples to demonstrate your point.

EXERCISE ■

1. **Choose one of the following topic sentences. Select an appropriate example and write the rest of the paragraph.**

    a. Sometimes a minor incident drastically changes a person's life.
    b. _____'s name exactly suits (her/his) personality.
    c. I still get embarrassed when I remember _____.
    d. Not all education goes on in the classroom.
    e. I learned the value of _____ the hard way.

2. **Explain why you would use one extended illustration, several shorter ones, or a whole series of examples to develop each of the following statements. Suggest appropriate illustrations.**

    a. Many parents I know think for their children.
    b. The hamburger isn't what it used to be.
    c. The ideal pet is small, quiet, and affectionate.
    d. Different college students view their responsibilities differently.
    e. The hotels in Gotham City run the gamut from sumptuous to seedy.
    f. Modern English includes any number of words taken directly from foreign languages.

ORGANIZING THE EXAMPLES

A single extended example often assumes the narrative form, presenting a series of events in time sequence. Sets of examples that trace trends also rely on time sequence, moving either forward or backward. This arrangement would work nicely for the paper on the growing permissiveness in child rearing.

On the other hand, a paper showing that different individuals exhibit some characteristic to different extents would logically be organized by order of climax (from the least to the greatest extent) or perhaps the reverse order. To demonstrate how salesclerks differ in their attitudes toward customers, you might first describe a hostile clerk, then a pleasant one, and finally an outstandingly courteous and helpful one.

Sometimes any arrangement will work equally well. Suppose you're showing that Americans are taking various precautions to ward off heart attacks. Although you might move from a person who exercises to one who diets and finally to one who practices relaxation techniques, no special order is preferable.

Large numbers of examples might first be grouped into categories and the categories then arranged in a suitable order. For example, the expressions from the world of gambling could be grouped according to types of gambling: cards, dice, horse racing, and the like. Depending upon the specific categories, one arrangement may or may not be preferable to another.

WRITING AN ILLUSTRATION

Planning and Drafting the Illustration

Assertions, unfamiliar topics, abstract principles, natural laws—as we've seen, all of these can form the foundation for your paper. If you have a choice, you should experience little difficulty finding something suitable. As always, the strategies on pages 12–19 can help generate some possibilities, which you can then evaluate by asking these questions.

Exactly what point am I trying to make? (Write it down in precise terms.)

Why do I want to make this point? To show how bad something is? To encourage something? To scare people into or away from something?

Who is my prospective audience?

Should I use one extended example, or will I need more? Why?

Once you've picked your topic, ask yourself, "What example(s) will work best with my audience?" Then brainstorm each one for supporting details. Use a chart patterned after the one below to help you.

Example 1	*Example 2*	*Example 3*
First supporting detail	First supporting detail	First supporting detail
Second supporting detail	Second supporting detail	Second supporting detail

Review your details carefully and add any new ones you think of; then make a new chart and re-enter the details into it, arranged in the order you intend to present them.

Your introduction should identify your topic and draw your reader into the paper. If you're illustrating a personal belief, you might indicate how you developed it. If you're trying to scare the reader into or away from something, you might open with an arresting statement.

Present your examples in the body of your paper. If you have a large number of very brief examples, perhaps group them into related categories for discussion. The paper on expressions from gambling, for instance, might devote one paragraph each to terms from the worlds of cards, dice, and horse racing. If you're dealing with a few relatively brief examples—say to show a trend—put each in its own paragraph. For a single extended example, use the entire body of the paper, suitably paragraphed. Thus, an extended example of someone with an eccentric life-style might include paragraphs on his mode of dress, living accommodations, and public behavior.

Conclude in whatever way seems most appropriate. You might express a hope or recommendation that the reader implement or avoid something, or you might issue a personal challenge that grows out of the point you've illustrated.

Revising the Illustration

Think about the following questions and the general guidelines in Chapter 3 as you revise your paper.

Exactly what idea am I trying to put across? Have I used the examples that best typify it?

Do my examples illuminate my idea without introducing irrelevant material?

Are my examples interesting?

Have I used an appropriate number of examples?

Have I organized my paper effectively?

EXAMPLE STUDENT ESSAY OF ILLUSTRATION

A Lesson from Nature

Mike Braendle

As I was growing up, my parents often passed   1
along little maximlike sayings to me. Most of these
have since slipped my mind, but I still remember the
exact words of my father's favorite: ''The door to
success is labeled Push.'' Although for a while these
were just words to me, I came to understand their true
meaning as I observed the struggles of a crayfish while
I was fishing one day.

There it lay, trapped in the small plastic   2
compartment of my steel tackle box, which was sitting
on the bank of the river. The sun had been shining for
some time and the plastic of the compartment

surrounding the crayfish intensified the heat. In fact, the heat had become so great that the skin covering the small hard-shelled body was beginning to wrinkle. Nevertheless, the pinching claws continually groped about, trying to find something to grasp, some means of escape. The hard and heavy shell, acting like an anchor, burdened the crayfish greatly. The two small eyes, always moving, searched wildly for some way out, but found none. The segmented tail, as large as the rest of the body, was constantly pushing, trying to hoist the heavy body over the edge of the compartment.

The eyes at last fell upon a possibility for escape: the back wall of the compartment was slightly lower than the other three walls. Sensing an advantage, the crayfish seemed to labor more deliberately. The tail, pushing vigorously, tried to lift the heavy shell out of the plastic compartment. As the tail struggled, the claws slashed savagely back and forth, searching for something to grab. 3

Finally, after some time and struggle, the crayfish grasped the back wall. As it pulled, with every muscle straining, the hard shell edged up and over the wall of the compartment. Stopping abruptly and gazing at its surroundings, the crayfish tried to orient itself. Off to one side in another compartment lay a strange-looking creature, unmoving. The crayfish did not recognize this odd-shaped thing as a fishing lure, but it did sense that the creature, with its bright metallic tint and protruding hooks, was not alive. 4

It took only a moment for the determined   5
crustacean to figure out which way to go. It moved, as
if driven by instinct, across this compartment and then
others, occasionally getting caught on a protruding
hook. These hooks slowed its progress, scratching
grooves and gouges in the hard shell.

As the crayfish moved steadily toward the edge of   6
the box, the thought of cold water seemed to excite it.
It moved faster, more deliberately now. When reaching
the edge of the box, it stopped for a moment, as if
pondering what to do next. Then, defiantly, it flopped
over the edge, landing on its hard shell. It stayed on
its back for some time but then turned over and dragged
itself to the water.

The crayfish lay there for a long time, soaking   7
in the cool and refreshing river. Then with a powerful
flap of its tail, it disappeared into the depths. Here,
where there was no threat of drying out, it could and
probably would recuperate from this tiring experience.

DISCUSSION QUESTIONS ■

1. What general statement does this essay illustrate?
2. Why is one extended iilustration effective here?
3. Explain the organization of the essay and why it is appropriate.
4. In paragraph 2, the writer says the crayfish "continually groped" and "searched wildly" with its tail "constantly pushing." How do these descriptions relate to the writer's purpose?
5. Point out specific sentences in paragraphs 3 and 4 that seem particularly effective in engaging the reader's interest.
6. Would a concluding paragraph which restated the main idea make this essay more effective? Why or why not?

DISCUSSION QUESTIONS

1. The essay illustrates the idea that "Dedicated effort is the key to accomplishing your goals." This can, of course, be phrased in various ways. In the essay we are told that "The door to success is labeled Push."
2. This single illustration is sufficient because the crayfish's struggle and eventual escape from the tackle box completely exemplify the writer's point. Additional examples would have been redundant.
3. Chronological organization is the only feasible way to present the series of events that make up the struggle.
4. Struggle, or "push," is the key to success. These phrases show the crayfish struggling for its objective: freedom.
5. The third and fourth sentences of paragraph 3 and the second sentence of paragraph 4 engage the reader's interest. These sentences offer vivid sight impressions that depict the struggle of the crayfish.
6. The illustration exemplifies the point effectively; a restatement of the idea would be superfluous.

SUGGESTIONS FOR WRITING ■   Use one of the ideas below or another that your instructor approves for your illustration essay. Select appropriate examples, determine how many you will use, and decide how you will organize them.

1. Americans are a wasteful people.
2. If you want something done, ask the busiest person around.
3. People often choose strange places to vacation.
4. Women are becoming increasingly prominent (in politics, business, sports, or some other field).
5. Dedication is the secret of success for many athletes (or use any other field or occupation).
6. People have many strange remedies for hangovers.
7. An adult never stands so tall as when stooping to help a child.
8. A good nurse must be compassionate, conscientious, and competent (or use another occupation with appropriate characteristics).
9. _____ is a demanding profession.
10. Many intelligent people lack common sense.
11. It does not (or does) pay to fight City Hall.
12. Successful people are often self-made.
13. "Doing your thing" does not always work out for the best.
14. _____ is the most (or least) effective teacher I have ever had.
15. Not to decide is to decide.

■ Chapter 8

Classification: Grouping into Categories

PERSPECTIVE

While we all classify our world into functional categories, students often find working with classification to be an abstract task. You can help them approach this strategy by reinforcing what the text points out: since they classify on a regular basis, they already have considerable experience with the method. Furthermore, some students find it difficult to think hierarchically in terms of categories divided into subcategories. By using drawings and charts, you can demonstrate the relationship among categories and prepare your students for writing.

Help Wanted, Situations Wanted, Real Estate, Personal. Do these terms look familiar? They do if you've ever scanned the classified ads of the newspaper. Ads are grouped into categories, and each category is then subdivided. The people who assemble this layout are *classifying*. Figure 8.1 shows the main divisions of a typical classified ad section and a further breakdown of one of them.

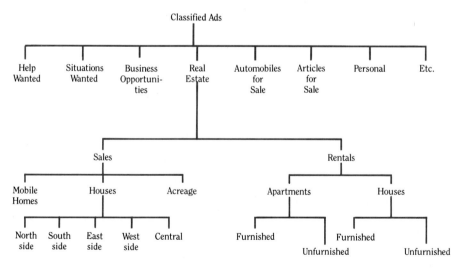

Figure 8.1

As this figure indicates, grouping allows the people who handle ads to divide entries according to a logical scheme and helps readers find what they are looking for. Imagine the difficulty of checking the real estate ads if all the entries were run in the order the ads were placed.

Our minds naturally sort information into categories. Within a few weeks

TEACHING STRATEGIES

1. Over a week's time have students record where they rely on classification, whether it is selecting a type of doctor, determining what store would have a coat, or finding a radio station that plays their kind of music.
2. Have students go to a local grocery store and see whether they can determine how the merchandise is classified. For example, some stores group health and beauty products together; some group them separately. Students could develop a list of the different categories, noting examples of the items in each one.
3. Have students examine popular writing and note any classifications that the writers use. Possibilities include types of parents, stereo systems, or food groups.
4. Classification can be a useful learning tool. Have students identify where direct or implied classification is used in their other courses. You might help them chart the classification system.

109

after their birth, infants can tell the faces of family members from those of outsiders. Later, toddlers learn to distinguish between cats, dogs, and rabbits. In both cases the classification rests solely on physical differences. As we mature we start classifying in more abstract ways, and by adulthood we are constantly sorting things into categories: dates or mates, eating places, oddballs, friends, investments, jobs, political views.

Classification also helps writers and readers come to grips with large or complex topics. It breaks a broad topic into categories according to some specific principle, presents the distinctive features of each category, and shows how the features vary among categories. Segmenting the topic simplifies the discussion by presenting the information in small, neatly sorted piles rather than in one jumbled and confusing heap.

Furthermore, classification helps people make choices. Identifying which groups of consumers—students, accountants, small business owners—are most likely to buy some new product allows the manufacturer to place ads in appropriate magazines. Knowing the engine size, maneuverability, seating capacity, and gas mileage of typical subcompact, compact, and intermediate-size cars helps customers decide which one to buy. Examining the features of term, whole-life, and endowment insurance enables prospective buyers to select the policy that best suits their needs. As you can see, classification plays an important role in our lives.

SELECTING CATEGORIES

People classify in different ways for different purposes, which generally reflect their interests. A clothing designer might classify women according to their fashion sense, a representative of the National Organization for Women according to their views on feminism, and the Secretary of Labor according to their occupations. A college's director of housing might classify students according to their type of residence, the dean of students according to their behavior problems, and the financial aid officer according to their sources of income.

When you write a classification paper, choose a principle of classification that's suited to your audience. To illustrate, if you are writing for students, don't classify instructors according to their religion, dietary choices, or investment habits. These breakdowns probably wouldn't interest most students and certainly wouldn't serve their needs. Instead, develop a more useful principle of classification—perhaps by teaching styles, grasp of subject matter, concern for students, or grading policies.

Sometimes it's helpful or necessary to divide one or more categories into subcategories. If you do, use just one principle of classification for each level. Both levels in Figure 8.2 meet this test because each reflects a single principle: place of origin for the first, number of cylinders for the second.

Now examine Figure 8.3. This classification is *improper* because it groups cars in two ways—by place of origin and by kind—making it possible for one car to end up in two different categories. For example, the British Triumph is both a

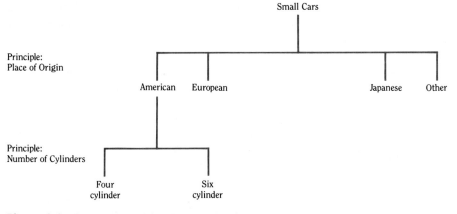

Principle:
Place of Origin

Principle:
Number of Cylinders

Figure 8.2   Proper Classification of Small Cars

Figure 8.3   Improper Classification of Small Cars

European car and a sports car. When categories overlap in this way, confusion reigns and nothing is clarified.

EXERCISE ■

1. **How would each of the following people be most likely to classify the families in Anytown, USA?**

   a. The bishop of the Roman Catholic diocese in which the city is located
   b. The state senator who represents the city
   c. A field worker for the NAACP
   d. The director of the local credit bureau

2. **The following lists contain overlapping categories. Identify the inconsistent item in each list and explain why it is faulty.**

Nurses	*Pictures*	*Electorate in Midville*
Surgical nurses	Oil paintings	Republicans
Psychiatric nurses	Magazine illustrations	Democrats
Emergency room nurses	Lithographs	Nonvoters
Terminal care nurses	Watercolors	Independents
Night nurses	Etchings	

2. Have students, working in groups, establish what classification systems would be helpful for marketing several new products or services to the student population. Possible services or products include a new tutoring service, pizza or newspaper delivery, research assistance, perfume, mini-refrigerators, stereo equipment.

EXERCISE ANSWERS

1. Classifying the families in Anytown, USA:
a. The Roman Catholic bishop would probably classify the families by religious preference: Catholic, Protestant, Jewish, Moslem, no religion.
b. The state senator would probably categorize the families by political preference: Democratic, Republican, Libertarian, independent.
c. The NAACP representative would probably categorize them by race: caucasian, black, oriental.
d. The director of the local credit bureau would probably categorize them by their credit ratings: good credit risks, questionable credit risks, poor credit risks.

You might remind students that in all cases the same group of people is being categorized. An individual might be a Catholic, a Republican, a black, and a good credit risk. In addition, these groupings might be expanded. The population of Anytown might include Buddhists, socialists, American Indians, and people who have no credit rating of any sort.

2. Identifying the overlapping category:
Nurses: The overlapping category is "night nurses"; these might work as surgical nurses, emergency room nurses, etc.

"SEE ME TOMORROW—I'M BUSY GRADING FINALS NOW."

Reprinted by permission of Richard N. Bibler

NUMBER OF CATEGORIES

Some classification papers discuss every category included within the topic. Others discuss only selected categories. Circumstances and purpose dictate the scope of the discussion. Suppose you work for the commerce department of your state and are asked to write a report that classifies the major nonservice industries in a certain city and assesses their strengths and weaknesses. Your investigation shows that food processing, furniture making, and the production of auto parts account for over 95 percent of all nonservice jobs. Two minor industries, printing and toy making, provide the rest of the jobs. Given these circumstances, you'd probably focus on the first three industries, mentioning the others only in passing. But if printing and toy making were significant industries, they too would require detailed discussion.

DEVELOPING CATEGORIES

Develop every category you include with specific, informative details that provide a clear picture of each one and help the reader grasp the distinctions and relationships among them. The following excerpt from a student paper classifying public restrooms for women discusses two of the writer's three categories.

TEACHING STRATEGY
You might point out that specific details help writers avoid stereotyping, particularly when the essay features types of people.

Luxurious restrooms are found in top-drawer business establishments such as fancy department stores, chic boutiques, and the better restaurants. This aristocrat of public facilities usually disdains the term ''restroom,'' masquerading instead under the alias of ''lounge'' or ''powder room.'' Upon entering its plush environs, the user is captivated by its elegance. Thick carpet reaches up to cushion tired feet, wood paneled or brocade velvet walls beckon invitingly, and dimly twinkling chandeliers or wall sconces soothe the eyes. Narrow little divans and gold-and-velvet tables add to the restful, welcoming atmosphere, and the latest issues of upscale magazines like Vogue, The New Yorker, and Vanity Fair entice resters into their pages. Mirrors in carved frames, designer lavatories with richly ornamented faucets, and creamy scented soap go hand in hand with the attendant who quietly dispenses thick, white towels as soft as suede. Her detached air deserts her only when she sneaks a furtive glance toward the silver tip dish as the patron passes it on the way out.

The adequate restroom offers utility without the swankiness of its lavish cousin. Typically located in a large shopping mall or mass-market department store, it is a stark world of hard, unadorned surfaces—tile floors, tile walls, and harshly glaring fluorescent lights recessed in the ceiling. For those who wish to rest, there is a garishly colored Naugahyde couch and next to it a battered metal or wood table holding a few tattered copies of Family Circle,

<u>People</u>, <u>Reader's Digest</u>, and similar publications. The mirrors have steel frames, the lavatories, set in a formica counter, have plain chrome faucets, and the soap dispenser emits a thin stream of unscented liquid. Paper toweling pulled from a wall-mounted metal holder replaces the cloth article, and no maid stands by to offer her help or to exact tips from departing visitors.

Student Unknown

The concrete details in these paragraphs effectively characterize each category and clearly distinguish between them. Imagine how vague and indistinct the categories would be without these details.

WRITING A CLASSIFICATION

Planning and Drafting the Classification

Any topic made up of categories is a potential candidate for classification. If you're selecting your own topic, use one or more of the narrowing strategies on pages 12–19 to help stimulate your thinking. As possibilities come to mind, examine each one in light of these questions.

What purpose will this classification serve?
Who is my audience and what will interest them?
What are the categories of this topic?
What features distinguish my categories from one another?

Next, determine whether you'll discuss every category or only selected ones, and then set up a classification chart similar to the one following.

Category 1
First distinguishing
  feature
Second distinguishing
  feature

Category 2
First distinguishing
  feature
Second distinguishing
  feature

Category 3
First distinguishing
  feature
Second distinguishing
  feature

TEACHING STRATEGY

Students often view writing a classification as a formal activity without a real purpose or audience. To correct this mistaken belief, you might specify both or guide students to do so. For example, students could classify the different types of sororities or fraternities for those thinking of pledging. A more challenging assignment is to have them research the different categories of jobs in their chosen fields (what are the different kinds of medical technicians or accountants?) in order to help others in the field select a specialty.

Such a chart helps you see the relationships among categories and provides a starting point for developing your specific details. Proceed by jotting down the details that come to mind for each distinguishing feature of every category. Then prepare a second chart with the distinguishing features and details arranged in the order you want to present them.

Begin your paper by identifying your topic and capturing your reader's attention in some way. A paper classifying hair dyes might point out their growing popularity among both men and women. One classifying snobs might offer an anecdote showing how far snobbery can go. Or you could cite a personal experience that relates to your topic. As always, circumstances dictate your choice.

In the body discuss your categories in whatever order best suits your purpose. Order of climax—least important, more important, most important—often works well. Or perhaps your topic will suggest arranging the categories by behavior, income, education, or physical characteristics. Whatever your arrangement, signal it clearly to your reader. Don't merely start the discussions of your categories by saying first . . . , second . . . , another . . . , next . . . , and the like. These words offer no hint of the rationale behind your order.

In addition, make sure the arrangement of material within the categories follows a consistent pattern. Recall the two categories of restrooms discussed on pages 113–114. In each case, after noting where the restroom can be found, the writer discusses its floor, walls, and lighting, moves to the furniture, and ends by discussing the lavatories, soap, and toweling.

The strategies for ending a classification paper are as varied as those for starting it. A paper on hair dyes might conclude by predicting their continued popularity. One on snobs might end with your recommendations for dealing with them. In other cases, you might express a hope of some kind or advise your reader to do something.

Revising the Classification

Revise your paper by following the guidelines in Chapter 3 as well as by pondering these questions.

Does my classification have a clear sense of purpose
    and audience?
Does my principle of classification accord with
    my purpose?
Do any of my categories overlap?
Have I chosen an appropriate number of categories?
Are these categories developed with sufficient details?
Are they arranged in an effective order?

EXAMPLE STUDENT ESSAY OF CLASSIFICATION

Undesirable Produce Market Customers

Clarence DeLong

You will find almost as large a variety of   1
customers at a produce market as you will find fruits
and vegetables. Undesirable produce market customers
fall into three main categories--those who squeeze the
fruit, those who complain constantly, and those who try
to cheat the market--and when you meet them all in one
day, you have one big headache. Perhaps you will
recognize these people as I describe them.

"Sammy Squeezer" is the least annoying of these   2
undesirables. He wants to make sure that everything he
buys is "just right." He pokes his thumbs into the top
of a cantaloupe. If they penetrate very deeply, he
won't buy this particular specimen, considering it to
be overripe. He squeezes the peaches, plums,
nectarines, and any other fruit he can get his hands on.
After ten of these people squeeze one piece of fruit, it
will surely be soft, even if it wasn't originally.
Moving on to the corn, Sammy carefully peels back the
husk to examine the kernels inside. If they don't suit
him, he doesn't bother to fold the husk back to protect
the kernels; he simply tosses the ear back into the
basket. The problems he creates for the employees are
primarily physical--removing the damaged items after
he leaves.

A more annoying customer is "Betty Bitcher." She   3

is never satisfied with the quality of the produce: the bananas are too green, the lettuce has brown spots, the berries are too ripe, and the potatoes have green spots. Sometimes you wonder if Betty would have been satisfied with the fruit grown in the Garden of Eden.

The produce has no monopoly on her complaints, 4 however. Betty also finds fault with the service she receives from the employees. Talking to other customers or directly to the clerks, she can be heard saying such things as "Why is this the only place I ever have to wait in line? They must have trouble getting good help here." Even as she leaves the market, which is none too soon, she must make one last complaint: "You mean I have to carry my own potatoes to the car?" The problems she creates for the employees are primarily mental—she can make your nerves quite active.

Perhaps the most annoying customer of all is 5 "Charlie Cheater." You have to keep your eye on him constantly because he knows all the tricks of cheating. He will add berries to an already full basket. He will take 6/79¢ oranges and tell you they're the 6/59¢ ones. He will put expensive grapes in the bottom of a sack and add cheaper ones on top. Then he'll tell you that they are all the cheaper variety. Likewise, he will put expensive nectarines in a sack, place a few cheaper peaches on top, and try to pass them all off as peaches. If he is caught, he usually says, "I don't know how that happened. My little girl (or boy) must have put them in there." The child usually looks dumbfounded.

The problem Charlie creates for the market is 6 twofold: financial and legal. If you don't catch him, your profits suffer. If you do catch him, you almost

have to prosecute, usually for amounts of only a dollar
or two, or you'll have every Charlie in town at your
door.

    Did you recognize any of these customers? If you   7
didn't and would like to see some of them in action,
stop in at Steve's Produce Market. That's where I work,
and that's where I meet them.

DISCUSSION QUESTIONS
1. The writer wants to show that different types of undesirable customers present different problems for the employees of the market. The second sentence in paragraph 1 introduces this purpose, and the last sentence in paragraphs 2 and 4 and all three sentences in paragraph 6 develop it further.
2. The writer uses order of climax. First, he discusses customers who are least annoying (paragraph 2), then those who are more annoying (paragraphs 3 and 4), and finally those who are most annoying (paragraphs 5 and 6).
3. Specific details in each category show that the squeezer, the bitcher, and the cheater do not overlap.
4. In paragraph 1, the writer says that undesirable customers fall into three "main" categories, thereby indicating that his classification won't encompass all types.

SUGGESTED INSTRUCTOR READING
Laruccia, J. A. "Stories Out of Eden: Reorganizing Naming as Rhetorical Strategy." College English 39 (1978): 979–84. An important approach to teaching the significance of classification is to have students experiment with the consequences of renaming.

DISCUSSION QUESTIONS ■

1. What is the writer's purpose in developing this classification? Where does he state it?
2. In what order has he arranged his categories? Refer to the essay when answering.
3. Demonstrate that the writer has avoided overlapping categories.
4. How do you know he hasn't discussed every category of undesirable customers?

SUGGESTIONS FOR WRITING ■

Write a classification paper on one of the topics below or one approved by your instructor. Determine your purpose and audience, select appropriate categories, decide how many you'll discuss, develop them with specific details, and arrange them in an effective order.

1. College teachers
2. Pet owners
3. House designs
4. Drivers
5. Churchgoers
6. Pocket calculators
7. Patrons of singles bars
8. Eating places
9. Parents
10. Sports announcers (or fans)
11. Television comedies
12. Attitudes toward death
13. Salesclerks
14. People waiting in line
15. Bores

■ Chapter 9

Comparison: Showing Relationships

Which candidate for senator should get my vote, Ken Conwell or Jerry Mander?

Let me know whether this new shipment of nylon thread meets specs.

Doesn't this tune remind you of a Kenny Rogers song?

How does high school in Australia stack up against high school in this country?

Everyone makes *comparisons*, not just once in a while but day after day. When we compare, we examine two or more items for likenesses, differences, or both.

Comparison often helps us choose between alternatives. Some issues are trivial: whether to plunk the first quarter into Star Wars or Space Ace, whether to order pizza or a sub sandwich. But comparison also influences our more important decisions. We weigh majoring in chemistry against majoring in physics, buying against renting, working for Apple Computer against working for IBM. An instructor may ask us to write a paper comparing the features of two word-processing systems. An employer may have us weigh two proposals for decreasing employee absenteeism and write a report recommending one of them.

Comparison also acquaints us with unfamiliar things. To help American readers understand the English sport of rugby, a sportswriter might compare its field, team, rules, and scoring system with those for football. To teach students about France's government, a political science textbook might discuss the makeup and election of its parliament and the method of picking its president and premier, using our own government as a backdrop. As you can see, comparison possibilities crowd our lives.

"WE'D LIKE TO TAKE YOU UPSTAIRS AND SHOW YOU THE REAL GRACIOUSNESS OF FRATERNITY LIFE, BUT IT'S SORT OF A RULE AROUND HERE TO WAIT UNTIL THE 'RUSHEE' IS PLEDGED."

Reprinted by permission of Richard N. Bibler

PERSPECTIVE

Purpose dictates the items selected for a comparison and also how they are developed. It is therefore crucial that students start and proceed with a clear purpose in mind.

TEACHING STRATEGIES

1. Without guidance students often lean toward superficial or self-evident comparisons—winter and summer, day and night—that produce inane generalities. Since such pointless papers serve neither students' interests nor yours, caution against them.
2. Using the subject matter in their other courses or the significant activities or events in their own lives as a basis, students could develop lists of possible purposes for writing comparisons and perhaps lists of points to include. This activity might be the starting point for actual papers.

SELECTING ITEMS FOR COMPARISON

Any items you compare must share some common ground. For example, you could compare two golfers on driving ability, putting ability, and sand play, or two cars on appearance, gas mileage, and warranty; but you can't meaningfully compare a golfer with a car, any more than you could compare guacamole with Guadalajara or chicken with charcoal. There's simply no basis for comparison.

Any valid comparison, on the other hand, presents many possibilities. Suppose you head the record and tape department of a large store and have two excellent salespeople working for you. The manager of the store asks you to prepare a one- or two-page report that compares their qualifications for managing the record department in a new branch store. Assessing their abilities becomes the guiding purpose that motivates and controls the writing. On the spot you can rule out points such as eye color, hair style, and religion, which have no bearing on job performance. Instead, you must decide what managerial traits the job will require and the extent to which each candidate possesses them. Your thinking might result in a list like this.

Points of Similarity or Difference	Pat	Mike
1. Ability to deal with customers, sales skills	Excellent	Excellent
2. Effort: regular attendance, hard work on the job	Excellent	Excellent
3. Leadership qualities	Excellent	Good
4. Knowledge of ordering and accounting procedures	Good	Fair
5. Musical knowledge	Excellent	Good

This list tells you which points to emphasize and suggests Pat as the candidate to recommend. You might briefly mention similarities (points 1 and 2) in an introductory paragraph, but the report would focus on differences (points 3, 4, and 5), since you're distinguishing between two employees.

EXERCISE ■ **Say you want to compare two good restaurants in order to recommend one of them. List the points of similarity and difference that you might discuss. Differences should predominate because you will base your decision on them.**

DEVELOPING A COMPARISON

Successful comparisons rest upon ample, well-chosen details that show just how the items under consideration resemble and differ from each other. Such support helps the reader grasp your meaning. Read the following two student paragraphs and note how the concrete details convey the striking differences between south and north 14th Street.

On 14th Street running south from P Street are opulent department stores, such as Woodward and Lothrop and Julius Garfinkle, and small but expensive clothing stores with richly dressed mannequins in the windows. Modern skyscraping office buildings harbor banks and travel bureaus on the ground floors and insurance companies and corporation headquarters in the upper stories. Dotting the

CLASSROOM ACTIVITY
Have students, working in small groups, brainstorm for details they might need to compare two jobs, two types of parents, or some other appropriate topic. Encourage them to consider the purpose of the details.

concretescape are high—priced movie theaters, gourmet restaurants, multilevel parking garages, bookstores, and candy—novelty—gift shops, all catering to the prosperous population of the city. This section of 14th Street is relatively clean: the city maintenance crews must clean up after only a nine—to—five populace and the Saturday crowds of shoppers. The pervading mood of the area is one of bustling wealth during the day and, in the night, calm.

Crossing P Street toward the north, one notes a gradual but disturbing change in the scenery of 14th Street. Two architectural features assault the eyes and automatically register as tokens of trouble: the floodlights that leave no alley or doorway in shadows and the riot screens that cage in the store windows. The buildings are old, condemned, decaying monoliths, each occupying an entire city block. Liquor stores, drugstores, dusty television repair shops, seedy pornographic bookstores that display photographs of naked bodies with the genital areas blacked out by strips of tape, discount stores smelling perpetually of stale chocolate and cold popcorn, and cluttered pawnshops——businesses such as these occupy the street level. Each is separated from the adjoining stores by a littered entranceway that leads up a decaying wooden stairway to the next two floors. All the buildings are three stories tall, all have most of their windows broken and blocked with boards or newspapers, and all reek of liquor, urine, and unidentifiable rot. And so the general atmosphere of this end of 14th Street is one of poverty and decay.

Student Unknown

Vivid details depict with stark clarity the economic differences between the two cultures.

ORGANIZING A COMPARISON

You can use either of two basic patterns to organize a comparison paper: block or alternating. The paper may deal with similarities, differences, or some combination of them.

The Block Pattern.   The block pattern first presents all of the points of comparison for one item and then all of the points of comparison for the other. Here is the comparison of the two salespeople, Pat and Mike, outlined according to the block pattern.

I.   Introduction: mentions similarities in sales skills and effort but recommends Pat for promotion.
II. Specific points about Mike
    A. Leadership qualities
    B. Knowledge of ordering and accounting procedures
    C. Musical knowledge
III. Specific points about Pat
    A. Leadership qualities
    B. Knowledge of ordering and accounting procedures
    C. Musical knowledge
IV. Conclusion: reasserts that Pat should be promoted.

The block pattern works best with short papers or ones that include only a few points of comparison. The reader can easily remember all the points in the first block while reading the second.

The Alternating Pattern.   The alternating pattern presents a point about one item, then follows immediately with a corresponding point about the other. Organized in this way, the Pat-and-Mike paper would look like this:

I.   Introduction: mentions similarities in sales skills and effort but recommends Pat for promotion.
II. Leadership qualities
    A. Mike's qualities
    B. Pat's qualities
III. Knowledge of ordering and accounting procedures
    A. Mike's knowledge
    B. Pat's knowledge
IV. Musical knowledge
    A. Mike's knowledge
    B. Pat's knowledge
V.   Conclusion: reasserts that Pat should be promoted.

For longer papers that include many points of comparison, use the alternating method. Discussing each point in one place highlights similarities and

PERSPECTIVE

While we usually find it easy to organize a comparison effectively, some students may not. They have difficulty juggling similarities and differences while maintaining a consistent pattern of organization. Reviewing student outlines can help overcome this difficulty.

TEACHING STRATEGY

Transitions are important in comparisons. Therefore, you might have students outline the comparison essays in the Reader, identify the key transition devices, and determine their contribution to the organization.

CLASSROOM ACTIVITY

In small groups students might brainstorm a comparison and then work out an effective outline, perhaps one that incorporates several similarities and differences. This activity could be the starting point for a paper.

EXERCISE ANSWER

Block Method

I. Introduction
II. Restaurant A
   A. Location
   B. Type and quality of food
   C. Decor
   D. Service
   E. Prices
III. Restaurant B
   A. Location
   B. Type and quality of food
   C. Decor
   D. Service
   E. Prices
IV. Conclusion: recommends one of the restaurants

Alternating Method

I. Introduction
II. Location
   A. Restaurant A
   B. Restaurant B
III. Type and quality of food
   A. Restaurant A
   B. Restaurant B
IV. Decor
   A. Restaurant A
   B. Restaurant B
V. Service
   A. Restaurant A
   B. Restaurant B
VI. Prices
   A. Restaurant A
   B. Restaurant B
VII. Conclusion: recommends one of the restaurants

PERSPECTIVE

Analogy can be seen as a key to creativity and effective problem solving. Insights often come from seeing the connections between two seemingly different things. And because an analogy shows a relationship between the familiar and unfamiliar, it is a powerful tool for explaining things.

differences; your reader doesn't have to pause and reread in order to grasp them. The alternating plan also works well for short papers.

Once you select your pattern, arrange your points of comparison in an appropriate order. Take up closely related points one after the other. Depending on your purpose, you might work from similarities to differences or the reverse. Often, a good writing strategy is to move from the least significant to the most significant point so that you conclude with punch.

EXERCISE ■   Using the points of comparison you selected for the exercise on page 121, prepare outlines for a paper organized according to the block and then the alternating pattern.

USING ANALOGY

An *analogy*, a special type of comparison, calls attention to one or more similarities underlying two different kinds of items that seem to have nothing in common. While some analogies stand alone, most clarify concepts in other kinds of writing. Whatever their role, they follow the same organizational pattern as ordinary comparisons.

An analogy often explains something unfamiliar by likening it to something familiar. Here is an example.

> The atmosphere of Earth acts like any window in serving two very important functions. It lets light in, and it permits us to look out. It also serves as a shield to keep out dangerous or uncomfortable things. A normal glazed window lets us keep our houses warm by keeping out cold air, and it prevents rain, dirt, and unwelcome insects and animals from coming in. . . . Earth's atmospheric window also helps to keep our planet at a comfortable temperature by holding back radiated heat and protecting us from dangerous levels of ultraviolet light.
>
> Lester del Ray, *The Mysterious Sky*

Conversely, an analogy sometimes highlights the unfamiliar in order to help illuminate the familiar. The following paragraph discusses the qualities and obligations of an unfamiliar person, the mountain guide, to shed light on a familiar practice—teaching:

> The mountain guide, like the true teacher, has a quiet authority. He or she engenders trust and confidence so that one is willing to join the endeavor. The guide accepts his leadership role, yet recognizes that success (measured by the heights that are scaled) depends upon the close cooperation and active participation of each member of the group. He has crossed the terrain before and is familiar with the landmarks, but each trip is new and generates its own anxiety and excitement. Essential skills must be mastered; if they are lacking, disaster looms. The situation

demands keen focus and rapt attention: slackness, misjudgment, or laziness can abort the venture.

Nancy K. Hill, "Scaling the Heights:
The Teacher as Mountaineer"

When you develop an analogy, keep these points in mind.

1. Your readers must be well acquainted with the familiar item. If they aren't, the point is lost.
2. The items must indeed have significant similarities. You could develop a meaningful analogy between a kidney and a filter or between cancer and anarchy but not between a flicker and a flapjack or a laser and limburger cheese.
3. The analogy must truly illuminate. Overly obvious analogies, such as one comparing a battle to an argument, offer few or no revealing insights.
4. Over-extended analogies can tax the reader's endurance. A multi-page analogy between a heart and a pump would likely overwhelm the reader with all its talk of valves, hoses, pressures, and pumping.

WRITING A COMPARISON

Planning and Drafting the Comparison

Don't discuss similarities and differences merely to fulfill an assignment. Instead, build your comparison around a clear sense of purpose. Do you want to show the superiority of one product or method over another? Do you want to show how sitcoms today differ from those twenty years ago? Purpose governs the details you choose and the organization you follow.

Whether you select your own topic or write on an assigned one, answer these questions.

What purpose will my comparison serve?
Who will be my audience and why will they want to read the essay?
What points of similarity or difference will I discuss?

To develop the comparison, draw up a chart similar to this one.

Item A	Item B
First point of comparison	First point of comparison
Second point of comparison	Second point of comparison

Next, brainstorm each point in turn, recording appropriate supporting details. When you finish, stand back and ask these questions.

Do all the details relate to my purpose?
Do any new details come to mind?
In what order should I organize the details?

When you decide upon an order, copy the points of comparison and the details, arranged in the order you will follow, into a chart like the one below.

Item A	*Item B*
First point of comparison	First point of comparison
First detail	First detail
Second detail	Second detail
Second point of comparison	Second point of comparison

Use the introduction to identify your topic and arouse the reader's interest. If you intend to establish the superiority of one item over the other, you might call attention to your position. If you're comparing something unfamiliar with something familiar, you might explain the importance of understanding the unfamiliar item.

Organize the body of your paper according to whichever pattern—block or alternating—suits its length and the number of points you're planning to take up. If you explain something familiar by comparing it with something unfamiliar, start with the familiar item. If you try to show the superiority of one item over another, proceed from the less to the more desirable one. Note that both of the Pat-and-Mike outlines (page 123) put Mike ahead of Pat, the superior candidate.

Write whatever kind of conclusion will round off your discussion effectively. Many comparison papers end with a recommendation or a prediction. A paper comparing two brands of stereo receivers might recommend purchasing one of them. A paper comparing a familiar sport, such as football, with an unfamiliar one, such as rugby, might predict the future popularity of the latter. Unless you've written a lengthy paper, don't summarize the likenesses and differences you've presented. If you've done a proper writing job, your reader already has them clearly in mind.

Revising the Comparison

Revise your paper in light of the general guidelines in Chapter 3 and the questions that follow.

Have I accomplished my purpose, whether to choose between alternatives or acquaint the reader with something unfamiliar?
For something unfamiliar, have I shown clearly just how it is like and unlike the familiar item?
Have I consistently written with my audience in mind?
Have I considered all points of similarity and difference that relate to my purpose?
Have I included appropriate supporting details?
Are my comparisons arranged effectively?

EXAMPLE STUDENT ESSAY OF COMPARISON

Different Shifts, Different Actions

Claire Mutter

The nursing team in a small hospital meets the   1
routine and special daily needs of patients. A
registered professional nurse usually leads the team,
and members often include registered and practical
nurses, nurse's aides, and attendants. Although all
nurses care for patients, the duties and working
conditions of team members on the first and second
shifts differ considerably.

The first shift begins at 7:00 A.M., when nurses   2
awaken patients and prepare them for laboratory tests,
X-rays, or medications. Additional nursing duties
include taking temperatures, pulses, and respirations
and giving enemas or preoperative injections. Team
members also serve breakfast and then administer
medications such as pain pills.

By this time doctors have arrived to visit their   3
patients. The nursing station swirls with activity.
Doctors write new orders at desks cluttered with their
patients' charts. Laboratory and X-ray technicians
explain test results. The pharmacist brings
medications and inquires about any new orders for
drugs. Inhalation and physical therapists check charts
for their new orders. The dietitian asks why Mr. Bowers
is not eating his prescribed foods. Telephones ring and
patients' signal lights flash continually. The members

of the nursing team, all with their own duties, try
desperately to keep up with these frenzied activities,
which leaves little time to spend with their patients.
This pace continues through most of the first shift.

Second shift team members, starting work at 3:00   4
P.M., usually can devote more attention to their
patients' personal needs. To prepare for supper,
nurses clear flowers and cards from tables, wash faces
and hands where necessary, and position patients for
eating comfort. After supper, when visitors have
departed, team members inform patients about their
conditions and teach them how to care for themselves
after discharge. For example, they show diabetic
patients how to administer insulin injections and to
care for their skin, and tell them what foods to eat.

To prepare patients for the night, nurses   5
straighten and change beds and give back rubs and last
medications. By 10:00 most patients are asleep.
Calmness and quiet prevail at the nursing station, with
only two or three nurses doing their charting—
recording how patients have tolerated treatment and
medication. Except for an occasional signal light from
a patient, activities cease for the night.

Although both shifts have the same   6
responsibilities, the care and welfare of the patient,
the second shift usually works in a much more relaxed
atmosphere. Fewer staff people and a slower pace result
in more personalized treatment.

DISCUSSION QUESTIONS

1. This phrase signals both the focus and the organization of the essay. The writer compares the first and second shifts on these two points of difference and in the indicated order.
2. Paragraphs 2–5 all contain effective supporting details. These details graphically show the differences between the two shifts.

DISCUSSION QUESTIONS ■

1. Comment on the significance of the phrase "the duties and working conditions" in paragraph 1.
2. Point out effective supporting details in the essay. What do they accomplish?

3. What pattern of organization does the writer use?

4. Explain why the writer ends the third sentence of paragraph 5 as follows: "recording how patients have tolerated treatment and medication." What can you learn from this explanation?

3. This essay uses the block pattern. Paragraphs 2 and 3 discuss the first shift, paragraphs 4 and 5 the second shift.

4. The writer ends her third sentence by explaining a specialized term. Students should learn that when they introduce a term or concept the reader may not know, they should clarify its meaning in order to ensure communication.

SUGGESTIONS FOR WRITING ■

1. **Write a comparison essay on one of the topics below or another that your instructor approves. Determine the points you will discuss and how you will develop and arrange them. Emphasize similarities, differences, or both.**

    a. A liberal arts versus a technical education
    b. The physical or mental demands of two jobs
    c. Two advertisements
    d. Parents versus teachers as educators
    e. Something natural and something artificial
    f. A novel and a movie that tell the same story
    g. Two instructors
    h. Two sportscasters or news commentators
    i. A television family and your family
    j. The business, residential, or slum districts of two cities or a wealthy and a working-class residential district in the same city
    k. A favorite social spot during the day and during the evening
    l. Suburban home life versus apartment life
    m. The effectiveness of two pieces of writing
    n. The working conditions on two jobs
    o. Two techniques for doing something in your field

2. **Develop an analogy based on one of the following sets of items or another set that your instructor approves. Proceed as you would for any other comparison.**

    a. The offerings in a college catalog and a restaurant
    b. A conquering army and a swarm of locusts
    c. An electric current and water flowing through a pipe
    d. A heart and a pump
    e. The structure of an atom and that of the solar system
    f. A teacher and a merchant
    g. Cancer and anarchy
    h. A parent and a farmer
    i. A brain and a telephone switchboard

j. Earth and a spaceship
k. A camera and the human eye
l. A workaholic and an alcoholic
m. A mob and a storm
n. A kidney and a filter
o. A cluttered attic and a disorderly mind

■ Chapter 10

Cause and Effect: Explaining Why

PERSPECTIVE

Cause-and-effect writing is certainly more conceptually difficult for students than, say, narration. Many writers have problems with causal analysis not only because of the writing but also because of the required thinking. Thus students often need special help in handling this strategy.

TEACHING STRATEGIES

1. Students aren't always sure what a cause is. You might explain, even demonstrate, a basic cause (putting a glass jar over a lighted candle) that produces a certain effect (putting out the candle).
2. Since simultaneously dealing with causes and effects taxes many students, have them concentrate either on one or the other.
3. Ask students to review newspaper articles or their textbooks and bring in examples of causes or effects.
4. You might help students gain experience in causal thinking by having them read about and discuss some familiar events or problems, such as the high dropout rate in the public schools or students' poor showing on standardized science and math tests. This type of exercise often helps students select writing topics.

"Dad, why do Mexican jumping beans jump?"

"I don't know, Lee."

"Well, then, why do zebras have stripes?"

"You've got me there, too."

"I wonder what happens inside the TV when I turn it on."

"Couldn't tell you. Lots of things, probably."

"Say, Dad, do you mind all these questions?"

"Of course not. If you don't ask questions, how'll you ever learn anything?"

People, of course, do learn lots of things without asking questions. This brief dialogue, for example, shows that *causation*, like a coin or record, has two sides. The first side, cause, probes the reasons why actions, events, attitudes, and conditions occur. Effect, the second side, examines their consequences. Causal analysis explains the operation of devices, the attitudes and actions of individuals and groups, as well as historical events and natural happenings.

All of us ask and answer questions of causation. Scott wonders why Susie *really* broke off their relationship, and Jennifer speculates on the consequences of changing her major. Your instructors ask you to write on topics such as the causes of the American Revolution, the consequences of the 1987 stock market crash, the reasons why so many couples are divorcing, or the effects of different fertilizers on plant growth. An employer may want a report on why a certain product malfunctions, what might happen if a community redesigns its traffic pattern, or how a school closing might affect business. Newspaper headlines proclaim "Oil Glut Drops Gas Prices" or "President Blames Fed for High Interest Rates," both echoing causal relationships. While watching a television documentary on AIDS, you speculate on how the disease has affected the sexual revolution. Thinking in terms of cause and effect goes on all the time.

PATTERNS IN CAUSAL ANALYSIS

Several organizational patterns are possible for a causal analysis. Sometimes, a single cause produces several effects. For instance, poor language skills prevent college students from keeping up with required reading, taking adequate notes, and writing competent papers and essay exams. To explore such a single cause–multiple effect relationship, construct an outline similar to the one following.

I.   Introduction: identifies cause
II. Body
    A. Effect number 1
    B. Effect number 2
    C. Effect number 3
III. Conclusion

Alternatively, you might discuss the cause after the effects are presented.

On the other hand, several causes may join forces to produce one effect. Zinc production in the United States, for example, has decreased over the last few years because it can be produced more cheaply abroad than it can here, it is being replaced on cars by plastics and lighter metals, and it cannot be recycled. Here's how you might organize a typical multiple cause–single effect paper.

I.   Introduction: identifies effect
II. Body
    A. Cause number 1
    B. Cause number 2
    C. Cause number 3
III. Conclusion

Sometimes discussion of the effect follows the presentation of causes.

At times a set of events forms a causal chain, with each event the effect of the preceding one and the cause of the following one. Interrupting the chain at any point halts the sequence. Such chains can be likened to a row of upright dominoes that fall one after the other when the first one is pushed. Belief in a domino theory, which held that if one nation in Southeast Asia fell to the communists all would, one after the other, helped bring about U.S. entry into the Vietnam War. Causal chains can also help explain how devices function and some social changes proceed. The following outline typifies the arrangement of a paper explaining a causal chain.

I.   Introduction
II. Body
    A. Cause
    B. Effect
    C. Cause
    D. Effect
III. Conclusion

Papers of this kind resemble process analyses, but process is concerned with *how* the events occur, cause and effect with *why*.

In many situations the sequence of causes and effects is too complex to fit the image of a chain. Suppose you are driving to a movie on a rainy night. You approach an intersection screened by bushes and, because you have the right-of-way, start across. Suddenly a car with unlit headlights looms directly in your path. You hit the brakes but skid on the slippery pavement and crash into the other car, crumpling its left fender and damaging your own bumper. Later, as you think about the episode, you begin to sense its complexities.

Obviously, the *immediate cause* of the accident was the other driver's failure to heed the stop sign. But other causes also played roles: the bushes and unlit headlights that kept you from seeing the other car sooner; the starts and stops, speedups and slowdowns that brought the two cars to the intersection at the same time; the wet pavement you skidded on; and the movie that brought you out in the first place.

You also realize that the effects of the accident go beyond the fender and bumper damage. After the accident, a police officer ticketed the other driver. As a result of the delay, you missed the movie. Further, the accident unnerved you so badly that you couldn't attend classes the next day and therefore missed an important writing assignment. Because of a bad driving record, the other driver lost his license for sixty days. Clearly, the effects of this accident rival the causes in complexity.

Here's how you might organize a multiple cause–multiple effect essay.

I.   Introduction
II. Body
    A. Cause number 1
    B. Cause number 2
    C. Cause number 3
    D. Effect number 1
    E. Effect number 2
    F. Effect number 3
III. Conclusion

In some situations, however, you might first present the effects, then turn to the causes.

type, you might point out that watering a houseplant is necessary because it would otherwise die. For survival, though, the plant also needs proper sunlight, drainage, nutrients, and temperature. To illustrate a contributory cause, you could note that high winds may intensify but can't start a brush fire and also that the fire might occur without any wind. To illustrate a sufficient cause, you could point out that a dose of potassium cyanide by itself will kill a person. Indicate that the great majority of causes are either necessary or contributory.

1. Folk societies	Settlement in villages, technological and organizational advances (effect)
Technological and organizational advances (cause)	Surplus of food (effect)
Feudal society, surplus of food (cause)	Specialization of labor, improved class structure (effect)
Specialization of labor, improved class structure (cause)	Irrigation systems, greater surplus of food (effect)

2. **a.** You might complain to the manager, become ill and have to cancel a shopping trip, scream and leave the restaurant, or remove the worm from the leaf and eat the salad.
   b. You might have to leave school for the remainder of the term, drop out of some kind of athletic competition, suffer complications that cause you to lose use of the arm, or, if the break is a simple one, merely miss a day's classes.
   c. You might lose your job, fail to find another one that pays as well, and have to settle for a less comfortable and desirable lifestyle; your boss might impose a two-week layoff without pay, forcing you to postpone or cancel the purchase of some household item; or you might convince your boss that the tardiness was unavoidable.

PERSPECTIVE

A vast amount of faulty thinking stems from inept causal analysis. It's rather alarming to hear students reason that since they did

EXERCISE ■

1. Read the following selection and then arrange the events in a causal chain.

Although some folk societies still exist today, similar human groups began the slow process of evolving into more complex societies many millennia ago, through settlement in villages and through advances in technology and organizational structure. This gave rise to the second level of organization: civilized preindustrial, or "feudal," society. Here there is a surplus of food because of the selective cultivation of grains—and also because of the practice of animal husbandry. The food surplus permits both the specialization of labor and the kind of class structure that can, for instance, provide the leadership and command the manpower to develop and maintain extensive irrigation systems (which in turn makes possible further increases in the food supply). . . .

Gideon Sjöberg, "The Origin and Development of Cities"

2. Trace the possible effects of the following occurrences:

a. You pick out a salad at the cafeteria and sit down to eat. Suddenly you notice a large green worm on one of the lettuce leaves.

b. As you leave your composition classroom, you trip and break your arm.

c. Your boss has warned you not to be late to work again. You are driving to work with ten minutes to spare when you get a flat tire.

REASONING ERRORS IN CAUSAL ANALYSIS

Ignoring Multiple Causes

An effect rarely stems from a single cause. The person who believes that permissive parents have caused the present upsurge of venereal disease or the one who blames television violence for the climbing numbers of emotionally disturbed children oversimplifies the situation. Permissiveness and violence perhaps did contribute to these conditions. Without much doubt, however, numerous other factors also played important parts.

Mistaking Chronology for Causation

Don't assume that just because one event followed another the first necessarily caused the second. This kind of faulty thinking feeds many popular superstitions. Horace walks under a ladder, later stubs his toe, and thinks that his path caused his pain. Sue breaks a mirror just before Al breaks their engagement; then she blames the cracked mirror. Many people once believed that the election of

Herbert Hoover as President in 1928 brought on the Great Depression in 1929. Today some people believe that the testing of atomic weapons has altered our weather patterns. Don't misunderstand: one event *may* cause the next; but before you go on record with your conclusion, make sure that you're not dealing with mere chronology.

Confusing Causes with Effects

Young children sometimes declare that the moving trees make the wind blow. Similarly, some adults may think that Pam and Paul married because they fell in love, when in reality economic necessity mandated the vows, and love came later. Scan your evidence carefully in order to avoid such faulty assertions.

EXERCISE ■

1. **Which of the following statements point toward papers that will focus on causes? Which point toward papers focusing on effects? Explain your answers?**

    a. Most of the problems that plague newly married couples are the direct outgrowth of timidity and pride.
    b. The Marshall Plan was designed to aid the economic recovery of Europe after World War II.
    c. The smoke from burning poison ivy can bring on a skin rash and lung irritation.
    d. Popularity in high school stems largely from good looks, a pleasing personality, participation in school activities, the right friends, and frequent dates.

2. **Identify which of the following paragraphs deals with causes, which with effects. List the causes and effects.**

    a.   Color filters offer three advantages in black-and-white photography. First, a particular color will be lightened by a filter of the same color. For example, in a photograph of a red rose in a dark blue vase, both will appear almost the same shade of gray if no filter is used. However, when photographed through a red filter, the rose will appear much lighter than the vase; and through a blue filter the vase will appear much lighter than the rose. This effect can be useful in emphasizing or muting certain objects in a photograph. Second, a particular color filter will darken its complementary color in the scene.

better on a test when they didn't study, why bother in the future? As part of our responsibility to teach students how to think about causes, we should help them identify such errors.

TEACHING STRATEGY

Ask students to record examples of faulty causal analysis that they find in their academic and personal lives. Have them write a short paper identifying such errors, explaining why they are errors and examining the consequences.

EXERCISE ANSWERS

1. **a.** The phrasing "are the direct outgrowth of" identifies timidity and pride as *causes* of marital discord.
   b. The phrasing "was designed to aid" denotes a paper that will deal with *effects*, concentrating on the ways in which the Marshall Plan aided European recovery.
   c. The phrasing "can bring on" denotes that a skin rash and lung irritation are the *effects* of exposure to burning poison ivy.
   d. This paper would explain the *causes* of high school popularity.
2. **a.** This paragraph deals with effects. These effects include making a color lighter by using a filter of the same color; making a color darker by using a filter of a complementary color; reducing or increasing atmospheric haze by the appropriate filter.
   b. This paragraph deals with causes. The causes include the overfeeding of children by their parents; the availability of fast foods; the advertising of snack foods on TV; psychological factors such as nervousness, boredom, loneliness, insecurity, discontent with life, and indolence.

Consequently, any orange object will appear darker than normal if a blue filter is used. Finally, color filters can reduce or increase atmospheric haze. For example, in a distant aerial shot there will often be so much haze that distant detail is obscured. To eliminate haze almost entirely, the photographer can use a deep red filter. On the other hand, if more haze is desired in order to achieve an artistic effect, varying shades of blue filters can be used.

Timothy Kelly

b.   Overeating, which has become a national pastime for millions of Americans, has several roots. For example, parents who are concerned that their children get enough to eat during the growing years overfeed them and thereby establish a lifetime overeating habit. The child who is constantly praised for cleaning up his plate experiences a sort of gratification later on as he cleans up all too many plates. The easy availability of so much food is a constant temptation for many people, especially the types of food served at fast food restaurants and merchandised in the frozen food departments of supermarkets. Equally tempting are all the snack foods constantly advertised on TV. But many people don't need temptation from the outside; their overeating arises from such psychological factors as nervousness, boredom, loneliness, insecurity, an overall discontent with life, or an aversion to exercise. Thus, overeating can actually be a symptom of psychological surrender to, or withdrawal from, the complexities and competition of modern life.

Kenneth Reichow

WRITING A CAUSAL ANALYSIS

Planning and Drafting the Causal Analysis

If you choose your own topic, perhaps your personal experience will suggest something promising. Topics such as "Why I Dislike (or Like) Foreign Cars" and "How My Father's (or Someone Else's) Death Has Changed My Life" might work well. Nonpersonal topics also offer writing possibilities. For instance, "What's Behind Teenage Suicides?" and "The Impact of Trade Tariffs on American Corporations" would allow you to draw on library resources.

The strategies on pages 12–19 can also help you find several topics. Answer these questions about each potential candidate.

What purpose will guide this writing?
Who is my audience? Will the topic interest them? Why or why not?
Shall I focus on causes, effects, or both?

Brainstorming your topic for supporting details should be easy. If you're dealing with causes, pose these questions about each one.

How significant is this cause?
Could it have brought about the effect by itself?
Does it form part of a chain?
Precisely how does it contribute to the effect?

For papers dealing with effects, substitute the following questions for the ones above.

How important is this effect?
What evidence will establish its importance?

Charting your results can help you prepare for writing the paper. To tabulate causes, use an arrangement like this one.

Cause	Contribution to Effect
First cause	Specific contribution
Second cause	Specific contribution

For effects, use this chart.

Effect	Importance
First effect	Why important
Second effect	Why important

ETHICAL ISSUES

Sometimes groups with vested interests issue reports that deliberately emphasize effects that support their position. Those opposed to a policy, for example, highlight its potentially negative effects, no matter how slim, and overlook the positive ones. Is this ethical? Does it make a difference if the report falsely pretends to be objective? What if the bias were overt? Is it ethical for a writer to oversimplify causes in order to lay blame on a particular individual or organization? Is it ethical for a gubernatorial candidate to attribute an increase in state crime to his/her opponent's policies, when in fact the nationwide crime rate rose by the same amount?

Once your items are tabulated, examine them carefully for completeness. Perhaps you've overlooked a cause or effect or have slighted the significance of one you've already mentioned. Think about the order in which you'd like to discuss your items and prepare a revised chart that reflects your decision.

Use the opening of your paper to identify your topic and indicate whether you plan to discuss causes, effects, or both. You can signal your intention in a number of ways. To prepare for a focus on causes, you might use the words *cause, reason,* or *stem from,* or you might ask why something has occurred. To signal a paper on effects, you might use *effect, fallout,* or *impact,* or you might ask what has happened since something took place. Read these examples:

Signals causes   Midville's recent increase in street crime stems primarily from its curtailed educational program, lack of job opportunities for young people, and high rate of drug addiction.

Signals effects   Since my marriage to Rita, how has my social life changed?

At times you may choose some dramatic attention-getter. For a paper on the effects of radon, a toxic radioactive gas present in many homes, you might note that "Although almost everyone now knows about the hazards associated with smoking, eating high-cholesterol foods, and drinking excessively, few people are aware that just going home could be hazardous to one's health." If you use an arresting statement, be sure the content of your paper warrants it.

How you organize the body of the paper depends on your topic. Close scrutiny may reveal that one cause was indispensable; the rest merely played supporting roles. If so, discuss the main cause first. In analyzing your automobile mishap, which fits this situation, start with the failure of the other driver to yield the right-of-way; then fan out to any other causes that merit mentioning. Sometimes you'll find that no single cause was essential but that all of them helped matters along. Combinations of this kind lie at the heart of many social and economic concerns: inflation, depression, and urban crime rates, to name just a few. Weigh each cause carefully and rank them in importance. If your topic and purpose will profit from building suspense, work from the least important cause to the most important. Otherwise, reverse the order. For analyzing causal chains, chronological order works effectively.

If space won't permit you to deal adequately with every cause, pick out the two or three you consider most important and limit your discussion to them. To avoid giving your reader an oversimplified impression, note that other causes exist. Even if length poses no problem, don't attempt to trace every cause to some more remote cause and then to a still more remote one. Instead, determine some sensible cutoff point that accords with your purpose, and don't go beyond it.

Treat effects as carefully as you do causes. Keep in mind that effects often travel in packs, and try to arrange them in some logical order. If they occur together, consider order of climax. If one follows the other in a chainlike sequence, present them in that fashion. If space considerations dictate, limit your discussion to the most interesting or significant effects.

Causal analyses can end in several ways. A paper discussing the effects of acid rain on America's lakes and streams might specify the grave consequences of failing to deal with the problem or express the hope that something will be done. Frequently, writers use their conclusions to evaluate the relative importance of their causes or effects.

Revising the Causal Analysis

Follow the guidelines in Chapter 3 and answer these questions as you revise your causal analysis.

Have I made the right decision in electing to focus on causes, effects, or both?
Have I ferreted out all important causes and effects? Mistakenly labeled something as an effect merely because it follows something else? Confused causes with effects?
Am I dealing with a causal chain? An immediate cause and several supporting causes? Multiple causes and effects?
Have I presented my causes and effects in an appropriate order?
Have I supported my discussion with sufficient details?

EXAMPLE STUDENT ESSAY OF CAUSE AND EFFECT

Backpacking

Student Unknown

For decades, Americans have been accepting John   1
Muir's invitation to "climb the Mountains; get their
glad tidings." Until fairly recently, the mountains
attracted only rugged individuals who were prepared to
face considerable hardship in order to hike and climb.
Since the early 1970s, however, the mountains have
changed from the sanctuary of the dedicated few to the
playground of the multitudes, as shown by the booming
backpacking-equipment industry and the crowded trails.
Why this sudden increase in the number of mountain-
climbing enthusiasts? I believe there are three

reasons--backpacking is inexpensive, provides exercise, and involves little physical discomfort.

In a decade that has seen the price of entertainment rise to outrageous levels, the mountains are a very economical place to vacation. A backpacker need spend only about two hundred and fifty dollars to obtain an outfit suitable for all seasons but winter. After that, the only expenses are for food and transportation. A reasonably economical shopper can buy a week's worth of high-nutrition, low-weight food from the local supermarket for about thirty to forty dollars, much less than the cost of eating in restaurants. Because backpackers travel under their own power, the only transportation expenses are those of driving to and from a trailhead. And because backpackers carry their own shelter, there are no motel bills--only the occasional camping permit or park entry fee. Overall, backpacking costs much less per day than most conventional forms of entertainment. Consequently, as compared to his tourist counterpart, the backpacker can "get away from it all" for more days without spending any more money.

Growing numbers of people are also coming to realize that backpacking provides very good exercise. Since mountain terrain varies from level meadows to sheer rock faces, the physical challenges in backpacking are boundless. Virtually anyone wanting exercise can participate--from those content with the mild exertion involved in exploring the meadows to those who crave the arduous task of scaling a high-altitude peak or pass.

2

3

But probably the major lure of the mountains for   4
today's backpackers is that conquering them involves
much less physical discomfort than it once did.
Technology has made it possible to be reasonably
comfortable in harsh weather if the proper gear is
used. A nylon tent or a tarpaulin will keep the rain
from dampening one's spirits or gear, a good frame pack
will comfortably carry everything needed for a few
days, a small gasoline stove will allow hot meals to be
cooked under almost any circumstances, and a well-
fitting pair of boots will keep the feet comfortable
and protect them too. All the items mentioned are so
light that one can be fully protected from the elements
without having to carry more than twenty pounds of
equipment.

When I first started backpacking about six years   5
ago, I encountered few people. Those who did backpack
made every effort to leave no trace of their presence
and treated the mountains with proper deference. But as
more people have taken to the mountains, trash,
defoliation, and erosion have increased. Let's hope
that as time passes, the new backpackers will also come
to respect the mountains.

DISCUSSION QUESTIONS ■

1. Does this paper focus on causes, effects, or both? Show how the opening paragraph signals the writer's intention.
2. Discuss the organization of the essay.
3. Explain how the conclusion supports the point made in the introduction to the paper.

DISCUSSION QUESTIONS

1. The paper focuses on causes. The next-to-the-last sentence in the opening paragraph makes this clear: "Why this sudden increase in the number of mountain-climbing enthusiasts?"

2. The last sentence of the opening paragraph signals the organization: "I believe there are three. . ." Paragraph 2 deals with the first reason, paragraph 3 the second one, and paragraph 4 the third one.

3. This conclusion cites one of the results of the popularity mentioned in the introduction. You might point out that while the body of the paper focuses on causes, the conclusion cites an effect.

SUGGESTED INSTRUCTOR READING

Buchan U. "Why and Because Method Really Works." Improving College and University Teaching 21 (1973): 273–74. Explains how a basic why-and-because question–answer strategy can be an effective teaching tool.

SUGGESTIONS FOR WRITING ■   Use one of the topics below, or another that your instructor approves, to develop a causal analysis. Determine which causes and/or effects to consider. Scrutinize your analysis for errors in reasoning, settle on an organization, and write the essay.

1. Reasons why students fail college
2. The effect of some friend, acquaintance, or public figure on your life
3. Causes behind some disciplinary action
4. Effects of some choice you made
5. Why you are a _____ major
6. Effects of living in a dormitory, in your own apartment, or at home
7. Reasons why you are a Democrat, a Republican, or an Independent
8. Effects of pollution in your hometown or some other familiar place
9. Effects of your choice of college or of your decision to go to college
10. Reasons why you have a particular habit or participate in a particular sport
11. Effects on your life of winning the grand prize in a state lottery
12. Reasons why _____ is a popular public figure
13. Effects of some family crisis on your life
14. Causes or effects or both of some disease
15. Causes or consequences or both of some decision made by you or your family

■ Chapter 11

Definition: Establishing Boundaries

That movie was egregious.

Once the bandage is off the wound, swab the proud flesh with the disinfectant.

Speaking on statewide television, Governor Blaine called his opponent a left-winger.

Do you have questions? You're not alone. Many people would question the sentences above: "What in the world does *egregious* mean?" "How can flesh be *proud*?" "What does the governor mean by *left-winger*? What specific policies does the opponent support that warrant this label?" To avoid puzzling and provoking your own readers, you'll often need to explain the meaning of some term. The term may be unfamiliar (egregious), used in an unfamiliar sense (proud flesh), or mean different things to different people (left-winger). Whenever you clarify the meaning of some term, you are *defining*.

Humans are instinctively curious. We start asking about meanings as soon as we can talk, and we continue to seek, as well as supply, definitions all through life. In school, instructors expect us to explain all sorts of literary, historical, scientific, technical, and social terms. An employer may ask us to define a term such as *corporate responsibility* or *product stewardship* for new employees. A newspaper story about a new earth-orbiting telescope may send us to a local astronomy buff for an explanation of *supernova, quasar*, or *black hole*. In our more reflective moments, we ponder the meaning of good and evil or the nature of God.

When you define, you identify the features that distinguish a term, thereby putting a fence around it, establishing its boundaries, and separating it from all others. Knowing these features enables both you and your reader to use the term appropriately.

Sometimes a word, phrase, or sentence will settle a definition question. To

CLASSROOM ACTIVITIES

1. To help students appreciate that precise definitions are essential to effective communication, write several abstract terms on the board (freedom, love, success) and have the class jot down, and then compare, their own definitions. They will see how differing attitudes can lead people to cross purposes.

2. Have the class, working in small groups, list terms that they use but their parents do not, and then develop definitions aimed at the parents.

clear up the mystery of "proud flesh," all you'd need to do is insert the parenthetical phrase (excessively swollen and grainy) after the word *proud*. But when you're dealing with new terms—*leveraged buyout, gene splicing,* and *computer virus* are examples—brief definitions won't provide the reader with enough information for proper understanding.

Abstract terms—those standing for things we can't see, touch, or otherwise detect with our five senses—often require extended definitions, too. It's impossible to capture the essence of *democracy* or *hatred* or *bravery* in a single sentence: the terms are too complex, and people have too many differing ideas about what they mean. The same holds true for some concrete terms—those standing for actions and things we can perceive with our five senses. Some people, for instance, limit the term *drug pusher* to full-time sellers of hard drugs like cocaine and heroin. Others, at the opposite extreme, extend the term to full- and part-time sellers of any illegal drug. Writing an argument recommending life sentences for convicted drug pushers would require you to tell just what you mean by the term so that the reader would have solid grounds for judging your position.

The many dimensions of the epithet *nurd*, captured in the following poster from the *National Lampoon*, suggest just how difficult defining can be.

TYPES OF DEFINITIONS

Three types of definitions—synonyms, essential definitions, and extended definitions—serve writers' needs. Although the first two seldom require more than a word or a sentence, an extended definition can run to several pages. The three types, however, are related. Synonyms and essential definitions share quarters between the covers of dictionaries, and both furnish starting points for extended definitions.

TEACHING STRATEGY

Have students, using dictionaries or thesauruses, select several synonyms for terms you provide and then determine contexts in which each synonym would be suitable. This activity offers an opportunity to distinguish between denotation and connotation.

Synonyms

Synonyms are words with very nearly the same meanings. *Lissome* is synonymous with *lithe* or *nimble*, and *condign* is a synonym of *worthy* and *suitable*. Synonyms let writers clarify meanings of unfamiliar words without using cumbersome explanations. To clarify the term *expostulation* in a quoted passage, all you'd have to do is add the word *objection*, in brackets, after it. Because synonyms are not identical twins, using them puts a slightly different shade of meaning on a message. For example, to "protest" and to "object" are certainly similar in many ways. Yet the claim that we "object" to the establishment of a nuclear power plant in our area fails to capture the active and sustained commitment implied in our willingness to "protest" against the same plant. Still, synonyms provide an easy, convenient means of breaking communications logjams.

nurd also **nerd** / nerd:/ n [ME, fr. OE *neord*, perforated earthen jar or gourd] : an adolescent male possessing any of a number of socially objectionable characteristics, including passivity, disregard for personal appearance, obsessive neatness, introversion, undue respect for authority, sexual ignorance, disinterest in athletics, fidgeting, kooties, anality, infantilism, orality, pusillanimity, obsequiousness, and using big words; *see:* TWINK, WONK, FINK, TWIT, [*greasy*], GRIND, FLAMER, WIMP, WEENIE, DINK, CREEP, FLYER, GEEK, DIP, LEMUR, Q-BALL, SIMP, TWIRP, DRIP, WOMBAT, ZOOMER, SCREAMER.

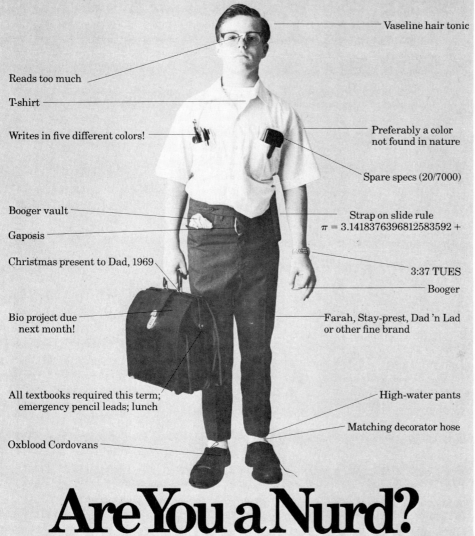

Vaseline hair tonic

Reads too much

T-shirt

Writes in five different colors!

Preferably a color not found in nature

Spare specs (20/7000)

Booger vault

Gaposis

Strap on slide rule
$\pi = 3.1418376396812583592 +$

Christmas present to Dad, 1969

3:37 TUES

Booger

Bio project due next month!

Farah, Stay-prest, Dad 'n Lad or other fine brand

All textbooks required this term; emergency pencil leads; lunch

High-water pants

Matching decorator hose

Oxblood Cordovans

Are You a Nurd?

...Let's hope not. But just in case you've begun to notice telltale signs, such as a reawakened fascination with word problems or scratching mosquito bites until they bleed, take this simple test. If you have less than five (5) of these dead giveaways, you're probably a cool guy. If you have eight (8) or more, you're just kind of flakey. Ten (10) or more? Check for a leper colony near you.

PERSPECTIVE

The structure of essential definitions dates back to the Greeks and particularly to Plato, who developed it most fully. Approaching ideas by fitting them into general categories and noting their distinguishing features is fundamental to Western analytic thought. Although most obvious in the sciences, this approach is crucial in every other field. Thus filmmakers use it to distinguish camera shots and bankers to categorize mortgages. Because nearly every idea they encounter will involve one or more essential definitions, students should appreciate the power of these definitions to organize the conceptual world.

TEACHING STRATEGIES

1. To help students grasp the need for essential definitions, have them review their previous papers and identify places where essential definitions would have been helpful. Next, ask them to find in other textbooks places where essential definitions are provided or needed, then gauge the effectiveness of the ones they find by checking them against the criteria in this chapter.
2. To follow up on item 1, you might point out that this chapter functions as an extended definition by providing several distinguishing features of the strategy it discusses.
3. Have students keep a record, over a week, of instances when others use flawed essential definitions. Ask them to watch especially for circular and overly broad definitions.
4. Not all terms, of course, have essential definitions. As Ludwig Wittgenstein pointed out in his *Philosophical Investigations*, often a term such as "game" can be used to describe so many things that at best there is only a family resemblance among the different uses. It's helpful if students can spot such fuzzy terms and recognize the difficulty of trying to define them.

Essential Definitions

An essential definition does three things: (1) names the item being defined, (2) places it in a broad category, and (3) distinguishes it from other items in that category. Here are three examples.

Item Being Defined	Broad Category	Distinguishing Features
A howdah	is a covered seat	for riding on the back of an elephant or camel.
A voiceprint	is a graphical record	of a person's voice characteristics.
To parboil	is to boil meat, vegetables, or fruits	until they are partially cooked.

Writing a good essential definition requires careful thought. Suppose your instructor has asked you to write an essential definition of one of the terms listed in an exercise, and you choose "vacuum cleaner." Coming up with a broad category presents no problem: a vacuum cleaner is a household appliance. The hard part is pinpointing the distinguishing features. The purpose of a vacuum cleaner is to clean floors, carpets, and upholstery. You soon realize, however, that these features alone do not separate vacuum cleaners from other appliances. After all, carpet sweepers also clean floors, and whisk brooms clean upholstery. What then does distinguish vacuum cleaners? After a little thought, you realize that, unlike the other items, a vacuum cleaner works by suction. You then write the following definition.

> A vacuum cleaner is a household appliance that uses suction to clean floors, carpets, and upholstery.

The same careful attention is necessary to establish the distinguishing features of any essential definition.

Limitations of Essential Definitions.   Essential definitions have certain built-in limitations. Because of their brevity, they often can't do full justice to abstract terms such as *cowardice, love, jealousy, power*. Problems also arise with terms that have several settled meanings. To explain *jam* adequately, you'd need at least three essential definitions: (1) a closely packed crowd, (2) preserves, and (3) a difficult situation. But despite these limitations, an essential definition can be useful by itself or as part of a longer definition. Writers often build an extended definition around an essential definition.

Pitfalls in Preparing Essential Definitions.   When you prepare an essential definition, guard against these flaws:

Circular definition. Don't define a term by repeating it or changing its form slightly. Saying that a psychiatrist is "a physician who practices psychiatry" will only frustrate someone who's never heard of psychiatry. Repress circularity and provide the proper insight by choosing terms the reader can relate to, for example, "A psychiatrist is a physician who diagnoses and treats mental disorders."

Overly broad definition. Shy away from definitions that embrace too much territory. If you define a skunk as "an animal that has a bushy tail and black fur with white markings," your definition is not precise. Many cats and dogs also fit this description. But if you add "and that ejects a foul-smelling secretion when threatened," you will clear the air, of any misconceptions at least.

Overly narrow definition. Don't hem in your definition too closely, either. "A kitchen blender is a bladed electrical appliance used to chop foods" illustrates this error. Blenders perform other operations, too. To correct the error, add the missing information. "A kitchen blender is a bladed electrical appliance used to chop, mix, whip, liquefy, or otherwise process foods."

Omission of main category. Avoid using "is where" or "is when" instead of naming the main category. Here are examples of this error. "A bistro is where food and wine are served" and "An ordination is when a person is formally recognized as a minister, priest, or rabbi." The reader will not know exactly what sort of thing (a bar? a party?) a *bistro* is and may think that *ordination* means a time. Note the improvement when the broad categories are named: "A bistro is a small restaurant where both food and wine are served" and "An ordination is a ceremony at which a person is formally recognized as a minister, priest, or rabbi."

EXERCISE ■

1. **Identify the broad category and the distinguishing traits in each of these essential definitions.**

   a. Gangue is useless rock accompanying valuable minerals in a deposit.
   b. A catbird is a small American songbird with a slate-colored body, a black cap, and a catlike cry.
   c. A soldier is a man or woman serving in an army.
   d. Myelin is a white fatty substance that forms a sheath around some nerve fibers.
   e. A gargoyle is a waterspout carved in the likeness of a grotesque animal or imaginary creature and projecting from the gutter of a building.
   f. A magnum is a wine bottle that holds about two-fifths of a gallon.

2. **Indicate which of the following statements are acceptable essential definitions. Explain what is wrong with those that are not. Correct them.**

   a. A scalpel is a small knife that has a sharp blade used for surgery and anatomical dissections.
   b. A puritan is a person with puritanical beliefs.
   c. A kraal is where South African tribespeople keep large domestic animals.
   d. A rifle is a firearm that has a grooved barrel and is used for hunting large game.

5. Students often believe that dictionary definitions are completely objective and unchanging. You might point out that dictionaries are compiled on the basis of common usage. It is interesting to compare the definitions of controversial words—"rebel" for instance—in dictionaries from several different historical periods. Students might also examine several definitions to determine any latent, and possibly questionable, assumptions. Those, for example, who have faith in astrology would dispute a definition calling it "a pseudoscience claiming that the relative positions of the stars, planets, sun, and moon can be used to foretell the future."

EXERCISE ANSWERS

1. Key: broad category // distinguishing traits
   a. Gangue is useless rock.// accompanying valuable minerals in a deposit.
   b. A catbird is a small American songbird//with a slate-colored body, a black cap, and a catlike cry.
   c. A soldier is a man or woman//serving in an army.
   d. Myelin is a white fatty substance//that forms a sheath around some nerve fibers.
   e. A gargoyle is a waterspout// carved in the likeness of a grotesque animal or imaginary creature and projecting from the gutter of a building.
   f. A magnum is a wine bottle// that holds about two-fifths of a gallon.
2. Identifying good and bad essential definitions and correcting the bad ones.
   a. This definition is good.
   b. This is a circular definition. A person who didn't know the meaning of "puritan" would not know the meaning of "puritanical." Change to "A puritan is a person with strict moral and religious views."

c. This definition does not name a broad category. Change to "A kraal is a fenced enclosure where South African tribes keep large domestic animals."

d. This definition is too narrow; rifles are used for other purposes besides hunting. Change to "A rifle is a firearm that has a grooved barrel and is used primarily for hunting large game and as a military weapon."

e. This definition is too broad; bicycles also fit the definition. Change to "A motorcycle is a two-wheeled vehicle powered by a gasoline engine and used mainly for human transportation."

f. This definition does not name a broad category. Change to "Fainting is a condition in which a person loses consciousness due to an inadequate flow of blood to the brain."

3. Writing essential definitions

a. A groupie is a girl who follows after rock bands or celebrities in the hope of forming a close attachment.

b. A happy hour is a period of time, usually from late afternoon to early evening, when a bar or restaurant sells alcoholic drinks at reduced prices.

c. A hit man is a criminal who specializes in assassinations.

d. A jock is a man or woman who is dedicated to athletic participation.

e. A pushover is a person who is easily swindled, defeated, or persuaded OR a pushover is anything that can be accomplished without significant effort.

f. A hard grader is an instructor who sets especially high standards for his or her students.

TEACHING STRATEGIES

1. Ask students to review materials or interview people in their field of study in order to determine key words requiring extended definitions. Students could also compile lists of other

e. A motorcycle is a two-wheeled vehicle used mainly for human transportation.

f. Fainting is when a person loses consciousness owing to inadequate flow of blood to the brain.

3. Write an essential definition for each of the following terms.

a. groupie   d. jock
b. happy hour   e. pushover
c. hit man   f. hard grader

Extended Definitions

Sometimes it's necessary to go beyond an essential definition and write a paragraph or whole paper explaining a term. New technical, social, and economic terms often require extended definitions. To illustrate, a computer scientist might need to define *data integrity* so that computer operators understand the importance of maintaining it. Terms with differing meanings also frequently require extended definitions. To let voters know just what he means by *left-winger*, Governor Blaine might detail the kinds of legislation his opponent favors and opposes. Furthermore, extended definition is crucial to interpretation of the law, as we see when courts clarify the meaning of concepts such as obscenity.

Extended definitions are not merely academic exercises; they are fundamental to your career and your life. A police officer needs to have a clear understanding of what counts as *reasonable grounds for search and seizure*; an engineer must comprehend the meaning of *stress*; a nuclear medical technologist had better have a solid grasp of *radiation*. And all of us are concerned with the definition of our basic rights as citizens.

Extended definitions are montages of other methods of development—narration, description, illustration, process analysis, classification, comparison, and cause and effect. Often, they also define by negation: explaining what a term *does not* mean. The following paragraphs show how one writer handled an extended definition of "sudden infant death syndrome." The student began by presenting a case history (illustration), which also incorporated an essential definition and two synonyms.

Jane and Dick Smith were proud, new parents of an eight-pound, ten-ounce baby girl named Jenny. One summer night, Jane put Jenny to bed at 8:00. When she went to check on her at 3:00 A.M., Jane found Jenny dead. The baby had given no cry of pain, shown no sign of trouble. Even the doctor did not know why she had died, for she was healthy and strong. The autopsy report confirmed the doctor's suspicion—the infant was a victim of the "sudden infant death syndrome," also known as SIDS or crib death. SIDS is the sudden and unexplainable death of an apparently healthy, sleeping infant. It is the number-one cause of death in infants after the first week of life and as a result has been the subject of numerous research studies.

DISCUSSION QUESTIONS ■

1. What synonyms does the writer use?
2. Which sentence presents an essential definition?

In the next paragraph, the writer turned to negation, pointing out some of the things that researchers have ruled out about SIDS.

Although researchers do not know what SIDS is, they do know what it is not. They know it cannot be predicted; it strikes like a thief in the night. Crib deaths occur in seconds, with no sound of pain, and they always happen when the child is sleeping. Suffocation is not the cause, nor is aspiration or regurgitation. Researchers have found no correlation between the incidence of SIDS and the mother's use of birth control pills or tobacco or the presence of fluoride in water. Since it is not hereditary or contagious, only a slim chance exists that SIDS will strike twice in the same family.

Finally, the student explored several proposed causes of SIDS as well as how parents may react to the loss of their child.

As might be expected, researchers have offered many theories concerning the cause of crib death. Dr. R. C. Reisinger, a National Cancer Institute scientist, has linked crib deaths to the growth of a common bacterium, E. coli, in the intestines of newborn babies. The organisms

words and ideas that are important to them, for example, words from the student conduct manual.

2. A common problem in student and professional writing is purposeful or accidental equivocation, that is, subtly changing the meaning of a term. In opposing the legalization of drugs, a writer might start by using "drugs" to refer to heroin, cocaine, and the like, but later, after establishing the danger of these drugs, shift the term so that it also covers marijuana. The arguments against legalizing marijuana then become the same as those directed against the harder drugs, despite the real differences between marijuana and the others. You could ask students to look for instances of equivocation in their own, and even professional, writing, or bring in illustrative examples yourself.

CLASSROOM ACTIVITIES

1. You might have the class work out an extended definition of some controversial term, such as "obscenity" or "hero," especially when the definition will help resolve a debate.

2. Have students read a Supreme Court decision and discuss how the Court reached its conclusion. Surprisingly, most decisions are extremely readable and usually hinge on an issue of definition establishing the essential character and limitations of specific rights.

3. A classroom discussion of a controversial issue—for example, should flag burning be banned?—can lead to questions of definition. What constitutes freedom of speech? What qualifies as a flag? Would a photograph count? A hand-colored representation on white paper? Such discussion can lead to definition papers with real purpose.

DISCUSSION QUESTIONS

1. The writer uses the synonym "crib death" for "sudden infant death syndrome."

2. The next-to-the-last one.

multiply in the intestines, manufacturing a toxin that is absorbed by the intestinal wall and passes into the bloodstream. Breast milk stops the growth of the organism, whereas cow's milk permits it. Therefore, Dr. Reisinger believes, bottle-fed babies run a higher risk of crib death than other babies. . . .

The loss of a child through crib death is an especially traumatic experience. Parents often develop feelings of guilt and depression, thinking they somehow caused the child's death. To alleviate such feelings, organizations have been established to help parents accept the fact that they did not cause the death.

Trudy Stelter

WRITING AN EXTENDED DEFINITION

Planning and Drafting the Extended Definition

If you choose your own topic, pick an abstract term or one that is concrete but unfamiliar to your reader. Why, for instance, define *table* when the discussion would likely ease the reader into the Land of Nod? On the other hand, a paper explaining *computer virus* might well prove interesting and informative. Use one of the strategies on pages 12–19 to unearth promising topics. Then answer these questions about them.

Which topic holds the most promise? Why?
What purpose will guide my writing? To clarify a technical or specialized concept? To show what the term means to me? To persuade the reader to adopt my attitude toward it? To discuss some neglected facet of it?
For what audience should I write?

Here's a helpful process to follow as you think your definition through. First, select a clear example that illustrates what you wish to define: the United States could exemplify *democracy*. Then brainstorm to uncover major identifying characteristics. For democracy your list might include majority rule, free elections, a separately elected chief executive, and basic human rights. Next, test these characteristics against other legitimate examples and retain only the characteristics that apply. Britain is clearly a democracy but doesn't have a separately elected chief executive. Finally, test the unfolding definition against a clear counter example, perhaps the Soviet Union. If the definition fits the example, something is wrong.

Now evaluate what methods you might use to develop your definition. Each method has its own set of special strengths, as the following list shows.

Narration. Tracing the history of a new development or the changing meaning of a term

Description. Pointing out interesting or important features of a device, an event, or an individual

Process. Explaining what a device does or how it is used, how a procedure is carried out, or how a natural event takes place

Illustration. Tracing changes in meaning and defining abstract terms

Classification. Pointing out the different categories into which an item or an event can be grouped

Comparison. Distinguishing between an unfamiliar and a familiar item

Cause and effect. Explaining the origins and consequences of events, conditions, problems, and attitudes

Negation. Placing limitations on conditions and events and correcting popular misconceptions

Examine your topic in light of this listing and select the methods of development that seem most promising. Don't hesitate to use a method for some purpose not mentioned here. If you think that a comparison will help your reader understand some abstract term, use it.

Chart the methods of development you'll use, and then brainstorm each method in turn to gather the details that will inform the reader. When you've finished, look everything over, rearrange the details as necessary, add any new ones you think of, and prepare a revised chart. The example below is for a paper utilizing four methods of development.

Narration	*Classification*	*Process*	*Negation*
First supporting detail	First supporting detail	First supporting detail	First supporting detail
Second supporting detail	Second supporting detail	Second supporting detail	Second supporting detail

Definition papers can begin in various ways. If you're defining a term with no agreed-upon meaning (for example, *conservatism*), you might note some differing views of it and then state your own. If the term reflects some new social, political, economic, or technological development (such as *macroengineering*), you might mention the events that brought it into being. A colloquial or slang term often lends itself nicely to an attention-getting opener. A paper defining

studying computers, might find that lay readers are confused about the nature of a "data base." Students should then indicate what they want to accomplish by writing their papers. Because students often concentrate on technique and shortchange purpose, have them draft a brief statement of purpose. Next, have them draft an audience profile detailing what the audience does and doesn't know about the concept. Only at this point are students ready to consider the appropriate strategies to use in developing their papers.

CLASSROOM ACTIVITY

Since most students will be interested in the personal characteristics addressed in the Reader—waiting, success, and charm—you could lead a class discussion that engages student interest in this type of writing. More controversial issues could also be introduced, such as ascertaining limitations on freedom of speech or determining whether assault rifles are included under our right to bear arms.

ETHICAL ISSUES

Many writers, particularly medical professionals, lawmakers, and bureaucrats, often use language that can't be understood by those directly affected by the diagnosis, law, or policy. Is such obfuscation ethical? What if a referendum is deliberately written to confuse voters? Sometimes writers distort a definition and count on an equivocation to sustain their argument. For example, a politician might exaggerate a definition of "liberal" or "conservative" and then apply it to an opponent who only marginally fits the embellished definition but who would, under more traditional uses of the term, be considered liberal or conservative. Are such equivocations ethical?

chutzpah might begin by illustrating the brash behavior of someone with this trait. Often an introduction includes a short definition, perhaps taken from a dictionary. If you do include a dictionary definition, use the dictionary's full name (*Webster's New World Dictionary* says . . .). Several dictionary titles include the word *Webster*, and unless you use the full name your reader won't know which one you mean. Draw on a dictionary definition, however, only as a last resort.

In writing the body of the paper, present the methods of development in whatever order seems most appropriate. A paper defining *drag racing* might first describe the hectic scene as the cars line up for a race, then classify the different categories of vehicles, and finally explain the steps in a race. One defining *intellectual* might start by showing the differences between intellectuals and scholars, then name several prominent intellectuals and note how their insights have altered our thinking, and conclude by trying to explain why many Americans hold intellectuals in low regard.

Definition papers can end, as well as begin, in a number of ways. If you're defining some undesirable condition or event (such as the sudden infant death syndrome), you might express hope for a speedy solution. If you're reporting on some new development (like macroengineering), you might predict its economic or social impact. Often, a summary of your main points is effective. Choose whichever type of ending best supports your main idea.

Revising the Extended Definition

Use the general guidelines in Chapter 3 and these specific questions as you revise your extended definition.

TEACHING STRATEGY

Given the difficult and often slippery nature of extended definitions, caution students to revise not only the form but also the substance of their drafts with great care. They could write out a revision plan that details appropriate questions they've asked and answered.

Are my purpose and audience clear and appropriate?
If I've used an essential definition, does it do what it should and avoid the common pitfalls?
Are the methods of development suitable for the topic?
Is the paper organized effectively?
Are there other factors or examples I need to consider?

EXAMPLE STUDENT ESSAY OF DEFINITION

The Food Chain

Michael Galayda

It is a truism that we must eat to stay alive and   1
that all the plants and animals we dine on must do the

same. How many of us, though, ever stop to consider whether or not any pattern underlies all the cross-dining that goes on? There is a pattern, and to understand it we must first familiarize ourselves with the concept of a food chain. Such a chain can be defined as a hierarchy of organisms in a biological community, or ecosystem, with each member of the chain feeding on the one below it and in turn being fed upon by the one above it. To put the matter more simply, a food chain starts with a great quantity of plant stuffs which are eaten by a large number of very hungry diners. These diners are then eaten by a lesser number of other animals, which in turn fall prey to an even smaller number of creatures. With the passage of time, the uneaten organisms die and become part of the soil for the plant to grow in.

To illustrate, let's look for a moment at one   2
particular biological community, a marshy ecosystem, and a few events that might take place there. First, there are the marsh grasses, with millions of grasshoppers busily feeding upon them. When one grasshopper isn't looking, a shrew sneaks up and eats it. This process is repeated many times as the day wears on. Later, toward sunset, as the stuffed and inattentive shrew is crossing an open stretch of ground, a hawk swoops out of the sky and eats the rodent. The food chain is completed when the marsh hawk dies and its corpse fertilizes the marsh grasses.

This illustration is not meant to suggest that   3
hawks eat only shrews or shrews eat only grasshoppers;

the cycle is much more complicated than that, involving what biologists call trophic levels--the different feeding groups in an ecosystem. For example, some creatures eat green plants and some eat meat. There are five major trophic levels. The beginning point for any food chain is green plants, known as producers, which absorb sunlight and through the process of photosynthesis turn carbon dioxide, water, and soil nutrients into food, especially carbohydrates, that animals can assimilate.

All of the other life forms subsist either directly or indirectly on the producers. Animals that feed directly on green plants are the herbivores, called primary consumers. This group includes, among other creatures, most insects, most rodents, and hooved animals. The secondary consumers are the carnivores and omnivores. The term "carnivore," meaning an animal that eats only flesh, is more familiar than the term "omnivore," which designates an animal that eats both green plants and flesh. Carnivores include such animals as lions, leopards, eagles, and hawks; whereas omnivores are represented by foxes, bears, humans, and so on.

The last feeding group in the food chain consists of the decomposers: bacteria and fungi. These microorganisms recycle the waste products of living animals and the remains of all dead things--plants, herbivores, omnivores, and carnivores alike--into fertilizers that plants, the producers, can use.

Obviously each trophic level must produce more energy than it transfers to the next higher level. With

4

5

6

animals, a considerable part of this energy is lost through body heat. The muscles that pump the lungs, continually pushing air out of the body and sucking it back in, consume energy. The muscles in the arms and legs sweat out energy. All of the life-supporting systems of the organism use energy to keep it going. Everything from worms to people lives in accordance with this law of energy loss. As long as life's fires burn, energy is lost, never to be regained.

Throughout history we humans have tried to manipulate the food chain so as to provide ever-greater outputs of energy. On the one hand, we have tried, by whatever means we could employ, to rid our fields of harmful birds, insects, and rodents, and our animals of diseases and parasites. On the other, we have constantly striven to produce healthier and more productive strains of plants and animals. Often these attempts have been spectacularly successful. Sometimes, though, the results have proved disastrous, as with the insecticide DDT.   7

Farmers first began using DDT on a large scale in 1946, right after it had proved its effectiveness in tropical military operations in World War II. As expected, the product proved equally effective as an agricultural pesticide, but there were some unexpected and disastrous side effects. The difficulties were caused by excessive DDT washing off crops, entering irrigation canals, and from there flowing to streams, rivers and lakes. All living creatures in the path of the chemical were contaminated--worms, fish, ducks, indeed all forms of aquatic life. Contaminated worms   8 poisoned songbirds, causing massive dieoffs of birds, and many humans developed serious health problems from eating contaminated aquatic animals. Although Congress has severely restricted the use of DDT in this country, the whole episode stands as a warning of what can happen when humans manipulate the food chain.

As time continues and the population grows, efforts will be made to further increase the food supply. Let us hope that in doing so we won't act in haste and create catastrophes of even greater magnitude.

9

DISCUSSION QUESTIONS

1. The essential definition occurs in paragraph 1: "Such a chain can be defined. . . ." The definition is proper because it names the chain, places it in a broad category ("a hierarchy of organisms"), and distinguishes it from other items (each member "feeding on the one below it and in turn being fed upon by the one above it.")

2. The writer shows the operation of the food chain in general terms. The chain assumes more concrete form later in the essay.

3. The writer uses the illustrations of the marsh grass, grasshopper, shrew, and marsh hawk to define the operation of the food chain. "To illustrate" at the start of the paragraph signals this method.

4. Paragraphs 3–5 rely primarily on process analysis. The food chain is traced from "The beginning point" (paragraph 3) to "The last feeding group" (paragraph 5), which starts the whole cycle over again. Illustrations and specific examples are also used to clarify the process. Students should note that two methods of development are often interwoven in an extended definition.

5. Brief definitions include "tropic levels" in paragraph 3 and "herbivore," "carnivore," and "omnivore" in paragraph 4.

DISCUSSION QUESTIONS ■

1. Identify the essay's essential definition and explain how it functions.
2. What is accomplished by the last three sentences in paragraph 1?
3. What method of development does the writer use in paragraph 2?
4. What methods of development are combined in paragraphs 3–5?
5. Cite three places in the essay where the writer uses brief definitions.

SUGGESTIONS FOR WRITING ■   Write an extended definition using one of the following suggestions or one approved by your instructor. The term you define may be new, misused, misunderstood, or may have a disputed meaning. Develop the essay by any combination of writing strategies.

1. Liberal arts (or vocational) education
2. 50s and 60s nostalgia
3. Routine
4. Culture
5. Stress
6. Charisma
7. Marriage
8. Boss
9. Greed in America

10. Computer virus
11. Macho man
12. Feminist
13. Angst
14. Fax communication
15. Some term from your field

■ Chapter 12

Argument: Convincing Others

"What did you think of that movie?"

"Great!"

"What do you mean, *great*? I thought the acting was wooden and the story completely unbelievable."

"That's about what I'd expect from you. You wouldn't know a good movie if it walked up and bit you."

"Oh yeah? What makes you think you're such a great. . . .?"

Argument or quarrel? Many people would ask, "What's the difference?" To them, the two terms convey the same meaning, both calling to mind two angry, red-faced people, shouting, trading insults, and sometimes slugging it out. In writing, however, *argument* stands for something quite different: a paper, grounded on logical, structured evidence, that attempts to convince the reader to accept an opinion, take some action, or do both.

We constantly attempt to win others over to our way of thinking. Children try to talk their parents into doing all sorts of things: taking them to the movies, buying them balloons or bicycles, letting them stay up beyond their usual bedtimes. Adults urge city councils to revise zoning ordinances, exhort their friends to change positions on drug testing or legalized gambling, or propose that a company change its billing system or buy some new piece of equipment.

As we press our own arguments, we are bombarded by those of others. Advertisers flood us with pitches for jeans and jackets, autos and albums, all the presumed necessities of a healthy, fulfilled life. Spouses press claims for lakeside vacations. Politicians vie for our votes. Rectors and rabbis try to enlist us on the side of righteousness. Mastering the skills of argument can help you gain your own ends, judge and accept effective presentations, and avoid the snares of unscrupulous persuaders.

Certain kinds of topics just aren't arguable. There's no point, for instance, in trying to tackle questions of personal preference or taste (is red prettier than blue?) Such contests quickly turn into "it is," "it isn't" exchanges that establish nothing except the silliness of the contenders. Questions of simple fact (Was Eisenhower first elected President in 1952?) don't qualify either; one side has all the ammunition. Bickering will never settle these issues; reference books quickly will.

Because argument involves conflict, there's always a chance we'll lose some contests. Our parents might turn thumbs down on the bike because they can't afford it. The city might claim that rezoning would upset long-range plans for commercial development. Our friends hear what we have to say but hold stubbornly to their original views. The boss refuses to buy the equipment, citing poor company profits. To score a win, we need to present a case more compelling than that of our opposition.

Most successful arguments rest on a firm, logical foundation. To supplement this rational base, writers often enlist emotion to arouse their readers' passions and sympathies. Furthermore, writers make ethical appeals by projecting favorable images of themselves.

THE RATIONAL APPEAL

When you appeal to reason, you appeal to the reader's ability to think logically. You say, in effect, "If you examine my thinking on this issue, you will agree with me." Logical thinking proceeds by leading the reader from some point that both reader and writer accept as true to other points that follow from it. Without such a starting point, the process can't get under way. Rational appeals include three reasoning strategies: induction, deduction, and analogy.

Induction

Induction moves from separate bits of evidence to a general observation. Suppose that on a hot, humid summer day you go to the kitchen to eat some potato chips from a bag opened the day before. As you start to munch, you make these observations:

Chip #1: limp and stale
Chip #2: limp and stale
Chip #3: limp and stale
Chip #4: limp and stale
Chip #5: limp and stale

At this point, you decide that the rest of the chips are probably stale too, and you stop eating. Inductive reasoning has led you, stale chip by stale chip, to a conclusion about the whole bag.

But probability is not proof. To prove something by induction, we must check every bit of evidence, and often that's just not practical or possible.

2. Ask students to review their textbooks, newspapers, and magazines to determine where authors are reaching conclusions based on inductive reasoning. If possible, have students test that reasoning to establish whether there is sufficient basis for the generalization.

3. Students often overgeneralize from induction. To correct this fault, you could have them list several inappropriate generalizations based on faulty induction. They might also consider how overgeneralization can give rise to superstitions. In this connection, a commonplace in psychology is the "superstitious rat." The rodent gains food by pushing a button and in the process happens to lift its leg accidentally. As a result, it believes it can't receive food if all four legs are on the ground.

CLASSROOM ACTIVITY

Any detective game now on the market can provide students with valuable practice in working with actual observations. Simply distribute lists of its clues and have students use them to determine the guilty person. They might defend their findings in a short paper.

Nonetheless, induction has great value for the conduct of human affairs. Say a food company has test marketed a new spaghetti sauce and now wants to decide whether it should start selling the product nationwide. A poll of 1,200 users, representing a cross section of the market, indicates that 78 percent rate the sauce "excellent." As a result, the company decides to go ahead. Induction has led them to conclude that future customers will favor the sauce as much as past customers did. Polls that sample political preferences and other public attitudes also operate inductively.

You have several options for organizing an inductive argument. You might begin by posing some direct or indirect question in order to snare your reader's interest, or you might simply state the position you will argue. The body of the paper provides the supporting evidence. In the conclusion you could reaffirm your position or suggest the consequences of that position. The following short example illustrates inductive argument.

Bologna is perhaps the most popular of all luncheon meats. Each day, thousands of individuals consume bologna sandwiches at noontime without ever considering the health consequences. Perhaps they should.

The sodium content of bologna is excessively high. On the average, three ounces contain over 850 milligrams, three times as much as a person needs in a single day. In addition, bologna's characteristic flavor and reddish color are caused by sodium nitrite, which is used to prevent the growth of botulism–causing organisms. Unfortunately, sodium nitrite combines with amines, natural compounds already in most foods, to form nitrosamines, which have been proven to cause cancer in laboratory animals. Finally, from a nutrition standpoint, bologna is terrible. The fat content is around 28 percent, the water content ranges upward from 50 percent, and the meat includes very little protein.

Health conscious people, then, will choose better fare for lunch.

Alison Russell

Deduction

Deduction is the reverse of induction. Instead of formulating a conclusion after considering pieces of evidence, you start with an observation that most people accept as true and then show how certain conclusions follow from that observation. For example, to convince a friend to study harder, you begin with the assumption that a profitable career requires a good education; proceed to argue that for a good education students must study diligently; and conclude that, as a result, your friend should spend more time with the books. Politicians who assert that we all want to act in ways beneficial to future generations, then point out how the policies they favor will ensure that outcome, argue deductively.

As with induction, you have several options when organizing a deductive argument. You might begin with the position you intend to prove, with a question that will be answered by the argument, or with a synopsis of the argument. The body of the paper works out the implications of your assumption. In the conclusion you could directly state (or restate, in different words) your position, suggest the consequences of adopting or not adopting that position, or pose a question that is easily answered after reading the argument. Here is a short example of deductive argument.

```
        The recent spot-checks of our rooms by the dorm's head

advisor are an unacceptable invasion of privacy. This

practice should stop immediately.

        The Constitution protects all citizens from

unreasonable search by police officers unless these

officers have adequate evidence. That is why the police need

a search warrant before they can search our home. If they

fail to obtain one, a case that ends up in court will likely

be thrown out. Our right to privacy, then, is guaranteed

unless adequate evidence suggests otherwise.

        If the police can't search our homes without good

reason, why should our head advisor spot-check our rooms for

signs of wrongdoing?

                                        Sammy Borchardt
```

Often, a deductive argument is built around a categorical syllogism, a set of three statements that follow a fixed pattern to ensure sound reasoning. The first statement, called the *major premise*, names a category of things and says that all or none of them share a certain characteristic. The *minor premise* notes that a thing or group of things belongs to that category. The *conclusion* states that the thing or group shares the characteristics of the category. Here are two examples.

PERSPECTIVE

Deductive reasoning is more common than most students recognize. When we draw conclusions from established values, apply scientific laws to a particular situation, or argue from any generally accepted principle, we use deduction. Unfortunately, our deductions rarely wear the clear markings of a syllogism, instead exhibiting only an inexact connection between assumed general principles and resulting conclusion. Depending on the class, you might spend time explaining how deduction is used. A dreadful contrast between inductive and deductive reasoning was apparent in the debate preceding the fatal Challenger lift-off that ended in an explosion. Management apparently favored the launch, arguing inductively that the O-rings had functioned without difficulty in several lift-offs under similar circumstances. Some engineers opposed the launch, arguing deductively about how the O-ring materials should behave in cold weather. Unfortunately, the engineers were correct.

TEACHING STRATEGIES

1. Some students tend to use shaky assumptions in their major premises and then move rather haphazardly to a conclusion. Caution against these flaws.
2. You could discuss the extent to which syllogisms are used in arguments, and why. Bring in and discuss syllogisms with a missing premise, a very common occurrence.
3. Have students record where they or others have argued deductively. Students could write down the major and minor premises, the conclusions, and the connections between them. Have them test the truth and validity of the syllogism.

CLASSROOM ACTIVITY
Starting from some agreed-upon premise, such as "Grading should be based only on the objective quality of course work," ask students to reach and justify reasonable conclusions. The validity of the conclusions could then be discussed in class.

Major premise	All persons are mortal.
Minor premise	Sue Davis is a person.
Conclusion	Therefore, Sue Davis is mortal.

Major premise	No dogs have feathers.
Minor premise	Spot is a dog.
Conclusion	Therefore, Spot does not have feathers.

Note that in each case both major and minor premise are true and the conclusion follows logically.

Syllogisms frequently appear in stripped-down form, with one of the premises or the conclusion omitted. The following example omits the major premise: "Because Wilma is a civil engineer, she has a strong background in mathematics." Here is the entire syllogism.

All civil engineers have strong backgrounds in mathematics.

Wilma is a civil engineer.

Therefore, Wilma has a strong background in mathematics.

Syllogistic Argument at Work.   A syllogism can occur anywhere in an essay: in the introduction to set the stage for the evidence, at various places in the body, even in the conclusion in order to pull the argument together. Here is an example that uses a syllogism in the introduction.

In 1966, when the Astrodome was completed in Houston, Texas, the managers concluded that it would be impossible to grow grass indoors. To solve their problem, they decided to install a ruglike synthetic playing surface that was fittingly called Astroturf. In the ensuing years, many other sports facilities have installed synthetic turf. Unfortunately, this development has been accompanied by a sharp rise in the number and severity of injuries suffered by athletes—a rise clearly linked to the surface they play upon. Obviously, anything that poses a threat to player safety is undesirable. Because synthetic turf does this, it is undesirable and should be replaced by grass.

Denny Witham

To support his position, the writer then notes that turf, unlike grass, often becomes excessively hot, tiring players and increasing their chances of injury; that seams can open up between sections of turf and lead to tripping and falling; that players can run faster on artificial turf and thus collide more violently; and that the extreme hardness of the turf leads to torn ligaments and tissues when players slam their toes into it.

In the following excerpt from Martin Luther King, Jr.'s, "Letter from Birmingham Jail," a syllogism is used to support part of the body of an essay. King wrote the letter after his arrest during a civil rights demonstration in Birmingham, Alabama. He addressed it to eight Birmingham clergymen who had published a letter that defended his war on racial discrimination but deplored his "nonviolent direct action" which included sit-ins and protest marches. In answering the clergymen, King draws a difference between just and unjust laws, then uses it to justify his willingness to defy segregation laws but not others.

> . . . How does one determine whether a law is just or unjust? A just law is a man-made code that squares with the moral law or the law of God. An unjust law is a code that is out of harmony with the moral law. To put it in the terms of St. Thomas Aquinas: An unjust law is a human law that is not rooted in eternal law and natural law. Any law that degrades human personality is unjust. All segregation statutes are unjust because segregation distorts the soul and damages the personality. It gives the segregator a false sense of superiority and the segregated a false sense of inferiority. . . . Thus it is that I can urge men to obey the 1954 decision of the Supreme Court, for it is morally right; and I can urge them to disobey segregation ordinances, for they are morally wrong.

Stated in syllogistic form, King's reasoning goes as follows:

All laws that degrade human personality are unjust.

All segregation laws are laws that degrade human personality.

Therefore, all segregation laws are unjust.

This syllogism is readily apparent and likely to win acceptance from the Birmingham clergymen because King enlists a religious authority to support his definitions of just and unjust laws. Indeed, most readers, not just these clergymen, would probably accept the syllogism.

Avoiding Misuse of Syllogisms.   Two cautions are in order. *First*, make sure any syllogism you use follows the proper order. The writer of the following passage has ignored this caution.

> And that's not all. Newton has stated openly that he favors federally funded abortions for the poor. Just the other day, the American Socialist party took this same stand. In my book, Newton's position puts him squarely in the Socialist camp. I strongly urge anyone supporting this man's candidacy to reconsider. . . .

Restated in syllogistic form, the writer's argument goes like this:

Socialists favor federally funded abortions for the poor.

Newton favors federally funded abortions for the poor.

Therefore, Newton is a Socialist.

The last two statements reverse the proper order, and as a result the syllogism proves nothing about Newton's politics: he may or may not be "in the Socialist camp."

Second, make sure the major premise of your syllogism is in fact true. Note this example.

All conservatives are opposed to environmental protection.

Mary is a conservative.

Therefore, Mary is opposed to environmental protection.

But is every conservative an environmental Jack the Ripper? In some communities, political conservatives have led fights against air and water pollution, and most conservatives agree that at least some controls are worthwhile. Mary's sympathies, then, may well lie with those who want to heal, rather than hack, the environment.

This type of flaw becomes much harder to detect when the syllogism omits the major premise:

Professor Snarf is a poor instructor; she grades her students so hard.

Expanding the statement into a full-blown syllogism exposes the shaky underpinnings of the original.

All instructors who grade hard are poor instructors.

Professor Snarf grades her students hard.

Therefore, Professor Snarf is a poor instructor.

Following this procedure with any stripped-down syllogism will quickly show whether it is trying to sneak across a faulty idea.

EXERCISE ANSWERS

1. Syllogism is faulty because its initial statement is untrue: Singers are not necessarily happy.
2. Syllogism is satisfactory.
3. Syllogism is faulty because the final two statements reverse the proper order.
4. Syllogism is faulty because its initial statement is untrue: Salespeople sometimes misrepresent the products they sell.

EXERCISE ■   Which of these syllogisms is satisfactory, which have false major premises, and which is faulty because the last two statements reverse the proper order?

1. All singers are happy people.
   Mary Harper is a singer.
   Therefore, Mary Harper is a happy person.
2. All cowards fear danger.
   "Chicken" Cacciatore is a coward.
   Therefore, "Chicken" Cacciatore fears danger.

3. All cats like meat.
   Towser likes meat.
   Therefore, Towser is a cat.
4. No salesperson would ever misrepresent a product to a customer.
   Sabrina is a salesperson.
   Therefore, Sabrina would never misrepresent a product to a customer.

Analogy in Argument

An analogy compares two unlike situations or things. Arguers often use analogies to contend that because two items share one or more likenesses, they are also alike in other ways. Familiar analogies assume that humans respond to chemicals as rats do and that success in school predicts success on the job.

Because its conclusions about one thing rest upon observations about some different thing, analogy is the weakest form of rational appeal. Analogies never prove anything. But they often help explain and show probability and therefore are quite persuasive.

For an analogy to be useful, its points of similarity must bear directly on the issue. Also, it must account for any significant differences between the two items. Here's an effective analogy, used to back an argument that a liberal education is the best kind to help us cope successfully with life.

> Suppose it were perfectly certain that the life and fortune of everyone of us would, one day or other, depend upon his winning or losing a game of chess. Don't you think that we should all consider it to be a primary duty to learn at least the names and the moves of the pieces; to have a notion of a gambit, and a keen eye for all the means of giving and getting out of check? Do you not think that we should look with a disapprobation amounting to scorn, upon the father who allowed his son, or the state which allowed its members, to grow up without knowing a pawn from a knight?
>
> Yet it is a very plain and elementary truth, that the life, the fortune, and the happiness of every one of us, and, more or less, of those who are connected with us, do depend upon our knowing something of the rules of a game infinitely more difficult and complicated than chess. It is a game which has been played for untold ages, every man and woman of us being one of the two players in a game of his or her own. The chessboard is the world, the pieces are the phenomena of the universe, the rules of the game are what we call the laws of Nature. The player on the other side is hidden from us. We know that his play is always fair, just, and patient. But also we know, to our cost, that he never overlooks a mistake, or makes the smallest allowance for ignorance. To the man who plays well, the highest stakes are paid, with that sort of overflowing generosity with which the strong shows delight in strength. And one who plays ill is checkmated—without haste, but without remorse. . . .

PERSPECTIVE

While an argument from analogy is never totally conclusive, it is extraordinarily common and, in some ways, unavoidable. We can't always do medical research on humans, and even when we do, it is often in controlled situations dissimilar to daily life. If we learn lessons from history, it can only be on the basis of analogy since historical situations are rarely identical. Economists, political scientists, and sociologists all regularly attempt to reach conclusions and make predictions on the basis of analogy. Indeed, any attempt to work from a scientific model implicitly relies on an analogy since few scientists confuse the model with the real world. More practically, when business executives review the potential for a marketing strategy based on the previous performance of other plans, they are probably drawing on an implicit analogy. For these reasons, students should understand, work with, and evaluate arguments from analogy.

TEACHING STRATEGIES

1. Both Reader essays on the legalization of drugs include analogies to prohibition. You might have students read the essays and evaluate the analogies. **2.** Ask students to review their textbooks and several newspaper editorials to observe where and how appropriately arguments from analogy were used.

Well, what I mean by Education is learning the rules of this mighty game. In other words, education is the instruction of the intellect in the law of Nature, under which name I include not merely things and their forces, but men and their ways; and the fashioning of the affections and of the will into an earnest and loving desire to move in harmony with those laws. For me, education means neither more nor less than this. Anything which professes to call itself education must be tried by this standard, and if it fails to stand the test, I will not call it education, whatever may be the force of authority, or of numbers, upon the other side.

Thomas Henry Huxley, "A Liberal Education and Where to Find It"

THE EMOTIONAL APPEAL

Although effective argument relies mainly on reason, an emotional appeal can lend powerful reinforcement. Indeed, emotion can win the hearts and the help of people who would otherwise passively accept a logical argument but take no action. Each Christmas, newspapers raise money for local charities by running stark case histories of destitute families. Organizations raise funds to fight famine by displaying brochures that feature skeletal, swollen-bellied children. Still other groups use emotion-charged stories and pictures to solicit support for environmental protection, to combat various diseases, and so on. Less benignly, advertisers use emotion to play upon our hopes, fears, and vanities in order to sell mouthwash, cars, clothes, and other products. Politicians paint themselves as God-fearing, honest toilers for the public good while lambasting their opponents as the uncaring tools of special interests. In evaluating or writing an argument, ask yourself whether the facts warrant the emotion. Is the condition of the destitute family truly cause for pity? Is any politician unwaveringly good, any other irredeemably bad?

The following paragraph from "Letter from Birmingham Jail" illustrates an appropriate use of emotion:

We have waited for more than 340 years for our constitutional and God-given rights. The nations of Asia and Africa are moving with jetlike speed toward gaining political independence, but we still creep at horse-and-buggy pace toward gaining a cup of coffee at a lunch counter. Perhaps it is easy for those who have never felt the stinging darts of segregation to say, "Wait." But when you have seen vicious mobs lynch your mothers and fathers at will and drown your sisters and brothers at whim; when you have seen hate-filled policemen curse, kick, and even kill your black brothers and sisters; when you see the vast majority of your twenty million Negro brothers smothering in an airtight cage of poverty in the midst of an affluent society; when you suddenly find your tongue twisted and your speech stammering as you seek to explain to your six-year-old daughter why she can't go to the public amusement park that has just been advertised on television, and see tears welling up in her eyes when she is told that Funtown is closed to colored children, and see ominous clouds of inferiority beginning to form in her little mental sky, and see her beginning to distort her personality by developing an unconscious bitterness toward white people; when you have to concoct an answer for a five-year-old son who is asking, "Daddy, why do white people treat colored people so mean?"; when you take a cross-country drive and find it necessary to sleep night after night in the uncomfortable corners of your automobile because no motel will accept you; when you are humiliated day in and day out by nagging signs reading "white" and "colored"; when your first name becomes "nigger," your middle name becomes "boy" (however old you are) and your last name becomes "John," and your wife and mother are never given the respected title "Mrs."; when you are harried by day and haunted by night by the fact that you are a Negro, living constantly at tiptoe stance, never quite knowing what to expect next, and are plagued with inner fears and outer resentments, when you are forever fighting a degenerating sense of "nobodiness"—then you will understand why we find it difficult to wait. There comes a time when the cup of endurance runs over, and men are no longer willing to be plunged into the abyss of despair. I hope, sirs, you can understand our legitimate and unavoidable impatience.

> Martin Luther King, Jr., "Letter from Birmingham Jail"

ETHICAL ISSUES

Is it acceptable to deliberately manipulate someone's emotional response in order to encourage a specific action? What if the manipulation is for the person's own good, as in ads stressing the risks of AIDS? What about cases where subliminal appeals are used?

THE ETHICAL APPEAL

Ethical appeals derive from the image a writer projects. Before logic can do its work, the audience must be willing to consider the argument. If a writer's tone offends the audience, the reasoning, however brilliant, will fail to penetrate. But if the writer comes across as pleasant, moral, fair-minded, decent, worthwhile, gaining reader support is much easier.

In "Letter from Birmingham Jail," King wisely enlists the force of ethical appeal, starting in the opening paragraph. King knows that his clergymen audience opposes his actions, if not his ends; that his wider audience includes many people who violently oppose the civil rights movement; and that he must therefore build a respectable character from the disadvantageous position of an inmate in a jail.

King first notes that his journey to Birmingham and activities there grew out of his desire for justice. In making this point, he draws a parallel between himself and biblical bearers of the gospel.

> . . . I am in Birmingham because injustice is here. Just as the prophets of the eighth century B.C. left their villages and carried their "thus saith the Lord" far beyond the boundaries of their home towns, and just as the Apostle Paul left his village of Tarsus and carried the gospel of Jesus Christ to the far corners of the Greco–Roman world, so am I compelled to carry the gospel of freedom beyond my own home town. Like Paul, I must constantly respond to the Macedonian call for aid.

King points out that he and his followers turned to direct action only after it had become clear that the city fathers would not negotiate in good faith. He further declares that he postponed his direct action program several times before finally putting it into effect. Then he defends his action as a necessary prelude to moral growth.

TEACHING STRATEGIES

1. Have students examine their own responses to arguments included in the Reader and in the news media. How do they evaluate the character of the author? How do those judgments influence their responses to the argument?
2. Many students are not sure of their ethical credibility; thus, they feel uncomfortable trying to demonstrate it. In discussing potential topics, have students write down the ethical appeals they would like to project and then suggest ways they might do so.
3. Some students have a tendency to come across as extremely judgmental, excessively rigid, and uncomfortably self-righteous, often because they have not explored their topic. Help them recognize this tendency by pointing out examples in their writing.

. . . I have earnestly opposed violent tension, but there is a type of constructive, nonviolent tension which is necessary for growth. Just as Socrates felt that it was necessary to create a tension in the mind so that individuals could rise from the bondage of myths and half-truths to the unfettered realm of creative analysis and objective appraisal, so must we see the need for nonviolent gadflies to create the kind of tension in society that will help men rise from the dark depths of prejudice and racism to the majestic heights of understanding and brotherhood.

Here King offers a needed explanation without sacrificing his dignity. He comes across as rational, religious, and peace-loving, a person who mirrors the qualities his audience would be most likely to accept.

SUPPORTING AN ARGUMENT

The heart of your argument is the evidence supporting your position. Evidence falls into several categories: established truths, opinions of authorities, statistical findings, and personal experience. The strongest arguments usually combine several types of evidence.

Established Truths

These are facts that no one can seriously dispute. Here are some examples.

Historical fact	The first amendment to the United States Constitution prohibits Congress from abridging freedom of the press.
Scientific fact	The layer of ozone in the earth's upper atmosphere protects us from the sun's harmful ultraviolet radiation.
Geographical fact	The western part of the United States has tremendous reserves of coal.

Established truths aren't arguable themselves but do provide strong backup for argumentative propositions. For example, citing the abundant coal supply in the western regions could support an argument that the United States should return to coal to supply its energy needs.

Some established truths, the result of careful observations and thinking over many years, basically amount to enlightened common sense. The notion that everyone possesses a unique combination of interests, abilities, and personality characteristics illustrates this kind of truth. Few people would seriously question it.

Opinions of Authorities

An authority is a recognized expert in some field. Authoritative opinions—the only kind to use—play a powerful role in winning readers over to your side. The views of metropolitan police chiefs and criminologists could support your

ETHICAL ISSUES

Is it ethical to fabricate a character or ethical credentials that are not yours? What if such fabrication is for the public good?

TEACHING STRATEGY

Some students quickly assume that a statement is an established truth when in fact it is merely opinion or easily contested. You might discuss the criteria that an established truth must meet. One technique is to envision how someone could legitimately object to the claim. If the objection seems reasonable, the student might reconsider the "truth." Or students might develop their own lists of established truths on a given topic and verify them.

CLASSROOM ACTIVITY

You could list so-called established truths on the board and have students discuss which ones qualify. Or students might develop their own list on a given topic, which could be discussed in class.

position on ways to control urban crime. Researchers who have investigated the effects of air pollution could help you argue for stricter smog control laws. Whatever your argument, don't settle for less than heavyweight authorities. And tell your reader just why those you cite are authorities.

The following paragraph, from an article arguing that extra-high-voltage electric transmission lines pose a health hazard, illustrates the use of authority.

> Robert Becker, a physician and director of the Orthopedic–Biophysics Laboratory at the Syracuse, New York, Veterans Administration Hospital—Upstate Medical Center, has been researching the effects of low-frequency electric fields (60 Hz) for fifteen years. Testifying at health and safety hearings for proposed lines in New York, he said that exposure to the fields can produce physiological and functional changes in humans—anything from increased irritability and fatigue to raised cholesterol levels, hypertension and ulcers. Studies of rats exposed to low-level electric fields showed tumor growths and abnormalities in development. Dr. Becker believes we are performing unauthorized medical experiments by exposing people to the electromagnetic fields surrounding the transmission lines.
>
> Kelly Davis, "Health and High Voltage: 765 KV Lines"

Beware of opinions from those who stand to profit if their views prevail. The agribusiness executive who favors farm price supports or the labor leader who opposes any restrictions on picketing may be writing merely to guard old privileges or garner new ones. Unless the opinion can stand especially close scrutiny, don't put it in your paper; it will just weaken your case with perceptive readers.

Because authorities don't always see eye to eye, their views lack the finality of established truths. Furthermore, their opinions will convince only if the audience accepts the authority *as* authoritative. Although advertisers successfully present football stars as authorities on shaving cream and credit cards, most people would not accept their views on the safety of nuclear energy.

Statistical Findings

Statistics—data showing how much, how many, or how often—can also buttress your argument. Most statistics come from books, magazines, newspapers, handbooks, encyclopedias, and reports, but you can use data from your own investigations as well.

Because statistics are often misused, many people distrust them, so any you offer must be reliable. First, make sure your sample isn't too small. Don't use a one-day traffic count to argue for a traffic light at a certain intersection. City Hall might counter by contending that the results are atypical. To make your case, you'd need to count traffic for perhaps two or three weeks. Take care not to push statistical claims too far. You may know that two-thirds of Tarrytown's factories pollute the air excessively, but don't argue that the same figures probably apply to your town. There's simply no carryover. Keep alert for biased statistics; they can cause as serious a credibility gap as biased opinions. Generally, recent data are better than old data, but either must come from a reliable source. Older information from the *New York Times* would probably be more accurate than current data from some publication that trades on sensationalism. Here's how one writer used statistics:

> The United States is losing its war against cocaine. Since this war is fought in the marketplace, percentages and statistics are needed to describe the dimensions of the defeat. The federal anti-drug budget grew by more than 300 percent from 1980 to 1988, but the cocaine supply multiplied tenfold in the same period. As a result, cocaine prices have plunged to barely 20 percent of what they were in 1980. In that year there were about 220,000 acres under coca cultivation in Peru, Bolivia, and Colombia; by 1984 the number had increased to 380,000, and by 1988, according to very conservative estimates, to at least 520,000. The supply of cocaine to the United States grew correspondingly: about 40 to 48 metric tons of cocaine entered the U.S. market in 1980, anywhere from 70 to 120 tons in 1984, and possibly as much as 350 to 400 tons in 1988. Plummeting prices reflected the supply glut: in 1980 the wholesale price at the port of entry was $50,000 to $55,000 a kilogram, by 1984 it had dropped to about $35,000, and in 1988 wholesale prices in Florida hit an all-time low of $10,000 to $12,000. . . .
>
> Gustavo A. Garroti, "How to Fight the Drug War"

TEACHING STRATEGY

Students seem to fall into two distinct groups: those who rely exclusively on and those who totally avoid personal experience. You might discuss when and where different kinds of personal experience can and cannot be used and also point out the criteria such experience must meet.

Personal Experience

Sometimes personal experience can deliver an argumentative message more forcefully than any other kind of evidence. Suppose that two years ago a speeder ran into your car and almost killed you. Today you're arguing for stiffer laws against speeding. Chances are you'll rely mainly on expert opinions and on statistics showing the number of people killed and injured each year in speeding accidents. However, describing the crash, the slow, pain-filled weeks in the hospital, and the months spent hobbling around on crutches may well provide the persuasive nudge that wins your reader over. Personal experience generally reinforces but does not replace other kinds of evidence. Unless it has other backup, readers may reject it as atypical or trivial.

CLASSROOM ACTIVITY

Bring in advertisements or political speeches and have students identify the fallacies and their intended effect on the reader. This exercise makes an excellent short writing assignment.

FERRETING OUT FALLACIES

Fallacies are lapses in logic that reflect upon your ability to think clearly, and therefore they weaken your argument. The fallacies described below are among the most common. Correct any you find in your own arguments, and call attention to those used by the opposition.

Hasty Generalization

Hasty generalization results when someone bases a conclusion on too little evidence. The student who tries to see an instructor during one of her office hours, finds her out, and goes away muttering, "She's never there when she should be" is guilty of hasty generalization. Perhaps the instructor was delayed by another student, attended a special department meeting, or went home ill. Even if she merely went shopping, that's not a good reason for saying she always shirks her responsibility. Several more unsuccessful office visits would be needed to make such a charge stick.

Non Sequitur

From the Latin "It does not follow," this fallacy draws unwarranted conclusions from seemingly ample evidence. Consider this example: "Bill's been out almost every night for the last two weeks. Who is she?" These evening excursions, however numerous, point to no particular conclusion. Bill may be studying in the library, participating in campus organizations, taking night classes, or walking. Of course, he *could* be charmed by a new date, but that conclusion requires other evidence.

Stereotyping

A person who commits this fallacy attaches one or more supposed characteristics to a group or one of its members. Typical stereotypes include "Latins make better lovers," "blondes have more fun," and "women are lousy drivers." Stereotyping racial, religious, ethnic, or nationality groups can destroy an argument. The images are often malicious and always offensive to fair-minded readers.

Either/Or Fallacy

The either/or fallacy asserts that only two choices exist when, in fact, several options are possible. A salesperson who wants you to buy snow tires may claim, "Either buy these tires or plan on getting stuck a lot this winter." But are you really that boxed in? You might drive only on main roads that are plowed immediately after every snowstorm. You could use public transportation when it snows. You could buy radial tires for year-round use. If very little snow falls, you might not need special tires at all.

Not all either/or statements are fallacies. The instructor who checks a student's record and then issues a warning, "Make at least a *C* on your final or you'll fail the course," is not guilty of a reasoning error. No other alternatives exist. Most situations, however, offer more than two choices.

Begging the Question

A person who begs the question asserts the truth of some unproven statement. Here is an example: "Vitamin A is harmful to your health, and all bottles should carry a warning label. If enough of us write the Food and Drug Administration, we can get the labeling we need." But how do we know Vitamin A does harm users? No evidence is offered. People lacking principles often use this fallacy to hit opponents below the belt: "We shouldn't allow a right-wing sympathizer like Mary

Dailey to represent us in Congress." Despite a lack of suitable evidence, voters often accept such faulty logic and vote for the other candidate.

Circular Argument

Circular argument, a first cousin to begging the question, supports a position merely by restating it. "Pauline is a good manager because she runs the company effectively" says, in effect, that "something is because something is." Repetition replaces evidence.

Arguing off the Point

The writer who commits this fallacy, which is sometimes called "ignoring the question" or "a red herring," sidetracks an issue by introducing irrelevant information. To illustrate: "The Ford Thunderbolt is a much better value than the Honda Harmony. Anyway, the Japanese are becoming too prominent in our country. They're buying up businesses and real estate on both the East and West Coasts. Many Americans don't want to work for a Japanese boss." The writer sets out to convince that the American car is superior in value but then abruptly shifts to Japanese ownership in America—a trend which has no bearing on the argument.

The Argument *Ad Hominem*

The Latin term "to the man" designates an argument that attacks an individual rather than that individual's opinions or qualifications. Note this example: "Sam Bernhart doesn't deserve promotion to Personnel Manager. His divorce was a disgrace, and he's always writing letters to the editor. The company should find someone more suitable." This attack completely skirts the real issue—whether Sam's job performance entitles him to the promotion. Unless his personal conduct has caused his work to suffer, it should not enter into the decision.

Appeal to the Crowd

An appeal of this sort arouses an emotional response by playing on the irrational fears and prejudices of the audience. Terms like *communists, fascists, bleeding hearts, right-winger, welfare chiselers*, and *law and order* are tossed about freely to sway the audience for or against something. Consider:

> The streets of our country are in turmoil. The universities are filled with students rebelling and rioting. Communists are seeking to destroy our country. Russia is threatening us with her might, and the public is in danger. Yes, danger from within and without. We need law and order. Yes, without law and order our nation cannot survive. Elect us, and we shall by law and order be respected among the nations of the world. Without law and order our republic shall fall.

Tapping the emotions of the crowd can sway large groups and win acceptance for positions that rational thinking would reject. Think what Adolf Hitler, the author of the foregoing excerpt, brought about in Germany.

Guilt by Association

This fallacy points out some similarity or connection between one person or group and another. It tags the first with the sins, real or imagined, of the second. The following excerpt from a letter protesting a speaker at a lecture series illustrates this technique:

> The next slated speaker, Dr. Sylvester Crampton, was for years a member of the Economic Information Committee. This foundation has very strong ties with other ultraright-wing groups, some of which have been labeled fascistic. When he speaks next Thursday, whose brand of Americanism will he be selling?

Post Hoc, ergo Propter Hoc

The Latin meaning, "after this, therefore because of this," refers to the fallacy of assuming that because one event follows another, the first caused the second. Such shoddy thinking underlies many popular superstitions ("If a black cat crosses your path, you'll have bad luck") and many connections that cannot be substantiated ("I always catch cold on Easter"). Sometimes one event does cause another: a sudden thunderclap might startle a person into dropping a dish. At other times, coincidence is the only connection. Careful thinking will usually lay farfetched causal notions to rest.

Faulty Analogy

This is the error of assuming that two circumstances or things are similar in all important respects, when in fact they are not. Here's an example. Harvey Thompson, high school football coach, tells his players, "Vince Lombardi won two Super Bowls by insisting on perfect execution of plays and enforcing strict disciplinary measures. We're going to win the conference championship by following the same methods." Thompson assumes that because he and Lombardi are coaches, he can duplicate Lombardi's achievements by using Lombardi's methods. Several important differences, however, mark the two situations:

1. Lombardi had very talented players, obtained through the player draft or trades; Thompson can choose only from the students in his high school.
2. Lombardi's players were paid professionals who very likely were motivated at least in part by the financial rewards that came from winning the Super Bowl; Thompson's players are amateurs.
3. "Perfect execution of plays" is probably easier to attain on the professional level than in high school because of the players' experience.
4. Despite Lombardi's rigid disciplinary measures, very few of his players quit,

EXERCISE ANSWER

1. A hasty generalization. Nancy has reached her conclusion after eating just one orange. Such a conclusion would be justified only after she had tried a number of oranges and found all of them rotten.

2. The either–or fallacy. Failure of the federal government to help poverty-stricken people would not necessarily cause starvation for all of them. Some might receive help from relatives or private charities, or state and local governments might provide financial assistance.

3. The *post hoc, ergo propter hoc* fallacy. The wife might have been unfaithful not because she had attended the X-rated movie but because she was angry with her husband or infatuated with the person with whom she was unfaithful.

4. Stereotyping and hasty generalization. The speaker has condemned all motorcycle riders because of the behavior of just one of them.

5. A *non sequitur*. Bill may love to eat, but we can't conclude that he will have a serious weight problem someday. He may be a person who never puts on weight regardless of his food intake, or he may alter his eating habits.

6. Begging the question. The statement assumes, without any supporting evidence, that no-fault divorce has caused the divorce rate to jump sharply.

7. A circular argument. The statement that the picture is "much more attractive than the others" essentially repeats the statement "This is the best-looking picture in the exhibit."

8. Argument *ad hominem*. Instead of attacking McAndrews' position on the bill, this critic attacks McAndrews' personality, which would seem irrelevant. Unless the critic can show that McAndrews' personality has led him to sponsor a faulty proposal (a task that would appear impossible), personality should not be mentioned.

perhaps because they were under contract. Could Thompson expect his players, essentially volunteers, to accept the kind of verbal and physical rigors Lombardi was famous for?

EXERCISE ■   Identify and explain the fallacies in the following examples. Remember that understanding the faulty reasoning is more important than merely naming the fallacy.

1. While eating a Golden Glow orange, Nancy discovers that it is rotten. "I'll never buy another Golden Glow product," she declares emphatically.

2. A campaigning politician states that unless the federal government appropriates funds to help people living in poverty, they will all starve.

3. A husband and wife see an X-rated movie called *Swinging Wives*. A week later the husband discovers that his wife, while supposedly attending an evening class, has been unfaithful to him. He blames the movie for her infidelity.

4. Look at those two motorcycle riders trying to pick a fight. All those cycle bums are troublemakers.

5. Bill really loves to eat. Some day he'll have a serious weight problem.

6. Because no-fault divorce is responsible for today's skyrocketing divorce rate, it should be abolished.

7. This is the best-looking picture in the exhibit; it's so much more attractive than the others.

8. I do not support this school millage proposal. It's sponsored by James McAndrews, who's about the most ill-tempered, quarrelsome person I've ever met. I'd never favor anything he supports.

9. My position on social and economic issues is easy to state. I am against wooly-brained do-gooders and big-spending, pie-in-the-sky welfare programs that have brought us to the brink of social disaster. I stand foursquare behind our free enterprise system, which has given us a standard of living the whole world envies, and if elected, I will defend it with everything at my command.

10. I am against the proposed ban on smoking in public places. As long as I don't inhale and I limit my habit to 8–10 cigarettes a day, my health won't suffer.

WRITING AN ARGUMENT

Planning and Drafting the Argument

Some instructors assign argumentative topics, and some leave the choice of topic to you. If you will be choosing, many options are available. Interesting issues—some local, some of broader importance—crowd our newspapers, magazines, and TV airways, vying for attention. Because several of them have probably piqued your interest, there's a good chance you won't have to rely on the strategies on pages 12–19 for help.

Some students approach an argument with such strong attitudes that they ignore evidence that contradicts their thinking. Don't make this mistake. Instead, maintain an open mind as you research your issue. Often, several possible positions exist. On the question of whether handguns should be banned, the positions might include (1) banning the possession of handguns by anyone except law officers and military personnel, (2) eliminating all restrictions on handgun possession, (3) banning handguns for persons with criminal records or a history of mental problems, and (4) banning certain types of handguns, such as "Saturday night specials" and all-plastic handguns. Even if you don't shift your position, knowing the opposition's strengths allows you to counter or neutralize them, and thus enhance your argument. Suppose you favor the first position. You need to know that half of our state constitutions grant citizens the right to own guns. Unless you acknowledge and somehow counter this fact, your case will suffer and perhaps even founder.

As you investigate the various positions, ask and answer the following questions about each:

> What kinds of evidence support it?
> How substantial is the evidence?
> If the evidence includes statistics and authoritative opinions, are they reliable? Flawed for some reason?
> What are the objections to each position, and how can they be countered?
> If the issue involves taking some action, what might be its consequences?

To help with this stage of the process, prepare a chart that summarizes your findings for each position; then examine it carefully to pick the position you'll argue for. The example below illustrates a three-position issue.

Position 1	Position 2	Position 3
Evidence and evaluation	Evidence and evaluation	Evidence and evaluation
Objections and how countered	Objections and how countered	Objections and how countered
Consequences	Consequences	Consequences

Imagine that your audience is a group of readers who are neutral or opposed to your position; there's no point in preaching to the converted. Take a little time to analyze these readers so that you can tailor your arguments appropriately. Pose these questions as you proceed.

> What are the readers' interests, expectations, and needs concerning this issue?
> What evidence is most likely to convince them?
> What objections and consequences would probably weigh most heavily with them?
> How can I answer the objections?

9. Appeal to the crowd. This statement attempts to sway its readers by playing upon their dislike of "wooly-brained do-gooders" and "big spending, pie-in-the-sky welfare programs," as well as upon their favorable attitudes toward our free-enterprise system.

10. Arguing off the point and also begging the question. The writer sets out to argue against the ban on public smoking and then abruptly shifts to his own health—an entirely different matter. Furthermore, he asserts that his health won't suffer but cites no evidence.

PERSPECTIVE

Some students, confused by the controversy surrounding an issue, are eager to reach a conclusion even when they don't have much support. Encourage students to collect and evaluate evidence for the different positions and consider potential objections to each. A few might need special attention as they confront a particularly difficult issue.

CLASSROOM ACTIVITIES

1. You might ask students, working in small groups, to discuss their tentative propositions and supporting evidence. Peers should adopt a critic's role and prompt any necessary re-evaluation. Students could also be shown how to act on peer criticism by refuting it in an argument.

2. Have students brainstorm the different interests of specific readers—lawmakers, police officers, parents—envisioned as a possible audience for a topic in order to determine the appropriate appeals.

To convince an audience of farmers that the federal school lunch program needs expanding, you might stress the added income they would gain. For nutritionists, you might note the health benefits that would result, and for school officials, the improved class performance of the students.

A typical introduction arouses the reader's interest and may also present the proposition. A *proposition* is a special thesis statement that names the issue and indicates which position the writer will take. It can declare that something is a fact, call for a certain action, or assert that something has greater value than something else. Here are examples.

1. Carron College does not provide adequate recreational facilities for its students. (*declares something is fact*)
2. Because the present building is overcrowded and unsafe, the people of Midville should vote funds for a new junior high school. (*calls for action*)
3. The new photocopier provides sharper, cheaper photocopies than those from the machine we now have. (*asserts value*)

Any of the techniques on pages 208–210 can launch your paper. For example, in arguing for stepped-up AIDS education, you might jolt your reader by describing a dying victim. If your issue involves unfamiliar terms, you might define them up front, and if the essay will be long, you could preview its main points.

After the introduction comes the evidence, arranged in whatever order you think will work best. If one of your points is likely to arouse resistance, hold it back and begin by making points your reader can more easily accept. Argument always goes more smoothly if you first establish some common ground of agreement that recognizes the values of your reader. Where strong resistance is not a factor, you could begin or end with your most compelling piece of evidence.

The strategies discussed in earlier chapters can help you develop an argument. Some papers incorporate one strategy, while others rely on several. Let's see how you might combine several in an argument against legalized casino gambling. You might open with a brief *description* of the frantic way an all-too-typical gambling addict keeps pulling the lever of a slot machine, his eyes riveted on the spinning dials, his palms sweating, as flashing lights and wailing sirens announce winners at other machines. Next, you could offer a brief *definition* of gambling fever so that the writer and reader are on common ground, and, to show the dimensions of the problem, *classify* the groups of people who are especially addicted. Then, after detailing the negative *effects* of the addiction, you might end by *comparing* gambling addiction with drug addiction, noting that both provide a "high" and both kinds of addicts know their habits hurt them.

Whatever strategies you use, make sure that substantiating evidence is embedded within them. Strategies by themselves won't convince. To illustrate, in discussing the negative effects of gambling, you might cite statistics that show the extent and nature of the problem. An expert opinion might validate your classification of addicts. Or you might use personal experience to verify gambling's addictive effects.

Besides presenting evidence, use this part of your paper to refute; that is, to point out weaknesses or errors in the opposing position. You can sprinkle refutations throughout the body of the paper or group them together just ahead of the conclusion. Whatever you decide, don't adopt a gloating or sarcastic tone that will alienate a fair-minded reader. Resist the urge to engage in *straw man* tactics—calling attention to imaginary or trivial weaknesses of the opposing side so that you can demolish them. Shrewd readers easily spot such ploys. Finally, don't be afraid to concede secondary or insignificant points to the opposition. Arguments have two or more sides; you can't have all the ammunition on your side. (If you discover you must concede major points, however, consider switching sides.) Here is a sample refutation from a student paper.

> Not everyone agrees with workplace drug testing for employees in public transportation companies, electric utilities, nuclear power plants, and other industries involving public safety. Critics assert that such tests invade privacy and therefore violate one of our cherished freedoms. While the examination of one's urine does entail inspection of something private, I believe such a test is a reasonable compromise because it helps ensure public safety and calm public fears. The individual's privacy should be tempered by concern for the community—a concern that benefits all of us.
>
> Annie Louise Griffith

Conclude in a manner that will sway the reader to your side. Depending on the argument, you might restate your position, summarize your main points, predict the consequences if your position does or doesn't prevail, or make an emotional appeal for support or action.

Revising the Argument

Review the guidelines in Chapter 3 and ponder these questions as you revise your argument paper.

- Is my topic controversial? Have I examined all of the main positions? Assessed the evidence supporting each one? Considered the objections to each position and how they can be countered? Weighed the consequences if a position involves taking some action?
- Is the paper aimed at the audience I want to reach? Have I tailored my argument to appeal to that audience?
- Is my evidence sound, adequate, and appropriate to the argument? Are my authori-

ties qualified? Have I established their expertise? Are they biased? Will my audience accept them as authorities? Do my statistics adequately support my position? Have I pushed my statistical claims too far?

If I've used analogy, are my points of comparison pertinent to the issue? Have I noted any significant differences between the items being compared?

If I've included an emotional appeal, does it center on those emotions most likely to sway the reader?

Have I made a conscious effort to present myself in a favorable light?

Is my proposition clearly evident and of the appropriate type; that is, one of fact, action, or value? If the proposition takes the form of a syllogism, is it sound? If faulty, have I started with a faulty premise? Reversed the last two statements of the syllogism?

Is my evidence effectively structured? Have I adequately refuted opposing arguments? Developed my position with one or more writing strategies?

Is my argument free of fallacies?

EXAMPLE STUDENT ESSAY OF ARGUMENT

TEACHING STRATEGY

If you teach this essay, you might generate a class discussion by asking whether the right to bear arms includes the right to purchase assault rifles and armor-piercing bullets.

ETHICAL ISSUES

Are there circumstances when it is ethical to deliberately (1) engage in card stacking, i.e., emphasize all the positive evidence and completely ignore any other? (2) exaggerate or fabricate evidence to support a position? (3) use a fallacy to trick unwary readers? (4) misrepresent an opponent's position in order to more easily refute it?

The Right to Bear Arms

Brenda Buehrle

The right of citizens to bear arms is often   1
discussed in heated tones and emotional language.
Political assassinations, for example, inevitably
spark an outcry for control of firearms, as do soaring
crime statistics. These appeals are frequently
countered by jingles such as "When guns are outlawed,
only outlaws will have guns." If we bypass such purely
emotional pleas and examine the issue objectively, we
find that there is ample legal justification for the
right to bear arms.

The first thing we should consider is the   2
original intent of the Second Amendment to the United
States Constitution, which states: "A well-regulated
militia being necessary to the security of a free

State, the right of the people to keep and bear arms shall not be infringed." When the purpose of any constitutional provision or law is in question, a good procedure is to return to the thoughts and words of those who originally framed it. For the Second Amendment, it is necessary to examine the ideas of George Mason, the Virginia constitutionalist. Mason wrote several specific safeguards of individual rights into the Virginia constitution of 1776. The Bill of Rights--that is, the first ten amendments added to the United States Constitution in 1791--incorporates many of Mason's safeguards. R.A. Rutland's edition of Mason's papers reveals clearly that his conception of the militia--that group empowered by law to bear arms-- went far beyond an organized group of men in uniform. During a debate in Richmond on June 16, 1788, Mason rhetorically said: "I ask who are the militia?" and then answered his own question with these words: "They consist now of the whole people, except a few public officials." There can be little doubt that George Mason, "Father of the Bill of Rights," never intended to restrict the right to bear arms to a relatively few men in uniform. Therefore, the original concept of the Second Amendment was that the militia consisted of all people; and to ensure security of a free country, the people had the right to keep and bear arms.

Early in this century Congress interpreted the   3
militia more narrowly than Mason did. On January 23, 1903, Congress defined the militia as all able-bodied male citizens more than eighteen and less than forty-five years of age. These men were divided into two classes: the organized militia, to be known as the

National Guard of the State, Territory, or District of
Columbia, and the remainder, to be known as the Reserve
Militia. Thus, the Congress classified all males
within certain age limits, and not in the National
Guard, as members of the militia. These men would now
seem to be the "people to keep and bear arms" whose
right to firearms "shall not be infringed" under the
Second Amendment. Furthermore, under the broad
doctrine of equal rights, it would appear that women
should also be included, if they fall into the proper
age groups eligible for military service.

Since no definite laws in the United States   4
Constitution define the rights of gun owners
throughout the fifty states, the state constitutions
certainly would seem to be the highest law in such
cases, as provided in the Ninth and Tenth Amendments.
These reserve, to the states and the people, all rights
and powers not spelled out in the United States
Constitution. Because the Second Amendment does not
definitely state the rights of gun owners, the federal
government cannot alter the rights that are defined in
individual state constitutions. At least half of these
state constitutions go beyond the Second Amendment by
spelling out that the right to bear arms is an
individual right for personal protection or defense of
home and property and has nothing to do with a "well—
regulated militia." Among these states are Arizona,
Michigan, and Pennsylvania. For example, Arizona's
constitution states, "The right of the individual
citizen to bear arms in defense of himself or the State
shall not be impaired. . . ." Michigan's says, "Every

person has a right to keep and bear arms for the defense of himself and the State." Pennsylvania's constitution is emphatic: "The right of the citizens to bear arms in defense of themselves and the State shall not be questioned." Given such declarations, the states with these and similar provisions could not possibly prohibit ownership of handguns or any other arms.

It should be clear that the Second Amendment was   5
not originally intended to apply only to militia, but to the "whole people." In addition, Congress has indicated that the militia consists of all able-bodied young and middle-aged males (and now perhaps females also). Furthermore, 50 percent of the state constitutions define and protect the rights of individual gun owners. Is it not evident that the right to bear arms is rooted in solid legal precedent?

DISCUSSION QUESTIONS ■

1. Identify the writer's proposition. Is it one of fact, action, or value?
2. In paragraph 1, the writer cites two approaches to the issue. What are they? Could they have been presented in reverse order? Why or why not?
3. What type of evidence does the writer use in her argument?
4. Reread the last two sentences in paragraph 3. Indicate why the phrasing "would now seem" and "it would appear" is appropriate here.
5. What type of conclusion does the writer use? Why is the question that ends it effective?

DISCUSSION QUESTIONS
1. The proposition, one of fact, is the final sentence in paragraph 1.
2. The writer cites emotional and objective approaches. They could not have been reversed. She introduces, and then bypasses, the emotional approaches in favor of her objective approach, which ends the first paragraph and sets up her arguments to follow.
3. She uses established truths and authoritative opinions.
4. The writer suggests her position rather than insisting upon it. You might point out that a writer who tries to force something on the reader will probably generate backlash. Note the difference if she had said "Only a fool couldn't see. . . ."
5. This conclusion summarizes the main points. The concluding question is effective because, in view of the evidence, the answer will probably be "yes," prompting the reader to acknowledge the strength of the argument.

SUGGESTIONS FOR WRITING ■   Write an argument on some topic you feel strongly about. Study all sides of the issue so you can argue effectively and appeal to a particular audience. Support your proposition with logical evidence. Here are some possibilities to consider if your instructor gives you a free choice.

1. Compulsory composition courses in college
2. Unmarried couples living together
3. Banning whale hunting

4. Requiring students to pass a general competency test in order to graduate from high school
5. Some aspect of native American affairs
6. Capital punishment
7. Government funding of noncommercial television
8. Gay rights
9. Legislation banning throwaway bottles
10. Bilingual instruction in schools
11. Legalizing prostitution (or gambling)
12. Mandatory airbags in cars
13. Guardian Angels patrolling city streets
14. Sobriety checklanes for nabbing drunk drivers
15. A local or campus issue

■ Chapter 13

Mixing the Writing Strategies

PERSPECTIVE

One of our goals is to offer students a variety of conceptual and writing tools that they can use to handle more complex writing projects. Students should understand that using the proper combination of strategies offers a way of approaching many writing situations, including the research paper assignment. When students discover that they have already blended various strategies in earlier papers and that complex writing tasks can be broken down into segments, any apprehension they may have about mixing the strategies should be lessened considerably.

TEACHING STRATEGIES

1. Have students go over their previous essays to determine and annotate where they used more than one strategy. They might find that in an earlier narrative, for example, they implicitly referred to a cause and explicitly used description.
2. Ask students to review a number of professional pieces of writing (perhaps even a proposal or a business report), establish the writer's purpose, and then determine what strategies were used and why. This could also be a classroom activity with the material presented on an overhead.
3. You might help inexperienced students gradually build up a more complex piece of writing by breaking assignments into several guided segments. Students could start by describing a college problem and illustrating it with specific examples, possibly even narratives. This writing could be collected and evaluated before students undertake the second step, which might be determining causes of the problem. Next, they could identify a possible solution, detail a process by which it might be implemented, and describe the probable effects of that solution. Such a step-by-step approach enables students to learn how to use the strategies to produce a complex report. In the process, they have also learned a method for tackling difficult assignments.

WHY AND HOW TO MIX STRATEGIES

Up to this point, we've focused on the different writing strategies. These strategies, however, seldom occur in pure form. Writers nearly always mix them in assorted combinations for various purposes, not just in papers of definition and argument, as we've noted in Chapters 11 and 12, but also in papers of narration, description, process analysis, illustration, classification, comparison, and cause and effect. An essay that is primarily narration might contain descriptive passages or note an effect. A comparison might include illustrations or carry an implied argument. The purpose, audience, and occasion of the individual essay dictate the mixture, which can't be predetermined. Your best bet is to familiarize yourself with the individual strategies and use them as needed.

Let's see how you'd go about combining the various strategies in an actual writing situation. Suppose you've been assigned a description paper, and you decide to write about the place your family vacationed last year. You might start your essay by noting what *caused* you to pick that locale and offering a brief *comparison* between it and previous vacation spots. You could then *narrate* your activities on a typical day and conclude by indicating the *effects* the whole experience had on you. Note that not all the strategies are used—only the ones that suit your purpose.

Mixing the writing strategies occurs outside your composition course as well. Your political science professor might ask for a paper which evaluates the advantages of a democratic state over a totalitarian one. You could open with contrasting *definitions* of the two forms of government and then, to make them more concrete, offer XYZ as an *illustration* of a typical democracy, ABC as a typical totalitarian state. After *describing* the key characteristics of each type, you might

Here are *possible* approaches to the writing situations.

1. You'd probably begin by *defining* the problem and offering a few *illustrations* of it. Then you might suggest its *causes* and *effects*, *compare* the alternative solutions, and *argue* for (recommend) implementing one of them.

2. You might begin by examining the reasons why (*causes*) the old equipment is obsolete and projecting the beneficial *effects* if new equipment is purchased. After *comparing* the features of several competing brands, you could review the *process* of operation for one of them and then *argue* for (recommend) its purchase.

3. For starters, you might mention the reasons (*causes*) that led to your choice. Next, you could *classify* your duties, *narrate* a typical work day, and finally move to *effects* by noting how your occupation benefits the public. You might enhance your account with plenty of enticing *descriptive* details.

compare their social, economic, and religious effects on their citizens. Without question, one strategy, presented in pure form, would not be as effective.

EXERCISE ■   Suggest what combination of writing strategies you might use in each of the situations below.

1. The company you work for, school you attend, or club you belong to has a serious morale problem. You have been asked to evaluate its various dimensions, propose feasible solutions, and then make a recommendation to the appropriate person.

2. Your company, school, or club is about to purchase some specific type of new equipment. You have been asked to write a report examining the available brands and recommending one.

3. Your local newspaper has asked you to write about your college major or occupation and how you regard it. The article will help high school students decide whether this major or occupation would be appropriate for them.

4. Your general science instructor has asked you to study and report on some industrial chemical. The report must answer typical questions a layperson would likely ask about the chemical.

The margin notes on the following essay show the interplay of several writing strategies.

BRUCE JAY FRIEDMAN

Eating Alone in Restaurants

Bruce Jay Friedman (born 1930) is a native of New York City and a 1951 graduate of the University of Missouri, where he majored in journalism. Between 1951 and 1953, he served in the U.S. Air Force and for the next decade was editorial director of a magazine management company. He now freelances. A versatile writer, Friedman has produced novels, plays, short stories, and nonfiction, earning critical acclaim as a humorist. In our selection, taken from The Lonely Guy's Book of Life *(1979), he offers the urban male who must dine out alone witty advice on coping with the situation.*

Illustration in narrative form

1   Hunched over, trying to be as inconspicuous as possible, a solitary diner slips into a midtown Manhattan steakhouse. No sooner does he check his coat than the voice of the headwaiter comes booming across the restaurant.

2   "Alone again, eh?"

3   As all eyes are raised, the bartender, with enormous good cheer, chimes in: "That's because they all left him high and dry."

4   And then, just in case there is a customer in the restaurant who isn't yet aware of the situation, a waiter shouts out from the buffet table: "Well, we'll take care of him anyway, won't we fellas!"

5   *Haw, haw, haw,* and a lot of sly winks and pokes in the ribs.

6   Eating alone in a restaurant is one of the most terrifying experiences in America.

7   Sniffed at by headwaiters, an object of scorn and amusement to couples, the solitary diner is the unwanted and unloved child of Restaurant Row. No sooner does he make his appearance than he is whisked out of sight and seated at a thin sliver of a table with barely enough room on it for an hors d'oeuvre. Wedged between busboy stations, a hair's breadth from the men's room, there he sits, feet lodged in a railing as if he were in Pilgrim stocks, wondering where he went wrong in life.

| Definition |
| Description |
| Effect |

8   Rather than face this grim scenario, most Lonely Guys would prefer to nibble away at a tuna fish sandwich in the relative safety of their high-rise apartments.

9   What can be done to ease the pain of this not only starving but silent minority—to make dining alone in restaurants a rewarding experience? Absolutely nothing. But some small strategies *do* exist for making the experience bearable.

■ Before You Get There

| Step in process |

10   Once the Lonely Guy has decided to dine alone at a restaurant, a sense of terror and foreboding will begin to build throughout the day. All the more reason for him to get there as quickly as possible so that the experience can soon be forgotten and he can resume his normal life. Clothing should be light and loose-fitting, especially around the neck—on the off chance of a fainting attack during the appetizer. It is best to dress modestly, avoiding both the funeral-director-style suit as well as the bold, eye-arresting costume of the gaucho. A single cocktail should suffice; little sympathy will be given to the Lonely Guy who tumbles in, stewed to the gills. (The fellow who stoops to putting morphine in his toes for courage does not belong in this discussion.) En route to the restaurant, it is best to play down dramatics, such as swinging the arms pluckily and humming the theme from *The Bridge on the River Kwai.*

| Description |

■ Once You Arrive

| Step in process |

11   The way your entrance comes off is of critical importance. Do not skulk in, slipping along the walls as if you are carrying some dirty little secret. There is no need, on the other hand, to fling your coat arrogantly at the hatcheck girl, slap the headwaiter across the cheeks with your gloves and demand to be seated immediately. Simply walk in with a brisk rubbing of the hands and approach the headwaiter. When asked how many are in your party, avoid cute responses such as "Jes lil ol' me." Tell him you are a party of one; the Lonely Guy who does not trust his voice can simply lift a finger. Do not launch into a story about how tired you are of taking out fashion models, night after night, and what a pleasure it is going to be to dine alone.

| Comparison |

12   It is best to arrive with no reservation. Asked to set aside a table for one, the restaurant owner will suspect either a prank on the part of an ex-waiter, or a terrorist plot, in which case windows will be boarded up and the kitchen bombswept. An advantage of the "no reservation" approach is that you will appear to have just stepped off the plane from Des Moines, your first night in years away from Marge and the kids.

| Effect |

13   All eyes will be upon you when you make the promenade to your table. Stay as close as possible to the headwaiter, trying to match him step for step. This will reduce your visibility and fool some diners into thinking you are a member of the staff. If you hear a generalized snickering throughout the restaurant, do not assume automatically that you are being laughed at. The other diners may all have just recalled an amusing moment in a Feydeau farce.

14   If your table is unsatisfactory, do not demand imperiously that one for eight people be cleared immediately so that you can dine in solitary grandeur. Glance around discreetly and see if there are other possibilities. The ideal table will allow you to keep your back to the wall so that you can see if anyone is laughing at you. Try to get one close to another couple so that if you lean over at a 45-degree angle it will appear that you are a swinging member of their group. Sitting opposite a mirror can be useful; after a drink or two, you will begin to feel that there are a few of you.

Definition

15   Once you have been seated, and it becomes clear to the staff that you are alone, there will follow The Single Most Heartbreaking Moment in Dining Out Alone—when the second setting is whisked away and yours is spread out a bit to make the table look busier. This will be done with great ceremony by the waiter—angered in advance at being tipped for only one dinner. At this point, you may be tempted to smack your forehead against the table and curse the fates that brought you to this desolate position in life. A wiser course is to grit your teeth, order a drink and use this opportunity to make contact with other Lonely Guys sprinkled around the room. A menu or a leafy stalk of celery can be used as a shield for peering out at them. Do not expect a hearty greeting or a cry of "huzzah" from these frightened and browbeaten people. Too much excitement may cause them to slump over, curtains. Smile gently and be content if you receive a pale wave of the hand in return. It is unfair to imply that you have come to help them throw off their chains.

Effect

16   When the headwaiter arrives to take your order, do not be bullied into ordering the last of the gazelle haunches unless you really want them. Thrilled to be offered anything at all, many Lonely Guys will say "Get them right out here" and wolf them down. Restaurants take unfair advantage of Lonely Guys, using them to get rid of anything from withered liver to old heels of roast beef. Order anything you like, although it is good to keep to the light and simple in case of a sudden attack of violent stomach cramps.

Step in process

■ Some Proven Strategies

Effect

17   Once the meal is under way, a certain pressure will begin to build as couples snuggle together, the women clucking sympathetically in your direction. Warmth and conviviality will pervade the room, none of it encompassing you. At this point, many Lonely Guys will keep their eyes riveted to the restaurant paintings of early Milan or bury themselves in a paperback anthology they have no wish to read.

18   Here are some ploys designed to confuse other diners and make them feel less sorry for you.

Classification

19   • After each bite of food, lift your head, smack your lips thoughtfully, swallow and make a notation in a pad. Diners will assume you are a restaurant critic.

20   • Between courses, pull out a walkie-talkie and whisper a message into it. This will lead everyone to believe you are part of a police stake-out team, about to bust the salad man as an international dope dealer.

21   • Pretend you are a foreigner. This is done by pointing to items on the menu with an alert smile and saying to the headwaiter: "Is good, no?"

22   • When the main course arrives, brush the restaurant silverware off the table and pull some of your own out of a breastpocket. People will think you are a wealthy eccentric.

23   • Keep glancing at the door, and make occasional trips to look out at the street, as if you are waiting for a beautiful woman. Half-way through the meal, shrug in a world-weary manner and begin to eat with gusto. The world is full of women! Why tolerate bad manners! Life is too short.

■ The Right Way

Step in process

24   One other course is open to the Lonely Guy, an audacious one, full of perils, but all the more satisfying if you can bring it off. That is to take off your dark glasses, sit erectly, smile broadly at anyone who looks in your direction, wave off inferior wines, and begin to eat with heartiness and enormous confidence. As outrageous as the thought may be—enjoy your own company. Suddenly, titters and sly winks will tail off, the headwaiter's disdain will fade, and friction will build among couples who will turn out to be not as tightly cemented as they appear. The heads of other Lonely Guys will lift with hope as you become the attractive center of the room.

Implied argument

25   If that doesn't work, you still have your fainting option.

SUGGESTED INSTRUCTOR READINGS

Larson, R. "Structure and Form in Non-Narrative Prose." Ten Bibliographic Essays. Ed. G. Tate. Fort Worth: Texas Christian UP, 1987. 39–82. Discusses contemporary paragraph theory, including Larson's own theory.

Shaughnessy, M. P. Errors and Expectations: A Guide for the Teacher of Basic Writing. New York: Oxford UP, 1977. While this book is best known for its helpful discussion of how to deal with grammatical errors, the chapter "Beyond the Sentence" provides practical advice on helping basic writers understand the paragraph.

■ Chapter 14

Paragraphs

Some paragraphs launch, others wrap up pieces of writing; still others establish links between parts. Paragraphs can break long discussions of one idea into segments that provide rest stops for readers. Paragraphs can also consolidate several briefly developed ideas into a single reading unit. Occasionally, a paragraph stands by itself as an essay in miniature. Most paragraphs, though, are blocks of sentences that develop and clarify one idea. As the major units in an essay, paragraphs relate to one another and reflect the controlling purpose of the whole piece.

CHARACTERISTICS OF EFFECTIVE PARAGRAPHS

TEACHING STRATEGIES

1. Select several different kinds of essays, perhaps from the Reader, and have students examine the unity in various paragraphs to determine how each sentence relates to the controlling idea and to identify any sentences that seem out of place.
2. Students could review their own essays, testing the unity of each paragraph. Revising those that are faulty helps create an awareness of unified writing.

Unity

A paragraph with unity develops one, and only one, key controlling idea. To ensure unity, edit out any stray ideas that don't belong and fight the urge to take interesting but irrelevant side trips; they only create confusion about your destination.

The following paragraph *lacks unity:*

The psychiatric nurse deals with dangerous mental patients, pathological personalities who may explode into violence at any moment. Sigmund Freud was one of the first doctors to study mental disorders. Today psychotherapy is a well established medical discipline.

What exactly is this writer trying to say? We can't tell. Each sentence expresses a different, undeveloped idea:

1. Job of the psychiatric nurse
2. Freud's pioneering work in studying mental disorders
3. Present status of psychotherapy

In contrast, the following paragraph develops and clarifies only one central idea: the professional responsibilities of a psychiatric nurse.

> The psychiatric nurse deals with dangerous mental patients, pathological personalities who may explode into violence at any moment. For this reason, the nurse must remain on guard at all times. When a patient displays anger or violence, she cannot respond in kind but must instead show tolerance and understanding. Furthermore, she must be able to recognize attempts at deception. Sometimes a mentally ill person, just prior to launching an attack, will act in a completely normal way in order to deceive the intended victim. The nurse must recognize this behavior and be alert for any possible assault.
>
> Peggy Feltman

Because no unrelated ideas sidetrack the discussion of characteristics, the paragraph has unity.

EXERCISE ■   **After reading the next two paragraphs, answer the questions that follow.**

---

1.   The legend—in Africa—that all elephants over a large geographical area go to a common "graveyard" when they sense death is approaching led many hunters to treat them with special cruelty. Ivory hunters, believing the myth and trying to locate such graveyards, often intentionally wounded an elephant in the hopes of following the suffering beast as it made its way to the place where it wanted to die.

The idea was to wound the elephant seriously enough so that it thought it was going to die but not so seriously that it died in a very short time. All too often, the process resulted in a single elephant being shot or speared many times and relentlessly pursued until it either fell dead or was killed when it finally turned and charged its attackers. In any case, no wounded elephant ever led its pursuers to the mythical graveyard with its hoped-for booty of ivory tusks.

Kris Hurrell

2.   When I was growing up, I spent many happy hours with my brothers and sisters playing jungle games in the woodlot behind our farm home. This lot, ten acres of dense-set poplars and birches standing amidst the blackened stumps of an old pine forest, provided a perfect setting for our jungle adventures. At times we acted out African versions of cowboys and Indians; at others we sought the long-lost treasures of fabled diamond mines. Often our adventures pitted Tarzan against tomb robbers and poachers. Besides serving as a playground, our woodlot furnished most of the fuel for the iron stoves in our kitchen and living room. I can still remember the back-breaking work of chopping up stumps and fallen trees and hauling them to the house. In the winter, the woodlot offered fine small-game hunting. In the summer, it provided a cool refuge from the heat that blistered the fields and farmhouse. Today, farm and woodlot are gone, swallowed up by a sprawling suburb. I wonder whether the children who live there ever want to play jungle games or regret that there's no place for them.

Student Unknown

1. Which of these paragraphs lacks unity? Refer to the paragraphs when answering.
2. How would you improve the paragraph that lacks unity?

The Topic Sentence

The topic sentence states the main idea of the paragraph. Think of the topic sentence as a rallying point, with all supporting sentences developing the idea it expresses. A good topic sentence helps you gauge what information belongs in a paragraph, thus ensuring unity. At the same time, it informs your reader about the point you're making.

Placement of the topic sentence varies from paragraph to paragraph, as the following examples show. As you read each, note how supporting information develops the topic sentence, which is italicized.

Topic Sentence Stated First.   Many paragraphs open with the topic sentence. The writer reveals the central idea immediately and then builds from a solid base.

> *Starting about one million years ago, the fossil record shows an accelerating growth of the human brain.* It expanded at first at the rate of one cubic inch of additional gray matter every hundred thousand years; then the growth rate doubled; it doubled again; and finally it doubled once more. Five hundred thousand years ago the rate of growth hit its peak. At that time, the brain was expanding at the phenomenal rate of ten cubic inches every hundred thousand years. No other organ in the history of life is known to have grown as fast as this.
>
> Robert Jastrow, *Until the Sun Dies*

Topic Sentence Stated Last.   In order to emphasize the support and build gradually to a conclusion, a topic sentence can end the paragraph. This position creates suspense as the reader anticipates the summarizing remark.

> An experience of my own comes handily to mind. Some years ago, when the Restaurant de la Pyramide in Vienne was without question one of the best half-dozen restaurants in the world, I visited it for the first time. After I had ordered my meal, the sommelier [wine steward] appeared to set before me a wine list of surpassing amplitude and excellence. But as I cast my eyes down this unbelievable offering of the world's most tantalizing wines, the sommelier bent over me and pointed out a wine of which I had never heard, ticketed at a price one-fifth that of its illustrious neighbors. "Monsieur," said the sommelier, "I would suggest this one. It is a local wine, a very good wine. It is not a great wine, but after all, monsieur, you are likely to pass this way only once. The great wines you will find everywhere; this wine you will find only in Vienne. I would like you to try it, while you have the opportunity." *This, to my mind, was true sophistication—on the part of M. Point for having the wine and on the part of the waiter for offering it.*
>
> Stephen White, "The New Sophistication: Defining the Terms"

Topic Sentence Stated First and Last.   Some paragraphs lead with the main idea and then restate it, usually in different words, at the end. This technique allows the writer to repeat an especially important idea.

> *Everything is changing.* . . . This is a prediction I can make with absolute certainty. As human beings, we are constantly in a state of change. Our bodies change every day. Our attitudes are constantly evolving. Something that we swore by five years ago is now almost impossible for us to imagine ourselves believing. The clothes we wore a few years ago now look strange to us in old photographs. The things we take for granted as absolutes, impervious to change, are, in fact, constantly doing just that. Granite boulders become sand in time. Beaches erode and shape new shorelines. Our buildings become outdated and are replaced with modern structures that also will be torn down. Even those things which last thousands of years, such as the Pyramids and the Acropolis, also are changing. This simple insight is very important to grasp if you want to be a no-limit person, and are desirous of raising no-limit children. *Everything you feel, think, see, and touch is constantly changing.*
>
> Wayne Dyer, *What Do You Really Want for Your Children?*

Topic Sentence Stated in the Middle.   On occasion, the topic sentence falls between one set of sentences that provides background information and a follow-up set that develops the central idea. This arrangement allows the writer to shift the emphasis and at the same time preserve close ties between the two sets.

> Over the centuries, China has often been the subject of Western fantasy. In their own way, a number of scholars, journalists, and other travelers have perpetuated this tradition in recent years, rushing to rediscover the country after its long period of isolation. Some of these visitors, justifiably impressed by the Communists' achievements in eliminating the exploitative aspects of pre-1949 mandarin society, propagated the view that the revolution, after its initial successes, had continued to "serve the people," and that China was "the wave of the future"—a compelling alternative to the disorder and materialism of contemporary Western society. Human rights were not at issue, they argued, because such Western concepts were inapplicable to China. *In the past year, however, the Chinese have begun to speak for themselves, and they are conveying quite a different picture.* In the view of many of its own people, China is a backward and repressive nation. "China is Asia's Gulag Archipelago," an elderly Chinese scholar said to me shortly after I had arrived in China last spring. "I was in Germany right after the Second World War, and I saw the horrors of Buchenwald and other concentration camps. In a way—in its destruction of the human spirit these past two decades—China has been even worse."
>
> David Finkelstein, "When the Snow Thaws"

Topic Sentence Implied.   Some paragraphs, particularly in narrative and descriptive writing, have no topic sentence. Rather, all sentences point toward a main idea that readers must grasp for themselves.

> [Captain Robert Barclay] once went out at 5 in the morning to do a little grouse shooting. He walked at least 30 miles while he potted away, and then after

dinner set out on a walk of 60 miles that he accomplished in 11 hours without a halt. Barclay did not sleep after this but went through the following day as if nothing had happened until the afternoon, when he walked 16 miles to a ball. He danced all night, and then in early morning walked home and spent a day partridge shooting. Finally he did get to bed—but only after a period of two nights and nearly three days had elapsed and he had walked 130 miles.

John Lovesey, "A Myth Is as Good as a Mile"

The details in this paragraph collectively suggest a clear central idea: that Barclay had incredible physical endurance. But writing effective paragraphs without topic sentences challenges even the best writers. Therefore, control most of your paragraphs with clearly expressed topic sentences.

EXERCISE ■   Identify the topic sentences in each of the following paragraphs and explain how you arrived at your decisions. If the topic sentence is implied, state the central idea in your own words.

1.   Last winter, while leafing through the Guinness Book of World Records, I came across an item stating that the tallest sunflower ever had been grown by G. E. Hocking, an Englishman. Fired by a competitive urge, I planted a half acre of sunflower seeds. That half acre is now a magnificent 22,000 square feet of green and gold flowers. From the elevated rear deck of my apartment, I can look out over the swaying mass of thick, hairy green stalks and see each stalk thrusting up through the darker heart-shaped leaves below and supporting an ever-bobbing imitation of the sun. In this dwarf forest, some of the flower heads measure almost a foot in diameter. Though almost all my plants are now blooming, none will top the sixteen feet, two inches reached by Hocking's plant. My tallest is just thirteen feet even, but I don't think that's too bad for the first attempt. Next year, however, will be another matter. I plan to have an automatic watering system to feed my babies.

Joseph Wheeler

EXERCISE ANSWERS

1. The topic sentence is the third sentence of the paragraph. The first two sentences explain why the writer started to grow sunflowers. The four sentences following the topic sentence develop the idea that the plot is magnificent. The last two sentences talk about the writer's plans for next season.

2. The topic sentence is the last sentence in the paragraph. The preceding sentences deal with two things Susskind's mother never told her: that time flies and sex can be fun. These sentences provide specific examples that support the general point made in the final sentence.
3. The first sentence is the topic sentence. The remaining sentences point out reasons for the widening gap.
4. This paragraph has an implied topic sentence. A suitable topic sentence might be "The terrorists, ignoring all efforts to negotiate the release of the passengers, began carrying out their threat to execute hostages."

2.   What my mother never told me was how fast time passes in adult life. I remember, when I was little, thinking I would live to be at least as old as my grandmother, who was dynamic even at ninety-two, the age at which she died. Now I see those ninety-two years hurtling by me. And my mother never told me how much fun sex could be, or what a discovery it is. Of course, I'm of an age when mothers really didn't tell you much about anything. My mother never told me the facts of life.

Joyce Susskind, "Surprises in a Woman's Life"

3.   In fact, the separation between the scientists and non-scientists is much less bridgeable among the young than it was even thirty years ago. Thirty years ago the cultures had long ceased to speak to each other: but at least they managed a kind of frozen smile across the gulf. Now the politeness has gone, and they just make faces. It is not only that the young scientists now feel that they are part of a culture on the rise while the other is in retreat. It is also, to be brutal, that the young scientists know that with an indifferent degree they'll get a comfortable job, while their contemporaries and counterparts in English or History will be lucky to earn 60 percent as much. No young scientist of any talent would feel that he isn't wanted or that his work is ridiculous, as did the hero of *Lucky Jim;* and in fact, some of the disgruntlement of Amis and his associates is the disgruntlement of the under-employed arts graduate [Kingsley Amis is the author of the novel *Lucky Jim*].

C. P. Snow, *The Two Cultures: A Second Look*

4.   The first hostage to be brought off the plane was a dark little man with a bald head and a moustache so thick and black that it obliterated his mouth. Four of the masked terrorists were guarding him closely, each with a heavy rifle held ready for fire. When the group was about fifty feet from the plane, a second hostage, a young woman in flowered slacks and a red blouse, was brought out in clear view by a single terrorist, who held a pistol against the side of her head. Then the first four pushed the dark little man from them and instructed him to kneel on the pavement. They looked at him as they might an insect. But he sat there on his knees, seemingly as indifferent as if he had already taken leave of his body. The shots from the four rifles sounded faintly at the far end of the field where a group of horrified spectators watched the grisly proceedings.

Bradley Willis

EXERCISE ■   **Develop one of the ideas below into a topic sentence. Then write a unified paragraph that is built around it.**

1. The career (or job or profession) I want is _____.
2. The one quality most necessary in my chosen field is _____.
3. The most difficult aspect of my chosen field is _____.
4. One good example of the American tendency to waste is _____.
5. The best (or worst) thing about fast-food restaurants is _____.
6. The college course I find most useful (or interesting) is _____.
7. Concentration (or substitute your own term here) is an important part of a successful golf game (or substitute your own sport).
8. The one place where I feel most at home is _____.
9. More than anything else, owning a pet (or growing a garden) involves _____.

Write a topic sentence that would control a paragraph on each of the following:

1. Preparations for traveling away from home
2. Advantages of having your own room
3. Some landmark of the community in which you live
4. The price of long-distance telephone calls
5. Registering for college courses
6. A cherished memento or souvenir
7. High school graduation
8. New Year's resolutions

Adequate Development

Students often ask for guidelines on paragraph length: "Should I aim for fifty to sixty words? Seven to ten sentences? About one-fourth of a page?" The questions are natural, but the approach is wrong. Instead of targeting a particular length, ask yourself what the reader needs to know. Then supply just enough information to make your point clearly. Inadequate development results in fuzziness, forcing the reader to grope for understanding. A swollen paragraph, on the other hand, dilutes emphasis. Why load up with four or five examples when two or three will do?

The details you supply can include facts, figures, thoughts, observations, steps, lists, examples, and personal experiences. Individually, these bits of information may mean little, but added together they clearly illustrate your point. Keep in mind, however, that development isn't an end in itself but instead advances the purpose of the entire essay.

Here are two versions of a paragraph, the first inadequately developed.

PERSPECTIVE

The amount of development needed varies according to the situation. Students, for various reasons, consistently underdevelop their paragraphs. Students simply may not take the time to gather the necessary information. Or they may be afraid of going into too much detail "for fear of boring the reader." (The short, pithy paragraphs of the popular press and of advertising reinforce this tendency.) Finally, some students just don't know how to develop their paragraphs. How to address the problem depends of course on its cause.

Underdeveloped Paragraph

Most of the delegates to the Constitutional Convention of 1787 feared too much democracy. As a result, they drafted the Constitution as a document outlining a limited democracy. Indeed, some of the provisions were simply undemocratic. But despite reflecting the delegates' distrust of popular rule, the Constitution did provide a framework in which democracy could evolve.

Adequately Developed Paragraph

Most of the delegates to the Constitutional Convention of 1787 feared too much democracy. As a result, they drafted the Constitution as a document outlining a limited democracy. Indeed, some of the provisions were simply undemocratic: *universal suffrage was denied; voting qualifications were left to the states; and women, blacks, and persons without property were denied the federal franchise. Until the passage of the Seventeenth Amendment in 1913, senators were not popularly elected but were chosen by state legislators.* But despite reflecting the delegates' distrust of popular rule, the Constitution did provide a framework in which democracy could evolve.

The first paragraph lacks examples of undemocratic provisions, whereas the second one provides the needed information.

Readability also helps set paragraph length. Within a paper, paragraphs signal natural dividing places, allowing the reader to pause and absorb the material presented up to that point. Too little paragraphing overwhelms the reader with long blocks of material. Too much creates a choppy Dick-and-Jane effect that may seem simplistic, even irritating. To counter these problems, writers sometimes use several paragraphs for an idea that needs extended development, or they combine several short paragraphs into one.

EXERCISE ■

1. **Indicate where the ideas in this long block of material divide logically; explain your choices.**

   During the summer following graduation from high school, I could hardly wait to get to college and "be on my own." In the first weeks of my freshman year at State University, however, I found that independence can be tough and painful. I had expected raucous good times and a carefree collegiate life, the sort depicted in old beach

movies and suggested by the selective memories of
sentimental alumni. Instead, all I felt at first was the
burden of increasing responsibilities and the loneliness of
"a man without a country." I discovered that being
independent of parents who kept at me to do my homework and
expected me to accomplish certain household chores did not
mean I was free to do as I pleased. On the contrary, living
on my own meant that I had to perform for myself all the
tasks that the family used to share. Studying became a full-
time occupation rather than a nightly duty to be
accomplished in an hour or two, and my college instructors
made it clear that they would have little sympathy for
negligence or even for my inability to do an assignment. But
what was more troubling about my early college life than
having to do laundry, prepare meals, and complete stacks of
homework, was the terrifying sense of being entirely alone.
I was independent, no longer a part of the world that had
seemed to confine me, but I soon realized that confinement
had also meant security. I never liked the feeling that
people were watching over me, but I knew that my family and
friends were also watching out for me--and that's a good
feeling to have. At the university no one seemed
particularly to be watching, though professors constantly
evaluated the quality of my work. I felt estranged from
people in those first weeks of college life, desperately
needing a confidant but fearful that the new and tenuous
friendships I had made would be damaged if I were to confess
my fears and problems. It was simply too early for me to feel
a part of the university. So there I was, independent in the
fullest sense, and thus "a man without a country."

2. The following short, choppy units are inadequately developed. List some details you could use to expand one of them into a good paragraph.

> I like living in a small town because the people are so friendly. I can always get the latest gossip from the local busybody. In addition, there's always the telephone party line.
>
> In a big city, people are afraid to get too friendly. Everything is very private, and nobody knows anything about anybody else.

3. Scan the compositions you have written in other classes for paragraphs that are over- or underdeveloped. Revise any you find.

Organization

An effective paragraph unfolds in a clear pattern of organization so that the reader can easily follow the flow of ideas. The options span a wide range:

1. The strategies discussed in Chapters 4–12
2. Coordination, subordination, or a combination of the two
3. Order of climax

The choice you make depends upon your material and purpose in writing.

Writing Strategies.   These include all of the following patterns:

Time sequence (narration)
Space sequence (description)
Process analysis
Illustration
Classification
Comparison
Cause and effect
Definition
Argument

Four example paragraphs follow. The first, organized by *time sequence,* traces the final years of the Model T Ford, concluding with a topic sentence that sums up its impact.

> In 1917 the Model T lost much of its attraction when its exterior appearance was drastically altered. The famous flat-sided brass radiator disappeared and the new style featured (in the words of the catalogue) "The stream-line hood, large radiator and enclosed fan, crown fenders, black finish and nickel trimmings" ("crown fenders" would be described in England as domed mudguards). Electric lighting and starting followed in 1919, and the model then continued with little alteration until 1927, when it was finally withdrawn. After a considerable pause it was replaced by the Model A, a very conventional machine with wire wheels, three-speed gearbox and four-wheel brakes (the "T" had never made this concession to progress and continued

to the last with two minute brake drums on the back wheels only). While it was in preparation, others had taken the lead and the "A" never replaced the immortal "T" in the public fancy. Indeed, the "Tin Lizzy" or "Flivver" had become almost a national characteristic, and at the end of its eighteen years in production the total number sold was fifteen million.

Cecil Clutton and John Stanford,
The Vintage Motor-Car

SUGGESTED INSTRUCTOR READING

Christensen, F. "A Generative Rhetoric of the Paragraph." College Composition and Communication 16 (1965): 144–56. Advances a theory of paragraph development for sentences that are connected by coordination and subordination.

The next paragraph, organized by *space sequence*, describes a ceramic elf, starting from the bottom and working up to the top. Other common spatial arrangements include top to bottom, left to right, right to left, nearby to far away, far away to nearby, clockwise, and counterclockwise.

> The ceramic elf in our family room is quite a character. His reddish-brown slippers, which hang over the mantel shelf, taper to a slender point. Pudgy, yellow-stockinged legs disappear into a wrinkled tunic-style, olive-green jacket, gathered at the waist with a thick brown belt that fits snugly around his roly-poly belly. His short, meaty arms hang comfortably, one hand resting on the knapsack at his side and the other clutching the bowl of an old black pipe. An unkempt, snow-white beard, dotted by occasional snarls, trails patriarch-fashion from his lower lip to his belt line. A button nose capped with a smudge of gold dust, mischievous black eyes, and an unruly snatch of hair peeking out from under his burnt-orange stocking cap complete Bartholomew's appearance.

> Maria Sanchez

Although descriptive paragraphs, like those developed by narration, often lack topic sentences, our example leads off with the central idea.

Here is a paragraph showing *process* development.

> Making beer nuts is a quick, simple procedure that provides a delicious evening snack. You'll need six cups of raw peanuts, three cups of sugar, and one-and-one-half cups of water. To begin, combine the sugar and water in a two-quart saucepan and stir to dissolve the sugar. Next, add the

peanuts and stir again until all of the peanuts are covered by the sugar—water solution. Leave the pan, uncovered, on a burner set at medium—high heat for ten to twelve minutes, until the sugar crystallizes and coats the peanuts thoroughly. Stay at the stove during the heating process and stir the mixture every two or three minutes to ensure even coating of the nuts. When the peanuts are thoroughly coated, pour them onto an ungreased cookie sheet and bake at 350 degrees for about thirty minutes, stirring and lightly salting at ten—minute intervals. Serve your beer nuts fresh out of the oven or eat them at room temperature.

Kimberlee Walters

Again, the topic sentence comes first.

The final example illustrates development by *comparison* and also proceeds from an opening topic sentence.

There is an essential difference between a news story, as understood by a newspaperman or a wire-service writer, and the newsmagazine story. The chief purpose of the conventional news story is to tell what happened. It starts with the most important information and continues into increasingly inconsequential details, not only because the reader may not read beyond the first paragraph but because an editor working on galley proofs a few minutes before press time likes to be able to cut freely from the end of the story. A newsmagazine is very different. It is written to be read consecutively from beginning to end, and each of its stories is designed, following the critical theories of Edgar Allan Poe, to create one emotional effect. The news, what happened that week, may be told in the beginning, the middle, or the end; for the purpose is not to throw information at the reader but to seduce him into reading the whole story, and into accepting the dramatic (and often political) point being made.

Otto Friedrich, "There are 00 Trees in Russia"

Coordination and Subordination.   Another good way of looking at a paragraph is to see its sentences as coordinate or subordinate. In a coordinate paragraph, all the supporting sentences carry the same weight. Together, they form a sort of list, with each developing a different facet of the main idea. Often, though not always, all follow the same grammatical form. Here's an example of a coordinate paragraph. To help you see the structure, we've indented, numbered, and stacked the supporting sentences.

1. As he opens the door to the crowded gymnasium, Dave is blasted by the familiar noises of the junior varsity basketball game.

   2. Hundreds of voices blend together to form one huge roar, which reaches a peak whenever the home team makes a basket.

   2. Suddenly, a shrill whistle silences the crowd, and then a stabbing buzzer signals a time out.

   2. With a break in the action, the pep band strikes up the school fight song.

   Mike Hogan

This paragraph opens with a topic sentence that focuses on the noises of the basketball game. Each of the supporting sentences then describes a different noise.

In a paragraph developed by subordination, each of the supporting sentences throws light on something in the sentence just ahead of it. Of all the supporting sentences, only the first one has a direct connection to the topic sentence. Here's an example:

1. The microorganisms that seem to have it in for us in the worst way—the ones that really appear to wish us ill—turn out on close examination to be rather more like bystanders, strays, strangers in from the cold.

   2. They will invade and replicate if given the choice, and some of them will get into our deepest tissues and set forth in our blood, but it is our response to their presence that makes the disease.

      3. Our arsenals for fighting off bacteria are so powerful, and involve so many different defense mechanisms, that we are in more danger from them than from the invaders.

         4. We live in the midst of explosive devices; we are mined.

         Lewis Thomas, *Lives of a Cell:*
Notes of a Biology-Watcher

They, them, and *their* in the second sentence refer to *microorganisms* in the topic sentence. The phrases *arsenals for fighting off bacteria* and *defense mechanisms* in the third sentence are linked to *response to their presence* in the second. *Explosive devices* and *mined* in the final sentence tie in with *danger* in the next-to-last sentence. As we move from one supporting sentence to the next, the link with the topic sentence becomes more and more indirect.

Many paragraphs mix coordinate and subordinate sentences, the subordinate sentences adding depth to the coordinate.

1. My roommate Leonard is the most high-strung person I've ever met.

2. Spending one evening with him is about all that most people can take.

   3. At the supper table, Leonard constantly drums his fingers on the table in a staccato beat, pausing only occasionally to gulp down some hunks of food.

      4. Those hunks are no doubt well churned in the most active stomach west of Walla Walla.

   3. Later, when it's time for a few hands of cards before cracking the books, you'd swear Leonard is shuffling the spots right off the cards.

      4. Nobody ever asks to cut the deck when he deals.

   3. These nervous mannerisms carry over into his studying.

      4. It's a unique experience to watch Leonard pace the floor, turn abruptly, and mutter something like "suburb located right outside city limits, exurb located farther out."

   3. Only when this bundle of nerves winds down and goes to bed does peace come to our room.

Steve Lintemuth

Here each of the four coordinate sentences, identified by the number 3, ties back to the second sentence of the paragraph, and each deals with a separate evening activity. Each of the fourth-level sentences supplements the point made in the sentence immediately preceding.

Order of Climax.   Climactic order creates a crescendo pattern, starting with the least emphatic detail and progressing to the most emphatic. The topic sentence can begin or end the paragraph, or it can remain implied. This pattern holds the reader's interest by building suspense. On occasion, writers reverse the order, landing the heaviest punch first; but such paragraphs can trail off, leaving the reader dissatisfied.

Here is a paragraph illustrating climactic order:

The speaking errors I hear affect me to different degrees. I'm so conditioned to hearing "It don't make any

difference" and "There's three ways to solve the problem"
that I've almost accepted such usage. However, errors such
as "Just between you and I, Arnold loves Edna" and "I'm
going back to my room to lay down" still offend my
sensibility. When hearing them, I usually just chuckle to
myself and walk away. The "Twin I's"--<u>irrevelant</u> and
<u>irregardless</u>--are another matter. More than any other
errors, they really grate on my ear. Whenever I hear "that
may be true, but it's irrevelant" or "Irregardless of how
much I study, I still get <u>C</u>'s," I have the urge to correct
the speaker. It's really surprising that more people don't
clean up their language act.

Valerie Sonntag

EXERCISE ■   **From a magazine or newspaper article, select
four paragraphs that illustrate different patterns of organization.
Identify the topic sentence in each case; or if it is implied, state
it in your own words. Point out the organization of each
paragraph.**

Coherence

Coherent writing flows smoothly and easily from one sentence and paragraph to another, clarifying the relationships among ideas and thus allowing the
reader to grasp connections. Because incoherent writing fails to do this, it confuses, and sometimes even irritates, the reader.

Here is a paragraph that lacks coherence:

> I woke up late. I had been so tired the night before that I had forgotten to set
> the alarm. All I could think of was the report I had stayed up until 3 A.M. typing, and
> how I could possibly get twenty copies ready for next morning's 9 o'clock sales
> meeting. I panicked and ran out the door. My bus was so crowded I had to stand.
> Jumping off the bus, I raced back up the street. The meeting was already underway.
> Mr. Jackson gestured for me to come into the conference room. Inserting the first
> page of the report into the copier, I set the dial for twenty copies and pressed the
> print button. The sign started flashing CALL KEY OPERATOR. The machine was out
> of order. Mr. Jackson asked whether the report was ready. I pointed to the flashing
> red words. Mr. Jackson nodded grimly without saying anything. He left me alone
> with the broken machine.

PERSPECTIVE

Incoherence assumes several
forms. Individual sentences
might not make sense; they
might not be linked by a common idea; some might shift the
point too radically; essential information may be missing; or
there might be an organization
problem. It's easy to see how
such problems arise. Sometimes
students don't really understand
their topic, or they haven't adequately thought it through. Often, they omit material they take
for granted, assuming that because they can fill in the gaps,
readers can too. On the other
hand, some students expect too
much from transitions. To demonstrate that connectors will not
make complete nonsense into
coherent writing, you might reproduce the following passage.

It is always important for us to consider the will of the populace. Certainly, we can find that the populace is by nature popular. But is the popular willful? This is an issue we need to carefully consider since the will of the populace is often a diet soft drink. The populace, after all, is comprised of lost cows in a meadow. Further, the populace is comprised of wolves baying at the moon. With these definitions of the populace, we have to doubt their will and go off willynilly to our own picnic.

TEACHING STRATEGIES

1. As they study coherence in individual paragraphs, you might remind students that body paragraphs are interconnected units developed in relation to some overall essay purpose, not a string of discrete units that exist in a vacuum.

2. Many students probably use most of these transitions in their paragraphs. You can help them diversify by having them review their writing, identify these techniques, and circle those they repeat excessively.

3. Advise students to deal with coherence problems primarily during the revision stage. They should read their drafts as a stranger would, particularly noting places where someone might be confused.

4. All of us have encountered students who have problems with coherence. In some cases, the material in each paragraph seems linked by free association rather than logic. Problems can occur because students are anxious or depressed about the thought of writing, or because they simply lack experience with any logical discipline. Such problems need to be addressed in an individual conference. In some cases, students may need to change topics. In others, they

This paragraph has some degree of unity: most of its sentences relate to the writer's disastrous experience with the sales report. Unfortunately, though, its many gaps in logic create rather than answer questions, and in very bumpy prose, at that. Note the gap between the third and fourth sentences. Did the writer jump out of bed and rush right out the door? Of course not, but the reader has no real clue to the actual sequence of events. Another gap occurs between the next two sentences, leaving the reader to wonder why the writer had to race up the street upon leaving the bus. And who is Mr. Jackson? The paragraph never tells, but the reader will want to know.

Now read this rewritten version, additions italicized:

> I woke up late *because* I had been so tired the night before that I had forgotten to set the alarm. All I could think of was the report I had stayed up until 3 A.M. typing, and how I could possibly get twenty copies ready for next morning's 9 o'clock sales meeting. *When I realized it was 8:30,* I panicked. *Jumping out of bed, I threw on some clothes, grabbed the report,* and ran out the door. My bus was so crowded I had to stand *and could not see out the window. Two blocks beyond my stop, I realized I should have gotten off. "Stop!" I cried and,* jumping off the bus, raced back up the street. *When I reached the office, it was 9:15, and* the meeting was already underway. Mr. Jackson, *the sales manager, saw me and* gestured for me to come into the conference room. *"One moment," I said as calmly as I could and hurried to the copier.* Inserting the first page of the report into it, I set the dial for twenty copies and pressed the print button. *Immediately,* the sign started flashing CALL KEY OPERATOR. The machine was out of order. *The next thing I knew,* Mr. Jackson *was at my side* asking whether the report was ready. I pointed to the flashing red words*, and* Mr. Jackson nodded grimly without saying anything. *Turning on his heel,* he *walked away and* left me alone with the broken machine.

As this example shows, correcting an incoherent paragraph may call for anything from a single word to a whole sentence or more.

Coherence derives from a sufficient supply of supporting details and your firm sense of the way your ideas go together. If you brainstorm your topic thoroughly and think carefully about the relationships between sentences, incoherence isn't likely to haunt your paragraphs.

As you write, and especially when you revise, signal connections to the reader by using *transitions*—devices that link sentences to one another. These are the most common transitional devices:

1. Connecting words and phrases
2. Repeated key words
3. Pronouns and demonstrative adjectives
4. Parallelism

You can use them to furnish links both within and between paragraphs.

Connecting Words and Phrases. These connectors clarify relationships between sentences. The following list groups them according to function:

Showing similarity: in like manner, likewise, moreover, similarly

Showing contrast: at the same time, but, even so, however, in contrast, instead, nevertheless, still, on the contrary, on the other hand, otherwise, yet

Showing results or effects: accordingly, as a result, because, consequently, hence, since, therefore, thus

Adding ideas together: also, besides, first (second, third . . .), furthermore, in addition, in the first place, likewise, moreover, similarly, too

Drawing conclusions: as a result, finally, in brief, in conclusion, in short, to summarize

Pointing out examples: for example, for instance, to illustrate

Showing emphasis and clarity: above all, after all, again, as a matter of fact, besides, in fact, in other words, indeed, nonetheless, that is

Indicating time: at times, after, afterward, from then on, immediately, later, meanwhile, next, now, once, previously, subsequently, then, until, while

Conceding a point: granted that, of course, to be sure, admittedly

Don't overload your paper with connectors. In well-planned prose, your message flows clearly with only an occasional assist from them.

In the following excerpt, which clarifies the difference between workers and workaholics, the connectors are italicized.

> My efforts to define workaholism and to distinguish workaholics from other hard workers proved difficult. *While* workaholics do work hard, not all hard workers are workaholics. Moonlighters, *for example,* may work 16 hours a day to make ends meet, but most of them will stop working when their financial circumstances permit. Accountants, *too,* seem to work non-stop, but many slow down after the April 15 tax deadline. Workaholics, *on the other hand,* always devote more time and thought to their work than their situation demands. Even in the absence of deadlines to meet, mortgages to pay, promotions to earn, or bosses to please, workaholics still work hard. What sets them apart is their attitude toward work, not the number of hours they work.
>
> Marilyn Machlowitz, "Workaholism: What's Wrong with Being Married to Your Work?"

DISCUSSION QUESTIONS ■

1. What ideas does each of the italicized words and phrases connect?
2. What relationship does each show?

Repeated Key Words.   Repeating key words, especially those that help convey a paragraph's central idea, can smooth the reader's path. The words may appear in different forms, but their presence keeps the main issues before the reader. In the following paragraph, the repetition of *majority, minority,* and *will* aids coherence, as does the more limited repetition of *government* and *interests.*

> Whatever fine-spun theories we may devise to resolve or obscure the difficulty, there is no use blinking the fact that the *will* of the *majority* is not the same thing as

---

may need practice with exercises that require them to arrange pre-sèlected sentences under appropriate topic headings and discard those that don't fit.

CLASSROOM ACTIVITY

Bring in several paragraphs that lack coherence. Have students identify the reasons for the incoherence and suggest ways to correct the problem.

SUGGESTED INSTRUCTOR READINGS

Bamberg, B. "What Makes a Text Coherent?" College English 34 (1983): 417–30. Elaborates on the role meaning plays in determining coherence.

Markels, R. B. A New Perspective on Cohesion in Expository Paragraphs. Carbondale, IL: Southern Illinois UP, 1984. Details both the semantic and syntactic considerations that produce cohesion.

DISCUSSION QUESTIONS

In this paragraph, *while* picks up the contrast suggested in the first sentence and provides a link to the specific contrast in the sentence in which it appears. *For example* links the illustration presented in its sentence with the general idea stated in the second. *Too* in the fourth sentence indicates that the writer is adding another example to illustrate her point. *On the other hand,* in the fifth sentence, sets up the contrast between hard workers and workaholics that is at the heart of the paragraph.

the *will* of all. *Majority* rule works well only so long as the *minority* is *willing* to accept the *will* of the *majority* as the *will* of the *nation* and let it go at that. Generally speaking, the *minority* will be *willing* to let it go at that so long as it feels that its essential *interests* and rights are not fundamentally different from those of the current *majority,* and so long as it can, in any case, look forward with confidence to mustering enough votes within four or six years to become itself the *majority* and so redress the balance. But if it comes to pass that a large *minority* feels that it has no such chance, that it is a fixed and permanent *minority* and that another group or class with rights and *interests* fundamentally hostile to its own is in permanent control, then *government* by *majority* vote ceases in any sense to be *government* by the *will* of the people for the good of all, and becomes *government* by the *will* of some of the people for their own *interests* at the expense of the others.

Carl Becker, *Freedom and Responsibility in the American Way of Life*

EXERCISE ■   **Write a paragraph using one of the following sentences as your topic sentence. Insert the missing key word and then repeat it in your paragraph to help link your sentences together.**

1. _____ is my favorite relative.
2. I wish I had (a, an, some, more) _____.
3. _____ changed my life.
4. _____ is more trouble that it's worth.
5. A visit to _____ always depresses me.
6. Eating _____ is a challenge.
7. I admire _____.

Pronouns and Demonstrative Adjectives.   Pronouns stand in for nouns that appear earlier in the sentence or in previous sentences. Mixing pronouns and their nouns throughout the paragraph prevents monotony and promotes clarity. We have italicized the pronouns in the following excerpt from an article about Dolores Huerta and Cesar Chavez, two leaders of The United Farm Workers union.

A book could be written on *their* [Huerta's and Chavez's] complex relationship. *Both* are stubborn and opinionated. *She* is notorious in the union for combativeness. (Stories are told of growers begging to face anyone at the negotiating table except Huerta.) Chavez jokes of "unleashing Dolores"; but *he* respects *her* opinions and *they* generally agree on larger issues. Dolores says *they* fight a lot because "*he* knows *I'*ll never quit, so *he* uses *me* to let off steam; *he* knows *I'*ll fight back anyway." Chavez, a traditionalist in *his* own home life, is said to privately disapprove of Dolores's divorces, *her* living now with *his* brother Richard, and *her* chaotic way of raising *her* kids. But *he* knows that the union is the center of *her* life, just as *it* is with *his*. "Dolores is absolutely fearless, physically and emotionally," *he* says.

Judith Coburn, "Dolores Huerta: La Pasionaria of the Farm Workers"

Except for *it* in the second sentence from the end, all the pronouns refer to Huerta, Chavez, or both.

Four demonstrative adjectives—*this, that, these,* and *those*—also help hook ideas together. Demonstratives are special adjectives that identify or point out nouns rather than describe them. Here is an example from the Declaration of Independence:

> We hold *these* truths to be self-evident, that all men are created equal, that they are endowed by their Creator with certain unalienable Rights, that among *these* are Life, Liberty, and the pursuit of Happiness. That to secure *these* rights, Governments are instituted among Men, deriving their just powers from the consent of the governed. That whenever any Form of Government becomes destructive of *these* ends, it is the Right of the People to alter or to abolish it, and to institute new Government, laying its foundation on such principles and organizing its power in such form, as to them shall seem most likely to effect their Safety and Happiness.

EXERCISE ■   **In a magazine, newspaper, textbook, or some other written source, find two paragraphs that use pronouns and demonstrative adjectives to increase coherence. Copy the paragraphs, underline the pronouns and demonstrative adjectives, and explain what each refers to.**

Parallelism.   Parallelism uses repetition of grammatical form to express a series of equivalent ideas. Besides giving continuity, the repetition adds rhythm and balance to the writing. Note how the following italicized constructions tie together the unfolding definition of poverty.

> *Poverty is staying* up all night on cold nights to watch the fire, knowing one spark on the newspaper covering the walls means your sleeping children die in flames. In summer *poverty is watching* gnats and flies devour your baby's tears when he cries. The screens are torn and you pay so little rent you know they will never be fixed. *Poverty means* insects in your food, in your nose, in your eyes, and crawling over you when you sleep. *Poverty is hoping* it never rains because diapers won't dry when it rains and soon you are using newspapers. *Poverty is seeing* your children forever with runny noses. Paper handkerchiefs cost money and all your rags you need for other things. Even more costly are antihistamines. *Poverty is cooking* without food and cleaning without soap.
>
> Jo Goodwin Parker, "What Is Poverty?"

PARAGRAPHS WITH SPECIAL FUNCTIONS

Special-function paragraphs include introductions, transitional paragraphs, and conclusions. One-paragraph introductions and conclusions appear in short, multiparagraph essays. Transitional paragraphs occur primarily in long compositions.

TEACHING STRATEGY
Have students review the introductions, conclusions, and transitions used in a variety of essays. They might note how type of writing, purpose, and audience influence the choice.

Introductions

A good introduction acquaints and coaxes. It announces the essay's topic and may directly state the thesis. In addition, it sets the tone—somber, light-hearted, angry—of what will follow. An amusing anecdote would not be an appropriate opening for a paper about political torture.

With essays, as with people, first impressions are important. If your opening rouses interest, it will draw the reader into the essay and pave the way for your ideas. If, instead, you'd like to try your hand at turning the reader away, search for a beginning that is mechanical, plodding, and dull. Your success will astonish you. Here are some bad openings.

In this paper I intend to . . .

Wars have always afflicted mankind.

As you may know, inflation is a problem for many of us.

In the modern world of today . . .

How would you respond to these openings? Ask yourself that same question about every opening you write.

Gear the length of the introduction to that of the essay. Although longer papers sometimes begin with two or more introductory paragraphs, generally the lead-in for a short essay is a single paragraph. Here are some possibilities for starting an essay. The type you select depends on your purpose, subject, audience, and personality.

A Directly Stated Thesis.   This is a common type of opening, orienting the reader to what will follow. After providing some general background, the writer of our example narrows her scope to a thesis that previews the upcoming sections of her essay.

An increasing number of mid–life women are reentering the workforce, pursuing college degrees, and getting more involved in the public arena. Several labels besides "mid-life" have been attached to this type of person: the mature woman, the older woman, and, more recently, the reentry woman. By definition, she is between thirty–five and fifty-five years old and has been away from the business or academic scene anywhere from fifteen to thirty years. The academic community, the media, marketing people, and employers are giving her close scrutiny, and it is apparent that she is having a greater impact on our society than she realizes.

                                                    Jo Ann Harris

A Definition.   This kind of introduction works particularly well in a paper that acquaints the reader with an unfamiliar topic.

> You are completely alone in a large open space and are struck by a terrifying, unreasoning fear. You sweat, your heart beats, you cannot breathe. You fear you may die of a heart attack, although you do not have heart disease. Suppose you decide you will never get yourself in this helpless situation again. You go home and refuse to leave its secure confines. Your family has to support you. You have agoraphobia—a disabling terror of open spaces.
>
>   "Controlling Phobias Through Behavior
>   Modification"

A Quotation.   A beginning quotation, particularly from an authority in the field, can be an effective springboard for the ideas that follow. Make sure any quote you use relates clearly to your topic.

> The director of the census made a dramatic announcement in 1890. The Nation's unsettled area, he revealed, "has been so broken into by isolated bodies of settlement that there can hardly be said to be a frontier line." These words sounded the close of one period of America's history. For three centuries before, men had marched westward, seeking in the forests and plains that lay beyond the settled areas a chance to begin anew. For three centuries they had driven back the wilderness as their conquest of the continent went on. Now, in 1890, they were told that a frontier line separating the settled and unsettled portions of the United States no longer existed. The west was won, and the expansion that had been the most distinctive feature of the country's past was at an end.
>
>   Ray Allen Billington, "The Frontier Disappears"

An Anecdote or Personal Experience.   A well-told personal anecdote or experience can lure readers into the rest of the paper. Like other introductions, this kind should bear on what comes afterward. Engle's anecdote, like the stories she reviews, demonstrates that "women also have dark hearts."

> My mother used to have a little china cream and sugar set that was given to her by a woman who later killed her children with an axe. It sat cheerfully in the china cabinet, as inadequate a symbol as I have ever seen of the dark mysteries within us. Yet at least it was there to remind us that no matter how much Jesus wanted us for a sunbeam, we would still have some day to cope with a deeper reality than common sense could explain. It stood for strange cars not to get into, running shoes to wear when you were out alone at night and the backs of Chinese restaurants you were not supposed to go into.
>
>   Marian Engle, review of *The Goddess and Other
>   Women* by Joyce Carol Oates

An Arresting Statement.   Sometimes you can jolt the reader into attention, using content, language, or both, particularly if your essay develops an unusual or extreme position.

> It's like Pearl Harbor. The Japanese have invaded, and the U.S. has been caught short. Not on guns and tanks and battleships—those are yesterday's weapons—but on mental might. In a high-tech age where nations increasingly compete on brainpower, American schools are producing an army of illiterates. Companies that cannot hire enough skilled workers now realize they must do something to save the public schools. Not to be charitable, not to promote good public relations, but to survive.
>
> Nancy Perry, "Saving the Schools: How Business Can Help"

Interesting Details.   These details pique curiosity and draw the reader into the paper.

> It is Friday night at any of the ten thousand watering holes of the small towns and crossroads hamlets of the South. The room is a cacophony of the ping-pong-ding-dingding of the pinball machine, the pop-fizz of another round of Pabst, the refrain of "Red Necks, White Socks and Blue Ribbon Beer" on the juke box, the insolent roar of a souped-up engine outside and, above it all, the sound of easy laughter. The good ole boys have gathered for their fraternal ritual—the aimless diversion that they have elevated into a life-style.
>
> Bonnie Angelo, "Those Good Ole Boys"

A Question.   A provocative question can entice the reader into the essay to find the answer.

> When you leave your apartment or house, do you begin to feel better? If you leave for a week-long trip, do you find your head clears, your migraine disappears, dizziness stops, your aches and pains subside, depression fades away, and your entire attitude is better? If so, chemical pollution of the atmosphere in your home may be making you ill.
>
> Marshall Mandell, "Are You Allergic to Your House?"

EXERCISE ■

1. **Explain why each of the preceding introductions interests or does not interest you. Does your response stem from the topic or the way the author introduces it?**
2. **Find magazine articles with effective introductory paragraphs illustrating at least three different techniques. Write a paragraph explaining why each impresses you.**

Transitional Paragraphs

In the midst of a lengthy essay, you may need a short paragraph that announces a shift from one group of ideas to another. Transitional paragraphs summarize previously explained ideas, repeat the thesis, or point to ideas that follow. In our example, Bruno Bettelheim has been discussing a young boy named Joey who has turned into a kind of human machine. After describing Joey's assorted delusions, Bettelheim signals his switch from the delusions to the fears that caused them.

> What deep-seated fears and needs underlay Joey's delusional system? We were long in finding out, for Joey's preventions effectively concealed the secret of his autistic behavior. In the meantime we dealt with his peripheral problems one by one.
>
> Bruno Bettelheim, "Joey: 'A Mechanical Boy' "

The following transitional paragraph looks back as well as ahead.

```
     Certainly these three factors--exercise, economy,
convenience of short-cuts--help explain the popularity of
bicycling today. But a fourth attraction sometimes
overrides the others: the lure of the open road.

                                        Mike Bernstein
```

Conclusions

A conclusion rounds out a paper and signals that the discussion has been completed. Not all papers require a separate conclusion; narratives and descriptions, for example, generally end when the writer finishes the story or concludes the impression. But many essays benefit from a conclusion that drives the point home a final time. To be effective, a conclusion must mesh logically and stylistically with what comes earlier. A long, complex paper often ends with a summary of the main points, but any of several other options may be used for shorter papers with easy-to-grasp ideas. Most short essays have single-paragraph conclusions; longer papers may require two or three paragraphs.

Here are some cautions about writing your conclusion:

1. Don't introduce new material. Draw together, round out, but don't take off in a new direction.
2. Don't tack on an ending in desperation when the hour is late and the paper is due tomorrow—the so-called midnight special. Your reader deserves better than "All in all, skiing is a great sport" or "Thus we can see that motorcycle racing isn't for everyone."
3. Don't apologize. Saying that you could have done a better job makes a reader wonder why you didn't.
4. Don't moralize. A preachy conclusion can undermine the position you have established in the rest of your composition.

The following examples illustrate several common types of conclusions.

Restatement of the Thesis.   The following conclusion reasserts Jordan's thesis that "a mood of antisocial negativism is creeping through the structure of American life, corroding our ideals, and suffocating the hopes of poor people and minorities."

> There is room for honest differences about each of these key issues, but the new negativism's overt greed and the implicit racism of its loud "No" to minority aspirations indicate that this is a poisonous movement that denies the moral ideals and humane values that characterize the best in America's heritage.
>
> Vernon E. Jordan, Jr., "The New Negativism"

A Summary.   A summary draws together and reinforces the main points of a paper.

> There are, of course, many other arguments against capital punishment, including its high cost and its failure to deter crime. But I believe the most important points against the death penalty are the possibility of executing an innocent man, the discriminatory manner in which it is applied, and the barbaric methods of carrying it out. In my opinion, capital punishment is, in effect, premeditated murder by society as a whole. As the old saying goes, two wrongs don't make a right.
>
> Diane Trathen

A Question.   The paragraph below concludes an argument that running should not be elevated to a religion, that its other benefits are sufficient. A final question often prompts the reader to think further on the topic. If your essay is meant to be persuasive, be sure to phrase a concluding question so that the way a reasonable person would answer emphasizes your point of view.

> Aren't those gifts enough? Why ask running for benefits that are plainly beyond its capacity to bestow?
>
> James Fixx, "What Running Can't Do for You"

A Quotation.   A quotation can capture the essence of your thought and end the essay with authority.

> "We had no idea of the emotional involvement and the commitment of these women," Richard says. "Suddenly a constituency arose. Suddenly there are thou-

sands and thousands of women who don't care about your moral position or mine—they want a baby."

> David Zimmerman, "Are Test-Tube Babies the Answer for the Childless?"

Ironic Twist or Surprising Observation.   These approaches prompt the reader to think further about a paper's topic. The following paragraph points out the ironic refusal of the government to confront poverty that exists a mere ten blocks away from its offices.

> Thus, a stark contrast exists between the two cultures of 14th Street, which appears to be like an earthworm with half of its body crushed by poverty but the other half still alive, wriggling in wealth. The two are alike only in that each communicates little with the other because of the wide disparity between the lives of the people and the conditions of the environments. The devastating irony of the situation on 14th Street lies in the fact that only ten blocks away sit the very governmental institutions that could alleviate the poverty—the Senate, the House of Representatives, and the White House.
>
> Student Unknown

Clever or Lighthearted Ending.   In our example, the writer, capitalizing on the essay's topic, ends by exaggerating the fault being criticized.

> Because using clichés is as easy as falling off a log, it goes without saying that it would be duck soup to continue in this vein till hell freezes over. However, since that would be carrying coals to Newcastle, let's ring down the curtain and bid adieu to the fair topic of the cliché. (No use beating a dead horse.)
>
> Student Unknown

Personal Challenge.   A challenge often prompts the reader to take some action.

> And therein lies the challenge. You can't merely puff hard for a few days and then revert to the La-Z-Boy

recliner, smugly thinking that you're "in shape." You must
sweat and strain and puff regularly, week in and week out.
They're your muscles, your lungs, your heart. The only
caretaker they have is you.

Monica Duvall

Hope or Recommendation. Both a hope and a recommendation may restate points already made in the essay or suggest actions to take in order to arrive
at a solution.

Periodically my pilot and I climb into our aircraft and head out over the
Minnesota wilderness, following a succession of electronic beeps that lead to some of
the last remaining wolves in the lower 48 states. We hope that the data we collect
will provide a better understanding of the wolf. We especially hope that our work will
help guide authorities into a management program that will insure the perpetuation
of the species in the last vestiges of its former range.

L. David Mech, "Where Can the Wolves Survive?"

I who am blind can give one hint to those who can see—one admonition to
those who would make full use of the gift of sight: Use your eyes as if tomorrow you
would be stricken blind. And the same method can be applied to the other senses.
Hear the music of voices, the song of the bird, the mighty strains of an orchestra, as
if you would be stricken deaf tomorrow. Touch each object you want to touch as if
tomorrow your tactile sense would fail. Smell the perfume of flowers, taste with
relish each morsel, as if tomorrow you could never smell and taste again. Make the
most of every sense; glory in all the facets of pleasure and beauty which the world
reveals to you through the several means of contact which Nature provides. But of all
the senses, I am sure that sight must be the most delightful.

Helen Keller, "Three Days to See"

EXERCISE ■

1. **Explain why each of the foregoing conclusions does or does not
interest you. Does your response stem from the topic or from the
author's handling of it?**
2. **Copy effective concluding paragraphs, illustrating at least three
different techniques, from magazine articles. Then write a paragraph explaining why each impresses you.**

■ Chapter 15

Effective Sentences

PERSPECTIVE

Most of us agree that a sentence comprises a subject and a verb or verb phrase and that it makes sense by itself. At times, of course, the subject may be implied, as in the sentence "Stop." Sentences play a much less prominent role in speech than they do in writing. Thus we can appropriately respond to the query, "Do you want tea or coffee?" by merely replying "Coffee." Some students have sentence problems because they fail to recognize the distinctions between writing and speaking. For this reason, referring to spoken discourse to help students decide whether something is a sentence is not always appropriate. In some contexts "John" might, to students, seem a sentence, while "He is trying" might not because the missing pronoun reference makes the sentence seem incomplete.

CLASSROOM ACTIVITY

Present students with a list of sentences and non-sentences. Have them indicate which they do and do not consider sentences and then formulate criteria that serve to define a sentence. For example: Stop. Running harder than before. She is sleeping. There is time enough to finish. Is he here? Smart!

A sentence is a group of words that begins with a capital letter, ends with a period, question mark, or exclamation point, and makes sense by itself. The elements that comprise sentences include subjects, predicates, direct objects, indirect objects, subject complements, object complements, phrases, and clauses. These elements are discussed on pages 541–569.

Sentences take many forms, some straightforward and unadorned, others intricate and ornate, each with its own stylistic strengths. Becoming familiar with these forms and their uses gives you the option to

- ▋ emphasize or deemphasize an idea
- ▋ combine ideas into one sentence or keep them separate in more than one sentence
- ▋ make sentences sound formal or informal
- ▋ emphasize the actor or the action
- ▋ achieve rhythm, variety, and contrast.

Effective sentences bring both exactness and flair to your writing.

SENTENCE STRATEGIES

Effective sentences stem, at least in part, from selecting the right word order for independent clauses, coordinating and subordinating effectively, correctly positioning movable modifiers, using parallel structures, choosing the right verb voice, and avoiding fragments except for particular effects. Usually it's best to work on these different strategies as you revise rather than pausing to refine each sentence after you write it.

PERSPECTIVE

You will probably encounter students with widely differing sentence skills. While some will write fairly effective and complex sentences, others will have trouble avoiding fragments. As a result, not all students will be able to achieve the same level of sentence maturity at the same time. Furthermore, even when all have similar skills, some students will improve slowly, while the sentences of others will quickly start showing more variety and flexibility.

Word Order in Independent Clauses

TEACHING STRATEGIES
1. You can teach any of these sentence strategy sections as a separate unit. If you choose this option, don't be surprised by the results. Sometimes when students are introduced to sentence structure, they make more errors as they try to understand new options. Furthermore, some students, baffled by an abstract account of what they have done unconsciously, will simply ignore your instruction.
2. Have students review several types of writing to see what word order predominates. They will probably discover that academic writing tends to include many expletives, and poetic writing contains more inverted-order sentences than do other types. Otherwise, standard subject–verb–object patterns predominate.
3. To demonstrate the importance of word order in English, you might select a paragraph, scramble the word order in several of its sentences, then have students read the paragraph and indicate why they are having problems. Students could then try to reconstruct the scrambled sentences and note how their changes improve clarity.

Most independent clauses follow a similar arrangement. First comes the subject, then the verb, and finally any other element needed to convey the main message.

> Barney blushed. *(subject, verb)*
>
> They built the dog a kennel. *(subject, verb, indirect object, direct object)*
>
> Samantha is an architect. *(subject, verb, subject complement)*

This arrangement puts the emphasis on the subject, right where it's usually wanted.

But the pattern doesn't work in every situation. Occasionally, a writer wants to emphasize some element that follows the verb, create an artistic effect, or give the subject unusual emphasis. Enter inverted order and the expletive construction.

Inverted Order. To invert a sentence, move to the front the element you want to emphasize. Sometimes the rest of the sentence follows in regular subject-then-verb order; sometimes the verb precedes the subject.

> Lovable he isn't. *(subject complement, subject, verb)*
>
> This I just don't understand. *(direct object, subject, verb)*
>
> Tall grow the pines in the mountains. *(subject complement, verb, subject)*

Sentences that ask questions typically follow an inverted pattern.

> Is this your coat? *(verb, subject, subject complement)*
>
> Will you let the cat out? *(verb, subject, verb, direct object)*

Most of your sentences should follow normal order: readers expect it and read most easily through it. Furthermore, don't invert a sentence if the result would sound strained and unnatural. A sentence like "Fools were Brett and Amanda for quitting college" will only hinder communication.

Expletives. An expletive fills a vacancy in a sentence without contributing to the meaning. English has two common expletives, *there* and *it*. Ordinarily, *there* functions as an adverb, *it* as a pronoun, and either can appear anywhere in a sentence. As expletives, however, they alter normal sentence order by beginning sentences and anticipating the real subjects or objects.

Expletives are often used unnecessarily, as in the following example:

> There were twenty persons attending the sales meeting.

This sentence errs on two counts: its subject needs no extra emphasis, and it is very clumsy. Notice the improvement without the expletive and the unneeded words:

Twenty persons attended the sales meeting.

When the subject or object needs highlighting, leading off with an expletive will, by altering normal order, call it more forcefully to the reader's attention.

Normal order	A fly is in my soup. He seeks her happiness.
Expletive construction	There is a fly in my soup. *(expletive anticipating subject)* It is her happiness he seeks. *(expletive anticipating object)*

Once in a while you'll find that something just can't be said unless you use an expletive.

There is no reason for such foolishness.

No other construction can express exactly the same thought.

EXERCISE ■ **Indicate which of these sentences follow normal order, which are inverted, and which have expletive constructions. Rewrite so that all will be in normal order.**

1. Dick Lewis is a true friend.
2. It was her cat in the ditch.
3. An intelligent person is she.
4. May I go to the movie with you?
5. A sadder but wiser man he became.
6. There are many dead fish on the beach.
7. The instructor gave the class a long reading assignment.
8. The Willetts have bought a new house.
9. It is Marianne's aim to become a lawyer.
10. Harry works at a supermarket.

Coordination and Subordination

Coordination and subordination are ways to rank ideas in sentences. Coordination makes ideas equal; subordination makes them unequal. To understand coordination and subordination, you need to know about four kinds of sentences: simple, compound, complex, and compound–complex.

EXERCISE ANSWERS

1. Normal order.
2. Inverted order. Her car was in the ditch.
3. Inverted order. She is an intelligent person.
4. Inverted order. Rewriting the sentence in normal order ("I may go to the movies with you.") converts it from a question to a statement.
5. Inverted order. He became a sadder but wiser man.
6. Expletive construction. Many dead fish are on the beach.
7. Normal order.
8. Normal order.
9. Expletive order. Marianne aims to become a lawyer.
10. Normal order.

PERSPECTIVE

Coordination and subordination are not merely important ways of structuring sentences. Encouraging students to coordinate or subordinate helps them understand the logical relationship among their ideas. Sentence combining is an effective way of exposing students to more mature syntax. Although sentence-combining texts are available, exercises are easy to prepare: simply break any more complicated sentence into basic simple sentences. Two cautions, however, need mentioning. First, sentence combining can result in excessively cumbersome sentences; students should always evaluate the quality of those they produce in light of clarity and stylistic effectiveness. Second, students who attempt more complex structures probably will commit the errors associated with them. Reassure students that these errors stem from the attempt to grow and are only temporary.

TEACHING STRATEGY

Using sentence-combining techniques, start with simple sentences that have a relationship which can be demonstrated through coordination and subordination. Ask the class to determine ways of establishing the relationship, and then introduce the structure you wish to teach. For example, "The ball was over. Arthur collapsed on the sofa." might become "After the ball was over, Arthur collapsed on the sofa." Have students try to explain what is gained conceptually and stylistically by the new sentence.

SUGGESTED INSTRUCTOR READING

O'Hare, F. Sentence-Combining: Improving Student Writing Without Formal Grammar Instruction. Urbana, IL: NCTE, 1973. Perhaps the most effective introduction to the sentence-combining technique.

Simple Sentences.   A simple sentence has one subject and one predicate. Some simple sentences consist merely of a single noun and a single verb.

> Millicent shouted.

Others can include elements such as compound subjects, compound verbs, direct objects, indirect objects, and subject complements.

> Jim and Sue have bought a car. *(compound subject, direct object)*
>
> Lucretia Borgia smiled and mixed her guests a cocktail. *(compound verb, indirect object, direct object)*
>
> Autumn is a sad season. *(subject complement)*

Most simple sentences are rather short and easy to understand. This trimness can add punch to your writing, but it can also make your writing sound childish and may waste words.

> The audience was young and friendly. It was responsive. It cheered for each speaker.

Combined into a single simple sentence, the information is easier to follow and more interesting to read:

> The young, friendly, responsive audience cheered for each speaker.

Compound Sentences.   A compound sentence contains two or more independent clauses, each holding the same (coordinate) rank. As a result, the idea in the first clause receives the same emphasis as the idea in the second.

In some cases, a comma and a coordinating conjunction *(and, but, or, nor, for, yet, so)* link successive clauses.

> Name the baby Huey, *or* I'll cut you out of my will.
>
> The audience was young, friendly, and responsive, *so* it cheered for each speaker.

In others, a semicolon and a conjunctive adverb *(for example, however, in fact, likewise, meanwhile, instead,* and the like) furnish the connection.

> Tod wants to see the play; *in fact,* he's talked about it for weeks.
>
> Today, many young women do not rush into marriage and motherhood; *instead,* they spend several years establishing careers.

Finally, a writer may omit any connecting word and separate the clauses with a semicolon.

> The sky grew pitch black; the wind died; an ominous quiet hung over the whole city.

Be sure to read this Hemingway novel; it suggests how to cope gracefully with pressure.

As the preceding sentences show, compound sentences allow writers to express simple relationships among simple ideas. However, such sentences have one important limitation: it is impossible to highlight one particular idea. To do this, we need to use complex sentences.

Complex Sentences.   A complex sentence has one independent clause and one or more dependent clauses. Relegating an idea to a dependent clause shows that the writer wishes it to receive less emphasis than the idea in the main clause.

Because the young, friendly audience was responsive, it cheered for each speaker.

After the ball was over, Arthur collapsed on the sofa.

Once they had reached the lakeshore, the campers found a level spot *where they could pitch their tent.*

Unlike compound sentences, complex ones allow writers to vary the emphasis of ideas.

While I watered the grass, I discussed stock options with Liz.

I watered the grass while I discussed stock options with Liz.

The first sentence emphasizes the talk with Liz, the second watering the lawn.
Often, shifting sights allows a writer to make changes in meaning as well as in emphasis.

While his bicycle was damaged, Pat walked to work.

While Pat walked to work, his bicycle was damaged.

Furthermore, complex sentences signal *how* ideas relate. Note the various relationships in the following sentences:

Because she was swimming well, Millicent did 200 laps today. *(reason)*

The Sears Tower is taller *than the Empire State Building. (extent).*

Ms. Yoshira is the executive *for whom I am working. (relationship between persons)*

Compound–Complex Sentences.   This type of sentence features two or more independent clauses and one or more dependent clauses. Here are two examples with the dependent clauses italicized.

Ms. Harris works as an investment manager, and Mr. Williams, *who lives next door to her,* owns a jewelry store.

A. 1. This is a simple sentence and so has one independent clause.
2. This is a complex sentence with two dependent clauses: "Because its bag was too full" and "than it had been before."
3. This is a simple sentence and so has one independent clause.
4. This is a compound–complex sentence with one dependent clause, "When Tom arrived home," and two independent clauses, "his roommate . . . gone" and "six hours . . . library."
5. This is a compound sentence with two independent clauses: "my orange trees blossomed last week" and "the grapefruit trees have withered." The word group following "withered" is a phrase.
6. This is a compound–complex sentence. The independent clauses are "kites make good gifts for children" and "a second will come in handy." The two dependent clauses are "even if a child already has a kite" and "if the first one becomes tangled in a tree."
7. This is a complex sentence. The independent clause is "It's risky to confide in a co-worker." The rest of the sentence consists of two dependent clauses: "because you can never be sure" and "that the confidence will be kept."
8. This is a compound–complex sentence. The first independent clause is "I think I know" and the second consists of everything following the colon. The dependent clause is "why he moved here." (Note: some instructors would classify this sentence as compound because the dependent clause serves as a direct object in the first independent clause.)

If you are to communicate properly, your thoughts must be clear and correct; thoughts are wasted when *language is muddled*.

Compound–complex sentences allow writers to present more intricate relationships than do other kinds of sentences. In the following example, three sentences—one compound and two simple—have been rewritten as a compound–complex sentence. Notice how subordination improves the compactness and smoothness of the final version.

Mary hated to be seen in ugly clothing, but she wore an ugly dress with red polka dots. She had received the dress as a Christmas present. Her Aunt Ida had given it to her.

Although Mary hated to be seen in ugly clothing, she wore an ugly red-polka-dot dress that her Aunt Ida had given her for Christmas.

The second version condenses thirty-five words to twenty-six.

EXERCISE ■

A. Label the independent and dependent clauses in the sentences below. Then identify each sentence as simple, compound, complex, or compound–complex.

1. A career in broadcasting requires good verbal skills, an extensive wardrobe, and a pleasant smile.
2. Because its bag was too full, the vacuum cleaner backfired, leaving the room dirtier than it had been before.
3. Leave your boots in the back hall, please.
4. When Tom arrived home, his roommate asked him where he had really gone; six hours seemed too long a time to spend in the library.
5. My orange tree blossomed last week; however, the grapefruit trees have withered, probably because of the freeze last month.
6. Kites make good gifts for children; even if a child already has a kite, a second one will come in handy if the first one becomes tangled in a tree.
7. It's risky to confide in a co-worker because you can never be sure that the confidence will be kept.
8. I think I know why he moved here: he likes having the only dental practice in this part of the state.
9. The pencil and the stapler are on the table next to the window in Mr. Brigg's office.
10. Don't add bleach to your load of colored shirts; the colors will fade and the fibers will weaken.

B. Using coordination and subordination, rewrite the following passages to reduce words and improve smoothness.

1. He played the piano. He played the organ. He played the French horn. He did not play the viola.

2. The weather was icy cold and windy. Lee was wearing only a T-shirt and athletic shorts.

3. Life on Venus may be possible. It will not be the kind of life we know on Earth. Life on Mars may be possible. It will not be the kind of life we know on Earth.

4. He felt his classmates were laughing at his error. He ran out of the room. He vowed never to return to that class.

5. Albert lay in bed. He stared at the ceiling. Albert thought about the previous afternoon. He had asked Kathy to go to dinner with him. She is a pretty, blonde-haired woman. She sits at the desk next to his. They work at Hemphill's. She had refused.

6. I went to the store to buy a box of detergent. I saw Bill there, and we talked about last night's game.

7. Tim went to the newsstand. He bought a magazine there. While he was on the way home, he lost it. He had nothing to read.

Positioning of Movable Modifiers

Movable modifiers can appear on either side of the main statement or within it.

Modifiers After Main Statement.   Sentences that follow this arrangement, frequently called *loose sentences,* occur more commonly than either of the others. They mirror conversation, in which a speaker first makes a statement and then adds on further thoughts. Often, the main statement has just one modifier.

Our company will have to file for bankruptcy *because of this year's huge losses. (phrase as modifier)*

Or it can head up a whole train of modifiers.

He burst suddenly into the party, *loud, angry, obscene. (words as modifiers)*

The family used to gather around the hearth, *doing such chores as polishing shoes, mending ripped clothing, reading, chatting, always warmed by one another's presence as much as by the flames. (words and phrases as modifiers)*

Sally stared in disbelief, and then she smiled, *slowly, tremulously, as if she couldn't believe her good fortune. (words and clause as modifiers)*

There are three essential qualities for buzzard country: *a rich supply of unburied corpses, high mountains, a strong sun. (noun-base groups as modifiers)*

John D. Stewart, "Vulture Country"

A sentence may contain several layers of modifiers. In the following example, we've indented and numbered to show the different layers.

9. This is a simple sentence and so has one independent clause.

10. This is a compound sentence. The first independent clause precedes the semi-colon; the second one follows it.

B. 1. He played the piano, organ, and French horn but not the viola.

2. Although the weather was icy cold and windy, Lee was wearing only a T-shirt and athletic shorts.

3. Life on Venus and Mars may be possible, but it will not be the kind of life we know on earth.

4. Feeling that his classmates were laughing at his error, he ran out of the room, vowing never to return to that class.

5. Albert lay in bed, staring at the ceiling and thinking about the previous afternoon when he had asked Kathy, the pretty blonde who sits at the desk next to him at Hemphill's, to go to dinner with him. She had refused.

6. While buying a box of detergent at the store, I saw Bill, and we talked about last night's game.

7. Tim bought a magazine at the newsstand, but on the way home he lost it, so he had nothing to read. OR On the way home from the newsstand, Tim lost the magazine he had bought there, so he had nothing to read.

TEACHING STRATEGIES

1. You might review different kinds of writing with students, first observing what modifier structures are employed and then discussing the results of each approach. Have students review their own writing to determine how and where they place modifiers and whether they might vary their word order.

2. Francis Christensen argues that having students add modifiers to simple sentences is an effective way of getting them to generate richer sentences of their own. This is an easy approach to teach. Give students fill-in-the-blank sentences and ask them to provide effective modifiers. For example: We have had to postpone our trip to London _____. _____, Marvin and Mary have become committed environmentalists. Harry Travis, _____, signed a three-year contract with the Boston Celtics.

SUGGESTED INSTRUCTOR READING

Christensen, F. "A Generative Rhetoric of the Sentence." College Composition and Communication 14 (1963): 155–61.

EXERCISE ANSWERS

1. Interrupted order. Rewritten as a periodic sentence: Cast out by family and friends, without the strength to make a new life in a new place, Victoria calmly and carefully injected the lethal drug into her thigh.

2. Periodic. Rewritten as a loose sentence: The woman gasped when told she had to have her spleen removed.

3. Loose. Rewritten as a periodic sentence: Because his wife had forgotten to set the alarm after she got up and he had cut himself several times shaving, Tom missed the bus.

4. Periodic. Rewritten in interrupted order: The best things—good health, warm friends, a beautiful summer evening—cannot be purchased.

5. Interrupted. Rewritten as a periodic sentence: Red-faced and perspiring, a customer stormed up to the claims desk.

6. Periodic. Rewritten in interrupted order: The freight train, stopping just short of the tunnel entrance, avoided a collision with the crowded commuter train stalled inside.

1. The men struggled to the top of the hill,
    2. thirsty,
    2. drenched in sweat,
    2. and cursing in pain
        3. as their knapsack straps cut into their raw, chafed shoulders
            4. with every step.

In this sentence, the terms numbered 2 refer back to *men* in the item numbered 1. Item 3 is linked to *cursing* in the preceding item 2, and item 4 is linked to *cut* in item 3.

The modifiers-last arrangement works well for injecting descriptive details into narratives and also for qualifying, explaining, and presenting lists in other kinds of writing.

Modifiers Before Main Statement.   Sentences that delay the main point until the end are called *periodic.* In contrast to loose sentences, they lend a formal note to what is said, slowing its pace, adding cadence, and making it more serious.

> *If you can keep your head when everyone around you is panicking,* you probably don't understand the situation. *(clauses as modifiers)*

> *From the onset of his journey to the heart of darkness,* Marlow witnesses many incidents that reveal the human capacity for evil. *(phrases as modifiers)*

> *The danger of sideswiping another vehicle, the knowledge that a hidden bump or hole could throw me from the dune buggy,* both of these things added to the thrill of the race. *(noun plus phrase and noun plus clause as modifiers)*

> *When so large a percentage of our college students admits to cheating, when so many professors practice grade inflation, when administrators fail to face up to these problems,* our colleges are in serious trouble. *(clauses as modifiers)*

1. *When the public protests,*
    2. *confronted with some obvious evidence of the damaging results of pesticide applications,* it is fed little tranquilizing pills of half truth. *(clause and phrase as modifiers)*

Rachel Carson, *Silent Spring*

As shown in the Carson example, periodic sentences can also have layers of modifiers.

Positioning the modifiers before the main point throws the emphasis upon the end of the sentence, adding force to the main point. The delay also lets the writer create sentences that, like the first example, carry stings, ironic or humorous, in their tails.

Modifiers Within Main Statement.   Inserting one or more modifiers into a main statement creates a sentence with *interrupted order.* The material may come between the subject and the verb or between the verb and the rest of the predicate.

The young girl, *wearing a tattered dress and looking anything but well-off herself,* gave the beggar a ten-dollar bill. *(phrases between subject and verb)*

Dewey declared, *in a loud, happy voice,* that the concert was the best he'd ever heard. *(phrase between verb and rest of predicate)*

The bedsprings, *bent and rusted, festooned with spider webs,* lay on top of the heap. *(words and phrase between subject and verb)*

The evolutionists, *piercing beneath the show of momentary stability,* discovered, *hidden in rudimentary organs,* the discarded rubbish of the past. *(one phrase between subject and verb, another between verb and rest of predicate)*

By stretching out the main idea, inserted modifiers slow the forward pace of the sentence, giving it some of the formality and force of a periodic sentence.

EXERCISE ■   Identify each sentence as loose, periodic, or interrupted. Rewrite each as one of the other kinds.

1. Victoria, cast out by family and friends, without the strength to make a new life in a new place, calmly and carefully injected the lethal drug into her thigh.
2. When told that she had to have her spleen removed, the woman gasped.
3. Tom missed the bus because his wife had forgotten to reset the alarm after she got up and he had cut himself several times while shaving.
4. Good health, warm friends, a beautiful summer evening—the best things cannot be purchased.
5. A customer, red-faced and perspiring, stormed up to the claims desk.
6. Stopping just short of the tunnel entrance, the freight train avoided a collision with the crowded commuter train stalled inside.
7. The new kid hammered away at the fading champ, determination in his eyes and glory in his fists.
8. The new tract house sparkled in the sunlight, pink and trim, its lawn immaculate, its two bushes and newly planted crab apple tree, by their very tininess, making the yard look vaster than its actual size.
9. Bright red and skin stinging after a day at the beach, Steve will remember the tanning oil next time.
10. Saloons, gaudily painted and beckoning with promises of extraordinary pleasures, lined the town's main street.
11. In being whisked from Lyons, France, to Tel Aviv to Sri Lanka for location shots, the Hollywood star gave new force to the phrase "international celebrity."
12. The first graders stood in line, talking and giggling, pushing at one another's caps and pencil boxes and kicking one another's shins, unmindful of the drudgery that awaited them within the old schoolhouse.

Using Parallelism

Parallelism presents equivalent ideas in grammatically equivalent form. Dressing them in the same grammatical garb calls attention to their kinship and

7. Loose. Rewritten as a periodic sentence: Determination in his eyes and glory in his fists, the new kid hammered away at the fading champ.

8. Loose. Rewritten as a periodic sentence: Pink and trim, its lawn immaculate, its two bushes and newly planted crab apple tree making by their very tininess the yard look vaster than its actual size, the new tract house sparkled in the sunlight.

9. Periodic. Rewritten in interrupted order: Steve, bright red and skin stinging after a day at the beach, will remember the tanning oil next time.

10. Interrupted. Rewritten as a periodic sentence: Gaudily painted and beckoning with promises of extraordinary pleasures, saloons lined the town's main street.

11. Periodic. Rewritten as a loose sentence: The Hollywood star gave new force to the phrase "international celebrity" in being whisked from Lyons, France, to Tel Aviv, to Sri Lanka for location shoots.

12. Loose. Rewritten as a periodic sentence: Talking and giggling, pushing at one another's caps and pencil boxes, kicking one another's shins, unmindful of the drudgery that awaited them within the old schoolhouse, the first graders stood in line.

PERSPECTIVE
The attempt to produce parallel structures can prompt students to ask a rhetorical "What else?" and expand one modifier into a parallel series. As a result, "He cleared the table" can become "He cleared the table, washed the dishes, then put his daughter to bed." In attempting to achieve parallelism, however, students can strain syntax and verb forms. Encourage them to check parallel structures for other faults.

TEACHING STRATEGY

You can encourage students to generate parallel sentences by providing them with fill-in-the-blank exercises like the following: ___ and ___ are essential to every college student. To gain victory our team will ___, ___, and even ___. Today we celebrate our victories, but tomorrow ___.

adds smoothness and polish. The following sentence pairs demonstrate the improvement that parallelism brings:

Nonparallel	James's outfit was *wrinkled, mismatched,* and *he needed to wash it.* *(words and independent clause)*
Parallel	James's outfit was *wrinkled, mismatched,* and *dirty. (words)*
Nonparallel	Oscar likes *reading books, attending plays,* and *to search for antiques. (different kinds of phrases)*
Parallel	Oscar likes *reading books, attending plays,* and *searching for antiques. (same kind of phrases)*
Nonparallel	Beth performs her tasks *quickly, willingly,* and *with accuracy. (words and phrase)*
Parallel	Beth performs her tasks *quickly, willingly,* and *accurately. (words)*
Nonparallel	The instructor complimented me *for taking part in class discussions* and *because I had written a superb theme. (phrase and clause)*
Parallel	The instructor complimented me *for taking part in class discussions* and *for writing a superb theme. (phrases)*

As the examples show, revising nonparallel sentences smooths out bumpiness while binding the ideas together more closely and lending them a more finished look.

Parallelism doesn't always stop with a single sentence. Writers sometimes use it in a series of sentences:

> He had never lost his childlike innocence. He had never lost his sense of wonder. He had never lost his sense of joy in nature's simplest gifts.

For an example of parallelism that extends over much of a paragraph, see page 207.

Repeating a structure through several sentences of a paragraph beats a tattoo that drums the points home more forcefully and adds rhythm to the prose. But don't overuse the technique, or it will lose its impact and seem irritating and artificial.

Balance, a special form of parallelism, positions two grammatically equivalent ideas on opposite sides of some pivot point, such as a word or punctuation mark.

Hope for the best, and prepare for the worst.

Many are called, but few are chosen.

When I'm right, nobody ever notices; when I'm wrong, nobody ever forgets.

The sheep are in the meadow, and the cows are in the corn.

Like regular parallel sentences, balanced sentences sometimes come in series:

> The tension in this city is not between white people and Negro people. The tension is, at bottom, between justice and injustice, between the forces of light and the forces of darkness. And if there is a victory, it will be a victory not merely for fifty thousand Negroes, but a victory for justice and the forces of light.

> Martin Luther King, Jr., "Pilgrimage
> to Nonviolence"

Balance works especially well for pitting contrasting or clashing ideas against each other. It sharpens the difference between them while achieving compactness and lending an air of insight to what is said.

EXERCISE ▧   **Identify each sentence as nonparallel, parallel, or balanced; then rewrite each nonparallel sentence to make it parallel.**

1. Professor Bartlett enjoys helping students, counseling advisees, and participation in faculty meetings.
2. I can still see Aunt Alva striding into the corral, cornering a cow against a fencepost, try to balance herself on a one-legged milking stool, and butt her head into the cow's belly.
3. The city plans on building a new fishing pier and on dredging the channel of the river.
4. Elton plans on vacationing in New York, but Noreen wants to raft down the Colorado River.
5. Being half drunk and because he was already late for work, Tom called his boss and said he was too ill to come in that day.
6. The novel's chief character peers through a tangle of long hair, slouches along in a shambling gait, and gets into trouble constantly.
7. You can take the boy out of the country, but you can't take the country out of the boy.
8. Joe's problem is not that he earns too little money but spending it foolishly.
9. The room was dark, gloomy, and everything was dusty.
10. The apparition glided through the wall, across the room, and up the fireplace chimney.

EXERCISE ANSWERS
  1. Nonparallel.   Professor Bartlett enjoys helping students, counseling advisees, and participating in faculty meetings.
  2. Nonparallel. I can still see Aunt Alva striding into the corral, cornering a cow against a fencepost, trying to balance herself on a one-legged milking stool, and butting her head into the cow's belly.
  3. Parallel.
  4. Balanced.
  5. Nonparallel. Because he was half-drunk and because he was already late for work, Tom called his boss and said he was too ill to come in that day.
  6. Parallel.
  7. Balanced.
  8. Nonparallel. Joe's problem is not that he earns too little money but that he spends it foolishly. OR Joe's problem is not earning too little money but spending it foolishly.
  9. Nonparallel. The room was dark, gloomy, and dusty.
10. Parallel.

Choosing the Right Verb Voice

A sentence's verb voice derives from the relationship between the subject and the action. A sentence in the *active voice* has a subject that does something plus a verb that shows action.

The boy hit the target.

The girl painted the garage.

This pattern keeps the key information in the key part of the sentence, making it strong and vigorous and giving the reader a close-up look at the action.

The *passive voice* reverses the subject–action relationship by having the subject receive, rather than perform, the action. It is built around a form of the verb *to be*; for example, *is, are, was, were*. Some sentences identify the actor by using a prepositional phrase; others don't mention the actor at all.

The target was hit by the boy. *(actor identified)*

The federal debt limit is to be increased. *(actor unidentified)*

Demoting or banishing the actor dilutes the force of the sentence, puts greater distance between the action and the reader, and almost always adds extra words to the message.

Most writers who overuse the passive voice simply don't realize its effects on their writing. Read the following paragraph, written mainly in the passive voice.

Graft becomes possible when gifts are given to police officers or favors are done for them by persons who expect preferential treatment in return. Gifts of many kinds may be received by officers. Often free meals are given to them by the owners of restaurants on their beats. During the Christmas season, they may be given liquor, food, or theater tickets by merchants. If favored treatment is not received by the donors, no great harm is done. But if traffic offenses, safety code violations, and other infractions are overlooked by the officers, corruption results. When such corruption is exposed by the newspapers, faith is lost in law enforcement agencies.

This impersonal, wordy passage plods across the page and therefore lacks any real, persuasive impact. Now note the livelier, more forceful tone of this rewritten version.

Graft becomes possible when police officers accept gifts or favors from persons who expect preferential treatment in return. Officers may receive gifts of many kinds. Restaurant owners often provide free meals for officers on the beat. During the Christmas season, merchants may give them liquor, food, or theater tickets. If donors do not receive favored treatment, no great harm is done. But if officers overlook traffic offenses, safety code violations, and other infractions, corruption results. When the newspapers expose such corruption, citizens lose faith in law enforcement agencies.

Don't misunderstand: the passive voice does have its uses. It can mask identities—or at least try to. A child may try to dodge responsibility by saying "Mother, while you were out, the living room lamp got broken." Less manipulatively, reporters may use it to conceal the identity of a source.

Technical and scientific writing customarily uses the passive voice to explain processes.

```
In the production of steel, iron ore is first

converted into pig iron by combining it with limestone and

coke and then heating the mixture in a blast furnace. Pig
```

iron, however, contains too many impurities to be useful to industry, and as a result must be refined and converted to steel. In the refining process, manganese, silicon, and aluminum are heated with the pig iron in order to degas it, that is, to remove excess oxygen and impurities from it. The manganese, silicon, and aluminum are vaporized while the iron remains in the liquid state and the impurities are carried away by the vapors. Once this step has been completed, the molten steel is poured into ingots and allowed to cool. The steel is now ready for further processing.

Greg Langford

Putting such writing in the passive voice provides a desirable objective tone and puts the emphasis where it's most important: on the action, not the actor.

On occasion, everyday writing also uses the passive voice.

The garbage is collected once a week, on Monday.

These caves were formed about 10 million years ago.

In the first case, there's no need to tell who collects the garbage; obviously, garbage collectors do. In the second, the writer may not know what caused the formation, and saying "Something formed these caves about 10 million years ago" would sound ridiculous. In both situations, the action, not the actor, is paramount.

Unless special circumstances call for the passive voice, however, use the active voice.

EXERCISE ■ **After determining whether each sentence below is in active or passive voice, rewrite the passive sentences as active ones.**

1. Mary's parents gave her a sports car for her sixteenth birthday.
2. Fires were left burning by negligent campers.
3. The new ice arena will be opened by the city in about two weeks.
4. Harry left the open toolbox out in the rain.
5. Corn was introduced to the Pilgrims by friendly American Indians.
6. Maude took a trip to Sante Fe, New Mexico.
7. We have just installed a new computer in our main office.
8. The club president awarded Tompkins the Order of the Golden Mace.

EXERCISE ANSWERS

1. Active.
2. Passive. Negligent campers left fires burning.
3. Passive. The city will open the new ice arena in about two weeks.
4. Active.
5. Passive. Friendly American Indians introduced the pilgrims to corn.
6. Active.
7. Active.
8. Active.

9. Passive. As they floated down the river, the missionaries heard the sound of war drums.
10. Passive. Some members of the legislature objected to the ratification of the proposed amendment.

9. The sound of war drums was heard by the missionaries as they floated down the river.
10. Objections were raised by some members of the legislature to the ratification of the proposed amendment.

Using Fragments

A fragment is a part of a sentence that is capitalized and punctuated as if it were a complete sentence.

Although fragments are seldom used in formal prose, they form the backbone of most conversations. Here's how a typical bit of dialogue might go:

"Where are you going tonight?" *(sentence)*
"To Woodland Mall." *(fragment)*
"What for?" *(fragment)*
"To buy some shoes." *(fragment)*
"Alone?" *(fragment)*
"No, with Maisie Perkins." *(fragment)*
"Can I come too?" *(sentence)*
"Sure." *(fragment)*

As with most conversations, the sprinkling of complete sentences makes the fragments clear.

Writers of nonfiction use fragments to create special effects. In the following passage, the fragment emphasizes the importance of the question it asks and varies the pace of the writing:

> Before kidney transplants, people had an ethical unease about renal dialysis—the artificial kidney machine. Unquestionably it was a great technical advance making it possible to treat kidney dysfunctions from which thousands die. But the machine was, and is, expensive and involves intensive care of the patient by doctors and nurses. For whom the machine? In the United States the dilemma was evaded but not solved by having lay panels, like juries, making life-or-death choices. In Britain, where the National Health Service entitles everyone, rich or poor, to have access to any necessary treatment, the responsibility rests on the medical staff. It was (and still is) a difficult decision.
>
> Lord Ritchie-Calder, "The Doctor's Dilemma"

Once in a while, as in the following examples, a writer will use a whole series of fragments. In the Ciardi selection, the fragments heighten the ironic effect. In the other one, they create a kaleidoscopic effect that mirrors the kaleidoscopic impressions offered by the Jazz Age itself.

> Or look at any of the women's magazines. There, as Bernard DeVoto once pointed out, advertising begins as poetry in the front pages and ends as pharmacopoeia and therapy in the back pages. The poetry of the front matter is the dream of perfect beauty that must be hers. These, the flawless teeth. This, the baby skin that

must be hers. This, the perfumed breath she must exhale. This, the sixteen-year-old figure she must display at forty, at fifty, at sixty, and forever.

John Ciardi, "What Is Happiness?"

The Jazz Age offers a kaleidoscope of shifting impressions. Of novelties quickly embraced and quickly discarded. Of flappers flaunting bobbed hair and short skirts. Of hip flasks and bootleg whisky, fast cars and coonskin coats, jazz and dancing till dawn. And overall a sense of futility, an uneasy conviction that all the gods were dead.

Elliott L. Smith and Andrew W. Hart, *The Short Story: A Contemporary Looking Glass*

Before using any fragment in your own writing, think carefully about your intended effect and explore other ways of achieving it. Unless only a fragment will serve your needs, don't use one; fragments are likely to be viewed as unintentional—and thus errors—in the work of inexperienced writers.

EXERCISE ■   Each of the following passages includes one or more fragments. Identify each and explain its function.

1.   Anthropologists came to Indian country only after the tribes had agreed to live on reservations and had given up their warlike ways. Had the tribes been given a choice of fighting the cavalry or the anthropologists, there is little doubt as to whom they would have chosen. In a crisis situation, men always attack the biggest threat to their existence. A warrior killed in battle could always go to the happy hunting grounds. But where does an Indian laid low by an anthro go? To the library?

Vine Deloria, Jr., "Custer Died for Your Sins"

2.   He [Richard Wagner] wrote operas; and no sooner did he have the synopsis of a story, but he would invite—or rather summon—a crowd of his friends to his house and read it aloud to them. Not for criticism. For applause. When the complete poem was written, the friends had to come again, and hear *that* read aloud. Then he would publish the poem, sometimes years before the music that went with it was written. He played the piano like a composer, in the worst sense of what that implies, and he would sit down at the piano before parties that included some of the finest pianists of his time, and play for them, by the hour, his own music, needless to say. He had a composer's voice. And he would invite eminent vocalists to his house, and sing them his operas, taking all the parts.

Deems Taylor, "The Monster"

BEYOND THE SINGLE SENTENCE

What makes a team successful? Skilled players, to be sure, but teamwork as well. Most sentences are part of a team; and unless they work in harmony, the composition will suffer, however good each of them may be.

Harmony—the rhythmic interplay of sentences—demands, first of all, sentences of different lengths. If all your sentences drag on and on, your reader may bog down and lose the train of thought. If all are clipped, the ideas may seem simplistic, and the sentences will jerk along like a car with a misfiring engine. And if all of them are middling long, their plodding, monotonous pace may bring boredom and inattention.

Content sets the pattern of sentence lengths, and often your ideas will lead naturally to the proper mix of long and short sentences. But don't count on it. Chances are, you will need to make adjustments. Once you have finished a draft of your paper, read it over, see how its rhythms strike your inner ear, and put check marks by stretches that "sound" wrong. For instance, you might need to condense a set of jolting primer-book sentences into one or two sentences that present their ideas in a series:

Original Version

Members of the Unification Church actively recruit converts. They do it in shopping malls. College campuses are also recruiting sites. They talk about the benefits of world unity and sell books as well as records. Donations are also solicited. Listeners receive invitations to a dinner. There the guests learn more about the sect.

Revised Version

Members of the Unification Church recruit converts in such places as shopping malls and college campuses. They talk about the benefits of world unity, sell books and records, ask for donations, and invite listeners to a dinner to learn more about the sect.

If a key point is submerged in a long sentence, highlight it as a separate thought, thereby giving it the recognition it deserves. Here is an example:

Original Version

Employers find mature women to be valuable members of their organizations. They are conscientious, have excellent attendance records, and stay calm when things go awry, *but unfortunately many employers exploit them.* Despite their desirable qualities, most remain mired in clerical, sales, and elementary teaching positions. On the average they earn two-thirds as much as men.

Revised Version

Employers find mature women to be valuable members of their organizations. They are conscientious, have excellent attendance records, and stay calm when things go awry. *Unfortunately, though, many employers exploit them.* Despite their desirable qualities, most remain mired in clerical, sales, and elementary teaching positions. On the average they earn two-thirds as much as men.

In the following paragraph, the sentences differ considerably in length.

> To protest that some fairly improbable people, some people who could not possibly respect themselves, seem to sleep easily enough is to miss the point entirely, as surely as those people miss it who think that self-respect has necessarily to do with not having safety pins in one's underwear. There is a common superstition that "self-respect" is a kind of charm against snakes, something that keeps those who have it locked in some unblighted Eden, out of strange beds, ambivalent conversations, and trouble in general. It does not at all. It has nothing to do with the face of things, but concerns instead a separate peace, a private reconciliation.
>
> Joan Didion, "On Self-Respect"

Much of the appealing rhythm of this passage stems from varied sentence length. The first two rather long sentences (49 and 36 words) are followed by the very brief "It does not at all," which gains emphasis by its position. The last sentence adds variety by means of its moderate length (19 words), quite apart from its interesting observation on the real nature of self-respect.

Look to the structures of your sentences as well as their length. Do they resemble a streetful of row houses built from the same blueprint? If they are all simple, with few modifiers, your readers may underrate the importance of your message. To correct row-house sentences, draw upon the patterns you learned about earlier in this chapter. Try inverting sentence order or positioning modifiers at different points. Combine sentences. Turn a statement into a question. Build from several blueprints. Try anything as long as the structures go together and you don't warp meanings.

The following example illustrates how sentence combining adds smoothness and interest to a piece of writing.

Original Version

Before deaf children can speak, they must learn the speech sounds of the English language. This is a process that requires them to practice breath control, to mouth vowels, and to study the speech positions of the mouth and tongue for many hours. A speech specialist helped my brother do these things. The specialist started with him before he was two years old. She built up his vocabulary by teaching him a series of related words. Each of these words identified something in his environment. My brother proved to be an apt student. He soon learned to talk.

Revised Version

Before deaf children can speak, they must learn the speech sounds of the English language, a process that requires them to practice breath control, mouth vowels, and study the speech positions of the mouth and tongue for many hours. A speech specialist helped my brother do these things. Starting before he was two years old, she built up his vocabulary by teaching him a series of related words, each identified with something in his environment. My brother proved to be an apt student and soon learned to talk.

EXERCISE ANSWERS

1. Andrew Carnegie came to America from Scotland. Working as a factory hand, a telegrapher, and a railway clerk, he invested his savings from these jobs in oil and later in the largest steel works in the country. Historians do not agree in their assessment of Carnegie, some considering him a cruel taskmaster and others a benevolent benefactor. Regardless of how he is viewed, however, his contributions to American society, particularly the libraries he established all across the country and his efforts in promoting peace, cannot be denied. Good or bad, he ranks as one of our country's most noteworthy nineteenth-century immigrants.

2. She went to the seashore to hunt for seashells. Whenever she found one, she picked it up and placed it in the basket she carried with her. As soon as she had a whole basketful of shells, she hurried home. Dumping her burden on a dinette table, she grabbed her jeweler's tools and began piercing holes in each of the shells. Then, when all the shells were pierced, she strung them on small gold and silver chains. Eventually she had twenty small necklaces, nineteen of which she was able to sell for $10 apiece. With the $175 profit she netted, she went off to the shore again. This time she was able to stay for a week.

EXERCISE ■   Revise the following passages to improve their style.

1.   Andrew Carnegie came to America from Scotland. He worked as a factory hand, a telegrapher, and a railway clerk to support himself. His savings from these jobs were invested in oil and later in the largest steel works in the country. Historians do not agree in their assessments of Carnegie. Some have considered him as a cruel taskmaster and others as a benevolent benefactor. His contributions to American society, however, cannot be denied. He established public libraries all across the country and spent much time in promoting peace. Good or bad, he ranks as one of our most noteworthy nineteenth-century immigrants.

2.   She went to the seashore. She found some seashells. She picked up the seashells. She put the seashells into a basket. She had a whole basketful of seashells. She went home with the basket. She took the shells out of the basket. She put the shells on a dinette table. She brought jeweler's tools to the table. She pierced holes in the shells. She strung the shells on small chains. The chains were gold and silver. She made twenty necklaces. The selling price of the necklaces was $10 apiece. She earned $175 profit. She used her profits to go to the shore again. She could afford to stay for a week this time.

■ Chapter 16

Diction,
Tone,
Style

PERSPECTIVE

While helping students improve their writing style, we should be wary of laying down excessively absolute rules such as "Never start a sentence with 'and,' 'but,' or 'because' " and "Always keep sentences short." Such rules must often be violated if writing is to be effective. Instead, we might well guide students to more effective choices in diction, tone, and style while helping them understand how to adapt their style to specific writing situations.

Your decisions about words and sentences set the tone and style of your writing. Not only do you choose sentence strategies for correctness and effectiveness, but you also choose words for accuracy and effect. Sentences must be clear and effective; so must words. Diction deals broadly with words, not in isolation but as parts of sentences, paragraphs, and essays. Every time you write and revise, diction comes into play.

PERSPECTIVE

Student vocabularies include words they can (1) understand only in context, (2) understand out of context but not explain, (3) understand and explain, (4) use productively. We should encourage students to learn new words and help them understand the nuances and appropriate contexts of those they already know.

TOWARD CLEAR DICTION

Clear diction stems from choosing words with the right meanings, using abstract and concrete words appropriately, and picking terms that are neither too specific nor too general. Dictionaries and thesauruses can help guide your choices.

TEACHING STRATEGIES

1. Have students review their essays, circle any words that are improperly used, and then make appropriate substitutions.
2. Ask students to record in their journals new words they encounter, along with their contexts and definitions.

Word Meanings

Make sure the words you use mean what you think they do, so that inaccurate words will not distort your message. Sound-alike word pairs often trip up unwary writers. Take "accept" and "except" for example. "Accept" means "to approve." "Except," when used as a verb, means "to exclude or omit." If you want to indicate approval but you say "The following new courses were *excepted* by the committee," think of the obvious consequences. Likewise, consider the distinction between "continual" (frequently or regularly repeated) and "continuous" (uninterrupted). If you illustrate your popularity by saying "My phone rings *continuously,*" your reader will wonder why you never answer it and how you ever sleep. Pages 638–661 present a list of commonly confused words. Study this list, refer to it as you

SUGGESTED INSTRUCTOR READINGS

Halliday, M. A. K. Learning How to Mean: Explorations in the Development of Language. London: Arnold, 1975. A seminal account of how we acquire mastery over language.

Smith, F. Writing and the Writer. New York: Holt, 1982. Provides a good psycholinguistic account of the writing process. Chapters 4 and 5 concentrate on the nature of language and language learning.

revise your writing, and use a dictionary if you have the slightest doubt about meaning.

Concrete and Abstract Words

A concrete word names or describes something that we can perceive with one or more of our five senses. A thing is concrete if we can weigh it, measure it, hold it in our hands, photograph it, taste it, sniff it, add salt to it, drop it, smash into it, or borrow it from a neighbor. If it's abstract, we can't do any of these things. *Bob Seger* is a concrete term, as are *Swiss cheese, petroleum, maple syrup,* and *Dallas.* On the other hand, *jealousy, power, conservatism, size,* and *sadness* are abstract terms.

Concrete words evoke precise, vivid mental images and thus help convey a message. The images that abstract terms create differ from person to person. Try this test: ask several of your friends to describe what comes to mind when they think of *joy, hatred, fear,* or some other abstract term. To illustrate, the word *hatred* might call up images of a person with cold, slitted eyes, a grimly set jaw, and tightly clenched fists. As you can see, concrete terms help us specify what we mean and thus enhance communication.

In the following passage, the concrete diction is italicized:

> To do without self-respect . . . is to be an unwilling *audience of one* to an interminable *documentary* that details one's failings, both real and imagined, with *fresh footage spliced* in for every *screening.* There's *the glass you broke* in anger, there's *the hurt on X's face; watch now, this next scene, the night Y came back from Houston,* see how you muff this one. To live without self-respect is to *lie awake some night,* beyond the reach of *warm milk, phenobarbital,* and *the sleeping hand on the coverlet,* counting up the sins of commission and omission, the trusts betrayed, the promises subtly broken, the gifts irrevocably wasted through sloth or cowardice or carelessness. However long we postpone it, we eventually lie down alone in that notoriously *uncomfortable bed,* the one we make ourselves. Whether or not we sleep in it depends, of course, on whether or not we respect ourselves.
>
> Joan Didion, "On Self-Respect"

Now note how vague and colorless the passage becomes without the concrete diction.

> To do without self-respect is to be continuously aware of your failings, both real and imagined. Incidents stay in your mind long after they are over. To live without self-respect means being bothered by intentional or unintentional failings, trusts betrayed, promises subtly broken, and gifts irrevocably wasted through sloth or cowardice or carelessness. However long we postpone it, we eventually must come to terms with who we are. How we respond to this situation depends, of course, on whether or not we respect ourselves.

EXERCISE ■   Underline the concrete terms in the following passage.

> The fog which rises from the river has no color, no texture, no taste, smell, or sound. It is sheer vision, a vision of purity, a slow, mesmeric, inexorable erasure of the slate. You see fog mushrooming along the river's course. Gently, it obliterates the alders tangled on the banks, wipes out the road. Buildings without foundations, trees without trunks, hang in the air like mirages. Sun may be shining brightly on them, or rain drenching them, or stars twinkling above or among them. Slowly the fog reaches higher and spreads. Ridgepoles, small topmost branches, and your own dooryard vanish. There is nothing left now but shining mist. It is all, and you float on it, utterly alone, as one imagines he might in empty space if flung off by earth; as the mind does, drifting into sleep; as the spirit does, having escaped its mortal frame.
>
> Gladys Hasty Carroll, *Sing Out the Glory*

Specific and General Terms

One concrete term can be more specific or more general than another. As we move from *Lassie* to *collie* to *dog* to *mammal* and finally to *animal*, we become less and less specific, ending with a term that encompasses every animal on earth. With each step we retain only those features that fit the more general term. Thus, when we move from *collie* to *dog,* we leave out everything that makes collies different from terriers, greyhounds, and other breeds.

The more specific the term, the less difference among the images it calls to mind. If you say *animal* to a group of friends, one may think of a dog, another of a horse, and a third of a gorilla. *Collie,* on the other hand, triggers images of a large, long-haired, brown and white dog with a pointed muzzle.

Ask yourself how specific you need to be and then act accordingly. Often, the more specific term will be the better choice. If, for instance, you're describing a wealthy jet-setter, noting that he drives a Ferrari, not just a car, helps establish his character. But if you're writing a narrative about your flight to New Orleans and your experience at Mardi Gras, nothing is gained by naming the make of car you rented and used uneventfully during your stay.

EXERCISE ■

1. Arrange each set of words from less specific to more specific.

    a. man, ex-President, human being, Ronald Reagan, American
    b. Forest Hills Apartments, building, structure, condominium, dwelling

2. Expand each of the following words into a series of four or more that become progressively more specific. Use 1a or 1b as a pattern.

a. activity	c. political party	e. device
b. event	d. institution	f. reading matter

Dictionaries and Thesauruses

Get the dictionary habit and learn to use a thesaurus. They'll increase your vocabulary as well as your skill at using words you already know.

Dictionaries.   Dictionaries are storehouses of word meanings. In general, dictionary makers do not try to dictate how words should be used. Instead, they note current and past meanings. When a word gains or loses a meaning or a newly minted word enjoys wide circulation, dictionary makers observe and record. Most users, however, regard dictionaries as authorities on correctness.

Dictionaries supply much more than word meanings. Figure 16.1, an annotated entry from a college-level dictionary, shows what they can provide. Some dictionary entries include other information as well.

Idioms.   Idioms express meanings that differ from those of the words that make them up. Here are two examples.

I won't *put up with* any foolishness.

The dowager *gave me the cold shoulder.*

Put up with means "tolerate"; *gave me the cold shoulder* means "snubbed me." Looking up the most prominent word of an unfamiliar idiom may lead you to a listing and a definition.

Irregular forms.   Any irregular forms are indicated. In *Webster's New World Dictionary,* the entry for the verb *spring* notes that the other forms are *sprang, sprung,* and *springing.* This information helps you use correct forms in your writing.

Usage labels.   Usage labels help you determine whether a word suits the circumstances of your writing. Here are the most common labels:

Label	*Meaning*
Colloquial	Characteristic of informal writing and speaking; should not be considered nonstandard.
Slang	Informal, newly coined words and expressions, or old expressions with new meanings.
Obsolete	No longer in use but found in past writing.
Archaic	Still finds restricted use; for example, in legal documents; otherwise not appropriate.
Poetic	Used only in poetry and in prose with a poetic tone.
Dialect	Used regularly only in a particular geographical location such as the southeastern United States or the Scottish Lowlands.

Supplementary information.   While focusing primarily on individual words, college-level dictionaries often provide several other kinds of information. These may include a history of the language, lists of standard abbreviations and of colleges and universities, biographical notes on distinguished individuals, and geographical notes on important locations.

Spelling, Syllabication. When a word has variant spellings, some dictionaries indicate a preferred version. Alphabetically close variants appear in the same entry. Dots or hyphens separate syllables and tell where to divide a word written on two lines.

Parts of Speech. Each word is classified by grammatical function. Usually, abbreviations such as *n* (noun), *adj.* (adjective), and *vt.* (transitive verb) identify the part of speech.

Pronunciation. Dictionaries indicate preferred as well as secondary pronunciations. Accent marks (') show which syllable gets the primary stress and which the secondary stress, if any. To determine the pronunciation, follow the key at the bottom of the page.

Etymology. This term means the origin and development of words. Most college dictionaries limit the entry to the root (original) word and an abbreviation for the original language. The abbreviation key near the front of the dictionary identifies the language.

man·i·fold (man′ə fōld′) *adj.* [ME. < OE. *manigfeald:* see MANY & -FOLD] **1.** having many and various forms, features, parts, etc. *[manifold wisdom]* **2.** of many sorts; many and varied; multifarious; used with a plural noun *[manifold duties.]* **3.** being such in many and various ways or for many reasons *[a manifold villain]* **4.** comprising, consisting of, or operating several units or parts of one kind: said of certain devices —*n.* **1.** something that is manifold **2.** a pipe with one inlet and several outlets or with one outlet and several inlets, for connecting with other pipes, as, in an automobile, for conducting exhausts from each cylinder into a single exhaust pipe —*vt.* **1.** to make manifold; multiply **2.** to make more than one copy of *[to manifold* a letter with carbon paper*]* —*SYN.* see MANY — **man′i·fold′er** *n.* —**man′i·fold′ly** *adv.* —**man′i·fold′ness** *n.*

MANIFOLD
(A. manifold; B. cylinders)

Additional Word Formations. These are words derived from the one being defined. Their parts of speech are also indicated. Because they have the same basic meaning as the parent word, definitions are omitted.

Meanings. Meanings are grouped by parts of speech. Sometimes usage is briefly illustrated (*manifold* duties). Some dictionaries list meanings in historical order, others according to frequency of use. The front part of the dictionary specifies the arrangement.

Synonyms. These are words close in meaning to the one being defined. Although no synonym carries exactly the same meaning as the original, the two may be interchangeable in some situations.

3. Parts of speech:
before (adverb, preposition, conjunction)
deep (adjective, noun, adverb)
fair (adjective, adverb, noun)
here (adverb, interjection, noun)
separate (verb, adjective, noun)
then (adverb, adjective, noun)
to (preposition, adverb); also serves as sign of infinitive (*to* run)
where (adverb, conjunction, pronoun)

4. Etymology:
carnival—based on the French *carnaval* or Italian *carnevale*, which in turn are derived from the Middle Latin *carnelevarium*, meaning "to remove meat."
fiduciary—based on the Latin *fiducarius*, which is derived from the Latin *fiducia*, meaning "trust" and "thing held in trust." *Fiducia* in turn derives from the Latin *fidere*, meaning "to trust."
Icarian—based on the Latin *Icarus*, which is derived from the Greek *Ikaros*.
lethargy—based on the Middle English *litarge*, which is derived from the late Latin *lethargia*. This term in turn derives from the Greek *lethargos*, meaning "forgetful."
phenomenon—based on the late Latin *phaenomenon*, which is derived from the Greek *phainesthai*, meaning "to appear." The latter word is related to the Greek *phainein*, meaning "fantasy."
sabotage—based on the French word *sabot*, which designates a kind of wooden shoe. In the past, workers used sabots to damage machines during times of labor strife, hence the present meaning of *sabotage*.
supercilious—based on the Latin *supercilium*, meaning "eyebrow." The term refers to the raised eyebrows of someone who is prideful or contemptuous of others.

Figure 16.1 From *Webster's New World Dictionary of the American Language, Second College Edition.*

While any dictionary is better than none, some clearly outrank others in usefulness. A pocket dictionary is handy but not as comprehensive as a desk dictionary. Excellent desk-sized dictionaries include the following:

The American Heritage Dictionary
Funk and Wagnall's Standard College Dictionary

tawdry—based on the name St. Audrey, with special reference to the cheap laces sold at St. Audrey's fair in Norwich, England.

5. Idiomatic phrases:

beat: beat (about, back, down, it, off, out, up [on], the band, on the beat)

ear: be all ears, bend an ear, fall on deaf ears, lend an ear, keep an ear to the ground, have someone's ear, in one ear and out the other, play (it) by ear, set on its ear, turn a deaf ear

get: get (about, across, after, along, around, around to, at, to, away, away with, back at, behind, by, down [to, from], in, together, it, nowhere, off, on with, out of, over, through, up

high: high and dry, high and low, high and mighty, high on, high, wide, and handsome, on high

jump: jump (a claim, at, bail, in with both feet, off, on [all over], the track, get the jump on)

make: make (a fool of, a meal on, as if, away with, believe, do, it, like, off [with], or break, out, over, up, up to, with, on the make)

put: put (about, across, ahead, aside, away, back, down, forth, forward, in [for], in on, over [on], it there, off, on [to], out, through, up, upon, up with

set: set (about, against, apart, aside, back, down, forth, in, off, out, straight, to, up, upon, all set)

6. Synonyms: attack (assail, assault, beset, bombard, storm);
distress (agony, anguish, suffering);
ghastly (grim, grisly, gruesome, horrible, macabre, terrible);
keep (reserve, retain, withhold);
mercy (charity, clemency, kindness, leniency);

The Random House Dictionary of the English Language
Webster's Ninth New Collegiate Dictionary
Webster's New World Dictionary of the American Language

Unabridged (complete) dictionaries such as *Webster's Third New International Dictionary* and the *Oxford English Dictionary* can be found in college and public libraries. There you'll also find a variety of specialized dictionaries. Your librarian can direct you to dictionaries that list terms in particular fields.

EXERCISE ■   **Use a good desk dictionary to look up the specified information for each of the following lists of words.**

1. Variant spellings:

airplane	aesthete	gray	tornadoes
color	gaily	theater	usable

2. Syllabication and the syllable that receives the main stress:

anacrusis	cadenza	harbinger	misanthrope
baccalaureate	exclamation	ionize	sequester

3. Parts of speech:

before	fair	separate	to
deep	here	then	where

4. Etymology:

carnival	Icarian	phenomenon	supercilious
fiduciary	lethargy	sabotage	tawdry

5. Idiomatic phrases:

beat	get	jump	put
ear	high	make	set

6. Synonyms:

attack	ghastly	mercy	plot
distress	keep	object	range

Thesauruses.   Thesauruses list synonyms for words but omit the other elements in dictionary entries. Figure 16.2 shows a typical entry. Note that the items are grouped according to parts of speech, and some are cross-indexed.

A thesaurus will help you find a word with just the right shade of meaning or a synonym when you want to avoid repetition. But synonyms are never exactly equal, nor are they always interchangeable. To illustrate, *old* means "in existence or use for a long time"; *antiquated* conveys the notion that something is old-fashioned or outdated. Therefore, use the thesaurus along with the dictionary. Only then can you tell which synonym fits a specific sentence.

247. FORMLESSNESS

.1 NOUNS **formlessness, shapelessness**; amorphousness, amorphism, amorphia; **chaos**, confusion, messiness, orderlessness; disorder 62; entropy; anarchy 740.2; **indeterminateness, indefiniteness**, indecisiveness, vagueness, mistiness, haziness, fuzziness, blurriness, unclearness, obscurity.

.2 unlicked cub, diamond in the rough.

.3 VERBS **deform, distort** 249.5; unform, unshape; disorder, jumble, mess up, muddle, confuse; obfuscate, obscure, fog up, blur.

.4 ADJS **formless, shapeless**, featureless, characterless, nondescript, inchoate, lumpen, blobby or baggy [both informal], inform: amorphous, amorphic, amorph(o)-: **chaotic, orderless**, disorderly 62.13, unordered, unorganized, confused, anarchic 740.6; kaleidoscopic; **indeterminate, indefinite**, undefined, indecisive, vague, misty, hazy, fuzzy, blurred or blurry, unclear, obscure.

.5 **unformed, unshaped**, unshapen, unfashioned, unlicked; uncut, unhewn.

object (demur, expostulate, protest, demonstrate);
plot (cabal, conspiracy, intrigue, machination, scheme);
range (compass, gamut, reach, scope, spectrum).

PERSPECTIVE

It's obvious which students excessively and indiscriminately use a thesaurus because their writing lurches from one misapplied word to the next. Students should understand the importance of knowing the actual meaning of words they use and their appropriateness in different contexts.

TEACHING STRATEGY

Provide students with a writing example in which one or more nouns, verbs, or adjectives are excessively repeated. Have them use a thesaurus to correct this problem and achieve greater precision.

Figure 16.2   From *Roget's International Thesaurus*, 4th edition, Robert L. Chapman. Copyright © 1977 by Harper & Row, Publishers, Inc. Reprinted by permission of the Publishers.

Excellent guides to synonyms include the following:

Roget's Thesaurus
Webster's New Dictionary of Synonyms
Modern Guide to Synonyms and Related Words

TOWARD RHETORICAL EFFECT

Rhetorical effect refers to the response that the manner of writing, not the message, generates in the reader. Successful writers create a desired response through the level of their diction and the tone of their writing.

Level of Diction

What level of diction is best? The answer depends upon the writer's audience and purpose. Think about a safety engineer who investigates a serious industrial accident on which she must write two reports, one for the safety director of the

PERSPECTIVE

Most students will eventually write in a variety of circumstances requiring a number of different levels of diction. Therefore we should ensure that they can select and use the proper level for any writing occasion. Students who speak and write nonstandard English pose special problems; fortunately several helpful techniques are available. If students are inexperienced writers who lack fluency, you might allow them to write early journal entries and the first couple of papers in nonstandard English to ease their introduction to writing. It's frequently counterproductive to treat a dialect as wrong, as this often results in a backlash that hinders learning. Explain that because standard English is the dialect used in school and business, students must master it to compete effectively. Sometimes it's helpful to have students mimic the speech of an instructor. Another good approach is to compare the rules that govern standard and nonstandard English. In especially difficult cases, students can benefit from reading a passage in standard English and deliberately stressing the constructions that differ from those in their dialect.

TEACHING STRATEGY

Have students write different versions of one short assignment, directing them at different audiences and using different levels of diction. If they write about some college problem, one version (informal and colloquial) might be directed to friends at home, a second (informal) to their parents, and a third (formal) to the college president.

SUGGESTED INSTRUCTOR READINGS

Davis, A. L., ed. Culture, Class, and Language Variety. Urbana, IL: NCTE, 1972. This collection of essays on a variety of dialects also classifies key problem areas.

Labov, W. The Study of Nonstandard English. Urbana, IL: NCTE, 1970. Documents the rule-governed nature of nonstandard English, argues for allowing some work in student dialects to help them gain fluency, and provides mechanisms for helping students acquire standard English.

company, who represents a technical audience, and another for the local newspaper, read by a general audience. Although the two accounts would deal with the same matter, clearly they would use very different language: specialized and formal in the first case, everyday and more relaxed in the second. In each case, the language would reflect the background of the audience. As you write, always choose language suited to your audience and purpose.

Standard English, the language that educated people use in both formal and informal settings, follows the familiar grammatical rules. Generally, everything you write should be in Standard English. *Nonstandard English* refers to any version of the language that deviates from these rules. Here is an example from Mark Twain's famous novel *The Adventures of Huckleberry Finn.*

> You don't know about me without you have read a book by the name of *The Adventures of Tom Sawyer;* but that ain't no matter. That book was made by Mr. Mark Twain, and he told the truth, mainly. There was things which he stretched, but mainly he told the truth. That is nothing. I never seen anybody but lied one time or another, without it was Aunt Polly, or the widow, or maybe Mary. Aunt Polly—Tom's Aunt Polly, she is—and Mary, and the Widow Douglas is all told about in that book, which is mostly a true book, with some stretchers, as I said before.

Nonstandard English does have a place in writing. Fiction writers use it to narrate the talk of characters who, if real, would speak that way. Journalists use it to report eyewitness reactions to accidents and crimes, and people who compile oral histories use it to record the recollections of people they interview. But avoid it in other writing.

Standard English includes three levels of usage: formal, informal, and technical.

Formal Level.   The formal level, dignified and serious, is suitable for important political, business, and academic occasions. Its vocabulary is marked by many abstract and multisyllabic words, but no slang or contractions. Long sentences and deliberately varied sentence patterns help give it a strong, rhythmic flow. Sentences are often periodic, and many have parallel or balanced structures. (See pages 222 and 223–225.) Overall, formal prose impresses the reader as authoritative, stately, and graceful.

The following excerpts from John F. Kennedy's inaugural address illustrate the formal level.

> Now the trumpet summons us again—not as a call to bear arms, though arms we need; not as a call to battle, though embattled we are; but a call to bear the burden of a long twilight struggle, year in and year out, "rejoicing in hope, patient in tribulation," a struggle against the common enemies of man: tyranny, poverty, disease, and war itself. . . .
>
> In the long history of the world, only a few generations have been granted the role of defending freedom in its hour of maximum danger. I do not shrink from this responsibility; I welcome it. I do not believe that any of us would exchange places with any other people or any other generation. The energy, the faith, the devotion

which we bring to this endeavor will light our country and all who serve it, and the glow from that fire can truly light the world.

And so, my fellow Americans, ask not what your country can do for you; ask what you can do for your country.

John F. Kennedy, "Inaugural Address"

The first sentence opens with parallelism to show contrast: "not as a call to bear arms, though arms we need" and "not as a call to battle, though embattled we are." In the second paragraph, parallelism in the second sentence shows contrast; in the last sentence it does not. Except for the second sentence in paragraph 2, all of the sentences are periodic rather than loose. Thus, not until the end of the opening sentence do we learn the nature of the "long twilight struggle" to which the "trumpet summons us." Time and again Kennedy uses elevated diction— polysyllabic words like *embattled, rejoicing, tribulation, tyranny, poverty, gener- ations, devotion,* and *endeavor,* along with shorter abstract words like *hope, freedom,* and *faith.* These carefully controlled sentence patterns, along with this wording, lend rhythmical dignity to the whole passage.

Informal Level. Informal writing resembles orderly, intelligent conversa- tion. Earmarked by relatively ordinary words, loose sentences, and numerous shorter, less varied sentence structures than formal prose, informal writing may include contractions or even slang, and it is more likely than formal writing to use the pronouns *I, me, my, you,* and *yours.* Casual and familiar rather than dignified and rhythmic, informal writing does not usually call attention to itself. Neverthe- less, the language is precise and effective. Here is an example:

There was a distressing story in the paper a few months ago. I wish I'd clipped it out and saved it. As it is, I can only hope I remember it fairly accurately. There was a group of people who wanted a particular dictionary removed from the shelves of the local library because it contained a lot of obscenity. I think they said there were sixty- five or so dirty words in it. Some poor woman who was acting as a spokesman for the group had a list of offending words, which she started to read aloud at a hearing. She managed to read about twenty of them before she started sobbing uncontrollably and couldn't continue.

Thomas H. Middleton, "The Magic Power
of Words"

Unlike the Kennedy excerpt, this one has relatively uncomplicated sen- tences. Three of them—the fourth, sixth, and seventh—are loose rather than periodic. The passage includes two contractions, *I'd* and *couldn't,* one casual expression, *a lot of,* and the pronoun *I.* Most of the words are very short, and none would be out of place in an ordinary conversation.

Formal–Informal Level. As life has become less formal, informal diction has become increasingly widespread. Today many articles and books, even ones on relatively serious topics, mix informal and formal elements. Here is an example:

. . . faith in sports has been vigorously promoted by industry, the military, government, the media. The value of the arena and the locker room has been imposed on our national life. Coaches and sportswriters are speaking for generals and businessmen, too, when they tell us that a man must be physically and psychologically "tough" to succeed, that he must be clean and punctual and honest, that he must bear pain, bad luck, and defeat without whimpering or making excuses. A man must prove his faith in sports and the American Way by whipping himself into shape, playing by the rules, being part of the team, and putting out all the way. If his faith is strong, he will triumph. It's his own fault if he loses, fails, remains poor.

Robert Lipsyte, *Sports World*

All these sentences except the next to last are loose. Two are quite long, four quite short, and only two have parallel phrases or clauses. Although a few expressions—"bear," "the American Way," "triumph"—echo formal diction, most of the words have an informal ring, and two expressions, "whipping himself into shape" and "putting out all the way," skirt the edges of slang.

Technical Level.   A specialist writing for others in the same field or for sophisticated nonspecialists writes on the technical level, a cousin to the formal level. Technical language uses specialized words that may be unfamiliar to a general audience. Its sentences tend to be long and complex, but unlike formal diction it doesn't lean toward periodic sentences, parallelism, and balance. Read this example from the field of entomology, the study of insects:

> The light organs of fireflies are complex structures, and recent studies using the electron microscope show them to be even more complex than once supposed. Each is composed of three layers: an outer "window," simply a transparent portion of the body wall; the light organ proper; and an inner layer of opaque, whitish cells filled with granules of uric acid, the so-called "reflector." The light organ proper contains large, slablike light cells, each of them filled with large granules and much smaller, dark granules, the latter tending to be concentrated around the numerous air tubes and nerves penetrating the light organ. These smaller granules were once assumed by some persons to be luminous bacteria, but we now know that they are mitochondria, the source of ATP [adenosine triphosphate] and therefore of the energy of light production. The much larger granules that fill most of the light cells are still of unknown function; perhaps they serve as the source of luciferin.
>
> Howard Ensign Evans, *Life on a Little-Known Planet*

Note the specialized vocabulary—*granules, uric acid, mitochondria,* and *luciferin*—as well as the length and complexity of the sentences. Five sentences make up the passage, the shortest having twenty-four words. None is periodic, and none has a parallel or balanced structure.

Every field has *jargon,* specialized terms or inside talk that provides a convenient shorthand for communication among its members. For an audience of biologists, you may write that two organisms have a *symbiotic relationship,* meaning "mutually beneficial"; for psychology majors, you might use *catalepsy* instead of "a temporary loss of consciousness and feeling, often accompanied by muscular rigidity." As a general rule, use technical terms only if your audience will know their meanings. If you must use unfamiliar words when writing for a general audience, define them the first time they appear.

Colloquial Language and Slang. *Colloquial* originally meant "the language of ordinary conversation between people of a particular region." *Slang,* according to *Webster's Ninth New Collegiate Dictionary,* is "an informal nonstandard vocabulary composed typically of coinages, changed words, and extravagant, forced, or facetious figures of speech." These two categories shade into each other, and even authorities sometimes disagree on whether to label a term *colloquial* or *slang.* The word *bender,* meaning "a drinking spree," seems firmly in the colloquial camp, and *bummer,* a term recently used by young people to mean "a bad time," is just as clearly slang. *Break a leg* is theater slang used to wish a performer success. But what about *guy* and *kid*? Once they were slang, but so many people have used them for so long that they have now become colloquial.

Regardless of their labels, colloquial and slang terms are almost never appropriate in formal writing. They sometimes serve a useful purpose in informal writing by creating a special effect or increasing audience appeal. Even so, careful writers use them sparingly. Some readers may not understand some colloquial language, and slang usually becomes dated quickly. The following paragraph uses colloquial and slang expressions successfully:

> . . . When I was just a kid on Eighth Avenue in knee pants . . . [Big Bill] was trying to get himself killed. He was always in some fight with a knife. He was always cutting or trying to cut somebody's throat. He was always getting cut or getting shot. Every Saturday night that he was out there, something happened. If you heard on Sunday morning that somebody had gotten shot or stabbed, you didn't usually ask who did it. You'd ask if Big Bill did it. If he did it, no one paid much attention to it, because he was always doing something like that. They'd say, "Yeah, man. That cat is crazy."
>
> Claude Brown, *Manchild in the Promised Land*

Kid, yeah, and *cat* reflect the speech of Brown's characters and thus add authenticity to his account. Despite the informal diction, Brown uses parallelism in the second, third, and fourth sentences; repetition of "he was always" emphasizes the single-minded self-destructiveness of Big Bill's behavior.

EXERCISE ■   Indicate whether each of the following passages is an example of formal, informal, or technical diction. Support your answers with examples from the passages. Point out slang or colloquial expressions.

1. We may now recapitulate the reasons which have made it necessary to substitute "space-time" for space and time. The old separation of space and time rested upon the belief that there was no ambiguity in saying that two events in distant places happened at the same time; consequently it was thought that we could describe the topography of the universe at a given instant in purely spatial terms. But now that simultaneity has become relative to a particular observer, this is no longer possible. What is, for one observer, a description of the state of the world at a

given instant, is, for another observer, a series of events at various different times, whose relations are not merely spatial but also temporal.

Bertrand Russell, *The ABC of Relativity*

2. This is formal–informal diction. Informal elements include loose sentences that, except for sentences 6 and 9, are relatively short; the use of the pronouns *I*, *me*, and *my*; and the colloquial expressions *yells* and *tough*. Formal elements include parallelism ("I am" in sentences 1–3, and "I have" in sentences 5 and 7–9) and the absence of contractions.

3. This is formal diction. The language is dignified and serious, lacks contractions and slang, and includes many abstract and polysyllabic words. The sentences are long and their patterns varied. Sentence 3 is periodic, sentence 5 interrupted, and the remaining ones are loose. Sentence 3 begins with a series of three parallel elements ("Whatever be," "whether he," "whether he"), while sentences 1, 4, 5, and 6 show parallelism by beginning with "A quibble."

4. This is informal diction. The language is casual, familiar, and frantic rather than stately and serious. The passage includes two original and highly figurative examples of slang—"short-circuiting themselves into hot little twitching death balls" and "charred in-the-flankers"—as well as such less flamboyant slang and colloquial expressions as "gets them queer," "hot-in-the-pants," "God knows where else," and "winds up." The first and third sentences are long, but the remaining five are relatively short. All are loose rather than periodic, and none of them shows parallelism or balanced construction. Although Wolfe uses one term, "ethology," which even a sophisticated audience might not know, he defines it for his readers.

2. In some ways I am an exceptionally privileged woman of thirty-seven. I am in the room of a private, legal abortion hospital, where a surgeon, a friend of many years, is waiting for me in the operating room. I am only five weeks pregnant. Last week I walked out of another hospital, unaborted, because I had suddenly changed my mind. I have a husband who cares for me. He yells because my indecisiveness makes him anxious, but basically he has permitted the final choice to rest in my hands: "It would be very tough, especially for you, and it is absolutely insane, but yes, we could have another baby." I have a mother who cares. I have two young sons, whose small faces are the most moving arguments I have against going through with this abortion. I have a doctorate in psychology, which among other advantages, assures me of the professional courtesy of special passes in hospitals, passes that at this moment enable my husband and my mother to stand in my room at a nonvisiting hour and yell at each other over my head while I sob.

Magda Denes, *In Necessity and Sorrow: Life and Death in an Abortion Hospital*

3. A quibble [pun] is to Shakespeare what luminous vapours are to the traveller; he follows it at all adventures, it is sure to lead him out of his way, and sure to engulf him in the mire. It has some malignant power over his mind, and its fascinations are irresistible. Whatever be the dignity or profundity of his disquisition, whether he be enlarging knowledge or exalting affection, whether he be amusing attention with incidents, or enchaining it in suspense, let but a quibble spring up before him, and he leaves his work unfinished. A quibble is the golden apple for which he will always turn aside from his career, or stoop from his elevation. A quibble, poor and barren as it is, gave him such delight, that he was content to purchase it, by the sacrifice of reason, propriety, and truth. A quibble was to him the fatal Cleopatra for which he lost the world, and was content to lose it.

Samuel Johnson, *Preface to The Plays of William Shakespeare*

4. I have just spent two days with Edward T. Hall, an anthropologist, watching thousands of my fellow New Yorkers short-circuiting themselves into hot little twitching death balls with jolts of their own adrenalin. Dr. Hall says it is overcrowding that does it. Overcrowding gets the adrenalin going, and the adrenalin gets them queer, autistic, sadistic, barren, batty, sloppy, hot-in-the-pants, charred-in-the-flankers, leering, puling, numb—the usual in New York, in other words, and God knows where else. Dr. Hall has the theory that overcrowding has already thrown New York into a state of behavioral sink. Behavioral sink is a term from ethology, which is the study of how animals relate to their environment. Among animals, the sink winds up with a "population collapse" or "massive die-off." O rotten Gotham.

Tom Wolfe, *The Pump House Gang*

Tone

Tone reveals the author's attitude toward the topic and the reader. Every piece of writing has a tone, intended or otherwise, which stems from the meanings and connotations of words, the sentence patterns, and the rhythm of the prose.

Denotation and Connotation.

The denotation of a word is its direct, essential meaning: what the word always stands for. The word *book,* for example, denotes "a set of printed or blank sheets bound together along one edge to form a volume." This definition is objective and neutral: it does not assign any special value or convey any particular attitude toward the word or what the word stands for. Connotations are the values and emotional associations that accompany a word. When the self-made man snorts "book learnin' " at his better-educated junior partner, he assigns a value and an attitude—that he ranks experience higher than the knowledge gained from books.

Some words—*death,* for instance—almost always carry strong connotations or emotional associations. *Webster's Ninth New Collegiate Dictionary* defines it as "a permanent cessation of all vital functions" or "the end of life," but it means much more. All of us have hopes, fears, and memories about death, feelings that color our responses whenever we hear or read the word. Likewise, we have personal responses to words like *sexy, cheap, radical, politician,* and *mother.* Experience, to a considerable extent, conditions how we think and feel about a word. To an Olympic swimmer who has won a gold medal, *swimming* may stir pleasant memories of the victory and the plaudits that went with it. The victim of a near-drowning, however, might react to the same word with something approaching horror.

Nonetheless, cultural connotations are more important than personal ones. Cultural connotations develop the way individual ones do, but on a much larger scale, growing out of the common experiences of many speakers and writers and changing with usage and circumstances.

Context, the parts of a passage that precede and follow a word, also affects connotation. Note, for instance, the different associations of *dog* in these sentences.

That movie is a real dog.

I sure am putting on the dog!

It's a dog-eat-dog world.

Your dog-in-the-manger attitude makes you very unpopular.

Denotation is sometimes called the language of science and technology; connotation, the language of art. But we need both to communicate effectively. Denotation allows us to convey precise, essential meanings. Connotation adds richness, warmth, and bite. Without these qualities our language would be bland and sterile, our lives bleak and mechanical.

Objective Tone.   An objective tone keeps the writer's personality and opinions out of the message. Here is an example.

```
Myopia is a condition of the eye which makes distant vision
blurry. In brief, the myopic individual is nearsighted.
When the eye is normal, rays of light pass through it and
come to focus on the retina, located at the back of the eye.
With the myopic eye, however, the rays of light come
together a little in front of the retina. As a result, the
distant image is not seen clearly. Myopia may result from
the eye itself being too long or the lens of the eye being
too flat. In either case, the rays converge in front of the
retina, and the nearsighted individual is likely to have
difficulty making out distant objects.
```

Janine Neumann

This tone suits a popular explanation of a medical condition. The prose is businesslike and authoritative, the sentence patterns uncomplicated, and nothing reveals the person behind the words.

Other Attitudes.   Sometimes you write merely to inform, sometimes to persuade. In persuasive writing, let your attitude toward your topic set the tone. Decide how subtle, flamboyant, or formal your writing should be and what special tone—satiric, cynical, serious, mock pompous, bawdy, playful—will win your reader over.

Every essay has combined characteristics that give it a special tone. The following excerpts illustrate some of tone's many dimensions.

> Unless you have led an abnormally isolated adulthood, the chances are excellent that you know many people who have at one time or another committed an act, or consorted with someone who was committing an act, for which they might have been sent to prison. We do not consider most of these people, or ourselves, criminals; the act is one thing, the criminality of it quite something else. Homicide, for example, is in our law not a crime; murder only is proscribed. The difference between the two is the intention, or to be more accurate, society's decision about the nature of that intention.

Bruce Jackson, "Who Goes to Prison: Caste and
Careerism in Crime"

Here we have a sophisticated and rather formal tone. Terms like *consorted* and *proscribed,* while exactly suited to Jackson's meaning, do not form part of most people's word kits. The complexity of the first sentence and the varied patterns of the others add to the air of sophistication. The emphatic *quite*, meaning "entirely," is cultivated usage; and along with *society's decision,* it lends the tone a wry touch.

> Cans. Beer cans. Glinting on the verges of a million miles of roadways, lying in scrub, grass, dirt, leaves, sand, mud, but never hidden. Piels, Rheingold, Ballantine, Schaeffer, Schlitz, shining in the sun or picked by moon or the beams of headlights at night; washed by rain or flattened by wheels, but never dulled, never buried, never destroyed. Here is the mark of savages, the testament of wasters, the stain of prosperity.
>
> Who are these men who defile the grassy borders of our roads and lanes, who pollute our ponds, who spoil the purity of our ocean beaches with the empty vessels of their thirst? Who are the men who make these vessels in millions and then say, "Drink and discard"? What society is this that can afford to cast away a million tons of metal and to make a wild and fruitful land a garbage heap?
>
> Marya Mannes, "Wasteland"

Rhythm and word choice contribute equally to the tone of this passage. The excerpt opens with imagistic sentence fragments that create a panoramic word picture of our littered roadways. Then complete sentences and somber commentary follow. Words and patterns are repeated, mixing the dignified language of epic and religion with common derogatory terms—*testament, purity, vessels,* and *fruitful* set against *savages, wasters, defile,* and *garbage heap*—to convey the contradictions Mannes deplores. The rhetorical questions, used instead of accusations, add a sense of loftiness to her outrage, helping create a tone both majestic and disdainful.

> *Erethizon dorsatus,* an antisocial character of the Northern U.S. and Canadian forest, commonly called a porcupine, looks like an uncombed head, has a grumpy personality, fights with his tail, hides his head when he's in trouble, attacks backing up, retreats going ahead, and eats toilet seats as if they were Post Toasties. It's a sad commentary on his personality that people are always trying to do him in.
>
> R. T. Allen, "The Porcupine"

The tone of this passage is affectionately humorous. Allen sets this tone by noting the porcupine's tousled appearance, testy personality, and peculiar habits, such as eating outdoor toilet seats (for their salt content, as Allen later explains). The net effect is to personify porcupines, making them seem like the eccentric reprobate human that others regard with amused toleration.

The final passage begins by referring to a "promissory note": the Constitution and the promise of life, liberty, and the pursuit of happiness spelled out in the Declaration of Independence:

> It is obvious today that America has defaulted on this promissory note insofar as her citizens of color are concerned. Instead of honoring this sacred obligation, America has given the Negro people a bad check; a check which has come back marked "insufficient funds." But we refuse to believe that the bank of justice is bankrupt. We refuse to believe that there are insufficient funds in the great vaults of opportunity in this nation. So we have come to cash this check—a check that will

give us upon demand the riches of freedom and the security of justice. We have also come to this hallowed spot to remind America of the fierce urgency of *now*. This is no time to engage in the luxury of cooling off or to take the tranquilizing drug of gradualism. *Now* is the time to make real the promises of Democracy. *Now* is the time to rise from the dark and desolate valley of segregation to the sunlit path of racial justice. *Now* is the time to open the doors of opportunity to all of God's children. *Now* is the time to lift our nation from the quicksands of racial injustice to the solid rock of brotherhood.

Martin Luther King, Jr., "I Have a Dream"

This writing speaks passionately for freedom and justice. Its most obvious rhetorical strategy is metaphor, first the extended one of the promissory note, then brief separate metaphors that make the same point. The repetition of *now* sharpens the insistent tone. Eloquence comes through parallelism, repetition, and words like *sacred* and *hallowed*, vividness through figures of speech like "vaults of opportunity" and "sunlit path of racial justice." Like George Orwell, Mark Twain, Joseph Conrad, and other masters of tonal effects whose work appears in this book, King uses both rhythm and diction to create a tone that infuses and invigorates his message.

EXERCISE ■   **Characterize the tone of each of the following paragraphs. Point out how word choice, sentence structure, rhythm, and other elements contribute to it.**

EXERCISE ANSWERS

1. This passage is elegiac but undespairing. Eiseley establishes his elegiac tone by first likening the glade in which the drama is played out to a cathedral and by calling the raven "the black bird at the heart of life." This tone is sustained by the strongly rhythmic and repetitious pattern of the sentences ("It was then I saw the judgment. It was the judgment of life against death. I will never see it again so forcefully presented. I will never hear it again in notes so tragically prolonged."). Much of the impact of the passage stems from its allegorical character: like Eiseley's sparrows, all of us exist "under the brooding shadow of the raven" and, again like them, have no choice except to sing in the shadow of death.

2. The tone here is one of deeply felt anger at people who produce the shoddy goods. The anger comes through strongly in the expressions "schlock," "shoddy goods," and, most notable of all, "the sanitary-fill schlock heaps that are the feces of our Gross (and how!) National Product."

1.   When I awoke, dimly aware of some commotion and outcry in the clearing, the light was slanting down through the pines in such a way that the glade was lit like some vast cathedral. I could see the dust motes of wood pollen in the long shaft of light, and there on the extended branch sat an enormous raven with a red and squirming nestling in its beak.

The sound that awoke me was the outraged cries of the nestling's parents, who flew helplessly in circles around the clearing. . . . And he, the murderer, the black bird at the heart of life, sat there, glistening in the common light, formidable, unperturbed, untouchable. The sighing died. It was then I saw the judgment. It was the judgment of life against death. I will never see it again so forcefully presented. I will never hear it again in notes so tragically prolonged. For in the midst of protest, they forgot the violence. There, in that clearing, the crystal note of a song sparrow lifted hesitantly in the hush. And, finally, after painful fluttering, another took the song, and then another, the song passing from one bird to another, doubtfully at first, as though some evil thing was being slowly forgotten. Till suddenly they took heart and sang from many throats joyously together as birds are known to sing. They sang under the brooding shadow of the raven. In simple truth they had forgotten the raven, for they were the singers of life, and not of death.

Loren Eiseley, "The Judgment of the Birds"

2.   America, which leads the world in almost every economic category, leads it above all in the production of schlock. Christmas toys broken before New Year's, wash-n-wear suits that neither wash well nor wear well, appliances that expire a

month after the guarantee, Barbie dolls, frozen pizza—these are but a few of the shoddy goods whose main contribution to our civilization, apart from a momentary satisfaction to the purchaser, is to swell the sanitary-fill schlock heaps that are the feces of our Gross (and how!) National Product.

Robert Claiborne, "Future Schlock"

3. Babe Ruth was ∗∗∗ The Sultan of Swat ∗∗∗
    Babe Ruth was ∗∗∗ THE BAMBINO ∗∗∗
    Babe Ruth was what you came to see!!!!

It was like going to a carnival, with Babe as both the star performer and the side-show attraction. Hell, that's what we called him: "You big ape." He was what a home-run hitter was supposed to look like. Wide, flat nose. Big feet. Little ankles. Belly hanging over his belt. All he had to do was walk on to the field and everybody would applaud. The air became charged with electricity. You just felt that something great was going to happen.

He'd twirl that big 48-ounce bat around in little circles up at the plate as if he were cranking it up for the Biggest Home Run Ever Hit—*you felt that*—and when he'd hit one he would hit it like nobody has hit it before or since. A mile high and a mile out. I can see him now, as I did so many times, just look up, drop the bat and start to trot, the little pitter-patter pigeon-toed, high-bellied trot that seemed to say, I've done it before and I'll do it again, but this one was for you.

Leo Durocher, *Nice Guys Finish Last*

SPECIAL STYLISTIC TECHNIQUES

The style of a piece of writing is its character or personality. Like people, writing can be many things: dull, stuffy, discordant, sedate, lively, flamboyant, eccentric, and so on. Figurative language, puns, and irony can contribute to your own distinctive writing style.

Figurative Language

Figurative language uses concrete words in a nonliteral way to create sharply etched sensory images that catch and hold the reader's attention. Besides energizing the writing, figurative language helps to strengthen the reader's grip on its ideas. Five figurative devices are especially important: simile, metaphor, personification, overstatement, and understatement.

Simile and Metaphor.   A *simile* directly compares two unlike things by the use of *like* or *as*. "Todd is as restless as an aspen leaf in a breeze" and "Her smile flicked on and off like a sunbeam flashing momentarily through a cloudbank" are similes. A *metaphor* also compares unlike things, but indirectly rather than directly. Some metaphors include a linking verb (*is, are, were,* and so on); others do not. "The moon was a wind-tossed bark" and "The curtain of darkness fell over

3. This passage conveys a strong sense of excitement and adulation, aroused in the opening short, pithy sentences with their stars, capitalized words, and exclamation points. Durocher then sustains this tone by invoking the carnival atmosphere of the games in which Ruth played and by his behavior when he got a hit. The language is highly informal—short sentences, slang and colloquialisms, and contractions—and adds to the excitement of the passage.

PERSPECTIVE

While stylistic techniques create more memorable prose, they also convey meaning that cannot be captured in a more literal fashion. Metaphors help us draw connections between apparently dissimilar ideas and establish a link between abstract ideas and our physical contact with the world. Modern physicists who talk of light as a wave or space as curved speak metaphorically. Overstatement and understatement are bound to our fundamental notion of character; the British traditional understatement and emphasis on a "stiff upper lip" are examples. Irony establishes an outlook that distrusts appearances and envisions a world fraught with contradictions.

TEACHING STRATEGIES

1. Have students record the metaphors and similes they use daily. They should discover that, like most of us, they often think in terms of metaphors and similes without deliberately trying to create them.

2. Students sometimes mistakenly believe that metaphors and similes belong exclusively to more literary writing. To correct this impression, have students review scientific and technical writing for examples of metaphors and then determine whether they were employed for stylistic effect or to help present an idea.

3. Students can be spurred to write effective metaphors and similes by completing unfinished statements, then evaluating the results in terms of stylistic effectiveness and the insights provided. For example: Education today is _____. My life _____ (concrete verb) like _____ (concrete but correlated object). Time _____ our days. Love _____ like a _____ in us. His voice _____.

DISCUSSION QUESTIONS

1. The passage has two similes: "like a shallow trough with paper-thin sides" and "like short bristly hairs." They help the reader to visualize unfamiliar things, the curvature of the grass blade and its ridges and valleys, by comparing them to familiar things, a shallow trough and hairs.

2. There are also two metaphors. The first, "a sea of deep, dark green," points out the vast expanse of the field by likening it to a huge body of water. The second, "a dark green spear. . . ." adds vividness to the overall image of the blade.

PERSPECTIVE

Personification comes naturally to us; we all tend to project human qualities onto other objects. Far from a rhetorical flourish, personification is often our first response to an obstinate motor that refuses to turn over or a computer that is too smart for its own good. The trick is for students to master their impulse to personify instead of wildly exaggerating.

the land" are both metaphors. Here is an excerpt that contains similes and metaphors.

> The field is a sea of deep, dark green, a sea made up of millions of small blades of grass blended together as one. Each blade is a dark green spear, broad at the bottom and narrowing to a needle point at the tip. Its full length is arched so that, viewed from one end, it looks like a shallow trough with paper-thin sides. On the inner side of this trough, small ridges and shallow valleys run from base to tip. To a finger rubbed across them, they feel like short, bristly hairs.
>
> Daniel Kinney

DISCUSSION QUESTIONS ■

1. Locate the similes in this passage and explain how they help the reader.
2. Locate the metaphors and point out how each heightens the sensory impact of the writing.

Writers too often snatch hastily at the first similes and metaphors that come to mind and end up strewing their pages with overused and enfeebled specimens. Johnny is "as blind as a bat," Mary runs around "like a chicken with its head cut off"—and the writing slips into trite gear. Other comparisons link items that are too dissimilar. For example, "The wind whistled through the trees like a herd of galloping horses" would only puzzle a reader.

Personification. This is a special sort of metaphor that assigns human qualities or traits to something nonhuman: a plant, an abstraction, a nonliving thing. Here are some examples.

The vine clung stubbornly to the trunk of the tree.

May fortune smile upon you.

The waves lapped sullenly against the base of the cliff.

Each of these sentences assigns its subject a different emotional quality—stubbornness, friendliness, gloom—each figurative rather than literal: vines aren't stubborn, fortune doesn't smile, and waves aren't sullen.

Personification sometimes extends beyond a single sentence. To illustrate, the following passage carries a single image through two paragraphs:

> "I figured when my legislative program passed the Congress," [Lyndon] Johnson said in 1971, "that the Great Society had a real chance to grow into a beautiful woman. And I figured her growth and development would be as natural and inevitable as any small child's. In the first year, as we got the laws on the books, she'd begin to crawl. Then in the second year, as we got more laws on the books, she'd begin to walk, and the year after that, she'd be off and running, all the time growing bigger and healthier and fatter. And when she grew up, I figured she'd be so big and beautiful that the American people couldn't help but fall in love with her, and once they did, they'd want to keep her around forever, making her a permanent part of American life, more permanent than the New Deal.
>
> "But now Nixon has come along and everything I've worked for is ruined. There's a story in the paper every day about him slashing another one of my Great Society programs. I can just see him waking up in the morning, making that victory sign of his and deciding which program to kill. It's a terrible thing for me to sit by and watch someone else starve my Great Society to death. She's getting thinner and thinner and uglier and uglier all the time; now her bones are beginning to stick out and her wrinkles are beginning to show. Soon she'll be so ugly that the American people will refuse to look at her; they'll stick her in a closet to hide her away and there she'll die. And when she dies, I too will die."
>
> Doris Kearns, "Who *Was* Lyndon Baines Johnson?"

Through personification, Johnson expresses affection for his social program, disapproval of Nixon's policies, and sorrow over the coming demise of the "child" he has so carefully nurtured.

Personification works best when it is used in moderation and doesn't make outrageous comparisons. Dishes don't run away with spoons except in nursery rhymes.

Overstatement.   Overstatement, sometimes called hyperbole, deliberately and drastically exaggerates in order to make a point. An example is "Wilfred is the world's biggest fool."

One of the best examples of sustained overstatement is Mark Twain's essay "Fenimore Cooper's Literary Offences." In it, Twain claims, "In one place in *Deerslayer,* and in the restricted space of two-thirds of a page, Cooper has scored 114 offences against literary art out of a possible 115." Twain also asserts, "There have been daring people in the world who claimed that Cooper could write English, but they are all dead now. . . . " Through such exaggerations, Twain mocks the shortcomings of Cooper's novels.

Used sparingly, overstatement is emphatic, adding real force to an event or situation. Writers who consistently exaggerate, however, risk losing their credibility.

Understatement.   Understatement makes an assertion in a humble manner without giving something its due, as when a sportscaster calls a team's 23–2

TEACHING STRATEGIES

1. Have students keep track of when and why they personify and determine whether or not the personifications are appropriate and helpful.
2. Have students examine the Johnson passage to determine why the personification is effective. The key lies in the way the passage plays on our sympathies by drawing a parallel between human life and the life of Johnson's Great Society program, based upon their shared traits of growth and decay.
3. To help students learn to create effective personifications, have them list a number of traits that people might share with education, the night, winter, or a stream, and then construct several personifications, each based upon one of the traits.

**SUGGESTED
INSTRUCTOR READINGS**

Lakoff, G. and M. Johnson. Metaphors We Live By. Chicago: U of Chicago P, 1980. Demonstrates how and why metaphors underlie most of our everyday language.
Ortony, A. ed. Metaphor and Thought. Cambridge, England: Cambridge UP, 1979. Includes some interesting theoretical accounts of the ways we think metaphorically.

TEACHING STRATEGIES

1. Fed a steady diet of media hype which discovers a crisis in even modest events, many students overstate, not for any particular effect but because they don't realize how shrill they sound. Have them read newspapers for examples of overstatements and then discuss the effects on readers.
2. Have students review their own writing for instances of overstatement and tone down any inappropriate examples they find.

3. Have students attempt to turn the following statements into effective overstatements: Students have some mechanical errors in their papers; It can be difficult to register for the class you want; Dorms may be noisy in the evening; Dorm food can occasionally be unappetizing.

TEACHING STRATEGY

Have students attempt to turn the following statements into effective understatements: College can be extremely expensive; This class will be terribly difficult; A serious illness will result in extensive medical bills.

EXERCISE ANSWERS

1. Personification.
2. Metaphor.
3. Overstatement.
4. Simile.
5. Metaphor.
6. Understatement.
7. Overstatement.
8. Personification.
9. Understatement.
10. Simile.

record "pretty fair." By drawing attention to the thing it appears to slight, this soft-spoken approach offers writers an effective strategy. Here is an example:

> To assume that Heidi Mansfield lacks the qualifications for this position is not unwarranted.

Without ever actually calling Mansfield unqualified, the statement suggests that she is. Similarly, when a meat company executive says, "It is not unlikely that beef prices will jump ten cents a pound in the next two months," we might as well count on spending another dime. As these statements show, understatement not infrequently has an ulterior motive.

EXERCISE ■ **Identify the similes, metaphors, personifications, overstatements, or understatements in these sentences.**

1. The old table greedily sucked up the linseed oil.
2. Russia's social and economic system is a giant staircase that leads nowhere.
3. Stanley has the bile of human meanness by the quart in every vein.
4. Their music sounds like the drumming of an infant's fists against the sides of a crib.
5. The foundations of our divorce are as strong as ever.
6. It is not unlike Muriel to be late.
7. You're the world's biggest liar!
8. "Fashion, though folly's child, and guide of fools, Rules e'en the wisest, and in learning rules."
9. Einstein's theories have had some impact on modern science.
10. I'm as tired as a horse at sunset.

TEACHING STRATEGIES

1. Have the class bring in examples of puns they spot in one week's reading and discuss whether they are or are not effective.

2. Have students see if they can generate puns to enliven the following titles: "Chickens stolen from farm," "Rotten fish smell up downtown area," "Heat wave to continue for the next week."

TEACHING STRATEGIES

1. Because students often fail to recognize that they use irony, you might provide them with relevant examples. "Oh, it was a wonderful date. He fascinated

Puns. A pun is a play on words. Generally, the same word has a double-barreled meaning, as in "The president of the Rockville Gun Club has blasted the state's plans to shorten the deer-hunting season." But on occasion, a pun juggles two words with identical or similar sounds but different meanings. The title "The Mourning After" for a paper on hangover remedies suggests that time when the effects of overdrinking come to a head. Don't use a pun that seems forced or is in bad taste. Few readers would probably object to "One current problem for Americans is the rising cost of electrical energy." But many would groan at "The professional tennis racket is one that people should avoid." And nearly all would rightly feel distaste if a paper about capital punishment talked about condemned prisoners "dying for news that the governor had commuted their sentences."

Irony. Irony occurs when a writer intentionally states one thing but actually means something different or even opposite. A certain point is thus highlighted. The sportswriter who refers to the "ideal conditions" for a tennis tournament when rain has drenched the courts and forced cancellation of matches speaks ironically. Here is a longer example of the same sort of irony:

The baron, though a small man, had a large soul, and it swelled with satisfaction at the consciousness of being the greatest man in the little world about him. He loved to tell long stories about the dark old warriors whose portraits looked grimly down from the walls around, and he found no listeners equal to those that fed at his expense. He was much given to the marvellous, and a firm believer in all those supernatural tales with which every mountain and valley in Germany abounds. The faith of his guests exceeded even his own; they listened to every tale of wonder with open eyes and mouths, and never failed to be astonished, even though repeated for the hundredth time. Thus lived the Baron Von Landshort, the oracle of his table, the absolute monarch of his little territory, and happy, above all things, in the persuasion that he was the wisest man of the age.

Washington Irving, "The Spectre Bridegroom"

Irving never directly states the baron's shortcomings. Rather, suggestive details such as the swelling of the baron's soul, his belief in the supernatural, and his deception by the sponging guests portray one who, far from being "the wisest man of the age," is pompous, superstitious, and gullible.

ELIMINATING FLAWED DICTION

These flaws include wordiness, euphemisms, clichés, mixed metaphors, and sexist language. As you revise, stay alert for these culprits and eliminate any that you find.

Wordiness

Wordiness is verbal obesity, and like physical obesity it has more than one cause. Some writers overnourish their prose to make it sound more impressive, some to pad an assignment, and some simply because they don't realize they're doing it. Whatever the reason, the results are the same: ponderous, slow-moving papers that lack punch. To inject vigor, strip your prose down to fighting weight by cutting out every word that doesn't serve a purpose. If five words are doing the work of one, drop four.

The two major forms of wordiness, deadwood and gobbledygook, often occur together. *Deadwood,* which does nothing but take up space and clutter the writing, is bracketed in the following sentence:

Responsible parents [of today] neither allow their children [to have] absolute freedom [to do as they please] nor severely restrict their children's activities.

Now read the sentence without the deadwood.

Responsible parents neither allow their children absolute freedom nor severely restrict their children's activities.

Careful revision has increased the clarity and reduced the words from twenty-three to fourteen.

me hour after hour with a detailed account of his high school exploits. He was so interesting I never had to say a thing. And what a big spender; he treated me to a meal at McDonald's." Have students record examples of irony they have heard or inadvertently produced themselves.
2. Have students attempt to respond to the following prompts with effective irony: A teacher who never gives a grade higher than a C; A student who attempts to get better grades by sleeping more and studying less; A summer day that never gets above 50°; A fairly unimportant member of the administration of a small college who sees himself as the key to the future.

PERSPECTIVE
Sometimes only a fine line separates excessive wordiness and essential elaboration. Although students need to cut excess verbiage, encourage them to supply helpful qualifications and useful technical terms. In some kinds of writing, especially legal documents, writers must follow established precedent. As they look for deadwood to chop, students should also check for places where they need to supply qualifications and modifiers to make their writing clearer.

TEACHING STRATEGIES
1. Have students review magazine articles and their textbooks for examples of seeming verbosity and then determine if cutting is needed.
2. Have students review their own writing for deadwood and gobbledygook which can be cut.

Gobbledygook consists of long, abstract, or technical words that help create unnecessarily long and complex sentences. Some people who write it mistakenly believe it "dignifies" their thoughts. Others want to conceal their meanings by clouding their statements. And some naively think that long words are better than short ones. All of these writers use gobbledygook, but none of their readers appreciate it. Here are some samples of gobbledygook followed by revised versions in plain English:

Original Version	*Revised Version*
The fish exhibited a 100 percent mortality response.	All of the fish died.
We have been made cognizant of the fact that the experiment will be terminated in the near future.	We have learned that the experiment will end soon.

Euphemisms

Euphemisms take the sting out of something unpleasant or add stature to something humble. Familiar expressions include *pass away* for *die, preowned* for *used, sanitation engineer* for *garbage collector,* and *exceptional* for *retarded* or *physically handicapped.*

In most cases, the writer simply intends to cushion reality. But euphemisms also have grisly uses. Mobsters don't *beat up* merchants who refuse *protection* (itself a euphemism); they *lean on* them. Hitler didn't talk about *exterminating the Jews* but about *the final solution to the Jewish problem.* These euphemisms don't just blur reality; they blot out images of horror. Of merchants with broken limbs and bloodied faces. Of cattle cars crammed with men, women, and children enroute to death camps. Of barbed wire and gas ovens and starved corpses in the millions.

Any euphemism, however well-intentioned, probably obscures an issue. On occasion you may need one in order to protect the sensitive reader, but usually you will serve readers best by using direct expressions that present reality, not a tidied-up version.

Clichés and Mixed Metaphors

Clichés. Clichés are expressions that have become flat and stale from overuse. Rather than responding to experience with their own perceptions, writers sometimes resort to oft-repeated words or phrases that stem from patterned thinking. Dullness follows. Daily conversation abounds with stale, trite expressions because talk is unplanned, but writing allows you time to find invigorating and effective language. Your individual response is what draws the reader's interest, and only fresh thinking will produce that response. The following list of clichés barely "scratches the surface."

acid test	easier said than done	no sooner said than
almighty dollar	fast and furious	done
apple of his eye	goes without saying	perfect specimen
beat a hasty retreat	green with envy	picture of health
better late than never	hit the nail on the	put in an appearance
black sheep	head	rears its ugly head
blind as a bat	honesty is the best	set the world on fire
budding genius	policy	sick as a dog
burn the midnight oil	innocent as a lamb	slowly but surely
chip off the old block	in the last analysis	strike while the iron is
clear as a bell	last but not least	hot
conspicuous by its	make hay while the	when my ship comes in
absence	sun shines	wine, women, and song
cool as a cucumber	nipped in the bud	worse for wear
each and every		

Mixed Metaphors. Clichéd writing often suffers as well from mixed metaphors—inappropriate combinations that startle or amuse the reader. How would you respond if you came across this example?

> When he opened that can of worms, he bit off more than he could chew.

Can you visualize someone chewing a mouthful of worms? The point is obvious.

Sexist Language

Sexist language assigns roles to people according to sex. It is offensive because it demeans women or reinforces erroneous beliefs that limit the roles they can play. Deliberate or accidental, sexist language must be eliminated from your writing. These guidelines will help you do just that.

1. Don't unnecessarily mention a woman's appearance, husband, or family.

Sexist   The attractive new loan officer at the Godfather Finance Company is a real hit with customers.

Sexist   Monica Helmond, wife of local restauranteur Samuel Helmond, won election to the Beal City Board of Education.

Sexist   After eight years of attending college part time, Angelica Denham, a three-time grandmother, was awarded a Bachelor of Science degree.

Nonsexist   The efficient new loan officer at the Godfather Finance Company is a real hit with the customers.

Nonsexist   Monica Helmond, principal of Oakwood Growth Enterprise, won election to the Beal City Board of Education.

PERSPECTIVE

However one regards the recent proscriptions against sexist language, it is essential to recognize that all government agencies, most businesses, and most academic publications prohibit it. Students should learn how to avoid inadvertent sexism without producing unacceptably clumsy writing.

TEACHING STRATEGY

Have students review their own writing to identify sexist language, then make the appropriate revisions.

Nonsexist   After eight years of attending college part time, Angelica Denham was awarded a Bachelor of Science degree.

Note how, in each case, the sentence has been rewritten to include only relevant information.

2. Use the pronouns *he, him, his,* and *himself* only when referring to antecedents that are clearly masculine.

Sexist   Each tourist must carry *his* passport with *him* at all times.

Sexist   If anyone doesn't understand the instructions, *he* should see me right away.

Correct this type of error by substituting plural antecedents and pronouns for the singular ones or by rewriting the sentence to eliminate the pronouns.

Nonsexist   Tourists must carry *their* passports with *them* at all times.

Nonsexist   Anyone who doesn't understand the instructions should see me right away.

For additional information on eliminating this kind of sexist language, see pages 577–579.

3. Don't use occupational labels that imply the positions are held only by men.

Sexist	*Nonsexist*
chairman	chair
draftsman	drafter
fireman	fire fighter
policeman	police officer
postman	letter carrier
weatherman	weather reporter

A word of caution here. To avoid sexism, some writers substitute the suffix *-person* for *-man* in many job titles (such as *handyperson* for someone who does odd jobs). Such attempts, however, often create awkward expressions that you should avoid.

EXERCISE ■   The following sentences are flawed by wordiness, euphemisms, clichés, mixed metaphors, and sexist language. When you have identified the faults, revise the sentences.

1. The American eagle will never, in the face of foreign threats, pull in its horns or draw back into its shell.
2. Last summer, I was engaged in the repair of automobiles.
3. You're looking as bright as a button this morning.
4. My mother was called to her heavenly reward last winter.

5. Any student wishing to attend summer school must pay his tuition one week before registration day.
6. My brother is in the process of pursuing a curriculum of industrial chemistry.
7. The ball's in your court, and if you strike out, don't expect me to pick up the pieces.
8. The blonde, sultry voiced clerk quickly filled the order.
9. Winning first prize for her essay was a real feather in Peggy's cap.
10. Our company plans to confer retirement on 200 employees by year's end.

---

5. Sexist language. Any students wishing to attend summer school must pay their tuition one week before registration day.

6. Wordiness. My brother is majoring in industrial chemistry.

7. Mixed metaphor. The ball is in your court (the matter is in your hands), and if you fail to handle things properly don't expect any help from me.

8. Sexist language. The efficient clerk quickly filled the order.

9. Cliché. Winning first prize for her essay was a real accomplishment for Peggy.

10. Wordiness. Our company plans to retire 200 employees by year's end.

■ Chapter 17

The Essay Examination

Instructors use essay examinations to gauge your grasp of ideas, noting how well you apply, analyze, challenge, compare, or otherwise handle them. Facts and figures, on the other hand, are more often tested by objective examinations. Writing essay answers under pressure and with minimal time to rethink and revise differs from writing at home. Instructors expect reasonably complete and coherent answers but not models of style or neatness. They do expect legibility. An effective presentation increases your chances for success; the skills learned in composition class can help you achieve it. A plan, a thesis, specific support, staying on track, and the pointers presented in this chapter—all are grade boosters.

STUDYING FOR THE EXAMINATION

Here are some pointers for studying:

1. Allow adequate preparation time. For a comprehensive test, start reviewing several days in advance. For one that covers a small segment of the course, a day or two should be enough.
2. Reread the key points you've marked in your class notes and textbook. Use them to develop a set of basic concepts.
3. Make up a set of sample questions related to these concepts and do some free-writing to answer them. Even if none of the questions appears on the test, your efforts will ease pretest jitters and supply insights that apply to other questions.
4. Answer your questions by drawing upon your concepts and supplying details from your notes and textbook.

TYPES OF TEST QUESTIONS

Some instructors favor narrow, highly focused test questions with detailed answering instructions. Others like broad items, perhaps with simple directions such as "write for twenty minutes." The sample questions below range from very broad to very narrow. Note how when answering them you can often use the writing strategies discussed in Chapters 4–12.

1. Analyze the influences of the industrial revolution on European society.
2. Discuss the most important causes of the Spanish–American War.
3. Compare and contrast the David statues of Michelangelo and Bernini.
4. Select three different camera shots used in the movie *Batman*. Identify at least one scene that illustrates each shot; then explain how each shot functions by describing the relationship between the shot and the action or dialogue.
5. Discuss the stock market crash of October 1987. Consider the major factors involved, such as the collapse of the Japanese bond market, the decline in the value of the dollar, and the wide spread between interest rates and stock yields, and how the different factors interacted. Use a thesis statement that signals the points you will discuss.

A highly focused question such as item 5 suggests how to organize and develop the essay. If you know the answer, you can begin writing quickly. In contrast, item 1 forces you to focus and narrow the subject before you respond. Answering this type of item requires careful planning.

PREPARING TO WRITE

You can't get from Pocatello to Poughkeepsie without knowing and following an appropriate route. The same principle applies to exam writing. Often students fail to read general directions or to answer what is asked. Low grades follow. To avoid penalizing yourself, scan the test items, noting how many must be answered and which ones, if any, are optional. When you have a choice, select the questions you can answer most thoroughly. Pay attention to any suggestions or requirements concerning length (one paragraph, two pages) or relative weight (25 points, 30 minutes, 40 percent), and budget your time accordingly.

The first requirement for most essay tests is to read the question for *key words*. Does the instructor want you to analyze, compare, criticize, defend, describe, discuss, evaluate, illustrate, explain, justify, trace, or summarize? If you are asked to explain how Darwin's theory of evolution affected nineteenth-century thinking, do just that; you won't like your grade if, instead, you summarize the theory. Merely putting ideas on paper, even perceptive ideas, does not substitute for addressing the question.

EXERCISE ■ **Indicate what each of the following questions calls for. What is required? By what methods—arguing, describing, or the like—would you develop the answer?**

1. Distinguish between mild depression and severe depression. You might focus on the nature, the symptoms, or the potential treatments of each condition.
2. Support or refute the following statement: Because waste incineration generates stack gases and ash that contain high levels of toxic substances, it is not an acceptable solution to waste-disposal problems.
3. Explain how to clean an automobile carburetor.
4. Briefly relate the events in the Book of Job and then explain the significance of the tale. Could the tale be called symbolic? Why or why not?

When you have the essay question clearly in mind, don't immediately start writing. A jack-rabbit start spells trouble. Instead, take a few moments to plan your answer. Following these steps will help you do this.

1. Jot down specific supporting information from your reading and lecture notes.
2. Make a rough outline that sketches the main points you'll cover and an effective order for presenting them.
3. Prepare a thesis statement that responds to the question and will control your answer.

Writing an essay exam, like writing an essay, is a front-end-loaded process. Much of the brain work occurs before you put your answer on paper. You won't get to Poughkeepsie just by starting to drive.

WRITING THE EXAMINATION ANSWER

Here are some guidelines that will help you write a successful exam.

1. Position your thesis statement at the beginning of your answer. Make sure each paragraph is controlled by a topic sentence tied to the thesis statement.
2. Don't become excessively concerned about your wording. Focus on content and, if time permits, make stylistic changes later.
3. Fight the impulse to jot down everything you know about the general subject. The grader doesn't want to plow through verbiage to arrive at your answer.

The following essay illustrates these guidelines.

Question:	Discuss the various appeals described by classical rhetoric that an orator can use. Give a brief example of each kind of appeal.
Answer: *Thesis statement previews focus and order of answer*	Classical rhetoric defines three major appeals—logical, emotional, and ethical—that orators may use to win support from their audience.

Topic sentence   Most rhetoricians agree that any argument must be based on logic; that is, it must appeal to the intellect of the listeners.

Example 1   Unless it does, the orator will fail to convince them. For example, if a speaker who is urging the election of a candidate presents the candidate's voting record, she is appealing to logic. She asks the audience to understand that the voting record predicts how the candidate will continue to vote if elected.

Example 2   Likewise, a candidate for public office who describes how a tax cut will stimulate the economy and create new jobs is using a logical appeal.

Topic sentence   In addition to logic, emotional appeals are a powerful means of swaying people, especially groups. Though emotional appeals work along with logical appeals, they are quite different, because they are directed at the listener's hopes, fears, and sympathies.

Example 1   When a presidential candidate indicates that a vote for his opponent is a vote to escalate the arms race and risk

Example 2   nuclear holocaust, he is making an emotional appeal. So, too, is the candidate who asserts that inflation can be whipped and American industry revitalized and that our country can assume its rightful place as economic leader of the free world.

Topic sentence   The ethical appeal is more subtle than either of the other two, but probably just as important. The orator must strike the audience as a sensible, good person if they are to believe the

Example 1   message. Sometimes the speaker's logic and also the tone— moderate, sensible, or wise—will convey sufficient ethical ap-

Example 2   peal. At other times, a speaker will use statements that are deliberately intended to create ethical appeal. "In developing this program, I will work closely with both houses of the legislature, including the members of both political parties" and "Despite our differences, I believe my opponent to be a decent, honest person" are examples of such statements.

Restatement of   In any speech, all these appeals—logical, emotional, and
thesis   ethical—work together to convince an audience.

Student Unknown

TEACHING STRATEGY
Have students bring in previously written exams and revise them as necessary according to the suggestions in this section. If students have no sample exams, you could follow the same practice with one you hand out.

In contrast, the next two responses to the same question illustrate common faults of examination essays.

Answer A

There are three basic appeals that a speaker can make to captivate his   1
audience. These are the ethical appeal, the logical appeal and the emotional appeal.

The first of these—the ethical appeal—includes all the speaker's efforts   2
to have his audience regard him as rational, wise, good, and generous. Needless to say, the ethical appeal is very important. Without it, no one would pay attention to the speaker's argument.

The second appeal—logical—is also extremely important. It carries the 3
burden of the argument from speaker to listener and appeals to the intellect of
the audience.

Emotional appeal—the third and final one—is made to the passions 4
and feelings of the listeners. The significance of such an appeal is obvious.

A speaker often uses all three appeals to win an audience over. 5

Answer *A* starts with a thesis statement and includes brief definitions of the
three appeals; however, it omits any concrete examples and includes no specific
details. As a result, the significance of the emotional appeal is not "obvious," as
paragraph 4 claims, nor does the answer offer any hints as to why the other
appeals are important. This response resembles an outline more than an answer
and suggests the student lacked the knowledge to do a good job.

Answer B

Orators may make three different kinds of appeals to win favor from an 1
audience: emotional appeal, logical appeal, and ethical appeal.

Let's start with emotional appeal because this is the one that is not 2
essential to a speech. Logical and ethical appeals are always included; emotional appeal may be used to help sway an audience, but without logical and
ethical appeals no argument is accepted. This simply makes sense: if there is
no logic, there is no argument; and if the speaker doesn't come across as an
ethical person—someone to be relied upon—then no one will accept what he
or she says. But emotional appeal is different. Unemotional arguments may be
accepted.

Nevertheless, emotional appeal is important. It includes whatever a 3
speaker does to move the feelings of the audience. The speaker asks, "Don't
you want to protect your families?" In doing so, he or she appeals emotionally.
A speaker may appeal to the prejudices or biases of listeners. Someone at a Ku
Klux Klan rally does that. So does a minister who exhorts people to be "saved."
Both speakers address the emotions of the groups they talk to.

There is a very fine use of emotional appeal in the "Letter from 4
Birmingham Jail" by Martin Luther King, Jr. At one point King asks his
audience of white clergy how they would feel if, like blacks, they had to deny
their children treats such as amusement parks and had to fear for the lives of
their families, and so on. He also describes the bombings and burnings that
blacks are subjected to. All the details move readers emotionally, so that they
come to sympathize with blacks who live in fear.

Logical appeal, as noted earlier, is crucial. The speaker must seem to 5
have an intelligent plan. The listeners want the plan to meet their needs.

The other appeal is the ethical one. It is made when a speaker makes 6
him- or herself seem generous, good and wise.

All three appeals can be used in one speech, although the logical and 7
ethical appeals are essential to it.

Although the writer opens with an acceptable thesis statement, this answer
shows little evidence of advance planning. Does it make sense to begin in

paragraph 2 with an appeal tagged "not essential"? And note how the paragraph drifts from the emotional appeal to the other two types, despite its topic sentence. Paragraphs 3 and 4 do focus on the emotional appeal and ironically, through specific examples, make a good case for its importance. Paragraphs 5 and 6 shortchange logical and ethical appeals by saying next to nothing about them. The essay contradicts itself: if logical and ethical appeals are the essential ones and emotional appeals "not essential," why is more than half of the essay about emotional appeal?

EXERCISE ■

1. **Read the examination questions and answers below. Then respond to the questions that follow the answers.**

A. Question

Living organisms are composed of cells. On the basis of structure, biologists categorize cells into two groups: the prokaryotic cells and the eukaryotic cells. What are the major differences between prokaryotic cells and eukaryotic cells, and in which living organisms are these cells found?

Answer

Eukaryotic cells have a true nucleus and their genetic material, the DNA-containing chromosomes, is located within this nucleus, which is surrounded by a nuclear membrane. Prokaryotic cells lack a true nucleus, and their genetic material lies free in the cytoplasm of the cell.   1

Eukaryotic cells are also much more complex than prokaryotic cells. Eukaryotic cells commonly contain organelles such as mitochondria, a Golgi complex, lysosomes, an endoplasmic reticulum, and in photosynthetic cells, chloroplasts. These organelles are typically lacking in the simpler prokaryotic cells.   2

Prokaryotic cells make up the structure of all bacteria and the blue-green algae. These are the simplest of all known cellular organisms. All other cellular organisms, including humans, are composed of eukaryotic cells.   3

Scott Wybolt

a. Does the response answer the question that was asked? Discuss.

ANSWER TO EXAM QUESTION

The student is asked to (1) distinguish between eukaryotic and prokaryotic cells and (2) tell where each is found. The response notes (1) that the first type has a true nucleus containing its genetic material while the second has no nucleus and dispersed genetic material and (2) that the first type is found in all life forms except bacteria and blue-green algae, which have the second type. Thus the student has addressed both parts of the question.

B. Question

Analyze the significant relationships between imagination and reality in Coleridge's "This Lime-Tree Bower My Prison." In your answer, you might consider some of the following questions. What is the importance of setting in the poem? Is the speaker's mind a form of setting? How is reality implicitly defined in the poem? How, and through what agencies, can reality be transmitted? What relationship is finally

a. The student uses the importance of setting as a springboard for her discussion. After noting the power of imagination to control one's perception of reality and the form the poem takes, she turns her attention to the setting, the lime tree bower "prison" in which the speaker finds himself. Paragraph 3 discusses his reactions to the bower, which lead to imaginative participation in his friends' walks, while paragraph 4 notes his newfound appreciation of the bower itself. Setting has triggered his imaginative faculties and transformed his perception of the setting itself.

b. Indirectly, the answer suggests that the speaker's mind is a sort of setting in which he walks imaginatively with his friends. Reality is defined as being not just what we perceive with our eyes but what we imagine and how we regard our circumstances. Although the answer does not explain *how* friendship triggers the insights revealed in the poem, it does suggest that friendship plays a role in stimulating the imagination: it's unlikely that one could as easily participate imaginatively in the activities of strangers or casual acquaintances.

c. The thesis statement is the first sentence in the answer. Everything that follows supports its contention that imagination shapes reality and is itself a sort of reality. Paragraph 3 notes that imagination allows the speaker to share his friends' reality. Paragraph 4 points out that imagination transforms the speaker's perceptions of his surroundings, and paragraph 5 shows that the reality of imagination is as valid as the reality of one's actual location.

perceived between the spiritual and the concrete? How does friendship or fellow-feeling trigger the essential insights revealed in the poem?

Answer

Coleridge's "This Lime-Tree Bower My Prison" shows imagination to be a powerful force that can control one's perception of reality and that is, in itself, a kind of reality—perhaps the most important reality. Thus, imagination and reality are more intimately linked and more similar in Coleridge's poem than they are ordinarily thought to be. 1

The relationship between imagination and reality is revealed by the speaker of "Lime-Tree Bower," although he doesn't openly state it. The technique for revelation is dramatic monologue, with the speaker seemingly talking spontaneously as his situation gives rise to a series of thoughts. 2

As the poem begins, the speaker finds himself "trapped" at home in his lime-tree bower, while his friends go on a walk he had hoped to take with them. This situation at first bothers the speaker, causing him to feel imprisoned. As the poem progresses, however, the speaker begins to imagine all the places his friends are visiting on their walk. Though he laments not being with them, he shows excitement as he describes the scenes his friends are viewing: the "roaring dell," the sea, and so on. Thus the speaker recognizes that he is able to participate imaginatively in the walk and, in doing so, to escape his "prison" reality and enter the reality of his friends. 3

The moment of recognition occurs at the beginning of stanza three: "A delight / Comes sudden on my heart, and I am glad / As I myself was there!" Interestingly, however, this point marks a turn in the speaker's thoughts. Once again he realizes where he actually is—the lime-tree bower. But now he appreciates its beauties. The natural beauties he imagined have taught him to appreciate the beauties of nature right before him. He has learned that there is "No plot so narrow, be but Nature there." The lime-tree bower is no longer a prison, but a rich and beautiful, if somewhat small, world. 4

Imagination has again shaped the speaker's perceptions of reality. It controls the perception of circumstances—whether one views a place as a prison or a microcosm of a larger world, with beauties and possibilities in its own right. The use of imagination can teach one about reality, as it has Coleridge's speaker. And, if one surrenders to it completely—as the speaker does when he envisions the world of the walkers—imagination is a delightful reality, as valid as the reality of the place in which one sits. 5

Imagination and reality are merged in "This Lime-Tree Bower My Prison," and though this identification is apparently temporary, one may learn through imagination how to cope with and enjoy reality. Thus, imagination is intimately involved in shaping the perception of reality. 6

Lori McCue

a. Which of the possible approaches suggested in the question does the student select?

b. Which of the other questions does she indirectly answer? Which ones are not addressed?

c. Identify the thesis statement and explain how it controls the answer.
d. Show how the answer demonstrates careful planning.
e. Point out some effective supporting details.

2. Read the following answers to the examination question "What factors account for the rise of Methodism in eighteenth-century England?" Explain specifically why each answer is good or poor.

Answer A

Methodism, a cult that became a religion, was founded in eighteenth-century England by John Wesley, with the aid of his brother Charles and of George Whitefield. The features of Methodism that accounted for its great success can best be understood by contrasting them with the features of Anglicanism, the state religion of England.

The eighteenth-century Anglican church was characterized by extreme complacency. Perhaps the religious traumas during the previous century encouraged the de-emphasizing of religious fervor that might stir up new trouble. Perhaps philosophical and scientific developments led to a decline of active interest in the church. And perhaps, finally, the new wealth and worldliness of the period worked against religious development within the state church. Whatever the reason or reasons might have been, most intellectuals and authorities were content to let the church be a quiet, social institution. Granted, the Anglican church was no place for the sort of religious enthusiasm that John Wesley tried to bring to it. But for a long time he did try to work within the church, turning his cult into a new religion only after years of effort to revitalize the Anglican church.

Wesley's attitudes seem somewhat contradictory; he believed in personal and immediate salvation through Christ, the sort of conversion that brought weeping, wailing, gnashing of teeth, and hysterical joy; at the same time, Wesley was a stern, ascetic individual, who did not even believe in play for children. Yet these seemingly contradictory attitudes indicate a depth of religious emotion that was out of place in the comfortable, even-keeled, socially oriented Anglican church and that was regarded with distaste by party-line clergymen.

Typically, Anglican clergymen were very different from Wesley and his colleagues. They were gentlemanly and, on the whole, they adopted a subdued approach in the pulpit. The Wesleys and Whitefield, on the other hand, preached provocatively, stirring the emotions more than the intellects of their audiences.

The typical Anglican church and churchmen appealed to educated upper- and middle-class people. And they continued to hold the allegiance of rural people, whose need for community was satisfied by their extended families, their friends, and their lifelong ties to their birthplace. But the rise of industrialism during the eighteenth century produced a large group of people to whom the spiritual and emotional community of Methodism appealed.

d. The answer begins with a thesis sentence which indicates what the writer will discuss and in what order. Then she explains her first point and her second point, using an inductive organization: first she discusses a specific situation and set of reactions, then draws general conclusions. The conclusion reiterates the two points stated in the thesis.
e. Paragraph 3 supports the statement that "the speaker begins to imagine all the places his friends are visiting. . . . " The speaker "shows excitement" in describing the scenery viewed by his friends: a "roaring dell" and "the sea." The two quotations cited in paragraph 4 support the student's comments about the relationship between imagination and reality.

ANSWERS TO EXAM QUESTION

Answer A is carefully planned. Paragraph 1 notes the origins of Methodism and provides a thesis statement which sets up a contrast. Paragraph 2 asserts that 18th century Anglicanism was complacent and then notes several possible reasons why. The next two paragraphs contrast Wesley's fervor with the subdued character of the Anglican clergymen. The next-to-last paragraph contrasts the kinds of people drawn to the two religions and accounts for their choice, while the final paragraph summarizes the central conclusion.

These were the poor, uprooted individuals and nuclear families who had been forced to leave their birthplace, migrate to crowded, unsanitary cities, and labor long hours under sweatshop conditions. They needed something to hold on to and to inspire them, but the state church spoke dispassionately and over their heads. Wesley spoke to their hearts and won them over, usually with just one sermon.

Thus, traditional needs of people, combined with new social, political, 6 philosophical, and religious situations, encouraged the development of Methodism. For certain people in eighteenth-century England (especially poor city workers), John Wesley's religion met the needs that the dominant religion no longer satisfied.

Answer B

Methodism began and grew with amazing rapidity during the eigh- 1 teenth century in England. It was founded by John Wesley, with the help of Charles Wesley and George Whitefield.

One of the factors in the rise of Methodism was the movement of many 2 people to cities to take jobs in industry. These people were no longer secure in their surroundings and could not rely on parish priests for help. Thus, they were ripe for conversion to Methodism.

John Wesley was a stern man who loved organization and who could 3 develop a strong church. He might seem grim to us because he opposed games and treats, even coming out against play for children. He believed equally strongly in salvation. He could get people to see sin and salvation as he did and thus get them to convert to his faith.

The Anglican church during this period was not active. People went to 4 church, but only out of duty. Ministers were more interested in scholarship or socializing or hunting than in their jobs. Thus, the church declined.

Imagine hearing a moving sermon on the horrible qualities of sin or 5 one on the joys of going to heaven. Thinking such thoughts, you can easily imagine how John Wesley's and George Whitefield's hearers felt.

The Age of Reason caused Methodism to rise, too. The state church was 6 a victim in the philosophical and scientific drive toward reason. The church became reasonable. But churches are supposed to be emotional supports, and reason and faith are different ways of knowing. Methodism appealed to faith. Thus, it rose.

For all the reasons given above, Methodism prospered in eighteenth- 7 century England.

Answer B shows a lack of planning. The first paragraph touches upon the origins of Methodism but lacks any thesis statement. As a result, the reader has no idea of what to expect. Paragraph 2 offers a reason for the rise of Methodism but instead of following up with a second reason, the writer shifts abruptly in paragraph 3 to a discussion of Wesley's character. Paragraph 4 signals a second abrupt shift in thought, this time to the nature of the 18th century Anglican church. With paragraph 5 there is a sharp shift in both tone and subject matter: the reader is now asked to imagine how a Wesley sermon affected its audience. After this three-paragraph digression, the student offers a second reason for the rise of Methodism and then ends with a weak one-sentence paragraph. A number of the paragraphs are underdeveloped. Paragraph 2, for example, doesn't adequately explain the conditions that drove urban workers to Methodism. Although dealing with some of the ideas presented in the first essay, the second essay fails to communicate them in an effective and orderly way.

■ Chapter 18

Writing About Literature

PERSPECTIVE

While writing about literature builds on and uses the skills and strategies students already know, it is nevertheless a specialized form of writing that utilizes a specific vocabulary and particular analytic skills. As a result, some students who are proficient in other types of writing may have difficulty with this type. In any event, effective performance usually occurs only after extensive discussion and several writing assignments.

TEACHING STRATEGIES

1. Response journals allow students to gain practice in responding to literature and to accumulate information that might be used in later assignments. In a personal response journal, students informally explore various reactions to a work—their feelings about the plot or understanding of the setting, for example. A directed journal features a more structured response to specific questions such as "In what ways did the main character change and why?"

2. A class discussion can help prepare students for the content of a literary work. To illustrate, before reading "The Bride Comes to Yellow Sky," students might discuss the nature of the wild west, what a sheriff and gunslinger were like, and so on.

Teachers of literature generally expect you to write about what you've read. Typically they might ask you to

- show how an author handled one element of a short story, play, or poem
- compare how two different works treat a particular element
- weigh several elements and then determine the writer's intention
- air your reactions to some work.

Writing about literature offers several benefits. Weighing and recording your thoughts on the different elements sharpen your critical thinking ability. Literary papers also pay artistic dividends, as careful reading and subsequent writing deepen your appreciation of the writer's craft. Furthermore, you'll feel a sense of accomplishment as you coherently express your perceptions. Finally, writing a literature paper offers yet another opportunity to apply the writing guidelines discussed in Chapters 1–3. Focusing, gathering information, organizing, writing, revising and editing—the old familiar trail leads to success here too.

THE ELEMENTS OF LITERATURE

Most writing assignments on literature will probably feature one or more of the following elements:

Plot	Symbols
Point of view	Irony
Character	Theme
Setting	

Depending on the work, some of these will be more important than others. Read the following story by Stephen Crane, "The Bride Comes to Yellow Sky." The discussions that follow it point out the basic features of each element and offer useful writing suggestions.

The Bride Comes to Yellow Sky

Stephen Crane

I

The great Pullman was whirling onward with such dignity of motion that a glance from the window seemed simply to prove that the plains of Texas were pouring eastward. Vast flats of green grass, dull-hued spaces of mesquit and cactus, little groups of frame houses, woods of light and tender trees, all were sweeping into the east, sweeping over the horizon, a precipice.

A newly married pair had boarded this coach at San Antonio. The man's face was reddened from many days in the wind and sun, and a direct result of his new black clothes was that his brick-colored hands were constantly performing in a most conscious fashion. From time to time he looked down respectfully at his attire. He sat with a hand on each knee, like a man waiting in a barber's shop. The glances he devoted to other passengers were furtive and shy.

The bride was not pretty, nor was she very young. She wore a dress of blue cashmere, with small reservations of velvet here and there, and with steel buttons abounding. She continually twisted her head to regard her puff sleeves, very stiff, straight, and high. They embarrassed her. It was quite apparent that she had cooked, and that she expected to cook, dutifully. The blushes caused by the careless scrutiny of some passengers as she had entered the car were strange to see upon this plain, under-class countenance, which was drawn in placid, almost emotionless lines.

They were evidently very happy. "Ever been in a parlor-car before?" he asked, smiling with delight.

"No," she answered; "I never was. It's fine, ain't it?"

"Great! And then after a while we'll go forward to the diner, and get a big lay-out. Finest meal in the world. Charge a dollar."

"Oh, do they?" cried the bride. "Charge a dollar? Why, that's too much—for us—ain't it, Jack?"

"Not this trip, anyhow," he answered bravely. "We're going to go the whole thing."

Later he explained to her about the trains. "You see, it's a thousand miles from one end of Texas to the other; and this train runs right across it and never stops but four times." He had the pride of an owner. He pointed out to her the dazzling fittings of the coach; and in truth her eyes opened wider as she contemplated the sea-green figured velvet, the shining brass, silver, and glass, the wood that gleamed as darkly brilliant as the surface of a pool of oil. At one end a bronze figure sturdily held a support for a separated chamber, and at convenient places on the ceiling were frescos in olive and silver.

To the minds of the pair, their surroundings reflected the glory of their marriage that morning in San Antonio; this was the environment of their new estate; and the man's face in particular beamed with an elation that made him appear ridiculous to the negro porter. This individual at times surveyed them from afar with an amused and superior grin. On other occasions he bullied them with skill in ways that did not make it exactly plain to them that they were being bullied. He subtly used all the manners of the most unconquerable kind of snobbery. He oppressed them; but of this oppression they had small knowledge, and they speedily forgot that infrequently a number of travelers covered them with stares of derisive enjoyment. Historically there was supposed to be something infinitely humorous in their situation.

"We are due in Yellow Sky at 3:42," he said, looking tenderly into her eyes.

"Oh, are we?" she said, as if she had not been aware of it. To evince surprise at her husband's statement was part of her wifely amiability. She took from a pocket a little silver watch; and as she held it before her, and stared at it with a frown of attention, the new husband's face shone.

"I bought it in San Anton' from a friend of mine," he told her gleefully.

"It's seventeen minutes past twelve," she said, looking up at him with a kind of shy and clumsy coquetry. A passenger, noting this play, grew excessively sardonic, and winked at himself in one of the numerous mirrors.

At last they went to the dining car. Two rows of negro waiters, in glowing white suits, surveyed their entrance with the interest, and also the equanimity, of men who had been forewarned. The pair fell to the lot of a waiter who happened to feel pleasure in steering them through their meal. He viewed them with the manner of a fatherly pilot, his countenance radiant with benevolence. The patronage, entwined with the ordinary deference, was not plain to them. And yet, as they returned to their coach, they showed in their faces a sense of escape.

To the left, miles down a long purple slope, was a little ribbon of mist where moved the keening Rio Grande. The train was approaching it at an angle, and the apex was Yellow Sky. Presently it was apparent that, as the distance from Yellow Sky grew shorter, the husband became commensurately restless. His brick-red hands were more insistent in their prominence. Occasionally he was even rather absent-minded and far-away when the bride leaned forward and addressed him.

As a matter of truth, Jack Potter was beginning to find the shadow of a deed weigh upon him like a leaden slab. He, the town marshal of Yellow Sky, a man known, liked, and feared in his corner, a prominent person, had gone to San Antonio to meet a girl he believed he loved, and there, after the usual prayers, had actually induced her to marry him, without consulting Yellow Sky for any part of the transaction. He was now bringing his bride before an innocent and unsuspecting community.

Of course people in Yellow Sky married as it pleased them, in accordance with a general custom; but such was Potter's thought of his duty to his friends, or of their idea of his duty, or of an unspoken form which does not control men in these matters, that he felt he was heinous. He had committed an extraordinary crime. Face to face with this girl in San Antonio, and spurred by his sharp impulse, he had gone headlong over all the social hedges. At San Antonio he was like a man hidden in the dark. A knife to sever any friendly duty, any form, was easy to his hand in that remote city. But the hour of Yellow Sky—the hour of daylight—was approaching.

He knew full well that his marriage was an important thing to his town. It could only be exceeded by the burning of the new hotel. His friends could not forgive

3. Perhaps start with a general question which leads to a particular insight into the story: "Why do you think Scratchy Wilson backed down?" Student responses can be followed by questions that ask for more detail: "In what ways does this action seem consistent or inconsistent with his character?" "What clues in the text led to your conclusion?"

4. Ask students to identify or explain specific features. For example: "The drummer is calmed by gazing at 'various zinc and copper fittings that bore a resemblance to armorplate.' "What do you think these fittings symbolize?"

5. Some instructors prefer to ask imaginative questions that call for speculation about what happens after the ending. You might ask students what they think the future holds for Scratchy Wilson and Potter. After they respond, ask what clues in the story led to their conclusion or how their views fit the themes of the story.

him. Frequently he had reflected on the advisability of telling them by telegraph, but a new cowardice had been upon him. He feared to do it. And now the train was hurrying him toward a scene of amazement, glee, and reproach. He glanced out of the window at the line of haze swinging slowly in toward the train.

Yellow Sky had a kind of brass band, which played painfully, to the delight of the populace. He laughed without heart as he thought of it. If the citizens could dream of his prospective arrival with his bride, they would parade the band at the station and escort them, amid cheers and laughing congratulations, to his adobe home.

He resolved that he would use all the devices of speed and plainscraft in making the journey from the station to his house. Once within that safe citadel, he could issue some sort of vocal bulletin, and then not go among the citizens until they had time to wear off a little of their enthusiasm.

The bride looked anxiously at him. "What's worrying you, Jack?"

He laughed again. "I'm not worrying, girl; I'm only thinking of Yellow Sky."

She flushed in comprehension.

A sense of mutual guilt invaded their minds and developed a finer tenderness. They looked at each other, with eyes softly aglow. But Potter often laughed the same nervous laugh; the flush upon the bride's face seemed quite permanent.

The traitor to the feelings of Yellow Sky narrowly watched the speeding landscape. "We're nearly there," he said.

Presently the porter came and announced the proximity of Potter's home. He held a brush in his hand, and, with all his airy superiority gone, he brushed Potter's new clothes as the latter slowly turned this way and that way. Potter tumbled out a coin and gave it to the porter, as he had seen others do. It was a heavy and muscle-bound business, as that of a man shoeing his first horse.

The porter took their bag, and as the train began to slow they moved forward to the hooded platform of the car. Presently the two engines and their long string of coaches rushed into the station of Yellow Sky.

"They have to take water here," said Potter, from a constricted throat and in mournful cadence, as one announcing death. Before the train stopped his eye had swept the length of the platform, and he was glad and astonished to see there was none upon it but the station-agent, who, with a slightly hurried and anxious air, was walking toward the water-tanks. When the train had halted, the porter alighted first, and placed in position a little temporary step.

"Come on, girl," said Potter, hoarsely. As he helped her down they each laughed on a false note. He took the bag from the negro, and bade his wife cling to his arm. As they slunk rapidly away, his hang-dog glance perceived that they were unloading the two trunks, and also that the station-agent, far ahead near the baggage-car, had turned and was running toward him, making gestures. He laughed, and groaned as he laughed, when he noted the first effect of his marital bliss upon Yellow Sky. He gripped his wife's arm firmly to his side, and they fled. Behind them the porter stood, chuckling fatuously.

II

The California express on the Southern Railway was due at Yellow Sky in twenty-one minutes. There were six men at the bar of the Weary Gentleman saloon.

One was a drummer[1] who talked a great deal and rapidly; three were Texans who did not care to talk at that time; and two were Mexican sheep-herders, who did not talk as a general practice in the Weary Gentleman saloon. The barkeeper's dog lay on the boardwalk that crossed in front of the door. His head was on his paws, and he glanced drowsily here and there with the constant vigilance of a dog that is kicked on occasion. Across the sandy street were some vivid green grass-plots, so wonderful in appearance, amid the sands that burned near them in a blazing sun, that they caused a doubt in the mind. They exactly resembled the grass mats used to represent lawns on the stage. At the cooler end of the railway station, a man without a coat sat in a tilted chair and smoked his pipe. The fresh-cut bank of the Rio Grande circled near the town, and there could be seen beyond it a great plum-colored plain of mesquit.

Save for the busy drummer and his companions in the saloon, Yellow Sky was dozing. The new-comer leaned gracefully upon the bar, and recited many tales with the confidence of a bard who has come upon a new field.

"—and at the moment that the old man fell downstairs with the bureau in his arms, the old woman was coming up with two scuttles of coal, and of course—"

The drummer's tale was interrupted by a young man who suddenly appeared in the open door. He cried: "Scratchy Wilson's drunk, and has turned loose with both hands." The two Mexicans at once set down their glasses and faded out of the rear entrance of the saloon.

The drummer, innocent and jocular, answered: "All right, old man. S'pose he has? Come in and have a drink, anyhow."

But the information had made such an obvious cleft in every skull in the room that the drummer was obliged to see its importance. All had become instantly solemn. "Say," said he, mystified, "what is this?" His three companions made the introductory gesture of eloquent speech; but the young man at the door forestalled them.

"It means, my friend," he answered, as he came into the saloon, "that for the next two hours this town won't be a health resort."

The barkeeper went to the door, and locked and barred it; reaching out of the window, he pulled in heavy wooden shutters, and barred them. Immediately a solemn, chapel-like gloom was upon the place. The drummer was looking from one to another.

"But say," he cried, "what is this, anyhow? You don't mean there is going to be a gun-fight?"

"Don't know whether there'll be a fight or not," answered one man, grimly; "but there'll be some shootin'—some good shootin'."

The young man who had warned them waved his hand. "Oh, there'll be a fight fast enough, if any one wants it. Anybody can get a fight out there in the street. There's a fight just waiting."

The drummer seemed to be swayed between the interest of a foreigner and a perception of personal danger.

"What did you say his name was?" he asked.

"Scratchy Wilson," they answered in chorus.

"And will he kill anybody? What are you going to do? Does this happen often? Does he rampage around like this once a week or so? Can he break in that door?"

[1]Traveling salesman

"No; he can't break down that door," replied the barkeeper. "He's tried it three times. But when he comes you'd better lay down on the floor, stranger. He's dead sure to shoot at it, and a bullet may come through."

Thereafter the drummer kept a strict eye upon the door. The time had not yet been called for him to hug the floor, but, as a minor precaution, he sidled near to the wall. "Will he kill anybody?" he said again.

The men laughed low and scornfully at the question.

"He's out to shoot, and he's out for trouble. Don't see any good in experimentin' with him."

"But what do you do in a case like this? What do you do?"

A man responded: "Why, he and Jack Potter—"

"But," in chorus the other men interrupted, "Jack Potter's in San Anton'."

"Well, who is he? What's he got to do with it?"

"Oh, he's the town marshal. He goes out and fights Scratchy when he gets on one of these tears."

"Wow!" said the drummer, mopping his brow. "Nice job he's got."

The voices had toned away to mere whisperings. The drummer wished to ask further questions, which were born of an increasing anxiety and bewilderment; but when he attempted them, the men merely looked at him in irritation and motioned him to remain silent. A tense waiting hush was upon them. In the deep shadows of the room their eyes shone as they listened for sounds from the street. One man made three gestures at the barkeeper; and the latter, moving like a ghost, handed him a glass and a bottle. The man poured a full glass of whisky, and set down the bottle noiselessly. He gulped the whisky in a swallow, and turned again toward the door in immovable silence. The drummer saw that the barkeeper, without a sound, had taken a Winchester from beneath the bar. Later he saw this individual beckoning to him, so he tiptoed across the room.

"You better come with me back of the bar."

"No, thanks," said the drummer, perspiring: "I'd rather be where I can make a break for the back door."

Whereupon the man of bottles made a kindly but peremptory gesture. The drummer obeyed it, and, finding himself seated on a box with his head below the level of the bar, balm was laid upon his soul at sight of various zinc and copper fittings that bore a resemblance to armorplate. The barkeeper took a seat comfortably upon an adjacent box.

"You see," he whispered, "this here Scratchy Wilson is a wonder with a gun—a perfect wonder; and when he goes on the wartrail, we hunt our holes—naturally. He's about the last one of the old gang that used to hang out along the river here. He's a terror when he's drunk. When he's sober he's all right—kind of simple—wouldn't hurt a fly—nicest fellow in town. But when he's drunk—whoo!"

There were periods of stillness. "I wish Jack Potter was back from San Anton'," said the barkeeper. "He shot Wilson up once—in the leg—and he would sail in and pull out the kinks in this thing."

Presently they heard from a distance the sound of a shot, followed by three wild yowls. It instantly removed a bond from the men in the darkened saloon. There was a shuffling of feet. They looked at each other. "Here he comes," they said.

III

A man in a maroon-colored flannel shirt, which had been purchased for purposes of decoration, and made principally by some Jewish women on the East Side of New York, rounded a corner and walked into the middle of the main street of Yellow Sky. In either hand the man held a long, heavy, blue-black revolver. Often he yelled, and these cries rang through a semblance of a deserted village, shrilly flying over the roofs in a volume that seemed to have no relation to the ordinary vocal strength of a man. It was as if the surrounding stillness formed the arch of a tomb over him. These cries of ferocious challenge rang against walls of silence. And his boots had red tops with gilded imprints, of the kind beloved in winter by little sledding boys on the hillsides of New England.

The man's face flamed in a rage begot of whisky. His eyes, rolling, and yet keen for ambush, hunted the still doorways and windows. He walked with the creeping movement of the midnight cat. As it occurred to him, he roared menacing information. The long revolvers in his hands were as easy as straws; they were moved with an electric swiftness. The little fingers of each hand played sometimes in a musician's way. Plain from the low collar of the shirt, the cords of his neck straightened and sank, straightened and sank, as passion moved him. The only sounds were his terrible invitations. The calm adobes preserved their demeanor at the passing of this small thing in the middle of the street.

There was no offer of fight—no offer of fight. The man called to the sky. There were no attractions. He bellowed and fumed and swayed his revolvers here and everywhere.

The dog of the barkeeper of the Weary Gentleman saloon had not appreciated the advance of events. He yet lay dozing in front of his master's door. At sight of the dog, the man paused and raised his revolver humorously. At sight of the man, the dog sprang up and walked diagonally away, with a sullen head, and growling. The man yelled, and the dog broke into a gallop. As it was about to enter an alley, there was a loud noise, a whistling, and something spat the ground directly before it. The dog screamed, and, wheeling in terror, galloped headlong in a new direction. Again there was a noise, a whistling, and sand was kicked viciously before it. Fear-stricken, the dog turned and flurried like an animal in a pen. The man stood laughing, his weapons at his hips.

Ultimately the man was attracted by the closed door of the Weary Gentleman saloon. He went to it and, hammering with a revolver, demanded drink.

The door remaining imperturbable, he picked a bit of paper from the walk, and nailed it to the framework with a knife. He then turned his back contemptuously upon this popular resort and, walking to the opposite side of the street and spinning there on his heel quickly and lithely, fired at the bit of paper. He missed it by a half-inch. He swore at himself, and went away. Later he comfortably fusilladed the windows of his most intimate friend. The man was playing with this town; it was a toy for him.

But still there was no offer of fight. The name of Jack Potter, his ancient antagonist, entered his mind, and he concluded that it would be a glad thing if he should go to Potter's house, and by bombardment induce him to come out and fight. He moved in the direction of his desire, chanting Apache scalp-music.

When he arrived at it, Potter's house presented the same still front as had the other adobes. Taking up a strategic position, the man howled a challenge. But this house regarded him as might a great stone god. It gave no sign. After a decent wait, the man howled further challenges, mingling with them wonderful epithets.

Presently there came the spectacle of a man churning himself into deepest rage over the immobility of a house. He fumed at it as the winter wind attacks a prairie cabin in the North. To the distance there should have gone the sound of a tumult like the fighting of two hundred Mexicans. As necessity bade him, he paused for breath or to reload his revolvers.

IV

Potter and his bride walked sheepishly and with speed. Sometimes they laughed together shamefacedly and low.

"Next corner, dear," he said finally.

They put forth the efforts of a pair walking bowed against a strong wind. Potter was about to raise a finger to point the first appearance of the new home when, as they circled the corner, they came face to face with a man in a maroon-colored shirt, who was feverishly pushing cartridges into a large revolver. Upon the instant the man dropped his revolver to the ground and, like lightning, whipped another from its holster. The second weapon was aimed at the bridegroom's chest.

There was a silence. Potter's mouth seemed to be merely a grave for his tongue. He exhibited an instinct to at once loosen his arm from the woman's grip, and he dropped the bag to the sand. As for the bride, her face had gone as yellow as old cloth. She was a slave to hideous rites, gazing at the apparitional snake.

The two men faced each other at a distance of three paces. He of the revolver smiled with a new and quiet ferocity.

"Tried to sneak up on me," he said. "Tried to sneak up on me!" His eyes grew more baleful. As Potter made a slight movement, the man thrust his revolver venomously forward. "No; don't you do it, Jack Potter. Don't you move a finger toward a gun just yet. Don't you move an eyelash. The time has come for me to settle with you, and I'm goin' to do it my own way, and loaf along with no interferin'. So if you don't want a gun bent on you, just mind what I tell you."

Potter looked at his enemy. "I ain't got a gun on me, Scratchy," he said. "Honest, I ain't." He was stiffening and steadying, but yet somewhere at the back of his mind a vision of the Pullman floated: the seagreen figured velvet, the shining brass, silver, and glass, the wood that gleamed as darkly brilliant as the surface of a pool of oil—all the glory of the marriage, the environment of the new estate. "You know I fight when it comes to fighting, Scratchy Wilson; but I ain't got a gun on me. You'll have to do all the shootin' yourself."

His enemy's face went livid. He stepped forward, and lashed his weapon to and fro before Potter's chest. "Don't tell me you ain't got no gun on you, you whelp. Don't tell me no lie like that. There ain't a man in Texas ever seen you without no gun. Don't take me for no kid." His eyes blazed with light, and his throat worked like a pump.

"I ain't takin' you for no kid," answered Potter. His heels had not moved an inch backward. "I'm takin' you for a damn fool. I tell you I ain't got a gun, and I ain't.

If you're goin' to shoot me up, you better begin now; you'll never get a chance like this again."

So much enforced reasoning had told on Wilson's rage; he was calmer. "If you ain't got a gun, why ain't you got a gun?" he sneered. "Been to Sunday-school?"

"I ain't got a gun because I've just come from San Anton' with my wife. I'm married," said Potter. "And if I'd thought there was going to be any galoots like you prowling around when I brought my wife home, I'd had a gun, and don't you forget it."

"Married!" said Scratchy, not at all comprehending.

"Yes, married. I'm married." said Potter, distinctly.

"Married?" said Scratchy. Seemingly for the first time, he saw the drooping, drowning woman at the other man's side. "No!" he said. He was like a creature allowed a glimpse of another world. He moved a pace backward, and his arm, with the revolver, dropped to his side. "Is this the lady?" he asked.

"Yes; this is the lady," answered Potter.

There was another period of silence.

"Well," said Wilson at last, slowly, "I s'pose it's all off now."

"It's all off if you say so, Scratchy. You know I didn't make the trouble." Potter lifted his valise.

"Well, I 'low it's off, Jack," said Wilson. He was looking at the ground. "Married!" He was not a student of chivalry; it was merely that in the presence of this foreign condition he was a simple child of the earlier plains. He picked up his starboard revolver, and, placing both weapons in their holsters, he went away. His feet made funnel-shaped tracks in the heavy sand.

Plot

Plot factors. Plot is the series of events that moves a narrative along. The opening of a story with a conventional plot introduces important characters and sets the stage for what happens. Then one or more conflicts develop, some pitting person against person, others setting characters against society, nature, fate or themselves. Action gradually builds to a climax, where events take a decisive turn. The ending can do a number of things—clear up unanswered questions, hint at the future, state a theme, or reestablish some sort of relationship between two foes. In "The Bride," Potter experiences two conflicts: one with Scratchy Wilson and the other within himself over his marriage. The climax comes when Potter and Scratchy meet face to face, and Scratchy learns about his old adversary's marriage. As Scratchy walks away, we sense that the two old foes have had their last confrontation, that Potter's marriage has altered forever the relationship between them.

To organize plots, writers use a number of techniques. In foreshadowing, for example, the writer hints at later developments, thus creating interest and building suspense. In H. H. Munro's short story "The Open Window," a visitor to a country house observes that "An undefinable something about the room seemed to suggest masculine habitation." Yet he accepts the story of a young girl that her

TEACHING STRATEGIES

1. To help students appreciate the importance of plot, have them discuss how the story would change if key plot elements were altered. What would have happened if Potter had arrived an hour earlier? If the men in the saloon had come to watch the showdown?

2. To help students appreciate the different devices of plot organization, have them discuss the effects if significant changes were made in plot structure. For example, how would the story differ if it were told as a flashback from the time Potter confronts Scratchy Wilson?

uncle, the man of the house, had lost his life in a bog three years before. Because he ignores his observation and accepts the girl's story at face value, the visitor is terrified by the sudden appearance of the uncle, who seems to be a ghost. The careful reader, however, senses what's coming and enjoys the trick more for having been in on it.

When using a flashback, another organizational technique, the writer interrupts the flow of events to relate one or more happenings that occurred before the point at which the story opened, then resumes the narrative at or near the point of interruption. Ernest Hemingway's short story "The Short Happy Life of Francis Macomber" provides an illustration. As the story opens, we meet characters who hint that Macomber displayed cowardice by running from, rather than shooting, a charging, wounded lion. A bit later the story flashes back to detail the actual incident. Flashbacks supply essential information and either create or resolve suspense.

Not every plot unfolds in clear stages. Many modern stories lack distinct plot divisions and focus on psychological, not physical, conflicts. In extreme cases, writers may abandon the traditional plot structure and present events in a disorganized sequence that helps accomplish some literary purpose, such as reflecting a character's disturbed state of mind. Joyce Carol Oates's short story "How I Contemplated the World from the Detroit House of Correction and Began My Life Over Again" fits this mold. To dramatize her chief character's mental turmoil, Oates presents the story as a series of notes for an English composition. These notes, labeled "Events," "Characters," "Sioux Drive," "Detroit," and "That Night," are internally disorganized and arranged in a jumbled sequence.

A poem sometimes includes a series of actions and events, as Edwin Arlington Robinson's "The Miller's Wife" illustrates.

> The miller's wife had waited long,
>   The tea was cold, the fire was dead;
> And there might yet be nothing wrong
>   In how he went and what he said:
> "There are no millers any more,"
>   Was all that she had heard him say:
> And he had lingered at the door
>   So long that it seemed yesterday.
>
> Sick with a fear that had no form
>   She knew that she was there at last;
> And in the mill there was a warm
>   And mealy fragrance of the past.
> What else there was would only seem
>   To say again what he had meant;
> And what was hanging from a beam
>   Would not have heeded where she went.
>
> And if she thought it followed her,
>   She may have reasoned in the dark

That one way of the few there were
    Would hide her and would leave no mark;
Black water, smooth above the weir
    Like starry velvet in the night,
Though ruffled once, would soon appear
    The same as ever to the sight.

Most poems, however, present a series of images, building statements that make a philosophical point rather than tell a conventionally plotted story.

Writing about plot. Unless your instructor asks for a plot summary, don't merely repeat what happens in the story. Instead, help your reader understand what's special about the plot and how it functions. Does it build suspense, mirror a character's confusion, shape a conflict, show how different lives can intersect, or help reveal a theme?

Before starting to write, answer the following questions:

What are the key events of the story? Do they unfold in conventional fashion or deviate from it in some way?
Does the writer use foreshadowing or flashback? If so, for what purpose?
Is the plot believable and effective, or does it display weakness of some sort?
Does it include any unique features?
Is it similar to the plot of another story or some type of story?
What plot features could I write about? What examples from the story would support my contentions?

TEACHING STRATEGY

You might ask students to answer, perhaps as short journal assignments, some of the plot questions posed in the text. This exercise helps them develop an understanding of plot and ingrains the habit of specific textual support.

As you prepare your analysis, determine the important events and how they relate to your topic. If the story is disjointed or incoherent, arrange the events so that they make sense and ask yourself why the writer chose that sequence. To mirror the main character's disordered state of mind? To show that life is chaotic and difficult to understand? Similarly, assess the reason for any use of foreshadowing or flashback. Does it build, create, or resolve suspense?

Not all plots are successful. A character's actions may not fit his or her personality or the situation. The plot might be too hard to follow or fail to produce the desired effect, as in a mystery where the clues are too obvious to create suspense. Or a writer might rely on chance or coincidence to resolve a conflict or problem: it's unacceptable to have the cavalry charge in gallantly out of nowhere and rescue the hero.

If there's something unique about the plot—perhaps a surprise event that works well—describe it and tell how it functions in the story, or perhaps you can compare the plot with one in another story in order to show how both develop some key insight.

The organization of a paper on plot is simple: you'll either present a thesis and then support it with examples taken from the text, or you'll write a comparison. Writing about "The Bride Comes to Yellow Sky," you could show how foreshadowing moves the story toward an inevitable showdown. As support, you could cite the deliberate, forward motion of the train, the repeated emphasis on clocks and time, the repeated suggestions of Potter's anxiousness, and Scratchy's ongoing conflict with Potter. As a more ambitious project, you might compare the plot of "The Bride" to that of a conventional western showdown, noting any important differences and what they accomplish. A more critical approach would be to argue that the plot is implausible, citing Potter's unplanned marriage and the coincidence of his return to Yellow Sky precisely when Scratchy Wilson was drunk and shooting up the town.

EXERCISE ■   **In a short story with a strong plot line, identify conflicts and climax and tell what the ending accomplishes. Point out any use of foreshadowing or flashback.**

Point of View

Point-of-view factors.   The point of view is the vantage point from which the writer of a literary work views its events. A writer may adopt either a first-person or a third-person point of view. In *first-person* narration, someone in the work tells what happens and is identified by words like *I, me, mine,* and *my.* A *third-person* narrator stays completely out of the story and is never mentioned in any way. "The Bride Comes to Yellow Sky" illustrates third-person narration.

The most common form of first-person narration features a narrator who takes part in the action. This technique puts the readers directly on the scene and is excellent for tracing the growth or deterioration of a character. Instead of participating in the action, the narrator may view it from the sideline, an approach that preserves on-the-scene directness and allows the narrator to comment on the characters and issues. The narrator, however, cannot enter the mind and reveal the unspoken thoughts of anyone else.

Third-person narrators don't participate in the action but can survey the whole literary landscape and directly report events that first-person narrators would know only by hearsay. Most third-person narrators reveal the thoughts of just one character. Others, with *limited omniscience,* can enter the heads of several characters, while still others display *full omniscience* and know everything in the literary work, including all thoughts and feelings of all characters. Omniscience allows the narrator to contrast two or more sets of thoughts and feelings and draw general conclusions from them. The narrator of Stephen Crane's "The Open Boat" is fully omniscient. The story is about four shipwrecked sailors adrift in a lifeboat, and the narrator, knowing what they all think, traces their developing awareness that nature is completely indifferent to their plight.

Yet another type of third-person narration, *dramatic,* has emerged in contemporary fiction. A dramatic narrator, like a motion-picture camera, moves about recording the characters' actions and words but without revealing anyone's thoughts. Stories with surprise endings often use this technique.

Writing about point of view.   For a paper about point of view, ask and answer these questions.

What point of view is used? Why is it used?

Is it suitable for the situation? Why or why not?

If the story uses first-person narration, is the narrator reliable? What textual evidence supports my answer?

What focus would produce an effective paper? What textual evidence could support its discussion?

Various reasons might prompt the choice of a particular point of view. For example, an author might use the first person to show a character's mental deterioration. A third-person narrator might enter two minds to contrast opposing attitudes toward some incident or enter no minds at all, in order to heighten the emotional impact of a story's climax.

If a point of view seems unsuitable, say so and suggest why. Suppose a man is planning an elopement that will create a surprise ending. A point of view that revealed the man's thoughts would give away that ending.

First-person narrators are sometimes unreliable; that is, they offer the reader a warped view of things. To gauge reliability, compare the narrator's version of the facts with what the work otherwise reveals. The narrator may come off as stupid, psychologically warped, or too biased to view events fairly. If so, speculate on the reasons. A mentally unreliable narrator may be meant, for example, to heighten the horror of events.

Although organization can vary, papers on point of view basically follow a cause-and-effect format, first identifying the point of view used and then demonstrating, with examples, its effect on the story and reader. In "The Bride," the third-person point of view allows Crane to shift from Potter and his new wife to the men in the saloon to the rampaging Scratchy and then to Potter and Scratchy as they confront each other. Shifting scenes in this way builds a sense of impending conflict, which would be difficult to produce with a first-person narrator, who could not move about in this fashion.

EXERCISE ■   Read the following two excerpts and answer the questions that follow them.

He had burned several times to enlist. Tales of great movements shook the land. . . . He had read of marches, sieges, conflicts, and he had longed to see it all. His busy mind had drawn for him large pictures, extravagant with color, lurid with breathless deeds.

But his mother had discouraged him. She had affected to look with some contempt on the quality of his war ardor and patriotism. She would calmly seat herself, and with no apparent difficulty give him many hundreds of reasons why he was of vastly more importance on the farm than he was on the field of battle. She had had certain ways of expression that told him that her statements on the subject came from a deep conviction. Moreover, on her side, was his belief that her ethical motive in the argument was impregnable.

Stephen Crane, *The Red Badge of Courage*

2. The first-person approach allows the reader to enter the mind of the story's main character, a small boy, and learn first-hand the impact that viewing a mysterious, ghostly train has had upon him. A third-person narrator could have told the reader what the boy thought and how he felt, but presenting these reactions directly strengthens their impact on the reader.

PERSPECTIVE

Students tend to react more strongly to literary characters than to any other element. For that reason, you might begin your analysis with a discussion of the characters and then have students write about them. Students should understand, however, the distinction between actual persons and literary characters that serve a function.

TEACHING STRATEGIES

1. Have students develop, in stages, a comprehensive analysis of a particular character's role. They might first note all the information they can about the character, next identify elements in the text that suggest these traits, and then detail how other characters perceive that character. Finally, they should consider how the character is important to the story, perhaps linking him or her to the plot or themes.
2. Inexperienced readers of literature tend to overemphasize the importance of verisimilitude. You could discuss where it is and isn't important for characters to be realistic. Students might identify the ways in which a character is unrealistic and then show how that character serves the function of the story.

Daddy helped me up onto the line and we hurried home. He said, "That was strange. What train was that, I wonder? And I didn't know the driver either." Then he didn't say any more.

I was shaking all over. That had been for me—for my sake. I guessed what it meant. It was all the fear which would come to me, all the unknowns; all that Daddy didn't know about and couldn't save me from. That was how the world would be for me. . . .

Pär Lagerkvist, "Father and I"

1. In Crane's third person stance, the narrator enters the son's mind but not the mother's. How does he convey the mother's attitude toward her son's desire to enlist?
2. What does Lagerkvist accomplish by using the first-person point of view?

Character

Character factors. The characters in a literary work function in various ways. Some are centers of physical and mental action. Others furnish humor, act as narrators, provide needed information, act as *foils* who highlight more important characters by contrast, serve as symbols, or simply populate the landscape. In "The Bride," the drummer helps funnel information to the reader. He asks questions, the bartender answers them, and the reader learns all about Scratchy.

Writers present character in several ways. Some tell the reader point-blank that a person is brave, stupid, self-serving, or the like. But most authors take an indirect approach by indicating how their characters look and act, what they think and say, how they live, and how other characters regard them.

Beware of uncritically accepting Character X's assessment of Character Y. X may be prejudiced, simple-minded, a deliberate liar, or too emotionally involved or disturbed to be objective. To illustrate, Scratchy Wilson, despite the bartender's fearful comments, proves to be something less than a real terror. He makes no real attempt to break down any doors and toys with, rather than shoots, the dog and Potter.

In picturing Potter, Crane first notes his appearance and self-conscious behavior, then delves into his mind to show the turmoil his marriage has stirred. Somewhat later, the bartender adds his brush strokes to Potter's portrait. At the confrontation, we again observe Potter's thoughts and behavior, as well as what he says to Scratchy. From all this, Potter emerges not as a mere one-dimensional lawman but as someone with a recognizably lifelike personality.

Some characters remain static; others mature, gain insight, or deteriorate in some telling way. Potter changes. As the story unfolds he abandons his doubts about the course he's charted and ends up fully committed to "the environment of the new estate." Scratchy, on the other hand, ends just as he started, "a simple child of the earlier plains."

Writing about character. Start the process by asking yourself these questions.

What characters offer the potential for a paper?

What are their most important features, and where in the story are these features revealed?

Do the characters undergo any changes? If so, how and why do the changes occur?

Are the characters believable, true to life? If not, why?

What focus would produce an effective paper?

What textual evidence could support the discussion?

Usually, you'll write about the main character, but at times you might choose the chief adversary or some minor character. For a lesser character, point out how that person interacts with the main one.

Most main characters change; most lesser ones do not. But sometimes a main character remains frozen, allowing the writer to make an important point. To show that a certain social group suffers from paralysis of the will, an author might create a main character who begins and ends weak and ineffectual. Whatever the situation, when you determine what purpose your character serves, tell the reader.

Think hard about your character's credibility. Ask yourself if he or she is true to life. Cruel stepmothers, brilliant but eccentric detectives, mad scientists, masked seekers after justice—these and other stereotyped figures don't square with real-life people, who are complex mixtures of many traits. Inconsistent acts of unexplained and unmotivated personality changes don't ring true: most people behave the same in similar situations and change only when properly motivated. Not every character needs to be a full-dress creation, but all require enough development to justify their roles.

Start your paper by identifying your character's role or personality; then back your contention with illustrations that support it, possibly following the sequence in which the writer presents them. If a character changes, say so, tell why, and indicate the results of the change, again using supporting examples. Such a paper is usually a cause-and-effect analysis. Papers that evaluate two characters are essentially comparisons.

For an example of a paper analyzing a character, see pages 291–293.

TEACHING STRATEGIES

1. For inexperienced students it is best to give assignments that require thought yet provide some structure, perhaps a comparison of two characters or a cause-and-effect analysis of character change. As students gain experience, increase the complexity of the assignments to include some evaluation. For example: "Is Scratchy Wilson's retreat believable given the way he is characterized?"

2. To help students see the range of options in writing about character, you might start a class discussion centered on possible approaches and how each would be developed.

EXERCISE ■   Write a paragraph describing the personality of the character in the following passage.

> The thousand injuries of Fortunato I had borne as I best could, but when he ventured upon insult, I vowed revenge. You, who so well know the nature of my soul, will not suppose, however, that I gave utterance to a threat. *At length* I would be avenged; this was a point definitely settled—but the very definiteness with which it was resolved precluded the idea of risk. I must not only punish, but punish with impunity. A wrong is unredressed when retribution overtakes its redresser. It is equally unredressed when the avenger fails to make himself felt as such to the one who has done the wrong.

> Edgar Allan Poe, "The Cask of Amontillado"

EXERCISE ANSWER

The speaker is vindictive, cunning, and without conscience. He's irrevocably committed to revenge, clever and calculating in plotting it, and shows no remorse over his impending act.

Setting

Setting factors. Setting locates characters in a time, place, and culture so they can think, feel, and act against this background. Writers can generate feelings and moods by describing settings. Sunny spring landscapes signal hope or happiness, dark alleys are foreboding, and thunderstorms suggest violent possibilities. Poetry, especially, uses setting to create mood. In the sonnet "Composed upon Westminster Bridge," William Wordsworth evokes the serenity and grandeur of London as the sun breaks over the sleeping city:

> Earth has not anything to show more fair:
> Dull would he be of soul who could pass by
> A sight so touching in its majesty:
> This city now doth, like a garment, wear
> The beauty of the morning: silent, bare,
> Ships, towers, domes, theaters, and temples lie
> Open unto the fields, and to the sky;
> All bright and glittering in the smokeless air.
> Never did sun more beautifully steep
> In his first splendor, valley, rock, or hill;
> Ne'er saw I, never felt, a calm so deep!
> The river glideth at his own sweet will:
> Dear God! the very houses seem asleep;
> And all that mighty heart is lying still!

Setting can also help reveal character. In this excerpt from Sinclair Lewis's novel *Babbitt,* the contents and atmosphere of the library mirror the stiff, self-satisfied formality of its banker-owner:

> . . . The books were most of them standard sets, with the correct and traditional touch of dim blue, dim gold, and glossy calf-skin. The fire was exactly correct and traditional; a small, quiet, steady fire, reflected by polished fire-irons. The oak desk was dark and altogether perfect; the chairs were gently supercilious.

Settings sometimes function as symbols, reinforcing the workings of the other elements. A broad, slowly flowing river may stand for time or fate, a craggy cliff for strength of character, a blizzard-swept plain for the overwhelming power of nature. The following section, a discussion of symbols, points out some symbolic settings in "The Bride."

At times, setting provides a clue to some observation about life. At one point in Stephen Crane's story "The Open Boat," the men spot a nearby flock of seagulls sitting comfortably on the turbulent waves. Juxtaposing the complacent gulls and the imperiled men suggests the philosophical point of the story: that the universe is indifferent to human aspirations and struggles.

Shifts in setting often trigger shifts in a character's emotional or psychological state. Jack Potter, typically calm and assured in Yellow Sky, displays great awkwardness and embarrassment in the unfamiliar environment of the Pullman car.

Writing about setting. Begin your search for a topic by identifying the settings in the story and then asking these questions about each one.

What are its key features?
What does it accomplish? Create a mood? Reveal a character? Serve as a symbol? Reinforce the story's point? How does it accomplish these things?
In what ways does it support or interfere with the story?
Does the setting seem realistic? If not, why not?
What focus would produce an effective paper? What textual evidence would support it?

Check the impact of setting on mood by seeing how well the two match up for each setting. Sometimes, as in "The Bride," the two bear little or no relationship to each other. In other cases, the two intertwine throughout the work.

Try to establish connections between settings and characters. If an emotionally barren individual always appears against backdrops of gloomy furnished rooms, cheerless restaurants, and decaying slums, you can assume that the writer is using setting to convey character. Look for links between changes in characters and changes in settings. If the setting remains the same, point out any shifts in the way the character views it.

Occasionally, a writer drums home settings so insistently that they overpower the characters and story line. A novel about the super rich may linger so lovingly over their extravagant surroundings that the plot lacks force and the characters seem mere puppets. If the setting hobbles the other elements, identify this flaw in your analysis.

When you write about setting, describe it and discuss its impact on the story's other elements, supporting your claims with specific examples. In writing about "The Bride," you might argue that Crane used as his chief setting a pulp fiction cliché of a western town in order to heighten the atypical nature of the showdown. As support, you could cite such stock features as the train station, saloon, dog, and dusty streets, all of which point toward an actual shootout rather than Scratchy Wilson's backdown.

EXERCISE ■ What mood does the following description of a room generate? What does it suggest about the situation of the room's inhabitants, two women in an Old Ladies' Home?

Marian stood enclosed by a bed, a washstand, and a chair; the tiny room had altogether too much furniture. Everything smelled wet—even the bare floor. She held onto the back of the chair, which was wicker and felt soft and damp. . . . How dark it was! The window shade was down, and the only door was shut. Marian looked at the ceiling. . . . It was like being caught in a robbers' cave. . . .

Eudora Welty, "A Visit of Charity"

EXERCISE ANSWER

The description of the small, dark, closed-in, wet-smelling and overcrowded room generates a gloomy mood. The room bears a strong resemblance to a jail cell, and the description suggests that its inhabitants are, like prisoners in a jail, hopelessly trapped creatures.

Symbols

TEACHING STRATEGIES

1. It helps to start your discussion with common symbols known to all students. The school mascot often provides a good, and sometimes humorous, example. Once students understand the array of symbols in their world, you could turn to literary symbols.

2. To help students begin to think about literary symbols, have them draw a network, just as in any brainstorming activity, which includes all the associations they see in the text for any potential symbol. Students might view a symbol not merely as an image that "stands for something else" but also as a knot that ties together a wide range of associations.

Symbol factors. To strengthen and deepen their messages, writers use symbols: names, persons, objects, places, colors, or actions that have a significance beyond their surface meaning. A symbol may be very obvious—as a name like Mr. Grimm, suggesting the person's character—or quite subtle, as an object representing a universal human emotion.

Some symbols are private and others conventional. A private symbol has special significance within a literary work but not outside it. Conventional symbols are deeply rooted in our culture, and almost everyone knows what they represent. We associate crosses with Christianity and limousines with wealth and power. In "The Bride," the plains pouring eastward past the Pullman windows, Scratchy's eastern clothing, and the mirage-like grass plots in front of the saloon are all private symbols that stand for the passing of the Old West. Because people of Crane's time associated Pullman cars with an urbane, eastern life-style, the Pullman is a conventional symbol that represents the new order of things. Like the Pullman, a symbol may appear more than once in a literary work.

Whether or not a recurring item is a symbol depends upon its associations. In Ernest Hemingway's novel *A Farewell to Arms,* rain may fairly be said to symbolize doom because it consistently accompanies disasters, and one of the main characters says that she has visions of herself lying dead in the rain. But if rain is randomly associated with a rundown lakeside resort, a spirited business meeting, a cozy weekend, and the twentieth-anniversary celebration of a happy marriage, the writer probably intends no symbolism.

PERSPECTIVE

Students are often much less successful writing about symbols than about plot, characters, setting, or themes. They experience difficulty pulling their ideas together into something more than a trite survey of the symbols.

TEACHING STRATEGIES

1. Examination of a professional or student paper that successfully discusses the symbols in some literary work can help students understand their function. Have students identify the paper's purpose, the writing strategies used to develop it, and the places where the writer points out connections between the symbols and the story's other elements.

2. Point out that discussions of symbols often support an interpretation of a work's themes rather than function as the central focus of a piece of writing.

Writing about symbols. When you examine the symbols in a literary work, think about these questions.

> What symbols are used and where do they appear?
> Are they private or conventional?
> What do they appear to mean?
> Do any of them undergo a change in meaning? If so, how and why?
> Which symbol(s) could I discuss effectively?
> What textual evidence would support my interpretation?

To locate symbols, read the literary work carefully, looking for items that seem to have an extended meaning. You might, for example, discover that the cracked walls of a crumbling mansion symbolize some character's disordered mental state or that a voyage symbolizes the human journey from birth to death. Several symbols often mean the same thing; writers frequently use them in sets. In "Bartleby the Scrivener," for instance, Herman Melville uses windows that look upon walls, a folding screen, and a prison to symbolize Bartleby's alienated condition, that is, his mental separation from those around him. Determining whether each symbol is private or conventional can provide clues to its meaning.

Sometimes a symbol changes meaning during the course of a work. A woman who regards her lover's large, strong hands as symbols of passion may, following an illness that leaves him a dangerous madman, view them as symbols of danger and brute strength. Note any changes you discover, and suggest what they signify.

A word of caution: don't let symbol hunting become an obsession. Before you assert that something has a different and deeper meaning than its surface application, make sure the evidence in the work backs your claim.

For each symbol you discuss, state what you think it means and then support your position with appropriate textual evidence. You could argue, for example, that the Pullman car in "The Bride" symbolizes the Eastern civilization that is encroaching on the West, offering as evidence the car's "figured velvet . . . shining brass, silver, and glass" and darkly gleaming wood appointments.

EXERCISE ■   Read the following excerpts from Edward Fitzgerald's *The Rubáiyát of Omar Khayyám* and answer the questions that follow.

> Strange, is it not? that of the myriads who
> Before us passed the door of Darkness through,
> Not one returns to tell us of the Road,
> Which to discover we must travel too.
>
> The Moving Finger writes; and, having writ,
> Moves on: nor all your Piety nor Wit
> Shall lure it back to cancel half a line,
> Nor all your Tears wash out a Word of it.

1. What does the door of Darkness symbolize? The Road? The Moving Finger?
2. What messages are these symbols meant to convey?

Irony

Irony factors.   Irony features some discrepancy, some difference between appearance and reality, expectation and outcome. Sometimes a character says one thing but means something else. The critic who, tongue in cheek, says that a clumsy dancer is "poetry in motion" speaks ironically.

Irony also results when the reader or a character recognizes something as important, but another character does not. In "The Bride" this situation occurs when Potter, not knowing that Scratchy is on a rampage, flees the station agent, who tries to let him know. A character's behavior sometimes offers ironic contrasts, too. There's high irony in the contrast between Potter's unflinching face-off with Scratchy and his fear of telling the townsfolk about his marriage.

At times the ending of a work doesn't square with what the reader expects: the confrontation between Potter and Scratchy ends not in a fusillade of bullets but a flurry of words. To add to the irony, Potter wins because he is armed with a new and unfamiliar weapon—his wife. The emotional impact of an ironic ending depends upon the circumstances of plot and character. As Scratchy walks off, we're likely to view matters with amusement. In other cases, we might register joy, horror, gloom, or almost anything else.

Writing about irony. Start by answering these questions.

Where does irony occur?
What does it accomplish?
What could my thesis be, and how could I support it?

In probing for irony, check for statements that say one thing and mean something else, situations in which one character knows something that another doesn't, and contrasts between the ways characters should and do behave. Review the plot to see whether the outcome matches the expectations.

To prove that irony is intended, examine the context in which the words are spoken or the events occur. Also, tell the reader what the irony accomplishes. In "The Bride," it is ironic that someone as wild as Scratchy Wilson would be awed by, and retreat from, Potter's wife, yet this irony is central to the idea that the Old West, despite its violence, was no match for the civilizing forces of the East.

EXERCISE ■ Discuss the irony in this poem.

Richard Cory
Edwin Arlington Robinson

Whenever Richard Cory went down town,
We people on the pavement looked at him:
He was a gentleman from sole to crown,
Clean favored, and imperially slim.

And he was always quietly arrayed,
And he was always human when he talked;
But still he fluttered pulses when he said,
"Good-morning," and he glittered when he walked.

And he was rich—yes, richer than a king—
And admirably schooled in every grace:
In fine, we thought that he was everything
To make us wish that we were in his place.

So on we worked, and waited for the light,
And went without the meat, and cursed the bread;
And Richard Cory, one calm summer night,
Went home and put a bullet through his head.

Theme

Theme factors. The theme of a literary work is its controlling idea, some observation or insight about life or the conditions and terms of living, such as the prevalence of evil, the foolishness of pride, or the healing power of love. Many literary works suggest several themes: sometimes one primary motif and several related ones, sometimes a number of unrelated motifs. Theme is central to a work of literature: frequently all of the other elements help develop and support it.

On occasion, the writer or a character states the theme directly. Mrs. Alving, the main character in Henrik Ibsen's play *Ghosts,* notes that the dead past plays a powerful and evil role in shaping human lives.

> . . . I am half inclined to think that we are all ghosts, Mr. Manders. It is not only what we have inherited from our fathers and mothers that exists again in us, but all sorts of old dead ideas and all kinds of old dead beliefs and things of that kind. They are not actually alive in us; but there they are dormant, all the same, and we can never be rid of them.

Ordinarily, though, the theme remains unstated and must be deduced by examining the other elements of the literary work.

Writing about theme. Before you begin writing, ask and answer these questions.

> What are the themes of this work? Which of these should I write about? Are they stated or unstated?
> If stated, what elements support them?
> If unstated, what elements create them?
> What, if any, thematic weaknesses are present?

Check the comments of the characters and the narrator to see whether they state the themes directly. If they don't, assess the interaction of characters, events, settings, symbols, and other elements to determine them.

Let's see how the elements of Nathaniel Hawthorne's short story "Young Goodman Brown" work together to yield the primary theme. The story has four characters—Goodman Brown; his wife, Faith; Deacon Gookin; and Goody Cloyse—whose names symbolically suggest that they are completely good. Another symbol, Faith's pink hair ribbon, at first suggests innocence and later its loss. The story relates Brown's nighttime journey into a forest at the edge of a Puritan village and subsequent attendance at a baptismal ceremony for new converts to the Devil. He proceeds into the forest, suggestive of mystery and lawlessness, during a dark night, suggestive of evil, where he meets his guide, the Devil in the guise of his grandfather. As he proceeds, Goodman vacillates between reluctance to join the Devil's party and fascination with it. Innocent and ignorant, he is horrified when he finds that the deacon and Goody seem to be in league with the Devil. Goodman tries to preserve his pure image of his wife, Faith, but her pink ribbon falls out of a tumultuous sky seemingly filled with demons, and Goodman sees her at the baptismal ceremony. He shrieks out to her to "resist the wicked one" and is suddenly alone in the woods, not knowing whether she obeyed. The end of the story finds Brown back in his village, unable to view his wife and neighbors as anything but totally evil.

In light of these happenings, it's probably safe to say that the primary theme of the story is somewhat as follows:

PERSPECTIVE

Since we read literature not simply as an art form but also for insights into life, much of the writing about literature is about theme. Students, however, experience problems when approaching this element. First, many of them see works as having only one theme. Instead, of course, it is the endless suggestiveness that allows us to go back to the best works repeatedly. Second, students tend to reduce theme to a simple generalization rather than recognize that it emerges from the actual dynamics of the story and how it is developed.

TEACHING STRATEGIES

1. Have students explain in a journal or as a class how the story either confirmed or changed their view of the world. Then have them articulate how that attitude might be a theme and, in turn, how it is realized in the text.
2. After students have identified a theme, have them list some of the associated themes and identify how these themes are developed in the text. Students tend to suppress the conflicts and contradictions in a theme in order to reduce it to the simplest form. Encourage them to note any conflicts and where they are resolved. For example, in "The Bride," there is a clear conflict between eastern society and the wild west.

Human beings are a mixture of good and evil, but some individuals can't accept this fact. Once they realize that "good" people are susceptible to sin, they decide that everyone is evil, and they become embittered for life.

Point out any thematic weakness that you find. Including a completely innocent major character in a story written to show that people are mixtures of good and evil would contradict the writer's intention.

A paper on theme is basically an argument, first presenting your interpretation and then supporting it with textual evidence. You might argue that the primary theme of "The Bride" is the demise of the Old West under the civilizing influence of the East. You could cite the luxurious Pullman car in contrast to the drab town, Potter's uncomfortable submission to the waiter and porter, and Scratchy Wilson's retreat at the story's end. In addition, you could suggest a related theme: people out of their element often founder—sometimes even appear ridiculous. As support, you might point to Potter's behavior on the train, the drummer's subdued attitude when Scratchy's arrival is imminent, and Scratchy's reaction when told about Potter's wife.

EXERCISE ANSWER

The poem offers the observation that time provides us with the opportunity to engage in meaningful or trivial pursuits. The observation emerges through the imagery of the muffled and dumb daughters of time who bring diadems (symbolizing the opportunity for meaningful pursuits) and fagots (symbolizing the opportunity for trivial pursuits). The final sentence presents the point of the poem: that it is shameful to opt for trivial pursuits. When the narrator hastily takes "a few herbs and apples," he earns the scorn of their bearer.

EXERCISE ■   **Ralph Waldo Emerson's "Days" offers an observation on how people should occupy their time. Read the poem carefully, checking any unfamiliar words in your dictionary. Then state Emerson's observation in your own words.**

Daughters of Time, the hypocritic Days,
Muffled and dumb like barefoot dervishes,
And marching single in an endless file,
Bring diadems and fagots in their hands.
To each they offer gifts after his will,
Bread, kingdom, stars, and sky that holds them all.

I, in my pleachéd garden, watched the pomp,
Forgot my morning wishes, hastily
Took a few herbs and apples, and the Day
Turned and departed silent. I, too late,
Under her solemn fillet saw the scorn.

WRITING A PAPER ON LITERATURE

PERSPECTIVE

You can help students write a paper about literature by giving them some sense of purpose and audience. If a class discussion of some work has raised questions of interest to your students,

Focusing, gathering information, organizing, writing, revising and editing—the same procedure leads to success in a literature paper as in any other type.

First, make sure you *understand the assignment.* Let's assume you have been asked to do the following:

Write a 750-word essay that analyzes one of the elements in Stephen Crane's "The Bride Comes to Yellow Sky." Take into account all the pertinent factors of whatever element(s) you choose.

For this assignment you could focus on plot, point of view, character, setting, symbols, irony, theme, or some meaningful combination of two or more of these elements.

Next, *decide upon a suitable topic.* For papers on literature, your best approach is to reread the work carefully and then reflect on it. As you do this for "The Bride" assignment, you rule out a paper centering on plot, setting, irony, point of view, or theme. Because your class has discussed the first three so thoroughly, you doubt you can offer anything more. The matter of the narrator stumps you; you can understand why Crane uses a third-person narrator who airs Potter's thoughts, but you can't see what's accomplished by the brief looks into other characters' minds. Regarding theme, you doubt you can do justice to the topic in 750 words. As you mentally mine character and symbolism for possible topics, your thoughts turn to the many gunfighters you've watched in the movies and read about in western fiction. Because gunfighters have always fascinated you and Scratchy Wilson seems an intriguing example of the breed, you decide to analyze his character.

To complete the next stage, *gathering information,* reread the story again and as you do, list all pertinent information about Scratchy that might help develop a character analysis. Your efforts might yield these results.

1. Scratchy "a wonder with a gun."
2. "about the last one of the old gang that used to hang out along the river here."
3. "He's a terror when he's drunk," the opposite otherwise.
4. Potter "goes out and fights Scratchy when he gets on one of these tears."
5. Has shot Scratchy once, in the leg.
6. Does nothing to stop "tears" from happening.
7. On street, Scratchy, "in a rage begot of whisky." Neck works angrily.
8. Utters "Cries of ferocious challenge."
9. Moves with "the creeping movement of the midnight cat."
10. Guns move "with an electric swiftness."
11. Clothes—maroon shirt, gilded red-topped boots—not adult western garb.
12. Doesn't shoot dog.
13. Doesn't try breaking down doors.
14. Warns Potter not to go for gun rather than shooting him.
15. Says he'll hit Potter with gun, not shoot him if Potter doesn't "mind what I tell you."
16. Only sneers when Potter calls him "damn fool," and when Potter says, "If you're goin' to shoot me up, you better begin now; you'll never get a chance like this again."
17. Backs down and walks away when confronted with Potter's marriage.

List in hand, you are now ready to *organize your information.* As you examine your items and answer the questions about character on page 281, you start to realize that Scratchy is not merely a one-dimensional gunslinging menace. To reflect your discovery, you prepare a formal topic outline.

clearly the purpose of their writing should be to share their insights. In general, students will write better if they see themselves helping an actual reader gain a new perspective on a work of literature.

TEACHING STRATEGY

An interesting discussion of the work can establish the context for writing assignments. Furthermore, students benefit if you discuss the range of papers they might possibly write and the ways they could approach them. Finished papers might be copied or exchanged as a way of carrying on the discussion.

   I. Bartender's assessment
     A. Evidence that Scratchy is a menace
        1. A wonder with a gun
        2. Former outlaw gang member
        3. A terror when drunk
     B. Contradictory evidence
        1. Mild when sober
        2. Only one actual shootout with Potter
  II. Scratchy's behavior
     A. Evidence that Scratchy is a menace
        1. Rage
        2. Wary movements
        3. Skillful handling of guns
     B. Contradictory evidence
        1. Mode of dress
        2. Failure to shoot dog
        3. Failure to try breaking down doors
        4. Behavior during confrontation
        5. Final retreat

The next stage, *developing a thesis statement,* presents few difficulties. After examining the outline and thinking about its contents, you draft the following sentence:

> A close look at Scratchy Wilson shows that he has much more
>
> depth than his pulp fiction counterparts.

Drawing on your notes and following your outline, you now *write a first draft* of your essay, and then follow up with the necessary revising and editing. In addition, you review the story and verify your interpretation.

As you *prepare your final draft,* follow these guidelines.

Handling quotations.   Like aspirin, quotations should be used when necessary, but not to excess. Cite brief, relevant passages to support key ideas, but fight the urge to quote huge blocks of material. Place short quotations, less than five lines long, within quotation marks and run them into the text. For longer quotes, omit the quotation marks and indent the material ten spaces from the left-hand margin. When quoting poetry, use a slash mark (/) to show the shift from one line to the other in the original: "A honey tongue, a heart of gall,/ Is fancy's spring, but sorrow's fall." Pages 340–343 provide added information on handling quotes.

Documentation.   Document ideas and quotations from outside sources by following the guidelines on pages 333–340.

If your instructor wants you to document quotations from the work you're writing about, include the information within parentheses following the quotations. For fiction, cite the page number on which the quote appeared: (83). For poetry, cite the word "line" or "lines" and the appropriate numbers: (lines 23–24). For plays, cite act, scene, and line numbers, separated by periods: (1.3.18–19). When discussing a work of fiction not in your textbook, identify the book you used as your source. Your instructor can then easily check your information. With short papers like the one below, internal documentation is often omitted.

Tense.   Write your essay in the present rather than the past tense. Say "In *The Sound and the Fury,* William Faulkner uses four narrators, each of whom provides a different perspective on the events that take place," not ". . . William Faulkner used four narrators, each of whom provided a different perspective on the events that took place."

EXAMPLE STUDENT ESSAY ON LITERATURE

Scratchy Wilson: No Cardboard Character

Wendell Stone

Stephen Crane's "The Bride Comes to Yellow Sky" is artful on several counts. For one thing, the story is rich in irony. It makes use of an elaborate set of symbols to get its point across. It is filled with vivid language, and in Jack Potter and Scratchy Wilson it offers its readers two very unusual characters. Potter's actions and thoughts clearly show that he is a complex person. In fact, his complexity is so conspicuous that it becomes easy to regard Scratchy as nothing more than a one-dimensional badman. But this judgment is mistaken. A close look at Scratchy shows that he, like Potter, has much more depth than his pulp fiction counterparts.

Nothing in what the bartender says about Scratchy hints that there is anything unusual about the old outlaw. We learn that Scratchy is "a wonder with a gun," that he is "about the last one of the old gang that used to hang out along the river here," and that "He's a terror when he's drunk" but mild-mannered and pleasant at other times. One thing may strike the careful reader as a little odd, though. Although Potter "goes out and fights Scratchy when he gets on one of these tears," he has wounded Scratchy just once, and then only in the leg. Apparently, Potter has been able to talk the supposed terror out of a shootout each of the other times. Nor has Potter apparently tried doing anything to stop Scratchy's "tears."

As he steps onto the main street of Yellow Sky, Scratchy seems every bit as menacing as the bartender has described him. His face flames "in a rage begot of whisky," the cords in his neck throb and bulge with anger, and he hurls "cries of ferocious challenge" at the barricaded buildings. Scratchy is clearly no stranger to either weapons or shootouts. He walks with "the creeping movement of the midnight cat," moves his revolvers with "an electric swiftness," and keeps constantly on the alert for an ambush.

Nevertheless, Scratchy comes across as less than totally menacing. For one thing, his maroon shirt and gilded, red-topped boots make him look not like a westerner but like some child's notion of one. When he sees the dog, he deliberately shoots to frighten rather than to kill it. And in spite of all his bluster, he makes no real attempt to break down any doors and get at the people hiding behind them. Scratchy's clothing shows that eastern ways have touched even this "child of the earlier plains." But one could easily argue that eastern gentleness has had some slight softening influence on him, too. Be that as it may, it seems evident that

Scratchy, perhaps without quite realizing it himself, is mainly play-acting when he goes on his rampages and that Potter knows this.

During the whole final confrontation, Scratchy seems more of an actor than a gunman wanting revenge against his "ancient antagonist." Instead of shooting when Potter makes a slight movement, Scratchy warns him not to go for a gun and says that he intends to take his time settling accounts, to "loaf along with no interferin'." Significantly, he threatens to hit Potter with a gun, not shoot him, if the marshal does not "mind what I tell you." Even when Potter, recovered from his brief fright, calls Scratchy a "damn fool" and says "If you're goin' to shoot me up, you better begin now; you'll never get a chance like this again." Scratchy does nothing except sneer. This confrontation, like all but one of the others, ends with no shots fired. But one thing is different. Potter's marriage has forced Scratchy to realize that something unstoppable is changing the Old West forever. When he drops his revolver to his side, stands silent for awhile, and then says, "I s'pose it's all off now," we sense that he means not just this episode but any future clashes as well.

Scratchy is not a cardboard creation. His behavior is by no means as easily explainable as it at first seems, and he is capable of some degree of insight. Nonetheless, Scratchy remains very much a creature of the past, something that time has passed by. As he leaves, his feet make funnel-shaped tracks, reminiscent of hourglasses, in the sand. Soon these tracks, along with Scratchy and his way of life, will disappear.

EXERCISE ANSWER

The student should note that Campion presents a highly idealized image of the woman he writes about. Shakespeare presents a much more realistic assessment of his mistress, yet asserts, in the final two lines of the poem, that his love (mistress) is every bit as precious as any woman (she) lied about (belied) through false comparison.

SUGGESTED INSTRUCTOR READINGS

Biatt, G. T., and L. M. Rosen. "The Writing Response to Literature." The Journal of Reading 28 (1984): 8–12. Reviews how writing can serve as an important vehicle for understanding literature.

Lodge, D., ed. 20th Century Criticism. London: Longman, 1972. Contains many of the key twentieth century essays on literary criticism. While no substitute for reading Richards, Empson, Brooks, and others, it provides an effective overview of many of the key issues in contemporary criticism.

Moran, C. "Teaching Writing/ Teaching Literature." College Composition and Communication 32 (1981): 21–29. Gives helpful suggestions for effectively combining the teaching of writing and the teaching of literature.

Rosenblatt, L. The Reader, The Text, The Poem: The Transactional Theory of the Literary Work. Carbondale, IL: Southern Illinois UP, 1978. Provides helpful insights into how students read literature and experience the literary work.

Scott, P. G. "Flowers in the Path of Science: Teaching Composition Through Traditional High Literature." College English 42 (1980): 1–9. Reviews the important reasons that literature can sometimes be an important ingredient for a successful composition class.

EXERCISE ■ Using the guidelines offered in this chapter, write a short essay comparing and contrasting the two writers' assessments of the women in the poems below. (You might find it helpful to review pages 119-126 on comparison.) Limit your focus and back any general statements you make with appropriate support from the poems.

There Is a Garden in Her Face
Thomas Campion (1617)

There is a garden in her face,
Where roses and white lilies grow;
A heavenly paradise is that place,
Wherein all pleasant fruits do flow.
There cherries grow which none may buy
Till "Cherry ripe" themselves do cry.

Those cherries fairly do inclose
Of orient pearl a double row,
Which when her lovely laughter shows,
They look like rosebuds filled with snow;
Yet them nor peer nor prince can buy,
Till "Cherry ripe" themselves do cry.

Her eyes like angels watch them still;
Her brows like bended bows do stand,
Threat'ning with piercing frowns to kill
All that attempt with eye or hand
Those sacred cherries to come nigh,
Till "Cherry ripe" themselves do cry.

Sonnet 130
William Shakespeare (1609)

My mistress' eyes are nothing like the sun;
Coral is far more red than her lips red;
If snow be white, why then her breasts are dun;
If hairs be wires, black wires grow on her head.
I have seen roses damask'd, red and white,
But no such roses see I in her cheeks;
And in some perfumes there is more delight
Than in the breath that from my mistress reeks.
I love to hear her speak, yet well I know
That music hath a far more pleasing sound;
I grant I never saw a goddess go;
My mistress, when she walks, treads on the ground.
And yet, by heaven, I think my love as rare
As any she belied with false compare.

Chapter 19

The Library Research Paper

Scene: A dark, sinister-looking laboratory. In the center of the stage stands a large laboratory bench crowded with an array of mysterious chemistry apparatus. Tall, cadaverous, and foreboding, Dr. Frankenslime leers as he pours the contents of a tube through a funnel and into a bubbling flask. A short, hunchbacked figure looks on with interest. Suddenly the doctor spreads his arms wide and flashes a sardonic smile.

Frankenslime: Igor! At last! At last I've got it! With this fluid, I can control. . . .

Research yes. But not all researchers are mad scientists, or scientists, or even mad. You aren't any of these things, but no doubt you'll be asked to prepare a *library research paper* for your composition class. This assignment calls for you to gather information from a variety of sources and then to focus, organize, and present it in a formal paper that documents the sources. The experience you gain will carry over and help you meet the research demands of other courses and perhaps your job. You'll become familiar with the mechanics of documentation. And when you finish the project, you'll have a good grasp of your topic and can point proudly to your accomplishment.

LEARNING ABOUT YOUR LIBRARY

Before starting a library research paper, take time to familiarize yourself with your library. Many college libraries offer guided tours, and almost all of them display floor plans that show where and how the books are grouped. If your library doesn't have tours, browse through it on your own and scan its contents. As you do, note the following features:

PERSPECTIVE

The reports of the research paper's demise have been, of course, greatly exaggerated; the research paper is still the key assignment in many courses. Furthermore, many professionals do on-the-job research-report writing: businesspeople detail new production methods, social workers explore the effects of a new law, and hospital pharmacists relate developments in their field. To advance in many fields, students must be able to research, synthesize, and report on published information affecting their occupation.

TEACHING STRATEGY

Students often believe that research papers are busywork. To counter this notion, have them interview faculty or working professionals in their fields to determine the role of research writing and then report back to the class. If this is too impractical, you could have students review publications in their fields to determine what kinds of reports are written and why.

PERSPECTIVE

Students often know little about researching in the library. Some don't understand how to use a card catalog. Most are unfamiliar with periodical indexes. Hardly any know how to use the more specialized indexes and resources. And yet the ability to find essential information is important, even crucial, to their academic, professional, and personal lives. Rather than regarding libraries as academic torture chambers, students should see them as useful resources that provide information they'll need in order to complete college and on-the-job writing assignments and resolve personal problems such as a landlord who refuses to make repairs.

TEACHING STRATEGY

You might develop an extensive library assignment that requires students to find a wide-ranging variety of information on such matters as the side effects of medication or the toxic waste sites located in their state. Depending on your students' abilities, you can specify the source and call numbers, just the source, the type of source, or provide no assistance at all. Students might be assigned to work in teams (since they will anyway). It's helpful to spend some time in the library with students when they are doing such assignments.

TEACHING STRATEGIES

1. Since few students are experienced in selecting suitable research topics, you might provide some guidelines. An assignment that specifies purpose and audience is often helpful. For instance, after discussing problems of concern to your state or local area, you could have each student write a research report for the governor or mayor, detailing one particular problem and arguing for some solution.
2. One way of teaching the research paper is to have everyone participate in a larger research

Stacks: These are the bookshelves that hold books and bound periodicals (magazines and newspapers). Stacks are either open or closed. Open stacks allow you to go directly to the books you want, take them off the shelf, and check them out. Closed stacks do not allow you direct access to shelved material. Instead, someone on the library staff brings you what you want.

Circulation Desk: Here's where you check materials in and out, renew books you want to keep longer, and pay overdue fines. If you can't find something you want, the desk clerk will tell you whether it's missing, on reserve, or checked out to someone else. If it's out, fill out a hold card, and the library will notify you when the other borrower returns it.

Reserve Area: This area contains books that instructors have asked the library to remove from general circulation so students can use them for particular courses. Ordinarily, you can keep these books for only a few hours or overnight.

Reference Area: This area houses the library's collection of encyclopedias, periodical indexes, almanacs, handbooks, dictionaries, and other research tools that you'll use as you investigate your topic. You'll also find here one or more reference guides—Eugene P. Sheehy's *Guide to Reference Books* (1979) is an example—that direct you to useful reference tools. To ensure that these books are always available, they must be used in the library. Someone is always on duty to answer questions.

Periodical Area: Here you'll find current and recent issues of magazines and newspapers. If your topic calls for articles that have appeared within the last few months, you're likely to find them in this area.

Microfilm and Microfiche Files: Microfilm is a filmstrip bearing a series of photographically reduced printed pages. Microfiche is a small card with a set of photographically reduced pages mounted on it. Often, most of a library's magazine and newspaper collection is on film. Ask a librarian how to work the viewing machines. Once you can run them, you'll have access to many library resources.

Card Catalog: The card catalog, located close to the circulation desk, indexes all the library's books and often most of the other holdings as well. Libraries classify and arrange books by either the Library of Congress system or the Dewey Decimal system. Each labels the cards with call numbers that enable you or a librarian to locate items quickly. The card catalog is discussed in detail on pages 301–303.

Computer Terminals: These may include terminals for computerized card catalogs and data bases. Ask the librarian how to use the terminals. There may be a small fee for using them.

CHOOSING A TOPIC

Instructors take different approaches in assigning library research papers. Some want explanatory papers, others want papers that address a two-sided question, and still others allow students a free choice. An explanatory paper takes no position but provides information that gives the reader a better grasp of the topic. For example, it may explain the key advantages of solar heating, thereby clearing up popular misconceptions. An argument paper, on the other hand, attempts to sway the reader toward one point of view—for instance, that solar heat is commercially feasible. Some instructors specify not only the type of paper but also the topic. Others restrict students to a general subject area, ask them to pick topics from lists, or give them free choice. If you have little to say in the selection, look at the bright side: at least you won't have to fret and fume over discovering a topic.

Whatever the circumstances, it's a good idea to follow a pacing schedule that establishes completion dates for the various stages of your paper. Such a timetable encourages you to plan your work, clarifies both your progress and the work remaining, and provides an overview of the entire project. You can use the following sample schedule as a guide, modifying the stages or adding other ones as necessary.

Sample schedule for a library research paper

Activity	Targeted Completion Date
Topic Selection	_____
Working Bibliography	_____
Tentative Thesis	_____
Note Taking	_____
Working Outline	_____
First Draft	_____
Revised Drafts	_____ _____ _____
Date Due:	_____

Topics to Avoid

If you have free rein to pick your topic, how should you proceed? To begin, rule out certain types of topics:

- Those based entirely on personal experience or opinion such as "The Thrills I Have Enjoyed Waterskiing" or "Colorado Has More [or Less] Scenic Beauty than New Mexico." Such topics can't be supported by library research. Don't hesitate, however, to include personal judgments and conclusions that emerge from your reading.

- Those fully explained in a single source. An explanation of a process, such as cardiopulmonary resuscitation, or the description of a place, such as the Gobi Desert, does not require coordination of materials from various sources. Although you may find several articles on such topics, basically they will repeat the same information.

- Those that are brand new. Often it's impossible to find sufficient source material about such topics.

- Those that are overly broad. Don't try to tackle such elephant-sized topics as "The Causes of World War II" or "Recent Medical Advances." Instead, slim them down to something like "The Advent of Jet Fighters" or "Eye Surgery with Laser Beams." The techniques discussed on pages 12–19 can help you reduce a topic to manageable size.

- Those that have been worked over and over, such as abortion and the legalization

project. The class might select a major problem, such as prison overcrowding, and then, after some initial reading, break this problem down into smaller projects that individual students take up according to their interests. One student might explore the success of alternative punishment programs; another might consider whether we should spend funds on early prevention; a third could evaluate the effects of overcrowding on prisoners. When the project is finished, student reports could be bound into a document and used as a teaching tool for future classes.
3. A pacing schedule helps guard against the tendency of some students to procrastinate, especially on a project of this magnitude. Depending on your class, you could specify the dates or have students determine their own. The latter option teaches students to budget their time effectively. This type of schedule helps deter plagiarism, particularly if you inspect the work at each stage and ask students to revise according to your suggestions.

TEACHING STRATEGIES

1. To help students avoid dead-end topics, specify that papers must either recommend a solution to a problem or argue one side of a controversial issue. Significant problems and issues are rarely personal or found in a single source. More importantly, you instill the notion that students should utilize their sources for a purpose rather than merely collect and display them.
2. You might show students how to generalize personal or recent topics and restrict broad ones. While "How last night's riot got started" is obviously too current, it might be acceptable if recast as "What causes student riots at sporting events, and how can these riots be prevented?" While "The home computer revolution" is clearly too broad, it could be narrowed to "How are home computers actually being used?"

of marijuana. Why bore your reader with information and arguments that are all too familiar already?

EXERCISE ▪ Using the advice on topics to avoid, explain why each of the following would or would not be suitable for a library research topic.

1. Genetic counseling
2. Neoconservatism
3. The home computer revolution
4. How last night's riot got started
5. Building a rock garden
6. A third world hot spot as described on the evening news
7. Reforming the financing of presidential election campaigns

Drawing on Your Interests

Let your interests guide your choice. A long-standing interest in baseball might suggest a paper on the Black Sox Scandal of 1919. An instructor's lecture might spark your interest in a historical event or person, an economic crisis, a scientific development, a sociological trend, a medical milestone, a political scandal, or the influences on an author. An argument with a friend might spur you to investigate latch-key children. A television documentary might arouse your curiosity about a group of primitive people. A recent article or novel might inspire you to explore the occult or some taboo.

Be practical in selecting a topic. Why not get a head start on a particular aspect of your major field by researching it now? Some management, marketing, or advertising strategy; the beginnings of current contract law; medical ethics— all of these topics, and many others, qualify. Think about your audience, the availability of information, and whether you can fit it into the guidelines for your paper.

CASE HISTORY ▪

Christine Harding was a freshman composition student when she wrote the library research paper at the end of this chapter. Christine's instructor had limited the class to writing on some recent technological development. After watching a TV rerun of the move *Star Wars*, she decided to explore some aspect of robots. Because her focus was fuzzy, she decided to sharpen it by doing some brainstorming and background reading in order to explore the many possibilities. Christine brainstormed by drafting a series of questions suggested by the writing strategies she learned about in Chapters 4–12. Perhaps these questions could lead to a focus for her paper.

Could I <u>narrate</u> a brief history of robots?

Could I <u>describe</u> a typical robot?

Could I <u>classify</u> robots into categories?

Could I <u>compare</u> robots to anything?

Could I explain a typical <u>process</u> that a robot performs?

What <u>causes</u> led to the development of robots?

What <u>effects</u> are robots likely to have?

What model or example best <u>illustrates</u> a robot?

Is there a widely accepted <u>definition</u> of ''robot''?

Could I <u>argue</u> for or against greater industrial use of
    robots?

These writing strategies can often help you narrow a subject to a manageable topic.

For her background reading, Christine turned to two general encyclopedias: the *Encyclopedia Americana* and the *Encyclopaedia Britannica*, where she skimmed the articles on robots. Next, she decided to search out a couple of other general articles in more specialized publications. Not knowing how to proceed, she consulted a reference room librarian who acquainted her with the *McGraw-Hill Encyclopedia of Science and Technology* and *Van Nostrand's Scientific Encyclopedia*.

This reading suggested several areas of focus: the history of robots, the factors involved in designing them, and their possible impact on industry. After a little thought, she elected the third possibility. Unlike the first one, it interested her greatly, and she felt it would also interest her audience—fellow students at the vocationally oriented school she attended. Unlike the second focus, it would not require highly technical source material, which she might not understand.

This case history continues on pages 309–310.

2. Encourage students to transform their topic ideas into questions. Questions call for responses, especially when related ones are clustered. For example, Christine might draft this series of questions: What are robots? Where are they used? Are they effective? Do they replace workers? Have students turn in sets of research questions for topics they have selected.
3. To keep students on track, you might require them to turn in an early prospectus. In it they should identify their topic, why it interests them, their potential audience and purpose, the initial research questions, what they know about the topic, and their next step in the project.

This same general procedure—brainstorming with the writing strategies and skimming encyclopedia articles and other background material—is helpful in approaching almost any research topic. Other background material depends on your topic: for a historical figure, there are the *Dictionary of American Biography* (for deceased American figures), the *Dictionary of National Biography* (for deceased British figures), and the *McGraw-Hill Encyclopedia of World Biography*. Librarians can suggest appropriate background books.

More often than not, things won't fall neatly into place when you probe for a topic. False starts and blind alleys are part of the process. Don't be discouraged when you encounter them.

ASSEMBLING A WORKING BIBLIOGRAPHY

Once you have a topic, you're ready to see whether the library has the resources you'll need to complete the project. This step requires you to check additional reference tools and compile a working bibliography—a set of cards that list promising sources of information. This section discusses these reference tools and how to use them.

Encyclopedias

What they are.   Encyclopedias fall into two categories, general and specialized. General encyclopedias, the *Encyclopedia Americana* and the *Encyclopaedia Britannica,* for instance, offer general articles on a wide range of subjects. Specialized encyclopedias cover one particular field, such as advertising or human behavior. Here's a sampling of specialized encyclopedias:

> *Encyclopedia of Advertising*
> *Encyclopedia of Education*
> *Encyclopedia of Environmental Science*
> *Encyclopedia of Human Behavior: Psychology, Psychiatry, and Mental Health*
> *Encyclopedia of Social Work*
> *Encyclopedia of World Art*
> *Harper's Encyclopedia of Science*
> *International Encyclopedia of the Social Sciences*
> *McGraw-Hill Encyclopedia of Science and Technology*

How to use them.   Encyclopedias are a convenient launching pad for your investigation because they provide an overview of the broad field your topic fits into. For a nonspecialized topic, like the impact of commercial television during the 1950s, check the articles on television in one or more general encyclopedias. For a specialized aspect of television, say the development of the picture tube, consult one or more specialized encyclopedias, such as *Harper's Encyclopedia of Science* and the *McGraw-Hill Encyclopedia of Science and Technology*, along with the general encyclopedias. During this search you'll re-encounter material you scanned while trying to focus on a topic.

Some instructors allow you to acknowledge encyclopedias as a source, others prohibit their use, and still others allow material from specialized, but not general, encyclopedias. As always, follow your instructor's wishes.

If you will be using encyclopedia sources, jot down the following information for each note you take:

Title of article
Author(s) of article (Not always available. Sometimes only initials at the end of an article identify an author. In that case, check the list of contributors at the front of the first volume for the full name.)
Name of encyclopedia
Year of publication

Furthermore, check for bibliographies at the ends of articles and copy down any reference that looks promising.

When you've finished your exploratory reading in encyclopedias, turn to the card catalog and periodical indexes—the prime sources of information for library research papers.

lege library while home for the weekend? Encourage students to assess the strengths of their college library and capitalize on them. If it has an inadequate selection of scholarly periodicals but a large collection of popular magazines, encourage students to consider current topics for their papers.

The Card Catalog

What it is.   The card catalog, a file of 3×5-inch cards, indexes all of the books in the library. In some libraries, it also lists magazines, newspapers, government documents, college catalogs, records, and tape recordings. In others, these materials are cataloged separately. Your librarian will help you locate any other listings.

The card catalog contains three kinds of cards—author, title, and subject—for each nonfiction item cataloged. Fiction has author and title cards only. Except for the top line, which differs for the different types of cards, all cards for the same book are identical. The cards are arranged alphabetically, and the three kinds may be filed together, separately, or in some other manner; for example, title and author cards together, subject cards elsewhere. In alphabetizing the cards, librarians follow certain standard practices.

1. Title and subject cards are filed alphabetically according to the first word that is not an article (*a, an, the*).
2. Cards are filed word by word rather than strictly letter by letter. To illustrate, note the following series:
   Chicken and Turkey Tapeworms
   Chicken Beacon
   Chicken Every Sunday
   Chicken Raising Made Easy
   The Chickenbone Special
   Chickens, Chickens, Chickens
   Chickens Come Home to Roost
3. "Mc" names are filed under "Mac."
4. Numbers and abbreviations are filed alphabetically as if they were spelled out. For example, the title card for the novel *Mr. Bridge* is filed under "Mister."
5. Names of people precede identical names of places and things. Thus, "Snow, C. P., *The Masters*" comes before "*Snow at Evening.*"

Knowing these conventions will lessen tedious thumbing through the cards.

The card catalog allows you to gauge your library's holdings on a subject or

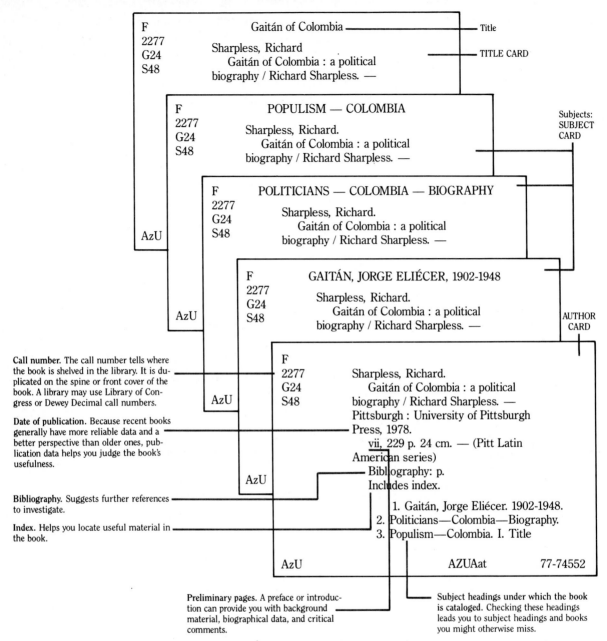

F
2277
G24
S48
Gaitán of Colombia ———————— Title

Sharpless, Richard
    Gaitán of Colombia : a political
biography / Richard Sharpless. —   TITLE CARD

F
2277
G24
S48
POPULISM — COLOMBIA

Sharpless, Richard.
    Gaitán of Colombia : a political
biography / Richard Sharpless. —   Subjects:
SUBJECT
CARD

F
2277
G24
S48
POLITICIANS — COLOMBIA — BIOGRAPHY

Sharpless, Richard.
    Gaitán of Colombia : a political
biography / Richard Sharpless. —

F
2277
G24
S48
GAITÁN, JORGE ELIÉCER, 1902-1948

Sharpless, Richard.
    Gaitán of Colombia : a political
biography / Richard Sharpless. —   AUTHOR
CARD

AzU

AzU

Call number. The call number tells where the book is shelved in the library. It is duplicated on the spine or front cover of the book. A library may use Library of Congress or Dewey Decimal call numbers.

Date of publication. Because recent books generally have more reliable data and a better perspective than older ones, publication data helps you judge the book's usefulness.

Bibliography. Suggests further references to investigate.

Index. Helps you locate useful material in the book.

F
2277
G24
S48
Sharpless, Richard.
    Gaitán of Colombia : a political
biography / Richard Sharpless. —
Pittsburgh : University of Pittsburgh
Press, 1978.
    vii, 229 p. 24 cm. — (Pitt Latin
American series)
    Bibliography: p.
    Includes index.

        1. Gaitán, Jorge Eliécer. 1902-1948.
    2. Politicians—Colombia—Biography.
    3. Populism—Colombia. I. Title

AzU   AZUAat   77-74552

Preliminary pages. A preface or introduction can provide you with background material, biographical data, and critical comments.

Subject headings under which the book is cataloged. Checking these headings leads you to subject headings and books you might otherwise miss.

Figure 19.1

by an author. The cards themselves also provide helpful information, as Figure 19.1 illustrates.

    How to Use It. Start your search for useful books by looking up any book titles gleaned from encyclopedia bibliographies. Next, draw up a list of subject headings that seem likely to yields useful material; then check the headings in the card catalog. If you're investigating satanic cults, your headings might include *devil worship, satanism, diabolism,* and *cult.*

When a check of your subject headings yields nothing, don't give up. Perhaps your list doesn't include any headings that are actually used. To find the right headings, turn to the publications that your library uses in cataloging books. These publications are the *Library of Congress Subject Heading Guide* and, for libraries that follow the Dewey Decimal system, Sears' *List of Subject Headings.* Say you're researching the impact of America's entry into World War I on citizens with German roots. You've come up with the subject headings "World War I" and "First World War" but have not found catalog entries for either of them. Your library uses Dewey Decimal call numbers. Check "World War I" in Sears' *List of Subject Headings* and you'll discover that the books you want are cataloged under "European War, 1914–1918."

For each promising title you turn up, record the following information on a 3 × 5-inch card:

Author(s)

Title

Editor(s) and translator(s), as well as author(s) of any supplementary material

Total number of volumes (if more than one) and the number of the specific volume that you want to use

City of publication

Name of publisher

Date of publication

Also, copy the book's call number in the upper left-hand corner of the card.

Next, scan the books themselves. If your library stacks are closed, give the librarian a list of your call numbers and ask to see the books. If you can enter the stacks, locate the general areas where your books are shelved. Once you find a number range that includes one of your call numbers, follow the trail of guides on the book spines until you find your book. Spend a few extra minutes browsing in the general area of each book; you may discover useful sources that you overlooked in the card catalog.

Skim each book's table of contents and any introductory material, such as a preface or introduction, to determine scope and approach. Also check the index and note the pages with discussions that relate to your topic. Finally, thumb through any portions that look promising. If the book won't help you, throw away the card.

Sometimes you may be unable to find a book you're searching for. Don't assume that its lost or not available. Ask the librarian whether it's been checked out or placed on reserve by some instructor. If it's on reserve, go to the reserve section and examine it there. If someone has checked it out, find out when it's due back. When that date is some time away, ask the librarian to contact the borrower and try to speed up the return.

Computerized Card Catalogs

Some libraries are now using computerized card catalogs. A terminal consists of a viewing screen and a keyboard on which the user enters requests for information. To determine what the library has on William Faulkner, for example, the user types Faulkner's name or its coded equivalent. Likewise, entering a subject heading produces a screen display of all the titles cataloged under that heading. In some systems, the screen also provides additional information, such as whether a book has been checked out and if so, the return date.

Instead of computerized catalogs, other libraries have their card catalogs on microfiche cards or microfilm, which are read with a special viewing device.

EXERCISE ■

1. **Select five of the following topics. Go to the card catalog and find one book about each. List each book's call number, author, title, publisher, and date of publication. Because subject headings may vary, investigate related categories, if necessary, to find an entry. To illustrate, if you find nothing under *mountaineering*, check *mountain climbing* or *backpacking*.**

   1. Adolescence
   2. Balkan Peninsula
   3. Child abuse
   4. Flying saucers
   5. Mohandas Gandhi
   6. Heraldry
   7. Doris Lessing
   8. Mass transit
   9. Mountaineering
   10. Origami
   11. Pearl Harbor
   12. Parapsychological research
   13. Regional planning
   14. Bertrand Russell
   15. Spin fishing
   16. Taxidermy
   17. Telecommunication
   18. Underwater exploration
   19. Volcanoes
   20. Zen Buddhism

2. **Provide your instructor with a list of the books you found that appear useful for developing your paper's topic. For each book, furnish the information specified in Part 1 above, along with a brief note indicating why you think the book will be useful.**

Periodical Indexes

What they are.   Periodical indexes catalog articles appearing in magazines and newspapers. Most indexes list entries by subject and author; some also list by title. Paperback segments of printed indexes appear biweekly or monthly, and their contents are later combined in hardback volumes spanning six months or a year.

Periodical indexes provide access to material that won't find its way into books for several years, if ever. Their listings allow you to examine newer topics, keep up with the latest developments in older topics, and explore different facets of your topic in greater depth than you could by using books alone. In short, articles help you avoid a superficial paper.

The *Reader's Guide to Periodical Literature* (1900–date) indexes articles that have appeared in widely circulated magazines: *Harper's, Newsweek, Scientific American, Vital Speeches,* and the like. The *Guide* covers over 150 magazines, listing nonfiction articles by subject and author, and other categories by title and author. It is especially useful for locating material on historical events (say the Korean War or the Iran hostage crisis) and on current social, political, and economic developments (the designer jean fad, the nuclear freeze movement). It doesn't, however, index many scientific, technical, or literary articles.

The first pages of the *Guide* identify the abbreviations used for the magazines indexed. Figure 19.2 shows the arrangement of the index and the "see also" cross-references that direct you to related subject headings.

Several periodical indexes are cataloged on microfilm or microfiche cards. *The Magazine Index,* on microfilm, deserves special mention. Indexing 400 popular publications by subject, author, and title, each monthly issue covers the past five years and includes coded references to articles no more than two weeks old. The viewing machines that hold the film resemble small television sets and

Subject heading

Europe and the United States
  See also
  Europe, Western—Foreign opinion—American
  United States—Foreign opinion—European

Cross-references

European American Bancorp
  A six-sided stalemate at European American Bank. il *Bus Week* p88-9 F 20 '84
European artificial satellites *See* Artificial satellites, European
European communications satellites *See* Communications satellites, European
European Economic Community
  Close to collision on trade. il *Bus Week* p22-3 Mr 12 '84
  Deficits may force Buy Europe policy [aerospace trade] M. Feazel. il *Aviat Week Space Technol* 120:135+ F 13 '84
  Economics in the Common Market. R. Ball. *Current* 260:34-9 F '84
  EEC commissioners ratify plan to relax fare, capacity limits [airlines] *Aviat Week Space Technol* 120:30 Mr 5 '84
  Europe eyes U.S. model on joint research rules. D. Dickson. *Science* 223:377 Ja 27 '84
  Europe moves to ease regulation [airlines] M. Feazel. *Aviat Week Space Technol* 120:28-9 Ja 30 '84
  Europe seeks joint computer research effort [Esprit program] D. Dickson. il *Science* 223:28-30 Ja 6 '84
  European farmers have troubles of their own. A. Zanker. il *U S News World Rep* 96:72 Mr 12 '84
  Europeans back computer plan [Esprit] D. Dickson. *Science* 223:1159 Mr 16 '84
  Test of wills in the Common Market. N. Gelb. il *New Leader* 67:5-7 Ja 9 '84

Subject subheading

Conferences
  Battling against a breakdown [agricultural policy] M. McDonald. il *Macleans* 97:32 Mr 26 '84
  The Community faces a crisis [Britain's contribution] M. McDonald. il *Macleans* 97:41 Ap 2 '84

Title of article

Author

Notation indicating article is illustrated

Name of magazine

Page number of article

Volume number of magazine

Date

Bracketed notation indicating topic

Figure 19.2

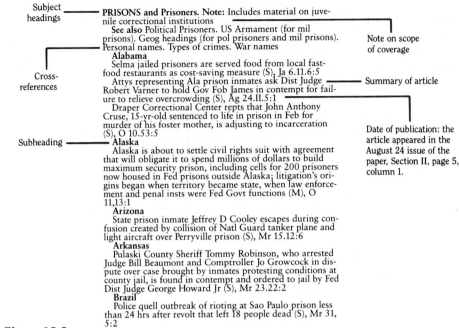

Figure 19.3

have motorized controls that allow you to move rapidly through the filmstrip and arrive at your subject. Accompanying the viewer are coded reels of microfilm containing the indexed articles, together with a reader/printer that allows you to read them and to obtain printed copies. Your librarian will demonstrate how these machines work. The producers of the index also publish a listing of recent articles on twenty to thirty current topics.

The *National Newspaper Index* covers five national papers: the *Christian Science Monitor,* the *Los Angeles Times,* the *New York Times,* the *Wall Street Journal,* and the *Washington Post.* Each monthly microfilm issue includes three years of references and is read on the same kind of viewer as *The Magazine Index.*

Two newspaper indexes, *The New York Times Index* and *News Bank,* come in printed form and refer readers to photographically reduced materials. *The New York Times Index* (1913–date) lists news articles, book reviews, commentaries, and features that have appeared in the *Times,* a paper with an international reputation for comprehensive coverage of events. The index entries refer to the "Late City Edition" of the paper, the one most libraries have on microfilm. If your library subscribes to a regional edition, an article may appear on another page or not at all. Figure 19.3 is a sample entry from this index.

For a topic of local, state, or regional interest (say the Great Lakes fishing rights of Michigan Indians), *News Bank* may be your best bet. This publication indexes articles from over 150 papers in all fifty states. It appears monthly in looseleaf notebook form; the articles themselves are supplied on microfiche cards.

Specialized indexes are also available. Here is a brief sampling of some of them. They list articles appearing in scholarly journals rather than popular magazines.

Applied Science and Technology Index, 1958–date (indexed by subject)
Education Index, 1929–date (indexed by subject and author)
Humanities Index, 1974–date (indexed by subject and author)
International Index to Periodicals, 1907–1964 (indexed by subject and author; entitled *Social Sciences and Humanities Index*, 1965–1974, and then separated into the *Humanities Index* and the *Social Science Index*)
Social Sciences and Humanities Index, 1965–1974 (indexed by subject and author)
Social Sciences Index, 1975–date (indexed by subject and author)

Figure 19.4 typifies the contents of the *Applied Science and Technology Index*.

How to use them.   Start your search for articles by checking general indexes; then move to appropriate specialized indexes. Each time you unearth a promising reference, copy the following information on a 3 × 5 inch note card:

Author(s), if identified
Title of article
Name of periodical
Volume or issue number (for professional and scholarly journals only)
Date of periodical
The page range of the entire article

Next, examine any articles referenced in *The Magazine Index* by using the coded microfilms and a viewing machine. Check topic sentences of the paragraphs for the article's essential points and scan any accompanying abstract or summary. If the article looks promising, check to see whether it has a bibliography, which

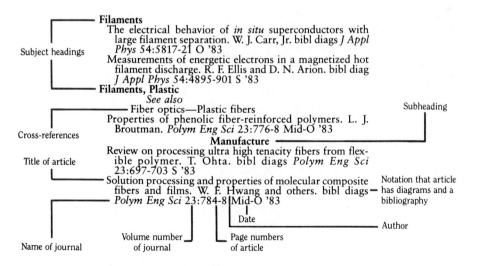

Figure 19.4

From *Applied Science and Technology Index*, March, 1984, Copyright © 1984 by the H. W. Wilson Company. Reproduced by permission.

might include additional useful sources. Keep the cards that list promising sources, and throw away the others.

Take the remaining cards—and any periodical references that you found in encyclopedia bibliographies—to whatever catalog your library uses for periodicals. There you can determine whether the library subscribes to what you want and, if it does, where the periodicals are shelved. Libraries frequently keep current issues in a periodical room or some other special section. Back issues of magazines are often kept on microfilm or bound into hardcover volumes and shelved. Most newspapers are on microfilm. Check these articles in the same manner that you checked the others.

EXERCISE ▨   **Select five of the following topics and find one magazine article about each. Use at least three different periodical indexes to locate the articles. List the author, if given, the title of the article, the name of the magazine, its date, the page range, and the name of the index used.**

1. Acting schools	11. Investment trusts
2. Aeronautical research	12. Leveraged buyouts
3. Black holes	13. Nuclear fusion
4. Campaign funds	14. Oral history
5. Collective bargaining	15. Perestroika
6. Dow Chemical Company	16. Television industry
7. Dwight David Eisenhower	17. Unemployment
8. Fiber optics	18. Vegetarianism
9. Fundamentalism	19. X-ray astronomy
10. Holography	20. Yale University

Data Bases

Many libraries subscribe to data bases, computerized periodical indexes that provide extensive listings of articles. Updated weekly or monthly, these listings give you access to the most recent material. Depending upon the particular base, the information may be recorded on compact discs supplied to the library or transmitted by wire to a library terminal. In some cases, terminals are intended for student operation; others are operated by library personnel. Some data bases will provide complete copies of articles and index them as well. If your search for information is stymied or you need up-to-date sources, consider asking your librarian to make a data base search, or if you have access to the terminal, do it yourself. You might be charged a service fee, but it's likely to be modest.

Other Reference Tools and Sources of Information

To beef up your preliminary bibliography, take a look at one or more of these reference tools or sources of information.

Essay and general literature index. Some articles appear in edited collections that are issued in book form. To find these articles, consult the *Essay and General Literature Index* (1900–date), an annual publication that indexes, by author, title, and subject, articles appearing in several hundred anthologies. Check far enough back to uncover everything useful. Then go to the card catalog to see whether the library has the books.

Interlibrary loans. Sometimes you'll discover sources your library doesn't own. If the source appears promising, check nearby libraries. If that search proves unsuccessful, think about an interlibrary loan. Two special reference books can help you locate libraries that have your source. The first, the *Union List of Serials in Libraries in the United States and Canada* indexes, by periodical, the magazine and newspaper holdings of major libraries. The second, the *National Union Catalog*, provides similar information about book holdings.

Adjusting Your Topic

After finishing your search for sources, you may need to adjust the scope and emphasis of your topic. If your start with "America's First Nuclear-Powered Submarine" but fail to turn up enough sources, you might expand your emphasis to "America's First Nuclear-Powered Warships." On the other hand, if you're working with "America's First Nuclear-Powered Warships" and find yourself floundering in an ocean of sources, you might zero in on one type of vessel. Gathering evidence helps to develop your judgment about how many sources you need to do the job.

CASE HISTORY ■ *(Continued from page 299)*

Once Christine Harding targeted a focus for her paper on robots, she began compiling her working bibliography. First, she reread the encyclopedia articles she had already skimmed, but found them uninformative.

Next, Christine turned to the card catalog and checked the listings under the headings "Robots" and "Robots, Industrial." The first heading yielded a cross-reference directing her to the headings "Androids," "Automata," and "Automation"; the second revealed a listing of seven books. A check of all four headings turned up fourteen books, four of which proved upon examination to contain material that looked useful.

Her search for periodical articles took Christine to four indexes: the *Reader's Guide to Periodical Literature*, the *Magazine Index*, the *Applied Science and Technology Index*, and the *National Newspaper Index*. The result: twenty-five articles with promising titles. Of these, sixteen were available in the college library, and eleven appeared useful for her purpose.

TEACHING STRATEGIES

1. After students have examined their working bibliographies, ask them if they need to revise their research questions in light of their findings.

2. At this point students might write brief progress reports specifying any problems they are having and outlining their plans for further research. Such reports allow you to provide helpful suggestions.

Suspecting that the library might have helpful government documents, Christine checked the library's document catalog after having a librarian explain how to use it. Her search led to a single promising publication.

Satisfied that ample information was available, Christine now returned to her sources for a closer look in order to carefully evaluate their content. Her instructor had suggested that one good way to approach a topic is to pose a question about it and then draft a *tentative* answer, if possible. Here's how Christine proceeded.

```
Q: What impact are robots likely to have on industry?

A: Despite the misgivings of some people, robots will

probably have a beneficial effect on industry and its work

force.
```

Her answer provided Christine with a *tentative thesis*, an informed opinion that guided her later note taking, giving her a sense of direction and indicating what information would likely prove useful and what useless. Tentative theses are just that—tentative—and can be altered slightly or changed completely if necessary. If later reading indicated that robots would likely prove a mixed blessing, Christine could alter her tentative thesis accordingly.

This case history continues on pages 318—319.

TAKING NOTES

To take notes, read your references carefully and record significant information. Notes are the raw materials for your finished product, so develop them accurately.

Evaluating Your Sources

Evaluate your sources by considering these factors.

The expertise of the author. Judge an author's expertise by examining his or her professional status. Say you're searching for information on some new cancer-treating drug. An article by the director of a national cancer research center would be a better bet than one by a staff writer for a magazine. Similarly, a historian's account of a national figure will probably have more balance and depth than a novelist's popularized account of that person's life. Gauging a writer's credentials poses no serious difficulties. Articles in periodicals often note authors' job titles along with their names. Some even supply thumbnail biographies. For a book, check its title page, preface, or introduction, and—if it's been left on—the dust jacket. Finally, notice whether the writer has other publications on this general subject. If your sources contain two or more items by one person or if that person's name keeps cropping up as you take notes, you're probably dealing with an expert in that field.

2. Using such articles, have students evaluate not only the author and the publication but also the material the author presents—the opinions of any authorities cited, the results of studies, the testimony of eye witnesses.

The credibility of the publication. A book's credibility hinges on its approach and its reception by reviewers. Cast a cautious eye on books that take a popular rather than a scholarly approach. For research papers, scholarly treatments provide more solid fare. Weigh what reviewers said when a book first appeared. Two publications excerpt selected reviews and provide references to others. The *Book Review Digest* (1905–date) deals mainly with nontechnical works, while the *Technical Book Review Index* (1935–date) covers technical and scientific books. Turn first to the volume for the year the book came out. If you don't find any reviews, scan the next year's index. Often books published in the fall are not reviewed until the following year.

Periodical articles can also take a scholarly or popular tack. Editors of journals in specialized fields and of some wide-circulation magazines—for example, *Scientific American* and *The New Yorker*—publish only in-depth, accurate articles. Most newsstand publications, however, popularize to some extent, and some deliberately strive for sensationalism. Popularizing may result in broad, general statements, skimpy details, and a sensational tone.

Don't automatically reject a source because the writer lacks expertise or offers a popularized treatment. Often, especially when writing about a current topic, you'll need to use material that falls short in some way. By recognizing and taking into account the shortcomings, you can make the information serve your purpose nicely.

Mechanics of Note Taking

Copy each note on a 4 × 6-inch card. That way you won't confuse the cards with the smaller bibliography cards. Record only one note per card, even when you take several notes from a single page: you may use the notes at different points. If you can't fit a note on a single card, continue the note on a second card and use a paper clip or staple to keep the two together. Cards allow you to test different arrangements of notes and use the best one. Copying notes in a notebook will prevent you from shuffling them into the proper order.

Before you take a note, indicate its source at the bottom of the card. You will then have all the details necessary for documenting the information if you use it in your paper. Usually, the author's last name and the page number suffice, since

TEACHING STRATEGY

Encourage students to include on their cards not only notes but also their personal reactions to them. Students must of course clearly distinguish between their borrowing and their commentary.

the bibliography card contains all other details. To distinguish between two authors with the same last name or between two works by the same author, add initials or partial titles. *Don't forget to include the page number or numbers for each note.* Otherwise, you'll have to waste time looking them up when you cite your sources in the paper.

Summarize briefly the contents of the note at the top of the card. Later, when you construct an outline, these notations will help you sort your cards into categories and subcategories.

Types of Notes

A note can be a summary, paraphrase, or quotation. *Whenever you use any kind of note in your paper, give proper credit to your source. Failure to do so results in plagiarism—that is, literary theft—a serious offense even when committed unintentionally.* Pages 343–345 discuss plagiarism, and pages 324–340 explain proper documentation of sources.

TEACHING STRATEGY

As an exercise, you might have students, working in groups, summarize all or part of one of the essays in the Reader. Then have them compare the different versions and prepare a final version.

Summary. A summary condenses original material, presenting its core ideas *in your own words.* By using summaries, you demonstrate that you have a good grasp of the information. You may include brief quotations if you enclose them in quotation marks. A properly written summary presents points in their original order without distorting their emphasis or meaning, and it omits supporting details and repetition. Summaries serve up the heart of the matter and help you write a shorter paper.

Begin the summarizing process by asking yourself, "What points does the author make that have an important bearing on my topic and purpose?" To answer, note especially the topic sentences in the original. Often, though not always, they provide essential information. Copy the points, following the order in the original. That done, condense and rewrite them in your own words. Figure 19.5 is a summary of the Bertrand Russell passage that follows. We have underscored key points in the original.

Under the influence of the romantic movement, a process began about a hundred and fifty years ago, which has continued ever since—a process of revaluing the traditional virtues, placing some higher on the scale than before, and others lower. The tendency has been to exalt impulse at the expense of deliberation. The virtues that spring from the heart have come to be thought superior to those that are based upon reflection: a generous man is preferred to a man who is punctual in paying his debts. *Per contra,* deliberate sins are thought worse than impulsive sins: a hypocrite is more harshly condemned than a murderer. The upshot is that we tend to estimate virtues, not by their capacity for providing human happiness, but by their power of inspiring a personal liking for the possessors, and we are not apt to include among the qualities for which we like people, a habit of reflecting before making an important decision.

> ## Necessity for law
>
> About a century and a half ago, there began a still-existing preference for impulsive actions over deliberate ones. Those responsible for this development believed that people are naturally good but institutions have perverted them. Actually, unfettered human nature breeds violence and brutality, and law is our only protection against anarchy. The law assumes the responsibility for revenge and settles disputes equitably. It frees people from the fear of being victimized by criminals and provides a means of catching them. Without it, civilization could not endure.
>
> Russell, pp. 63-65

Figure 19.5

The men who started this movement were, in the main, gentle sentimentalists who imagined that, when the fetters of custom and law were removed, the heart would be free to display its natural goodness. Human nature, they thought, is good, but institutions have corrupted it; remove the institutions and we shall all become angels. Unfortunately, the matter is not so simple as they thought. Men who follow their impulses establish governments based on pogroms, clamour for war with foreign countries, and murder pacifists and Negroes. Human nature unrestrained by law is violent and cruel. In the London Zoo, the male baboons fought over the females until all the females were torn to pieces; human beings, left to the ungoverned impulse, would be no better. In ages that have had recent experience of anarchy, this has been obvious. All the great writers of the middle ages were passionate in their admiration of the law; it was the Thirty Years' War that led Grotius to become the first advocate of international law. Law, respected and enforced, is in the long run the only alternative to violent and predatory anarchy; and it is just as necessary to realize this now as it was in the time of Dante and Grotius.

What is the essence of law? On the one hand, it takes away from private citizens the right of revenge, which it confers upon the government. If a man steals your money, you must not steal it back, or thrash him, or shoot him; you must establish the facts before a neutral tribunal, which inflicts upon him such punishment as has seemed just to the disinterested legislators. On the other hand, when two men have a dispute, the law provides a machinery for settling it, again on principles laid down in advance by neutrals. The advantages of law are many. It diminishes the amount of private violence, and settles disagreements in a manner more nearly just than that which would result if the disputants fought it out by private war. <u>It makes it possible for men to work without being perpetually on the watch against bandits. When a crime has been committed it provides a skilled machine for discovering the criminal.</u>

<u>Without law, the existence of civilized communities is impossible.</u> In international law, there is as yet no effective law, for lack of an international police force capable of overpowering national armies, and it is daily becoming more evident that this defect must be remedied if civilization is to survive. Within single nations there is a dangerous tendency to think that moral indignation excuses the extra-legal punishment of criminals. In Germany an era of private murder (on the loftiest grounds) preceded and followed the victory of the Nazis. In fact, nine-tenths of what appeared as just indignation was sheer lust for cruelty; and this is equally true in other countries where mobs rob the law of its functions. In any civilized community, toleration of mob rule is the first step towards barbarism.

Bertrand Russell, "Respect for Law," *San Francisco Review*, Winter 1958, 63–65.

EXERCISE ■

A.   Prepare summary note cards for the following passages.

1.   This is a report about islands, but it's not about calypso or Mai Tais or hula dancers or hot dogs. The islands I'm interested in are off the coasts of Georgia and South Carolina, and their names are Hilton Head, Seabrook, Sea Island, St. Simons, Fripp and Kiawah—not the sort of names you're ever going to hear on an afternoon game show.

The islands, different as they are individually, share any number of common virtues. All have great beaches—large, romantic beaches free, for the most part, of high-rises and free of anything suggesting honky-tonk. All of the islands, moreover, have been developed in a manner that has preserved the basic environmental character of the land, has kept the trees standing where possible and has left unspoiled the nesting groups of the many types of wild birds that breed there. A 10-minute walk from any of the lodgings on just about any of the islands puts you in the middle of a wilderness.

But what is most appealing about these islands, I think, is that they generate much the same low-keyed atmosphere that prevails at vacation retreats populated by only the very rich, while, at the same time, offering leisure opportunities—tennis in particular—on a scale, a variety, and a quality simply not found at most vacation home retreats.

Barry Tarshis, "Islands of Tennis: Where to Vacation in the Southeast"

2.   There are currents of change on the public scene which I believe will have profound implications for education. This is a time in which the expectations for schools are at an all-time high and support is, at best, confused. This confusion threatens to destroy our system of public education.

EXERCISE ANSWERS

1. The islands that lie near Georgia and South Carolina abound in desirable features. Their beaches are excellent and lack any traces of trashiness, and developers have taken pains to preserve the islands' forests and wildlife. Visitors can enjoy a splendid array of leisure activities in a restrained atmosphere.
2. Although the public expects more of our schools than ever before, it often appears unwilling to provide them with the proper support. This reluctance is the direct result of inflation, which pinches wage earners and causes them to withhold funding that they were formerly willing to provide. To correct this situation, the federal government must provide one-third of the monies needed to operate our local school system while leaving control of the systems in local hands.

What's more, it is my belief that there's a good deal more at stake than a simple concept of education. For just as surely as the loss of free speech would destroy our ability to maintain our freedom and democracy, the loss of public education would destroy our ability to preserve that freedom and to regenerate it across the years.

Furthermore, loss of universal, public education would tend to stimulate the kind of class divisions which have torn apart so many other nations throughout the world.

Why are our public schools being threatened? Because our economy has become sick. Costs of all things continue to rise, and inflation puts every citizen under the economic gun. So, whatever way a wage earner can find to save money in such trying times becomes much more attractive than it does at other times. And being what we are, all too often we become penny-wise and pound-foolish, willing to risk long-term disaster in exchange for short-term relief.

Today, unfortunately, too many Americans seem willing to risk sacrificing the very foundation of our future as a free people—our public schools—in order to achieve financial relief. But we all know the problem does not lie with the schools; the problems lies with our system for financing them.

The facts are that property taxes are inequitable and that inflation has robbed our salaries of much of their value. But teachers are taxpayers too—and property owners as well. We share in these problems just like everyone else. We have no desire whatever to bleed the taxpayers of our nation. Nor, on the other hand, do we intend to subsidize the increased costs of education by absorbing the effects of inflation in already inadequate salaries. We do want for education a fair share of funding in order that we can bring to all Americans the full opportunities that only universal, public education can bring. To achieve that, there must be a transfusion of federal funds into locally controlled public school systems. For many years, NEA has called for one-third federal funding of education. That proposal has taken on greater importance in this day of inflation and taxpayer revolt.

John Ryor, "Save Our Schools"

B. Submit summaries of three pieces of information that you plan to use in writing your paper; also submit photocopies of the original information.

Paraphrase.   To paraphrase is to restate material *in your own words* without attempting to condense it. Unlike a summary, a paraphrase allows you to present an essentially complete version of the original material. A note of caution, however: Don't copy the original source nearly verbatim, changing only a word here and there. To do so is to plagiarize. To avoid this offense, follow a read, think, and write-without-looking-at-the-original strategy when you take notes so that you concentrate on recording the information in your own words. Then verify the accuracy of your notes by checking them against the original source. Here is a sample passage, and Figure 19.6 is its paraphrase.

Acceptable

The initiators of this movement were "sentimentalists" who believed that people, when no longer bound by social and legal constraints, would behave decently. People, they felt, were naturally decent but debased by institutions. Without institutions, everyone will behave justly.

Unacceptable

The men who began this movement were gentle sentimentalists who believed that when the restraints of custom and law were removed, the human heart would display its natural goodness. Human nature, they believed, is good; it is institutions that have corrupted it.

Over time, more and more of life has become subject to the controls of knowledge. However, this is never a one-way process. Scientific investigation is continually increasing our knowledge. But if we are to make good use of this knowledge, we must not only rid our minds of old, superseded beliefs and fragments of magic, but also recognize new superstitions for what they are. Both are generated by our wishes, our fears, and our feelings of helplessness in difficult situations.

Margaret Mead, "New Superstitions for Old," *A Way of Seeing.* New York: McCall, 1970. 266.

Combatting Superstitions

As time has passed, knowledge has asserted its sway over larger and larger segments of human life. But the process cuts two ways. Science is forever adding to the storehouse of human knowledge. Before we can take proper advantage of its gifts, however, we must purge our minds of old and outmoded convictions, while recognizing the true nature of modern superstitions. Both stem from our desires, our apprehensions, and our sense of impotence under difficult circumstances.

Mead, p. 266

Figure 19.6

EXERCISE ■ **Paraphrase a short passage from one of your textbooks. Make a copy of the passage to hand in with the assignment.**

Quotation. A quotation is a copy of original material. Since your paper should demonstrate that you've mastered your sources, don't rely extensively on quotations. You need practice in expressing yourself. As a general rule, avoid quotations except when

  ▌ the original displays special elegance or force
  ▌ you really need support from an authority
  ▌ you need to back up your interpretation of a passage from a literary work

Paraphrasing a passage as well-written as the one below would rob it of much of its force.

Man is himself, like the universe he inhabits, like the demoniacal stirring of the ooze from which he sprang, a tale of desolation. He walks in his mind from birth to death the long resounding shores of endless disillusionment. Finally, the commitment to life departs or turns to bitterness. But out of such desolation emerges the awful freedom to choose beyond the narrowly circumscribed circle that delimits the rational being.

Loren Eisely, *The Unexpected Universe*

Special rules govern the use of quotations. If, for clarity, you need to add an explanation or substitute a proper name for a personal pronoun, enclose the addition in *brackets* (see page 616).

The Declaration of Independence asserts that "the history of the present King of Great Britain [George III] is a history of repeated injuries and usurpations. . . ."

If your typewriter cannot type brackets, insert them neatly with a dark pen.

Reproduce any grammatical or spelling errors in a source exactly as they appear in the original. To let your reader know that the original author, not you, made the mistake, insert the Latin word *sic* (meaning "thus") within brackets immediately after the error.

As Wabash notes, "The threat to our enviroment [sic] comes from many directions."

If you exclude an unneeded part of a quotation, show the omission with an ellipsis—three spaced periods. Indicate omissions *within sentences* in the following way:

Writing in *Step by Step, 1936–1939*, Winston Churchill observed, "To France and Belgium the avalanche of fire and steel which fell upon them twenty years ago . . . [was] an overpowering memory and obsession."

When an omission comes *at the end of a sentence* and what is actually quoted can also stand as a complete sentence, use an unspaced period followed by an ellipsis.

In his second inaugural address, Lincoln voiced his hopes for the nation: "With malice toward none, with charity for all, with firmness in the right as God gives us to see the right, let us strive on to finish the work we are in. . . ."

Do the same when you drop *a whole sentence* within a quoted passage.

According to newspaper columnist Grace Dunn, "Williamson's campaign will undoubtedly focus primarily on the legalized gambling issue because he hopes to capitalize on the strong opposition to it in his district. . . . Nonetheless, commentators all agree he faces an uphill fight in his attempt to unseat the incumbent."

Don't change or distort when you delete. Tampering like the following violates ethical standards:

Original passage   This film is poorly directed, and the acting uninspired; only the cameo appearance by Laurence Olivier makes it truly worth seeing.

Distorted version   This film is . . . truly worth seeing.

You can summarize or paraphrase original material but retain a few words or phrases to add vividness or keep a precise shade of meaning. Simply use quotation marks but no ellipsis.

Because of the "passionate advocacy" of its supporters, the push to roll back property taxes has been gaining momentum across the country.

When you copy a quotation onto a note card, put quotation marks at the beginning and the end so you won't mistake it for a paraphrase or a summary when you write the paper. If the quoted material starts on one page and ends on the next, use a slash mark (/) to show exactly where the shift comes. Then if you use only part of the quotation in your paper, you'll know whether to use one page number or two.

Don't expect to find a gold mine of information on every page you read. Sometimes one page will yield several notes, another page nothing. If you can't immediately gauge the value of some material, take it down. Useless information can be discarded later. Place a rubber band around your growing stack of note cards. Store them in a large envelope closed with a snap or string and labeled with your name and address. Submit them with your completed paper if your instructor requests.

Using a word processor.   You can copy your summaries, paraphrases, and quotations, along with the bibliographic references for them, into a word processor for later expansion and reorganization. If your unit has a bibliographic function, enter individual references as you go along and then print out the entire bibliography at the end of the project.

TEACHING STRATEGIES

1. After students have done extensive reading but before they make an outline, you might give them a chance to pull their material together. Have them set aside their notes and write down what they know about their topics; what position, if any, they want to take and why; what questions still need answering; and how they plan to organize their papers. Such an assess-

CASE HISTORY ■   *(Continued from page 310)*

Working bibliography in hand, Christine Harding began taking notes for her paper. Most were in summary form, but in a few cases she chose quotations because of the importance of the source, the significance of the material, or the force with which it was presented. One quotation offered the Robot Institute of America's definition of the term *robot*. Several spoke optimistically of the impact of robots, while yet another related a landmark agreement between General Motors and the United Auto Workers on the retraining of displaced workers.

As she read, Christine realized that she should focus on (1) the benefits that robots promise and (2) the steps being taken to lessen their harmful effects, while giving passing attention to (3) the history of robots and (4) the fears they have caused. A plan started to emerge: the paper would begin with a historical overview, touch lightly on the fears aroused by robots, and then deal in depth with the other two matters.

This case history continues on pages 321—322.

ment gives students an overview of their projects. It also helps you spot problems, detect potential plagiarists, and place procrastinators on notice. Students could draft this document in class while you review their note cards.

2. Alternatively, have students report on and answer questions about their research, either to the entire class or in small groups. Such a presentation requires them to pull everything together.

ORGANIZING AND OUTLINING

Next comes your formal outline, the blueprint that shows the divisions and subdivisions of your paper, the order of your ideas, and the relationships between ideas and supporting details. An outline is a tool that benefits both writer and reader.

A formal outline follows the pattern shown below:

I.
  A.
  B.
    1.
    2.
      a.
      b.
II.

You can see the significance of an item by its numeral, letter, or number designation and by its distance from the left-hand margin; the farther it's indented, the less important it is. All items with the same designation have roughly the same importance.

TEACHING STRATEGY
Before students construct a formal outline, you might have them draft a more general plan, perhaps just a list of questions to be answered or issues to be addressed. They can then add to or reorganize the plan as they build it into a formal outline.

Developing Your Outline

Developing an outline is no easy job. It involves arranging material from various sources in an appropriate manner. Sorting and re-sorting your note cards is a good way to proceed. First, determine the main divisions of your paper by checking the summarized notations at the tops of your cards, and then make one stack of cards for each division. Next, review each stack carefully to determine further subdivisions and sort it into smaller stacks. Finally, use the stacks to prepare your outline.

There are two types of formal outlines: *topic* and *sentence*. A topic outline presents all entries as words, short phrases, or short clauses. A sentence outline presents them as complete sentences. To emphasize the relationships among elements, items of equal importance have parallel phrasing. Although neither is *the* preferred form, a sentence outline includes more details and also your attitude toward each idea. The following segments of a topic and a sentence outline for a paper on tranquilizer dependence illustrate the difference between the two.

Topic Outline

II. The abuse problem
    A. Reasons for the problem
        1. Over-promotion
        2. Over-prescription
        3. Patient's misuse
           a. Dosage
           b. Length of usage
    B. Growth of the problem

Sentence Outline

II. Tranquilizers are widely abused.
    A. Several factors account for the abuse of tranquilizers.
        1. Drug companies over-promote their product.
        2. Doctors often unnecessarily prescribe tranquilizers.
        3. Patients often do not follow their doctors' instructions.
           a. Some patients take more than prescribed doses.
           b. Some continue to use tranquilizers beyond the prescribed time.
    B. The problem of tranquilizer abuse appears to be growing.

Note that the items in the sentence outline are followed by periods, but those in the topic outline are not.

Keying Your Note Cards to Your Outline

When your outline is finished, key your note cards to it by writing at the top of each card the letters and numbers—such as IIA or IIIB2—for the appropriate outline category. Now arrange the cards into one stack, following the order shown in the outline. Finally, start with the top card in the stack and number all of them consecutively. If they later fall off the table or slide out of place, you can easily put them in order again. You might have a few stragglers left over when you complete this keying. Some of these may be worked into your paper as you write or revise it.

CASE HISTORY ■   *(Continued from page 319)*

Sorting and re-sorting was challenging and at times frustrating for Christine. Since some of her material could be arranged in different ways, she found herself experimenting, evaluating, and rearranging as she tested various options. After much thought and some trial and error, the following *initial draft* of her outline evolved.

I.   History of robots

    A. Origin of the term "robot"

    B. Who started the robot revolution?

    C. Who were the first purchasers of robots?

    D. Present status of robots and their future prospects

II. Fears about robots

    A. Company managers' fears

    B. Fears of people not working for companies

III. What benefits will robots bring?

    A. Past benefits of automation

    B. Company benefits

    C. What workers can expect

        1. More interesting jobs

        2. Shorter workweek

        3. There will be fewer workers being injured.

IV. The unemployment threat

    A. Reassignment of displaced workers to other jobs

    B. Where displaced workers will be retrained

        1. By industry

        2. By colleges

        3. By others

This version is marked by nonparallelism, poor phrasing, and inadequate attention to some points. Despite these weaknesses, her tentative outline provided an adequate blueprint for the first draft of Christine's paper.

This case history continues on pages 345–369.

WRITING YOUR RESEARCH PAPER

TEACHING STRATEGY

As students draft their papers, you might set aside class time to discuss problems they are experiencing. Since some students forget their initial audience and purpose, ask the class to redefine both. Sometimes the initial outline won't work, and changes are necessary.

Some students think of a library research paper as a series of quotations, paraphrases and summaries, one following the other throughout the paper. Not so. Without question, you use the material of others, but *you* select and organize it according to *your purpose. You* develop insights, and *you* draw conclusions about what you've read. You can best express your conclusions by setting your notes aside, stepping back to gain some perspective, and then expressing your sense of what you've learned.

Writing the First Draft

Your final research results will be expressed in a thesis. You've already drafted a tentative thesis (see page 310), and now you'll probably refine or revise it to accommodate any change in perspective. Position the thesis in your introduction unless you're analyzing a problem or recommending a solution; then you might hold the thesis back until the conclusion. If you do hold it back, state the problem clearly at the outset. Because of the paper's length, it's a good idea to reveal your organizational plan in the introduction.

Write the paper section by section, following the divisions of your outline. Link the material on your note cards with transitional elements and your own assessments. Don't fret if the style bumps along or connections aren't always clear. These problems can be smoothed out when you revise.

You will, of course, need to properly credit the sources you use. The section entitled "Acknowledging and Handling your Sources Properly (MLA and APA Formats)" details appropriate guidelines.

On occasion you may want to include supplementary information that would interrupt the flow of thought if you placed it in the paper. When this happens, use an *explanatory note.*[1] A typical explanatory note might clarify or elaborate upon a point, discuss some side issue, or define a term used in a specialized way.

When you finish writing, let this version sit for a day or two. Then revise it, just as you would with a shorter essay. Keep track of all sources so that preparing the bibliography will go smoothly.

---

[1] This is an explanatory note. Position it at the bottom of the page, spaced four lines away from the main text. If more than one note occurs on a page, double-space between them. If the note carries over to the next page, separate it from your text with a solid, full-length line. Put two spaces above the line and two spaces below it.

Preparing Your Finished Copy

Follow the revision guidelines in Chapter 3. In addition, verify that you have

- ▌ included all key information
- ▌ clearly organized your material
- ▌ not overloaded your paper with quotations
- ▌ worked in your own observations
- ▌ put in-text documentation and source information in proper form

TEACHING STRATEGY
You might comment on student drafts in conference sessions. The scope of their projects often makes such sessions particularly helpful to students.

Prepare your final draft with a typewriter or word-processor printer that produces dark, readable copy. Don't use a dot-matrix printer. Double-space throughout, including indented block quotations and the list of works you used to prepare the paper.

For the MLA system, number every page in the upper right-hand corner one-half inch from the top, and precede each number with your last name. Beginning one inch from the top of the first page, type your full name, the instructor's name, the course designation, and the date, all flush with the left-hand margin. Two lines below this, center the title, then double-space before starting your first paragraph. Leave one-inch margins on all four sides except at the top of the first page. Indent the first line of each paragraph five spaces.

The MLA system does not require a title page. However, if your instructor wants one, include the title of the paper, centered about two inches below the top of the sheet; your name, centered in the middle of the sheet; and the course designation, instructor's name, and date, centered about two inches from the bottom. Use capital and lowercase letters for everything on the page. Repeat the title, again in capital and lowercase letters, on the first text page, positioning it about two inches from the top.

Papers that follow the APA system require a title page. Center the title about four inches from the top and position your name, similarly centered, two spaces below the title. About three-fourths of the way from the top of the page, provide the course designation, the name of your instructor, and the date, typed flush with the right-hand margin. Two inches from the bottom of the page, type the words "Running Head," without quotation marks, then a colon and a word or phrase that identifies the paper's topic. Center these items. Use capital and lowercase letters for all items on the title page except the identifying word or phrase, which should be typed in capital letters. Number every page of the text in the upper right-hand corner, beginning with the number "2," without quotation marks. Position a shortened form of the title about one and one-half inches from the top of the page and, two spaces below it, the page number. Use one-and-one-half-inch margins at the bottom and at both sides of each page. Indent the first line of each paragraph five spaces.

The bibliography follows the text of the paper. It begins on a new page and lists all the sources you actually used. If your paper follows the MLA system, head your bibliography "Works Cited." For the APA system, substitute "References."

List each entry alphabetically according to the author's last name or, if no author is given, by the first significant word in the title. For a work with more than one author, alphabetize by the name that comes first. If you include more than one entry for an author and follow the MLA system, substitute three unspaced hyphens, followed by a period and a double space, for the second and subsequent entries. For the APA system, repeat the names. Begin the first line of each entry at the left-hand margin, and indent any subsequent lines five spaces for the MLA system and three spaces for the APA system.

ACKNOWLEDGING AND HANDLING YOUR SOURCES PROPERLY (MLA AND APA FORMATS)

To give proper credit to your sources, you must know how to (1) prepare source information, (2) document sources within your text, (3) handle quotations, and (4) avoid plagiarism.

Preparing Accurate Source Information

Your bibliography cards will help you when it comes time to list all the sources you used in writing your paper. Two systems of acknowledging sources are commonly used: the Modern Language Association (MLA) system, favored by many English and humanities instructors, and the American Psychological Association (APA) system, used by many social science and psychology instructors. The entries below illustrate basic conventions. For more information, consult the *MLA Handbook for Writers of Research Papers,* 3rd ed., 1988, and *The Publication Manual of the American Psychological Association,* 3rd. ed., 1983.

Source information for books.   The basic bibliographic reference for a book includes the name of the author, the title of the book, the place of publication, the name of the publisher, and the date of publication. Other information is added as necessary. The order of presentation depends upon which system of listing sources, the MLA or APA, is used.

A Book with One Author

MLA

Wilk, Max. <u>Every Day's a Matinee</u>. New York: Norton, 1975.

APA

Wilk, Max. (1975). <u>Every Day's a Matinee</u>. New York: W. W. Norton.

A Book with Two Authors

MLA

Bolt, A. B., and M. E. Wardle. <u>Communicating with a Computer</u>. Cambridge, Eng.: Cambridge UP, 1970.

Bolt, A. B., & Wardle, M. E. Communicating with a Computer.

    (1970). Cambridge: Cambridge University Press.

APA

Note that the APA system reverses the name of the second author and uses "&" instead of "and" between the names.

A Book with More than Three Authors

Alder, Roger William, et al. Mechanisms in Organic Chemistry.

    New York: Wiley, 1971.

MLA

Alder, Roger William, et al. (1971). Mechanisms in Organic

    Chemistry. New York: John Wiley.

APA

The MLA system used "et al." for four or more authors, the APA system for more than five.

A Book with Corporate Authorship

United Nations, Public Administration Division. Local

    Government Training. New York: UN, 1968.

MLA

United Nations, Public Administration Division. (1968). Local

    Government Training. New York: Author.

APA

When the author of the work is also the publisher, the APA system uses the word "Author" following the place of publication. If the work is published by another organization, its name replaces "Author."

An Edition Other than the First

MLA

Turabian, Kate L. A Manual for Writers of Term Papers, Theses,

    and Dissertations. 4th ed. Chicago: U of Chicago P, 1973.

Turabian, Kate L. (1973). A Manual for Writers of Term Papers,

    Theses, and Dissertations. (4th ed.). Chicago: University

    of Chicago Press.

APA

A Book in Two or More Volumes

MLA Hicks, John D., et al. History of American Democracy. 2 vols.
      Boston: Houghton, 1970.

APA Hicks, John D., et al. (1970). History of American Democracy. (2
      vols.). Boston: Houghton Mifflin.

A Reprint of an Older Work

MLA Matthiessen, F.O. American Renaissance: Art and Expression in
      the Age of Emerson and Whitman.' 1941. New York: Oxford
      UP, 1970.

APA Matthiessen, F. O. American Renaissance: Art and Expression in
      the Age of Emerson and Whitman. (1970). New York: Oxford
      University Press. (Originally published, 1941).

A Book with an Editor Rather than an Author

MLA Deetz, James, ed. Man's Imprint from the Past: Readings in the
      Methods of Archaeology. Boston: Little, 1971.

APA Deetz, James. (ed.)., (1971). Man's Imprint from the Past:
      Readings in the Methods of Archaeology. Boston: Little
      Brown.

A Book with Both an Author and an Editor

MLA Melville, Herman. The Confidence Man. Ed. Hershel Parker. New
      York: Norton, 1971.

APA Melville, Herman. (1971). The Confidence Man. (Herschel
      Parker, Ed.). New York: W. W. Norton. (Originally
      published, 1857).

A Translation

MLA Beauvoir, Simone de. All Said and Done. Trans. Patrick
      O'Brian. New York: Putnam, 1974.

Beauvoir, Simone de. (1974). <u>All Said and Done</u>. (Patrick

O'Brian, Trans.). New York: G. P. Putnam. (Originally

published, 1972).

APA

An Essay or Chapter in a Collection of Works by One Author

Woolf, Virginia. "The Lives of the Obscure." In her <u>The Common</u>

<u>Reader, First Series</u>. New York: Harcourt, 1925. 111–18.

MLA

Woolf, Virginia. (1925). The Lives of the Obscure. In Woolf,

Virginia, <u>The Common Reader, First Series</u> (pp. 111–18). New

York: Harcourt Brace Jovanovich.

APA

An Essay or Chapter in a Collection Containing Several Authors' Contributions Complied by an Editor

Angell, Roger. "On the Ball." <u>Subject and Strategy</u>. Ed. Paul

Eschholz and Alfred Rosa. New York: St. Martin's, 1981.

34–41.

MLA

Angell, Roger. (1981). On the Ball. In Paul Eschholz and

Alfred Rosa (Eds.), <u>Subject and Strategy</u> (pp. 34–41). New

York: St. Martin's Press.

APA

Source information for periodicals.   The basic information for a periodical article includes the name of the article's author, the name of the periodical, the title of the article, the date of publication, the page range of the entire article, and, for scholarly journals, the volume number of the periodical. Again, the order of presentation depends on the documentation system used.

An Article in a Scholarly Journal Consecutively Paged Through the Entire Volume

Alvord, John A. "Literature and Law in Medieval England." <u>PMLA</u>

<u>92</u> (1977): 941–51.

MLA

Alvord, John A. (1977). Literature and Law in Medieval

England. <u>PMLA</u>, 92, 941–51.

APA

An Article in a Scholarly Journal That Pages Each Issue Separately

MLA

Block, Joel W. "Sodom and Gomorrah: A Volcanic Disaster."

Journal of Geological Education 23.5 (1976): 74–77.

APA

Block, Joel W. (1976, May). Sodom and Gomorrah: A Volcanic

Disaster. Journal of Geological Education, 23, 74–77.

An Article in a Periodical

MLA

Kraft, Joseph. "Letter from Saudi Arabia." New Yorker 20 Oct.

1975: 111–39.

APA

Kraft, Joseph. (1975, October 20). Letter from Saudi Arabia.

New Yorker, pp. 111–39.

A Signed Article in a Daily Newspaper

MLA

Walker–Lynn, Joyce. "The Marine Corps Now Is Building Women,

Too." Chicago Tribune 30 Oct. 1977:I5.

APA

Walker–Lynn, Joyce. (1977, October 30). The Marine Corps Now

Is Building Women, Too. Chicago Tribune, sec. I, p. 5.

An Unsigned Article in a Daily Newspaper

MLA

"Lawmakers Unite on Mileage Rules." Detroit Free Press 21 Oct.

1975: B3.

APA

Lawmakers Unite on Mileage Rules. (1975, October 21). Detroit

Free Press, sec. B, p. 3.

Source information for encyclopedia articles. The basic information includes the name of the article's author, the title of the article, the name of the encyclopedia, and the date of the edition. Here too the order of presentation differs for the MLA and APA systems.

MLA

Davis, Harold S. "Team Teaching." The Encyclopedia of

Education. 1974 ed.

Davis, Harold S. (1974 ed.). Team Teaching. The Encyclopedia
    of Education.

    APA

    For an unsigned article, the reference begins with the title of the article:

"Hydrography." The American People's Encyclopedia. 1965 ed.

    MLA

Hydrography. (1965 ed.). The American People's Encyclopedia.

    APA

Source information for other sources. The information presented and
the order of presentation depend on the type of source and the documentation
system.

Book Reviews

Koenig, Rhoda. "Billy the Kid." Rev. of Billy Bathgate, by E.
    L. Doctorow. New York 20 Feb. 1989: 20–21.

    MLA

Koenig, Rhoda. Billy the Kid. (Review of Billy Bathgate by E.
    L. Doctorow). New York, 1989, February 20, 20–21.

    APA

If the review is unsigned but titled, begin with the title and follow the above
formats for the rest of the citation. If the review is both untitled and unsigned, use
the formats that follow.

Rev. of Billy Bathgate, by E. L. Doctorow. New York 20 Feb.
    1989: 20–21.

    MLA

Rev. of Billy Bathgate by E. L. Doctorow. New York, 1989,
    February 20, 20–21.

    APA

Interviews

    MLA

Noriega, Manuel. Interview. "A Talk with Manuel Noriega." By
    Felipe Hernandez. News Report 20 March 1987: 28–30.

    APA

Noriega, Manuel. A Talk with Manuel Noriega. (Interview with
    Felipe Hernandez). News Report, 1987, March 20, pp. 28–30.

If the interview in untitled, use the word "Interview," without quotation marks or underlining, for the MLA system. For the APA system, follow the example above, omitting any mention of a title. If you conducted the interview yourself, start with the name of the person interviewed and follow it with the kind of interview and the date conducted.

MLA   Newman, Paul. Personal interview. 19 May 1985.

APA   Newman, Paul. (Personal interview). 19 May 1985.

Films

MLA   Frankenstein. Dir. James Whale. With Boris Karloff, John

        Boles, Colin Clive, and Mae Clarke. Universal, 1931.

If you are interested in the contribution of a particular person, start with that person's name.

MLA   Whale, James, dir. Frankenstein. With Boris Karloff, John

        Boles, Colin Clive, and Mae Clarke. Universal, 1931.

In the APA system, the citations begins with an individual's name and his or her contribution to the film.

APA   Whale, James. (Director). (1931). Frankenstein. With Boris

        Karloff, John Boles, Colin Clive, and Mae Clarke, Hollywood:

        Universal.

Television and Radio Programs

MLA   Murder, She Wrote. With Angela Lansbury, David McCallum, and

        Peter Donat. CBS. WZZM, Grand Rapids. 26 Feb. 1989.

If you are focusing on the work of some individual connected with the program, begin the entry with his or her name.

APA   Anderson, Lindsay, dir. Glory! Glory! With Richard Thomas,

        Ellen Greene, and James Whitmore. HBO, Detroit. 19, 20 Feb.

        1989.

When citing one episode out of a series, start with its title, in quotation marks.

MLA

"Forgive Us our Debts." Miami Vice. With Don Johnson, Edward

    James Olmos, and Olivia Brown. NBC. WOTV, Grand Rapids.

    20 April 1987.

The APA system does not include a documentation format for television and radio programs.

Record Albums and Tapes

Smith, Bessie. The World's Greatest Blues Singer. Columbia, GP

MLA

    33, 1948.

If you mention the name of a particular item on the record or tape, set it off with quotation marks and position it as shown.

Smith, Bessie. "Down Hearted Blues." The World's Greatest

MLA

    Blues Singer. Columbia, GP 33, 1948.

The APA system calls for these formats.

Smith, Bessie. (Singer). (1948). The World's Greatest Blues

APA

    Singer. (Record No. GP 33). New York: Columbia.

Smith, Bessie. (Singer). (1948). Down Hearted Blues. The

APA

    World's Greatest Blues Singer. (Record No. GP 33). New

    York: Columbia.

Computer Software Programs

Southwell, Michael G., and John Fox. GrammarLab. Computer

MLA

    Software. Applied Logic Consultants, 1985. IBM PC, 48

    KB, Disk.

Southwell, Michael G., & Fox, John. (1985). GrammarLab.

APA

    (Computer program). New York: Applied Logic Consultants. IBM

    PC, 48 KB, Disk.

EXERCISE ANSWERS

1. Dow Chemical Company. *Gas Conditioning Fact Book*. Midland, Michigan: Dow, 1962.

2. "Justices Restrict Action by Courts in Nuclear Cases." *The Wall Street Journal* 5 April 1982: 2.

3. Mills, C. Wright. "The Competitive Personality." *Power, Politics, and People*. Ed. Irving Louis Horowitz. New York: Ballantine, 1963. 263–73.

4. "Where Do We Go From Here?" *U.S. News and World Report* 4 Oct. 1982: 30–33.

5. Theroux, Paul. *The Kingdom by the Sea*. Boston: Houghton, 1983.

6. Chopin, Kate. *The Awakening*. Ed. Margaret Culley. New York: Norton, 1976.

7. Schmerdler, Gertrude. "Parapsychology." *International Encyclopedia of the Social Sciences*. 1968 ed.

8. Willcox, Christopher. "Right-to-Die Bill Sparks Hot Debate." *Detroit Free Press* 28 Feb. 1983: 2.

9. Ember, Carol R., and Melvin Ember. *Anthropology*. New York: Appleton, 1973.

10. Descola, Jean. *A History of Spain*. Trans. Elaine P. Halperin. New York: Knopf, 1962.

11. Flanagan, John T., and Raymond L. Grimer. "Mexico in American Fiction to 1850." *Hispania* 23 (1940): 307–18.

EXERCISE ■

A. Using the MLA system, write a proper reference for each of the following sets of information.

1. A book titled Gas Conditioning Fact Book. The book was published in 1962 by Dow Chemical Company in Midland, Michigan. No author is named.

2. An unsigned article titled Justices Restrict Action by Courts in Nuclear Cases. The article was published in the April 5, 1982, issue of the Wall Street Journal. It appears on page 2.

3. An essay written by C. Wright Mills and titled The Competitive Personality. The essay appeared in a collection of Mill's writings entitled Power, Politics, and People. The collection was published in 1963 by Ballantine Books in New York. The book is edited and introduced by Irving Louis Horowitz. The essay appears on pages 263 through 273.

4. An unsigned article titled Inflation: Where Do We Go from Here? The article was published in the October 4, 1982, issue of U.S. News and World Report. It appears on pages 30 to 33.

5. A book written by Paul Theroux and titled The Kingdom by the Sea. The book was published in 1983 by the Houghton Mifflin Company in Boston.

6. A book written by Kate Chopin and titled The Awakening. The book, edited by Margaret Culley, was published in 1976 by W. W. Norton and Company in New York.

7. An article written by Gertrude R. Schmerdler and titled Parapsychology. The article appears in volume 11 of the International Encyclopedia of the Social Sciences, published in 1968. It appears on pages 386 through 398.

8. An article written by Christopher Willcox and titled Right-to-Die Bill Sparks Hot Debate. The article was published in the February 28, 1983, issue of the Detroit News. It appears on page 2 of Section B.

9. A book written by Carol R. Ember and Melvin Ember and titled Anthropology. The book was published in 1973 by Appleton-Century-Crofts in New York.

10. A book written by Jean Descola and titled A History of Spain. The book, translated by Elaine P. Halperin, was published in 1962 by Alfred A. Knopf in New York.

11. An article written by John T. Flanagan and Raymond L. Grimer and titled Mexico in American Fiction to 1850. The article was published in 1940 in a journal called Hispania. It appears on pages 307 through 318. The volume number is 23.

12. A book written by Babette Deutsch and titled Poetry in Our Time. The second edition of the book was published in 1956 by Columbia University Press in New York.

13. A book written by Joseph Blotner and titled Faulkner: A Biography. The book was published in two volumes in 1974 by Random House in New York.

14. An article written by Jerome L. Singer and titled Fantasy: The Foundation of Serenity. The article was published in the July 1983 issue of Psychology Today. It appears on pages 32 through 37.

15. A book written by Thomas Beer and titled Stephen Crane: A Study in American Letters. The book was published in 1923 and reprinted in 1972 by Octagon Books in New York.

16. A review of a book written by Jacques Barzun and titled The Culture We Deserve. The review, by Beth Winona, appeared in the March 1989 issue of American Issues magazine and was titled Barzun and Culture. It appeared on pages 46 through 50.

17. An interview of play producer Joseph Papp. The interview was titled Joseph Papp on the New York Theater and appeared in the August 21, 1989, issue of the Long Island News, on page C3-4. The interviewer was Mary Barnes.

18. A Film titled Casablanca. The film was directed by Michael Curtiz and starred Humphrey Bogart, Ingrid Bergman, Claude Rains, and Paul Henreid. It was released in 1942 by Warner Brothers.

19. A television program titled Wolf. It starred Jack Scalia, Joseph Sirola, Mimi Kuzyk, and Nicholas Surovy. It appeared on WNTR, New York, on September 13, 1989. The station is part of the CBS network.

20. A song titled I've Been Alone Too Long. It appeared in an album titled B. J. Thomas Songs. The designation of the album is PAS 6052. The album, by Paramount Records, appeared in 1973.

21. A computer software program titled SpelHelp. The program was written by Andras DuKlos. It was produced in 1988 by United Computek for IBM personal computers. It has a 96 KB capacity and is available in cassette form.

B. Prepare a proper MLA entry for each of the works you plan to use in writing your paper.

Handling In-Text Citations

Both the MLA and APA systems use notations that appear within the text and are set off by parentheses. The systems are illustrated by the following examples.

Basic citation form.   For the MLA system, the citation consists of the last name of the author and the page numbers of the publication in which the material originally appeared. The APA system adds the year to the citation. At the writer's option, the items may be grouped together or separated, as shown in the following examples.

Bibliographic Reference

Bryan, Christopher.   "Big Steel's Winter of Woes."   Time 24 Jan.

    1983: 58.

---

12. Deutsch, Babette. *Poetry in Our Time*. 2nd ed. New York: Columbia UP, 1956.

13. Blotner, Joseph. *Faulkner: A Biography*. 2 vols. New York: Random, 1974.

14. Singer, Jerome L. "Fantasy: The Foundation of Serenity." *Psychology Today* July 1983: 32–37.

15. Beer, Thomas. *Stephen Crane: A Study in American Letters*. 1923. New York: Octagon, 1972.

16. Winona, Beth. "Barzun and Culture." Review of *The Culture We Deserve*, by Jacques Barzun, *American Issues* March 1989: 46–50.

17. Papp, Joseph. "Joseph Papp on the New York Theater." With Mary Barnes. *Long Island News* 21 Aug. 1989: C3-4.

18. *Casablanca*. Dir. Michael Curtiz. With Humphrey Bogart, Ingrid Bergman, Claude Rains, and Paul Henreid. Warner Brothers, 1942.

19. *Wolf*. With Jack Scalia, Joseph Sirola, Mimi Kuzyk, and Nicholas Surovy. CBS. WNTR, New York. 13 Sept. 1989.

20. Thomas. B.J. "I've Been Alone Too Long." *B. J. Thomas Songs*. Paramount Records, PAS 6052, 1973.

21. DuKlos, Andras. *SpelHelp*. Computer software. United Computek, 1988. IBM PC, 96 KB, cassette.

Passage and Citation

MLA	Steel workers in this country make an average of twenty-four dollars an hour, including benefits, whereas Japanese workers make just over eleven dollars an hour (Bryan 58).
MLA	Bryan notes that steel workers in this country make an average of twenty-four dollars an hour, including benefits, whereas Japanese workers make just over eleven dollars an hour (58).
APA	. . . make just over eleven dollars an hour (Bryan, 1983, p. 58).
APA	Bryan (1983) notes that . . . Japanese workers make just over eleven dollars an hour (58).

Bibliographic Reference

Weider, Benjamin, and David Hapgood.   The Murder of Napoleon.
      New York: Congdon, 1982.

Passage and Citation

MLA	Four different autopsy reports were filed. All the reports agreed that there was a cancerous ulcer in Napoleon's stomach, but none of them declared that the cancer was the cause of death. Nevertheless, cancer has become accepted as the cause (Weider and Hapgood 72).
APA	. . . Nevertheless, cancer has become accepted as the cause (Weider & Hapgood, 1982, p. 72).

If a source has more than three authors (more than five for the APA), use et al., meaning "and others," for all but the first-named one.

Bibliographic Reference

Baugh, Albert C., et al. <u>A Literary History of England</u>. New
    York: Appleton, 1948.

Passage and Citation

Although no one knows for certain just when Francis Beaumont
and John Fletcher started collaborating, by 1610 they were
writing plays together (Baugh et al. 573).

| MLA |

    . . . writing plays together (Baugh et al., 1948, p. 573).

| APA |

Authors with the same last name.   If your notes include authors with the
same last name, use the initials of their first names to distinguish them.

Bibliographic Reference

Adler, Jerry. "Search for an Orange Thread." <u>Newsweek</u> 16 June
    1980: 32–34.

Adler, William L. "The Agent Orange Controversy." <u>Detroit Free
    Press</u> 18 Dec. 1979: B2.

Passage and Citation

As early as 1966, government studies showed that dioxin-
contaminated 2,4,5-T caused birth defects in laboratory
animals. Later studies also found that this herbicide was to
blame for miscarriages, liver abscesses, and nerve damage
(J. Adler 32).

| MLA |

    . . . miscarriages, liver abscesses, and nerve damage (J.
Adler, 1980, p. 32).

| APA |

Separate works by the same author.   If your references include two or
more works by the same author, add shortened forms of the titles to your in-text
citation if you follow the MLA system. Underline shortened book titles and use

quotation marks around article and essay titles. For the APA system, use the conventional name-date-page number entry.

Bibliographic Reference

```
Mullin, Dennis.  "After U.S. Troops Pull Out of Grenada."  U.S.
      News & World Report 14 Nov. 1983: 22–25.

———.  "Why the Surprise Move in Grenada——and What Next."  U.S.
      News & World Report 7 Nov. 1983: 31–34.
```

Passage and Citation

```
          As the rangers evacuated students, the marines launched
MLA       another offensive at Grand Mal Bay, then moved south to
          seize the capital and free the governor (Mullin, "Why the
          Surprise" 33).
```

```
APA           . . . and free the governor (Mullin, 1983b, p. 33).
```

If the two works appeared in the same year, put an "a" or a "b," without quotes, after the date to identify whether you are referring to the first or second entry for that author in the bibliography.

Two separate sources for the same citation. If two sources provide essentially the same information and you wish to mention both in one parenthetical citation, group them together with a semicolon between them and position them as you would any other citation.

Bibliographic Reference

```
Bryce, Bonnie.  "The Controversy over Funding Community
      Colleges."  Detroit Free Press 13 Nov. 1988: A4.
Warshow, Harry.  "Community College Funding Hits a Snag."  Grand
      Rapids Press 15 Nov. 1988: A2.
```

Passage and Citation

```
MLA       In contending that a 3 percent reduction in state funding
          for community colleges would not significantly hamper their
```

operations, the governor overlooks the fact that community college enrollment is expected to jump by 15 percent next year (Bryce A4; Warshow A2).

APA

In contending that a 3 percent reduction in state funding for community colleges would not significantly hamper their operations, the governor overlooks the fact that community college enrollment is expected to jump by 15 percent next year (Bryce, 1988, p. A4; Warshow, 1988, p. A2).

Unsigned references. When you use a source for which no author is given, the in-text citation consists of all or part of the title, the appropriate page numbers, and, for the APA system, the date.

Bibliographic Reference

"Reform in Sight for People's Right to Know." American
    Libraries 4 (1975): 540.

Passage and Citation

In 1974, Congress proposed several amendments to the Freedom of Information Act, only to have President Ford reject them on the grounds that they were "unconstitutional and unworkable." But while Ford was out of the country in early 1975, Congress voted overwhelmingly to enact them into law ("Reform in Sight" 540).

MLA

. . . overwhelmingly to enact them into law ("Reform in Sight," 1975, p. 540).

APA

Citing quotations. When the quotation is run into the text, position the citation as shown below.

Bibliographic Reference

Verney, Thomas, M.D., and John Kelly. The Secret Life of the
    Unborn Child. New York: Simon, 1981.

Passage and Citation

MLA

Investigators who have studied mother-child bonding have found that "women who bond become better mothers, and their babies almost always are physically healthier, emotionally more stable and intellectually more acute than infants taken from their mothers right after birth" (Verney and Kelly 146).

APA

. . . mothers right after birth" (Verney & Kelly, 1981, p. 146).

With longer, indented quotations, skip two horizontal spaces after the end punctuation and type the reference in parentheses.

Bibliographic Reference

Newhouse, John. "The Diplomatic Round: A Freemasonry of Terrorism." <u>New Yorker</u> 8 July 1985: 46-63.

Passage and Citation

MLA

One commentator offers this assessment of why foreign terrorist groups don't operate in this country:

> The reason that America has been spared so far, apparently, is that it is less vulnerable than Europe, especially to Middle Eastern extremists. Moving in and out of most European countries isn't difficult for non-Europeans; border controls are negligible. But American customs and immigration authorities, being hyper-alert to drug traffic, tend to pay attention to even marginally doubtful people, and a would-be terrorist . . . could come under surveillance for the wrong reason. (Newhouse 63)

. . . come under surveillance for the wrong reason.

(Newhouse, 1985, p. 63).

APA

Indirect citations.   If you use a quotation from person A that you obtained from a book or article written by person B, or you paraphrase such a quotation, put "qtd. in" before the name of the publication's author in the parenthetical reference.

Bibliographic Reference

Klein, Joe.   "Ready for Rudy."   New York 6 Mar. 1989: 30–37.

Passage and Citation

U.S. attorney Rudolph Giuliani favors the death penalty for

"the murder of a law-enforcement officer, mass murder, a

particularly heinous killing" but would impose it only

"when there is certainty of guilt well beyond a reasonable

doubt" (qtd. in Klein 37).

MLA

". . . there is certainty of guilt well beyond a reasonable

doubt" (qtd. in Klein, 1989, p. 37).

APA

Authors identified in text.   Sometimes you'll want to introduce a paraphrase, summary, or quotation with the name of its author. In this case the page number may be positioned immediately after the name or follow the material cited.

Bibliographic Reference

Jacoby,Susan.   "Waiting for the End: On Nursing Homes."   New

York Times Magazine 31 March 1974: 80.

Passage and Citation

Susan Jacoby (80) sums up the grim outlook of patients in

bad nursing homes by noting that they are merely waiting to

die.

MLA

MLA

Susan Jacoby sums up the grim outlook of patients in bad nursing homes by noting that they are merely waiting to die (80).

APA

Susan Jacoby (1974, p. 80) sums up . . .

APA

Susan Jacoby (1974) sums up . . . waiting to die (p. 80).

EXERCISE ■ **Using the MLA system, write a proper in-text citation for each of the bibliographic references you prepared for parts A and B on pages 332–333. Assume that you have not used the author's name to introduce the material you cite.**

Handling Quotations

Set off quotations fewer than five lines long (fewer than forty words long for the APA system) with quotation marks and run them into the text of the paper. For longer quotes, omit the quotation marks and indent the material ten spaces from the left-hand margin (four spaces for the APA system). Double-space the typing. If you quote part or all of one paragraph, don't further indent the first line. If you quote two or more consecutive paragraphs, indent each one's first line three additional spaces. Use single quotation marks for a quotation within a shorter quotation and double marks for a quotation within a longer, indented quotation. The following examples illustrate the handling of quotations. The documentation and indentation follow the MLA guidelines.

Short Quotation

Ellen Goodman offers this further observation about writers who peddle formulas for achieving success through selfishness: "They are all Doctor Feelgoods, offering placebo prescriptions instead of strong medicine. They give us a way to live with ourselves, perhaps, but not a way to live with each other." (16).

Quotation Within Short Quotation

The report further stated, "All great writing styles have their wellsprings in the personality of the writer. As Buffon said, 'The style is the man.'" (Duncan 49).

Quotation Within Longer, Indented Quotation

> Barbara Tuchman's <u>The Proud Tower</u> presents a somewhat
> different view of the new conservative leaders:
>
> > Besides riches, rank, broad acres, and ancient
> > lineage, the new government also possessed, to
> > the regret of the liberal opposition, and in the
> > words of one of them, "an almost embarrassing
> > wealth of talent and capacity." Secure in
> > authority, resting comfortably on their
> > electoral majority in the House of Commons and on
> > a permanent majority in the House of Lords, of
> > whom four-fifths were conservatives, they were in
> > a position, admitted the same opponent, "of
> > unassailable strength" (4).

Always provide some context for material that you quote. Various options exist. When you quote from a source for the first time, you might provide the author's full name and the source of the quotation, perhaps indicating the author's expertise as well. The passage just above omits the author's expertise; the passage below includes it.

> Writing in <u>Newsweek</u> magazine, Riena Gross, chief
> psychiatric social worker at Illinois Medical Center in
> Chicago, said, "Kids have no real sense that they belong
> anywhere or to anyone as they did ten or fifteen years ago.
> Parents have loosened the reins, and kids are kind of
> floundering" (74).

Or you might note the event prompting the quotation and then the author's name.

> Addressing a seminar at the University of Toronto, Dr.
> Joseph Pomeranz speculated that "acupuncture may work by
> activating a neural pain suppression mechanism in the
> brain" (324).

On other occasions you might note only the author's full name and expertise.

> Economist Richard M. Cybert, President of Carnegie—Mellon University, offers the following sad prediction about the steel industry's future: "It will never be as large an industry as it has been. There are a lot of plants that will never come back and many laborers that will never be rehired" (43).

When quoting from a source with no author given, introduce the quotation with the name of the source.

> Commenting upon the problems that law enforcement personnel have in coping with computer crime, Credit and Financial Management magazine pointed out that "A computer crime can be committed in three hundredths of a second, and the criminal can be thousands of miles from the 'scene,' using a telephone" ("Computer Crime" 43).

After first citing an author's full name, use only the last name for subsequent references.

> In answering the objections of governmental agencies to the Freedom of Information Act, Wellford commented, "Increased citizen access should help citizens learn of governmental activities that weaken our First Amendment freedoms. Some administrative inconvenience isn't too large a price to pay for that" (137).

Page numbers are not helpful when you cite passages from plays and poems since these literary forms are available in many editions. When you quote from a play, identify the act, scene, and line numbers. Use Arabic numbers separated by periods. Here's how to cite Act 2, Scene 1, lines 258–263 of Shakespeare's *Othello*:

> That Cassio loves her, I do well believe it;
>
> That she loves him, 'tis apt, and of great credit:
>
> The Moor, how be it that I endure him not,
>
> Is of a constant, loving, noble nature;
>
> And I dare think he'll prove to Desdemona
>
> A most dear husband. (Othello 2.1. 258–263)

When quoting from a short poem, use "line" or "lines" and the line number(s):

> In "Dover Beach," Matthew Arnold offers this melancholy
>
> assessment of the state of religion:
>
> > The Sea of Faith
> >
> > Was once, too, at the full, and round earth's
> >
> > shore
> >
> > Lay like the folds of a bright girdle furl'd.
> >
> > But now I only hear
> >
> > Its melancholy, long, withdrawing roar.　(lines
> >
> > 21–26)

In quoting poetry that has been run into the text, use a slash mark (/) to indicate the shift from one line to another in the original:

> In his ode "To Autumn," Keats says that Autumn is the
>
> "Season of mists and mellow fruitfulness,/Close bosom—
>
> friend of the maturing sun" (lines 1–2).

Avoiding Plagiarism

Plagiarism occurs when a writer uses another person's material without properly acknowledging the debt. Sometimes plagiarism is deliberate, but often it happens because students simply don't understand what must be acknowledged and documented. Deliberate or not, plagiarism is absolutely unacceptable. *Any summary, paraphrase, or quotation you include in your paper must be documented.* The only types of information escaping this requirement are those listed below.

1. Common Knowledge. Common knowledge is information that most educated people would know. For instance, there's no need to document a statement that the Disney theme parks in California and Florida attract thousands of visitors each year. However, if you include precise daily, monthly, or yearly figures, then documentation is necessary.
2. Your own conclusions. As you write your paper, you'll incorporate your own conclusions at various points. (See the margin notes accompanying Christine Harding's library research paper, pages 359, 363, and 365, for example.) Such comments require no documentation. The same holds true for your own research. If you polled students on a campus issue, simply present the findings as your own.

PERSPECTIVE

The sad fact of plagiarism, intentional or otherwise, cannot be ignored. Advertisements in many school papers offer to sell term papers, students write them for a fee, and fraternities and sororities often keep "A" models on file. There are, however, several ways of coping with the problem.

TEACHING STRATEGIES

1. Have students bring in the appropriate original sources and proofread in class for instances of unintentional plagiarism in their papers. This activity reinforces the message that plagiarism is unacceptable and also gives students an opportunity to detect and redress problems.

2. Have students turn in the paper in stages—working bibliography, note cards, rough outline, different drafts, and the like. If students are asked to revise according to your responses, they can't simply turn in a pre-written paper. Refuse to accept a finished draft on an entirely new topic "because the old one just wasn't working out."

3. You might add unique requirements that serve as plagiarism fingerprints, such as including faculty interviews (on their topic) in the paper.

**SUGGESTED
INSTRUCTOR READING**

Galles, G. "Psst, Kid! Wanna Buy a Term Paper?" Christian Science Monitor 25 Sept. 1989: 19. Analyzes the operation of term paper mills and the difficulties teachers face in dealing with them. In a separate listing, Galles details some creative "Barriers to Plagiarism" that instructors might like to consider.

3. Facts found in many sources. Facts such as the year of Shakespeare's death, the size of the 1990 national budget deficit, and the location of the Taj Mahal need not be documented.

Any piece of information not set off with quotation marks must be in your own words. Otherwise, even though you name your source, you plagiarize by stealing the original phrasing.

The following passages illustrate the improper and proper use of source material.

Original Passage

One might contend, of course, that our country's biological diversity is so great and the land is so developed—so criss-crossed with the works of man—that it will soon be hard to build a dam anywhere without endangering some species. But as we develop a national inventory of endangered species, we certainly can plan our *necessary* development so as to exterminate the smallest number possible . . .

James L. Buckley, "Three Cheers for the Snail Darter," *National Review,* September 14, 1979: 1144–45.

Plagiarism

Our country's biological diversity is so great and the land is so developed that it will soon be hard to build a dam anywhere without endangering some species. But as we develop a national inventory of endangered species, we certainly can plan our necessary development so as to exterminate the smallest number possible.

This writer clearly plagiarizes. The absence of Buckley's name and the failure to enclose his words in quotation marks create the impression that this passage is the student's own work.

Plagiarism

Our country's biological diversity is so great and the land so developed that in the near future we may pose a threat to some creature whenever we construct a dam. By developing a national inventory of endangered species, however, we can plan necessary development <u>so as to</u> preserve as many species

as possible (Buckley 1144).

This version credits the ideas to Buckley, but the student has plagiarized by failing to put quotation marks around the phrasing (underlined above) that was copied from the original. As a result, readers will think that the passage represents the student's own wording.

Proper Use of Original

America has so many kinds of plants and animals, and it is so

built up, that in the near future we may pose a threat to

some living thing whenever we construct a dam. If, however,

we knew which of our nation's plants and animals were

threatened, we could use this information to preserve as

many species as possible (Buckley 1144).

This student has identified the author and used her own words. As a result, no plagiarism occurs.

Plagiarism is a serious offense because it robs the original wrier of recognition. Students caught plagiarizing risk failure in the course or perhaps suspension from school. Whenever you are unsure whether material requires documentation, supply a reference. And always handle direct quotations by following the guidelines beginning on page 340.

EXAMPLE RESEARCH PAPER

CASE HISTORY ■ *(Concluded)*

Using her outline and thesis statement as a guide, Christine prepared a first draft of her paper, following the MLA format required by her instructor. After setting it aside for two days, she revised it carefully. Because her instructor required both a topic and a sentence outline, she revised the topic outline she had previously prepared and then followed it while drafting the sentence version. These two outlines appear on pages 346–349, and the two drafts of the paper, with "Rough Draft" on the left and "Final Draft" on the right for easy comparison, are on pages 350–369. The notes to the right of the final draft highlight the more important changes Christine made and also direct your attention to noteworthy features.

Topic Outline

Thesis Statement: Despite the misgivings of some people, robots will probably have beneficial effects on industry and its workforce.

I.   History of robots

    A. Origin of term "robot"

    B. Launchers of the robot revolution

    C. First purchasers of robots

    D. Present status of robots

    E. Future prospects for robots

II. Fears concerning the impact of robots

    A. Fears of corporate management

        1. Financial fears

        2. Unemployment fears

    B. Fears of noncorporate persons

III. Benefits resulting from robots

    A. Past benefits of automation

        1. The first automobile assembly line

        2. The Hargreaves spinning jenny

    B. Benefits for corporate managers

        1. Greater efficiency

        2. Lower operational costs

    C. Benefits for workers

        1. More interesting jobs

        2. Shorter workweek

        3. Safer workplace

IV. Robots and the unemployment threat

    A. Reassignment of displaced workers to other jobs

    B. Retraining of displaced workers

        1. By industry

        2. By colleges

            a. In Michigan

            b. Nationwide

        3. By government and other organizations

Sentence Outline

Thesis Statement: Despite the misgivings of some people, robots will probably have beneficial effects on industry and its workforce.

I.   Robots have a short but highly successful history.
     A. Karel Capek, a Czech writer, coined the term "robot."
     B. George C. Devol and Joseph F. Engelberger launched the robot revolution.
     C. The first robots were sold to automakers.
     D. Robots are now firmly established in American industry.
     E. Robots will continue to become more sophisticated and important to American industry.
II. Many people fear the impact that robots will have.
     A. Corporate management often looks with disfavor on robots.
        1. Some managers fear their financial impact.
        2. Some worry about unemployment.
     B. Some people outside of corporations also worry about unemployment.
III. Robots are another form of mechanization, and mechanization is beneficial, not harmful.
     A. Historical evidence points up the benefits of automation.
        1. The introduction of the assembly line into the auto industry caused manufacturing costs and car prices to plummet and sales and employment to leap.
        2. The invention of the Hargreaves spinning jenny benefited employment in Britain's textile industry.

    B. Robots offer corporate managers a number of advantages.

        1. They are more efficient than human workers.

        2. They are more economical than human workers.

    C. Robots offer advantages to workers as well as managers.

        1. Jobs become more interesting and challenging.

        2. Workers will spend less time on the job.

        3. Workers will face fewer health and safety risks.

IV. Robots do not pose a serious unemployment threat.

    A. Most displaced workers will move into jobs directly or indirectly associated with robots.

    B. Efforts are now underway to provide the specialized training these workers will need.

        1. Industry is initiating training programs.

        2. Colleges are also rising to the challenge.

            a. Twelve Michigan colleges are offering or considering programs.

            b. Nationwide, over 30 colleges have programs.

        3. Government and private organizations may also play a role in training workers.

Robots in Industry

     In the beginning, industry relied upon the muscle power of workers, using a few hand tools, to perform its tasks. As time passed, these hand tools gave way to complicated machines. Today, robots have entered the picture and will replace many present machines.

     The Robot Institute of America says that a robot is "a reprogrammable multifunctional manipulator designed to move material, parts, tools, or specialized devices through variable programmed motions for the performance of a variety of tasks" (Rosenblatt 349). <u>Despite the misgivings of some people, robots will probably have beneficial effects on industry and its workforce.</u>

     The term "robot" was coined by Karel Capek, a Czech writer. He was writing a play and needed a name for the machine in the script, which resembled people but worked twice as hard (Rosenblatt 348). It was George C. Devol who developed the basic technology that made the robot industry possible. In 1956, Devol met Joseph Engelberger, a physics student. He (Devol) shared his dream of when robots would be widely used in industry. Engelberger founded and became president of a company that produced the first robots that industry bought (Feder F6).

Christine Harding

Professor Reinking

English 113

May 7, 1990

Final Draft

Robots in Industry: A Boon for Everyone

Title reflects main thrust of paper

Historically, industry has relied on humans to perform its tasks. In the beginning, productivity depended upon the sheer muscle power of workers, augmented by a few hand—operated devices. With the Industrial Revolution, these devices gave way to ever— larger, ever—more—complicated machines that made modern factories possible and multiplied enormously the production capacity of their workers. Now technological advances have ushered in a new Industrial Revolution, one in which robots will take over many of the operations now carried out by conventional machines and their human attendants.

New information smoothes writing, points to robots' impact

Exactly what is a robot? The Robot Institute of America defines it as "a reprogrammable multifunctional manipulator designed to move material, parts, tools, or specialized devices through variable programmed motions for the performance of a variety of tasks" (Rosenblatt 349). A robot consists essentially of a manipulator arm, a pair of grippers, an electrical control unit, and a power pack to move the mechanical arm (McElroy 43). Currently, efforts are underway to develop robots that can "see" and "feel" so that they can respond to changes in the environment without expensive human assistance (Rosenblatt, 350, 352). Although the rapid

Context provided for short, run-in quote within quotation marks

More about robots, future capabilities

■ **Rough Draft**

General Motors bought the first robots. It used them to weld 1969 Vega automobiles. The factory where they were produced was in Lordstown, Ohio. By 1975, Ford was using robots for many welding operations in Kansas City. This facility was recognized as the world's most technically advanced auto assembly plant (Weisel 19).

Robots have now become firmly established in many industries, where they do welding, machine tool loading and unloading, forging, shot blasting, and painting (Weisel 18). Future prospects for robots seem good. By 1990, many robots will be able to see and feel and be controlled by computers (McElroy 43). Robots will do a considerable share of all welding, material handling, and assembly (Rosenblatt 360).

growth in robot technology has aroused some fears of its consequences, robots will actually benefit everyone, and efforts are being made to lessen any harmful impact upon the work force.

As Rosenblatt notes, the term "robot" was coined in 1921 by Karel Capek, a Czech writer, who used it to designate the humanoid factory workers in his satirical play R.U.R., or Rosson's Universal Robots (348). George C. Devol, an engineer, developed the basic technology that made the robot industry possible. In 1956, Devol met Joseph F. Engelberger, a physics student at Columbia University, and shared with him his dream of a day when robots would be used for a broad spectrum of industrial tasks. Engelberger, an avid disciple of Devol, went on to become the founder and president of Unimation, Inc., which produced the first robots industry was to buy (Feder 6F).

These first robots were sold to auto makers. The pioneer purchaser, General Motors, installed a robot welding line in its Lordstown, Ohio, auto plant, where it was used in respot welding on the 1969 Vega automobile. By 1975, Ford was using robots for a whole range of welding operations, and its Kansas City facility was recognized as the world's most technically advanced auto assembly plant (Weisel 19).

Robots have become firmly established in many industries. By 1982, 29 percent of all automated factories were using robots, 19 percent were planning to install them very soon, and 44 percent were considering them for a later time ("Robot Productivity" 53). Specific functions now performed by robots in automobile plants and elsewhere include die casting, arc and spot

---

■ **Final Draft**

Thesis statement truer to content and organization

Cites play, corrects grammar, adds history, improves writing

Corrects phrasing, describes use at GM and Ford

One paragraph now two; statistics, forecasts of functions and sales add interest, depth

Many people fear the effects that robots will have. Many corporate managers are afraid to invest in them. They reason that workers are plentiful, and the high cost of robots as well as the long payback period could hurt the company (Rosenblatt 360). Other people outside the corporate fold worry about robots too. They include Harley Shaiken, a labor analyst at the Massachusetts Institute of Technology (Skrzycki 25), and William Wimpisinger, of the International Association of Machinists (Cromie 16). Both have made strongly worded negative statements about the impact of robots. Shaiken said, "What of the worker in Flint, Mich.? He's being asked to commit economic suicide so GM can return to profitability" (Skrzycki 26). Wimpisinger went so far as to declare that "The union worker is the endangered species in the robot revolution" (Cromie 16).

welding, machine tool loading and unloading, forging, shot blasting, and spray painting (Weisel 18).

As time passes, robots will become more sophisticated, and their industrial role will continue to enlarge. The Robot Institute of America forecasts that by 1990, 25 percent of all robots will have "vision," 20 percent will be able to "feel," and 88 percent will be controlled by computers (McElroy 43). At that time, the Institute says, the nation's robot population will number between 75,000 and 100,000 (Hunt and Hunt 3). Robots will do 15 to 20 percent of all arc welding, 30 to 35 percent of all materials handling, and 35 to 40 percent of all assembly work in our factories (Rosenblatt 360). Annual sales of industrial robots in the United States will be as much as $2.5 billion, as compared to 1984 sales of $190 million (Stepanek 4B). Similarly, annual sales of service robots are expected to top $2 billion by 1995, up from 1987's $120 billion (Bylinsky 82).

The swift industrial inroads made by robots have led many people to fear their impact on industry as well as on the overall economy. Corporate management is often reluctant to invest in robots, reasoning that workers are plentiful and that the high initial cost and long payback period could jeopardize the financial position of their companies. Many managers also fear that robots may bring about massive unemployment (Rosenblatt 360). Others outside the corporate fold have criticized the impact of robots upon the employment picture. Thus Harley Shaiken, a labor analyst at the Massachusetts Institute of Technology, wonders, "What of the worker in Flint, Mich.? He's being asked to commit economic suicide so GM can return to profitability" (qtd. in Skrzycki 25). William Wimpisinger, of the International Association of

■ **Final Draft**

Corrects strung-out phrasing; reinforces thrust with views of management and labor on cost and job loss; cites figures

These fears would shrink or disappear if people realized that robots are merely another form of automation or mechanization. History shows that automation is good for employment. Henry Ford proved this when he started using assembly lines and mass production. By so doing, he increased the productivity of his workers and reduced the number of hours needed to produce each car. The increase amounted to 8.5 percent per year and the decrease to 56 percent. The average price of a car dropped over 62 percent, ten times as many cars were sold, and the number of workers in the Ford factory jumped from 37,000 to 206,000. All of this took place in just one decade (Vedder 26). Some 140 years earlier, the invention of the Hargreaves spinning jenny helped the British textile industry, too (Deane 90–91).

Machinists, goes so far as to declare that "The union worker is the endangered species in the robot revolution" (qtd. in Cromie 16). At first glance, this gloomy assessment of the impact of robotics on the work force seems only too well-founded since, Skrzycki notes, robots may eliminate 1.3 million jobs by the year 2000 (25).

These fears would shrink or disappear if the people holding them would only stop to realize that robots are merely another form of automation or mechanization. Historical evidence shows that automation leads to more, not less, employment. Consider, for example, Henry Ford's introduction of the assembly line and mass production into the automobile industry. This innovation proved spectacularly successful, boosting the productivity of the work force by 8.5 percent a year and reducing by 56 percent the number of hours needed to build each vehicle. As a result, the average price of a Ford car dropped by more than 62 percent, sales increased tenfold, and the employment of assembly workers in the Ford factory jumped from 37,000 to 206,000 in just one decade (Vedder 26).

Some 140 years earlier, the invention of the Hargreaves spinning jenny brought about much the same happy outcome in Britain's textile industry. This invention made it possible for one spinner to do as much in a day as 200 could have done previously. But instead of creating mass unemployment, the jenny led to a sharp jump in the work force—from approximately 100,000 in 1770 to 350,000 in 1800 (Deane 90-91). As more and more industries become highly robotized, we can expect this

■ Final Draft

Short quotations put in context, enclosed in quotation marks

Expansion to two paragraphs likens benefits of robots to those of assembly line and spinning jenny; writing tightened and honed

■ **Rough Draft**

Robots offer corporate managers a number of advantages over human workers. Robots require less instruction and can outperform people. They can be reassigned and reprogrammed instantly, too (Cromie 13). A survey found that over 30 percent of the average workday is lost because of human frailty (Weisel 18). Sickness, vacations, physical disabilities, injuries, carelessness, and boredom also cut into productivity. Robots surpass human capabilities by working in hot, dirty, noisy, dangerous, and fume-filled areas without any type of safety equipment (Chamberlin 32).

Robots cost a lot but are much more economical than human workers. The Robot Institute of America says that an average human assembly-line worker costs management about $17 an hour. In contrast, a robot costs about $5-6 (Cromie 13). Often the cost of a robot can be recovered in two years, a small fraction of its working life ("Robots Are Coming" 75).

pattern of falling prices and surging sales to repeat
itself.

Robots offer corporate managers a number of
advantages over human workers. To begin, robots require
much less instruction and can outperform even the best
humans by working around the clock with precision and at
high speed. Furthermore, robots, unlike humans, can be
reassigned and reprogrammed for new jobs instantly
(Cromie 13). Adopting robots also allows management to
avoid production losses that stem from human frailty. A
survey cited by Walter Weisel found that 30 percent of the
workday is lost because of scheduling problems,
misunderstood assignments, improper staffing, and poor
discipline (18). Other sources have pointed out the
extent to which sickness, vacations, physical
disabilities, injuries, carelessness, and boredom cut
into productivity. Robots have none of these
shortcomings. In fact, they surpass human capabilities by
working in hot, dirty, noisy, dangerous, fume-filled
areas without any type of safety equipment (Chamberlin
32).

Not surprisingly, robots, despite their high
initial cost, are much more economical than human
workers. According to the Robot Institute of America, an
average human assembly-line worker costs management
about $17 per hour in wages, fringe benefits, and the
expenses associated with absenteeism, work stoppages,
and so on. In contrast, the cost of a robot--including
maintenance charges, indirect labor support costs,
depreciation, and property tax liabilities--works out to
be $5 to $6 per hour (Cromie 13). Often the costs of a

■ **Final Draft**

Independent conclusion;
no reference necessary

Clarifies robots'
advantages, immunity to
specific human frailties;
writing level raised

More sophisticated topic
sentence; compares costs
of humans and robots

■ **Rough Draft**

Robots offer important advantages to workers as well as management. The introduction of robots into a plant makes it necessary for workers to tend them more carefully. The workers must also show more ability to plan, beside exercising good judgment. The result is more interesting and challenging work (Mueller et al. 14–15).

> Most of the skilled workers doing 4–7% of American jobs that could be taken over by robots by 1990 should welcome their incursion. Robots will have to be taught to do their jobs and be supervised while they work. American companies are discovering that few people can teach or supervise a robot better than the man who did the job before. Although fewer people are needed in the trade as a whole . . . the skilled people in factories where robots are welcomed generally get more interesting jobs. . . . Joblessness is created in firms that fail to welcome robots. ("Robots Are Coming" 75)

Besides having more interesting jobs, employees in plants with robots will have to work fewer hours—possibly only a four-day-week—and will earn more money (McElroy 43). A significant number of workers may well use the extra time creatively and usefully. This could lead to an improvement in the quality of American life.

robot can be recovered in two years, a small fraction of its working life ("Robots Are Coming" 75).

Robots offer important advantages to workers as well as to corporate management. The introduction of robots into a plant makes it necessary for workers to tend their charges more carefully as well as to show more ability to plan and to exercise good judgment. The result: more interesting and mentally challenging work (Mueller et al. 14–15). Here's what The Economist of London says about this matter:

Writing has been polished and context provided for quotation

> Most of the skilled workers doing 4–7% of American jobs that could be taken over by robots by 1990 should welcome their incursion. Robots will have to be taught to do their jobs and be supervised while they work. American companies are discovering that few people can teach or supervise a robot better than the man who did the job before. Although fewer people are needed in the trade as a whole . . . the skilled people in factories where robots are welcomed generally get more interesting jobs.
>
> . . . Joblessness is created in firms that fail to welcome robots. ("Robots Are Coming" 75).

Extended quotation, indented ten spaces, without quotation marks, double-spaced

Omission within sentence, ellipsis

Omission at end of sentence, period and ellipsis

Besides having more interesting jobs, employees in plants with robots will have to work fewer hours—— possibly only a four-day week——and will earn more money (McElroy 43). When this happens, a significant number of workers may well use the extra time in creative and socially useful ways——painting, carpentry, restoring antiques, and becoming involved in public issues such as conservation, for example. If enough of them do so, the

Specific, not general, comments on leisure

Workers will face fewer health and safety risks. In many factories, robots are now doing welding, spray painting, and other hazardous tasks. Efforts are also being made to develop robots that will perform other dangerous tasks. The mining industry is developing robots to excavate and haul coal and bolt mine roofs. The electrical industry is developing robots that walk up poles and search out flaws in power plants. The construction industry is developing robots that dig around natural gas lines and install tunnel liners (Armstrong 6). By 1995, the Society of Manufacturing Engineers says, robots should bring about a 41 percent decrease in factory injuries (McElroy 44).

Robots have not created an unemployment problem, nor should they have a significant impact on future employment. Government studies show that by 1990 robots will reduce the overall employment level by less than 1 percent. Many displaced workers will move into robot-related jobs (Hunt and Hunt 82, 139).

result could be a noticeable improvement in the quality
of American life.

Thanks to robots, workers will face fewer on-the-job
health and safety risks. In many factories robots have
already taken over welding, spray painting, and other
heavy or hazardous work, and efforts are now underway to
develop robots that will take over other dangerous tasks.
Several robots are on the drawing board for the mining
industry, including those that excavate, haul coal, and
bolt mine roofs. The nuclear power industry is developing
robots that walk up poles and search out flaws in power
plants. For the construction industry, robots that dig
around natural gas lines and install tunnel liners are in
the offing (Armstrong 6). By 1995, the Society of
Manufacturing Engineers says, robots should bring about a
41 percent decrease in factory injuries (McElroy 44).

Despite predictions to the contrary, robots have not
created an unemployment problem, nor should they have a
significant direct impact on the nation's employment
level in the future. Government studies show that by 1990
robots will reduce the overall employment level by less
than 1 percent. Many displaced workers will move into jobs
building, installing, programming, and serving robots.
Still others will become involved in designing and
engineering them, while some will provide a backup cadre
of clerical workers and managers (Hunt and Hunt 82, 139).

To handle these jobs, workers will have to be more
highly trained than in the past. Over one half of the jobs
created by robot technology will require two or more
years of college, while others will require extensive
on-the-job training. Industry has risen to the

■ **Final Draft**

Independent conclusion;
no reference needed

No new information but
rewriting is more polished

Transitional phrase added
to topic sentence;
examples of jobs that will
open up to displaced
workers

Topic sentence added;
writing refined

Over half of the jobs created by robot technology
will require two or more years of college. Other jobs will
require extensive on-the-job training. Industry has set
up a number of training programs. General Motors and the
United Auto Workers have agreed that "In view of the
corporation's interest in affording maximum opportunity
for employes to progress with advancing technology, the
Corporation shall make available short-range,
specialized training programs for those employees who
have the qualifications to perform the new and changed
work, where such programs are reasonable and
practicable." The company has agreed to provide $80
million annually (Hunt and Hunt 156-57).

A number of colleges are putting in programs to
train robot technicians. In 1983, Hunt and Hunt report,
four Michigan colleges were offering such programs and
eight more were considering them. At one school, 600
students enrolled for the first semester. Over 80C
students enrolled for the second semester (159-160).
Nationwide, over 30 colleges and universities have
robotics programs. Some of these are such famous
institutions as the Massachusetts Institute of
Technology and Pittsburgh's Carnegie-Mellon University.
The salaries obtained by graduates are $30,000 or more
(Rosenblatt, 360).

challenge by initiating training programs to provide the
needed technical and scientific know-how. In this
connection, General Motors and the United Auto Workers
have endorsed a "Statement on Technological Progress,"
which states that

> In view of the corporation's interest in
> affording maximum opportunity for employes
> [sic] to progress with advancing technology,
> the Corporation shall make available short-
> range, specialized training programs for those
> employees who have the qualifications to
> perform the new or changed work, where such
> programs are reasonable and practicable. (qtd.
> in Hunt and Hunt 156-57)

To implement training, GM is providing $80 million
annually. This development reflects industry's awareness
of the problems workers face from robots and a
willingness to help cope with them.

A number of colleges are now instituting programs to
train robot technicians. In 1983, Hunt and Hunt report,
four Michigan junior colleges were offering such
programs, and eight others were considering them. These
programs have proved extremely popular; at one school,
600 students enrolled in the semester that the program
began, and over 900 enrolled the second semester
(159-60). Nationwide, over 30 colleges and universities
have robotics programs, including such prestigious
institutions as the Massachusetts Institute of
Technology and Pittsburgh's Carnegie-Mellon University.
Graduates can expect salaries ranging upward from $30,000

■ Final Draft

Context provided for quotation

Bracketed "sic" marks misspelling

Extended quotation now indented ten spaces without quotation marks

Independent conclusion; no reference needed

Authors' names noted, only page numbers in citation

Improved phasing

■ **Rough Draft**

Government may also play a role in helping workers displaced by robots by helping pay the costs of retraining workers. It could also distribute labor market information, not to mention reshaping vocational education programs with the aim of having them meet the needs of industry (Vedder 20). In time, help may come from other sources too.

Robots are entrenched in industry. They have greatly altered the manufacture of many products. In the future their impact will continue to grow. Robots will also have an effect on the world outside the factory. They will perform many household tasks and may do such jobs as fire fighting and ditch digging. Because of robots, the world will never be the same.

(Rosenblatt 360).

Government can also play a role in retraining the victims of robotization for different jobs. Help could, for example, be provided in the form of vouchers to cover the costs of retraining in private or public schools. In addition, government could distribute labor market information and help reshape vocational educational programs to meet the needs of industry (Vedder 20). As time passes, help may come from other sources. Labor unions, for instance, might establish their own retraining programs. Other organizations--churches, service clubs, charitable groups--might also offer some retraining or help displaced workers find jobs unconnected with robots.

> Improved phrasing explains government's and other sources' aid in retraining

Robots are firmly and irreversibly entrenched in industry. Already they have greatly altered the manufacture of many products, and in the coming years they could transform the world of work as greatly as did the first Industrial Revolution in the 18th century. But even greater potential exists. As technology advances, we can expect robots to move out of the factory and into the wider world. Someday, household robots may vacuum our floors, feed our dog, cook our meals, take out our trash, balance our checkbook, and then, for relaxation, challenge us to checkers or chess. Out-of-the-home mechanical servants may include robot security officers, fire fighters, ditch diggers, trash collectors, and salesclerks, to name just a few possibilities. Whatever the future of robots, we can be sure of one thing: the world will never be the same as before they arrived on the scene.

> Independent conclusion; no reference needed

> Stresses future of robots; reinforces revolutionary aspect

Works Cited

Armstrong, Scott. "Hard-Hat Robots May Take Risk Out of

   Dangerous Jobs." Christian Science Monitor 30 Aug. 1983:

   6.

Bylinsky, Gene. Invasion of the Service Robots." Fortune 14

   Sept. 1987: 81-88.

Chamberlin, Leslie J. "Facing up to Robotation." USA Today Nov.

   1982: 31-33.

Cromie, William J. "Robots: A Growing, Maturing Population."

   Sciquest Mar. 1981: 12-16.

Deane, Phyllis. The First Industrial Revolution. Cambridge,

   Eng.: Cambridge UP, 1979.

Feder, Barnaby J. "He Brought the Robot to Life." New York Times

   21 Mar. 1982: F6.

Hunt, H. Allan, and Timothy L. Hunt. Human Resource

   Implications of Robotics. Kalamazoo, MI: The W.E. Upjohn

   Institute for Employment Research, 1983.

McElroy, John. "Industrial Robot Growth: How Experts See It."

   Automotive Industries Sept. 1982: 43-45.

Mueller, Eva, et al. Technological Advance in an Expanding

   Economy. Ann Arbor: U of Mich P, 1969.

"Robot Productivity." Production Engineering May 1982: 52-55.

"Robots are Coming to Industry's Service." The Economist 29

   Aug. 1981: 71-75.

Rosenblatt, Jean. "The Robot Revolution." Editorial Research

   Reports 14 May 1982: 347-62.

Skrzycki, Cindy. "Will Robot's Bring More Jobs—Or Less?" U.S.

   News & World Report 5 Sept. 1983: 25.

Entry for newspaper article

Entry for periodical article with one author

Entry for book with one author

Entry for book with two authors

Entry for book with multiple authors

Entries for periodical journal articles with no author given

Entry for popular magazine article

Stepanek, Marcia. "Automotive Leader Directs Invasion of a
　　　Cutthroat Industry." <u>Detroit Free Press</u> 28 May 1984: B1,
　　　4.

Vedder, Richard K. <u>Robotics and the Economy</u>. Subcommittee on
　　　Monetary and Fiscal Policy, Joint Economic Committee, U.S.
　　　97th Cong. 26 Mar. 1982.

Weisel, Walter K. "The Robot's Role in Productivity."
　　　<u>Production Engineering</u> Dec. 1981: 18–19.

Entry for government
document.

369

Business Letters and Résumés

Business people aren't the only ones who write business letters. You write quite a few yourself, or soon will, especially to request information, place orders, register complaints, and apply for jobs. There's nothing mysterious or difficult about business correspondence. True, it follows its own special format, but otherwise it breaks no new writing ground. As always, deciding what to say and how to say it is vital to your success.

LETTER LANGUAGE

Effective letter language weaves conciseness, informality, and courtesy into a three-strand finished fabric. Concise writing avoids word clutter and gets directly to the point, saving the reader time and enlivening the message. As you write and revise, guard against two kinds of wordiness: deadwood and gobbledygook. *Deadwood* repeats the same thing or uses excess words to deliver its message. Here are some examples of deadwood and ways of correcting them.

Deadwood	*Correction*
in the view of the fact that. due to the fact that	because
had the effect of causing	caused
would you be kind enough to	would you please
I want to take this opportunity to thank you	thank you
in the event that	if
personally, I believe	I believe
I want to make it clear that	[simply state what you want known]

Gobbledygook uses inflated, elaborately polite expressions that make writing stiff, stuffy, and distant. Note how the corrections soften the standoffish tone.

Gobbledygook	**Correction**
enclosed please find	I am enclosing
pursuant to the purchase of your	after buying your
in accordance with the terms of your warranty	your warranty provides
reference is made herewith	I am referring to
the said lawnmower	this lawnmower

Informal language is everyday language. Friendly and relaxed, it has the air of face-to-face conversation between writer and reader. To achieve it, use simple words and sentence structures; personal pronouns like *I, me, you,* and *your* are appropriate. At the same time, though, don't go overboard and resort to slang or overly casual expressions. Saying "When you guys packed my radio, you must have goofed; when I got it, it was busted" raises questions about your seriousness.

In your business letters, as in direct dealings with others, courtesy plays a key part in helping you gain your ends. Here are some tips to help you avoid antagonizing the reader.

1. Avoid insults and sarcasm.

   Sarcastic Do you think you could possibly send me the correct size this time?

   Courteous Would you please replace the dress with one of the correct size?

2. Avoid curt demands

   Blunt I want you to send me . . . , I need a copy of . . .

   Courteous Would you please send me . . .

3. Avoid negative implications. The first example below suggests that the reader will automatically disagree.

   Negative I take the position that . . .

   Courteous I think you'll find that . . .

As you prepare your letter, try changing places with your reader. How would you react to the message? If you're pleased with what you see, courtesy should be no problem.

If you hadn't been so foolish, you wouldn't have had the problems you describe. The hydrochloric acid you used in the wash had the effect of damaging both your clothes and your washer. In the future, you would be well advised to use only bleach and standard detergents as per instructions. This will protect your machine in the future.

Revised Version

We are sorry to hear about the damage to your new Maelstrom washing machine and your clothes. Unfortunately, our warranty does not cover the damage, as it was caused by the hydrochloric acid you used in your machine. This strong acid is dangerous and should not be used with any Maelstrom product.

In the future, to protect your washing machine and clothes, please follow the instructions in the owner's manual and use only standard detergents and bleaches.

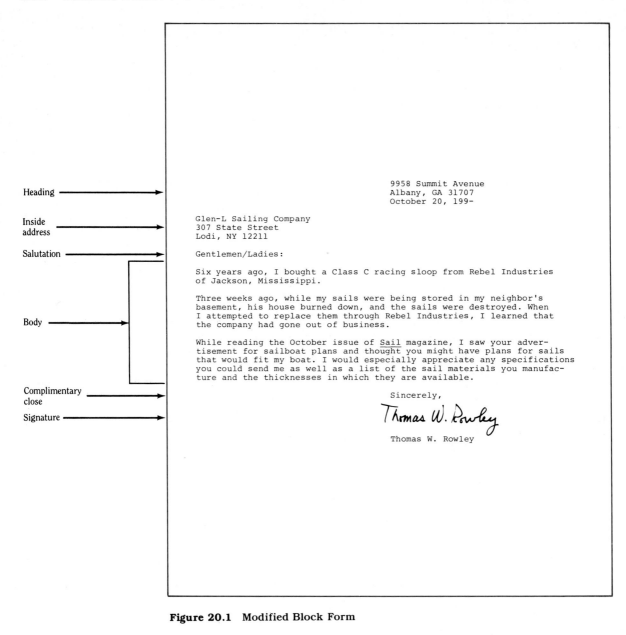

Heading ——————→

Inside address ——————→

Salutation ——————→

Body ——————→

Complimentary close ——————→

Signature ——————→

```
                                        9958 Summit Avenue
                                        Albany, GA 31707
                                        October 20, 199-

Glen-L Sailing Company
307 State Street
Lodi, NY 12211

Gentlemen/Ladies:

Six years ago, I bought a Class C racing sloop from Rebel Industries
of Jackson, Mississippi.

Three weeks ago, while my sails were being stored in my neighbor's
basement, his house burned down, and the sails were destroyed. When
I attempted to replace them through Rebel Industries, I learned that
the company had gone out of business.

While reading the October issue of Sail magazine, I saw your adver-
tisement for sailboat plans and thought you might have plans for sails
that would fit my boat. I would especially appreciate any specifications
you could send me as well as a list of the sail materials you manufac-
ture and the thicknesses in which they are available.

                                        Sincerely,

                                        Thomas W. Rowley

                                        Thomas W. Rowley
```

Figure 20.1 Modified Block Form

PARTS OF THE BUSINESS LETTER

PERSPECTIVE
The letters in this chapter follow
the same format. You might tell
students that other formats are
used and that they will be expected to use whichever one
their company has adopted.

The letter in Figure 20.1, labeled to show the parts of a business letter, is set
up in the modified block format, a very common one for business correspondence.

Heading. Spell out every word except for the two-letter state abbreviation
used by the postal service. Begin the heading at the center of the sheet.

Inside address. *Ms.* is an acceptable personal title for both married and single women. If you don't know the name of the person you want to reach, begin the inside address with the job title or name of the department, for example, *Vice-president for Research* or *Sales Department*. If you don't know the job title or department, start with the company name. Use abbreviations only if they are part of the company name. Begin the inside address two spaces below the heading in long letters and three to eight spaces in shorter letters. The shorter the letter, the more space should be left.

Salutation. Address an individual by title and name. If the inside address begins with a job title or the name of a department, use that title or department name for the salutation, for instance *Vice-president for Research* or *Sales Department*. If the inside address begins with the name of the company, use the salutation *Gentlemen/Ladies*. The letters on pages 372, 375, 377, and 379 show these kinds of salutations. The salutation comes two spaces below the inside address.

Body. Most letters are one page or less. Try to keep your paragraphs short— about seven lines at most. Begin the body two spaces below the salutation. If the letter contains only one brief paragraph, double-space the typing. Otherwise use single spacing with double spacing between paragraphs.

Complimentary close. Acceptable closings are *Sincerely yours, Sincerely,* and *Yours truly.* Type the complimentary close two spaces below the last line of the body and line it up with the center of the sheet.

Signature. Both typewritten and handwritten signatures are necessary. Leave four spaces between the complimentary close and the typed signature. Line the typed signature up with the center of the sheet.

Enclosure notation. The abbreviation *Enc.,* used in several of our sample letters, indicates that a brochure, drawing, check, money order, or other document accompanies the letter. It starts at the left-hand margin. If more than one item accompanies a letter, the notation should indicate how many there are. Important documents are often named:

Enc. 3
Enc. Money Order

Type business letters on 8½ × 11-inch unlined white paper and center them on the page. For full-page letters, make the side margins one inch wide; for shorter letters, make wider margins. In all cases, establish top and bottom margins of roughly equal width.

```
DJ ASSOCIATES
230 PARK AVE S
NEW YORK NY 10003-1502




                        MS SHARON CUSTOMER
                        806 S ARLINGTON MILL DRIVE APT 1A
                        ARLINGTON VA 22204-2921
```

Figure 20.2

PREPARATION FOR MAILING

To ensure that the Post Office's optical scanners can read your envelope, type the address entirely in capital letters and without punctuation. Position the address between one-half and three inches from the bottom of the envelope and at least one inch from the right-hand edge. Figure 20.2 shows a properly typed address. Use the standard state abbreviations in the following list.

Standard State Abbreviations

AL	Alabama	KY	Kentucky	OH	Ohio
AK	Alaska	LA	Louisiana	OK	Oklahoma
AZ	Arizona	ME	Maine	OR	Oregon
AR	Arkansas	MD	Maryland	PA	Pennsylvania
CA	California	MA	Massachusetts	PR	Puerto Rico
CO	Colorado	MI	Michigan	RI	Rhode Island
CT	Connecticut	MN	Minnesota	SC	South Carolina
DE	Delaware	MS	Mississippi	SD	South Dakota
DC	District of Columbia	MO	Missouri	TN	Tennessee
		MT	Montana	TX	Texas
FL	Florida	NE	Nebraska	UT	Utah
GA	Georgia	NV	Nevada	VT	Vermont
HI	Hawaii	NH	New Hampshire	VA	Virginia
ID	Idaho	NJ	New Jersey	WA	Washington
IL	Illinois	NM	New Mexico	WV	West Virginia
IN	Indiana	NY	New York	WI	Wisconsin
IA	Iowa	NC	North Carolina	WY	Wyoming
KS	Kansas	ND	North Dakota		

Proofread your letter carefully, sign it, and then fold it neatly in thirds (Figure 20.3) so that it will fit into a number 10 size business envelope.

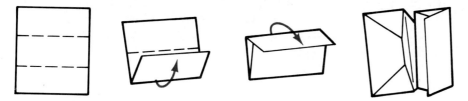

Figure 20.3

```
                              325 Darrin Hall
                              Prentice College
                              Barstow, ME 04611
                              January 3, 199-

Mr. John Antwerp
Antrim Industries, Inc.
6431 Honeysuckle Avenue
Modesto, CA 95355

Dear Mr. Antwerp:

Your article in the December issue of Modern Health, in which
you describe the features of your company's new comprehensive
medical program, greatly interested me.

I am an environmental health student investigating the benefits
that small companies have realized by instituting such programs.
Can you help me by answering the following questions?

     1. To what extent has the number of employees calling in
        sick increased or decreased since your program began?

     2. To what extent has the program affected worker
        productivity and efficiency?

     3. How do the costs of the program compare with those of
        the medical insurance you used to provide through a
        private insurance company?

Thank you for any information you can supply. If you wish, I will
be happy to send you a copy of my finished report.

                         Sincerely,

                         René M. Hewitt

                         René M. Hewitt
```

Figure 20.4 The Pointers Applied: Sample Inquiry Letter

TYPES OF LETTERS

Of the many kinds of business letters, the ones you'll most likely write are inquiries, orders, complaints, and job applications. Here are guidelines and models.

Letters of Inquiry

Your letters of inquiry may be written to request information about a vacation spot, a hobby, or a project that you are working on; or you may write for data to be used in a research paper. (See Figure 20.4.) Here's how to proceed:

1. Identify yourself, indicate the kind of information you're after, and explain why you need it.
2. To avoid inconveniencing your reader, keep your questions to a minimum, make them clear, and word them so they can be answered briefly.
3. If you have three or more questions, set them up in a numbered list, so the reader is less likely to miss answering one.
4. If you're using the information for a research paper and it's appropriate to do so, offer to supply a copy of your paper. Acknowledge the source of information when you write the paper.
5. Close by expressing appreciation for any help the reader can give.

EXERCISE ■ **Write a letter of inquiry that requests one of the following kinds of information.**

1. More details about a project reported in a magazine or newspaper article
2. Performance data for something you might buy
3. Detailed information about the credit policies of a company
4. Information for a research paper
5. Your congressional representative's, mayor's, or other public official's position on an issue you're concerned about
6. Membership information for a club or professional organization

Order Letters

Order letters, used to order sports equipment, hobby supplies, appliances, furniture, clothing, and the like, must be brief and to the point. (See Figure 20.5.) Write the letter as follows:

1. Identify the merchandise by name, model, or catalog number, size, weight, color, finish, or whatever else is needed.
2. To order a single item, write the letter in paragraph form. Otherwise set up a numbered list.

3. Specify how many items of each sort you want, the cost of a single item, and the total cost of the order.
4. Indicate when you wish to pay and how: by check, money order, or credit card. If you are enclosing payment, say so.
5. If you're ordering a gift to be shipped to someone at another address, be sure to include that address in the body of your letter.

Order Department:

Please ship me the professional ski bindings you recently advertised in <u>Outdoor World Magazine</u>. I would be pleased to pay C.O.D. or be billed at your convenience.

This vague letter must be revised to specify how many sets of bindings are wanted, their model number, and the cost.

Revised Version

Order Department:

Please ship me the following merchandise as advertised recently in <u>Outdoor World Magazine</u>.

2 Model A20 professional ski bindings

Unit price: $29.95 Total: $59.90

I would be pleased to pay C.O.D. or be billed at your convenience.

```
                                    420 Bayshore Drive
                                    Durham, NC 27701
                                    October 30, 199-

Order Department
Fitzpatrick Manufacturing Company
123 Getty Street
Philadelphia, PA 19141

Order Department:

Please ship the following merchandise as advertised in the
October 199- issue of Better Homes and Gardens:

     1 Model 979-14/ES Luxury Lady
       Kitchen Center. Unit price:
       $121.77.                              $121.77

     1 Model 5109/WN Whippet five-
       quart Automatic Oriental
       Wok. Unit price: $28.67.                28.67
     TOTAL                                   $150.44

Please send the order at your earliest convenience to the above
address. I have enclosed a check for the total amount.

                    Sincerely yours,

                    Cheryl A. Forrest

                    Cheryl A. Forrest

Enc. Check
```

Figure 20.5   The Pointers Applied: Sample Order Letter

EXERCISE ■ Write one of the following letters.

1. Order one or more pieces of furniture, household appliances, garden implements, or automobile accessories.
2. Order a gift to be shipped to a friend or relative.

Claim Letters

Writing a claim (complaint) letter is unpleasant but sometimes necessary. An improperly filled order, damaged or shoddy merchandise, a misunderstanding about prices—these and many other situations can result in claims. The letter points out the problem and asks that it be corrected.

When writing your letter, don't let anger make you discourteous. Remember, you're trying to settle a problem, not antagonize your reader. These guidelines will help you get a quick, favorable response.

1. If you are writing a large company and don't know the name of the department that handles claims, address your letter to "Customer Adjustments Department" or "Claims Department." For small companies, write to the sales department. Your letter should then quickly reach someone who can help you.
2. Begin the body of the letter by identifying the problem precisely. Tell what happened and when, giving size, colors, model numbers, prices—whatever the reader needs to investigate and make an adjustment.
3. If you've suffered serious inconvenience, mentioning it may speed the settlement.
4. Clearly state the adjustment you want.
5. Back your position with supporting evidence or arguments, positioned at whatever point in the letter seems most appropriate.
6. End courteously by expressing hope for a speedy settlement or offering any further information needed to reach that settlement.

Figure 20.6 shows a typical claim letter.

EXERCISE ■ Write a claim letter calling attention to one of the following.

1. An improperly or incompletely filled order
2. An order that was delivered late
3. Merchandise damaged in transit because of improper packing
4. Improper billing by a credit card company or utility

Job Application Letters

Once you've finished your academic preparation and started looking for a permanent job, you'll have to write one or more job application letters. In the

815 Buckaroo Lane
Dallas, TX 75226
July 10, 199-

Customer Relations Department
Carlson Craft
P.O. Box 87
Mankato, MN 56001

Customer Relations Department:

On June 12, I sent a check for $10.19 and an order for 150
imprinted white luncheon napkins, style 7219. These napkins
were intended for my wedding reception.

The napkins came today, but instead of saying "Kathleen and
Ward" they have the wrong imprint--"Kathleen and Lard." I am
enclosing one of them to show you the mistake.

My wedding is less than five weeks off, and I'd like to settle the
details of the reception well before then. Therefore, I'd appreciate
a replacement order as soon as possible.

My fiancé and I both hope you'll take care of this matter promptly.

Yours truly,

Kathleen M. Van Meer

Kathleen M. Van Meer

Enc.

Figure 20.6 The Pointers Applied: Sample Claim Letter

meantime, you may need to write one to apply for a summer job (see Figures 20.7 and 20.8).

Take great care to do a first-rate job. Companies scan applications carefully and immediately discard those that fail to measure up. Grammatical or punctuation errors, misspellings, strikeovers, obvious erasures, smudge marks, beverage stains—all can earn your letter a quick trip to the reject pile. Be sure to include enough information for the employer to evaluate your qualifications. Here are some guidelines.

then have the groups exchange papers and rank them. The discussion that accompanies the rankings will help illuminate the important features of a good cover letter and résumé.

Sample Biography

John Sims. Age 21. Sims will graduate from Ferris State University this summer with a BA in accounting. He minored in computer science and can program in COBOL, Pascal, and Assembly. His GPA is 2.4. While at Ferris, he has been the treasurer of his fraternity, Sigma Delta Alpha. He worked summers at Friendly Foods in Bangor, Michigan, first as a cashier, but for the last two summers as a bookkeeper. He graduated from Bangor High School four years ago but only with a 2.2 GPA.

Job Opening

Accountant wanted for Morton Foods, Inc. Person will need to be responsible for computerized payroll operations. Experience preferred.

2. Have students revise the following cover letter:

Dear Mr. Carter:

I hope you will hire me for a summer position as a sales representative at Beach Paper Products. I know summer is your best sales season since so many people go on picnics. I have also noticed that far too few stores in my neck of the woods sell your paper plates, napkins, and cups. I will do a slam-bang job for you. As you might guess, I am wonderful with people. As president of our college fraternity, I have been responsible for throwing parties, signing up new members, and making sure everyone gets along well. My college education is appropriate as well since I am getting a degree in marketing. As you probably guessed, I haven't much work experience. I have only had summer jobs as a

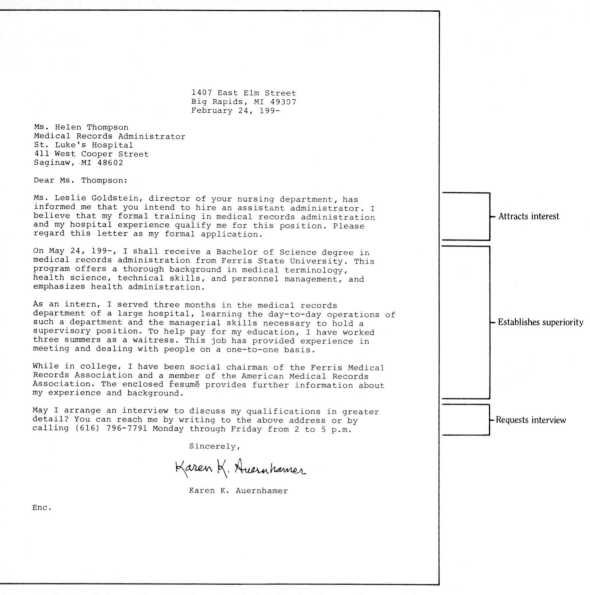

```
                        1407 East Elm Street
                        Big Rapids, MI 49307
                        February 24, 199-

Ms. Helen Thompson
Medical Records Administrator
St. Luke's Hospital
411 West Cooper Street
Saginaw, MI 48602

Dear Ms. Thompson:

Ms. Leslie Goldstein, director of your nursing department, has        ]— Attracts interest
informed me that you intend to hire an assistant administrator. I
believe that my formal training in medical records administration
and my hospital experience qualify me for this position. Please
regard this letter as my formal application.

On May 24, 199-, I shall receive a Bachelor of Science degree in
medical records administration from Ferris State University. This
program offers a thorough background in medical terminology,
health science, technical skills, and personnel management, and
emphasizes health administration.

As an intern, I served three months in the medical records           ]— Establishes superiority
department of a large hospital, learning the day-to-day operations of
such a department and the managerial skills necessary to hold a
supervisory position. To help pay for my education, I have worked
three summers as a waitress. This job has provided experience in
meeting and dealing with people on a one-to-one basis.

While in college, I have been social chairman of the Ferris Medical
Records Association and a member of the American Medical Records
Association. The enclosed résumé provides further information about
my experience and background.

May I arrange an interview to discuss my qualifications in greater    ]— Requests interview
detail? You can reach me by writing to the above address or by
calling (616) 796-7791 Monday through Friday from 2 to 5 p.m.

                        Sincerely,

                        Karen K. Auernhamer

                        Karen K. Auernhamer

Enc.
```

Figure 20.7 The Pointers Applied: Sample Job Application Letter [Permanent Job]

1. If you know an opening exists, begin by naming the position and how you heard of it—through an advertisement or from an instructor, for example. Using a name implies a recommendation by that person. If you're writing to ask whether an opening exists, specify exactly what position you're after. In either case, proceed by naming one or two of your qualifications or mentioning some service you can provide.
2. Establish your superiority over other candidates. Elaborate on the qualities mentioned at the start and present others that suit you for the position. If you have earned some or all of your college expenses or had on-the-job supervisory

```
                                    2439 South Lake Road
                                    Fenton, MI 48438
                                    March 27, 199-

Mr. Roger Updike
General Manager
Martin Buick-Olds, Inc.
Fenton, MI 48439

Dear Mr. Updike:

According to the weekly bulletin of the Drake College Placement Bureau,
you have several summer openings for automotive technicians. I believe
my academic training and practical experience have provided me with
the qualifications needed to fill one of these positions.

I am a second-year student in the automotive service program at Drake
College and expect to receive my Bachelor of Science degree in May 199-.
My overall academic average is 3.08 on a 4.0 scale.

I have worked nine months as a co-op auto mechanic, and I owned a lawn-
care service for one year. The co-op position has given me hands-on ex-
perience working with automobiles, and both positions have taught me
the value of teamwork. I am hardworking, responsible, and quick to learn,
and I will do an effective job for you.

If you desire further information concerning my background and qualifi-
cations, the Drake Placement Bureau can supply you with my college
transcripts. Just call (616) 892-2319, extension 2607, and request
them.

I will be happy to come in for an interview at some mutually convenient
time. My number is (616) 892-9531, or you can reach me at the above
address.

                         Sincerely yours,

                         Philip Thomas Dieck

                         Philip Thomas Dieck
```

Figure 20.8   The Pointers Applied: Sample Job Application Letter (Summer Job)

salesclerk at a local clothing store. But you can give me the break I need. Hire me and you won't regret it. Before long you will want to make me vice-president in charge of sales. I will be happy to hop up and see you at your convenience.

Revised Version

Dear Mr. Carter:

I believe I can help you improve your sales in the Cincinnati area. Your quality line of paper plates, napkins, and cups is not available in most of the area stores, even during the summer months, which are the peak sales period for such products. I would like to help you place your products in these stores by working for you as a sales representative from May to September.

I am experienced in sales, having worked the last four years as a salesclerk for John Atterbury's Clothing Shop. Because of that experience, I not only know sales but am also familiar with many of the area retailers who should be interested in your product. In addition, I will complete my degree in Marketing at Forham University next year. While at Forham, I served two years as the president of Sigma Delta Pi fraternity. As president, I was responsible for organizing charity and social functions, managing the affairs of the fraternity, and recruiting new members. These activities have helped prepare me to be an effective sales representative.

May I arrange an interview to discuss how I might use my sales ability to the benefit of your company? You can reach me by writing to the above address or by calling (616) 796-7791.

experience, note these facts; employers like candidates who are ambitious and possess leadership potential.

3. Don't take a "hard-sell" approach. Assertions such as "I'm just the person you're looking for" or "You'll be making a mistake if you bypass me" will likely backfire. On the other hand, don't sell yourself short with statements such as "Although I have little on-the-job experience, I think I can probably handle your job." Instead, say something like "I'm confident my academic training has prepared me to handle this job successfully." In short, don't cast yourself in a negative light; accentuate the positive without bragging.

4. Keep your letter short by referring the reader to your résumé for further information.
5. End by requesting an interview. Provide a phone number so the employer can contact you quickly. If you can be reached only at certain times, specify them.

RÉSUMÉS

The résumé, sent with the application letter, elaborates on the qualifications mentioned in that letter and presents others that the employer is likely to find useful (see Figure 20.9). Since it, like the letter, helps to sell you as a candidate, spare no effort to ensure that it's attractive, well-organized, and easy to read. Here are some tips.

1. Capitalize the main captions to make them stand out on the page.
2. To condense information, use phrases and clauses rather than complete sentences.
3. List your most recent education and employment experience first and then work backward so the employer can quickly gauge what you've done recently.
4. Don't try to cram too much material onto a page. Ample white space is important.
5. Center the heading at the top of the page.

Typically, information is grouped under the six headings below. If you are a recent graduate with little or no full-time work experience, list education before work experience. If you've worked for a number of years, however, reverse the order.

1. *Heading.* Include your address and phone number. Don't date the résumé; it will then become obsolete more quickly than it otherwise would.
2. *Employment Objective.* State your immediate work goal and the direction you hope your career will take. Avoid any impression that you will soon move on to another organization or try for the boss's job. If you can't specify your objective in a believable manner, leave it out.
3. *Education.* List pertinent facts of your college education. Note any academic honors, such as a good (above 3.0) grade-point average, a scholarship, or a certificate of commendation. If you've taken elective courses in your major or have a minor in a closely related field, so indicate. To demonstrate leadership and a strong commitment to your field of study, name any campus offices you have held or professional organizations to which you belong. Conclude by noting the basic facts of your high school education: date and place of graduation and your program.
4. *Employment Experience.* Highlight your full-time, part-time, volunteer, and summer work experience. If a job was seasonal, note this fact to avoid the impression that you were fired. Mention any promotions or raises you've received and any supervisory experience you've had. Don't mention any job duties unless they are similar to those of the job you're after.

```
                    Karen K. Auernhamer
                    1407 East Elm Street
                    Big Rapids, MI 49307
                    Telephone: (616) 796-7791


        EMPLOYMENT OBJECTIVE

        To work in a technical or an assistant managerial position in a
        medical records department, gain experience, and eventually
        assume an administrative position.


        EDUCATION

        May 1991, Bachelor of Science degree, medical records
        administration, Ferris State University, Big Rapids, MI 49307

        Academic Honors:
          3.85/4.0 G.P.A., medical records courses

        Extracurricular Activities:

          Social Chairman, Ferris Medical Records Association


        June 1987, graduated from Reese High School, Reese, MI 48757,
        college preparatory program.


        EMPLOYMENT EXPERIENCE

        June 1990 to August 1990        Technical trainee (internship
                                        program)
                                        Saginaw Osteopathic Hospital,
                                        Saginaw, MI 48602
                                        Assisted with technical duties in
                                        the medical records department.


        Summers of 1987, 1988, 1989     Waitress, Zehnder's of
                                        Frankenmuth,
                                        215 South Main Street,
                                        Frankenmuth, MI 48734

        PERSONAL AND PROFESSIONAL INTERESTS

        Member, American Medical Records Association. Enjoy tennis,
        reading, biking, skiing, ice skating, and arts and crafts.


        REFERENCES

        Will be furnished upon request.
```

Figure 20.9   The Pointers Applied: Sample Résumé

SUGGESTED INSTRUCTOR READING

Odell, L. and D. Goswami, eds. Writing in Nonacademic Settings. New York: Guilford, 1985. Includes a number of helpful essays on the kinds of nonacademic writing and the concerns and writing processes of nonacademic writers.

Many textbooks on business communication as well as guides for writing résumés and cover letters are available and can provide additional insights and teaching ideas.

5. *Personal and Professional Interests.* Cite membership in civic and noncampus professional organizations. In addition, note any special skills like training in life saving or fluency in a foreign language, as well as special interests.
6. *References.* List references only if you are answering an advertisement that asks for them. Otherwise, indicate that they will be furnished on request. Typical references include instructors, supervisors, and prominent community leaders who know you. Never use names of relatives or name anyone as a reference

without first obtaining permission. For each reference, give the person's name, including a personal title, position, business address, and telephone number. An example follows.

Ms. Brenda Pretzer
Director, Medical Records Department
Saginaw Osteopathic Hospital
515 North Michigan Avenue
Saginaw, MI 48602
Telephone: (517) 776-2682

EXERCISE ■

1. **Write a letter applying for an advertised job or one that someone has told you about.**
2. **Write a letter applying for a position for which there may or may not be a vacancy.**
3. **Prepare a résumé to accompany your letter.**

Reader

Narration

Of the four narrative essays, three have unstated points, and one offers an indirectly stated point. Two essays take a serious approach, one is permeated with light-hearted humor, and the remaining one ends with an ironic twist that adds a wry note of humor to an otherwise serious treatment. Two essays use extensive dialogue, another offers a few brief snatches of it, while the fourth contains only two comments by one person. Conflict is present in every essay and with one exception involves clashes between individuals rather than internal conflict. All essays are in the first person.

PERSPECTIVE

Dialogue is a prime way of developing conflict between and among individuals. Because this narrative focuses entirely on internal rather than external conflict, Thom uses almost no dialogue. You might point out that professional writers use narrative elements purposefully, not haphazardly.

JAMES ALEXANDER THOM

■ *The Perfect Picture*

James Alexander Thom (born 1933) is a native of Gosport, Indiana, where his parents were physicians, and a graduate of Butler University. Before becoming a freelance writer in 1973, he worked as an editor for the Indianapolis Star *and the* Saturday Evening Post. *In addition, he has been a lecturer at Indiana University. He has authored one volume of essays,* Let the Sun Shine *(1976), and three historical novels,* Long Knife *(1979),* Follow the River *(1981), and* From Sea to Shining Sea *(1984). He is a contributor to many popular magazines and an editor for* Nuggets *magazine. "The Perfect Picture," which first appeared in* Reader's Digest, *depicts an incident and an ethical dilemma that Thom experienced as a cub reporter.*

It was early in the spring about 15 years ago—a day of pale sunlight and trees just beginning to bud. I was a young police reporter, driving to a scene I didn't want to see. A man, the police-dispatcher's broadcast said, had accidentally backed his pickup truck over his baby granddaughter in the driveway of the family home. It was a fatality.

As I parked among police cars and TV-news cruisers, I saw a stocky white-haired man in cotton work clothes standing near a pickup. Cameras were trained on him, and reporters were sticking microphones in his face. Looking totally bewildered, he was trying to answer their questions. Mostly he was only moving his lips, blinking and choking up.

After a while the reporters gave up on him and followed the police into the small white house. I can still see in my mind's eye that devastated old man looking down at the place in the driveway where the child had been. Beside the house was a freshly spaded flower bed, and nearby a pile of dark, rich earth.

"I was just backing up there to spread that good dirt," he said to me, though I had not asked him anything. "I didn't even know she was outdoors." He stretched his hand toward the flower bed, then let it flop to his side. He lapsed

1 | Introduction: notes time, locale, and cause of action; first-person point of view

2 | Body: paragraphs 2–12; action begins

3 | Time signal
Key event

4 | Dialogue

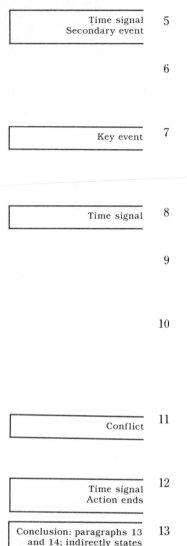

back into his thoughts, and I, like a good reporter, went into the house to find someone who could provide a recent photo of the toddler.

5   A few minutes later, with all the details in my notebook and a three-by-five studio portrait of the cherubic child tucked in my jacket pocket, I went toward the kitchen where the police had said the body was.

6   I had brought a camera in with me—the big, bulky Speed Graphic which used to be the newspaper reporter's trademark. Everybody had drifted back out of the house together—family, police, reporters and photographers. Entering the kitchen, I came upon this scene:

7   On a Formica-topped table, backlighted by a frilly curtained window, lay the tiny body, wrapped in a clean white sheet. Somehow the grandfather had managed to stay away from the crowd. He was sitting on a chair beside the table, in profile to me and unaware of my presence, looking uncomprehendingly at the swaddled corpse.

8   The house was very quiet. A clock ticked. As I watched, the grandfather slowly leaned forward, curved his arms like parentheses around the head and feet of the little form, then pressed his face to the shroud and remained motionless.

9   In that hushed moment I recognized the makings of a prize-winning news photograph. I appraised the light, adjusted the lens setting and distance, locked a bulb in the flashgun, raised the camera and composed the scene in the viewfinder.

10   Every element of the picture was perfect: the grandfather in his plain work clothes, his white hair backlighted by sunshine, the child's form wrapped in the sheet, the atmosphere of the simple home suggested by black iron trivets and World's Fair souvenir plates on the walls flanking the window. Outside, the police could be seen inspecting the fatal rear wheel of the pickup while the child's mother and father leaned in each other's arms.

11   I don't know how many seconds I stood there, unable to snap that shutter. I was keenly aware of the powerful story-telling value that photo would have, and my professional conscience told me to take it. Yet I couldn't make my hand fire that flashbulb and intrude on the poor man's island of grief.

12   At length I lowered the camera and crept away, shaken with doubt about my suitability for the journalistic profession. Of course I never told the city editor or any fellow reporters about that missed opportunity for a perfect news picture.

13   Every day on the newcasts and in the papers, we see pictures of people in extreme conditions of grief and despair. Human suffering has become a spectator sport. And sometimes, as I'm watching news film, I remember that day.

14   I still feel right about what I did.

DISCUSSION QUESTIONS ■

1. Thom notes in his opening paragraph that he is "driving to a scene I didn't want to see." How does this statement help explain what happens later?

2. Paragraph 10 contains numerous descriptive details. What bearing do these details have on Thom's decision?

3. Do you think that Thom made the right decision? Why or why not?

DISCUSSION QUESTIONS

1. Thom's statement shows him to be a sensitive person with empathy for the misfortunes of others. These characteristics lead him to pass up the picture that a more callous photographer would have eagerly snapped.

SUGGESTION FOR WRITING ■ **Write a personal narrative that features a conflict over a choice between an advantageous and a morally satisfying decision. State your point directly or indirectly and use time signals and dialogue as necessary.**

PHILIP ROSS

■ *The Boy and the Bank Officer*

Philip Ross (born 1939) has spent his writing career in New York, his birthplace, and in New Jersey. After earning degrees at Princeton (1961) and Columbia (1962), he worked for four years as a newspaper reporter. In 1965, he became a writer for the American Museum of Natural History, and in 1969 he turned to freelance writing, which he has done ever since. His writings include two book-length works: The Bribe *(1976), a nonfiction work about an unsuccessful attempt at municipal bribery, and* The Kreuzeck Coordinates *(1985), a spy thriller. He has contributed articles to* New York, Reader's Digest, New Times, *and the* New York Times. *Our Ross narrative details an episode with an unexpected and highly embarrassing outcome.*

I have a friend who hates banks with a special passion. "A bank is just a store like a candy store or a grocery store," he says, "except that a bank's merchandise happens to be money which is yours in the first place. If banks were required to sell wallets and money belts, they might act less like churches." 1

I began thinking about my friend the other day as I walked into a small, overlighted branch office on the West Side. I had come to open a checking account. 2

It was lunchtime and the only officer on duty was a fortyish black man with short, pressed hair, a pencil mustache, and a neatly pressed brown suit. Everything about him suggested a carefully groomed authority, an eager determination to define himself through his vaulted surroundings. 3

This officer was standing across a small counter from a young white boy who was wearing a crew-neck sweater, khakis, and loafers. He had sandy hair, and I think I was especially aware of him because he looked like he belonged more on the campus of a New England prep school than in a West Side bank. 4

The boy continued to hold my attention because of what happened next. 5

He was clutching an open savings-account book and wearing an expression of open dismay. "But I don't understand," he was saying to the officer. "I opened the account myself, so why can't I withdraw any money?" 6

"I've already explained to you," the officer told him, "that bank regulations prohibit someone who is fourteen years old from withdrawing any funds without a letter from his parents." 7

2. These details, while providing the makings of a perfect picture, also highlight the horror of what has happened and through their impact on his sensitivity help influence his decision.
3. Each person, of course, will have his or her own answer. You might pose this question to several students and generate a class discussion.

PERSPECTIVE

Unlike Thom's essay, this one, except for the relatively brief introduction which sets the stage, consists almost entirely of dialogue. The two conflicts noted in Discussion Question 4 are developed through this dialogue. Sometimes a narrator uses background information to help set up conflicts. But because the bank officer and the narrator have just met, no such background exists.

TEACHING STRATEGIES

1. Encourage your students to study this essay in order to learn the conventions of writing dialogue properly. Students should note that each shift from one speaker to another requires a new paragraph; when an expression like "he said" interrupts a sentence, it is set off by commas; when the expression comes between two complete quoted sentences, a period is used after the expression, and the first word of the second sentence is capitalized; commas and periods that come at the end of direct quotations are positioned inside the quotation marks.
2. Ask students to assume the role of a narrator who is favorably disposed toward the bank and then, beginning with paragraph 11, rewrite the dialogue between him and the bank officer as it might have unfolded. This exercise shows students how a participant's attitude can influence dialogue.

8   "But that doesn't seem fair," the boy said, his voice breaking. "It's my money. I put it in. It's my account."

9   "I know it is," the officer said, "but those are the rules. Now if you'll excuse me."

10   He turned to me with a smile. "May I help you, sir?"

11   I didn't think twice. "I was going to open a new account," I said, "but after seeing what's going on here, I think I've changed my mind."

12   "Excuse me?" he said.

13   "Look," I said, "if I understand what's going on here correctly, what you're saying is that this boy is old enough to deposit his money in your bank but he's not old enough to withdraw it. And since there doesn't seem to be any question as to whether it's his money or his account, the bank's so-called policy is patently ridiculous."

14   "It may seem ridiculous to you," he replied in a voice rising slightly in irritation, "but that is the bank's policy and I have no alternative but to abide by the rules."

15   The boy had stood hopefully next to me during this exchange, but now I was reduced to his helplessness. Suddenly I noticed that the open savings book he continued to grasp showed a balance of about $100. It also showed that there had been a series of small deposits and withdrawals.

16   I had my opening.

17   "Have you withdrawn money before by yourself?" I asked the boy.

18   "Yes," he said.

19   I moved in for the kill.

20   "How do you explain that away?" I zeroed in on the officer. "Why did you let him withdraw money before but not now?"

21   He looked exasperated. "Because the tellers were not aware of his age before and now they are. It's really very simple."

22   I turned to the boy with a pained shrug. "You're really getting ripped off," I said. "You ought to get your parents to come in here and protest."

23   The boy looked destroyed. Silently, he put his savings book in a rear-pocket and walked out of the bank.

24   The officer turned to me. "You know," he said, "you really shouldn't have interfered."

25   "Shouldn't have interfered?" I shouted. "Well, it damn well seemed to me that he needed someone to represent his interests."

26   "Someone was representing his interests," he said softly.

27   "And who might that be?"

28   "The bank."

29   I couldn't believe what this idiot was saying. "Look," I concluded, "we're just wasting each other's time. But maybe you'd like to explain exactly how the bank was representing that boy's interests?"

30   "Certainly," he said. "We were informed this morning that some neighborhood punk has been shaking this boy down for more than a month. The other guy was forcing him to take money out every week and hand it over. The poor kid was apparently too scared to tell anyone. That's the real reason he was so upset. He

DISCUSSION QUESTIONS

1. The attitude of the friend prejudices Ross against the bank officer and, together with the officer's stuffy appearance, prompts Ross to take the side of the boy. (The developing situation, "bullying" officer and young boy, and the discussion between Ross and the officer also set the reader's mind against banks and add to the surprise of the outcome.)

2. Incomplete sentences occur in paragraph 9 ("Now, if you'll excuse me."), paragraph 21

was afraid of what the other guy would do to him. Anyway, the police are on the case and they'll probably make an arrest today."

Uh.   31

"You mean there is no rule about being too young to withdraw funds from a savings account?"   32

"Not that I ever heard of. Now, sir, what can we do for you?"   33

DISCUSSION QUESTIONS ■

1. In his opening paragraph Ross cites a friend's attitude toward banks, and in the third paragraph he describes the bank officer. What does he accomplish by presenting these two aspects of the story?

2. Examine the dialogue in this essay and then point out examples of incomplete sentences and slang. Why are these included?

3. This story has very few time signals. Why are they unnecessary?

4. This narrative features two conflicts: the first between the boy and the bank officer, the second between the officer and the narrator. In which paragraphs does Ross present each conflict? Why does the second conflict receive more extended treatment?

5. Ross provides a good example of a narrative with an unstated point. What is the point? Refer to the story when answering.

SUGGESTION FOR WRITING ■   Narrate an experience whose outcome was not at all what you expected. Include material that points toward an ending different from the one that in fact occurred.

MAYA ANGELOU

■ *Momma's Encounter*[1]

Maya Angelou has earned a reputation as one of this country's foremost black writers. Born (1928) Marguerite Johnson in St. Louis, Missouri, she spent much of her childhood in Stamps, Arkansas, the locale of our selection, where her grandmother ran a general store. Angelou has written plays, poems, and a five-part autobiography that includes I Know Why the Caged Bird Sings *(1970),* Gather Together in My Name *(1974),* Singin' and Swingin'

[1]Editors' title.

("Because the tellers were not aware of his age before and now they are."), paragraph 28 ("The bank."), and the final paragraph ("Not that I ever heard of."). Slang expressions are found in paragraphs 22 ("ripped off") and 30 ("neighborhood punk," "shaking this boy down," "other guy," "poor kid"). Omitting these features, particularly the slang expressions in paragraph 30, would leave the dialogue sounding stilted and artificial.

3. Time signals are unnecessary because the action unfolds in an uninterrupted sequence which the reader can easily follow.

4. Paragraphs 4–9 deal with the first conflict and paragraphs 10–33 with the second. The latter conflict receives more extended treatment because it involves the narrator, and the point of the essay hinges on it. You might call attention to an offstage conflict: the one between the boy with the account and the one shaking him down.

5. The unstated point of this narrative is "appearances can be deceiving." Everything preceding paragraph 28 stamps the bank officer as a pompous bureaucrat with no concern for the boy's feelings. Then the writer springs his surprise, and we learn the truth about the teller.

PERSPECTIVE

As the answer to Discussion Question 2 indicates, the disrespectful upbringing of the "po-whitetrash" children foreshadows their confrontation with Momma. But race also plays a role in what happens. Because Momma and her family are black, they are regarded as inferior and are thus fair game for humiliation. Momma's reaction in turn is conditioned by the then-prevailing racial climate. Given her firm approach to discipline in her own family, she probably would not have tolerated the taunting words and antics in black children.

TEACHING STRATEGY

1. Initially you might point out that differences in status influence the ways people behave toward one another. Examples are plentiful: teachers who expect to be addressed as "Ms.," "Doctor," or "Professor" call students by their first names; bosses summon employees to their offices for conferences but not vice versa; people in a courtroom are asked to rise when the judge enters. With this point established, ask the class to read paragraphs 7–13 and discuss their function in the essay.

2. When writing narratives some students become so absorbed in relating events that they forget about creating and maintaining reader interest. You might discuss how Angelou keeps the reader involved. When students write their own narratives, have them exchange papers within peer groups, get some feedback on the interest level, and then revise accordingly.

and Gettin' Merry Like Christmas *(1976)*, The Heart of a Woman *(1981), and* All God's Children Have Traveling Shoes *(1986). She has acted in numerous plays and has served as a television narrator, interviewer, and host. In our selection, taken from her first volume of autobiography, Angelou tells about an encounter in which her grandmother, whom she calls Momma, triumphs over a pack of taunting neighborhood children.*

1 "Thou shall not be dirty" and "Thou shall not be impudent" were the two commandments of Grandmother Henderson upon which hung our total salvation.

2 Each night in the bitterest winter we were forced to wash faces, arms, necks, legs and feet before going to bed. She used to add, with a smirk that unprofane people can't control when venturing into profanity, "and wash as far as possible, then wash possible."

3 We would go to the well and wash in the ice-cold, clear water, grease our legs with the equally cold stiff Vaseline, then tiptoe into the house. We wiped the dust from our toes and settled down for schoolwork, cornbread, clabbered milk, prayers and bed, always in that order. Momma was famous for pulling the quilts off after we had fallen asleep to examine our feet. If they weren't clean enough for her, she took the switch (she kept one behind the bedroom door for emergencies) and woke up the offender with a few aptly placed burning reminders.

4 The area around the well at night was dark and slick, and boys told about how snakes love water, so that anyone who had to draw water at night and then stand there alone and wash knew that moccasins and rattlers, puff adders and boa constrictors were winding their way to the well and would arrive just as the person washing got soap in her eyes. But Momma convinced us that not only was cleanliness next to Godliness, dirtiness was the inventor of misery.

5 The impudent child was detested by God and a shame to its parents and could bring destruction to its house and line. All adults had to be addressed as Mister, Missus, Miss, Auntie, Cousin, Unk, Uncle, Buhbah, Sister, Brother and a thousand other appellations indicating familial relationship and the lowliness of the addressor.

6 Everyone I knew respected these customary laws, except for the powhitetrash children.

7 Some families of powhitetrash lived on Momma's farm land behind the school. Sometimes a gaggle of them came to the Store, filling the whole room, chasing out the air and even changing the well-known scents. The children crawled over the shelves and into the potato and onion bins, twanging all the time in their sharp voices like cigarbox guitars. They took liberties in my Store that I would never dare. Since Momma told us that the less you say to whitefolks (or even powhitetrash) the better, Bailey and I would stand, solemn, quiet, in the displaced air. But if one of the playful apparitions got close to us, I pinched it. Partly out of angry frustration and partly because I didn't believe in its flesh reality.

8 They called my uncle by his first name and ordered him around the Store. He, to my crying shame, obeyed them in his limping dip-straight-dip fashion.

My grandmother, too followed their orders, except that she didn't seem to   9
be servile because she anticipated their needs.

"Here's sugar, Miz Potter, and here's baking powder. You didn't buy soda last   10
month, you'll probably be needing some."

Momma always directed her statements to the adults, but sometimes, Oh   11
painful sometimes, the grimy, snotty-nosed girls would answer her.

"Naw, Annie. . ."—to Momma? Who owned the land they lived on? Who   12
forgot more than they would ever learn? If there was any justice in the world, God
should strike them dumb at once!—"Just give us some extry sody crackers, and
some more mackerel."

At least they never looked in her face, or I never caught them doing so.   13
Nobody with a smidgen of training, not even the worst roustabout, would look
right in a grown person's face. It meant the person was trying to take the words
out before they were formed. The dirty little children didn't do that, but they
threw their orders around the Store like lashes from a cat-o'-nine tails.

When I was around ten years old, those scruffy children caused me the   14
most painful and confusing experience I had ever had with my grandmother.

One summer morning, after I had swept the dirt yard of leaves, spearmint-   15
gum wrappers and Vienna-sausage labels, I raked the yellow-red dirt, and made
half-moons carefully, so that the design stood out clearly and mask-like. I put the
rake behind the Store and came through the back of the house to find Grandmother on the front porch in her big, wide white apron. The apron was so stiff by
virtue of the starch that it could have stood alone. Momma was admiring the
yard, so I joined her. It truly looked like a flat redhead that had been raked with a
big-toothed comb. Momma didn't say anything but I knew she liked it. She
looked over toward the school principal's house and to the right at Mr. McElroy's.
She was hoping one of those community pillars would see the design before the
day's business wiped it out. Then she looked upward to the school. My head had
swung with hers, so at just about the same time we saw a troop of the powhitetrash kids marching over the hill and down by the side of the school.

I looked to Momma for direction. She did an excellent job of sagging from   16
her waist down, but from the waist up she seemed to be pulling for the top of the
oak tree across the road. Then she began to moan a hymn. Maybe not to moan,
but the tune was so slow and the meter so strange that she could have been
moaning. She didn't look at me again. When the children reached halfway down
the hill, halfway to the Store, she said without turning, "Sister, go on inside."

I wanted to beg her, "Momma, don't wait for them. Come on inside with   17
me. If they come in the Store, you go to the bedroom and let me wait on them.
They only frighten me if you're around. Alone I know how to handle them." But of
course I couldn't say anything, so I went in and stood behind the screen door.

Before the girls got to the porch I heard their laughter crackling and   18
popping like pine logs in a cooking stove. I suppose my lifelong paranoia was
born in those cold, molasses-slow minutes. They came finally to stand on the
ground in front of Momma. At first they pretended seriousness. Then one of them
wrapped her right arm in the crook of her left, pushed out her mouth and started
to hum. I realized that she was aping my grandmother. Another said, "Naw,

Helen, you ain't standing like her. This here's it." Then she lifted her chest, folded her arms and mocked that strange carriage that was Annie Henderson. Another laughed, "Naw, you can't do it. Your mouth ain't pooched out enough. It's like this."

19   I thought about the rifle behind the door, but I knew I'd never be able to hold it straight, and the .410, our sawed-off shotgun, which stayed loaded and was fired every New Year's night, was locked in the trunk and Uncle Willie had the key on his chain. Through the fly-specked screen-door, I could see that the arms of Momma's apron jiggled from the vibrations of her humming. But her knees seemed to have locked as if they would never bend again.

20   She sang on. No louder than before, but no softer either. No slower or faster.

21   The dirt of the girls' cotton dresses continued on their legs, feet, arms and faces to make them all of a piece. Their greasy uncolored hair hung down, uncombed, with a grim finality. I knelt to see them better, to remember them for all time. The tears that had slipped down my dress left unsurprising dark spots, and made the front yard blurry and even more unreal. The world had taken a deep breath and was having doubts about continuing to revolve.

22   The girls had tired of mocking Momma and turned to other means of agitation. One crossed her eyes, stuck her thumbs in both sides of her mouth and said, "Look here, Annie." Grandmother hummed on and the apron strings trembled. I wanted to throw a handful of black pepper in their faces, to throw lye on them, to scream that they were dirty, scummy peckerwoods, but I knew I was as clearly imprisoned behind the scene as the actors outside were confined to their roles.

23   One of the smaller girls did a kind of puppet dance while her fellow clowns laughed at her. But the tall one, who was almost a woman, said something very quietly, which I couldn't hear. They all moved backward from the porch, still watching Momma. For an awful second I thought they were going to throw a rock at Momma, who seemed (except for the apron strings) to have turned into stone herself. But the big girl turned her back, bent down and put her hands flat on the ground—she didn't pick up anything. She simply shifted her weight and did a hand stand.

24   Her dirty bare feet and long legs went straight for the sky. Her dress fell down around her shoulders, and she had on no drawers. The slick pubic hair made a brown triangle where her legs came together. She hung in the vacuum of that lifeless morning for only a few seconds, then wavered and tumbled. The other girls clapped her on the back and slapped their hands.

25   Momma changed her song to "Bread of Heaven, bread of Heaven, feed me till I want no more."

26   I found that I was praying too. How long could Momma hold out? What new indignity would they think of to subject her to? Would I be able to stay out of it? What would Momma really like me to do?

27   Then they were moving out of the yard, on their way to town. They bobbed their heads and shook their slack behinds and turned, one at a time:

28   " 'Bye, Annie."

29   " 'Bye, Annie."

DISCUSSION QUESTIONS

1. This narrative has an unstated main point which might be rendered somewhat as follows: high standards of behavior are an important part of life, and one should not abandon them even under severe provocation. By maintaining her dignity when confronted with the rudeness of the "powhitetrash" children, Momma triumphs over them. The whole episode has a classic Christian outcome, as Momma's triumph comes through acting humbly and turning the other cheek.

2. Angelou's strict upbringing stresses cleanliness and respect for elders. Each night, even during the winter, she and the other children must wash in the ice-cold water of the well, and all adults have to be addressed by some title. In contrast, the "powhitetrash" children are so dirty that they change "the well-

" 'Bye, Annie." 30

Momma never turned her head or unfolded her arms, but she stopped 31
singing and said, " 'Bye, Miz Helen, 'bye, Miz Ruth, 'bye, Miz Eloise."

I burst. A firecracker July-the-Fourth burst. How could Momma call them 32
Miz? The mean nasty things. Why couldn't she have come inside the sweet, cool
store when we saw them breasting the hill? What did she prove? And then if they
were dirty, mean and impudent, why did Momma have to call them Miz?

She stood another whole song through and then opened the screen door to 33
look down on me crying in rage. She looked until I looked up. Her face was a
brown moon that shone on me. She was beautiful. Something had happened out
there, which I couldn't completely understand, but I could see that she was
happy. Then she bent down and touched me as mothers of the church "lay hands
on the sick and afflicted" and I quieted.

"Go wash your face, Sister." And she went behind the candy counter and 34
hummed, "Glory, glory, hallelujah, when I lay my burden down."

I threw the well water on my face and used the weekday handkerchief to 35
blow my nose. Whatever the contest had been out front, I knew Momma had won.

I took the rake back to the front yard. The smudged footprints were easy to 36
erase. I worked for a long time on my new design and laid the rake behind the
wash pot. When I came back in the Store, I took Momma's hand and we both
walked outside to look at the pattern.

It was a large heart with lots of hearts growing smaller inside, and piercing 37
from the outside rim to the smallest heart was an arrow. Momma said, "Sister,
that's right pretty." Then she turned back to the Store and resumed, "Glory, glory,
hallelujah, when I lay my burden down."

DISCUSSION QUESTIONS ■

1. Does this narrative have a stated or an unstated point? If it is stated, indicate where. If
   it is unstated, express it in your own words.

2. Point out the contrast between Angelou's upbringing and that of the "powhitetrash"
   children. How does this contrast prepare the reader for the events that follow?

3. Explain what Angelou means in paragraph 22 when she says ". . .but I knew I was as
   clearly imprisoned behind the scene as the actors outside were confined to their roles."

4. Discuss the significance of the dialogue in paragraphs 28–31.

5. Suggest the significance of the pattern of hearts that Angelou draws in the front yard.
   Of Momma singing "Glory, glory, hallelujah, when I lay my burden down."

6. Angelou recalls that she was "around ten years old" when the encounter took place.
   Explain why her age was significant. How would her perception have differed had she
   been, say, eighteen?

7. Angelou uses the first-person point of view. Explain why third-person narration would
   have been inappropriate for this narrative.

known scents" of the store
whenever they enter it. In the
store they show disrespect by
messing up the merchandise and
treating the proprietors disre-
spectfully, behavior that foreshadows their later abuse of
Momma.

3. Angelou is a prisoner of her
sociological and familial backgrounds. The first of these dictates deference to whites, and
the second prohibits her from
responding in kind to the taunts
of her grandmother's torment-
ers. Like Angelou, the "powhitetrash" children are prisoners of their upbringing. Reared
in a society that regards blacks
as inferior, and lacking any sense
of respect for adults, they behave
in a manner that fully accords
with their upbringing.

4. This dialogue marks the climax of the confrontation between Momma and her torment-
ers and points up her triumph
over them. Having survived their
insolent behavior with her dignity intact, she replies courteously
to their final taunting "bye's"
and in so doing signals their final defeat.

5. The pattern of concentric
hearts pierced by an arrow suggests the love that the 10-year-
old Angelou bears for her family
and perhaps the wish for love to
bind everyone together. Momma's "Glory, glory, hallelujah
. . ." reflects both her recognition of the difficulty of maintaining her standards of behavior
and her determination to do so
as long as she lives.

6. At 10, Angelou, as paragraph 35 indicates, realizes that
her grandmother has won the
contest with the girls but does
not understand why. At 18, the
reason would have been clear,
and Angelou would have recognized why the grandmother re-
acted as she did.

7. Third-person narration
would have been inappropriate
for two reasons. First, Angelou is
telling about a personal experience. Second, third-person narration could not have captured
so vividly the thoughts and feelings she experienced during the
confrontation.

SUGGESTION FOR WRITING ■ **Write a narrative that illustrates how a friend, an acquaintance, or a family member achieved a personal triumph through turning the other cheek.**

JAMES THURBER

■ *University Days*

James Thurber (1894–1961) is widely regarded as one of this country's finest twentieth-century humorists. A native of Ohio, Thurber attended Ohio State University and then worked as a reporter and columnist for several papers in this country and abroad. In 1927, he became associated with The New Yorker *and in the succeeding years produced a steady flow of stories, reminiscences, and cartoons for that magazine. Collections of his works include* The Owl in the Attic *(1931),* My Life and Hard Times *(1933),* Let Your Mind Alone! *(1937),* Fables for Our Times *(1940),* My World—And Welcome to It *(1942),* The Thurber Carnival *(1945), and* Thurber Country *(1952). The following selection, which originally appeared in* The New Yorker, *offers a humorous look at Thurber's difficulties in college.*

1 I passed all the other courses that I took at my university, but I could never pass botany. This was because all botany students had to spend several hours a week in a laboratory looking through a microscope at plant cells, and I could never see through a microscope. I never once saw a cell through a microscope. This used to enrage my instructor. He would wander around the laboratory pleased with the progress all the students were making in drawing the involved and, so I am told, interesting structure of flower cells, until he came to me. I would just be standing there. "I can't see anything," I would say. He would begin patiently enough, explaining how anybody can see through a microscope, but he would always end up in a fury, claiming that I could *too* see through the microscope but just pretended that I couldn't. "It takes away from the beauty of flowers anyway," I used to tell him. "We are not concerned with beauty in this course," he would say. "We are concerned solely with what I may call the *mechanics* of flars. " "Well," I'd say, "I can't see anything." "Try it just once again," he'd say, and I would put my eye to the microscope and see nothing at all, except now and again a nebulous milky substance—a phenomenon of maladjustment. You were supposed to see a vivid, restless clockwork of sharply defined plant cells. "I see what looks like a lot of milk," I would tell him. This, he claimed, was the result of my not having adjusted the microscope properly, so he would readjust it for me, or rather, for himself. And I would look again and see milk.

2 I finally took a deferred pass, as they called it, and waited a year and tried again. (You had to pass one of the biological sciences or you couldn't graduate.) The professor had come back from vacation brown as a berry, bright-eyed, and

eager to explain cell-structure again to his classes. "Well," he said to me, cheerily, when we met in the first laboratory hour of the semester, "we're going to see cells this time, aren't we?" "Yes, sir," I said. Students to right of me and to left of me and in front of me were seeing cells; what's more, they were quietly drawing pictures of them in their notebooks. Of course, I didn't see anything.

"We'll try it," the professor said to me, grimly, "with every adjustment of the microscope known to man. As God is my witness, I'll arrange this glass so that you see cells through it or I'll give up teaching. In twenty-two years of botany, I—" He cut off abruptly for he was beginning to quiver all over, like Lionel Barrymore,[1] and he genuinely wished to hold onto his temper; his scenes with me had taken a great deal out of him.

3

So we tried it with every adjustment of the microscope known to man. With only one of them did I see anything but blackness or the familiar lacteal opacity, and that time I saw, to my pleasure and amazement, a variegated constellation of flecks, specks, and dots. These I hastily drew. The instructor, noting my activity, came back from an adjoining desk, a smile on his lips and his eyebrows high in hope. He looked at my cell drawing. "What's that?" he demanded, with a hint of a squeal in his voice. "That's what I saw," I said. "You didn't, you didn't, you *didn't!*" he screamed, losing control of his temper instantly, and he bent over and squinted into the microscope. His head snapped up. "That's your eye!" he shouted. "You've fixed the lens so that it reflects! You've drawn your eye!"

4

Another course that I didn't like, but somehow managed to pass, was economics. I went to that class straight from the botany class, which didn't help me any in understanding either subject. I used to get them mixed up. But not as mixed up as another student in my economics class who came there direct from a physics laboratory. He was a tackle on the football team, named Bolenciecwcz. At that time Ohio State University had one of the best football teams in the country, and Bolenciecwcz was one of its outstanding stars. In order to be eligible to play it was necessary for him to keep up in his studies, a very difficult matter, for while he was not dumber than an ox he was not any smarter. Most of his professors were lenient and helped him along. None gave him more hints in answering questions or asked him simpler ones than the economics professor, a thin, timid man named Bassum. One day when we were on the subject of transportation and distribution, it came Bolenciecwcz's turn to answer a question. "Name one means of transportation," the professor said to him. No light came into the big tackle's eyes. "Just any means of transportation," said the professor. Bolenciecwcz sat staring at him. "That is," pursued the professor, "any medium, agency, or method of going from one place to another." Bolenciecwcz had the look of a man who is being led into a trap. "You may choose among steam, horse-drawn, or electrically propelled vehicles," said the instructor. "I might suggest the one which we commonly take in making long journeys across land." There was a profound silence in which everybody stirred uneasily, including Bolenciecwcz and Mr. Bassum. Mr. Bassum abruptly broke this silence in an amazing manner. "Choo-choo-choo," he said, in a low voice, and turned instantly scarlet. He

5

[1]A noted dramatic actor of the time.

glanced appealingly around the room. All of us, of course, shared Mr. Bassum's desire that Bolenciecwcz should stay abreast of the class in economics, for the Illinois game, one of the hardest and most important of the season, was only a week off. "Toot, toot, too-toooooot!" some student with a deep voice moaned, and we all looked encouragingly at Bolenciecwcz. Somebody else gave a fine imitation of a locomotive letting off steam. Mr. Bassum himself rounded off the little show. "Ding, dong, ding, dong," he said, hopefully. Bolenciecwcz was staring at the floor now, trying to think, his great brow furrowed, his huge hands rubbing together, his face red.

6   "How did you come to college this year, Mr. Bolenciecwcz?" asked the professor. "*Chuffa,* chuffa, *chuffa* chuffa."

7   "M'father sent me," said the football player.

8   "What on?" asked Bassum.

9   "I git an 'lowance," said the tackle, in a low, husky voice, obviously embarrassed.

10   "No, no," said Bassum. "Name a means of transportation. What did you *ride* here on?"

11   "Train," said Bolenciecwcz.

12   "Quite right," said the professor. "Now, Mr. Nugent, will you tell us—"

13   If I went through anguish in botany and economics—for different reasons—gymnasium work was even worse. I don't even like to think about it. They wouldn't let you play games or join the exercises with your glasses on and I couldn't see with mine off. I bumped into professors, horizontal bars, agricultural students, and swinging iron rings. Not being able to see, I could take it but I couldn't dish it out. Also, in order to pass gymnasium (and you had to pass it to graduate) you had to learn to swim if you didn't know how. I didn't like the swimming pool, I didn't like swimming, and I didn't like the swimming instructor, and after all these years I still don't. I never swam but I passed my gym work anyway, by having another student give my gymnasium number (978) and swim across the pool in my place. He was a quiet, amiable blond youth, number 473, and he would have seen through a microscope for me if we could have got away with it, but we couldn't get away with it. Another thing I didn't like about gymnasium work was that they made you strip the day you registered. It is impossible for me to be happy when I am stripped and being asked a lot of questions. Still, I did better than a lanky agricultural student who was cross-examined just before I was. They asked each student what college he was in—that is, whether Arts, Engineering, Commerce, or Agriculture. "What college are you in?" the instructor snapped at the youth in front of me. "Ohio State University," he said promptly.

14   It wasn't that agricultural student but it was another a whole lot like him who decided to take up journalism, possibly on the ground that when farming went to hell he could fall back on newspaper work. He didn't realize, of course, that that would be very much like falling back full-length on a kit of carpenter's tools. Haskins didn't seem cut out for journalism, being too embarrassed to talk to anybody and unable to use a typewriter, but the editor of the college paper assigned him to the cow barns, the sheep house, the horse pavilion, and the animal husbandry department generally. This was a genuinely big "beat," for it

took up five times as much ground and got ten times as great a legislative appropriation as the College of Liberal Arts. The agricultural student knew animals, but nevertheless his stories were dull and colorlessly written. He took all afternoon on each of them, on account of having to hunt for each letter on the typewriter. Once in a while he had to ask somebody to help him hunt. "C" and "L," in particular, were hard letters for him to find. His editor finally got pretty much annoyed at the farmer-journalist because his pieces were so uninteresting. "See here, Haskins," he snapped at him one day, "why is it we never have anything hot from you on the horse pavilion? Here we have two hundred head of horses on this campus—more than any other university in the Western Conference except Purdue—and yet you never get any real lowdown on them. Now shoot over to the horse barns and dig up something lively." Haskins shambled out and came back in about an hour; he said he had something. "Well, start it off snappily," said the editor. "Something people will read." Haskins set to work and in a couple of hours brought a sheet of typewritten paper to the desk; it was a two-hundred-word story about some disease that had broken out among the horses. Its opening sentence was simple but arresting. It read: "Who has noticed the sores on the tops of the horses in the animal husbandry building?"

Ohio State was a land grant university and therefore two years of military drill was compulsory. We drilled with old Springfield rifles and studied the tactics of the Civil War even though the World War was going on at the time. At 11 o'clock each morning thousands of freshman and sophomores used to deploy over the campus, moodily creeping up on the old chemistry building. It was good training for the kind of warfare that was waged at Shiloh but it had no connection with what was going on in Europe. Some people used to think there was German money behind it, but they didn't say so or they would have been thrown in jail as German spies. It was a period of muddy thought and marked, I believe, the decline of higher education in the Middle West.

As a soldier I was never any good at all. Most of the cadets were glumly indifferent soldiers, but I was no good at all. Once General Littlefield, who was commandant of the cadet corps, popped up in front of me during regimental drill and snapped, "You are the main trouble with this university!" I think he meant that my type was the main trouble with the university but he may have meant me individually. I was mediocre at drill, certainly—that is, until my senior year. By that time I had drilled longer than anybody else in the Western Conference, having failed at military at the end of each preceding year so that I had to do it all over again. I was the only senior still in uniform. The uniform which, when new, had made me look like an interurban railway conductor, now that it had become faded and too tight made me look like Bert Williams in his bellboy act.[2] This had a definitely bad effect on my morale. Even so, I had become by sheer practice little short of wonderful at squad maneuvers.

One day General Littlefield picked our company out of the whole regiment and tried to get it mixed up by putting it through one movement after another as fast as we could execute them: squads right, squads left, squads on right into line, squads right about, squads left front into line, etc. In about three minutes one

15

16

17

DISCUSSION QUESTIONS (p. 400)

1. Thurber may actually have experienced these incidents, but without much doubt he's gone beyond the bare facts. Most likely, no botany professor would "end up in a fury" (paragraph 1), begin "to quiver all over" (paragraph 3), or scream, "losing control of his temper instantly" (paragraph 4) if poor vision inhibited a student's work. Similarly, no economics professor, in front of a class, would say "Choo-choo-choo," "Ding, dong,

[2]A comedian who in one notable skit wore an overly tight bellboy's uniform.

ding, dong" (paragraph 5) or "Chuffa chuffa, chuffa chuffa" (paragraph 6). Finally, no general, when a cadet entered, would continue to swat flies abstractedly or forget the purpose of a summons (paragraph 18).

2. Thurber uses his well-known humor to poke fun at some of the people and the courses that he recalls from his university days. He doesn't intend this essay as an exacting account; rather, he tries to amuse by exaggerating.

3. The discussion of the botany course (paragraphs 1–4) is linked to that of the economics course (paragraphs 5–12) by "Another course that I didn't like" (paragraph 5). Economics is linked to gym in paragraph 13 by the first sentence in paragraph 13, and the "lanky agricultural student" in gym leads to a similar agricultural student in journalism (paragraph 14). And Haskins' order to start his story snappily leads to the "compulsory" (paragraph 15) nature of military drill (paragraphs 15–18). Students should note that there is a clear link between key events.

4. The main conflict pits the individual against the system, and the system is manifested primarily through college policies and customs: passing biological science and learning to swim in order to graduate, taking compulsory military drill, and stripping in order to register for gym. Thurber is also pitted against his insensitive botany instructor and General Littlefield.

5. Thurber's essay is not weakened by not having a separate concluding paragraph. In fact, any attempt to make a summary comment would probably have proven ineffective. The various recollections speak for themselves, and Thurber simply stops when he finishes the final one.

18

hundred and nine men were marching in one direction and I was marching away from them at an angle of forty degrees all alone. "Company, halt!" shouted General Littlefield. "That man is the only man who has it right!" I was made a corporal for my achievement.

The next day General Littlefield summoned me to his office. He was swatting flies when I went in. I was silent and he was silent too, for a long time. I don't think he remembered me or why he had sent for me, but he didn't want to admit it. He swatted some more flies, keeping his eyes on them narrowly before he let go with the swatter. "Button up your coat!" he snapped. Looking back on it now I can see that he meant me although he was looking at a fly, but I just stood there. Another fly came to rest on a paper in front of the general and began rubbing its hind legs together. The general lifted the swatter cautiously. I moved restlessly and the fly flew away. "You startled him!" barked General Littlefield, looking at me severely. I said I was sorry. "That won't help the situation!" snapped the General, with cold military logic. I didn't see what I could do except offer to chase some more flies toward his desk, but I didn't say anything. He stared out the window at the faraway figures of co-eds crossing the campus toward the library. Finally, he told me I could go. So I went. He either didn't know which cadet I was or else he forgot what he wanted to see me about. It may have been that he wished to apologize for having called me the main trouble with the university; or maybe he had decided to compliment me on my brilliant drilling of the day before and then at the last minute decided not to. I don't know. I don't think about it much any more.

DISCUSSION QUESTIONS ■

1. Do you get the feeling that Thurber is "telling it like it was" or that he is overstating the facts? Discuss, referring to relevant parts of the essay.

2. With your answer to the previous question in mind, how would you characterize Thurber's purpose?

3. How does he link the key events that he recalls from his university days? Cite appropriate examples when answering.

4. What conflicts do you see in this essay?

5. Thurber's piece has no conclusion that draws his various recollections together. Explain why this does or does not weaken his essay.

SUGGESTION FOR WRITING ■   Write an essay relating your failures or your successes as you worked on some job. Aim for a light, humorous tone.

Description

OVERVIEW OF DESCRIPTIVE ESSAYS

Two of the descriptive essays rely almost entirely on sight impressions, one details sound impressions, and one blends all five. Three are written from a fixed vantage point, the other from a moving vantage point. Two essays span intervals of only a few minutes, one covers a single day, and one covers about a week. Three culminate in a turning point or climax that brings with it either emotional release or some insight. All feature a strong dominant impression.

JOHN V. YOUNG

■ *When the Full Moon Shines Its Magic over Monument Valley*

John V. Young (born 1909) is a native of Oakland, California. After attending San Jose State Teachers College, he spent twelve years as a reporter and editor for several rural California newspapers, then held a series of personnel and public relations positions. In 1966, he became a full-time freelance writer, specializing in western travel pieces. His books include The Grand Canyon *(1969),* Ghost Towns of the Santa Cruz Mountains *(1979, 1984),* Hot Type and Pony Wire *(1980),* State Parks of New Mexico *(1984), and* State Parks of Arizona *(1986). His articles have appeared in the* New York Times *as well as numerous travel publications. In the article that follows, he focuses on the sensations generated first by his surroundings and then by the moonrise.*

1   We were camped here in early spring, by one of those open-faced shelters that the Navajos have provided for tourists in this part of their vast tribal park on the Arizona–Utah border, 25 miles north of Kayenta. It was cool but pleasant, and we were alone, three men in a truck.

> Introduction: paragraphs 1 and 2; identifies when, where, who, why
> Touch impression

2   We were here for a purpose; to see the full moon rise over this most mysterious and lonely of scenic wonders, where fantastically eroded red and yellow sandstone shapes soar to the sky like a giant's chess pieces and where people—especially white strangers—come quickly to feel like pretty small change indeed.

> Sight impression
> Comparisons

3   Because all Navajo dwellings face east, our camp faced east—toward the rising sun and the rising moon and across a limitless expanse of tawny desert, that ancient sea, framed by the towering nearby twin pinnacles called The Mittens. We began to feel the magic even before the sun was fully down. It occurred when a diminutive wraith of a Navajo girl wearing a long, dark, velvet dress gleaming with silver ornaments drifted silently by, herding a flock of ghostly sheep to a waterhole somewhere. A bell on one of the rams tinkled faintly, and then its music was lost in the soft rustle of the night wind, leaving us with an impression that perhaps we had really seen nothing at all.

> Body: paragraphs 3–8
> Fixed vantage point
> Sight impressions
>
> Time signal
>
> Sight impressions
>
> Sound impressions

401

Time signal
Sight impression
Comparison

4   Just then, a large woolly dog appeared out of the gloom, seeming to materialize on the spot. It sat quietly on the edge of the glow from our campfire, its eyes shining like mirrors. It made no sound but when we offered food, it accepted the gift gravely and with much dignity. The dog then vanished again, probably to join the girl and her flock. We were not certain it was not part of the illusion.

Time signal
Sight impressions
Comparison
Sight impressions

5   As the sun disappeared entirely, the evening afterglow brush tipped all the spires and cliffs with magenta, deepening to purple, and the sand ripples stood out like miniature ocean waves in darkening shades of orange. Off to the east on the edge of the desert, a pale saffron glow told us the moon was about to rise behind a thin layer of clouds, slashed by the white contrail of an invisible jet airplane miles away.

6   We had our cameras on tripods and were fussing with light meters, making casual bets as to the exact place where the moon would first appear, when it happened—instant enchantment. Precisely between the twin spires of The Mittens, the enormous globe loomed suddenly, seeming as big as the sun itself, behind a coppery curtain on the rim of creation.

Sight impressions
Comparison
Original language

Sight impressions

7   We were as totally unprepared for the great size of the moon as we were for its flaming color, nor could we have prepared ourselves for the improbable setting. We felt like the wizards of Stonehenge, commanding the planets to send their light through the magic orifices in line at the equinox. Had the Navajo medicine men contrived this for our benefit?

Comparison

Sight impressions

8   The massive disk of the moon seemed to rise very fast at first, an optical effect magnified by the crystalline air and the flatness of the landscape between us and the distant, ragged skyline. Then it seemed to pause for a moment, as if it were pinioned on one of the pinnacles or impaled on a sharply upthrusting rocky point. Its blazing light made inky shadows all around us, split by the brilliant wedge of the moon's path between the spires. The wind had stopped. There was not a sound anywhere, nor even a whisper. If a drum had sounded just then, it would not have been out of place, I suppose, but it would have frightened us half to death.

Original language

Absent sound
Impression

Conclusion: time signal;
renames dominant
impression

9   Before the moon had cleared the tops of The Mittens, the show was over and the magic was gone. A thin veil of clouds spread over the sky, ending the spell as suddenly as it had come upon us. It was as if the gods had decided that we had seen enough for mere mortals on one spring night, and I must confess it was something of a relief to find ourselves back on mundane earth again, with sand in our shoes and a chill in the air.

Notes writer's reaction

Touch impression

DISCUSSION QUESTIONS ■

1. How does the last sentence in paragraph 7 ("Had the Navajo medicine men contrived this for our benefit?") relate to the purpose of the essay?
2. This description takes the form of a narrative. Where does the climax occur and how does it affect the viewers?

SUGGESTION FOR WRITING ■ **Select a place you know well and describe it by conveying some dominant impression that emerges during daylight hours. Settle on an appropriate vantage point and either identify the impression or allow readers to determine it for themselves.**

---

when the moon suddenly looms between the twin spires of the mountain called "The Mittens." The men are awe-struck, and they liken their reactions to those of the ancient wizards at Stonehenge, in England, "commanding the planets to send their light through the magic orifices in line at the equinox."

ANNIE DILLARD

■ *A Total Eclipse*[1]

Annie Dillard was born in Pittsburgh (1945) and received her education at Hollins College in Virginia. Between 1965 and 1975, she lived in the Roanoke Valley of Virginia, where she investigated the world of nature and wrote about it. In 1975, she became Distinguished Visiting Professor at Western Washington State University and later became Writer-in-Residence at Wesleyan University. Dillard's first prose book, Pilgrim at Tinker Creek *(1974), was compared favorably with Thoreau's* Walden *and won her the 1974 Pulitzer Prize. Later books include* Teaching a Stone to Talk *(1982), from which "A Total Eclipse" is taken, and* An American Childhood *(1987). She has contributed to a variety of magazines, including* American Scholar, Atlantic Monthly, Chicago Review, Harper's, *and* Poetry. *In "A Total Eclipse" Dillard shares her perceptions about one of nature's most spectacular phenomena.*

TEACHING STRATEGIES

1. Dillard uses an extensive amount of figurative language to create her effect. Have students list separately the figurative language that is evocative and also the more direct descriptions of the eclipse. Have them suggest what is and isn't effective and why.
2. Using Dillard's account as a basis, have students describe the eclipse more objectively. Then discuss what is gained and lost.

It began with no ado. It was odd that such a well-advertised public event should have no starting gun, no overture, no introductory speaker. I should have known right then that I was out of my depth. Without pause or preamble, silent as orbits, a piece of the sun went away. We looked at it through welders' goggles. A piece of the sun was missing; in its place we saw empty sky.   1

I had seen a partial eclipse in 1970. A partial eclipse is very interesting. It bears almost no relation to a total eclipse. Seeing a partial eclipse bears the same relation to seeing a total eclipse as kissing a man does to marrying him, or as flying in an airplane does to falling out of an airplane. Although the one experience precedes the other, it in no way prepares you for it. During a partial eclipse the sky does not darken—not even when 94 percent of the sun is hidden. Nor does the sun, seen colorless through protective devices, seem terribly strange. We have all seen a sliver of light in the sky; we have all seen the crescent moon by day. However, during a partial eclipse the air does indeed get cold, precisely as if someone were standing between you and the fire. And blackbirds do fly back to their roosts. I had seen a partial eclipse before, and here was another.   2

---

[1]Editors' title.

Pages 89–93 from "A Total Eclipse" in *Teaching a Stone to Talk: Expeditions and Encounters* by Annie Dillard. Copyright © 1982 by Annie Dillard. Reprinted by permission of Harper & Row, Publishers, Inc.

3   What you see in an eclipse is entirely different from what you know. It is especially different for those of us whose grasp of astronomy is so frail that, given a flashlight, a grapefruit, two oranges, and fifteen years, we still could not figure out which way to set the clocks for Daylight Saving Time. Usually it is a bit of a trick to keep your knowledge from blinding you. But during an eclipse it is easy. What you see is much more convincing than any wild-eyed theory you may know.

4   You may read that the moon has something to do with eclipses. I have never seen the moon yet. You do not see the moon. So near the sun, it is as completely invisible as the stars are by day. What you see before your eyes is the sun going through phases. It gets narrower and narrower, as the waning moon does, and, like the ordinary moon, it travels alone in the simple sky. The sky is of course background. It does not appear to eat the sun; it is far behind the sun. The sun simply shaves away; gradually, you see less sun and more sky.

5   The sky's blue was deepening, but there was no darkness. The sun was a wide crescent, like a segment of tangerine. The wind freshened and blew steadily over the hill. The eastern hill across the highway grew dusky and sharp. The towns and orchards in the valley to the south were dissolving into the blue light. Only the thin river held a trickle of sun.

6   Now the sky to the west deepened to indigo, a color never seen. A dark sky usually loses color. This was a saturated, deep indigo, up in the air. Stuck up into that unworldly sky was the cone of Mount Adams, and the alpenglow was upon it. The alpenglow is that red light of sunset which holds out on snowy mountaintops long after the valleys and tablelands are dimmed. "Look at Mount Adams," I said, and that was the last sane moment I remember.

7   I turned back to the sun. It was going. The sun was going, and the world was wrong. The grasses were wrong; they were platinum. Their every detail of stem, head, and blade shone lightless and artificially distinct as an art photographer's platinum print. This color has never been seen on earth. The hues were metallic; their finish was matte. The hillside was a nineteeth-century tinted photograph from which the tints had faded. All the people you see in the photograph, distinct and detailed as their faces look, are now dead. The sky was navy blue. My hands were silver. All the distant hills' grasses were finespun metal which the wind laid down. I was watching a faded color print of a movie filmed in the Middle Ages; I was standing in it, by some mistake. I was standing in a movie of hillside grasses filmed in the Middle Ages. I missed my own century, the people I knew, and the real light of day.

8   I looked at Gary [her husband]. He was in the film. Everything was lost. He was a platinum print, a dead artist's version of life. I saw on his skull the darkness of night mixed with the colors of day. My mind was going out; my eyes were receding the way galaxies recede to the rim of space. Gary was light-years away, gesturing inside a circle of darkness, down the wrong end of a telescope. He smiled as if he saw me; the stringy crinkles around his eyes moved. The sight of him, familiar and wrong, was something I was remembering from centuries hence, from the other side of death: yes, *that* is the way he used to look, when we were living. When it was our generation's turn to be alive. I could not hear him; the wind was too loud. Behind him the sun was going. We had all started down a chute of time. At first it was pleasant; now there was no stopping it. Gary was

chuting away across space, moving and talking and catching my eye, chuting down the long corridor of separation. The skin on his face moved like thin bronze plating that would peel.

The grass at our feet was wild barley. It was the wild einkorn wheat which   9
grew on the hilly flanks of the Zagros Mountains, above the Euphrates valley, above the valley of the river we called *River*. We harvested the grass with stone sickles, I remember. We found the grasses on the hillsides; we built our shelter beside them and cut them down. That is how he used to look then, that one, moving and living and catching my eye, with the sky so dark behind him, and the wind blowing. God save our life.

From all the hills came screams. A piece of sky beside the crescent sun was   10
detaching. It was a loosened circle of evening sky, suddenly lighted from the back. It was an abrupt black body out of nowhere; it was a flat disk; it was almost over the sun. That is when there were screams. At once this disk of sky slid over the sun like a lid. The sky snapped over the sun like a lens cover. The hatch in the brain slammed. Abruptly it was dark night, on the land and in the sky. In the night sky was a tiny ring of light. The hole where the sun belongs is very small. A thin ring of light marked its place. There was no sound. The eyes dried, the arteries drained, the lungs hushed. There was no world. We were the world's dead people rotating and orbiting around and around, embedded in the planet's crust, while the earth rolled down. Our minds were light-years distant, forgetful of almost everything. Only an extraordinary act of will could recall to us our former, living selves and our contexts in matter and time. We had, it seems, loved the planet and loved our lives, but could no longer remember the way of them. We got the light wrong. In the sky was something that should not be there. In the black sky was a ring of light. It was a thin ring, an old, thin silver wedding band, an old, worn ring. It was an old wedding band in the sky, or a morsel of bone. There were stars. It was all over.

DISCUSSION QUESTIONS ■

1. Comment on the significance of the opening line: "It began with no ado."

2. In paragraph 2 Dillard observes that "seeing a partial eclipse bears the same relation to seeing a total eclipse as kissing a man does to marrying him, or as flying in an airplane does to falling out of an airplane." Point out why her comparisons are effective.

3. State in your own words what Dillard means when she says in paragraph 3 that "usually it is a bit of a trick to keep your knowledge from blinding you. But during an eclipse it is easy."

4. Explain how the plea "God save our life" at the end of paragraph 9 relates to the dominant impression that emerges from the essay. Cite specific details that help create this impression.

5. The essays of Dillard and John V. Young (pages 401–402) both deal with effects triggered by heavenly bodies. How do the two effects compare?

SUGGESTION FOR WRITING ■   **Select some event that had a profound impact on your life—perhaps the launch of a space shuttle or the devastation caused by a storm. Describe the event so that the reader clearly grasps the impression you experienced.**

JAMES TUITE

■ *The Sounds of the City*

James Tuite is a former sports editor at the New York Times *and a frequent contributor to sports magazines. His writings include not only articles but also three books:* Snowmobiles and Snowmobiling *(1973),* The Arthur Daly Years *(1975), and* How to Enjoy Sports on TV *(1976). In this essay Tuite turns from sports, focusing instead on the sounds that loom so large in New York's urban landscape.*

1   New York is a city of sounds: muted sounds and shrill sounds; shattering sounds and soothing sounds; urgent sounds and aimless sounds. The cliff dwellers of Manhattan—who would be racked by the silence of the lonely woods—do not hear these sounds because they are constant and eternally urban.

2   The visitor to the city can hear them, though, just as some animals can hear a high-pitched whistle inaudible to humans. To the casual caller to Manhattan, lying restive and sleepless in a hotel twenty or thirty floors above the street, they tell a story as fascinating as life itself. And back of the sounds broods the silence.

3   Night in midtown is the noise of tinseled honky-tonk and violence. Thin strains of music, usually the firm beat of rock 'n' roll or the frenzied outbursts of the discotheque, rise from ground level. This is the cacophony, the discordance of youth, and it comes on strongest when nights are hot and young blood restless.

4   Somewhere in the canyons below there is a shrill laughter or raucous shouting. A bottle shatters against concrete. The whine of a police siren slices through the night, moving ever closer, until an eerie Doppler effect [1] brings it to a guttural halt.

5   There are few sounds so exciting in Manhattan as those of fire apparatus dashing through the night. At the outset there is the tentative hint of the first-due company bullying his way through midtown traffic. Now a fire whistle from the opposite direction affirms that trouble is, indeed, afoot. In seconds, other sirens converging from other streets help the skytop listener focus on the scene of excitement.

---

[1] The apparent change in the frequency of sound or light waves as the source moves toward or away from an observer.

But he can only hear and not see, and imagination takes flight. Are the   6
flames and smoke gushing from windows not far away? Are victims trapped there,
crying out for help? Is it a conflagration, or only a trash-basket fire? Or, perhaps,
it is merely a false alarm.

The questions go unanswered and the urgency of the moment dissolves.   7
Now the mind and the ear detect the snarling, arrogant bickering of automobile
horns. People in a hurry. Taxicabs blaring, insisting on their checkered priority.

Even the taxi horns dwindle down to a precocious few in the gray and pink   8
moments of dawn. Suddenly there is another sound, a morning sound that taunts
the memory for recognition. The growl of a predatory monster? No, just garbage
trucks that have begun a day of scavenging.

Trash cans rattle outside restaurants. Metallic jaws on sanitation trucks   9
gulp and masticate the residue of daily living, then digest it with a satisfied groan
of gears. The sounds of the new day are businesslike. The growl of buses, so
scattered and distant at night, becomes a demanding part of the traffic bedlam.
An occasional jet or helicopter injects an exclamation point from an unexpected
quarter. When the wind is right, the vibrant bellow of an ocean liner can be
heard.

The sounds of the day are as jarring as the glare of a sun that outlines the   10
canyons of midtown in drab relief. A pneumatic drill frays countless nerves with
its rat-a-tat-tat, for dig they must to perpetuate the city's dizzy motion. After each
screech of brakes there is a moment of suspension, of waiting for the thud or
crash that never seems to follow.

The whistles of traffic policemen and hotel doormen chirp from all sides,   11
like birds calling for their mates across a frenzied aviary. And all of these sounds
are adult sounds, for childish laughter has no place in these canyons.

Night falls again, the cycle is complete, but there is no surcease from   12
sound. For the beautiful dreamers, perhaps, the "sounds of the rude world heard
in the day, lulled by the moonlight have all passed away," but this is not so in the
city.

Too many New Yorkers accept the sounds about them as bland parts of   13
everyday existence. They seldom stop to listen to the sounds, to think about
them, to be appalled or enchanted by them. In the big city, sounds are life.

DISCUSSION QUESTIONS ■

1. Why do you think Tuite repeats "sounds" seven times in his opening sentence?
2. Explain what the author means by the "cliff dwellers" he mentions in paragraph 1.
3. Tuite demonstrates considerable skill in using precise, exact words that capture the impressions he wishes to create. Cite some specific examples from different paragraphs.
4. Tuite says that "childish laughter has no place in these canyons" (paragraph 11). Explain why.

DISCUSSION QUESTIONS

1. Besides characterizing the qualities of the sounds encountered in Manhattan, the repetition creates a tattoo effect, driving home his point that Manhattan is a place of noises.
2. Tuite's image refers to the people who live in the high-rise apartments and who work in the skyscrapers.
3. A variety of answers are possible, of course, but some of the better examples include "racked" (paragraph 1), "broods" (paragraph 2), "frenzied" (paragraph 3), "slices" and "guttural" (paragraph 4), "bullying" (paragraph 5), "gushing" (paragraph 6), "snarling, arrogant bickering" (paragraph 7), "growl" (paragraph 8), "masticate," "groan of gears," "growl," and "exclamation point" (paragraph 9), and "chirp" (paragraph 11). You might want to discuss Tuite's use of animal imagery with your class.
4. The sounds that Tuite describes are, with few exceptions, associated with frenzied, violent, or dangerous activities or with the noisier sorts of workaday occupations. Midtown Manhattan is simply no place for childhood activities that would trigger the laughter of enjoyment.

5. Answers will vary, but the impression of "frenzy" is as good as any. Note that Tuite uses "frenzied" in paragraphs 3 and 11.

6. Tuite moves from night to day back to night again. The nighttime is introduced in the second sentence of paragraph 2, and the discussion of it continues through paragraph 7. Paragraph 8 takes up dawn, and paragraphs 9–11 discuss daytime noises. Paragraph 12 brings the reader back to night, where "the cycle is complete."

7. We've had good success teaching Tuite's essay in connection with "Once More to the Lake." White deals with a rural scene, Tuite an urban one; White includes most of the five senses, and Tuite concentrates primarily on sounds; White develops the peacefulness and tranquillity of his vacation retreat while Tuite suggests the frenzy of midtown Manhattan. Yet despite these differences both writers use precise, exact words to convey their thoughts.

5. Characterize the dominant impression of midtown Manhattan that emerges from this essay.

6. How does Tuite organize his description? Refer to the essay when answering.

7. What similarities and differences do you find when you compare Tuite's essay with "Once More to the Lake" (pages 408–413)?

SUGGESTION FOR WRITING ■ **Write an essay describing some aspect of an area you know well. Possibilities include a favorite shopping place, vacation home, or physical fitness area. Develop your dominant impression of the scene.**

E. B. WHITE

■ *Once More to the Lake*

E. B. White (1899–1985) was born in Mount Vernon, New York, and was a graduate of Cornell University. In 1927, he accepted a position with The New Yorker, *which had begun publication about two years before, and in the next several decades he produced a steady flow of short pieces for that magazine. Between 1937 and 1943, he also wrote a column, "One Man's Meat," for* Harper's. *He is the author of three children's books,* Stuart Little *(1945),* Charlotte's Web *(1952), and* The Trumpet of the Swan *(1970), and numerous works for adults, including* The Second Tree from the Corner *(1954),* The Essays of E. B. White *(1977), and* The Poems and Sketches of E. B. White *(1981). In "Once More to the Lake," White creates a vivid and memorable word picture of a summer vacation spot that had great meaning for him and that brought him a sobering insight.*

PERSPECTIVE

Narration figures more prominently in this essay than in any of the others in this section. White presents a series of events that cover about a week's time and culminate in a turning point together with its chilling insight. On the other hand, the essay lacks any dialogue or characterization of White's son.

1   One summer, along about 1904, my father rented a camp on a lake in Maine and took us all there for the month of August. We all got ringworm from some kittens and had to rub Pond's Extract on our arms and legs night and morning, and my father rolled over in a canoe with all his clothes on; but outside of that the vacation was a success and from then on none of us ever thought there was any place in the world like that lake in Maine. We returned summer after summer—always on August 1st for one month. I have since become a salt-water man, but sometimes in summer there are days when the restlessness of the tides and the fearful cold of the sea water and the incessant wind which blows across the afternoon and into the evening make me wish for the placidity of a lake in the woods. A few weeks ago this feeling got so strong I bought myself a couple of bass

"Once More to the Lake" from *Essays of E. B. White.* Copyright 1941; copyright renewed © 1969 by E. B. White. Reprinted by permission of Harper & Row, Publishers, Inc.

hooks and a spinner and returned to the lake where we used to go, for a week's fishing and to revisit old haunts.

I took along my son, who had never had any fresh water up his nose and who had seen lily pads only from train windows. On the journey over to the lake I began to wonder what it would be like. I wondered how time would have marred this unique, this holy spot—the coves and streams, the hills that the sun set behind, the camps and the paths behind the camps. I was sure the tarred road would have found it out and I wondered in what other ways it would be desolated. It is strange how much you can remember about places like that once you allow your mind to return into the grooves which lead back. You remember one thing, and that suddenly reminds you of another thing. I guess I remembered clearest of all the early mornings, when the lake was cool and motionless, remembered how the bedroom smelled of the lumber it was made of and the wet woods whose scent entered through the screen. The partitions in the camp were thin and did not extend clear to the top of the rooms, and as I was always the first up I would dress softly so as not to wake the others, and sneak out into the sweet outdoors and start out in the canoe, keeping close along the shore in the long shadows of the pines. I remembered being very careful never to rub my paddle against the gunwale for fear of disturbing the stillness of the cathedral.

The lake had never been what you would call a wild lake. There were cottages sprinkled around the shores, and it was in farming country although the shores of the lake were quite heavily wooded. Some of the cottages were owned by nearby farmers, and you would live at the shore and eat your meals at the farmhouse. That's what our family did. But although it wasn't wild, it was a fairly large and undisturbed lake and there were places in it which, to a child at least, seemed infinitely remote and primeval.

I was right about the tar: it led to within half a mile of the shore. But when I got back there, with my boy, and we settled into a camp near a farmhouse and into the kind of summertime I had known, I could tell that it was going to be pretty much the same as it had been before—I knew it, lying in bed the first morning, smelling the bedroom, and hearing the boy sneak quietly out and go off along the shore in a boat. I began to sustain the illusion that he was I, and therefore by simple transposition, that I was my father. This sensation persisted, kept cropping up all the time we were there. It was not an entirely new feeling, but in this setting it grew much stronger. I seemed to be living a dual existence. I would be in the middle of some simple act, I would be picking up a bait box or laying down a table fork, or I would be saying something, and suddenly it would be not I but my father who was saying the words or making the gesture. It gave me a creepy sensation.

We went fishing the first morning. I felt the same damp moss covering the worms in the bait can, and saw the dragonfly alight on the tip of my rod as it hovered a few inches from the surface of the water. It was the arrival of this fly that convinced me beyond any doubt that everything was as it always had been, that the years were a mirage and there had been no years. The small waves were the same, chucking the rowboat under the chin as we fished at anchor, and the boat was the same boat, the same color green and the ribs broken in the same places, and under the floor-boards the same fresh-water leavings and debris—the

2

3

4

5

TEACHING STRATEGIES

1. If you have students of different ages, say 10–15 years apart, ask them to discuss to what extent and why they can empathize with White's feelings and the philosophical point of the essay. Divergent views are likely.
2. Ask students why they think White ended the essay as he did rather than with actually leaving the lake at the conclusion of the trip.
3. Ask students to list the most memorable sensory details of their favorite vacation spot. The list might serve as the starting point for a descriptive essay.

CLASSROOM ACTIVITIES

1. Have students, working in small groups, exchange experiences that brought them an insight. Again, such a discussion might lead to a writing assignment.
2. White is a master at using emotionally evocative description. Have students, working in small groups, identify the descriptive passages that have emotional associations. The entire class could then discuss why. A writing assignment stressing emotionally evocative description could follow.

dead hellgramite,[1] the wisps of moss, the rusty discarded fishhook, the dried blood from yesterday's catch. We stared silently at the tips of our rods, at the dragonflies that came and went. I lowered the tip of mine into the water, tentatively, pensively dislodging the fly, which darted two feet away, poised, darted two feet back, and came to rest again a little farther up the rod. There had been no years between the ducking of this dragonfly and the other one—the one that was part of memory. I looked at the boy, who was silently watching his fly, and it was my hands that held his rod, my eyes watching. I felt dizzy and didn't know which rod I was at the end of.

6   We caught two bass, hauling them in briskly as though they were mackerel, putting them over the side of the boat in a businesslike manner without any landing net, and stunning them with a blow on the back of the head. When we got back for a swim before lunch, the lake was exactly where we had left it, the same number of inches from the dock, and there was only the merest suggestion of a breeze. This seemed an utterly enchanted sea, this lake you could leave to its own devices for a few hours and come back to, and find that it had not stirred, this constant and trustworthy body of water. In the shallows, the dark, water-soaked sticks and twigs, smooth and old, were undulating in clusters on the bottom against the clean ribbed sand, and the track of the mussel was plain. A school of minnows swam by, each minnow with its small individual shadow, doubling the attendance, so clear and sharp in the sunlight. Some of the other campers were in swimming, along the shore, one of them with a cake of soap, and the water felt thin and clear and unsubstantial. Over the years there had been this person with the cake of soap, this cultist, and here he was. There had been no years.

7   Up to the farmhouse to dinner through the teeming, dusty field, the road under our sneakers was only a two-track road. The middle track was missing, the one with the marks of the hooves and the splotches of dried, flaky manure. There had always been three tracks to choose from in choosing which track to walk in; now the choice was narrowed down to two. For a moment I missed terribly the middle alternative. But the way led past the tennis court, and something about the way it lay there in the sun reassured me; the tape had loosened along the backline, the alleys were green with plantains and other weeds, and the net (installed in June and removed in September) sagged in the dry noon, and the whole place steamed with midday heat and hunger and emptiness. There was a choice of pie for dessert, and one was blueberry and one was apple, and the waitresses were the same country girls, there having been no passage of time, only the illusion of it as in a dropped curtain—the waitresses were still fifteen; their hair had been washed, that was the only difference—they had been to the movies and seen the pretty girls with the clean hair.

8   Summertime, oh summertime, pattern of life indelible, the fade-proof lake, the woods unshatterable, the pasture with the sweetfern and the juniper forever and ever, summer without end; this was the background, and the life along the shore was the design, the cottages with their innocent and tranquil design, their tiny docks with the flagpole and the American flag floating against the white clouds in the blue sky, the little paths over the roots of the trees leading

[1] Insect used as bait.

from camp to camp and the paths leading back to the outhouses and the can of lime for sprinkling, and at the souvenir counters at the store the miniature birch-bark canoes and the post cards that showed things looking a little better than they looked. This was the American family at play, escaping the city heat, wondering whether the newcomers in the camp at the head of the cove were "common" or "nice," wondering whether it was true that the people who drove up for Sunday dinner at the farmhouse were turned away because there wasn't enough chicken.

It seemed to me, as I kept remembering all this, that those times and those summers had been infinitely precious and worth saving. There had been jollity and peace and goodness. The arriving (at the beginning of August) had been so big a business in itself, at the railway station the farm wagon drawn up, the first smell of the pine-laden air, the first glimpse of the smiling farmer, and the great importance of the trunks and your father's enormous authority in such matters, and the feel of the wagon under you for the long ten-mile haul, and at the top of the last long hill catching the first view of the lake after eleven months of not seeing this cherished body of water. The shouts and cries of the other campers when they saw you, and the trunks to be unpacked, to give up their rich burden. (Arriving was less exciting nowadays, when you sneaked up in your car and parked it under a tree near the camp and took out the bags and in five minutes it was all over, no fuss, no loud wonderful fuss about trunks.)

9

Peace and goodness and jollity. The only thing that was wrong now, really, was the sound of the place, an unfamiliar nervous sound of the outboard motors. This was the note that jarred, the one thing that would sometimes break the illusion and set the years moving. In those other summertimes all motors were inboard; and when they were at a little distance, the noise they made was a sedative, an ingredient of summer sleep. They were one-cylinder and two-cylinder engines, and some were make-and-break and some were jump-spark, but they all made a sleepy sound across the lake. The one-lungers throbbed and fluttered, and the twin-cylinder ones purred and purred, and that was a quiet sound too. But now the campers all had outboards. In the daytime, in the hot mornings, these motors made a petulant, irritable sound; at night, in the still evening when the afterglow lit the water, they whined about one's ears like mosquitoes. My boy loved our rented outboard, and his great desire was to achieve singlehanded mastery over it, and authority, and he soon learned the trick of choking it a little (but not too much), and the adjustment of the needle valve. Watching him I would remember the things you could do with the old one-cylinder engine with the heavy flywheel, how you could have it eating out of your hand if you got really close to it spiritually. Motor boats in those days didn't have clutches, and you would make a landing by shutting off the motor at the proper time and coasting in with a dead rudder. But there was a way of reversing them, if you learned the trick, by cutting the switch and putting it on again exactly on the final dying revolution of the flywheel, so that it would kick back against compression and begin reversing. Approaching a dock in a strong following breeze, it was difficult to slow up sufficiently by the ordinary coasting method, and if a boy felt he had complete mastery over his motor, he was tempted to keep it running beyond its time and then reverse it a few feet from the dock. It took a cool nerve,

10

because if you threw the switch a twentieth of a second too soon you would catch the flywheel when it still had speed enough to go up past center, and the boat would leap ahead, charging bull-fashion at the dock.

11   We had a good week at the camp. The bass were biting well and the sun shone endlessly, day after day. We would be tired at night and lie down in the accumulated heat of the little bedrooms after the long hot day and the breeze would stir almost imperceptibly outside and the smell of the swamp drift in through the rusty screens. Sleep would come easily and in the morning the red squirrel would be on the roof, tapping out his gay routine. I kept remembering everything, lying in bed in the mornings—the small steamboat that had a long rounded stern like the lip of a Ubangi, and how quietly she ran on the moonlight sails, when the older boys played their mandolins and the girls sang and we ate doughnuts dipped in sugar, and how sweet the music was on the water in the shining night, and what it had felt like to think about girls then. After breakfast we would go up to the store and the things were in the same place—the minnows in a bottle, the plugs and spinners disarranged and pawed over by the youngsters from the boys' camp, the fig newtons and the Beeman's gum. Outside, the road was tarred and cars stood in front of the store. Inside, all was just as it had always been, except there was more Coca-Cola and not so much Moxie and root beer and birch beer and sarsaparilla. We would walk out with a bottle of pop apiece and sometimes the pop would backfire up our noses and hurt. We explored the streams, quietly, where the turtles slid off the sunny logs and dug their way into the soft bottom; and we lay on the town wharf and fed worms to the tame bass. Everywhere we went I had trouble making out which was I, the one walking at my side, the one walking in my pants.

12   One afternoon while we were there at the lake a thunderstorm came up. It was like the revival of an old melodrama that I had seen long ago with childish awe. The second-act climax of the drama of the electrical disturbance over a lake in America had not changed in any important respect. This was the big scene, still the big scene. The whole thing was so familiar, the first feeling of oppression and heat and a general air around camp of not wanting to go very far away. In mid-afternoon (it was all the same) a curious darkening of the sky, and a lull in everything that had made life tick; and then the way the boats suddenly swung the other way at their moorings with the coming of a breeze out of the new quarter, and the premonitory rumble. Then the kettle drum, then the snare, then the bass drum and cymbals, then crackling light against the dark, and the gods grinning and licking their chops in the hills. Afterward the calm, the rain steadily rustling in the calm lake, the return of light and hope and spirits, and the campers running out in joy and relief to go swimming in the rain, their bright cries perpetuating the deathless joke about how they were getting simply drenched, and the children screaming with delight at the new sensation of bathing in the rain, and the joke about getting drenched linking the generations in a strong indestructible chain. And the comedian who waded in carrying an umbrella.

13   When the others went swimming my son said he was going in too. He pulled his dripping trunks from the line where they had hung all through the

shower, and wrung them out. Languidly, and with no thought of going in, I watched him, his hard little body, skinny and bare, saw him wince slightly as he pulled up around his vitals the small, soggy, icy garment. As he buckled the swollen belt suddenly my groin felt the chill of death.

DISCUSSION QUESTIONS ■

1. In paragraph 4 White says that while doing or saying things "suddenly it would be not I but my father who was saying the words or making the gesture." Explain what he means.

2. White supplies relatively little information about his son except to mention that his actions resemble White's own as a child. How do you account for this brief treatment?

3. What is the significance of the missing middle track of the road (paragraph 7) and the "nervous sound of the outboard motors" (paragraph 10)?

4. Throughout the essay White spices his descriptions with precise sensory impressions of sight, hearing, touch, taste, and smell. How do these sensory details enhance his writing?

5. On what audience would this essay likely have the largest impact?

6. White's final sentence provides an indirect statement of his main point. What is the point?

SUGGESTION FOR WRITING ■   Write an essay describing a place you have revisited after being absent for a number of years. Indicate what was similar and what was different and describe your reactions to the changes. Appeal to at least three of the five senses.

DISCUSSION QUESTIONS

1. Since the actions of White's son closely resemble his own actions as a child, White imagines himself to be his father.

2. White's son is not intended to be a fully drawn individual; he is there to trigger White's recognition of his own mortality. Time has passed since White himself engaged in similar boyhood activities, and incessantly it continues to move.

3. Both of these suggest to White that time in fact has not stood still. Both look forward to his chilling realization in the last sentence.

4. The reader is there—seeing, hearing, touching, smelling, tasting. Even if readers have never physically visited a Maine lake, White's description allows them to experience one imaginatively. Students should understand that effective sensory details can place readers on the scene and allow them to "soak up" its atmosphere.

5. Older readers, particularly those who are raising or have raised children, will feel a keen sense of identity with White's sentiments. It's important to point out, however, that the author's insight is universal; time rolls on, and one generation replaces another.

6. White realizes that despite indications to the contrary, time continues moving. Someday White's son and grandson will be reliving this same experience.

The first two process analysis essays offer directions for readers
who might carry out the procedures. The third tells how a
natural process unfolds, and the
fourth, directed at non-doers,
explains how a process is performed. Two of the essays use
formal–informal language and a
serious tone. A third uses informal language laced with colloquialisms and touched with light
humor. The fourth combines
formal–informal diction and
black, even macabre, humor.

Process Analysis

KATHY ROTH

◼ *How to Adopt a Stray*

*Kathy Roth is a cat fancier with special concern for the plight of homeless
animals. In this essay, which first appeared in* The Cat Catalog *(1976), she
tells how to go about turning a stray cat into a healthy, contented house cat.*

> Title indicates set of
> directions

> Introduction: paragraphs 1
> and 2

> Emotional appeal

> Notes rewards,
> requirements of adoption

> Body: paragraphs 3–13;
> uses polite commands,
> addressing reader as
> "you"

> First step and its actions

> Reasons for actions

1   Did you know that for every cat with a home there are twelve strays? We
have all seen them—huddled in doorways, foraging through garbage, frightened,
sick, unwanted. The average street cat has a limited life expectancy; poorly fed, he
risks death from untreated ailments, automobiles, and the cold. It is of no help to
think someone else will do something about the stray. In most cases no one does.
The A.S.P.C.A. can do no more than pick up some of them. What stay cats need
are *homes*.

2   Adopting a stray can be rewarding and fun for you and the cat, but be aware
before you bring the cat home of what the costs will be. Every stray will need at
least a check-up, shots and neutering as soon as possible after adoption. Many
veterinarians (not all, but many) will reduce fees if you tell them that the animal
you have adopted was a stray. If your veterinarian cannot help with costs, find one
who can—they do exist. Your local A.S.P.C.A or humane society can probably
make recommendations.

3   The first step in adopting a stray is, of course, getting him home. Approach
the cat slowly; talk to him reassuringly. Touch him, pet him. Pick him up by
placing your right hand under his rib cage between his two sets of legs, your left
hand around his rump supporting his back legs, and lifting gently. If you have a
distance to go, wrap him inside your coat or sweater, for a sudden noise on the
street might cause him to start and jump from your arms. Hold him close to your
body so that he will be comforted by your body heat.

4   The stray in need of help is often the most docile, the most trusting. The
seriously injured stray needs help most, yet because people dislike the problems
this situation creates, this is the cat most often ignored. Take the injured cat to a
veterinarian immediately. Even if it must be euthanized, it is far worse to walk
away and leave a cat to suffer.

Pregnant cats present other problems, particularly if they are strays. You will not help reduce the stray population by taking in the mother and then plan to abandon the newborn kittens. If you assume responsibility for a cat's welfare, you should be prepared to assume total responsibility. Therefore, if you are unable to deal with the difficulties of finding good homes for kittens (as anyone who has tried knows, it is nearly an impossible job), then it is best to have the kittens aborted.

5

Warning

If you are bringing the stray into a household where there is another cat, totally isolate the stray on arrival and until it has been examined by your vet. The most frequent health problems one confronts in strays are parasites—ear mites, worms and fleas. Although these can be treated quickly and effectively, they are easily transmitted to other cats. Strays may also suffer from upper respiratory ailments—symptoms are running eyes, sneezing and nasal discharge. Do not think of this as "just a cold." Upper respiratory ailments can kill cats.

6   Second step and its actions

Warnings

If you already have a cat, you probably know about feline distemper. This is a virus which may be fatal to cats. If your cat has been inoculated, he runs no risk of catching this virus from a stray (nor do you, since it affects only cats). During the past two years, I have rescued fourteen strays. None of these had distemper and only one died from an upper respiratory illness. Do not be overly concerned about the possibilities of the stray being seriously sick. Just follow two simple precautions: keep the stray isolated from other cats for the first few days and have him examined by a doctor as soon as possible.

7

Once treated for ailments and restored to good health, strays require no more special care than any other cat. Some people think that stray cats, like dogs, should be bathed. It is best to let the cat take care of himself unless he has gotten into some terrible mess that only a scrubbing, and not a self-licking, will clean up. Secure in a new home, even the dingiest stray will soon make himself shine again.

8

Stray cats, like all cats, do not need much training to be house-broken. Introduce the stray to the litter pan and he will quickly get the idea. If your stray seems slow catching on, put him in the pan and help him make digging motions in the litter with his front paws, as you would a kitten. One or two lessons should be sufficient.

9

Because of poor diet, strays often suffer from constipation or diarrhea when first picked up. If your cat is suffering from constipation, feed him a half-teaspoon of nonmedicated petroleum jelly. If he is suffering from diarrhea, mix a little cooked white rice with his food. If you notice blood in the cat's stool, it may be the result of the stray's having eaten bones or sharp objects or having gotten worms while living outside on the street. Don't panic; take a stool sample to your veterinarian to be analyzed.

10

The adoption of a stray should be enjoyable, but it is no fun living with a cat who has not been spayed or neutered. Adult males tend to spray furniture with urine; females cry all night long, particularly when in heat. Do not believe the old stories about how neutering or spaying will change the disposition of a cat. It does not, as your veterinarian will tell you.

11   Warning

Once you have provided the physical comforts and medical necessities of your new pet, you may begin to worry about his adjustments to his new life. The

12   Third step and its actions

best advice is not to worry. If this is your first cat, relax and enjoy getting to know him. He will be nervous and shy for a few days, but gradually he will begin to come to you for petting and play sessions. You are providing him with food and shelter, and in a short time he will begin to show his appreciation of your care. If you already have a cat, let the new cat adjust gradually. Do not try to force the cats to accept each other—they will want to maintain distance for a time. No matter how much explaining you do, your original cat will feel threatened and jealous. Reassure him by giving him extra attention. There will be growling and hissing, but ignore everything for at least three days. In most cases, by the end of this period the original cat usually tires of hostilities and beings to establish a negotiated peace.

Warning	

13   As soon as your new cat begins to feel at home, he will sleep a lot. A little food, a little quiet, and you may not see much of your new pet for a few days. I have known strays to sleep almost uninterruptedly for a week after being rescued from the rigors of street life. If the vet found the cat healthy, do not worry. Let him rest and, in a few days, he will feel more sociable.

Conclusion: corrects misconception	
Warning	

14   People often mistakenly think that cats who have lived on the streets must be permitted to go outside. A former street cat will quickly adjust to life in the home and come to depend on the food and comforts he has been deprived of for so long. To let your cat back out on the streets is to expose him once more to the risks of becoming a stray again. You are not breaking natural laws; you are establishing a new, happy life the stray deserves.

DISCUSSION QUESTIONS

1. The steps are presented in the order in which the actions are carried out, and any attempt to rearrange them would pose a difficult writing task as well as create a highly unnatural effect.
2. Roth's tone reflects a deep concern for the plight of homeless cats. This concern is apparent in the very first paragraph of the essay, in which she describes the desperate situation of strays and the dangers they face. It is further apparent in her directions for getting cats home and caring for them afterward. All of this serves as a powerful inducement to adopt a stray.
3. This question should provide an interesting class discussion.

DISCUSSION QUESTIONS ■

1. Explain why the steps in this process could or could not be arranged in a different order.
2. Characterize the tone (see pages 245–248) of Roth's essay.
3. After reading Roth's essay would you be more likely to adopt a stray cat? Does your answer stem from Roth's content, her manner of presentation, or both?

SUGGESTION FOR WRITING ■   **Write an essay that provides directions for selecting a riding horse, hunting dog, or household pet other than a cat. Be sure to include the reason for any action whose purpose is not obvious, and provide cautionary warnings whenever necessary.**

WALTER KIECHEL III

■ *How to Give a Speech*

Walter Kiechel III (born 1946) is a native of Nebraska but grew up in Alexandria, Virginia. In 1968, he graduated from Harvard University. After five years of naval service, he returned to Harvard where, in 1977, he received advanced degrees in law and business administration. That same year, he joined the staff of Fortune *as a reporter-researcher. Subsequently, he became an associate editor and writer, then was made a member of the magazine's board of editors, and finally was promoted to assistant managing editor. Kiechel writes a column titled "Office Hours" that deals with issues of managerial psychology and sociology and also edits the magazine's Money and Markets section. A collection of his "Office Hours" columns has been published under the title* Office Hours: A Guide to the Managerial Life. *In our selection, Kiechel offers neophyte speechmakers tips for improving their effectiveness.*

Looking for an easy way to reduce even a strong, self-confident manager to a nail-biting mass of insecurities? Just ask him to give a speech to an unfamiliar audience. If he can't get out of accepting, he'll probably devote several sweaty hours to writing out his remarks or, if he is senior enough, delegate the awful task of composition to some underling. When the hour of execution arrives, he will stride manfully to the podium, assume a quasi-fetal stance, and proceed to read his text word by droning word. Not for nothing does pop research indicate that the average American fears speaking before a group more than he fears death. As Paul Nelson, dean of Ohio University's college of communication, observes, "Death is faster."

Choose life, even if it means working to become a better speaker. Why don't more managers take up the challenge? "Most businessmen are worried that they're going to come across like someone else," argues Charles Windhorst, co-founder of Communispond. It's a firm that teaches executives that the trick in fact is to have all the mechanical stuff down so pat that the authentic, worth-listening-to you comes through undistorted. Learn the basics and get out of your own way.

The basics begin when you're invited to speak. While the folks asking may have a foggy idea of what they want you to talk on, their none-too-clear guidelines probably leave you ample room to set your own topic. Don't be in a hurry here. First, the experts universally agree, you should find out as much as you can about your audience.

Who are these people—what age, sex, and line of work—and why will they be assembled? If they're mostly women, you will want to use more examples that feature you know whom. Are they coming to hear you more or less voluntarily, or is their attendance required? Captive audiences are harder to grab. When are you supposed to talk to them? If it's right after a meal or at the end of the day, expect Coma City; leading off in the morning often means that you'll lose 15 minutes to your hosts' unavailing attempts to start on time. Maybe most important, why do they want to hear from *you,* of all people?

5   Much of this dope you can get by grilling the person who had the temerity to invite you. For the ultimate in analysis, though, nothing beats spending a little time with your prospective audience. Robert Waterman Jr., whose co-authorship of *In Search of Excellence* propelled him into big-time speakerdom, finds that if he's to exhort some company's troops, for example, it helps a lot to poke around the corporation for a day or so beforehand talking to everybody he can. He can then address their specific concerns.

6   Once you have a feel for your audience, consult your mental inventory of what interests you these days. Not just what you know or can amass facts on, but what you care about. Dale Carnegie said it 70 years ago, and the experts are still saying it: If you're not excited about your subject, you won't be able to excite your audience about it either. To find your topic, look for where your concerns intersect with their wants and needs. Decide on your purpose—whether to inform, persuade, or entertain. Then give your impending address what Max Wortman, a management professor at the University of Tennessee and a popular speaker, calls a "schmaltzy" title. Not "Current Realities and Future Trends in the Brake Shoe Industry"; rather "What the Future Holds, and Why We Probably Can't Get There From Here."

7   Now all you have to do is compose and deliver the sucker. In putting it together, bear in mind that this is an oral, not a written communication. This means you should use short, simple words, go long on personal pronouns—I, me, you, we—and repeat your main points, since the listener won't be able to go back and reread whatever puzzled him. To achieve the right effect, try composing initially with a Dictaphone or cassette recorder, says Fern Johnson, a professor of communication at the University of Massachusetts at Amherst. If others write the talk for you, make sure that they too observe the basic principle. Dorothy Sarnoff, a Manhattanite who has taught public speaking to many a celebrity, tells of asking 20 or so U.S. State Department speechwriters whether they ever spoke aloud the remarks they prepared for senior diplomats. None ever did. And you wondered why we're in trouble around the globe.

8   In thinking about how to structure what you say, go back to the purpose you decided on. As Communispond's Windhorst observes, the standard tell-'em-what-you're-gonna-tell-'em, tell-'em, and tell-'em-what-you-told-'em works fine if your goal is to inform. If you're out to persuade, though, you're probably better off laying out the problem, marshaling the evidence for your view, then ending with a call to action.

9   At the beginning of your remarks, you want to get the audience on your side—and fast. Research suggests that they make up their minds on whether to like you, and to listen to you, within a minute or two after you start out. Audacious you can, of course, attempt to win them over with a joke. Be careful, though: Make sure that you can actually tell a funny story—not everyone can— and that the joke leads naturally into the body of your speech. The best openers, the experts advise, are probably tales from your own experience: sometimes self-deprecating, not necessarily thigh-slappers, but calculated to show the audience that you're pretty much like them. Or worse.

The standard wisdom says you probably can't hope to put across more than three main points. Listeners should get a sense of movement, of progression, from one part of the speech to the next. Consider using rhetorical questions to alert them to transitions. You needn't be highfalutin, though. Some of the hottest speakers on the corporate circuit—Tom Peters, Waterman's co-author, for example—seem to do nothing but string together story after story.

In framing your conclusion, figure out precisely what you want your listeners to take away. An impulse to act? Lay out with gory specificity what they should do, whether it's writing their Congressman, selling more brake shoes, or razing Carthage. A better understanding of your subject? Summarize your main points. A warm, happy feeling? Leave 'em laughing. Time your remarks to run a bit shorter than the period allotted; besides surprising your listeners no end, this may cause them to want more, and to invite you back another time.

Once you know what you're going to say, put it into a form you can talk from. To keep you from reading, the Communispond firm recommends using your own miserably hand-drawn pictures, or ideographs, one for each major idea. If you simply must have the words in front of you, at least break down your text into natural five- or six-word phrases, one to a line, triple-spaced, with brackets to indicate the phrases that make up a single thought.

You can now attend to the truly mechanical. If you're going to use so-called visual aids—and you probably should if your audience is large—keep them simple, one phrase or idea per slide or overhead transparency. Determine in as much detail as possible how the room will be set up. Will there be a podium, for instance? How tall? If the answer is two inches below your height in stiletto heels, ask that other arrangements be made. Ensure that someone checks out the microphone before you go on.

Rehearse, but try to avoid getting it down so well that you're bored with it. A final pre-speaking tip from Ohio University's Nelson: Write your own introduction. The audience is going to form an impression about you so quickly that if Mr. It-Gives-Me-Great-Pleasure stumbles through your entire potted bio—the four degrees, the military service, the time you spent heading the Thule office—you may lose them before you stand up. Furnish him instead with a brief, down-to-earth account of yourself that stresses what you have in common with your listeners.

With appropriate fanfare, you take the podium. Stand up straight, look out at your audience, smile if it's appropriate, and then launch right in, with no boring "Thank you" or "Madam President, Mr. First Vice President. . ." Put more energy into talking than you usually do; this isn't the time or place for the stuffy nonsense that says that a good manager never raises his voice or gestures with his hands. Indeed, if you can just forget about those appendages, you may free them to do their own helpful thing, whether it's the grand sweep of a big idea, a short jab for emphasis, or the clenched fist of intensity.

Maintain eye contact with your audience. If you're a novice, and nervous, try to find two or three friendly faces, people who seem to be laughing at your stories and nodding along with your witty *aperçus*. When you look up from your text, look at them. As Dean Nelson notes, the nodders are more likely to be women, who aren't socialized like males to keep a poker face. As you grow more

10

11

12

13

14

15

16

DISCUSSION QUESTIONS (p. 420)

1. An activity that inspires such universal fear and trembling clearly requires directions for coping. Thus Kiechel establishes the rationale for his essay.

2. While the phrasing in paragraph 1 could have been handled differently and "businessmen" in paragraph 2 could have been "business people," little else in the essay suggests that women are slighted. Two women speaking authorities are cited in paragraph 7, the reference in paragraph 13 to the podium being "below your height in stiletto heels" obviously indicates a female manager, and in paragraph 15 Kiechel refers to "*Madame* President" and "*Mr.* First Vice President." Sandwiched in between these last two references is "*Mr.* It-Gives-Me-Great-Pleasure" in paragraph 14. For what it's worth, Kiechel takes a slap at *Tom* Peters for seeming "to do nothing but string together story after story" in paragraph 10.

3. The major steps, and the actions involved in each, are as follows: A. Assessing your audience: 1. Asking the person who invited you to talk; 2. Talking directly with the prospective audience. B. Choosing your subject: 1. Determining what interests you; 2. Relating your interests to your audience's wants and needs; 3. Choosing a title. C. Preparing to give the speech: 1. Choosing appropriate diction; 2. Structuring the speech; 3. Preparing the opening; 4. Choosing the main points; 5. Framing the conclusion; 6. Preparing speaking aids; 7. Checking features of the speaking place; 8. Rehearsing the speech. D. Giving the speech: 1. Creating a favorable first impression; 2. Speaking energetically; 3. Maintaining proper eye contact; 4. Maintaining audience interest; 5. Ending strongly.

4. Some noteworthy examples include the following: Paragraph 2: "Choose life, even if it means. . . ." and "the mechani-

cal stuff." Paragraph 4: "harder to grab" and "Coma City." Paragraph 5: "this dope," "exhort some company's troops," and "poke around." Paragraph 6: "these days" and "schmaltzy." Paragraph 7: "the sucker." Paragraph 8: "the standard tell-'em-what-you're-gonna-tell-'em. . . ." Paragraph 10: "high-falutin." Paragraph 11: "gory." Paragraph 14: "Mr. It-Gives-Me-Great-Pleasure" and "potted." Paragraph 15: "stuffy nonsense." Paragraph 16: "trot out." Paragraph 17: "sure-fire gag line."
5. We feel it's better to point out fragments to students before they call the "error" to our attention. Paragraph 6: "Not just what you know. . . ." and "Not 'current Realities and Future'. . . ." Paragraph 9: "Or worse." Kiechel uses the fragments intentionally as part of his humorous informality. Caution students against using fragments until they can handle correct sentences.
6. Expert opinions are cited in paragraphs 1–3 (universally), 5–9 (generally), 10, 12, 14, 16, and 17. Such opinions lend authority to the presentation and indicate that it has been well researched.
7. Although there are obvious differences, learning about your audience, being excited about your subject, determining your purpose, and creating a sense of progression from one part to the next are important in both speaking and writing.

experienced, you'll be able to sweep the room with your gaze, exchanging glances with the neutrals and eventually even with the hostiles. What you're looking for is not just encouragement, but also any sense that you may be losing the crowd. When you see them beginning to stare at the floor, react: Rephrase your last point to make it clearer, tell them again how vital your subject is to them, trot out one of your punchier anecdotes. You may also want to hasten to the close, dropping the lesser points that stand in your way.

17   Finish strong, not trailing off or adding another feeble "thank you." Give 'em a great quote, a passionate, punctuated request, or a sure-fire gag line. Leave the vivid air signed with your honor, to borrow Stephen Spender's phrase. Then sit down and just wait for the applause.

DISCUSSION QUESTIONS ■

1. Why do you think Kiechel begins by noting that both managers and the average American dread giving a speech?

2. In paragraph 1 Kiechel refers to a manager and the average American as "him" or "he." Do you think the essay slights women? Be specific.

3. What are the major steps of this process? The actions which make up these steps? Be specific.

4. No law decrees that a set of directions must be presented in a serious and formal manner. Point out several examples of humorous informality in Kiechel's essay.

5. Identify the two sentence fragments in paragraph 6 and the one in paragraph 9. How can you justify their inclusion?

6. Show where and explain why Kiechel cites expert opinions to support his ideas.

7. How are preparing a speech and preparing an essay similar?

SUGGESTION FOR WRITING ■ Write an essay that provides directions for some nail-biting activity, perhaps asking the boss for a raise or informing your spouse or parents that you caused major damage to the family car. Use humor if it seems appropriate.

ALEXANDER PETRUNKEVITCH

■ *From* The Spider and the Wasp

Alexander Petrunkevitch (1875–1964) was a professor of zoology at Yale University for over a third of a century. He was born in Russia and emigrated to the United States in 1903, holding teaching positions at several universities before going to Yale. He gained international recognition for his investiga-

tions of spiders and his writings on them, in particular his Index Catalogue of Spiders of North, Central, and South America *(1911) and* An Inquiry into the Natural Classification of Spiders *(1933). A man of wide-reaching interests, Petrunkevitch also produced historical and philosophical works as well as translations of Russian poetry. The following selection, excerpted from a 1952* Scientific American *article, describes a natural process and analyzes the behavior of its two participants.*

In the adult stage the [pepsis] wasp lives only a few months. The female produces but a few eggs, one at a time at intervals of two or three days. For each egg the mother must provide one adult tarantula, alive but paralyzed. The mother wasp attaches the egg to the paralyzed spider's abdomen. Upon hatching from the egg, the larva is many hundreds of times smaller than its living but helpless victim. It eats no other food and drinks no water. By the time it has finished its single Gargantuan meal and become ready for wasphood, nothing remains of the tarantula but its indigestible chitinous skeleton.

The mother wasp goes tarantula-hunting when the egg in her ovary is almost ready to be laid. Flying low over the ground late on a sunny afternoon, the wasp looks for its victim or for the mouth of a tarantula burrow, a round hole edged by a bit of silk. The sex of the spider makes no difference, but the mother is highly discriminating as to species. Each species of Pepsis requires a certain species of tarantula, and the wasp will not attack the wrong species. In a cage with a tarantula which is not its normal prey, the wasp avoids the spider and is usually killed by it in the night.

Yet when a wasp finds the correct species, it is the other way about. To identify the species the wasp apparently must explore the spider with her antennae. The tarantula shows an amazing tolerance to this exploration. The wasp crawls under it and walks over it without evoking any hostile response. The molestation is so great and so persistent that the tarantula often rises on all eight legs, as if it were on stilts. It may stand this way for several minutes. Meanwhile the wasp, having satisfied itself that the victim is of the right species, moves off a few inches to dig the spider's grave. Working vigorously with legs and jaws, it excavates—like a machine—a hole 8 to 10 inches deep with a diameter slightly larger than the spider's girth. Now and again the wasp pops out of the hole to make sure that the spider is still there.

When the grave is finished, the wasp returns to the tarantula to complete her ghastly enterprise. First she feels it all over once more with her antennae. Then her behavior becomes more aggressive. She bends her abdomen, protruding her sting, and searches for the soft membrane at the point where the spider's legs join its body—the only spot where she can penetrate the horny skeleton. From time to time, as the exasperated spider slowly shifts ground, the wasp turns on her back and slides along with the aid of her wings, trying to get under the tarantula for a shot at the vital spot. During all this maneuvering, which can last for several minutes, the tarantula makes no move to save itself. Finally the wasp corners it against some obstruction and grasps one of its legs in her powerful jaws. Now at last the harassed spider tries a desperate but vain defense. The two contestants roll over and over on the ground. It is a terrifying sight and the outcome is always the same. The wasp finally manages to thrust her sting into the soft spot and holds it there for a few seconds while she pumps in the poison. Almost immediately the tarantula falls paralyzed on its back. Its legs stop twitching; its heart stops beating. Yet it is not dead, as is shown by the fact that if taken from the wasp it can be restored to some sensitivity by being kept in a moist chamber for several months.

5   After paralyzing the tarantula, the wasp cleans herself by dragging her body around the ground and rubbing her feet, sucks the drop of blood oozing from the wound in the spider's abdomen, then grabs a leg of the flabby, helpless animal in her jaws and drags it down to the bottom of the grave. She stays there for many minutes, sometimes for several hours, and what she does all that time in the dark we do not know. Eventually she lays her egg and attaches it to the side of the spider's abdomen with a sticky secretion. Then she emerges, fills the grave with soil carried bit by bit in her jaws, and finally tramples the ground all around to hide any trace of the grave from prowlers. Then she flies away, leaving her descendant safely started in life.

6   In all this the behavior of the wasp evidently is qualitatively different from that of the spider. The wasp acts like an intelligent animal. This is not to say that instinct plays no part or that she reasons as man does. But her actions are to the point; they are not automatic and can be modified to fit the situation. We do not know for certain how she identifies the tarantula—probably it is by some olfactory or chemo-tactile sense—but she does it purposefully and does not blindly tackle a wrong species.

7   On the other hand, the tarantula's behavior shows only confusion. Evidently the wasp's pawing gives it no pleasure, for it tries to move away. That the wasp is not simulating sexual stimulation is certain because male and female tarantulas react in the same way to its advances. That the spider is not anesthetized by some odorless secretion is easily shown by blowing lightly at the tarantula and making it jump suddenly. What, then, makes the tarantula behave as stupidly as it does?

8   No clear, simple answer is available. Possibly the stimulation by the wasp's antennae is masked by a heavier pressure on the spider's body, so that it reacts as when prodded by a pencil. But the explanation may be much more complex. Initiative in attack is not in the nature of tarantulas; most species fight only when cornered so that escape is impossible. Their inherited patterns of behavior apparently prompt them to avoid problems rather than attack them. For example, spiders always weave their webs in three dimensions, and when a spider finds that there is insufficient space to attach certain threads in the third dimension, it leave the place and seeks another, instead of finishing the web in a single plane. This urge to escape seems to arise under all circumstances, in all phases of life, and to take the place of reasoning. For a spider to change the pattern of its web is as impossible as for an inexperienced man to build a bridge across a chasm obstructing his way.

9   In a way the instinctive urge to escape is not only easier but often more efficient than reasoning. The tarantula does exactly what is most efficient in all cases except in an encounter with a ruthless and determined attacker dependent for the existence of her own species on killing as many tarantulas as she can lay

DISCUSSION QUESTIONS

1. This process is divided into six steps: Hunting for a victim (paragraph 2), determining that the victim is the right species (first part of paragraph 3), digging the victim's grave (last part of paragraph 3), paralyzing the victim (paragraph 4), laying an egg on the victim (middle part of paragraph 5), and burying the victim (last part of paragraph 5). Point out to students that step 4 involves a series of substeps: feeling the victim all over once more, searching for a spot to insert the poison, battling the victim, and inserting the poison. Similarly, step 5 involves the wasp's cleaning herself, dragging the victim into the grave, and laying the egg.

2. Petrunkevitch's attitude is basically, but not entirely. objective. In a few places the writing reflects his emotional reactions. In paragraph 4, the wasp's enterprise is called "ghastly," and the sight of the two contestants rolling on the ground is "terrifying." In paragraph 7, the spider is said to behave "stupidly." These examples suggest that Petrunkevitch is sympathetic toward the spider.

eggs. Perhaps in this case the spider follows its usual pattern of trying to escape, instead of seizing and killing the wasp, because it is not aware of its danger. In any case, the survival of the tarantula species as a whole is protected by the fact that the spider is much more fertile than the wasp.

DISCUSSION QUESTIONS ■

1. Into how many steps is this natural process divided? In which paragraph or paragraphs is each discussed?

2. Characterize Petrunkevitch's attitude toward his topic. Is it completely objective, or does Petrunkevitch sometimes reveal his personal feelings? If he does, indicate where.

3. Petrunkevitch uses a number of transitional words and phrases to ensure a smooth flow of ideas. Indicate those transitional devices and the paragraphs in which they are found.

4. Where does the conclusion begin and what is its purpose?

SUGGESTION FOR WRITING ■   **Write an essay explaining some process you perform frequently. Possibilities include flossing your teeth, brewing a pot of coffee, or preparing for a date.**

---

3. Paragraph 3: "Meanwhile," "Now and again." Paragraph 4: "When the grave is finished," "First," "Then," "From time to time," "Finally," "Now at last," "Finally," "Almost immediately," "Yet." Paragraph 5: "After paralyzing," "then," "Eventually," "Then," "Finally," "Then." Most of these words and phrases simply signal the passage of time. However, "When the grave is finished" (paragraph 4), echoes "Meanwhile the wasp . . . moves off . . . to dig the spider's grave" (paragraph 3), and "Yet" (paragraph 4) signals a contrast between what precedes and what follows it.

4. Paragraphs 8 and 9 form the conclusion and try to account for the "stupid" behavior of the spider. The preceding two paragraphs contrast the behavior of the adversaries and set the stage for the conclusion.

JESSICA MITFORD

■ *Behind the Undertaker's Door*[1]

Jessica Mitford's roots are in the English nobility. Born in 1917 to Lord and Lady Redesdale, she was educated at home by her mother. In 1936, she left home and three years later moved to the United States, where she became a naturalized citizen. In the 1950s she became an investigative journalist whose exposés of fraud, greed, and injustice later caused Time *magazine to dub her the "Queen of Muckrakers." Mitford's first book,* Lifeitselfmanship, *appeared in 1956. It was followed by the autobiographical* Daughters and Rebels *(1960) and then a series of three investigative books:* The American Way of Death *(1963), an investigation of the funeral business;* The Trial of Dr. Spock *(1969), a look into the trial of the famous pediatrician for his activities on behalf of draft resisters during the Vietnam War; and* Kind and Usual Punishment *(1973), an attack on the American prison system. Other, more recent books include* A Fine Old Conflict *(1979), which details her involvement in left-wing politics, and* Poison Penmanship *(1979), a collection of*

---

[1] Editors' title.

articles that originally appeared in such magazines as Atlantic Monthly, The Nation, Esquire, *and* Harper's. *Our Mitford selection, taken from* The American Way of Death, *describes the process of embalming a body and readying it for viewing.*

1   Embalming is indeed a most extraordinary procedure, and one must wonder at the docility of Americans who each year pay hundreds of millions of dollars for its perpetuation, blissfully ignorant of what it is all about, what is done, how it is done. Not one in ten thousand has any idea of what actually takes place. Books on the subject are extremely hard to come by. They are not to be found in most libraries or bookshops.

2   In an era when huge television audiences watch surgical operations in the comfort of their living rooms, when, thanks to the animated cartoon, the geography of the digestive system has become familiar territory even to the nursery school set, in a land where the satisfaction of curiosity about almost all matters is a national pastime, the secrecy surrounding embalming can, surely, hardly be attributed to the inherent gruesomeness of the subject. Custom in this regard has within this century suffered a complete reversal. In the early days of American embalming, when it was performed in the home of the deceased, it was almost mandatory for some relative to stay by the embalmer's side and witness the procedure. Today, family members who might wish to be in attendance would certainly be dissuaded by the funeral director. All others, except apprentices, are excluded by law from the preparation room.

3   A close look at what does actually take place may explain in large measure the undertaker's intractable reticence concerning a procedure that has become his major *raison d'être*. Is it possible he fears that public information about embalming might lead patrons to wonder if they really want this service? If the funeral men are loath to discuss the subject outside the trade, the reader may, understandably, be equally loath to go on reading at this point. For those who have the stomach for it, let us part the formaldehyde curtain. . . .

4   The body is first laid out in the undertaker's morgue—or rather, Mr. Jones is reposing in the preparation room—to be readied to bid the world farewell.

5   The preparation room in any of the better funeral establishments has the tiled and sterile look of a surgery, and indeed the embalmer-restorative artist who does his chores there is beginning to adopt the term "dermasurgeon" (appropriately corrupted by some mortician-writers as "demisurgeon") to describe his calling. His equipment, consisting of scalpels, scissors, augurs, forceps, clamps, needles, pumps, tubes, bowls and basins, is crudely imitative of the surgeon's, as is his technique, acquired in a nine- or twelve-month post-high-school course in an embalming school. He is supplied by an advanced chemical industry with a bewildering array of fluids, sprays, pastes, oils, powders, creams, to fix or soften tissue, shrink or distend it as needed, dry it here, restore the moisture there. There are cosmetics, waxes and paints to fill and cover features, even plaster of Paris to replace entire limbs. There are ingenious aids to prop and stabilize the cadaver: a Vari-Pose Head Rest, the Edwards Arm and Hand Positioner, the Repose Block (to support the shoulders during the embalming), and the Throop Foot Positioner, which resembles an old-fashioned stocks.

Mr. John H. Eckels, president of the Eckels College of Mortuary Science, thus describes the first part of the embalming procedure: "In the hands of a skilled practitioner, this work may be done in a comparatively short time and without mutilating the body other than by slight incision—so slight that it scarcely would cause serious inconvenience if made upon a living person. It is necessary to remove the blood, and doing this not only helps in the disinfecting, but removes the principal cause of disfigurements due to discoloration."

6

Another textbook discusses the all-important time element: "The earlier this is done, the better, for every hour that elapses between death and embalming will add to the problems and complications encountered. . . . Just how soon should one get going on the embalming? The author tells us, "On the basis of such scanty information made available to this profession through its rudimentary and haphazard system of technical research, we must conclude that the best results are to be obtained if the subject is embalmed before life is completely extinct—that is, before cellular death has occurred. In the average case, this would mean within an hour after somatic death." For those who feel that there is something a little rudimentary, not to say haphazard, about this advice, a comforting thought is offered by another writer. Speaking of fears entertained in early days of premature burial, he points out, "One of the effects of embalming by chemical injection, however, has been to dispel fears of live burial." How true; once the blood is removed, chances of live burial are indeed remote.

7

To return to Mr. Jones, the blood is drained out through the veins and replaced by embalming fluid pumped in through the arteries. As noted in *The Principles and Practices of Embalming,* "every operator has a favorite injection and drainage point—a fact which becomes a handicap only if he fails or refuses to forsake his favorites when conditions demand it." Typical favorites are the carotid artery, femoral artery, jugular vein, subclavian vein. There are various choices of embalming fluid. If Flextone is used, it will produce a "mild, flexible rigidity. The skin retains a velvety softness, the tissues are rubbery and pliable. Ideal for women and children." It may be blended with B. and G. Products Company's Lyf-Lyk tint, which is guaranteed to reproduce "nature's own skin texture . . . the velvety appearance of living tissue." Suntone comes in three separate tints: Suntan; Special Cosmetic Tint, a pink shade "especially indicated for young female subjects"; and Regular Cosmetic Tint, moderately pink.

8

About three to six gallons of a dyed and perfumed solution of formaldehyde, glycerin, borax, phenol, alcohol, and water is soon circulating through Mr. Jones, whose mouth has been sewn together with a "needle directed upward between the upper lip and gum and brought out through the left nostril," with the corners raised slightly "for a more pleasant expression." If he should be bucktoothed, his teeth are cleaned with Bon Ami and coated with colorless nail polish. His eyes, meanwhile, are closed with flesh-tinted eye caps and eye cement.

9

The next step is to have at Mr. Jones with a thing called a trocar. This is a long, hollow needle attached to a tube. It is jabbed into the abdomen, poked around the entrails and chest cavity, the contents of which are pumped out and replaced with "cavity fluid." This done, and the hole in the abdomen sewn up, Mr. Jones's face is heavily creamed (to protect the skin from burns which may be caused by leakage of the chemicals), and he is covered with a sheet and left

10

unmolested for a while. But not for long—there is more, much more, in store for him. He has been embalmed, but not yet restored, and the best time to start the restorative work is eight to ten hours after embalming, when the tissues have become firm and dry.

11   The object of all this attention to the corpse, it must be remembered, is to make it presentable for viewing in an attitude of healthy repose. "Our customs require the presentation of our dead in the semblance of normality . . . unmarred by the ravages of illness, disease or mutilation," says Mr. J. Sheridan Mayer in his *Restorative Art.* This is rather a large order since few people die in the full bloom of health, unravaged by illness and unmarked by some disfigurement. The funeral industry is equal to the challenge: "In some cases the gruesome appearance of a mutilated or disease-ridden subject may be quite discouraging. The task of restoration may seem impossible and shake the confidence of the embalmer. This is the time for intestinal fortitude and determination. Once the formative work is begun and affected tissues are cleaned or removed, all doubts of success vanish. It is surprising and gratifying to discover the results which may be obtained."

12   The embalmer, having allowed an appropriate interval to elapse, returns to the attack, but now he brings into play the skill and equipment of sculptor and cosmetician. Is a hand missing? Casting one in plaster of Paris is a simple matter. "For replacement purposes, only a cast of the back of the hand is necessary; this is within the ability of the average operator and is quite adequate." If a lip or two, a nose or an ear should be missing, the embalmer has at hand a variety of restorative waxes with which to model replacements. Pores and skin texture are simulated by stippling with a little brush, and over this cosmetics are laid on. Head off? Decapitation cases are rather routinely handled. Ragged edges are trimmed, and head joined to torso with a series of splints, wires and sutures. It is a good idea to have a little something at the neck—a scarf or high collar—when time for viewing comes. Swollen mouth? Cut out tissue as needed from inside the lips. If too much is removed, the surface contour can easily be restored by padding with cotton. Swollen necks and cheeks are reduced by removing tissue through vertical incisions made down each side of the neck. "When the deceased is casketed, the pillow will hide the suture incisions . . . as an extra precaution against leakage, the suture may be painted with liquid sealer."

13   The opposite condition is more likely to present itself—that of emaciation. His hypodermic syringe now loaded with massage cream, the embalmer seeks out and fills the hollowed and sunken areas by injection. In this procedure the backs of the hands and fingers and the under-chin area should not be neglected.

14   Positioning the lips is a problem that recurrently challenges the ingenuity of the embalmer. Closed too tightly they tend to give a stern, even disapproving expression. Ideally, embalmers feel, the lips should give the impression of being ever so slightly parted, the upper lip protruding slightly for a more youthful appearance. This takes some engineering, however, as the lips tend to drift apart. Lip drift can sometimes be remedied by pushing one or two straight pins through the inner margin of the lower lip and then inserting them between the two front upper teeth. If Mr. Jones happens to have no teeth, the pins can just as easily be anchored in his Armstrong Face Former and Denture Replacer. Another method to maintain lip closure is to dislocate the lower jaw, which is then held in its new

position by a wire run through holes which have been drilled through the upper and lower jaws at the midline. As the French are fond of saying, *il faut souffrir pour être belle.*[2]

If Mr. Jones has died of jaundice, the embalming fluid will very likely turn   15
him green. Does this deter the embalmer? Not if he has intestinal fortitude. Masking pastes and cosmetics are heavily laid on, burial garments and casket interiors are color-correlated with particular care, and Jones is displayed beneath rose-colored lights. Friends will say, "How *well* he looks." Death by carbon monoxide, on the other hand, can be rather a good thing from the embalmer's viewpoint: "One advantage is the fact that this type of discoloration is an exaggerated form of a natural pink coloration." This is nice because the healthy glow is already present and needs but little attention.

The patching and filling completed, Mr. Jones is now shaved, washed and   16
dressed. Cream-based cosmetic, available in pink, flesh, suntan, brunette, and blond, is applied to his hands and face, his hair is shampooed and combed (and, in the case of Mrs. Jones, set), his hands manicured. For the horny-handed son of toil special care must be taken; cream should be applied to remove ingrained grime, and the nails cleaned. "If he were not in the habit of having them manicured in life, trimming and shaping is advised for better appearance—never questioned by kin."

Jones is now ready for casketing (this is the present participle of the verb   17
"to casket"). In this operation his right shoulder should be depressed slightly "to turn the body a bit to the right and soften the appearance of lying flat on the back." Positioning the hands is a matter of importance, and special rubber positioning blocks may be used. The hands should be cupped slightly for a more life-like, relaxed appearance. Proper placement of the body requires a delicate sense of balance. It should lie as high as possible in the casket, yet not so high that the lid, when lowered, will hit the nose. On the other hand, we are cautioned, placing the body too low "creates the impression that the body is in a box."

Jones is next wheeled into the appointed slumber room where a few last   18
touches may be added—his favorite pipe placed in his hand or, if he was a great reader, a book propped into position. (In the case of little Master Jones a Teddy bear may be clutched.) Here he will hold open house for a few days, visiting hours 10 A.M. to 9 P.M.

DISCUSSION QUESTIONS ■

1. What is Mitford's purpose in this excerpt? Does her writing include a thesis statement, or is the statement implied?

2. Even though the reader is not expected to carry out the process, Mitford includes a list of the tools and materials it requires. Explain why.

3. How do you know that Mitford assumes her audience has little knowledge of the embalming and restorative process?

[2]One must suffer to be beautiful.

DISCUSSION QUESTIONS

1. Mitford's purpose is to shock her audience, turn them against the process she details, and make them wonder "if they really want this service" (paragraph 3). The selection does not include a thesis statement; the implied statement might be stated as follows: "As practiced in America, preparing a body for burial is a gruesome process that has questionable value."

2. The extensive listing (in paragraph 5) helps point out the gruesome nature of the process and forms part of her attack on the funeral industry.

3. Paragraph 1 makes clear that she considers Americans "blissfully ignorant . . . ." Paragraph 2 mentions "the secrecy surrounding embalming," and paragraph 3 mentions "the undertaker's intractable reticence." Mitford's detailed explanation of the steps involved (see answer 4), in addition to satirizing the industry, also assumes little knowledge on the part of her audience.

4. She starts describing the process in paragraph 8. It includes two major steps: embalming and restoration. Embalming includes replacing the blood with embalming fluid, injecting "cavity fluid" into the body's trunk, and putting protective face cream on the body. Restoration includes supplying replacements for missing parts, correcting for swollen tissue and emaciation, positioning the lips, shaving, washing, and dressing the body, and "casketing."

5. Mitford is clearly here, as elsewhere, mounting an attack on morticians: they "have at" Jones, the needle is "jabbed" and "poked," and finally the corpse is left "unmolested."

6. Jones, common name that it is, suggests that this gruesome process is carried out on any man, woman, or child who dies.

7. The casual style and flip attitude of the last sentence is a fitting end to Mitford's humorous and sarcastic indictment of the funeral industry.

4. At what point does Mitford start discussing the actual process of preparing the body? Identify the major steps and tell what separate actions each includes.

5. Reread paragraph 10 and then cite appropriate language that suggests Mitford's attitude toward morticians.

6. What is the effect of tagging the corpse with the name "Jones"—"Mr. Jones," "Mrs. Jones," and "little Master Jones?"

7. Suggest why "Here he will hold open house for a few days, visiting hours 10 A.M. to 9 P.M." is an appropriate ending.

SUGGESTION FOR WRITING ■

Write an essay detailing a process you find distasteful. Possible topics might include slaughtering pigs or cattle, dressing a badly infected wound, or treating sewage in a municipal sewage plant. Aim for a tone that reflects your feelings.

Illustration

OVERVIEW OF ILLUSTRATION ESSAYS

Three of the four illustration essays offer multiple examples to make their point. One features a single extended example. Three are serious and one is humorous. Three use informal language, and the remaining one uses colloquial language. One has an unstated point, and the others have stated points.

JAMES THURBER

■ *Courtship Through the Ages*

A biographical sketch of James Thurber can be found on page 396. The following selection, which originally appeared in The New Yorker, *offers a humorous look at the difficulties encountered by the male of the species when a-wooing he would go.*

Surely nothing in the astonishing scheme of life can have nonplussed Nature so much as the fact that none of the females of any of the species she created really cared very much for the male, as such. For the past ten million years Nature has been busily inventing ways to make the male attractive to the female, but the whole business of courtship, from the marine annelids up to man, still lumbers heavily along, like a complicated musical comedy. I have been reading the sad and absorbing story in Volume 6 (Cole to Dama) of the *Encyclopaedia Britannica.* In this volume you can learn all about cricket, cotton, costume designing, crocodiles, crown jewels, and Coleridge but none of these subjects is so interesting as the Courtship of Animals, which recounts the sorrowful lengths to which all males must go to arouse the interest of a lady.

We all know, I think, that Nature gave man whiskers and a mustache with the quaint idea in mind that these would prove attractive to the female. We all know that, far from attracting her, whiskers and mustaches only made her nervous and gloomy, so that man had to go in for somersaults, tilting with lances, and performing feats of parlor magic to win her attention; he also had to bring her candy, flowers, and the furs of animals. It is common knowledge that in spite of all these "love displays" the male is constantly being turned down, insulted, or thrown out of the house. It is rather comforting, then, to discover that the peacock, for all his gorgeous plumage, does not have a particularly easy time in courtship; none of the males in the world do. The first peahen, it turned out, was only faintly stirred by her suitor's beautiful train. She would often go quietly to sleep while he was whisking it around. The *Britannica* tells us that the peacock actually had to learn a certain little trick to wake her up and revive her interest: he had to learn to vibrate his quills so as to make a rustling sound. In

1   Introduction: provides background

Point to be illustrated

2   Body: paragraphs 2–7

First examples: support main point, as do all examples

429

ancient times man himself, observing the ways of the peacock, probably tried vibrating his whiskers to make a rustling sound; if so, it didn't get him anywhere. He had to go in for something else; so, among other things, he went in for gifts. It is not unlikely that he got this idea from certain flies and birds who were making no headway at all with rustling sounds.

Second example; features different animal as do all examples, providing more evidence supporting paper's point

3   One of the flies of the family Empidae, who had tried everything, finally hit on something pretty special. He contrived to make a glistening transparent balloon which was even larger than himself. Into this he would put sweetmeats and tidbits and he would carry the whole elaborate envelope through the air to the lady of his choice. This amused her for a time, but she finally got bored with it. She demanded silly little colorful presents, something that you couldn't eat but that would look nice around the house. So the male Empis had to go around gathering flower petals and pieces of bright paper to put into his balloon. On a courtship flight a male Empis cuts quite a figure now, but he can hardly be said to be happy. He never knows how soon the female will demand heavier presents, such as Roman coins and gold collar buttons. It seems probable that one day the courtship of the Empidae will fall down, as man's occasionally does, of its own weight.

Third example

4   The bowerbird is another creature that spends so much time courting the female that he never gets any work done. If all the male bowerbirds became nervous wrecks within the next ten or fifteen years, it would not surprise me. The female bowerbird insists that a playground be built for her with a specially constructed bower at the entrance. This bower is much more elaborate than an ordinary nest and is harder to build; it costs a lot more, too. The female will not come to the playground until the male has filled it up with a great many gifts: silvery leaves, red leaves, rose petals, shells, beads, berries, bones, dice, buttons, cigar bands, Christmas seals, and the Lord knows what else. When the female finally condescends to visit the playground, she is in a coy and silly mood and has to be chased in and out of the bower and up and down the playground before she will quit giggling and stand still long enough even to shake hands. The male bird is, of course, pretty well done in before the chase starts, because he has worn himself out hunting for eyeglass lenses and begonia blossoms. I imagine that many a bowerbird, after chasing a female for two or three hours, says the hell with it and goes home to bed. Next day, of course, he telephones someone else and the same trying ritual is gone through with again. A male bowerbird is as exhausted as a night-club habitué before he is out of his twenties.

Fourth example

5   The male fiddler crab has a somewhat easier time, but it can hardly be said that he is sitting pretty. He has one enormously large and powerful claw, usually brilliantly colored, and you might suppose that all he had to do was reach out and grab some passing cutie. The very earliest fiddler crabs may have tried this, but, if so, they got slapped for their pains. A female fiddler crab will not tolerate any caveman stuff; she never has and she doesn't intend to start now. To attract a female, a fiddler crab has to stand on tiptoe and brandish his claw in the air. If any female in the neighborhood is interested—and you'd be surprised how many are not—she comes over and engages him in light badinage, for which he is not in the mood. As many as a hundred females may pass the time of day with him and go on about their business. By nightfall of an average courting day, a fiddler crab

Illustration   **431**

who has been standing on tiptoe for eight or ten hours waving a heavy claw in the air is in pretty sad shape. As in the case of the male of all species, however, he gets out of bed next morning, dashes some water on his face, and tries again.

The next time you encounter a male web-spinning spider, stop and reflect that he is too busy worrying about his love life to have any desire to bite you. Male web-spinning spiders have a tougher life than any other males in the animal kingdom. This is because the female web-spinning spiders have very poor eyesight. If a male lands on a female's web, she kills him before he has time to lay down his cane and gloves, mistaking him for a fly or a bumblebee who has tumbled into her trap. Before the species figured out what to do about this, millions of males were murdered by ladies they called on. It is the nature of spiders to perform a little dance in front of the female, but before a male spinner could get near enough for the female to see who he was and what he was up to, she would lash out at him with a flat-iron or a pair of garden shears. One night, nobody knows when, a very bright male spinner lay awake worrying about calling on a lady who had been killing suitors right and left. It came to him that this business of dancing as a love display wasn't getting anybody anywhere except the grave. He decided to go in for web-twitching, or strand-vibrating. The next day he tried it on one of the nearsighted girls. Instead of dropping in on her suddenly, he stayed outside the web and began monkeying with one of its strands. He twitched it up and down and in and out with such a lilting rhythm that the female was charmed. The serenade worked beautifully; the female let him live. The *Britannica's* spider-watchers, however, report that this system is not always successful. Once in a while, even now, a female will fire three bullets into a suitor or run him through with a kitchen knife. She keeps threatening him from the moment he strikes the first low notes on the outside strings, but usually by the time he has got up to the high notes played around the center of the web, he is going to town and she spares his life.

Even the butterfly, as handsome a fellow as he is, can't always win a mate merely by fluttering around and showing off. Many butterflies have to have scent scales on their wings. Hepialus carries a powder puff in a perfumed pouch. He throws perfume at the ladies when they pass. The male tree cricket, Oecanthus, goes Hepialus one better by carrying a tiny bottle of wine with him and giving drinks to such doxies as he has designs on. One of the male snails throws darts to entertain the girls. So it goes, through the long list of animals, from the bristle worm and his rudimentary dance steps to man and his gift of diamonds and sapphires. The golden-eye drake raises a jet of water with his feet as he flies over a lake; Hepialus has his powder puff, Oecanthus his wine bottle, man his etchings. It is a bright and melancholy story, the age-old desire of the male for the female, the age-old desire of the female to be amused and entertained. Of all the creatures on earth, the only males who could be figured as putting any irony into their courtship are the grebes and certain other diving birds. Every now and then a courting grebe slips quietly down to the bottom of a lake and then, with a mighty "Whoosh!" pops out suddenly a few feet from his girl friend, splashing water all over her. She seems to be persuaded that this is a purely loving display, but I like to think that the grebe always has a faint hope of drowning her or scaring her to death.

6 | Fifth example |

7 | Sixth example: discusses series of animals |

Conclusion: final example

8   I will close this investigation into the mournful burdens of the male with *Britannica's* story about a certain Argus pheasant. It appears that the Argus displays himself in front of a female who stands perfectly still without moving a feather. . . . The male Argus the *Britannica* tells about was confined in a cage with a female of another species, a female who kept moving around, emptying ashtrays and fussing with lampshades all the time the male was showing off his talents. Finally, in disgust, he stalked away and began displaying in front of his water trough. He reminds me of a certain male (*Homo sapiens*) of my acquaintance who one night after dinner asked his wife to put down her detective magazine so that he could read a poem of which he was very fond. She sat quietly enough until he was well into the middle of the thing, intoning with great ardor and intensity. Then suddenly there came a sharp, disconcerting *slap!* It turned out that all during the male's display, the female had been intent on a circling mosquito and had finally trapped it between the palms of her hands. The male in this case did not stalk away and display in front of a water trough; he went over to Tim's and had a flock of drinks and recited the poem to the fellas. I am sure they all told bitter stories of their own about how their displays had been interrupted by females. I am also sure that they all ended up singing "Honey, Honey, Bless Your Heart."

DISCUSSION QUESTIONS

DISCUSSION QUESTIONS ■

1. Thurber suggests throughout the essay that his primary interest is man, not animals. Paragraph 1: "the marine annelids up to man. . . ." Paragraph 2: His first illustration deals with man and "In ancient times man himself. . . ." Paragraphs 3 and 4: Thurber attributes human qualities to the fly and the bowerbird. Depending on the level of your class, you might introduce and discuss personification. Paragraph 6: The female spider strikes "with a flat-iron or a pair of garden shears" and "will fire three bullets into a suitor or run him through with a kitchen knife." Paragraph 7: "from the bristle worm and his rudimentary dance steps to man. . . ." and ". . . man [has] his etchings." Paragraph 8: Thurber's final illustration deals with man.

2. At the end of paragraph 2, Thurber indicates that the peacock got the idea of vibrating its quills from certain flies and birds. Paragraphs 3 and 4 then provide examples of a fly and a bird. Paragraph 4 ends by mentioning the exhaustion of the bowerbird; then paragraph 5 takes up the idea of exhaustion by mentioning the exhausting courtship rite of the fiddler crab. Paragraph 6 moves on to discuss the creature with the toughest courting problem of all those mentioned, and paragraph 7 moves away from a very ugly creature to a beautiful one. Students write more effectively if we reinforce the idea of coherence.

1. In paragraph 1 Thurber notes that he will be dealing with the courtship of animals, and the remainder of the selection appears to do just that. What evidence suggests that his main interest is not in the mating of animals at all?

2. Point out the linking techniques that Thurber uses in moving from paragraph 2 through paragraph 7.

3. Why do you think Thurber cites the *Encyclopaedia Britannica* in paragraphs 1, 2, 6, and 8?

4. Explain why the ending "Honey, Honey, Bless Your Heart" is or is not effective.

5. Is Thurber writing primarily to inform? To entertain? To do both? Discuss.

SUGGESTION FOR WRITING ■   Write an essay illustrating the ways that men court women or women court men. Provide at least three examples and aim for a light, humorous tone.

Illustration **433**

BERNARD SLOAN

■ *Old Folks at Home*

Bernard Sloan has had a long writing career. A graduate of Stanford University, he assumed a position of copywriter at a major New York advertising agency, where he became senior vice-president and the associate creative director. He is the author of several nonfiction books and many articles, and at 63 he continues an active career as a free-lance writer.

I once felt sorry for people in old-age homes. I accepted their portrayal on television specials as helpless innocents cast aside by their young, paying the price of growing old in America. I thought all these lonely old men and women were victims of the indifference and selfishness of the younger generation.

No more.

I have learned through personal experience why so many grandmothers and grandfathers end up in institutions for the aged, unwanted and unvisited. It isn't always their children who put them there. Sometimes they put themselves there.

These are the selfish, demanding elderly who are impossible to live with. Often they are people who were difficult to live with when they were younger, but now they have age on their side. Their families, torn with pain and guilt, spend months or years struggling to do "the right thing." Finally, they give up.

I have been through it. I have friends who are going through it. Caring, concerned sons and daughters who try, God knows they try, but the harder they try the harder it gets. Their elderly parents who should know better carp and criticize and complain. Instead of compromising, they constantly test their children, forever setting up new challenges for them to meet, assuming the one-sided game can go on forever.

It comes as a shock to them when the special privileges conferred by their age and relationship run out, and their son or daughter tolerates their tyranny no longer. "How can you do this to me?" the parent cries, bags packed.

It is not easy.

We have friends who spent a fortune remodeling their home to provide an apartment for the wife's aging mother. The daughter was determined to overcome their differences for the chance to be close to her mother, to give her mother the love of a family rather than the services of a mercenary. Instead, she provided herself and her family with a three-year nightmare, the old woman seizing every opportunity to demean her daughter's husband, criticize the children, and turn every family argument into a screaming fight.

"She's tearing our family apart," the daughter cries. "I'm going to be the villain by casting her out, but she has to go, or it's the end of my marriage."

Our friend is now searching for a suitable home. In her desperation she will settle for the best home available, which will not necessarily be the best home.

1
2
3
4
5
6
7
8
9
10

---

3. Thurber cites the *Encyclopaedia Britannica* to lend authority to his illustrations, which might otherwise seem made up. Of course, the *Encyclopaedia* does not attribute human behavior to its examples, as Thurber humorously does.
4. This ending is effective because it makes the same point the other illustrations do: despite rejections, the males will try again. This is Nature's law. But note also how Thurber suggests the irony in Nature's law.
5. While Thurber makes a point about the difficulties and frustrations of males, he seems mainly intent on entertaining us with his humorous approach.

PERSPECTIVE

Sloan displays bitterness and indignation, a reaction that probably stems from his disillusionment with his mother, and that is compounded by a sense of decency which makes him hate what he is forced to do. His feelings emerge strongly in paragraph 5, which points up the terrible situation faced by the caring children of selfish, demanding, elderly parents, and paragraph 17, where he takes parents to task for failing to observe the rules of common decency. This tone is entirely appropriate for the subject.

TEACHING STRATEGIES

1. Point out the parallelism in paragraph 1 and discuss its effect. Then have students locate other examples of parallelism in the essay.
2. Ask students to discuss the effectiveness of the fragments in paragraphs 2, 11, and 14. You could announce (or reiterate) at this point whether you'll accept fragments in student essays.
3. Ask students why they think Sloan began paragraph 17 with questions rather than statements.

CLASSROOM ACTIVITIES
1. Have students, working in small groups, determine which examples were and were not effective and why.
2. Have students, working in small groups, compile examples they would use in an illustration to counter the contentions in this essay.

11   Another friend not only brings her father-in-law cooked meals, she cleans his apartment every week. Not once has he thanked her. But he has managed to find fault with everything she does. How long will he be able to live by himself? Another year, perhaps. And then what? Who will he blame when he winds up in an institution? Not himself.

12   A business acquaintance makes solitary visits to his angry mother in her lonely apartment. His wife will no longer submit to the old woman's hostility. The old woman, an Italian Catholic, cannot forgive her son for marrying a French Catholic. Mixed marriages, she still proclaims regularly, don't work. Twenty-five years and three delightful children don't count.

13   Can't she read the handwriting on the wall? She is busy writing her own future.

14   When my mother became ill, I moved her from her Sun Belt apartment to our home so that she could spend her remaining time with her only family, her only grandchildren. Although she never approved of my wife (the wrong religion again), we were positive she would relinquish her prejudices in exchange for love and care. No such luck. Instead of making an attempt to adjust to our household, my mother tried to manipulate the four of us to center our lives around her.

15   My wife took her to the doctor regularly, supervised her medication, bought and prepared special foods for her—all while working full time—yet my mother found nothing right about anything she did. Our refrigerator could be bulging, but my mother managed to crave the one thing missing. We were made to feel guilty if we left her alone for an evening, and were maneuvered into quarrels if we stayed. After five months of this, we began to investigate "homes."

16   Even the most relentlessly cheerful were depressing. Amidst flowered walls and piped-in music ("Heaven, I'm in Heaven") old people stared at television or gathered in activity rooms where they were kept busy with the arts and crafts taught in the third grade. They were not bedridden, these people; they required no nursing, no special care. Although unable to shop, cook and take care of a home of their own, they were quite capable of participating in the life of a family. Yet they were separated from their families.

17   How many of these people had driven their families to drive them out? How many felt that reaching 60 or 70 or 80 entitled them to behave in a manner that would never be tolerated in the young? As if the very fact of being old excused them from the rules of common decency. As if the right to be demanding and complaining was conferred upon them along with half fares on buses and discount days at the market.

18   That cantankerous old man may be a laugh riot on the stage as he sends comic characters scurrying at his every command, but he is hell to live with. That feisty old lady may be hilarious when company comes, but she can drive a family crazy. They are candidates for being "put away" as soon as the family being destroyed gets up the courage.

19   I don't mean to suggest that there are not great numbers of old people who must live in institutions because they are victims—victims of infirmity and, yes, victims of callous, selfish children. But for our own sakes, and for our children, it is pointless to ignore the fact that many of the elderly bear some responsibility for

Illustration   **435**

their fate. After all, warm, loving, sharing people are a joy to live with whatever their age.

DISCUSSION QUESTIONS ■

1. What general idea does this essay illustrate? State it as a thesis sentence.

2. Why are several illustrations a good choice here?

3. Discuss the arrangement of these illustrations. Would it be more logical to reposition the final illustration earlier in the essay? Why or why not? How can you account for the greater length of the final illustration?

4. Point out the significance of the following statements, found at the start of paragraph 5: "I have been through it. I have friends who are going through it."

5. Write a sentence or two explaining why the title of this essay is effective.

SUGGESTION FOR WRITING ■   **Write a paper illustrating several characters who belong to some group—perhaps a fraternity, sorority, dormitory wing, or religious denomination— that you do. Make sure the general idea you wish to convey comes across clearly and arrange your illustrations in an effective order.**

MARK TWAIN

■ *Corn-Pone Opinions*

Samuel Langhorne Clemens (1835–1910), who later adopted the pen name Mark Twain, was born in Florida, Missouri, and grew up in the Mississippi River town of Hannibal, Missouri. After working as a printer, steamboat pilot, and western journalist, he turned to lecturing and fiction writing and soon achieved fame as a humorist. Today Twain is regarded as one of this country's foremost realistic writers and satirists. His reputation rests firmly on such works as The Adventures of Tom Sawyer *(1875),* The Prince and the Pauper *(1881),* The Adventures of Huckleberry Finn *(1884),* A Connecticut Yankee in King Arthur's Court *(1889), and* Life on the Mississippi *(1883), from which our selection comes. In this excerpt, Twain examines the way we form our opinions and finds it wanting.*

Fifty years ago, when I was a boy of fifteen and helping to inhabit a Missourian village on the banks of the Mississippi, I had a friend whose society was very dear to me because I was forbidden by my mother to partake of it. He   1

TEACHING STRATEGIES

1. This essay was published in 1923. You might have students discuss to what extent Twain's opinions are valid in the 1990s. The discussion might lead to an illustration essay.
2. Ask students to identify several examples of parallelism and discuss their effectiveness. Furthermore, depending on the sophistication of your class, you could have them comment on the distinguishing features of Twain's style.
3. Ask why Twain concludes with statements dripping with irony. The answer, of course, requires an understanding of the whole essay.

was a gay and impudent and satirical and delightful young black man—a slave—who daily preached sermons from the top of his master's woodpile, with me for sole audience. He imitated the pulpit style of the several clergymen of the village, and did it well, and with fine passion and energy. To me he was a wonder. I believed he was the greatest orator in the United States and would some day be heard from. But it did not happen; in the distribution of rewards he was overlooked. It is the way, in this world.

2   He interrupted his preaching, now and then, to saw a stick of wood; but the sawing was a pretense—he did it with his mouth; exactly imitating the sound the bucksaw makes in shrieking its way through the wood. But it served its purpose; it kept his master from coming out to see how the work was getting along. I listened to the sermons from the open window of a lumber room at the back of the house. One of his texts was this:

3   "You tell me whar a man gits his corn pone, en I'll tell you what his 'pinions is."

4   I can never forget it. It was deeply impressed upon me. By my mother. Not upon my memory, but elsewhere. She had slipped in upon me while I was absorbed and not watching. The black philosopher's idea was that a man is not independent, and cannot afford views which might interfere with his bread and butter. If he would prosper, he must train with the majority; in matters of large moment, like politics and religion, he must think and feel with the bulk of his neighbors, or suffer damage in his social standing and in his business prosperities. He must restrict himself to corn-pone opinions—at least on the surface. He must get his opinions from other people; he must reason out none for himself; he must have no first-hand views.

5   I think Jerry was right, in the main, but I think he did not go far enough.

6   1. It was his idea that a man conforms to the majority view of his locality by calculation and intention.

7   This happens, but I think it is not the rule.

8   2. It was his idea that there is such a thing as a first-hand opinion; an original opinion; an opinion which is coldly reasoned out in a man's head, by a searching analysis of the facts involved, with the heart unconsulted, and the jury room closed against outside influences. It may be that such an opinion has been born somewhere, at some time or other, but I suppose it got away before they could catch it and stuff it and put it in the museum.

9   I am persuaded that a coldly-thought-out and independent verdict upon a fashion in clothes, or manners, or literature, or politics, or religion, or any other matter that is projected into the field of our notice and interest, is a most rare thing—if it has indeed ever existed.

10   A new thing in costume appears—the flaring hoopskirt, for example—and the passers-by are shocked, and the irreverent laugh. Six months later everybody is reconciled; the fashion has established itself; it is admired, now, and no one laughs. Public opinion resented it before, public opinion accepts it now, and is happy in it. Why? Was the resentment reasoned out? Was the acceptance reasoned out? No. The instinct that moves to conformity did the work. It is our nature to conform; it is a force which not many can successfully resist. What is its seat? The inborn requirement of self-approval. We all have to bow to that; there

Illustration   **437**

are no exceptions. Even the woman who refuses from first to last to wear the hoopskirt comes under that law and is its slave; she could not wear the skirt and have her own approval; and that she *must* have, she cannot help herself. But as a rule our self-approval has its source in but one place and not elsewhere—the approval of other people. A person of vast consequences can introduce any kind of novelty in dress and the general world will presently adopt it—moved to do it, in the first place, by the natural instinct to passively yield to that vague something recognized as authority, and in the second place by the human instinct to train with the multitude and have its approval. An empress introduced the hoopskirt, and we know the result. A nobody introduced the bloomer, and we know the result. If Eve should come again, in her ripe renown, and reintroduce her quaint styles—well, we know what would happen. And we should be cruelly embarrassed, along at first.

The hoopskirt runs its course and disappears. Nobody reasons about it. 11 One woman abandons the fashion; her neighbor notices this and follows her lead; this influences the next woman; and so on and so on, and presently the skirt has vanished out of the world, no one knows how nor why, nor cares, for that matter. It will come again by and by and in due course will go again.

Twenty-five years ago, in England, six or eight wine glasses stood grouped 12 by each person's plate at a dinner party, and they were used, not left idle and empty; today there are but three or four in the group, and the average guest sparingly uses about two of them. We have not adopted this new fashion yet, but we shall do it presently. We shall not think it out; we shall merely conform, and let it go at that. We get our notions and habits and opinions from outside influences; we do not have to study them out.

Our table manners, and company manners, and street manners change 13 from time to time, but the changes are not reasoned out; we merely notice and conform. We are creatures of outside influences; as a rule we do not think, we only imitate. We cannot invent standards that will stick; what we mistake for standards are only fashions, and perishable. We may continue to admire them, but we drop the use of them. We notice this in literature. Shakespeare is a standard, and fifty years ago we used to write tragedies which we couldn't tell from—from somebody else's; but we don't do it any more, now. Our prose standard, three quarters of a century ago, was ornate and diffuse; some authority or other changed it in the direction of compactness and simplicity, and conformity followed, without argument. The historical novel starts up suddenly, and sweeps the land. Everybody writes one, and the nation is glad. We had historical novels before; but nobody read them, and the rest of us conformed—without reasoning it out. We are conforming in the other way, now, because it is another case of everybody.

The outside influences are always pouring in upon us, and we are always 14 obeying their orders and accepting their verdicts. The Smiths like the new play; the Joneses go to see it, and they copy the Smith verdict. Morals, religions, politics, get their following from surrounding influences and atmospheres, almost entirely; not from study, not from thinking. A man must and will have his own approval first of all, in each and every moment and circumstance of his life—even if he must repent of a self-approved act the moment after its commission, in

1. Twain notes, in paragraph 9, that ". . . a coldly-thought-out and independent verdict upon a fashion in clothes, or manners, or literature, or politics, or religion, or any other matter . . . is a most rare thing. . . ." Because no single example could illustrate the lack of independent thinking on all of these matters, a whole series of examples is required.

2. This essay has a nine-paragraph introduction that ends with Twain's thesis statement. This lengthy introduction allows Twain to present a detailed discussion of the character and views of his friend Jerry as well as to offer a criticism of the views that acts as a springboard for his own thoughts. At the time Twain wrote this essay, fashion favored a more leisurely style than is now in vogue. By conforming to the prevailing mode, Twain ironically and unintentionally lends support to his thesis.

3. Twain arranges his examples in a sequence that moves from trivial matters such as fashions in literature and clothing to more serious concerns—religion and political questions. This principle of presentation allows for some flexibility. Thus Twain might have reversed the order in which he discusses clothing and literature or religion and politics, but he could not logically have used an order intermingling trivial and serious concerns.

4. Twain is making the point that although he examined both questions carefully, he found no evidence that people arrived at their views concerning silver and tariffs through the exercise of logic.

order to get his self-approval *again:* but, speaking in general terms, a man's self-approval in the large concerns of life has its source in the approval of the peoples about him, and not in a searching personal examination of the matter. Mohammedans are Mohammedans because they are born and reared among the sect, not because they have thought it out and can furnish sound reasons for being Mohammedans; we know why Catholics are Catholics; why Presbyterians are Presbyterians; why Baptists are Baptists; why Mormons are Mormons; why thieves are thieves; why monarchists are monarchists; why Republicans are Republicans and Democrats, Democrats. We know it is a matter of association and sympathy, not reasoning and examination; that hardly a man in the world has an opinion upon morals, politics, or religion which he got otherwise than through his associations and sympathies. Broadly speaking, there are none but corn-pone opinions. And broadly speaking, corn-pone stands for self-approval. Self-approval is acquired mainly from the approval of other people. The result is conformity. Sometimes conformity has a sordid business interest—the bread-and-butter interest—but not in most cases. I think. I think that in the majority of cases it is unconscious and not calculated; that it is born of the human being's natural yearning to stand well with his fellows and have their inspiring approval and praise—a yearning which is commonly so strong and so insistent that it cannot be effectually resisted, and must have its way.

15   A political emergency brings out the corn-pone opinion in fine force in its two chief varieties—the pocketbook variety, which has its origin in self-interest, and the bigger variety, the sentimental variety—the one which can't bear to be outside the pale; can't bear to be in disfavor; can't endure the averted face and the cold shoulder; wants to stand well with his friends, wants to be smiled upon, wants to be welcome, wants to hear the precious words, *"He's on the right track!"* Uttered, perhaps by an ass, but still an ass of high degree, an ass whose approval is gold and diamonds to a smaller ass, and confers glory and honor and happiness, and membership in the herd. For these gauds many a man will dump his life-long principles into the street, and his conscience along with them. We have seen it happen. In some millions of instances.

16   Men think they think upon great political questions, and they do; but they think with their party, not independently; they read its literature, but not that of the other side; they arrive at convictions, but they are drawn from a partial view of the matter in hand and are of no particular value. They swarm with their party, they feel with their party, they are happy in their party's approval; and where the party leads they will follow, whether for right and honor, or through blood and dirt and a mush of mutilated morals.

17   In our late canvass half of the nation passionately believed that in silver lay salvation, the other half as passionately believed that that way lay destruction. Do you believe that a tenth part of the people, on either side, had any rational excuse for having an opinion about the matter at all? I studied that mighty question to the bottom—came out empty. Half of our people passionately believe in high tariff, the other half believe otherwise. Does this mean study and examination, or only feeling? The latter, I think. I have deeply studied that question, too—and didn't arrive. We all do no end of feeling, and we mistake it for thinking. And out

Illustration   **439**

of it we get an aggregation which we consider a boon. Its name is Public Opinion. It is held in reverence. It settles everything. Some think it the Voice of God.

DISCUSSION QUESTIONS ■

1. Why do you think Twain uses several examples rather than a single extended one?
2. What part of the essay constitutes the introduction? What is Twain's thesis?
3. Discuss the order in which Twain arranges his examples.
4. In paragraph 17, Twain says that after studying two important questions he "came out empty" and "didn't arrive." Explain what he means by these expressions.
5. How would you characterize the tone (see pages 245–248) of this essay? Refer to the text when answering.

SUGGESTION FOR WRITING ■   **Write a rebuttal to Twain by citing examples of friends and acquaintances who hold nonconformist views on such matters as religion, politics, family relationships, education, or recreation and who can rationally defend their positions.**

ELLEN GOODMAN

■ *The Company Man*

Ellen Goodman (born 1941) is a native of Massachusetts and a 1963 graduate of Radcliffe College. A journalist since graduation, she has worked as a researcher and reporter for Newsweek, *a feature writer for the* Detroit Free Press *and the* Boston Globe, *and a columnist for the Washington Post Writers Group, as well as a commentator on CBS Radio's* Spectrum *show and NBC-TV's* Today Show. *She has also contributed articles to* Ms., McCall's, *and the* Village Voice. *Book-length publications include* Turning Points *(1979) and two collections of newspaper columns,* Close to Home *(1979) and* At Large *(1981). In 1980, she received a Pulitzer Prize for commentary. Our selection, taken from* At Large, *depicts a workaholic whose total dedication to his job killed him.*

He worked himself to death, finally and precisely, at 3:00 A.M. Sunday morning.

The obituary didn't say that, of course. It said that he died of a coronary thrombosis—I think that was it—but everyone among his friends and acquain-

5. The tone of the essay reflects Twain's disillusionment with human beings. This attitude is perhaps most readily apparent in the thesis statement but finds expression at many other places in the essay. In paragraph 10, for example, Twain notes that "It is our nature to conform; it is a force which not many can successfully resist. What is its seat? The inborn requirement of self-approval. We all have to bow to that. . . ." In paragraph 13, he declares that "We cannot invent standards that will stick; what we mistake for standards are only fashions, and perishable." In paragraph 15, he declares that in order to avoid the stigma of being held in political disfavor, "a man will dump his life-long principles into the street, and his conscience along with them." And note the highly sarcastic words that end the essay.

PERSPECTIVE

Unlike the other writers in this section, Goodman uses a single extended example. Because her company man typifies the type A workaholic, no other examples are needed. The style is informal, the tone matter-of-fact, and because the topic does not lend itself to humor, there is none. The essay ends on an ironic note when Phil's boss, thinking about Phil's replacement, asks, "Who's been working the hardest?"

TEACHING STRATEGIES

1. Ask students to consider the whole essay and then comment on the curt statement at the end of paragraph 3.
2. Ask students to list the characteristics of a type B, or laid-back, personality. They might consider the person's approach to his or her job, family, recreation, and neighbors. This list could launch the writing suggestion that follows Goodman's essay.

tances knew it instantly. He was a perfect Type A, a workaholic, a classic, they said to each other and shook their heads—and thought for five or ten minutes about the way they lived.

3   This man who worked himself to death finally and precisely at 3:00 A.M. Sunday morning—on his day off—was fifty-one years old and a vice-president. He was, however, one of six vice-presidents, and one of three who might conceivably—if the president died or retired soon enough—have moved to the top spot. Phil knew that.

4   He worked six days a week, five of them until eight or nine at night, during a time when his own company had begun the four-day week for everyone but the executives. He worked like the Important People. He had no outside "extracurricular interests," unless, of course, you think about a monthly golf game that way. To Phil, it was work. He always ate egg salad sandwiches at his desk. He was, of course, overweight, by 20 to 25 pounds. He thought it was okay, though, because he didn't smoke.

5   On Saturdays, Phil wore a sports jacket to the office instead of a suit, because it was the weekend.

6   He had a lot of people working for him, maybe sixty, and most of them liked him most of the time. Three of them will be seriously considered for his job. The obituary didn't mention that.

7   But it did list his "survivors" quite accurately. He is survived by his wife, Helen, forty-eight years old, a good woman of no particular marketable skills, who worked in an office before marrying and mothering. She had, according to her daughter, given up trying to compete with his work years ago, when the children were small. A company friend said, "I know how much you will miss him." And she answered, "I already have."

8   "Missing him all these years," she must have given up part of herself which had cared too much for the man. She would be "well taken care of."

9   His "dearly beloved" eldest of the "dearly beloved" children is a hard-working executive in a manufacturing firm down South. In the day and a half before the funeral, he went around the neighborhood researching his father, asking the neighbors what he was like. They were embarrassed.

10   His second child is a girl, who is twenty-four and newly married. She lives near her mother and they are close, but whenever she was alone with her father, in a car driving somewhere, they had nothing to say to each other.

11   The youngest is twenty, a boy, a high-school graduate who has spent the last couple of years, like a lot of his friends, doing enough odd jobs to stay in grass and food. He was the one who tried to grab at his father, and tried to mean enough to him to keep the man at home. He was his father's favorite. Over the last two years, Phil stayed up nights worrying about the boy.

12   The boy once said, "My father and I only board here."

13   At the funeral, the sixty-year-old company president told the forty-eight-year-old widow that the fifty-one-year-old deceased had meant much to the company and would be missed and would be hard to replace. The widow didn't look him in the eye. She was afraid he would read her bitterness and, after all, she would need him to straighten out the finances—the stock options and all that.

Illustration   **441**

Phil was overweight and nervous and worked too hard. If he wasn't at the   14
office, he was worried about it. Phil was a Type A, a heart-attack natural. You
could have picked him out in a minute from a lineup.

So when he finally worked himself to death, at precisely 3:00 A.M. Sunday   15
morning, no one was really surprised.

By 5:00 P.M. the afternoon of the funeral, the company president had   16
begun, discreetly of course, with care and taste, to make inquiries about his
replacement. One of three men. He asked around: "Who's been working the
hardest?"

DISCUSSION QUESTIONS ■

1. Goodman says that Phil was "a perfect type A" (paragraph 2). After reflecting on her essay, explain the characteristics of this type.
2. Why do you think Goodman doesn't supply Phil's last name or the name of the company he works for?
3. What idea is Goodman trying to put across?
4. Unlike the essay by Thurber, Goodman's uses one longer illustration rather than several shorter ones. Why?
5. What is the significance of Phil's oldest son going "around the neighborhood researching his father, asking the neighbors what he was like" (paragraph 9)? Why were they embarrassed?
6. How do you account for Goodman's relatively short paragraphs?

SUGGESTION FOR WRITING ■   **Using one extended example, write an essay that illustrates the life-style of a laid-back employee or friend. Your paper need not, of course, feature a death.**

PERSPECTIVE

In making his classification, Berne almost totally ignores the largest category of humans, those who have "a fair mixture of brains, muscles, and inward organs." Why? Because his purpose is to acquaint readers with the personality quirks of three relatively uncommon types of individuals. Since the behavior patterns of the "mixture" category are more familiar, there is little need to discuss them.

Introduction: discusses development of three embryo layers	1

Body: paragraphs 2–14	2

Paragraphs 3–6: general characteristics, naming of three body types	3

Classification

ERIC BERNE

■ *Can People Be Judged by Their Appearance?*

Eric Berne (1910–1970) was born in Montreal, Quebec, and earned his medical degree at McGill University. Following graduation, he studied at the Yale Psychiatric Clinic and the New York Psychoanalytic Institute and became a U.S. citizen in 1943. During World War II, Berne served in the Army Medical Corps and later was a consultant to the Surgeon General. He also practiced psychiatry in New York and California. Berne was the author of several books on psychiatry, two of which, Games People Play *(1964) and* Layman's Guide to Psychiatry and Psychoanalysis *(1957, 1968), gained wide popular attention. In our selection, taken from the second edition of the latter book, Berne offers an explanation of why some people act the way they do.*

Everyone knows that a human being, like a chicken, comes from an egg. At a very early stage, the human embryo forms a three-layered tube, the inside layer of which grows into the stomach and lungs, the middle layer into bones, muscle, joints, and blood vessels, and the outside layer into the skin and nervous system.

Usually these three grow about equally, so that the average human being is a fair mixture of brains, muscles, and inward organs. In some eggs, however, one layer grows more than the others, and when the angels have finished putting the child together, he may have more gut than brain, or more brain than muscle. When this happens, the individual's activities will often be mostly with the overgrown layer.

We can thus say that while the average human being is a mixture, some people are mainly "digestion-minded," some "muscle-minded," and some "brain-minded," and correspondingly digestion-bodied, muscle-bodied, or brain-bodied. The digestion-bodied people look thick; the muscle-bodied people look wide; and the brain-bodied people look long. This does not mean the taller a man is the brainier he will be. It means that if a man, even a short man, looks long rather than wide or thick, he will often be more concerned about what goes on in his mind than about what he does or what he eats; but the key factor is slenderness and not height. On the other hand, a man who gives the impression of being thick rather than long or wide will usually be more interested in a good steak than in a good idea or a good long walk.

Medical men use Greek words to describe these types of body-build. For the man whose body shape mostly depends on the inside layer of the egg, they use the word *endomorph*. If it depends mostly upon the middle layer, they call him a *mesomorph*. If it depends upon the outside layer, they call him an *ectomorph*. We can see the same roots in our English words "enter," "medium," and "exit," which might just as easily have been spelled "ender," "mesium," and "ectit."   4

Since the inside skin of the human egg, or endoderm, forms the inner organs of the belly, the viscera, the endomorph is usually belly-minded; since the middle skin forms the body tissues, or soma, the mesomorph is usually muscle-minded; and since the outside skin forms the brain, or cerebrum, the ectomorph is usually brain-minded. Translating this into Greek, we have the viscerotonic endomorph, the somatotonic mesomorph, and the cerebrotonic ectomorph.   5

Words are beautiful things to a cerebrotonic, but a viscerotonic knows you cannot eat a menu no matter what language it is printed in, and a somatotonic knows you cannot increase your chest expansion by reading a dictionary. So it is advisable to leave these words and see what kinds of people they actually apply to, remembering again that most individuals are fairly equal mixtures and that what we have to say concerns only the extremes. Up to the present, these types have been thoroughly studied only in the male sex.   6

If a man is definitely a thick type rather than a broad or long type, he is likely to be round and soft, with a big chest but a bigger belly. He would rather eat than breathe comfortably. He is likely to have a wide face, short, thick neck, big thighs and upper arms, and small hands and feet. He has overdeveloped breasts and looks as though he were blown up a little like a balloon. His skin is soft and smooth, and when he gets bald, as he does usually quite early, he loses the hair in the middle of his head first.   7

> First category

The short, jolly, thickset, red-faced politician with a cigar in his mouth, who always looks as though he were about to have a stroke, is the best example of this type. The reason he often makes a good politician is that he likes people, banquets, baths, and sleep; he is easygoing, soothing, and his feelings are easy to understand.   8

His abdomen is big because he has lots of intestines. He likes to take in things. He likes to take in food, and affection and approval as well. Going to a banquet with people who like him is his idea of a fine time. It is important for a psychiatrist to understand the nature of such men when they come to him for advice.   9

If a man is definitely a broad type rather than a thick or long type, he is likely to be rugged and have lots of muscle. He is apt to have big forearms and legs, and his chest and belly are well formed and firm, with the chest bigger than the belly. He would rather breathe than eat. He has a bony head, big shoulders, and a square jaw. His skin is thick, coarse, and elastic, and tans easily. If he gets bald, it usually starts on the front of the head.   10

> Second category

Dick Tracy, Li'l Abner, and other men of action belong to this type. Such people make good lifeguards and construction workers. They like to put out   11 energy. They have lots of muscles, and they like to use them. They go in for adventure, exercise, fighting, and getting the upper hand. They are bold and unrestrained, and love to master the people and things around them. If the psychiatrist knows the things which give such people satisfaction, he is able to understand why they may be unhappy in certain situations.

| Third category | 12 |

The man who is definitely a long type is likely to have thin bones and muscles. His shoulders are apt to sag, and he has a flat belly with a dropped stomach, and long, weak legs. His neck and fingers are long, and his face is shaped like a long egg. His skin is thin, dry, and pale, and he rarely gets bald. He looks like an absent-minded professor and often is one.

13

Though such people are jumpy, they like to keep their energy and don't fancy moving around much. They would rather sit quietly by themselves and keep out of difficulties. Trouble upsets them, and they run away from it. Their friends don't understand them very well. They move jerkily and feel jerkily. The psychiatrist who understands how easily they become anxious is often able to help them get along better in the sociable and aggressive world of endomorphs and mesomorphs.

| Connection between body type, personality | 14 |

In the special cases where people definitely belong to one type or another, then, one can tell a good deal about their personalities from their appearance. When the human mind is engaged in one of its struggles with itself or with the world outside, the individual's way of handling the struggle will be partly determined by his type. If he is a viscerotonic he will often want to go to a party where he can eat and drink and be in good company at a time when he might be better off attending to business; the somatotonic will want to go out and do something about it, master the situation, even if what he does is foolish and not properly figured out, while the cerebrotonic will go off by himself and think it over, when perhaps he would be better off doing something about it or seeking good company to try to forget it.

| Conclusion: value of understanding three personalities | 15 |

Since these personality characteristics depend on the growth of the layers of the little egg from which the person developed, they are very difficult to change. Nevertheless, it is important for the individual to know about these types, so that he can have at least an inkling of what to expect from those around him, and can make allowances for the different kinds of human nature, and so that he can become aware of and learn to control his own tendencies, which may sometimes guide him into making the same mistakes over and over again in handling his difficulties.

DISCUSSION QUESTIONS

1. This essay is addressed to intelligent, well-educated lay people. The writing is relaxed, including figurative language ("when the angels have finished putting the child together"), homely phrasing ("He . . . looks as though he were blown up a little like a balloon," "His abdomen is big because he has lots of intestines"), and references to politicians, comic-strip characters, and absent-minded professors. The use of scientific

DISCUSSION QUESTIONS ∎

1. Even though Berne applies scientific labels to the three categories of people he discusses, the essay isn't written for scientists. What audience is Berne trying to reach? How do you know?

2. Point out the significance of the following sentence in paragraph 6: "So it is advisable to leave these words and see what kinds of people they actually apply to, remembering again that most individuals are fairly equal mixtures and that what we have to say concerns only the extremes."

3. In what order does Berne organize his categories? Would another order have worked as well? Why or why not?

4. How does Berne organize the discussion within each of his categories?

SUGGESTION FOR WRITING ■   **Write an essay that classifies your friends according to their political beliefs, taste in clothes, or preferences in movies.**

KATHLEEN FURY

■ *It's Only a Paper World*

Kathleen Fury (born 1941) is a native New Yorker and a graduate of Purdue University (1964). Since graduation Fury has worked as a writer and magazine editor. She has held editorships with Redbook, Ladies Home Journal, *and* Savvy, *and is currently a regular contributor to* Working Woman. *She is the author of a 1985 book,* Dear 60 Minutes. *In the essay we have chosen, Fury takes a lighthearted look at the different kinds of "paper pushers" in a modern office.*

Many experts claimed that the computer age heralded the advent of the paperless office. Clearly, this is not to be. If anything, offices are overwhelmed by even more paper, much of it now with sprocket holes. 1

Humankind is adapting, fortunately. According to the dictates of our varied individual natures, we have developed ways of coping with our changing ecosystem. 2

The beaver uses paper to build. It may not be exactly clear to observers just what she's building, but deep in her genetic code she knows. 3

On one side of the typical beaver's desk leans a foot-high stack of papers. Close by is a vertical file stuffed with bulging folders, some waving in the air, unable to touch bottom. In between, the beaver constructs a clever "dam" to prevent the entire structure from falling over: Her two-tier In/Out box supports the pile and allows movement of papers from one place to another. 4

Incredibly, to nonbeaver observers, the beaver has an uncanny ability to locate a two-month-old report buried within the pile. With deft precision, she can move her hand four millimeters down the pile and extract what she's looking for, confident that the dam will hold. 5

In this way, the beaver has evolved a protective mechanism that makes her invaluable within the organization, for nobody else, including her secretary, can find anything on her desk. When the beaver goes away on vacation, her department simply ceases work until she returns. She is thus assured that the cliché "nobody's indispensable" doesn't apply to her. 6

The squirrel's desk, by contrast, is barren. Throughout the year, in all kinds of weather, the squirrel energetically stores away what her brain tells her 7

---

terms is confined to paragraphs 4–6, after which these terms are abandoned in favor of terms like "thick type," "broad type," and "long type."

2. This sentence serves two purposes. First, it reminds us that most people don't fall into one of the three categories discussed in the essay. (This point is first mentioned in paragraph 2.) More important, it signals a shift from a general discussion of the three types to specific explanations and examples of each category.

3. He begins by describing the type of person that results when the inner layer of the embryo develops too much and ends by describing the type that develops when the outer layer develops too much. The progression is from physically oriented to mentally oriented people. It would seem disorganized to sandwich the mentally oriented type between the others.

4. The discussion begins with basic physical information about the type, offers examples, provides behaviorial information, and ends by pointing out the importance of the information to psychiatrists.

PERSPECTIVE

Like Thurber's "Courtship Through the Ages," this essay links humans and animals. Fury, however, compares humans to animals, while Thurber attributes human qualities to nonhuman creatures. Either approach helps achieve a comic effect. Some students may ask why many of Fury's paragraphs are so brief. Such paragraphs, of course, are common in newspapers and in articles appearing in magazines aimed at the mass market.

TEACHING STRATEGY

Fury's use of animal labels for her categories lends itself nicely to a writing assignment. Ask your class to evaluate, for example, the dress styles of their peers, teaching styles of their instructors, or shopping styles on display in a supermarket and then supply animal labels for different categories. Remind students not to become so absorbed in their labels that they lose sight of developing and planning their categories.

she may need someday. In her many file cabinets, drawers and bookcases she neatly stores memos, letters, printouts and receipts she believes will nourish her in the months and years to come.

8   Unlike her co-worker the beaver, the squirrel does not always know exactly where she has hidden a particular item. She knows she *has* it but is not skilled at remembering the exact location.

9   Like the maple tree, which produces enough seeds to reforest a continent, the squirrel illustrates nature's method of "overkill." By saving and storing everything, she increases her chance of retrieving something.

10   Of necessity, squirrels have developed the ability to move through a wide territorial range. When a squirrel moves on to another job, as she tends to do rather often due to lack of space, management must hire a special team of search-and-destroy experts to go through her files.

11   Nature's scavengers, her "clean-up crew," crows are regarded with wary admiration by squirrels and beavers, who recognize their contribution to keeping the corporate ecosystem tidy.

12   Crows are responsible for such paper-management advice as "Act on it—or throw it away." They are deeply drawn to paper shredders, trash compactors and outsized waste receptacles and will buy them if they happen to work in purchasing.

13   Crows belie the common epithet "birdbrained," for it has taken centuries of evolution to create a mind disciplined enough to know with certainty that it is OK to throw the CEO's Statement of Corporate Policy in the wastebasket after a glance.

14   Other species, who must adapt to the corporate food chain, quickly learn not to address any crow with a sentence that begins, "Do you have a copy of. . .?"

15   The clever bees are among the wonders of the corporate world. A bee neither hoards nor destroys paper; she redistributes it, moving from office to office as if between flowers.

16   Her methods are various and unpredictable, but there is no madness in them. Sometimes she arrives in an office with paper in hand and, distracting a colleague with conversation, simply leaves the paper inconspicuously on his desk. Sometimes she moves paper through seemingly legitimate channels, sending it through interoffice mail with ingenious notes like "Please look into this when you get a chance." More often, she employs the clever notation invented by bees, "FYI."

17   Whatever her method, she ensures that paper floats outward and does not return to her. Students of human behavior have come to call this cross-pollination "delegation," though to the bee it is simply a genetic imperative.

18   While others of the species hoard, distribute and destroy paper, the possum follows the evolutionary dictates of all marsupials and carries it with her.

19   Instead of a pouch, the office possum has a briefcase—in some cases, several. It is large and soft sided to accommodate her needs. Some possums, as an auxiliary system, carry handbags large enough to hold legal-size files. When a possum needs to retrieve paper, she goes not to a file cabinet or an In box but to her bags. She protects her paper by carrying it with her at all times—to her home, to the health club, to lunch.

Though she has no natural predators, the possum's habits create special 20
risks. She must spend considerable time at the lost-and-found department of
theaters and restaurants and knows by heart the telephone number of the taxi
commissioner. One of her arms is longer than the other.

But in nature, all things serve a purpose. And if the office burned down, the 21
lowly possum would be the sole possessor of the paper that is the raison d'être of
all the other animals.

DISCUSSION QUESTIONS ■

1. How would you explain the term "sprocket holes" in paragraph 1?

2. What does Fury mean in paragraph 17 when she refers to the bee's habit of distributing
   paper as a "genetic imperative"?

3. Speaking of the possum Fury says that "One of her arms is longer than the other"
   (paragraph 20). Why?

4. Point out the transitions that Fury uses to link her various categories.

5. Explain why you think Fury does or does not consider this to be a complete classification in which all categories are discussed.

6. Indicate why the concluding paragraph of the essay is effective.

7. Reflect on the essay and then suggest Fury's purpose in writing this classification.

SUGGESTION FOR WRITING ■   **Write an essay classifying
the members of some group that you encounter regularly. You
might, for example, classify the shoppers in a mall, the members
in a sports or entertainment group, or the members of your
church or synagogue.**

WILLIAM GOLDING

■ *Thinking as a Hobby*

*William Golding (born 1911) is a native of St. Columb Minor, Cornwall,
England, and a 1935 graduate of Brasenose College, Oxford, where he
received a B.A. Following graduation, he worked for a time in a settlement
house and as a teacher in a private school. After service in World War II,
Golding, who had previously produced a number of plays for the London
stage, became a full-time writer. Although his output includes poems, plays,
and essays, he is best known as a novelist, gaining particular fame for* Lord of
the Flies, *a novel depicting the descent into savagery of a group of shipwrecked English schoolboys. In 1983, his output earned him the Nobel Prize
for Literature. Our selection, which originally appeared in* Harper's, *distinguishes three levels of thinking and tells about Golding's relation to them.*

DISCUSSION QUESTIONS

1. "Sprocket holes" refer to
the perforated edges used to feed
the computer paper into a printer. With today's emphasis on
computer literacy, most students will be able to answer this
question.

2. Fury points out that in distributing paper from one desk to
another, the office bee is operating by instinct, much like her
insect counterpart who distrib-
utes pollen from flower to flower. Neither type can help itself.

3. Supposedly her arm has
been stretched by carrying paper
in one or more briefcases or
handbags.

4. Paragraph 7: "The squirrel's
desk, *by contrast.* . . ." Paragraph 11: ". . .crows are regarded with wary admiration by
squirrels and *beavers.* . . ."
Paragraph 15: "A bee neither
hoards [like the squirrel] nor
destroys [like the crow]. . . ."
Paragraph 18: "while others of
the species *hoard, distribute*
[like the bee] *and destroy.* . . ."

5. Fury probably intends her
essay to be a complete classification. "Humankind" in paragraph
2 suggests this as does "of all the
other animals" in paragraph 21.

6. By noting the relationship
between the possum and the
other office animals, Fury draws
all the elements of the essay together, giving it a sense of completeness.

7. Since offices today are
"overwhelmed" with paper, Fury
points out in humorous fashion
the ways that different types
handle this deluge.

PERSPECTIVE

Golding uses urbane, ironic
humor as a vehicle for making a
serious and disturbing observation: that only a very few individuals are capable of the highest
form of thought, which seeks to
answer the question "What is
truth?" To help make his case,
Golding offers several examples
of the different grades of thinkers as well as anecdotes that
characterize them. Golding's
humor, cutting when directed at
grade-three   and   grade-two

thinkers, turns gentle as he narrates his encounter with Einstein and then regains its sharpness as he considers his own efforts at grade-one thinking. This experience points up an important truth about grade-one thinking: its capacity, because of its originality, to alienate those who are comfortable with established institutions and beliefs.

TEACHING STRATEGY

Ask how many students have had teachers who taught them to think. Encourage students to discuss their answers. Such a discussion could lead to the Suggestion for Writing at the end of this essay.

CLASSROOM ACTIVITY

Divide students into small groups and have them exchange ideas about types of thinkers they have known. Ask them to characterize each type with appropriate examples. This activity might culminate in a classification essay.

1   While I was still a boy, I came to the conclusion that there were three grades of thinking; and since I was later to claim thinking as my hobby, I came to an even stranger conclusion—namely, that I myself could not think at all.

2   I must have been an unsatisfactory child for grownups to deal with. I remember how incomprehensible they appeared to me at first, but not, of course, how I appeared to them. It was the headmaster of my grammar school who first brought the subject of thinking before me—though neither in the way, nor with the results he intended. He had some statuettes in his study. They stood on a high cupboard behind his desk. One was a lady wearing nothing but a bath towel. She seemed frozen in an eternal panic lest the bath towel slip down any farther; and since she had no arms, she was in an unfortunate position to pull the towel up again. Next to her, crouched the statuette of a leopard, ready to spring down at the top drawer of a filing cabinet labeled A–AH. My innocence interpreted this as the victim's last, despairing cry. Beyond the leopard was a naked, muscular gentleman, who sat, looking down, with his chin on his fist and his elbow on his knee. He seemed utterly miserable.

3   Some time later, I learned about these statuettes. The headmaster had placed them where they could face delinquent children, because they symbolized to him the whole of life. The naked lady was the Venus of Milo. She was Love. She was not worried about the towel. She was just busy being beautiful. The leopard was Nature, and he was being natural. The naked, muscular gentleman was not miserable. He was Rodin's Thinker, an image of pure thought. It is easy to buy small plaster models of what you think life is like.

4   I had better explain that I was a frequent visitor to the headmaster's study, because of the latest thing I had done or left undone. As we now say, I was not integrated. I was, if anything, disintegrated; and I was puzzled. Grownups never made sense. Whenever I found myself in a penal position before the headmaster's desk, with the statuettes glimmering whitely above him, I would sink my head, clasp my hands behind my back and writhe one shoe over the other.

5   The headmaster would look opaquely at me through flashing spectacles.

6   "What are we going to do with you?"

7   Well, what *were* they going to do with me? I would writhe my shoe some more and stare down at the worn rug.

8   "Look up, boy! Can't you look up?"

9   Then I would look up at the cupboard, where the naked lady was frozen in her panic and the muscular gentleman contemplated the hindquarters of the leopard in endless gloom. I had nothing to say to the headmaster. His spectacles caught the light so that you could see nothing human behind them. There was no possibility of communication.

10   "Don't you ever think at all?"

11   No, I didn't think, wasn't thinking, couldn't think—I was simply waiting in anguish for the interview to stop.

12   "Then you'd better learn—hadn't you?"

13   On one occasion the headmaster leaped to his feet, reached up and plonked Rodin's masterpiece on the desk before me.

14   "That's what a man looks like when he's really thinking."

I surveyed the gentleman without interest or comprehension.   15

"Go back to your class."   16

Clearly there was something missing in me. Nature had endowed the rest   17
of the human race with a sixth sense and left me out. This must be so, I mused,
on my way back to the class, since whether I had broken a window, or failed to
remember Boyle's Law, or been late for school, my teachers produced me one,
adult answer: "Why can't you think?"

As I saw the case, I had broken the window because I had tried to hit Jack   18
Arney with a cricket ball and missed him; I could not remember Boyle's Law
because I had never bothered to learn it; and I was late for school because I
preferred looking over the bridge into the river. In fact, I was wicked. Were my
teachers, perhaps, so good that they could not understand the depths of my
depravity? Were they clear, untormented people who could direct their every
action by this mysterious business of thinking? The whole thing was incomprehensible. In my earlier years, I found even the statuette of the Thinker
confusing. I did not believe any of my teachers were naked, ever. Like someone
born deaf, but bitterly determined to find out about sound, I watched my teachers
to find out about thought.

There was Mr. Houghton. He was always telling me to think. With a   19
modest satisfaction, he would tell me that he had thought a bit himself. Then why
did he spend so much time drinking? Or was there more sense in drinking than
there appeared to be? But if not, and if drinking were in fact ruinous to health—
and Mr. Houghton was ruined, there was no doubt about that—why was he
always talking about the clean life and the virtues of fresh air? He would spread
his arms wide with the action of a man who habitually spent his time striding
along mountain ridges.

"Open air does me good, boys—I know it!"   20

Sometimes, exalted by his own oratory, he would leap from his desk and   21
hustle us outside into a hideous wind.

"Now, boys! Deep breaths! Feel it right down inside you—huge draughts of   22
God's good air!"

He would stand before us, rejoicing in his perfect health, an open-air man.   23
He would put his hands on his waist and take a tremendous breath. You could
hear the wind, trapped in the cavern of his chest and struggling with all the
unnatural impediments. His body would reel with shock and his ruined face go
white at the unaccustomed visitation. He would stagger back to his desk and
collapse there, useless for the rest of the morning.

Mr. Houghton was given to high-minded monologues about the good life,   24
sexless and full of duty. Yet in the middle of one of these monologues, if a girl
passed the window, tapping along on her neat little feet, he would interrupt his
discourse, his neck would turn itself and he would watch her out of sight. In this
instance, he seemed to me ruled not by thought but by an invisible and irresistible spring in his nape.

His neck was an object of great interest to me. Normally it bulged a bit over   25
his collar. But Mr. Houghton had fought in the First World War alongside both
Americans and French, and had come—by who knows what illogic?—to a settled

detestation of both countries. If either happened to be prominent in current affairs, no argument could make Mr. Houghton think well of it. He would bang the desk, his neck would bulge still further and go red. "You can say what you like," he would cry, "but I've thought about this—and I know what I think!

26   Mr. Houghton thought with his neck.

27   There was Miss Parsons. She assured us that her dearest wish was our welfare, but I knew even then, with the mysterious clairvoyance of childhood, that what she wanted most was the husband she never got. There was Mr. Hands—and so on.

28   I have dealt at length with my teachers because this was my introduction to the nature of what is commonly called thought. Through them I discovered that thought is often full of unconscious prejudice, ignorance and hypocrisy. It will lecture on disinterested purity while its neck is being remorselessly twisted toward a skirt. Technically, it is about as proficient as most businessmen's golf, as honest as most politicians' intentions, or—to come near my own preoccupation—as coherent as most books that get written. It is what I came to call grade-three thinking, though more properly, it is feeling, rather than thought.

29   True, often there is a kind of innocence in prejudices, but in those days I viewed grade-three thinking with an intolerant contempt and an incautious mockery. I delighted to confront a pious lady who hated the Germans with the proposition that we should love our enemies. She taught me a great truth in dealing with grade-three thinkers; because of her, I no longer dismiss lightly a mental process which for nine-tenths of the population is the nearest they will ever get to thought. They have immense solidarity. We had better respect them, for we are outnumbered and surrounded. A crowd of grade-three thinkers, all shouting the same thing, all warming their hands at the fire of their own prejudices, will not thank you for pointing out the contradictions in their beliefs. Man is a gregarious animal, and enjoys agreement as cows will graze all the same way on the side of a hill.

30   Grade-two thinking is the detection of contradictions. I reached grade-two when I trapped the poor, pious lady. Grade-two thinkers do not stampede easily, though often they fall into the other fault and lag behind. Grade-two thinking is a withdrawal, with eyes and ears open. It became my hobby and brought satisfaction and loneliness in either hand. For grade-two thinking destroys without having the power to create. It set me watching the crowds cheering His Majesty and King and asking myself what all the fuss was about, without giving me anything positive to put in the place of that heady patriotism. But there were compensations. To hear people justify their habit of hunting foxes and tearing them to pieces by claiming that the foxes liked it. To hear our Prime Minister talk about the great benefit we conferred on India by jailing people like Pandit Nehru and Gandhi. To hear American politicians talk about peace in one sentence and refuse to join the League of Nations in the next. Yes, there were moments of delight.

31   But I was growing toward adolescence and had to admit that Mr. Houghton was not the only one with an irresistible spring in his neck. I, too, felt the compulsive hand of nature and began to find that pointing out contradiction

could be costly as well as fun. There was Ruth, for example, a serious and attractive girl. I was an atheist at the time. Grade-two thinking is a menace to religion and knocks down sects like skittles. I put myself in a position to be converted by her with an hypocrisy worthy of grade three. She was a Methodist— or at least, her parents were, and Ruth had to follow suit. But, alas, instead of relying on the Holy Spirit to convert me, Ruth was foolish enough to open her pretty mouth in argument. She claimed that the Bible (King James Version) was literally inspired. I countered by saying that the Catholics believed in the literal inspiration of Saint Jerome's *Vulgate*,[1] and the two books were different. Argument flagged.

At last she remarked that there were an awful lot of Methodists, and they couldn't be wrong, could they—not all those millions? That was too easy, said I restively (for the nearer you were to Ruth, the nicer she was to be near to) since there were more Roman Catholics than Methodists anyway; and they couldn't be wrong, could they—not all those hundreds of millions? An awful flicker of doubt appeared in her eyes. I slid my arm around her waist and murmured breathlessly that if we were counting heads, the Buddhists were the boys for my money. But Ruth had *really* wanted to do me good, because I was so nice. She fled. The combination of my arm and those countless Buddhists was too much for her.   32

That night her father visited my father and left, red-cheeked and indignant. I was given the third degree to find out what had happened. It was lucky we were both of us only fourteen. I lost Ruth and gained an undeserved reputation as a potential libertine.   33

So grade-two thinking could be dangerous. It was in this knowledge, at the age of fifteen, that I remember making a comment from the heights of grade two, on the limitations of grade three. One evening I found myself alone in the school hall, preparing it for a party. The door of the headmaster's study was open. I went in. The headmaster had ceased to thump Rodin's Thinker down on the desk as an example to the young. Perhaps he had not found any more candidates, but the statuettes were still there, glimmering and gathering dust on top of the cupboard. I stood on a chair and rearranged them. I stood Venus in her bath towel on the filing cabinet, so that now the top drawer caught its breath in a gasp of sexy excitement. "A-ah!" The portentous Thinker I placed on the edge of the cupboard so that he looked down at the bath towel and waited for it to slip.   34

Grade-two thinking, though it filled life with fun and excitement, did not make for content. To find out the deficiencies of our elders bolsters the young ego but does not make for personal security. I found that grade two was not only the power to point out contradictions. It took the swimmer some distance from the shore and left him there, out of his depth. I decided that Pontius Pilate was a typical grade-two thinker. "What is truth?" he said, a very common grade-two thought, but one that is used always as the end of an argument instead of the beginning. There is still a higher grade of thought which says, "What is truth?" and sets out to find it.   35

But these grade-one thinkers were few and far between. They did not visit my grammar school in the flesh though they were there in books. I aspired to   36

[1]A fourth-century Latin Bible regarded as authoritative by the Roman Catholic Church.

37

38

DISCUSSION QUESTIONS

1. Golding's teachers, supposedly good thinkers, actually set bad examples of thinking; but Golding, being a boy and imagining that they were really thinking, compared them to himself and decided he really wasn't thinking.

2. The Venus of Milo, as Golding indicates, represents love, an emotion. It can therefore also be taken to represent an aspect of grade-three thinking, which, in Golding's words, "is feeling, rather than thought." The Leopard, a beast of prey, symbolizes grade-two thinking, whose practitioners hunt down and attack contradictions in the thinking of others. The "naked muscular gentleman . . . with his chin on his fist and his elbow on his knee" represents grade-one thinking, the type that seeks to discover truth and thus involves contemplation.

3. This statement reflects Golding's contempt for grade-three thinkers, whose need to band together and share sets of prejudices makes them the human equivalent of cows grazing in the same direction. Human beings are of course not cows but members of highly complex societies who must hold certain beliefs in common if the societies are to survive. Some students, recognizing this, may reject Golding's position as too extreme.

them, partly because I was ambitious and partly because I now saw my hobby as an unsatisfactory thing if it went no further. If you set out to climb a mountain, however high you climb, you have failed if you cannot reach the top.

I *did* meet an undeniably grade-one thinker in my first year at Oxford. I was looking over a small bridge in Magdalen Deer Park, and a tiny mustached and hatted figure came and stood by my side. He was a German who had just fled from the Nazis to Oxford as a temporary refuge. His name was Einstein.

But Professor Einstein knew no English at that time and I knew only two words of German. I beamed at him, trying wordlessly to convey by my bearing all the affection and respect that the English felt for him. It is possible—and I have to make the admission—that I felt here were two grade-one thinkers standing side by side; yet I doubt if my face conveyed more than a formless awe. I would have given my Greek and Latin and French and a good slice of my English for enough German to communicate. But we were divided; he was as inscrutable as my headmaster. For perhaps five minutes we stood together on the bridge, undeniable grade-one thinker and breathless aspirant. With true greatness, Professor Einstein realized that my contact was better than none. He pointed to a trout wavering in midstream.

He spoke: *"Fisch."*

My brain reeled. Here I was, mingling with the great, and yet helpless as the veriest grade-three thinker. Desperately I sought for some sign by which I might convey that I, too, revered pure reason. I nodded vehemently. In a brilliant flash I used up half of my German vocabulary.

"Fisch. Ja Ja."

For perhaps another five minutes we stood side by side. Then Professor Einstein, his whole figure still conveying good will and amiability, drifted away out of sight.

I, too, would be a grade-one thinker. I was irreverent at the best of times. Political and religious systems, social customs, loyalties and traditions, they all came tumbling down like so many rotten apples off a tree. This was a fine hobby and a sensible substitute for cricket, since you could play it all the year round. I came up in the end with what must always remain the justification for grade-one thinking, its sign, seal and charter. I devised a coherent system for living. It was a moral system, which was wholly logical. Of course, as I readily admitted, conversion of the world to my way of thinking might be difficult, since my system did away with a number of trifles, such as big business, centralized government, armies, marriage. . .

It was Ruth all over again. I had some very good friends who stood by me, and still do. But my acquaintances vanished, taking the girls with them. Young women seemed oddly contented with the world as it was. They valued the meaningless ceremony with a ring. Young men, while willing to concede the chaining sordidness of marriage, were hesitant about abandoning the organizations which they hoped would give them a career. A young man on the first rung of the Royal Navy, while perfectly agreeable to doing away with big business and marriage, got as rednecked as Mr. Houghton when I proposed a world without any battleships in it.

Had the game gone too far? Was it a game any longer? In those prewar days, I stood to lose a great deal, for the sake of a hobby.

Now you are expecting me to describe how I saw the folly of my ways and came back to the warm nest, where prejudices are so often called loyalties, where pointless actions are hallowed into custom by repetition, where we are content to say we think when all we do is feel.

But you would be wrong. I dropped my hobby and turned professional.

If I were to go back to the headmaster's study and find the dusty statuettes still there, I would arrange them differently. I would dust Venus and put her aside, for I have come to love her and know her for the fair thing she is. But I would put the Thinker, sunk in his desperate thought, where there were shadows before him—and at his back, I would put the leopard, crouched and ready to spring.

DISCUSSION QUESTIONS ■

1. As a boy, Golding concluded that he could not think at all (paragraph 1). Why?

2. Golding refers several times to the three statuettes in the headmaster's study. Explain the connection between these statuettes and the three grades of thinking.

3. At the end of paragraph 29, Golding asserts that "Man is a gregarious animal, and enjoys agreement as cows will graze all the same way on the side of a hill." Explain how this statement illustrates Golding's attitude toward grade-three thinking. Do you think the statement is effective? Why or why not?

4. Golding cites several specific examples of his own grade-two thinking in paragraph 30. What are these examples? Why are they effective?

5. Discuss the significance of Golding's encounter with Einstein. Explain why you think the encounter took place on a bridge.

6. In paragraph 48 Golding notes that he would arrange the statuettes differently. Explain how this altered arrangement reflects Golding's attitude toward the three types of thinking.

SUGGESTION FOR WRITING ■   Write an essay classifying your instructors or fellow students.

LEWIS THOMAS

■ *The Technology of Medicine*

Lewis Thomas (born 1913) has won widespread recognition as one of our most perceptive writers on medical topics. A native of Flushing, New York, he earned his medical degree at Harvard (1937) and then held positions as a

4. [45] [46] Golding was indulging in grade-two thinking when he looked askance at the crowds cheering the king, the people justifying fox hunting, the prime minister supporting the jailing of Indian dissidents, and American politicians talking about [47] [48] peace while rejecting membership in an organization designed to promote it. These illustrations are necessary to show what grade-two thinking is. Students should understand that illustrations help readers grasp abstract concepts.

5. Einstein is a grade-one thinker—the type Golding admires most. His admiration for Einstein is shown by his statement that "I would have given my Greek and Latin and French and a good slice of my English for enough German to communicate." The bridge—bridges are common symbols of transition—suggests the transition that Golding will undergo, from grade-two to grade-one thinker. Golding's desire to make the shift is apparent in his statement that he was a "breathless aspirant" for the new rank.

6. Golding's final arrangement of the statuettes reflects certain changes in their symbolic significance. The Venus of Milo, once suggestive both of grade-three thinking and of love, now appears to represent only love, something apart from thinking on any level. This separateness is shown in Golding's separation of the Venus from the other statuettes. Rodin's Thinker still represents grade-one thinking, but the leopard at his back now appears to represent both third- and second-grade thinkers, whose practitioners are prone to attack original thinking wherever it surfaces. You might in this connection point out that symbols often undergo changes in meaning.

pathologist and medical administrator at several universities. In 1973, he became president of the Sloan-Kettering Cancer Center in New York. In 1971, he started writing a column called "Notes of a Biology Watcher" for the New England Journal of Medicine. *These contributions became very popular, and in 1974 were collected in a book,* The Lives of a Cell: Notes of a Biology Watcher, *which won the National Book Award. A second collection of columns from the same journal,* The Medusa and the Snail: Further Notes of a Biology Watcher, *appeared in 1979. Most recent books include the autobiographical* The Youngest Science: Notes of a Medical Watcher *(1983) and* Late Night Thoughts on Listening to Mahler's Ninth Symphony *(1983). In our selection, originally published in the* New England Journal of Medicine, *Thomas classifies and evaluates three categories of medical technology.*

1   Technology assessment has become a routine exercise for the scientific enterprises on which the country is obliged to spend vast sums for its needs. Brainy committees are continually evaluating the effectiveness and cost of doing various things in space, defense, energy, transportation, and the like, to give advice about prudent investments for the future.

2   Somehow medicine, for all the $80-odd billion that it is said to cost the nation, has not yet come in for much of this analytical treatment. It seems taken for granted that the technology of medicine simply exists, take it or leave it, and the only major technologic problem which policy-makers are interested in is how to deliver today's kind of health care, with equity, to all the people.

3   When, as is bound to happen sooner or later, the analysts get around to the technology of medicine itself, they will have to face the problem of measuring the relative cost and effectiveness of all the things that are done in the management of disease. They make their living at this kind of thing, and I wish them well, but I imagine they will have a bewildering time. For one thing, our methods of managing disease are constantly changing—partly under the influence of new bits of information brought in from all corners of biologic science. At the same time, a great many things are done that are not so closely related to science, some not related at all.

4   In fact, there are three quite different levels of technology in medicine, so unlike each other as to seem altogether different undertakings. Practitioners of medicine and the analysts will be in trouble if they are not kept separate.

5   1. First of all, there is a large body of what might be termed "nontechnology," impossible to measure in terms of its capacity to alter either the natural course of disease or its eventual outcome. A great deal of money is spent on this. It is valued highly by the professionals as well as the patients. It consists of what is sometimes called "supportive therapy." It tides patients over through diseases that are not, by and large, understood. It is what is meant by the phrases "caring for" and "standing by." It is indispensable. It is not, however, a technology in any real sense, since it does not involve measures directed at the underlying mechanism of disease.

6   It includes the large part of any good doctor's time that is taken up with simply providing reassurance, explaining to patients who fear that they have

contracted one or another lethal disease that they are, in fact, quite healthy.

It is what physicians used to be engaged in at the bedside of patients with   7
diphtheria, meningitis, poliomyelitis, lobar pneumonia, and all the rest of the
infectious diseases that have since come under control.

It is what physicians must now do for patients with intractable cancer,   8
severe rheumatoid arthritis, multiple sclerosis, stroke, and advanced cirrhosis.
One can think of at least twenty major diseases that require this kind of
supportive medical care because of the absence of an effective technology. I would
include a large amount of what is called mental disease, and most varieties of
cancer, in this category.

The cost of this nontechnology is very high, and getting higher all the   9
time. It requires not only a great deal of time but also very hard effort and skill on
the part of physicians; only the very best of doctors are good at coping with this
kind of defeat. It also involves long periods of hospitalization, lots of nursing, lots
of involvement of nonmedical professionals in and out of the hospital. It represents, in short, a substantial segment of today's expenditures for health.

2. At the next level up is a kind of technology best termed "halfway   10
technology." This represents the kinds of things that must be done after the fact,
in efforts to compensate for the incapacitating effects of certain diseases whose
course one is unable to do very much about. It is a technology designed to make
up for disease, or to postpone death.

The outstanding examples in recent years are the transplantations of   11
hearts, kidneys, livers, and other organs, and the equally spectacular inventions
of artificial organs. In the public mind, this kind of technology has come to seem
like the equivalent of the high technologies of the physical sciences. The media
tend to present each new procedure as though it represented a breakthrough and
therapeutic triumph, instead of the makeshift that it really is.

In fact, this level of technology is, by its nature, at the same time highly   12
sophisticated and profoundly primitive. It is the kind of thing that one must
continue to do until there is a genuine understanding of the mechanisms
involved in disease. In chronic glomerulonephritis, for example, a much clearer
insight will be needed into the events leading to the destruction of glomeruli by
the immunologic reactants that now appear to govern this disease, before one
will know how to intervene intelligently to prevent the process, or turn it around.
But when this level of understanding has been reached, the technology of kidney
replacement will not be much needed and should no longer pose the huge
problems of logistics, cost, and ethics that it poses today.

An extremely complex and costly technology for the management of   13
coronary heart disease has evolved—involving specialized ambulances and hospital units, all kinds of electronic gadgetry, and whole platoons of new professional
personnel—to deal with the end results of coronary thrombosis. Almost everything offered today for the treatment of heart disease is at this level of technology,
with the transplanted and artificial hearts as ultimate examples. When enough
has been learned to know what really goes wrong in heart disease, one ought to
be in a position to figure out ways to prevent or reverse the process, and when
this happens the current elaborate technology will probably be set to one side.

14   Much of what is done in the treatment of cancer, by surgery, irradiation, and chemotherapy, represents halfway technology, in the sense that these measures are directed at the existence of already established cancer cells, but not at the mechanisms by which cells become neoplastic.

15   It is a characteristic of this kind of technology that it costs an enormous amount of money and requires a continuing expansion of hospital facilities. There is no end to the need for new, highly trained people to run the enterprise. And there is really no way out of this, at the present state of knowledge. If the installation of specialized coronary-care units can result in the extension of life for only a few patients with coronary disease (and there is no question that this technology is effective in a few cases), it seems to me an inevitable fact of life that as many of these as can be will be put together, and as much money as can be found will be spent. I do not see that anyone has much choice in this. The only thing that can move medicine away from this level of technology is new information, and the only imaginable source of this information is research.

16   3. The third type of technology is the kind that is so effective that it seems to attract the least public notice; it has come to be taken for granted. This is the genuinely decisive technology of modern medicine, exemplified best by modern methods of immunization against diphtheria, pertussis, and the childhood virus diseases, and the contemporary use of antibiotics and chemotherapy for bacterial infections. The capacity to deal effectively with syphilis and tuberculosis represents a milestone in human endeavor, even though full use of this potential has not yet been made. And there are, of course, other examples: the treatment of endocrinologic disorders with appropriate hormones, the prevention of hemolytic disease of the newborn, the treatment and prevention of various nutritional disorders, and perhaps just around the corner the management of Parkinsonism and sickle-cell anemia. There are other examples, and everyone will have his favorite candidates for the list, but the truth is that there are nothing like as many as the public has been led to believe.

17   The point to be made about this kind of technology—the real high technology of medicine—is that it comes as the result of a genuine understanding of disease mechanisms, and when it becomes available, it is relatively inexpensive, and relatively easy to deliver.

18   Offhand, I cannot think of any important human disease for which medicine possesses the outright capacity to prevent or cure where the cost of the technology is itself a major problem. The price is never as high as the cost of managing the same diseases during the earlier stages of no-technology or halfway technology. If a case of typhoid fever had to be managed today by the best methods of 1935, it would run to a staggering expense. At, say, around fifty days of hospitalization, requiring the most demanding kind of nursing care, with the obsessive concern for details of diet that characterized the therapy of that time, with daily laboratory monitoring, and, on occasion, surgical intervention for abdominal catastrophe, I should think $10,000 would be a conservative estimate for the illness, as contrasted with today's cost of a bottle of chloramphenicol and a day or two of fever. The halfway technology that was evolving for poliomyelitis in the early 1950s, just before the emergence of the basic research that made the vaccine possible, provides another illustration of the point. Do you remember

DISCUSSION QUESTIONS

1. Paragraphs 1 and 2 contrast the amount of technology assessment carried out in nonmedical scientific disciplines and in medicine. Paragraph 3 points out the difficulties that analysts will face when they do cope with the technology of medicine. Thomas uses the "funnel technique" to ease his readers into the categories.

2. The categories are arranged according to the level of technology involved in each, from the lowest level to the highest, from the least effective to the most effective. This is the most logical arrangement for Thomas to use. If he had begun by discussing the most highly technical category, everything following that discussion would have seemed anticlimactic. Furthermore, since Thomas ends with a plea for giving priority to the third category, it is logical that his discussion should lead up to that category.

3. In each case, Thomas begins by explaining and illustrating what he means by that level of technology and then moves to consider its costs.

4. Halfway technology involves no understanding of underlying disease mechanisms and is very costly. High technology is based on an understanding of disease mechanisms and is relatively inexpensive as well as relatively easy to administer.

Sister Kenny, and the cost of those institutes for rehabilitation, with all those ceremonially applied hot fomentations, and the debates about whether the affected limbs should be totally immobilized or kept in passive motion as frequently as possible, and the masses of statistically tormented data mobilized to support one view or the other? It is the cost of that kind of technology, and its relative effectiveness, that must be compared with the cost and effectiveness of the vaccine.

Pulmonary tuberculosis had similar episodes in its history. There was a sudden enthusiasm for the surgical removal of infected lung tissue in the early 1950s, and elaborate plans were being made for new and expensive installations for major pulmonary surgery in tuberculosis hospitals, and then INH and streptomycin came along and the hospitals themselves were closed up. 19

It is when physicians are bogged down by their incomplete technologies, by the innumerable things they are obliged to do in medicine when they lack a clear understanding of disease mechanisms, that the deficiencies of the health-care system are most conspicuous. If I were a policy-maker, interested in saving money for health care over the long haul, I would regard it as an act of high prudence to give high priority to a lot more basic research in biologic science. This is the only way to get the full mileage that biology owes to the science of medicine, even though it seems, as used to be said in the days when the phrase still had some meaning, like asking for the moon. 20

5. Basic research in biological science will allow scientists to discover the basic mechanisms underlying various diseases and to develop medicines—antibiotics, hormones, and the like—that will interrupt the mechanisms and thus stop the disease. Doing this will eliminate the need for and the expenses of the first two categories.

6. As the headnote indicates, this essay originally appeared in the *New England Journal of Medicine*, so obviously physicians form the audience. Nevertheless, Thomas uses language that an educated lay audience could easily understand. Generally, he cites diseases and illnesses with which such readers are familiar—diphtheria, arthritis, multiple sclerosis, coronary thrombosis—and he avoids complex medical terminology.

DISCUSSION QUESTIONS ■

1. Thomas classifies three different degrees of medical technology, yet he doesn't start to deal with these categories until paragraph 4. Why?
2. Discuss the arrangement of the categories in this essay. What is the basis for the arrangement? Why is this arrangement the most logical choice?
3. Study the discussions *within* each of the three categories, and then point out what type of information Thomas includes and the order in which he presents it.
4. What are the differences between "halfway technology" and "the real high technology"?
5. Why would Thomas "give high priority to a lot more basic research in biologic science" (paragraph 20)?
6. What audience do you think Thomas is trying to reach? Explain your answer.

OVERVIEW OF COMPARISON ESSAYS (pp. 458–470)

Four of the essays in this section are comparisons, and one is an analogy. Three comparisons are organized according to the alternating pattern. Two of them focus entirely on differences, and the other, while primarily concerned with differences, devotes some attention to similarities. The remaining comparison uses the block pattern and deals entirely with differences. Like all analogies, ours calls attention to the similarities that underlie two seemingly dissimilar things. In it, the writer likens the passage of grief to the return to a house that has withstood a cruel winter. One essay combines informal and colloquial diction, two fall into the formal–informal category, and two use devices like descriptive language, parallelism, and rhythmic sentences to give the writing a formal cast.

SUGGESTION FOR WRITING ■ **Write an essay classifying the levels of expertise in some profession or trade you know about. For example, you might classify the workers in a dental office, the nursing personnel in a hospital, the employees in an accounting department, or the personnel in a law firm.**

Comparison

BRUCE CATTON

■ *Grant and Lee: A Study in Contrasts*

Title sets up differences

Bruce Catton (1899–1978) was a nationally recognized expert on the Civil War. Born in Petoskey, Michigan, he attended Oberlin College, then worked as a reporter for several large newspapers. Between 1942 and 1948, he held several positions in the U.S. government, and then became an editor of American Heritage *magazine. His first book on the Civil War,* Mr. Lincoln's Army, *appeared in 1951 and was followed by* Glory Road *(1952) and* A Stillness at Appomattox *(1953). This last book won the Pulitzer Prize and the National Book Award and established Catton's reputation as a Civil War historian. In the years that followed, Catton continued to write other books on the Civil War, including a centennial trilogy:* The Coming Fury *(1961),* Terrible Swift Sword *(1962), and* Never Call Retreat *(1965). In 1972, he published the autobiographical* Waiting for the Morning Train: An American Boyhood *and followed it two years later with* Michigan: A Bicentennial History. *Our Catton selection comes from a collection of essays by eminent historians. In it, Catton points out differences as well as similarities in the two foremost military adversaries of the Civil War.*

Introduction: paragraphs
1–3; background;
significance of following
contrasts

1   When Ulysses S. Grant and Robert E. Lee met in the parlor of a modest house at Appomattox Court House, Virginia, on April 9, 1865, to work out the terms for the surrender of Lee's Army of Northern Virginia, a great chapter in American life came to a close, and a great new chapter began.

2   These men were bringing the Civil War to its virtual finish. To be sure, other armies had yet to surrender, and for a few days the fugitive Confederate government would struggle desperately and vainly, trying to find some way to go on living now that its chief support was gone. But in effect it was all over when Grant and Lee signed the papers. And the little room where they wrote out the terms was the scene of one of the poignant, dramatic contrasts in American history.

3   They were two strong men these oddly different generals, and they represented the strengths of two conflicting currents that, through them, had come into final collision.

Body: paragraphs 4–first
part, paragraph 16;
alternating pattern
throughout

4   Back of Robert E. Lee was the notion that the old aristocratic concept might somehow survive and be dominant in American life.

458

Lee was tidewater Virginia, and in his background were family, culture, and tradition . . . the age of chivalry transplanted to a New World which was making its own legends and its own myths. He embodied a way of life that had come down through the age of knighthood and the English country squire. America was a land that was beginning all over again, dedicated to nothing much more complicated than the rather hazy belief that all men had equal rights and should have an equal chance in the world. In such a land Lee stood for the feeling that it was somehow of advantage to human society to have a pronounced inequality in the social structure. There should be a leisure class, backed by ownership of land; in turn, society itself should be keyed to the land as the chief source of wealth and influence. It would bring forth (according to this ideal) a class of men with a strong sense of obligation to the community; men who lived not to gain advantage for themselves, but to meet the solemn obligations which had been laid on them by the very fact that they were privileged. From them the country would get its leadership; to them it could look for the higher values—of thought, of conduct, or personal deportment—to give it strength and virtue.

5

First difference
Paragraphs 4–6: Lee's
background, character

Lee embodied the noblest elements of this aristocratic ideal. Through him, the landed nobility justified itself. For four years, the Southern states had fought a desperate war to uphold the ideals for which Lee stood. In the end, it almost seemed as if the Confederacy fought for Lee; as if he himself was the Confederacy . . . the best thing that the way of life for which the Confederacy stood could ever have to offer. He had passed into legend before Appomattox. Thousands of tired, underfed, poorly clothed Confederate soldiers, long since past the simple enthusiasm of the early days of the struggle, somehow considered Lee the symbol of everything for which they had been willing to die. But they could not quite put this feeling into words. If the Lost Cause, sanctified by so much heroism and so many deaths, had a living justification, its justification was General Lee.

6

Grant, the son of a tanner on the Western frontier, was everything Lee was not. He had come up the hard way and embodied nothing in particular except the eternal toughness and sinewy fiber of the men who grew up beyond the mountains. He was one of a body of men who owed reverence and obeisance to no one, who were self-reliant to a fault, who cared hardly anything for the past but who had a sharp eye for the future.

7   Paragraphs 7–9: Grant's
background, character

These frontier men were the precise opposites of the tidewater aristocrats. Back of them, in the great surge that had taken people over the Alleghenies and into the opening Western country, there was a deep, implicit dissatisfaction with a past that had settled into grooves. They stood for democracy not from any reasoned conclusion about the proper ordering of human society, but simply because they had grown up in the middle of democracy and knew how it worked. Their society might have privileges, but they would be privileges each man had won for himself. Forms and patterns meant nothing. No man was born to anything, except perhaps to a chance to show how far he could rise. Life was competition.

8

Yet along with this feeling had come a deep sense of belonging to a national community. The Westerner who developed a farm, opened a shop, or set up in business as a trader could hope to prosper only as his own community prospered—and his community ran from the Atlantic to the Pacific and from Canada down to Mexico. If the land was settled, with towns and highways and

9

accessible markets, he could better himself. He saw his fate in terms of the nation's own destiny. As its horizons expanded, so did his. He had, in other words, an acute dollars-and-cents stake in the continued growth and development of his country.

Second difference
Lee's loyalty

10   And that, perhaps, is where the contrast between Grant and Lee becomes most striking. The Virginia aristocrat, inevitably, saw himself in relation to his own region. He lived in a static society which could endure almost anything except change. Instinctively, first loyalty would go to the locality in which that society existed. He would fight to the limit of endurance to defend it, because in defending it he was defending everything that gave his own life its deepest meaning.

Grant's loyalty

11   The Westerner, on the other hand, would fight with an equal tenacity for the broader concept of society. He fought so because everything he lived by was tied to growth, expansion, and a constantly widening horizon. What he lived by would survive or fall with the nation itself. He could not possibly stand by unmoved in the face of an attempt to destroy the Union. He would combat it with everything he had, because he could only see it as an effort to cut the ground out from under his feet.

Summary of significant
differences

12   So Grant and Lee were in complete contrast, representing two diametrically opposed elements in American life. Grant was the modern man emerging; beyond him, ready to come on the stage, was the great age of steel and machinery, of crowded cities and a restless burgeoning vitality. Lee might have ridden down from the old age of chivalry, lance in hand, silken banner fluttering over his head. Each man was the perfect champion of his cause, drawing both his strengths and his weaknesses from the people he led.

Transition paragraph
signals switch to
similarities

13   Yet it was not all contrast, after all. Different as they were—in background, in personality, in underlying aspiration—these two great soldiers had much in common. Under everything else, they were marvelous fighters. Furthermore, their fighting qualities were really very much alike.

First similarity

14   Each man had, to begin with, the great virtue of utter tenacity and fidelity. Grant fought his way down the Mississippi Valley in spite of acute personal discouragement and profound military handicaps. Lee hung on in the trenches at Petersburg after hope itself had died. In each man there was an indomitable quality . . . the born fighter's refusal to give up as long as he can still remain on his feet and lift his two fists.

Second similarity

15   Daring and resourcefulness they had, too; the ability to think faster and move faster than the enemy. These were the qualities which gave Lee the dazzling campaigns of Second Manassas and Chancellorsville and won Vicksburg for Grant.

Third similarity: notes
order of climax

16   Lastly, and perhaps greatest of all, there was the ability, at the end, to turn quickly from war to peace once the fighting was over. Out of the way these two men behaved at Appomattox came the possibility of a peace of reconciliation. It was a possibility not wholly realized, in the years to come, but which did, in the end, help the two sections to become one nation again . . . after a war whose bitterness might have seemed to make such a reunion wholly impossible. No part of either man's life became him more than the part he played in this brief meeting in the McLean house at Appomattox. Their behavior there put all

Conclusion: significance
of the meeting

succeeding generations of Americans in their debt. Two great Americans, Grant and Lee—very different, yet under everything very much alike. Their encounter at Appomattox was one of the great moments of American history.

DISCUSSION QUESTIONS ■

1. Where is Catton's thesis statement?
2. Summarize the way of life that Lee stood for, and then do the same for Grant.
3. Why do the differences between Grant and Lee receive more extended treatment than the similarities? Why are the similarities discussed last?
4. How would you characterize Catton's attitude toward the two men? Refer to the essay when answering.

SUGGESTION FOR WRITING ■   Write an essay comparing two past or present political or military figures—perhaps Abraham Lincoln and Jefferson Davis or Dwight Eisenhower and Erwin Rommel. Try for a balanced treatment and select an appropriate organization.

SUZANNE BRITT

■ *That Lean and Hungry Look*

Suzanne Britt is a native of Winston-Salem, North Carolina, and an alumna of Salem College and Washington University. Since college, she has made a career of journalism. Her writings have appeared in several major newspapers, including the Baltimore Sun, *the* Des Moines Register and Tribune, *the* Raleigh News and Observer, *and the* New York Times, *as well as in* Newsweek *magazine. In 1982, a collection of her essays appeared under the title* Show and Tell. *The following essay first appeared in* Newsweek *and was then made the basis of a book* Skinny People Are Dull and Crunchy Like Carrots. *In the essay, Britt draws a distinction between thin and fat people— and between two different philosophies of life.*

Caesar was right. Thin people need watching. I've been watching them for   1
most of my adult life, and I don't like what I see. When these narrow fellows spring at me, I quiver to my toes. Thin people come in all personalities, most of them menacing. You've got your "together" thin person, your mechanical thin

1. Paragraph 3 contains the thesis statement.
2. Lee stood for the aristocratic, chivalric tradition, loyalty to his locality, and a belief in a privileged leisure class destined to be leaders. Grant stood for just the opposite—democracy, self-reliance, loyalty to the nation, the chance to advance as far as ability would allow. (Catton's purpose is to contrast these two opposing outlooks.)
3. The differences between Grant and Lee (paragraphs 4–12) receive more extended treatment than the similarities because they represent the two conflicting currents that came into final collision with the outbreak of the Civil War. Similarities are discussed last because one of these similarities is the ability of both men to begin reconciliation and help the two sides "become one nation again."
4. Catton obviously admires, perhaps even eulogizes, the two men. Paragraphs 12 ("Each man was the perfect champion of his cause. . . .") through 16 ("Their behavior there put all succeeding generations of Americans in their debt.") suggest this attitude.

PERSPECTIVE

Students often assume that writing a humorous essay is easy. In fact, it is a demanding task that requires the careful choice of words, phrasing, and language devices needed to achieve just the right effect. Because Britt has clearly mastered the craft of humorous writing, you might explore with students how she makes us laugh.

TEACHING STRATEGIES

1. Follow up Discussion Question 4 by exploring the irony in paragraph 9. Britt's "one," "two," "three" methodical rationale for rejection is ironic in view of her statement in paragraph 4 that fat people let things "stay all blurry and hazy and vague." Furthermore, in paragraph 9 she says "The important thing is. . . ," yet note the last three sentences of paragraph 4.
2. Ask the class to identify some of the concrete details Britt uses to clarify her assertions about thin and fat people. Then ask what these details accomplish.
3. Point out the clichés and the sentence fragment in paragraph 7. Then ask why Britt uses them and whether they are effective.
4. Call attention to the alliteration in paragraph 12. Then ask students to discuss whether it is effective or overdone and to supply reasons for their answers.

CLASSROOM ACTIVITY

Have small groups of students generate contrasts between strict and non-strict parents or teachers, amusing and boring dates, health-conscious and non-health-conscious people, or other dissimilar groups. These contrasts might be presented as reports to the class and serve as the prelude to a writing assignment. Remind students to write with some clear purpose in mind and not merely to list contrasts.

2

3

4

5

6

7

8

9

person, your condescending thin person, your tsk-tsk thin person, your efficiency-expert thin person. All of them are dangerous.

In the first place, thin people aren't fun. They don't know how to goof off, at least in the best, fat sense of the word. They've always got to be adoing. Give them a coffee break, and they'll jog around the block. Supply them with a quiet evening at home, and they'll fix the screen door and lick S&H green stamps. They say things like "there aren't enough hours in the day." Fat people never say that. Fat people think the day is too damn long already.

Thin people make me tired. They've got speedy little metabolisms that cause them to bustle briskly. They're forever rubbing their bony hands together and eying new problems to "tackle." I like to surround myself with sluggish, inert, easygoing fat people, the kind who believe that if you clean it up today, it'll just get dirty again tomorrow.

Some people say the business about the jolly fat person is a myth, that all of us chubbies are neurotic, sick, sad people. I disagree. Fat people may not be chortling all day long, but they're a hell of a lot *nicer* than the wizened and shriveled. Thin people turn surly, mean and hard at a young age because they never learn the value of a hot-fudge sundae for easing tension. Thin people don't like gooey soft things because they themselves are neither gooey nor soft. They are crunchy and dull, like carrots. They go straight to the heart of the matter while fat people let things stay all blurry and hazy and vague, the way things actually are. Thin people want to face the truth. Fat people know there is no truth. One of my thin friends is always staring at complex, unsolvable problems and saying, "The key thing is . . ." Fat people never say that. They know there isn't any such thing as the key thing about anything.

Thin people believe in logic. Fat people see all sides. The sides fat people see are rounded blobs, usually gray, always nebulous and truly not worth worrying about. But the thin person persists. "If you consume more calories than you burn," says one of my thin friends, "you will gain weight. It's that simple." Fat people always grin when they hear statements like that. They know better.

Fat people realize that life is illogical and unfair. They know very well that God is not in his heaven and all is not right with the world. If God was up there, fat people could have two doughnuts and a big orange drink anytime they wanted it.

Thin people have a long list of logical things they are always spouting off to me. They hold up one finger at a time as they reel off these things, so I won't lose track. They speak slowly as if to a young child. The list is long and full of holes. It contains tidbits like "get a grip on yourself," "cigarettes kill," "cholesterol clogs," "fit as a fiddle," "ducks in a row," "organize" and "sound fiscal management." Phrases like that.

They think these 2,000-point plans lead to happiness. Fat people know happiness is elusive at best and even if they could get the kind thin people talk about, they wouldn't want it. Wisely, fat people see that such programs are too dull, too hard, too off the mark. They are never better than a whole cheesecake.

Fat people know all about the mystery of life. They are the ones acquainted with the night, with luck, with fate, with playing it by ear. One thin person I know once suggested that we arrange all the parts of a jigsaw puzzle into groups according to size, shape and color. He figured this would cut the time needed to complete the puzzle by at least 50 percent. I said I wouldn't do it. One, I like to muddle through. Two, what good would it do to finish early? Three, the jigsaw puzzle isn't the important thing. The important thing is the fun of four people (one thin person included) sitting around a card table, working a jigsaw puzzle. My thin friend had no use for my list. Instead of joining us, he went outside and mulched the boxwoods. The three remaining fat people finished the puzzle and made chocolate, double-fudged brownies to celebrate.

10   The main problem with thin people is they oppress. Their good intentions, bony torsos, tight ships, neat corners, cerebral machinations and pat solutions loom like dark clouds over the loose, comfortable, spread-out, soft world of the fat. Long after fat people have removed their coats and shoes and put their feet up on the coffee table, thin people are still sitting on the edge of the sofa, looking neat as a pin, discussing rutabagas. Fat people are heavily into fits of laughter, slapping their thighs and whooping it up, while thin people are still politely waiting for the punch line.

11   Thin people are downers. They like math and morality and reasoned evaluation of the limitations of human beings. They have their skinny little acts together. They expound, prognose, probe and prick.

12   Fat people are convivial. They will like you even if you're irregular and have acne. They will come up with a good reason why you never wrote the great American novel. They will cry in your beer with you. They will put your name in the pot. They will let you off the hook. Fat people will gab, giggle, guffaw, gallumph, gyrate and gossip. They are generous, giving and gallant. They are gluttonous and goodly and great. What you want when you're down is soft and jiggly, not muscled and stable. Fat people know this. Fat people have plenty of room. Fat people will take you in.

DISCUSSION QUESTIONS ■

1. Cite passages from Britt's essay to show that she is trying to entertain us.
2. Britt asserts that thin people have four shortcomings. What are they, and where is each discussed? In what order are these shortcomings arranged?
3. Why do you think Britt uses the alternating pattern rather than the block pattern to organize her essay?
4. In paragraph 11 Britt charges that thin people like to make "reasoned evaluation of the limitations of human beings." In what way is this statement ironic?

SUGGESTION FOR WRITING ■   Write an essay comparing the attitudes of two people, one efficient and organized, the other inefficient and disorganized. Focus your paper on three or four points of comparison and organize them in the alternating pattern.

AMY GROSS

■ *The Appeal of the Androgynous Man*

Amy Gross has been features editor at Vogue *magazine since 1983. A native of Brooklyn, New York, she earned a zoology degree at Connecticut College, then joined Condé Nast Publications where she served on the staffs of* Glamour *and* Mademoiselle. *After a period of freelancing, she became consulting editor for* Mademoiselle, *writing features every month, and then she moved to her present position at* Vogue. *She is currently coauthoring a book on women and surgery. In this selection, which first appeared in* Mademoiselle, *Gross compares androgynous men to "all-men" and finds the former preferable.*

1   James Dean was my first androgynous man.[1] I figured I could talk to him. He was anguished and I was 12, so we had a lot in common. With only a few exceptions, all the men I have liked or loved have been a certain kind of man: a kind who doesn't play football or watch the games on Sunday, who doesn't tell dirty jokes featuring broads or chicks, who is not contemptuous of conversations that are philosophically speculative, introspective, or otherwise foolish according to the other kind of man. He is more self-amused, less inflated, more quirky, vulnerable and responsive than the other sort (the other sort, I'm visualizing as the guys on TV who advertise deodorant in the locker room). He is more like me than the other sort. He is what social scientists and feminists would call androgynous: having the characteristics of both male and female.

2   Now the first thing I want you to know about the androgynous man is that he is neither effeminate nor hermaphroditic. All his primary and secondary sexual characteristics are in order and I would say he's all-man, but that is just what he is not. He is more than all-man.

3   The merely all-man man, for one thing, never walks to the grocery store unless the little woman is away visiting her mother with the kids, or is in the hospital having a kid, or there is no little woman. All-men men don't know how to shop in a grocery store unless it is to buy a 6-pack and some pretzels. Their ideas of nutrition expand beyond a 6-pack and pretzels only to take in steak, potatoes, scotch or rye whiskey, and maybe a wad of cake or apple pie. All-men men have absolutely no taste in food, art, books, movies, theatre, dance, how to live, what are good questions, what is funny, or anything else I care about. It's not exactly that the all-man's man is an uncouth illiterate. He may be educated, well-mannered, and on a first-name basis with fine wines. One all-man man I knew was a handsome individual who gave the impression of being gentle, affectionate, and sensitive. He sat and ate dinner one night while I was doing something endearingly feminine at the sink. At one point, he mutely held up his glass to indicate in a primitive, even ape-like, way his need for a refill. This was in 1967, before Women's Liberation. Even so, I was disturbed. Not enough to break the

---

[1]James Dean (1931–1955) was a 1950s film star who gained fame for his portrayals of restless, defiant young men.

glass over his handsome head, not even enough to mutely indicate the where-abouts of the refrigerator, but enough to remember that moment in all its revelatory clarity. No androgynous man would ever brutishly expect to be waited on without even a "please." (With a "please," maybe.)

The brute happened to be a doctor—not a hard hat—and, to all appear-ances, couth. But he had bought the whole superman package, complete with that fragile beast, the male ego. The androgynous man arrives with a male ego too, but his is not as imperialistic. It doesn't invade every area of his life and person. Most activities and thoughts have nothing to do with masculinity or femininity. The androgynous man knows this. The all-man man doesn't. He must keep a constant guard against anything even vaguely feminine (*i.e.*, "sissy") rising up in him. It must be a terrible strain.   4

Male chauvinism is an irritation, but the real problem I have with the all-man man is that it's hard for me to talk to him. He's alien to me, and for this I'm at least half to blame. As his interests have not carried him into the sissy, mine have never taken me very far into the typically masculine terrains of sports, business and finance, politics, cars, boats and machines. But blame or no blame, the reality is that it is almost as difficult for me to connect with him as it would be to link up with an Arab shepherd or Bolivian sandalmaker. There's a similar culture gap.   5

It seems to me that the most masculine men usually end up with the most feminine women. Maybe they like extreme polarity. I like polarity myself, but the poles have to be within earshot. As I've implied, I'm very big on talking. I fall in love for at least three hours with anyone who engages me in a real conversation. I'd rather a man point out a paragraph in a book—wanting to share it with me—than bring me flowers. I'd rather a man ask what I think than tell me I look pretty. (Women who are very pretty and accustomed to hearing that they are pretty may feel differently.) My experience is that all-men men read books I don't want to see paragraphs of, and don't really give a damn what I or any woman would think about most issues so long as she looks pretty. They have a very limited use for women. I suspect they don't really like us. The androgynous man likes women as much or as little as he likes anyone.   6

Another difference between the all-man man and the androgynous man is that the first is not a star in the creativity department. If your image of the creative male accessorizes him with a beret, smock and artist's palette, you will not believe the all-man man has been seriously short-changed. But if you allow as how creativity is a talent for freedom, associated with imagination, wit, empathy, unpredictability, and receptivity to new impressions and connections, then you will certainly pity the dull, thick-skinned, rigid fellow in whom creativity sets no fires.   7

Nor is the all-man man so hot when it comes to sensitivity. He may be true-blue in the trenches, but if you are troubled, you'd be wasting your time trying to milk comfort from the all-man man.   8

This is not blind prejudice. It is enlightened prejudice. My biases were confirmed recently by a psychologist named Sandra Lipsetz Bem, a professor at Stanford University. She brought to attention the fact that high masculinity in males (and high femininity in females) has been "consistently correlated with   9 lower overall intelligence and lower creativity." Another psychologist, Donald W. MacKinnon, director of the Institute of Personality Assessment and Research at the University of California in Berkeley, found that "creative males give more expression to the feminine side of their nature than do less creative men . . . [They] score relatively high on femininity, and this despite the fact that, as a group, they do not present an effeminate appearance or give evidence of increased homosexual interests or experiences. Their elevated scores on femininity indicate rather an openness to their feelings and emotions, a sensitive intellect and understanding self-awareness and wide-ranging interests including many which in the American culture are thought of as more feminine . . ."

10   Dr. Bem ran a series of experiments on college students who had been categorized as masculine, feminine, or androgynous. In three tests of the degree of nurturance—warmth and caring—the masculine men scored painfully low (painfully for anyone stuck with a masculine man, that is). In one of those experiments, all the students were asked to listen to a "troubled talker"—a person who was not neurotic but simply lonely, supposedly new in town and feeling like an outsider. The masculine men were the least supportive, responsive or humane. "They lacked the ability to express warmth, playfulness and concern," Bem concluded. (She's giving them the benefit of the doubt. It's possible the masculine men didn't express those qualities because they didn't possess them.)

11   The androgynous man, on the other hand, having been run through the same carnival of tests, "performs spectacularly. He shuns no behavior just because our culture happens to label it as female and his competence crosses both the instrumental [getting the job done, the problem solved] and the expressive [showing a concern for the welfare of others, the harmony of the group] domains. Thus, he stands firm in his opinion, he cuddles kittens and bounces babies and he has a sympathetic ear for someone in distress."

12   Well, a great mind, a sensitive and warm personality are fine in their place, but you are perhaps skeptical of the gut appeal of the androgynous man. As a friend, maybe, you'd like an androgynous man. For a sexual partner, though, you'd prefer a jock. There's no arguing chemistry, but consider the jock for a moment. He competes on the field, whatever his field is, and bed is just one more field to him: another opportunity to perform, another fray. Sensuality is for him candy to be doled out as lure. It is a ration whose flow is cut off at the exact point when it has served its purpose—namely, to elicit your willingness to work out on the field with him.

13   Highly masculine men need to believe their sexual appetite is far greater than a woman's (than a nice woman's). To them, females must be seduced: Seduction is a euphemism for a power play, a con job. It pits man against woman (or woman against man). The jock believes he must win you over, incite your body to rebel against your better judgment: in other words—conquer you.

14   The androgynous man is not your opponent but your teammate. He does not seduce: he invites. Sensuality is a pleasure for him. He's not quite so goal-oriented. And to conclude, I think I need only remind you here of his greater imagination, his wit and empathy, his unpredictability, and his receptivity to new impressions and connections.

DISCUSSION QUESTIONS ■

1. In paragraph 1 Gross refers to the androgynous man as "more quirky." State in your own words what you think she means. Where in the essay does she refer again (using a different term) to this trait?

2. Gross reveals in paragraph 3 that the all-man man never goes grocery shopping unless "the little woman" is gone and that her doctor acquaintance raised his glass in a "primitive, even ape-like" manner. What is the effect of these quoted phrases?

3. In paragraph 5 Gross tells us that it would be as difficult for her to relate to an all-man man "as it would be to link up with an Arab shepherd or Bolivian sandalmaker." Why do you think she uses this comparison?

4. Gross writes in a very informal style. Point out elements in the essay that contribute to this informality.

5. This essay uses the alternating pattern of organization. Point out how this choice relates to the author's purpose.

6. Gross makes a number of strong statements in her essay. Are you inclined to agree with most of them? Some of them? Discuss.

SUGGESTION FOR WRITING ■   Write an essay comparing a stereotyped attitude or life-style with a strongly contrasting one. For example, you might compare homemakers with career women or conventional youth with punkers. Use the block or alternating method of comparison and take sides in your essay.

MARK TWAIN

■ *Innocence and Experience: Different Views of the River*[1]

A biographical sketch of Mark Twain appears on page 435. In this excerpt from Life on the Mississippi *(1881), Twain compares how the Mississippi River appeared to him before and after he became a pilot.*

Now when I had mastered the language of this water, and had come to know every trifling feature that bordered the great river as familiarly as I knew the letters of the alphabet, I had made a valuable acquisition. But I had lost something, too. I had lost something which could never be restored to me while I lived. All the grace, the beauty, the poetry, had gone out of the majestic river! I still kept in mind a certain wonderful sunset which I witnessed when steamboating was new to me. A broad expanse of the river was turned to blood; in the

1

[1] Editors' title.

CLASSROOM ACTIVITY

Divide the class into small groups and have them contrast how they viewed college before enrolling and how they view it now. The discussions could lead to reports presented to the whole class and ultimately to a paper.

middle distance the red hue brightened into gold, through which a solitary log came floating, black and conspicuous; in one place a long, slanting mark lay sparkling upon the water; in another the surface was broken by boiling, tumbling rings, that were as many-tinted as an opal; where the ruddy flush was faintest, was a smooth spot that was covered with graceful circles and radiating lines, ever so delicately traced; the shore on our left was densely wooded, and the somber shadow that fell from this forest was broken in one place by a long, ruffled trail that shone like silver; and high above the forest wall a clean-stemmed dead tree waved a single leafy bough that glowed like a flame in the unobstructed splendor that was flowing from the sun. There were graceful curves, reflected images, woody heights, soft distances; and over the whole scene, far and near, the dissolving lights drifted steadily, enriching it every passing moment with new marvels of coloring.

2   I stood like one bewitched. I drank it in, in a speechless rapture. The world was new to me, and I had never seen anything like this at home. But as I have said, a day came when I began to cease from noting the glories and the charms which the moon and the sun and the twilight wrought upon the river's face; another day came when I ceased altogether to note them. Then, if that sunset scene had been repeated, I should have looked upon it without rapture, and should have commented upon it, inwardly, after this fashion: "This sun means that we are going to have wind to-morrow; that floating log means that the river is rising, small thanks to it; that slanting mark on the water refers to a bluff reef which is going to kill somebody's steamboat one of these nights, if it keeps on stretching out like that; those tumbling 'boils' show a dissolving bar and a changing channel there; the lines and circles in the slick water over yonder are a warning that that troublesome place is shoaling up dangerously; that silver streak in the shadow of the forest is the 'break' from a new snag, and he has located himself in the very best place he could have found to fish for steamboats; that tall dead tree, with a single living branch, is not going to last long, and then how is a body ever going to get through this blind place at night without the friendly old landmark?"

3   No, the romance and beauty were all gone from the river. All the value any feature of it had for me now was the amount of usefulness it could furnish toward compassing the safe piloting of a steamboat. Since those days, I have pitied doctors from my heart. What does the lovely flush in a beauty's cheek mean to a doctor but a "break" that ripples above some deadly disease? Are not all her visible charms sown thick with what are to him the signs and symbols of hidden decay? Does he ever see her beauty at all, or doesn't he simply view her professionally and comment upon her unwholesome condition all to himself? And doesn't he sometimes wonder whether he has gained most or lost most by learning his trade?

DISCUSSION QUESTIONS

1. Twain uses the block pattern. Since paragraph 1 presents one scene viewed at one particular time, it couldn't be fragmented. Paragraph 2 follows the sequence in paragraph 1, and thus it also can't be fragmented.
2. The key thrust of the comparison is the sense of losing "the grace, the beauty, the poetry" that Twain felt when he came to know the river well as a pilot. Twain draws attention to this loss by the repetition.
3. "Bewitched" suggested that Twain was under some type of spell, and indeed he was—the spell of "grace," "beauty," and "poetry" cast by the "majestic river."
4. In paragraph 1 the sun, the log, and the mark didn't "mean" or "refer" to anything. Twain simply enjoyed these items for their sensuous beauty. In paragraph 2 the items have become much more practical, helping Twain navigate the river as a pilot.

DISCUSSION QUESTIONS ∎

1. Does Twain use the block or alternating pattern to organize his comparison? Why is his choice appropriate?

2. Why does Twain begin and end with references to something lost?

3. Why is "bewitched" at the start of paragraph 2 an appropriate word to describe Twain's reaction to the sunset in paragraph 1?

4. In paragraph 2 Twain says that "This sun means . . . ," "that floating log means . . . ," and "that slanting mark on the water refers. . . ." Point out the significance of the verbs Twain uses.

5. How does the tone (see pages (245–248) of paragraphs 1 and 2 differ?

6. Why do you suppose that Twain concludes by comparing doctors and steamboat pilots?

SUGGESTION FOR WRITING ■ **Write an essay comparing your original perceptions of and current reactions to a place you've revisited after a period of time—for example, Las Vegas, Disneyland, or a national park.**

MARJORIE WATERS

■ *Coming Home*

Marjorie Waters was born and educated in upstate New York. A free-lance writer who works in Boston, she has authored numerous articles in popular and literary magazines, as well as one longer work, The Victory Garden Kids' Book (1988). *In the essay that follows, Ms. Waters draws an analogy between a house that has weathered a severe winter and an individual who has weathered a period of severe grief.*

After the cruelest of winters, the house still stood. It was pale, washed 1
clean by elements gone wild, and here and there a shutter dangled from a broken hinge. But the structure was sound; the corners had held. I walked around it slowly, studying every detail: the fine edge where window frame met clapboard, the slice of shadow across the roofline, the old wooden railing around the porch. When I climbed the stairs toward the door, I heard the floorboards groan beneath my weight as they had always done. Hello yourself, old friend, I said.

Inside, I made those rooms my own again, drew the curtains back, threw 2
open the window, pulled the covers from the furniture, slapped all the upholstery with my hands. I could feel fresh air move in through open windows, replacing a season's worth of staleness with a smell of moist earth, a hint of flowers. After all the months of darkness light poured again into the house, fell in familiar angled patterns across furniture, walls, and floors. Where light beams passed through moving air, even the dust seemed alive; I watched it swirl, dance, resettle.

I made myself at home, kicked off my shoes so I could feel the floors 3
beneath my feet again. I tilted my head, read the titles on the spines of all my books. I played old songs I hadn't heard in months, felt the summer music move through me as if my muscles were the strings. It carried me from room to room

CLASSROOM ACTIVITY

Divide the class into small groups and have them discuss possibilities for developing analogies based on some of the writing suggestions listed at the end of Chapter 9. These discussions might lead to a writing assignment.

DISCUSSION QUESTIONS

1. The house had been assaulted by the elements of nature and, despite showing some effects of this assault, was still basically sound. Similarly, as paragraphs 5 and 6 make clear, Waters herself had been assaulted by grief after an unexpected death. And despite experiencing some traumatic effects, she also had emerged from the grief intact and feeling like herself again. Thus in this sentence Waters starts to lay the foundation (although unannounced: see answer 2) for her analogy.
2. Waters wants readers of her first four paragraphs to concentrate on and understand only the house and how she acclimated to it. That done, she then introduces the analogy at the start of paragraph 5, confident that the reader will now comprehend it.
3. Who died is unimportant to understanding the writer's purpose: to point out similarities between the reopening of a closed house and the recovery from grief, whatever its source.
4. The "as . . . so . . ." (or just as . . . so also . . .) pattern is a common one in analogies because it clearly links the similarities. Students might well use this pattern when writing their own analogies.
5. Waters explains the somewhat unfamiliar (the recovery from grief) by likening it to the more familiar (the return to a house).
6. In paragraph 1 the phrase refers to the house; in paragraph 6 it refers to Waters' recovery from grief. Thus the two similarities under discussion are tied together.

4

while I swept away the mustiness of winter, shook the rugs, cleaned cobwebs out of corners, hung laundered linens on the line to whip dry in the outdoor air. I pulled closed boxes out of closets and unwrapped all my things, slowly, one by one. I held and turned them in my hands before I put them out again on shelves, in cupboards and drawers. And when I had each room all full of me again, I showered and washed away the last of winter's claims in hot lather and steam.

5

Night fell and brought a chill to the air outside. I built a fire in the stove, drank tea that smelled of oranges and spice. I warmed my fingers round the cup and thought of how my house would look to passers-by, drowsy and content, with soft rectangles of light on the ground below the windows, a breath of smoke from the chimney. She's come back, they would say as they walked through the dark night. She's home again.

For me, the end of grief was a homecoming like this one, a returning to myself made sweeter by the long separation. I remember well the months that had followed that most unexpected death, when I felt cut loose, caught in my own cold storm, far away from all that made me feel at home. I wondered if I would ever again belong to any time or place. People spoke to me of sadness and loss, as if they were burdens to carry in my hands. I nodded in agreement, afraid to tell them that I felt no burdens, only weightlessness. I thought the world had pulled itself away from me, that I would drift, beyond reach, forever.

6

But winter ends, and grief does pass. As I had reclaimed my house and made it my own again, so I slowly reclaimed my life. I resumed my small daily rituals: a cup of coffee with a friend, long walks at sunset. I felt like myself again, and when I laughed, it was my own laugh I heard, rich and full. I had feared that, in my absence, the space that I had left behind would close over from disuse, but I returned to find that my house still stood, even after the cruelest of winters.

DISCUSSION QUESTIONS ■

1. Consider the essay as a whole and then point out the significance of this sentence in paragraph 1: "But the structure was sound; the corners had held."

2. Waters does not introduce her analogy at the start of the essay. Suggest why. Where are we first aware of her analogy?

3. Why do you think Waters, in paragraph 5, doesn't identify the person who died?

4. Reread the "As . . . so . . . " sentence in paragraph 6. What can you learn from its structure that can help you write your own analogy?

5. Does this analogy further explain · the familiar by presenting information on the unfamiliar, or does it explain the unfamiliar by likening it to the familiar?

6. What does Waters accomplish by beginning and ending her essay with ". . . the cruelest of winters"?

SUGGESTION FOR WRITING ■   **Write an analogy which helps explain a time of great joy in your life. Feel free to either reveal or conceal the actual joy. Announce your analogy at the point which seems most effective.**

Cause and Effect

OVERVIEW OF CAUSE-
AND-EFFECT ESSAYS

Two of the four cause-and-effect essays explore causes, one explores effects, and one, while emphasizing causes, devotes some attention to effects. Three of the four writers draw upon personal experience. Of these three, one uses gentle irony to make a philosophical point, one displays an affectionate attitude, and one, as his ending makes clear, adopts a humorous approach. All three use informal language. The remaining writer relies on technical language and achieves an objective tone by citing case histories and statistics.

E. M. FORSTER

■ *My Wood*

E. M. Forster (1879–1970) was born in London and educated at King's College, Cambridge, where he received baccalaureate degrees in classics (1900) and history (1901). For the next eighteen years, he spent much of his time outside England, living in Greece and Italy, visiting India, and during World War I serving with the Red Cross in Egypt. After the war, Forster returned to England and, except for a brief stint in India as a Maharajah's private secretary, remained there the rest of his life. Forster's novels include Where Angels Fear to Tread *(1905),* The Longest Journey *(1907),* A Room with a View *(1908),* Howard's End *(1910), and* A Passage to India *(1924). His short stories have been collected in two volumes,* The Celestial Omnibus *(1911) and* The Eternal Moment *(1928). After 1928, Forster focused on nonfiction, producing, among other books,* Abinger Harvest *(1936), a collection of essays and literary criticism from which our selection comes. In it, Forster notes the effects that owning property had on him.*

PERSPECTIVE

Forster's views about ownership provide an interesting and enlightening contrast to many of the attitudes in evidence today. Advertising, upscale TV serials, and celebrity lifestyles lead many people to believe, at least subconsciously, that possessions bring status, romantic success, and happiness. Forster would disagree. Encourage students to examine their own attitudes toward property.

A few years ago I wrote a book which dealt in part with the difficulties of the English in India. Feeling that they would have had no difficulties in India themselves, the Americans read the book freely. The more they read it the better it made them feel, and a cheque to the author was the result. I bought a wood with the cheque. It is not a large wood—it contains scarcely any trees, and it is intersected, blast it, by a public foot path. Still, it is the first property that I have owned, so it is right that other people should participate in my shame, and should ask themselves, in accents that will vary in horror, this very important question: What is the effect of property upon the character? Don't let's touch economics; the effect of private ownership upon the community as a whole is another question—a more important question, perhaps, but another one. Let's keep to psychology. If you own things, what's their effect on you? What's the effect on me of my wood?

1 ⟶ Introduction: provides background

Signals essay of effects

471

Body: paragraphs 2–first
part, paragraph 7
First effect

2

In the first place, it makes me feel heavy. Property does have this effect. Property produces men of weight, and it was a man of weight who failed to get into the Kingdom of Heaven. He was not wicked, that unfortunate millionaire in the parable, he was only stout; he stuck out in front, not to mention behind, and as he wedged himself this way and that in the crystalline entrance and bruised his well-fed flanks, he saw beneath him a comparatively slim camel passing through the eye of a needle and being woven into the robe of God. The Gospels all through couple stoutness and slowness. They point out what is perfectly obvious, yet seldom realized: that if you have a lot of things you cannot move about a lot, that furniture requires dusting, dusters require servants, servants require insurance stamps, and the whole tangle of them makes you think twice before you accept an invitation to dinner or go for a bathe in the Jordan. Sometimes the Gospels proceed further and say with Tolstoy that property is sinful; they approach the difficult ground of asceticism here, where I cannot follow them. But as to the immediate effects of property on people, they just show straightforward logic. It produces men of weight. Men of weight cannot, by definition, move like the lightning from the East unto the West, and the ascent of a fourteen-stone[1] bishop into a pulpit is thus the exact antithesis of the coming of the Son of Man. My wood makes me feel heavy.

Second effect

3

In the second place, it makes me feel it ought to be larger.

4

The other day I heard a twig snap in it. I was annoyed at first, for I thought that someone was blackberrying, and depreciating the value of the undergrowth. On coming nearer, I saw it was not a man who had trodden on the twig and snapped it, but a bird, and I felt pleased. My bird. The bird was not equally pleased. Ignoring the relation between us, it took fright as soon as it saw the shape of my face, and flew straight over the boundary hedge into a field, the property of Mrs. Henessy, where it sat down with a loud squawk. It had become Mrs. Henessy's bird. Something seemed grossly amiss here, something that would not have occurred had the wood been larger. I could not afford to buy Mrs. Henessy out, I dared not murder her, and limitations of this sort beset me on every side. . . . A boundary protects. But—poor little thing—the boundary ought in its turn to be protected. Noises on the edge of it. Children throw stones. A little more, and then a little more, until we reach the sea. . . . And after all, why should even the world be the limit of possession? A rocket containing a Union Jack, will, it is hoped, be shortly fired at the moon. Mars. Sirius. Beyond which . . . But these immensities ended by saddening me. I could not suppose that my wood was the destined nucleus of universal dominion—it is so very small and contains no mineral wealth beyond the blackberries. Nor was I comforted when Mrs. Henessy's bird took alarm for the second time and flew clean away from us all, under the belief that it belonged to itself.

Third effect

5

In the third place, property makes its owner feel that he ought to do something to it. Yet he isn't sure what. A restlessness comes over him, a vague sense that he has a personality to express—the same sense which, without any vagueness, leads the artist to an act of creation. Sometimes I think I will cut down such trees as remain in the wood, at other times I want to fill up the gaps

[1]A stone is a British unit of weight equal to fourteen pounds.

between them with new trees. Both impulses are pretentious and empty. They are not honest movements toward money-making or beauty. They spring from a foolish desire to express myself and from an inability to enjoy what I have got. Creation, property, enjoyment form a sinister trinity in the human mind. Creation and enjoyment are both very good, yet they are often unattainable without a material basis, and at such moments property pushes itself in as a substitute, saying, "Accept me instead—I'm good enough for all three." It is not enough. It is, as Shakespeare said of lust, "The expense of spirit in a waste of shame": it is "Before, a joy proposed; behind, a dream." Yet we don't know how to shun it. It is forced on us by our economic system as the alternative to starvation. It is also forced on us by an internal defect in the soul. By the feeling that in property may lie the germs of self-development and of exquisite or heroic deeds. Our life on earth is, and ought to be, material and carnal. But we have not yet learned to manage our materialism and carnality properly; they are still entangled with the desire for ownership. . . .

And this brings us to our fourth and final point: the blackberries.   6

Blackberries are not plentiful in this meagre grove, but they are easily seen   7
from the public footpath which traverses it, and all too easily gathered. Foxgloves, too—people will pull up the foxgloves, and ladies of an educational tendency even grub for toad stools to show them on the Monday in class. Other ladies, less educated, roll down the bracken in the arms of their gentlemen friends. There is a paper, there are tins. Pray, does my wood belong to me or doesn't it? And, if it does, should I not own it best by allowing no one else to walk there? There is a wood near Lyme Regis, also cursed by a public footpath, where the owner has not hesitated on this point. He has built high stone walls on each side of the path, and has spanned it by bridges, so that the public circulate like termites while he gorges on the blackberries unseen. He really does own his wood, this able chap. . . . And perhaps I shall come to this in time. I shall wall in and fence out until I really taste the sweets of property. Enormously stout, endlessly avaricious, pseudo-creative, intensely selfish, I shall weave upon my forehead the quadruple crown of possession until those nasty Bolshies come and take it off again and thrust me aside into the outer darkness.

> Fourth effect

> Conclusion: humorously predicts effects of property on himself

DISCUSSION QUESTIONS ■

1. Where in paragraph 1 does Forster reveal his attitude toward the ownership of property?

2. In paragraph 1 Forster cautions, "Don't let's touch economics. . . . Let's keep to psychology." Why does he say this?

3. Forster refers to the bird in paragraph 4 as "My bird" and tells us that it flew away "under the belief that it belonged to itself." What point is he trying to make?

4. How does Forster arrange his discussion of effects? Why do you think he chose that arrangement?

5. Why do you think Forster's essay mentions the Bible, Tolstoy, and Shakespeare?

DISCUSSION QUESTIONS

1. After acknowledging that this is the first property he's owned, Forster says others should participate in his "shame" and ask themselves, in varying accents of "horror," about the effects of ownership. These two words foreshadow the negative effects that Forster details.

2. By avoiding any discussion of the economic aspects of property and focusing on what he calls "character" or "psychology," Forster limits the scope of his discussion. This is a wise decision as any adequate treatment of economics would have resulted in a very lengthy essay and done nothing to advance Forster's purpose—to explore the effects of property ownership on himself. Students should learn to tailor the scope of their topics to the length of their papers, thus avoiding overly general discussions, and to exclude material without any bearing on their purpose.

3. Forster shows that one effect of owning his wood is to make him greedy. At the end he muses that the bird was "under the belief that it belonged to itself," and of course it did.

4. Forster focuses first on the physical effect of owning property (the wood makes him feel heavy), then turns to three effects of ownership on attitude (the wood makes him become greedy, feel he should do something to the property, and become selfish). This arrangement seems natural and logical.

5. Forster mentions these references to lend authority to his insights.

6. These expressions include "blast it" and "Don't let's" (paragraph 1); "stuck out in front, not to mention behind," "wedged himself this way and that," "bruised his well-fed flanks," and "a lot" (paragraph 2); "blackberrying," "a loud squawk," and "poor little thing" (paragraph 4); and "grub," "gorges," "chap," and "nasty Bolshies" (paragraph 7).

7. Most Americans today probably would not share Forster's views, but this question might elicit some interesting responses from your class.

PERSPECTIVE

Crews' essay speaks to a universal reality—affection for a locale that holds pleasant associations, past or present. Twain expresses

6. Forster writes in a casual, informal style. Point out several examples of expressions that contribute to this informality.

7. To what extent do you think that most Americans today would agree with what Forster, an Englishman, said over fifty years ago about the effects that owning property had on him?

SUGGESTION FOR WRITING ■   **Write an essay explaining how some new possession, such as an automobile, a home computer, a videocassette player-recorder, or a new wardrobe affected your outlook and behavior. Try to maintain a light, playful tone.**

HARRY CREWS

■ *Why I Live Where I Live*

Harry Crews (born 1935) is a professor and novelist whose works, in the Southern Gothic tradition, feature strange settings, grotesque characters, and much violence. Born in Georgia, he received degrees from the University of Florida, where he has taught since 1962. He has written some one dozen novels along with two volumes of essays and short stories, and he contributes to literary journals and male-oriented national magazines. In our essay, Crews reveals how his surroundings influence his creativity.

1   I can leave the place where I live a couple of hours before daylight and be on a deserted little strip of sand called Crescent Beach in time to throw a piece of meat on the fire and then, in a few minutes, lie back sucking on a vodka bottle and chewing on a hunk of bloody beef while the sun lifts out of the Atlantic Ocean (somewhat unnerving but also mystically beautiful to a man who never saw a body of water bigger than a pond until he was grown) and while the sun rises lie on a blanket, brain singing from vodka and a bellyful of beef, while the beautiful bikinied children from the University of Florida drift down the beach, their smooth bodies sweating baby oil and the purest kind of innocent lust (which of course is the rankest sort) into the bright air. If all that starts to pall—and what *doesn't* start to pall?—I can leave the beach and be out on the end of a dock, sitting in the Captain's Table eating hearts-of-palm salad and hot boiled shrimp and sipping on a tall, icy glass of beer while the sun I saw lift out of the Atlantic that morning sinks into the warm, waveless Gulf of Mexico. It makes for a hell of a day. But that isn't really why I live in the north-central Florida town of Gainesville.

Nor do I live in Gainesville because seven blocks from my house there are two enormous libraries filled with the most courteous, helpful people you can imagine, people who, after explaining some of the more intricate mysteries of how the place works, including the purposes of numerous indices, will go ahead and cheerfully find what I cannot: for example, the car capacity of drive-in theaters in Bakersfield, California, in 1950. A man never knows when he may need a bit of information like that, but it isn't enough to keep him living in a little town in Florida as opposed to, say, Ann Arbor, Michigan.

I love the size of Gainesville. I can walk anywhere I want to go, and consequently I have very little to do with that abomination before the Lord, the car. It's a twenty-minute stroll to my two favorite bars, Lillian's Music Store and the Winnjammer; ten minutes to a lovely square of grass and trees called the Plaza of the Americas; less than ten minutes to the house of a young lady who has been hypnotizing me for six years. Some people get analyzed; I get hypnotized. It leaves me with the most astonishing and pleasurable memories. But there must be ten thousand towns like Gainesville in this country, and surely several hundred of them would have good places to drink and talk and at least one house where a young lady lived who would consent to hypnotize me into astonishing and pleasurable memories. So I cannot lean too heavily on walking and memories to justify being where I am.

The reason I live where I do is more complicated than the sorts of things I've been talking about thus far—more complicated and, I expect, ultimately inexplicable. Or, said another way: anyone other than I may find that the explanation does not satisfy. To start, I live right in the middle of town on three acres of land, land thick with pines a hundred feet tall, oak, wild plum trees, and all manner of tangled, unidentifiable underbrush. The only cleared space is the very narrow road leading down to the house. No lawn. (There are many things I absolutely refuse to do in this world, but the three things leading the list are: wash my car, shine my shoes, and mow a lawn.) The back wall of the room I work in at the rear of the house is glass, and when I raise my eyes from the typewriter I look past an enormous bull bay tree through a thin stand of reeds into a tiny creek, the banks of which are thick with the greenest fern God ever made. In my imagination I can follow that little creek upstream to the place where, after a long, circuitous passage, it joins the Suwannee River, and then follow the dark waters of the Suwannee upriver to the place where it rises in the nearly impenetrable fastness of the Okefenokee Swamp. Okefenokee: Creek Indian word for Land of the Trembling Earth, because most of the islands in the swamp—some of them holding hundreds of huge trees growing so thick that their roots are matted and woven as closely as a blanket—actually float on the water, and when a black bear crashes across one of them, the whole thing trembles.

I saw the Okefenokee Swamp long before I saw the Suwannee River, and the Suwannee River long before I saw the little creek I'm looking at as I write this. When I was a boy, I was in the swamp a lot, on the edges of it practically all the time that I was not in the fields working. I went deep into the Okefenokee with T. J., the husband of one of my first cousins. His left leg was cut off at the knee and he wore a peg, but he got along fine with it because we were usually in a

2 similar sentiments when reminiscing about the farm where he spent childhood vacations (see pages 79–80). Many students will be able to identify with the deep feelings Crews has for his community.

TEACHING STRATEGIES

3 **1.** You might have students discuss the type of language used in paragraph 1 and comment on its effectiveness.
2. In paragraph 8, Crews points out why he can't write in Georgia: ". . . it was all too much for me." Have students explain precisely what he means.
3. Ask why the concluding paragraph is effective. The answer of course depends on an understanding of the entire essay.

CLASSROOM ACTIVITY

4 Divide the class into small groups and have them exchange ideas about where they would like to settle and why. The discussions might lead to a writing assignment. Or have students discuss how they have been affected by their current surroundings.

5

flat skiff casting nets for crawfish, which he sold for fish bait at a penny apiece. I did not know enough then and do not know enough now to go into the deep middle swamp, but T. J. did; he knew the twisting maze of sloughs like his back yard, could read every sign of every living thing in the swamp, and made a good living with the crawfish nets and his string of traps and his gun. He sold alligator, wore alligator, and ate alligator. This was long before the federal government made the place a national wildlife refuge.

6   T. J. made his living out of the swamp, and I make mine now out of how the swamp shaped me, how the rhythms and patterns of speech in that time and place are still alive in my mouth today and, more important, alive in my ear. I feed off now and hope always to feed off the stories I heard told in the early dark around fires where coffee boiled while our clothes, still wet from stringing traps all day, slowly dried to our bodies. Even when I write stories not set in Georgia and not at all about anything in the South, that writing is of necessity still informed by my notions of the world and of what it is to be caught in it. Those notions obviously come out of South Georgia and out of everything that happened to me there, or so I believe.

7   Living here in North Florida, I am a little more than a hundred miles from where I was born and raised to manhood. I am just far enough away from the only place that was ever mine to still see it, close enough to the only people to whom I was ever kin in ways deeper than blood to still hear them. I know that what I have just written will sound precious and pretentious to many people. So be it. Let them do their work as they will, and I'll do mine.

8   I've tried to work—that is, to write—in Georgia, but I could not. Even under the best of circumstances, at my mama's farm, for instance, it was all too much for me. I was too deep in it, too close to it to use it, to make anything out of it. My memory doesn't even seem to work when I'm writing in Georgia. I can't seem to hold a story in my head. I write a page, and five pages later what I wrote earlier has begun to slide out of focus. If this is all symptomatic of some more profound malaise, I don't want to know about it and I certainly don't want to understand it.

9   Living here in Gainesville seems to give me a kind of geographic and emotional distance I need to write. I can't write if I get too far away. I tried to work on a novel in Tennessee once and after a ruined two months gave it up in despair. I once spent four months near Lake Placid in a beautiful house lent to me by a friend—perfect place to write—and I didn't do a damn thing but eat my guts and look out the window at the mountains.

10   And that, all of it, precious, pretentious, or whatever, is why I live where I live. And unless something happens that I cannot control, I plan to die here.

DISCUSSION QUESTIONS

1. The thesis statement is the first sentence of paragraph 4.
2. In paragraphs 1–3 Crews dismisses some plausible, but incorrect, reasons for living in Gainesville. Then in paragraph 4 he begins an extended discussion of the primary reason he does live (and plans to die) there: in order to write effectively, he needs to be close to his roots. You might point out how this structure helps explain the position of the thesis statement.
3. Crews explains in paragraph 6 that he now makes his living ". . . out of how the swamp shaped me, how the rhythms and patterns of speech in that time and place are still alive in my mouth today and, more important, alive in my ear." Thus mention of the swamp is intimately connected with his purpose.

DISCUSSION QUESTIONS ■

1. In this essay Crews explains why he lives in Gainesville. Identify his thesis statement.
2. How does Crews structure his discussion of reasons? Refer to the essay when answering.

3. The information about the Okefenokee swamp in paragraphs 4 and 5 appears to stray from the focus on reasons. Explain the connection between the swamp and Crews' purpose.

4. Consider the essay as a whole and then point out the significance of this sentence in paragraph 7: "I am just far enough away from the only place that was ever mine to still see it, close enough to the only people to whom I was ever kin in ways deeper than blood to still hear them."

5. What does Crews mean in paragraph 9 when he says "eat my guts"?

6. Composition students are generally advised not to enclose phrases or sentences within parentheses. How do you explain Crews' doing just that in paragraphs 1 and 4?

SUGGESTION FOR WRITING ■ **Write an essay explaining the reasons why you avoid a place that disturbs you.**

CARLL TUCKER

■ *Fear of Dearth*

Carll Tucker, a native of New York City, has reviewed books and movies for the Village Voice *and served as editor and columnist for the* Saturday Review. *Since 1983, he has edited the* Patent Trader *magazine. In this selection, he considers a contemporary paradox: the popularity of the unenjoyable activity of jogging.*

I hate jogging. Every dawn, as I thud around New York City's Central Park reservoir, I am reminded of how much I hate it. It's so tedious. Some claim jogging is thought conducive; others insist the scenery relieves the monotony. For me, the pace is wrong for contemplation of either ideas or vistas. While jogging, all I can think about is jogging—or nothing. One advantage of jogging around a reservoir is that there's no dry shortcut home.

From the listless looks of some fellow trotters, I gather I am not alone in my unenthusiasm: Bill-paying, it seems, would be about as diverting. Nonetheless, we continue to jog; more, we continue to *choose* to jog. From a practically infinite array of opportunities, we select one that we don't enjoy and can't wait to have done with. Why?

For any trend, there are as many reasons as there are participants. This person runs to lower his blood pressure. That person runs to escape the telephone or a cranky spouse or a filthy household. Another person runs to avoid doing anything else, to dodge a decision about how to lead his life or a realization that his life is leading nowhere. Each of us has his carrot and stick. In my case,

1

2

3

3. Look around the class and note any personal items, perhaps stone-washed jeans, tennis shoes, gold chains, that seem popular. Have the class discuss why the items are popular and then follow up with a writing assignment.

CLASSROOM ACTIVITY

This essay could prompt a paper exploring the effects of a vigorous exercise program—jogging, pumping iron, aerobics, or something similar. These effects might take the form of a causal chain. The initial effect, say a trimmer body, might cause the participant to replace large, bulky garments with more stylish ones and then to pursue a more active social life. Students could brainstorm possibilities in small groups and then use the discussions as the springboard for a paper. Remind students to check the third model outline in Chapter 10 for the organizational pattern of causal chains.

DISCUSSION QUESTIONS

1. Tucker uses the fragment intentionally to prepare for his focus on causes. Regarding fragments, we feel it's better to point them out to students than to have them call the "error" to our attention.
2. The reasons in paragraph 3 are relatively unimportant, and each is confined to relatively few people. Tucker gets these reasons out of the way before moving on to more important reasons.
3. Paragraph 5 discusses economic reasons, paragraph 6 discipline–obligation reasons, paragraph 7 theological reasons, and paragraph 9 "fear of dearth."

4

5

6

7

8

9

10

the stick is my slackening physical condition, which keeps me from beating opponents at tennis whom I overwhelmed two years ago. My carrot is to win.

Beyond these disparate reasons, however, lies a deeper cause. It is no accident that now, in the last third of the twentieth century, personal fitness and health have suddenly become a popular obsession. True, modern man likes to feel good, but that hardly distinguishes him from his predecessors.

With zany myopia, economists like to claim that the deeper cause of everything is economic. Delightfully, there seems no marketplace explanation for jogging. True, jogging is cheap, but then not jogging is cheaper. And the scant and skimpy equipment which jogging demands must make it a marketer's least favored form of recreation.

Some scout-masterish philosophers argue that the appeal of jogging and other body-maintenance programs is the discipline they afford. We live in a world in which individuals have fewer and fewer obligations. The work week has shrunk. Weekend worship is less compulsory. Technology gives us more free time. Satisfactorily filling free time requires imagination and effort. Freedom is a wide and risky river; it can drown the person who does not know how to swim across it. The more obligations one takes on, the more time one occupies, the less threat freedom poses. Jogging can become an instant obligation. For a portion of his day, the jogger is not his own man; he is obedient to a regimen he has accepted.

Theologists may take the argument one step further. It is our modern irreligion, our lack of confidence in any hereafter, that makes us anxious to stretch our mortal stay as long as possible. We run, as the saying goes, for our lives, hounded by the suspicion that these are the only lives we are likely to enjoy.

All of these theorists seem to me more or less right. As the growth of cults and charismatic religions and the resurgence of enthusiasm for the military draft suggest, we do crave commitment. And who can doubt, watching so many middle-aged and older persons torturing themselves in the name of fitness, that we are unreconciled to death, more so perhaps than any generation in modern memory?

But I have a hunch there's a further explanation of our obsession with exercise. I suspect that what motivates us even more than a fear of death is a fear of dearth. Our era is the first to anticipate the eventual depletion of all natural resources. We see wilderness shrinking; rivers losing their capacity to sustain life; the air, even the stratosphere, being loaded with potentially deadly junk. We see the irreplaceable being squandered, and in the depths of our consciousness we are fearful that we are creating an uninhabitable world. We feel more or less helpless and yet, at the same time, desirous to protect what resources we can. We recycle soda bottles and restore old buildings and protect our nearest natural resource—our physical health—in the almost superstitious hope that such small gestures will help save an earth that we are blighting. Jogging becomes a sort of penance for our sins of gluttony, greed, and waste. Like a hairshirt or a bed of nails, the more one hates it, the more virtuous it makes one feel.

That is why *we* jog. Why *I* jog is to win at tennis.

DISCUSSION QUESTIONS ■

1. Does Tucker focus on causes or effects? How does the sentence fragment that ends paragraph 2 relate to this focus?

2. What function does paragraph 3 serve?

3. Identify the causes or effects that Tucker discusses. In what order are they presented?

4. Explain the meaning of this sentence in paragraph 6: "Freedom is a wide and risky river; it can drown the person who does not know how to swim across it." Relate this sentence to the focus on causes or effects.

5. Explain how Tucker defends his contention in paragraph 9 that we are anticipating "the eventual depletion of all natural resources."

6. Why are "we" and "I" italicized in paragraph 10?

7. If you are a jogger or an exercise enthusiast, do you know why? If you are a couch potato, do you know why? Discuss.

SUGGESTION FOR WRITING ■   Write an essay explaining the causes or effects of the popular preoccupation with dieting, sleek cars, fashionable clothes, or something similar.

ALEX TAYLOR III

■ *Why Women Managers Are Bailing Out*

Alex Taylor III (born 1945) is a writer on business and finance at Time, Inc., where he is an associate editor of Fortune. *Before joining Time, Inc., he was a business news writer at the* Detroit Free Press *and a news reporter, producer, and anchorman at three Midwestern television stations. Born in Greenwich, Connecticut, Taylor graduated with a B.A. in history from Middlebury College and an M.A. in journalism from the University of Missouri. He is a member of the adjunct faculty of the Columbia Graduate School of Journalism. In this essay, Taylor examines a recent business phenomenon, the exodus of large numbers of women from the ranks of management.*

When the history of the last quarter of the 20th century in the U.S. is written, scholars may well conclude that the nation's most important social development has been the rise to positions of power and influence of its most   1

These reasons are arranged from least to most important. The economic reason is essentially dismissed, the discipline one is plausible, and the theological one goes "one step further." But in paragraph 9 he explains what drives us "even more."

4. Tucker means that people with too much free time have problems occupying that time. Regular jogging can become part of the answer.

5. The four sentences immediately following offer supporting evidence for the statement. You may want to point out the parallel structure of these sentences.

6. The "we" tend to jog for reasons related to survival; the "I" (Tucker) jogs for practical reasons.

7. This question should prompt an interesting and revealing discussion. It could be used as a springboard for a writing assignment.

PERSPECTIVE

The cause-and-effect essays demonstrate how purpose affects a piece of writing. Forster, Crews, and Tucker all present personal insights—with which others might disagree—on their topics. They write informally in the first person. In contrast, Taylor, who writes in the third person and uses technical language, has produced an objective report which is unlikely to trigger serious disagreement.

TEACHING STRATEGIES

1. Ask students to compare Taylor's essay with the one written by either Forster, Crews, or Tucker and try to account for the differences in language, content, point of view, and tone. Suggest that students consider these matters in light of the writers' purposes. The ensuing discussion can provide an excellent opportunity to discuss the role of purpose in shaping these elements.

2. Ask students to evaluate the audience Taylor has in mind and to defend their conclusions with references to the essay.

3. Taylor relies on a number of direct quotations. Ask students to locate some examples, point out how and why he establishes the qualifications of those quoted, and discuss the reasons for using quotations.

4. Ask students to comment on the effectiveness of Taylor's opening sentence and to indicate what they can learn from it.

5. To reinforce the notion of coherence, have students examine paragraphs 10–22 and point out how they are connected.

CLASSROOM ACTIVITY

Organize students into small groups and have them brainstorm some of the reasons people quit jobs—domineering bosses, unsafe conditions, poor pay, health considerations, burn out, and the like. Each group could present its conclusions in a report delivered to the entire class. A writing assignment might follow.

2

3

4
5

6

7

8

vigorous majority: American women. So many women have come flocking into the labor force—fully 70% of all American women aged 25 to 54 are today at work for pay or actively seeking jobs—that more Americans are now employed than ever before. . . .

But there is a cloud, no bigger than a woman's hand, on the horizon. Many women, including some of the best educated and most highly motivated, are dropping out of the managerial work force. A disquieting number of the dropouts are the pioneering women who have struggled so hard, often in the face of prejudice and economic adversity, to earn the valued passport to high executive rank in corporate America, the Master of Business Administration degree.

A decade ago scarcely one newly minted MBA in eight was a woman. Today the proportion has risen dramatically and hearteningly to one in three. Yet the fact that many of those who led the way ten years ago have begun to bail out presents worrisome auguries not only for the female MBAs, but also for women of all kinds in the work force. If the MBAs cannot find gratification there, can *any* women?

To take just two examples:

Earning a master's degree in management from Northwestern University's Kellogg School in 1976 represented a personal triumph for Kathleen Mattox. She attended classes at night while working full time as a sales representative, first for American Hospital Supply and then for Abbott Laboratories. This enabled her to pay about half the $24,000 cost of her degree. Upon graduation she went to work for Bristol-Myers as an associate product manager in its medical devices subsidiary, based in Warsaw, Indiana.

Mattox thrived on the heavy travel to such cities as Hong Kong, Singapore, and Sydney, but both she and her husband chafed at Warsaw's provincialism. When she was recruited by 3M to work in St. Paul, she leaped at the chance. But the job, supervising a 15-person marketing department for orthopedic products, proved too demanding. "I was the youngest person in that job and one of only two women holding jobs like it," she recalls. "I was working my buns off, and there was a lot of emotional pressure." Already rocky, the marriage, her second, failed.

In 1983 Mattox decided she had had enough of big companies. She quit 3M to start her own marketing consulting firm, catering to clients in the health-care business. Working out of a converted bedroom in her home, she still puts in long hours on occasion, but now she has what she wants. Says she: "There are no hassles and it's great. I just want to live in the style to which I've become accustomed as a self-employed person. I have no visions of grandeur."

Another member of the class of '76, Mary Beth Deyerle took her MBA from the University of Chicago and then got her first job at Texas Commerce Bank in Houston. She soon discovered that she was earning $500 a year less than a man with similar experience in the same job. "At first I was kind of angry, especially with this talk about equality," she says. "Finally I accepted it." Three years later she left the bank to have her first child, even though she was due a promotion to assistant vice president. "A lot of women MBAs feel guilty if they stay home. An MBA is an aggressive person. You want something for yourself—money, power, whatever. To give it all up is a cop-out in a way." For the first 18 months Deyerle missed her job, but now, after the birth of her second child, she has no plans to return. Says she: "I don't think you can both be a mother and work every day without it taking a big toll on you."

Not so long ago such defections would have gone unnoticed. Women were expected to work only a few years before marrying or having children. But times have radically changed, particularly with the awarding of substantial numbers of MBAs to women beginning in the mid-1970s. These women were supposed to lead the charge into the corridors of corporate power. Now many of these would-be leaders are retreating.

Fortune analyzed the career paths of men and women who received MBAs in 1976 from 17 of the most selective business schools. The analysis shows that of those whose first jobs were identifiable from school records, the same percentage of women MBAs as men—69%—went to work for large corporations or professional firms. Ten years later, of those who reported their current job situations on alumni questionnaires, about the same percentage—44% of the men and 43% of the women—still worked for such employers.

But there is one major difference between male and female MBAs. After ten years significantly more women than men have dropped off the management track. That is, they have left positions where they either managed other people or were clearly on their way to doing so. Fully 30% of the 1,039 women from the class of '76 reported they are either self-employed or unemployed or they listed no occupation. Men bail out too, but the percentage is much smaller. Some 21% of the 4,255 men listed either self-employment or no occupation on the alumni questionnaires.

Even those numbers probably understate the difference. Telephone interviews with a random sample of over 50 of the women in the 30% indicate that many work only part time out of their homes, or do not work at paying jobs at all. Phone interviews with 50 men chosen at random from the 21% found that 29 are in fact working for companies, 19 are self-employed, and only two are unemployed. . . .

This attrition in the managerial work force comes at a critical time for working women. Companies have had visible numbers of female managers for two decades or so. But the unspoken expectation back in the 1960s and early 1970s was that any women who had persevered and become managers had put child-rearing behind them or forgone families entirely. Women MBAs from 1976 and the classes that followed are among the first trying to juggle the demands of full-time jobs with family life. If these women decide their careers are not worth the struggle, their example may deter younger women coming along behind them. Corporations will lose a supply of talented executives.

Why are women dropping out? First, they find it hard to get ahead—harder, they think, than it is for men. Says Donald Johnson of the New York executive search firm of Johnson Smith & Knisely: "When they reach their mid-30s and early 40s, women feel the men surging ahead of them. They aren't winding up in the important jobs." Mary Anne Devanna, a research coordinator at Columbia's Graduate School of Business who has studied the careers of MBAs, observes: "Women are making rational decisions. The probability that they will make chairman of the board is less than that of men, so if higher responsibility isn't going to be forthcoming, now is the time to quit."

9

10

11

12

13

14

15   At the majority of companies, the most successful women still find themselves stuck just below the level of vice president. A new study by Korn/Ferry International, the executive recruiting firm, shows that at Fortune 500 industrial and service companies women account for only 2% of senior executives—defined as vice presidents and above, but excluding the president and chairman.

16   Women also suspect they are not paid as well as their male classmates. They are often right. Research at the University of Pittsburgh indicates that MBA women who joined accounting firms in 1973 were earning an average of $6,400 less than their male counterparts ten years later. Women who received MBAs from Pitt between 1973 and 1982 earned an average of $9,000 less in 1983 than men from the same graduating classes. When differences in work experience and job type were eliminated, women still made $2,200 less.

17   There are several theories to explain why women seem to feel more unhappiness with corporate life than men do. One is that women more often find themselves stifled by organizational rigidity. Ardis Burst left Harvard Business School in 1976 "fueled with rockets," she says. But after the birth of her first child, she quit her job at General Foods as an associate product manager in the Maxwell House division. Says she of life in a big company: "There's a lack of autonomy. The homogeneity is difficult to live with. They only real reward was money and, further down the line, power, but the trade-off didn't seem worth it." Burst is now writing a book on management, and says she will never go back to a large corporation.

18   A second theory holds that women are still shunted away from exciting operating assignments into staff jobs in the "three p's": purchasing, personnel, and public relations. Yet another theory maintains that the number of women managers has not yet reached the critical mass needed for them to function comfortably in the corporate world.

19   In their forthcoming book, *Success and Betrayal: The Crisis of Women in Corporate America*, authors Sarah Hardesty and Nehama Jacobs, who interviewed 100 women, contend that the level of discontent is far higher than generally acknowledged. They blame part of it on women's own unrealistic expectations, expectations buoyed by stories of individual successes and by the pronouncements of the women's movement about how fulfilling work outside the home supposedly is.

20   The demands of raising a family are probably the biggest factor driving women out of the corporation. Says Allan Cox, a Chicago executive recruiter: "We have more women than before who are having second thoughts about everything-for-the-career. When the baby comes along, the six-week maternity leave becomes a two-year maternity leave." The notion of the so-called superwoman who successfully manages job and family is far less popular than it was a few years ago. "My perception is that women have given up the goal of being superwomen because it is impossible," observes Eleanor G. May, A University of Virginia Business School professor. "Only a few people can cope, and if you talk to them you discover that they aren't coping satisfactorily, and the stress is greater than they should be handling."

21   Some research even suggests that having a family can hurt women's careers. In her study of Columbia MBAs from the classes of '69 through '72, Mary

Ann Devanna found that only 58% of the women were married, compared with 73% of the men. She concluded: "Women are still asked to pay a significant price for their economic success by limiting the probability that they will also marry." Josephine Olson, a researcher at the University of Pittsburgh, also observes that women who have a managerial career are less likely to have a husband and children. "Why is not clear," Olson says. "Do the MBAs consciously choose to make sacrifices in their personal lives for their careers? Or are the women who are less interested in being wives and mothers the ones who are most interested in being managers?"

No one knows the answer. But women's priorities change as they grow   22
older. The career-minded 25-year-old dynamo is often more concerned about marriage and a family a few years later. Brooke Banbury-Masland, a management specialist at Data General Corp., and Daniel Brass, a Penn State professor, studied 94 MBA women whose average age was 30. They found marriage had overtaken career as what the women valued most. The authors concluded: "As more of the women married, careers did not decrease in importance, but the importance of marriage increased significantly. In response to the statement, 'I feel that a career can take the place of marriage,' most of the sample strongly disagreed."

More and more women are deciding to leave companies to go to work for   23
themselves. The number of self-employed women surged from 2.1 million in 1980 to 2.6 million in 1985. The most popular areas to start businesses in are consulting, retail sales, and educational services, followed closely by public relations, real estate, and advertising. . . .

The two-career couple, a phenomenon that has become widespread, cre-   24
ates strains that can lead to work force defections. Consider the day-to-day life of Ilene Gordon, a graduate of M.I.T.'s Sloan School of Management and now a vice president of Packaging Corp. of America. Gordon operates on a schedule that would derail Amtrak. Both she and her husband, vice president with the Booz Allen consulting firm, travel frequently for work; sometimes they rendezvous at the airport and take a limo home together. Sunday is the only day of the week they eat dinner with their two small children. Gordon functions on six hours of sleep a night and seems to thrive. She concedes that "I'm probably missing out on some important moments in my daughter's life, but I think I'm getting plenty. Besides, my children have each other."

Even the best organized household can be thrown off-balance, though.   25
When the baby sitter does not arrive or a nursery closes down unexpectedly, parents are faced with a decision about who will stay home with the child. Opportunities for one spouse to change jobs or relocate can become traumatic decisions. Couples complain that they have everything except time together.

Most companies have been slow to change the aspects of corporate life that   26
drive women out. One problem is that corporations lack data on the phenomenon. Phyllis Silverman, who directed a study of corporate policies on parental leave for Catalyst, a research group that studies issues relating to women in the workplace, says: "Companies are not keeping statistics on how many women leave, how many come back, and how many remain a year after they return from maternity leave. Corporate information is all based on anecdotal evidence about 'that woman' who took maternity leave and never came back." Some executives

fear that figures showing an exodus of women due to frustration and lack of promotion could open the way to lawsuits for sex discrimination.

27   A number of organizations, though are beginning to awaken to the problem. . . . It has already become acute at certain Big Eight accounting firms, where more than half of new hires are women. At Touche Ross, for example, women have been leaving to work for client companies, where the hours and travel are more predictable. In response the firm is experimenting with a four-day workweek for mothers of young children who want to stay on the partnership track. The short-week path takes ten to 12 years rather than the traditional eight to ten years, but keeps women in the running. Touche Ross refuses to disclose how many women are partners now, and will say only that several junior women are using the short-week path.

28   At other companies women seeking to vary their work schedules are encouraged to cut their own deals with bosses. Corporations generally avoid formal policies on such arrangements as flexible working hours, work at home, shortened workweeks, or job sharing. Despite the publicity generated about telecommuting, for instance, only two companies—Pacific Bell and Mountain Bell—are known to have programs that allow managers to work at home on computer terminals. Lack of flexibility can hurt. Janie Witham, a 1976 Indiana University MBA, was on a managerial career track at IBM—legendary for its consideration of employees—for eight years. She ended up quitting, though, because the company would not allow her to work part time after the birth of her child. . .

29   Corporations will be under increasing pressure to develop better policies for child care. Many already provide referral services and some have supported independent day-care centers, but only a handful have opened their own on-premise facilities or provided financial assistance for at-home baby sitters.

30   One of the few major U.S. corporations with its own day-care center is Campbell Soup. Some 125 children—80 are on the waiting list—aged 2 months to 5 years spend their day in a center across the street from Campbell's Camden, New Jersey, headquarters. The company picks up half the weekly tab, which can total $95. Campbell President R. Gordon McGovern says the center cuts absenteeism, reduces distractions at work, and enables the company to hire people it could not hire before.

31   Consultants urge companies to survey employees to find out exactly what kind of child care they need. The simplest solution is to give workers more time off, such as when a child is sick. But that's tough to do with managers. Other possibilities include direct payments for child care through a flexible benefits system that also allows workers without children to direct the payments to other purposes. Such benefits are tax deductible to the employer and tax free to the employee, and would remain so under the tax reform bill. Some companies provide counseling on child care and steer parents toward community care programs, which they may also help subsidize. Most employers find they do not want their own day-care centers on the premises. For one thing, parents do not like to commute with their children. For another, the threat of lawsuits against child-care providers has sent insurance premiums spiraling.

DISCUSSION QUESTIONS

1. Taylor establishes the significance of his subject—the rise of America's women to positions of power and influence—and the size of the female work force: 70% of all women aged 25 to 54. These facts lead him to the cloud on the horizon (paragraph 2). **2.** These examples illustrate the nature and the severity of the problems that women managers face and how they are reacting. The cases not only lend credence to the contention that many women are leaving the ranks of management but also help us to understand why.

So what is a company to do? Corporate management is by its nature a consultative process, difficult to pull off unless all the managers are present. But efficient companies should be able to afford women managers more flexibility in their hours, particularly at the beginning and end of the workday. Establishing a separate career track for women to permit extended leaves of absence may seem like perpetuation of their treatment as persons apart. But it may be the only way to keep them in the corporate fold. Companies will have to recognize, too, that nowadays their best future executives are often married to other promising managers. These busy people may not be willing to relocate or work a 70-hour week.

The tougher challenge for corporations will be to overcome the remaining, sometimes extraordinarily subtle barriers to women's advancement. If employers are serious about treating women equitably, they obviously will have to put them in the same jobs, provide them with the same support, and give them the same power as men.

As Rosabeth Kanter [a professor at Harvard Business School] notes, companies have found a place in the managerial work force for the superwoman who came to the job unencumbered by outside obligations. Now, if they want the benefit of her brains, they will have to find a place for the woman with a family. The woman, in short, who is merely human.

32

33

34

3. Paragraphs 14–22 deal with the reasons women are dropping out. Note that the first sentence of paragraph 14 sets up the causes to follow. There are six causes: women find that it is difficult for them to attain the top management ranks (paragraphs 14 and 15), women are not paid as well as men (paragraph 16), women are stifled by organizational rigidity (paragraph 17), women are shunted into staff jobs rather than receiving more exciting operating jobs (paragraph 18), women have unrealistic expectations (paragraph 19), and family demands and the pull of marriage override the desire for corporate success (paragraphs 20–22). The causes seem to be arranged in order of climax, as the start of paragraph 20 notes that "The demands of raising a family are probably the biggest factor. . . ."

4. The effects that Taylor discusses are of two sorts: on the women and on their employers. First Taylor notes that more and more women are going to work for themselves (paragraph 23). Then, turning his attention to employers, he points out that Touche Ross is experimenting with a four-day work week for mothers of young children (paragraph 27), some companies encourage women to negotiate flexible work schedules (paragraph 28), and other companies have established day-care centers for the children of female employees (paragraphs 29 and 30) or are being urged to survey women about their child-care preferences (paragraph 31).

5. Taylor attempts to conclude with punch by using a fragment that calls attention to itself and highlights the situation of the woman who can't be manager, wife, and mother all at once. We always tell our students that even though professional writers sometimes use fragments, complete sentences are expected in freshman English.

6. These questions should prompt a spirited discussion.

DISCUSSION QUESTIONS ■

1. Besides starting the essay, what does Taylor accomplish in his opening paragraph?

2. What purpose do the two examples detailed in paragraphs 5–8 serve? Explain why the essay would have been less effective without these examples.

3. In what part of the essay does Taylor deal with causes? What are these causes? In what order are they arranged?

4. Where does Taylor deal with effects? What are these effects?

5. Note that Taylor concludes his essay with a sentence fragment. How would you justify this fragment?

6. Do you think it would be discriminating against men to grant women managers the special concessions the essay names? Why or why not?

SUGGESTION FOR WRITING ■   **Write an essay explaining why you changed your mind about some important matter. For example, you might tell why you altered a decision to attend a certain college or follow a certain career or why you switched your views on marriage, religion, or politics. End the essay by briefly noting one or more effects of the change.**

Three of the definition essays define abstract terms, and one defines a concrete term. In developing their topics, two writers use brief definitions in the form of metaphors (for example, "Waiting is a kind of suspended animation" and "True charm is an aura. . . ."), a third uses an essential definition, and the fourth uses a variant form of an essential definition that is presented as a question. All four essays employ formal–informal language, two with a pronounced formal slant, and all incorporate some of the other writing strategies.

PERSPECTIVE

Most students should be receptive to Morrow's essay since waiting—in cafeteria, registration, book-buying, and library checkout lines—is an all-too-familiar part of their college experience. Students, however, may not have viewed life's waits as burdensome, rendering us helpless and powerless.

> Introduction: notes negative aspects of waiting and some ways of coping

> Body: paragraphs 2–10

> Development by single example

Definition

LANCE MORROW

◼ *Waiting as a Way of Life*

Lance Morrow (born 1939) was born in Lewisburg, Pennsylvania, and attended Harvard University, graduating in 1963. After a short stint at the Washington Star, *he moved to* Time *magazine, where he is now a senior writer. His writings for* Time *include numerous cover stories and essays; and he has also authored one book,* The Chief: A Memoir of Fathers and Sons, *in which he explores his relationship with his father. In 1981, he received a National Magazine Award for his essays in* Time. *In our selection, Morrow explores the various facets of one of life's unpleasant necessities: waiting.*

1   Waiting is a kind of suspended animation. Time solidifies: a dead weight. The mind reddens a little with anger and then blanks off into a sort of abstraction and fitfully wanders, but presently it comes up red and writhing again, straining to get loose. Waiting casts one's life into a little dungeon of time. It is a way of being controlled, of being rendered immobile and helpless. One can read a book or sing (odd looks from the others) or chat with strangers if the wait is long enough to begin forming a bond of shared experience, as at a snowed-in airport. But people tend to do their waiting stolidly. When the sound system went dead during the campaign debate in 1976, Jerry Ford and Jimmy Carter stood in mute suspension for 27 minutes, looking lost.

2   To enforce a wait, of course, is to exert power. To wait is to be powerless. Consider one minor, almost subliminal form. The telephone rings. One picks up the receiver and hears a secretary say, "Please hold for Mr. Godot." One sits for perhaps five seconds, the blood pressure just beginning to cook up toward the red line, when Godot comes on the line with a hearty "How are ya?" and business proceeds and the moment passes, Mr. Godot having established that he is (subtly) in control, that his time is more precious than his callee's. (Incidentally, the only effective response to hearing the secretary's "Please hold for . . ." is to hang up without explanation. After two or three times, Mr. Godot himself will place the call, as he should have done at the start.)

But the "please hold" ploy is a mere flicker in the annals of great and horrible waiting. Citizens of the Soviet Union would think it bourgeois decadence to complain about such a trifle. The Soviets have turned waiting into a way of life. The numb wait is their negotiating style: a heavy, frozen, wordless impassivity designed to madden and exhaust the people across the table. To exist in the Soviet Union is to wait. Almost perversely, when Soviet shoppers see a line forming, they simply join it, assuming that some scarce item is about to be offered for sale. A study published by *Pravda* calculates that Soviet citizens waste 37 billion hours a year standing in line to buy food and other basic necessities. To bind an entire people to that kind of life is to do a little of the work of the Gulag in a different style.

Waiting is a form of imprisonment. One is doing time—but why? One is being punished not for an offense of one's own but often for the inefficiencies of those who impose the wait. Hence the peculiar rage that waits engender, the sense of injustice. Aside from boredom and physical discomfort, the subtler misery of waiting is the knowledge that one's most precious resource, time, a fraction of one's life, is being stolen away, irrecoverably lost.

Americans have ample miseries of waiting, of course—waits sometimes connected with affluence and leisure. The lines to get a passport in Manhattan last week stretched around the block in Rockefeller Center. Travelers waited four and five hours just to get into bureaucracy's front door. A Washington *Post* editorial writer reported a few days ago that the passengers on her 747, diverted to Hartford, Conn., on the return flight from Rome as a result of bad weather in New York City, were forced to sit on a runway for seven hours because no customs inspectors were on hand to process them.

The great American waits are often democratic enough, like traffic jams. Some of the great waits have been collective, tribal—waiting for the release of the American hostages in Iran, for example. But waiting often makes class distinctions. One of the more depressing things about being poor in America is the endless waiting in welfare or unemployment lines. The waiting rooms of the poor are forlorn, but in fact almost all waiting rooms are spiritless and blank-eyed places where it always feels like 3 in the morning.

One of the inestimable advantages of wealth is the immunity that it can purchase from serious waiting. The rich do not wait in long lines to buy groceries or airplane tickets. The help sees to it. The limousine takes the privileged right out onto the tarmac, their shoes barely grazing the ground.

People wait when they have no choice or when they believe that the wait is justified by the reward—a concert ticket, say. Waiting has its social orderings, its rules and assumptions. Otherwise peaceful citizens explode when someone cuts into a line that has been waiting a long time. It is unjust; suffering is not being fairly distributed. Oddly, behavioral scientists have found that the strongest protests tend to come from the immediate victims, the people directly behind the line jumpers. People farther down the line complain less or not at all, even though they have been equally penalized by losing a place.

Waiting is difficult for children. They have not yet developed an experienced relationship with time and its durations: "Are we there yet, Daddy?" There can be pleasant, tingling waits, of course, full of fantasies, and they are often

3 | Development by single example

4 | Development by cause and effect

5 | Development by two brief examples

6 | Paragraphs 6 and 7: development by comparison

7

8 | Development by cause and effect, comparison

9 | Development by comparison

connected with children: the wait for the child to arrive in the first place, the wait for Christmas, for summer vacation. Children wait more intensely than adults do. Sheer anticipation makes their blood jump in a lovely way.

| Development by comparison | 10 |

Waiting can have a delicious quality ("I can't wait to see her." "I can't wait for the party"), and sometimes the waiting is better than the event awaited. At the other extreme, it can shade into terror: when one waits for a child who is late coming home or—most horribly—has vanished. When anyone has disappeared, in fact, or is missing in action, the ordinary stress of waiting is overlaid with an unbearable anguish of speculation: Alive or dead?

| Conclusion: contains an ironic twist | 11 |

Waiting can seem an interval of nonbeing, the blank space between events and the outcomes of desires. It makes time maddeningly elastic: it has a way of seeming to compact eternity into a few hours. Yet its brackets ultimately expand to the largest dimensions. One waits for California to drop into the sea or for "next year in Jerusalem" or for the Messiah or for the Apocalypse. All life is a waiting, and perhaps in that sense one should not be too eager for the wait to end. The region that lies on the other side of waiting is eternity.

DISCUSSION QUESTIONS ■

1. What is Morrow's purpose in writing this definition? Cite specific parts of the essay to defend your answer.
2. For what audience does he write? How do you know?

SUGGESTION FOR WRITING ■   Write an essay that defines speed or efficiency as a way of life. Use the methods of development that seem most appropriate.

LAURENCE SHAMES

■ *The Sweet Smell of Success Isn't All That Sweet*

Laurence Shames (born 1951) is a native of Newark, New Jersey, and a graduate of New York University. After completing his education, he began a career as a nonfiction writer, contributing to such publications as Playboy, McCalls, Esquire, Vanity Fair, *and the* New York Times. *A 1986 book,* The Big Time: The Harvard Business School's Most Successful Class and How It Shaped America, *explores the contributions of the 1949 graduating class to the worlds of business and public service. Shames's writings reflect a strong concern for values, a concern apparent in the following selection, which attacks contemporary attitudes about success.*

DISCUSSION QUESTIONS

1. Morrow's purpose might be stated in this way: to wait is to be controlled, powerless, even imprisoned. Several parts of the essay convey this notion. Paragraph 1: "straining to get loose," "little dungeon of time," "way of . . . being rendered immobile and helpless." Paragraph 2: "exert power" and "to be powerless," "he is (subtly) in control." Paragraph 3: the Soviet "negotiating style" and the reference to "the Gulag." Paragraph 4: "form of imprisonment" and "stolen away, irrecoverably lost." Paragraphs 5–10 show various manifestations of waiting and the resultant helplessness.
2. Morrow writes for a general, intelligent audience, one that does not consist of a certain age group or is not marked by specialized knowledge or particular interests. His examples are drawn from all levels—children, rich, poor—and they will be familiar to most of us: traffic jams, American hostages in Iran, waiting for concert tickets. In addition, his sentences and words, as well as the notation that the essay originally appeared in *Time,* suggest this general, intelligent audience.

John Milton was a failure. In writing "Paradise Lost," his stated aim was to "justify the ways of God to men." Inevitably, he fell short of accomplishing that and only wrote a monumental poem. Beethoven, whose music was conceived to transcend Fate, was a failure, as was Socrates, whose ambition was to make people happy by making them reasonable and just. The inescapable conclusion seems to be that the surest, noblest way to fail is to set one's own standards titanically high.

The flip-side of that proposition also seems true, and it provides the safe but dreary logic by which most of us live: The surest way to succeed is to keep one's strivings low—or at least to direct them along already charted paths. Don't set yourself the probably thankless task of making the legal system better; just shoot at becoming a partner in the firm. Don't agonize over questions about where your talents and proclivities might most fulfillingly lead you; just do a heads-up job of determining where the educational or business opportunities seem most secure.

After all, if "success" itself—rather than the substance of the achievements that make for success—is the criterion by which we measure ourselves and from which we derive our self-esteem, why make things more difficult by reaching for the stars?

What is this contemporary version of success really all about?

According to certain beer commercials, it consists in moving up to a premium brand that costs a dime or so more per bottle. Credit-card companies would have you believe success inheres in owning their particular piece of plastic.

If these examples sound petty, they are. But take those petty privileges, weave them into a fabric that passes for a value system and what you've got is a national mood that has vast motivating power that can shape at least the near future of the entire company.

Under the flag of success, modern-style, liberal arts colleges are withering while business schools are burgeoning—and yet even business schools are having an increasingly hard time finding faculty members, because teaching isn't considered "successful" enough. Amid a broad consensus that there is a glut of lawyers and an epidemic of strangling litigation, record numbers of young people continue to flock to law school because, for the individual practitioner, a law degree is still considered a safe ticket.

The most sobering thought of all is that today's M.B.A.'s and lawyers are tomorrow's M.B.A.'s and lawyers: Having invested so much time and money in their training, only a tiny percentage of them will ever opt out of their early chosen fields. Decisions made in accordance with today's hothouse notions of ambition are locking people into careers that will define and also limit their activities and yearnings for virtually the rest of their lives.

Many, by external standards, will be "successes." They will own homes, eat in better restaurants, dress well and, in some instances, perform socially useful work. Yet there is a deadening and dangerous flaw in their philosophy: It has little room, little sympathy and less respect for the noble failure, for the person who ventures past the limits, who aims gloriously high and falls unashamedly short.

That sort of ambition doesn't have much place in a world where success is proved by worldly reward rather than by accomplishment itself. That sort of

1

2

3

4

5

6

7

8

9

10

ambition is increasingly thought of as the domain of irredeemable eccentrics, of people who haven't quite caught on—and there is great social pressure not to be one of them.

11   The result is that fewer people are drawn to the cutting edge of noncommercial scientific research. Fewer are taking on the sublime, unwinnable challenges of the arts. Fewer are asking questions that matter—the ones that can't be answered. Fewer are putting themselves on the line, making as much of their minds and talents as they might.

12   The irony is that today's success-chasers seem obsessed with the idea of *not settling*. They take advanced degrees in business because they won't settle for just a so-so job. They compete for slots at law firms and investment houses because they won't settle for any but the fastest track. They seem to regard it as axiomatic that "success" and "settling" are opposites.

13   Yet in doggedly pursuing the rather brittle species of success now in fashion, they are restricting themselves to a chokingly narrow swath of turf along the entire range of human possibilities. Does it ever occur to them that, frequently, success is what people settle for when they can't think of something noble enough to be worth failing at?

DISCUSSION QUESTIONS

1. Shames clearly signals his ironic intent by emphasizing the noble aims of Milton, Beethoven, and Socrates and by noting that although Milton failed to "justify the ways of God to men," he did produce a "monumental poem." Indeed, the fact that Shames cites men whose achievements have survived for centuries shows that he doesn't seriously consider them failures.

2. Shames is making the point that we define success by the trappings associated with financial advancement rather than by the actual accomplishment. The trappings include such things as the premium beer and credit cards mentioned in paragraph 5 and the homes, elegant meals, and fine clothing alluded to in paragraph 9. Because this distinction highlights the contemporary definition of success, Shames positions it ahead of the paragraphs that elaborate upon it.

3. The essay uses the following writing strategies: Paragraph 1: examples; paragraph 3: comparison; paragraph 5: examples and brief definitions; paragraph 7: comparison and examples; paragraph 9: comparison; paragraphs 10 and 11: cause (10) and effect (11); paragraphs 12 and 13: cause (12) and effect (13).

4. A rhetorical question produces a stronger emphasis than an assertion; thus it draws reader attention.

5. This question should prompt a stimulating discussion.

DISCUSSION QUESTIONS ■

1. In paragraph 1 Shames asserts that Milton, Beethoven, and Socrates were failures. How do you know that he doesn't intend these statements to be taken seriously?

2. Shames notes in paragraph 3 that " 'success' itself—rather than the substance of the achievements that make for success—" seems to be the touchstone by which we measure our worth. What do you think he means? Why is the distinction positioned at this point?

3. What writing strategies does Shames use to develop his essay? Where does he use them?

4. Why do you think Shames ends his essay with a rhetorical question, that is, one for which no answer is expected?

5. To what extent do you agree with Shames's idea of success? Discuss.

SUGGESTION FOR WRITING ■   Write a definition essay explaining how the popular view of responsibility, greed, marriage, single life, friendship, or some other concept needs redefining. Use whatever writing strategies advance your purpose.

LAURIE LEE

■ *Charm*

Laurie Lee (born 1914) was born in Gloustershire, England, and educated in Stroud, England. During World War II, he worked as a documentary film-maker for the Post Office and a publications editor for the Ministry of Information. His publications include several volumes of poetry; a verse play; an autobiographical memoir; and a collection of prose pieces, I Can't Stay Long *(1976), from which this essay is taken. In it, Lee develops an extended definition of charm that features a composite of many qualities, some abstract and some concrete.*

Charm is the ultimate weapon, the supreme seduction, against which there are few defences. If you've got it, you need almost nothing else, neither money, looks, nor pedigree. It's a gift, only given to give away, and the more used the more there is. It is also a climate of behaviour set for perpetual summer and thermostatically controlled by taste and tact.

True charm is an aura, an invisible musk in the air; if you see it working, the spell is broken. At its worst, it is the charm of the charity duchess, like being struck in the face with a bunch of tulips; at its best, it is a smooth and painless injection which raises the blood to a genial fever. Most powerful of all, it is obsessive, direct, person-to-person, forsaking all others. Never attempt to ask for whom the charm-bells ring; if they toll for anyone, they must toll for you.

As to the ingredients of charm, there is no fixed formula; they vary intuitively between man and woman. A whole range of mysteries goes into the cauldron, but the magic remains the same. In some cases, perhaps, the hand of the charmer is lighter, more discreet, less overwhelming, but the experience it offers must be absolute—one cannot be "almost" or "partly" charmed.

Charm in a woman is probably more exacting than in a man, requiring a wider array of subtleties. It is a light in the face, a receptive stance, an air of exclusive welcome, an almost impossibly sustained note of satisfaction in one's company, and regret without fuss at parting. A woman with charm finds no man dull, doesn't have to pretend to ignore his dullness; indeed, in her presence he becomes not just a different person but the person he most wants to be. Such a woman gives life to his deep-held fantasies and suddenly makes them possible, not so much by flattering him as adding the necessary conviction to his long suspicion that he is king.

Of those women who have most successfully charmed me in the past, I remember chiefly their eyes and voices. That swimming way of looking, as though they were crushing wine, their tone of voice, and their silences. The magic of that look showed no distraction, nor any wish to be with anyone else. Their voices were furred with comfort, like plumped-up cushions, intimate and enveloping. Then the listening eyes, supreme charm in a woman, betraying no concern with any other world than this, warmly wrapping one round with total attention and turning one's lightest words to gold. Looking back, I don't pretend

1

2

3

4

5

that I was in any way responsible; theirs was a charm to charm all men, and must have continued to exist, like the flower in the desert, when there was nobody there to see it.

6   A woman's charm needn't always cater to such extremes of indulgence—though no man will complain if it does. At the least, she spreads round her that particular glow of well-being for which any man will want to seek her out, and by making full use of her nature, celebrates the fact of his maleness and so gives him an extra shot of life. Her charm lies also in the air of timeless materialism, that calm and pacifying presence, which can dispel a man's moments of frustration and anger and salvage his failures of will.

7   Charm in a man, I suppose, is his ability to capture the complicity of a woman by a single-minded acknowledgment of her uniqueness. Here again it is a question of being totally absorbed, of forgetting that anyone else exists—but *really* forgetting, for nothing more fatally betrays than the suggestion of a wandering eye. Silent devotion is fine, but seldom enough; it is what a man says that counts, the bold declarations, the flights of fancy, the uncovering of secret virtues. Praise can be a jewel, but the gift must be personal, the only one of its kind in the world; while flattery itself will never be thought excessive so long as there's no suspicion that it's been said before.

8   A man's charm strikes deepest when a woman's imagination is engaged, with herself as the starting point; when she is made a part of some divine extravaganza, or mystic debauch, in which she feels herself both the inspirer and ravished victim. A man is charmed through his eyes, a woman by what she hears, so no man need be too anxious about his age. As wizened Voltaire once said: "Give me a few minutes to talk away my face and I can seduce the Queen of France."

9   No man, even so, will wish to talk a woman to death; there is also room for the confessional priest, a role of unstinted patience and dedication to the cause, together with a modest suspension of judgment. "You may have sinned, but you couldn't help it, you were made for love. . . . You have been wronged, you have suffered too much. . . ." If man has this quality, it is as much a solace to a woman as his power to dilate her with praise and passion.

10   But charm, after all, isn't exclusively sexual, it comes in a variety of cooler flavours. Most children have it—till they are told they have it—and so do old people with nothing to lose; animals, too, of course, and a few outdoor insects, and certain sea-creatures if they can claim to be mammals—seals, whales, and dolphins, but not egg-laying fish (you never saw a fish in a circus). With children and smaller animals it is often in the shape of the head and in the chaste unaccusing stare; with young girls and ponies, a certain stumbling awkwardness, a leggy inability to control their bodies. The sullen narcissism of adolescents, product of over-anxiety, can also offer a ponderous kind of charm. But all these are passive, and appeal to the emotions simply by capturing one's protective instinct.

11   Real charm is dynamic, an enveloping spell which mysteriously enslaves the senses. It is an inner light, fed on reservoirs of benevolence which well up like a thermal spring. It is unconscious, often nothing but the wish to please, and cannot be turned on and off at will. Which would seem to cancel the claims of some of the notorious charmers of the past—Casanova, Lawrence of Arabia,

Rubirosa—whose talent, we suspect, wasn't charm at all so much as a compulsive need to seduce. Others, more recent, had larger successes through being less specific in their targets—Nehru, for instance, and Yehudi Menuhin, Churchill, and the early Beatles. As for the women—Cleopatra, Mata Hari, Madame du Barry—each one endowed with superb physical equipment; were they charmers, too?—in a sense they must have been, though they laid much calculated waste behind them.

You recognize charm by the feeling you get in its presence. You know who   12
has it. But can you get it, too? Properly, you can't, because it's a quickness of spirit, an originality of touch you have to be born with. Or it's something that grows naturally out of another quality, like the simple desire to make people happy. Certainly, charm is not a question of learning palpable tricks, like wrinkling your nose, or having a laugh in your voice, or gaily tossing your hair out of your dancing eyes and twisting your mouth into succulent love-knots. Such signs, to the nervous, are ominous warnings which may well send him streaking for cover. On the other hand, there is an antenna, a built-in awareness of others, which most people have, and which care can nourish.

But in a study of charm, what else does one look for? Apart from the ability   13
to listen—rarest of all human virtues and most difficult to sustain without vagueness—apart from warmth, sensitivity, and the power to please, what else is there visible? A generosity, I suppose, which makes no demands, a transaction which strikes no bargains, which doesn't hold itself back till you've filled up a test-card making it clear that you're worth the trouble. Charm can't withhold, but spends itself willingly on young and old alike, on the poor, the ugly, the dim, the boring, on the last fat man in the corner. It reveals itself also in a sense of ease, in casual but perfect manners, and often in a physical grace which springs less from an accident of youth than from a confident serenity of mind. Any person with this is more than just a popular fellow, he is also a social healer.

Charm, in the abstract, has something of the quality of music: radiance,   14
balance, and harmony. One encounters it unexpectedly in odd corners of life with a shock of brief, inexplicable ravishment: in a massed flight of birds, a string of running horses, an arrangement of clouds on the sea; wooded islands, Tanagra figures, old balconies in Spain, the line of a sports car holding a corner, in the writings of Proust and Jane Austen, the paintings of Renoir and Fragonard, the poetry of Herrick, the sound of lute and guitar. . . . Thickets of leaves can have it, bare arms interlocking, suds of rain racing under a bridge, and such simplicities as waking after a sleep of nightmares to see sunlight bouncing off the ceiling. The effect of these, like many others, is to restore one's place in the world; to reassure, as it were, one's relationship with things, and to bring order to the wilderness.

But charm, in the end, is flesh and blood, a most potent act of behaviour,   15
the laying down of a carpet by one person for another to give his existence a moment of honour. Much is deployed in the weaponry of human dealings: stealth, aggression, blackmail, lust, the urge to possess, devour, and destroy. Charm is the rarest, least used, and most invincible of powers, which can capture with a single glance. It is close to love in that it moves without force, bearing gifts like the growth of daylight. It snares completely, but is never punitive, it disarms

by being itself disarmed, strikes without wounds, wins wars without casualties—though not, of course, without victims. He who would fall in the battle, let him fall to charm, and he will never be humbled, or know the taste of defeat.

16   In the armoury of man, charm is the enchanted dart, light and subtle as a hummingbird. But it is deceptive in one thing—like a sense of humour, if you think you've got it, you probably haven't.

DISCUSSION QUESTIONS ■

1. Why do you think Lee began with the statement "Charm is the ultimate weapon . . . "?
2. Explain this apparent contradiction in paragraph 1: "It's a gift, only given to give away, and the more used the more there is."
3. What significance do you attach to the opening words of paragraph 3: "As to the ingredients of charm, there is no fixed formula . . . "?
4. What method of development does Lee use in paragraphs 4–9? 14?
5. Show that Lee attributes a certain magical aura to the quality of charm by citing specific examples from the essay.
6. Lee makes some sweeping statements in this essay: "A man is charmed through his eyes, a woman by what she hears, so no man need be too anxious about his age" (paragraph 8) and "The ability to listen [is the] rarest of all human virtues . . . " (paragraph 13). Do you agree with these statements? Why or why not?

SUGGESTION FOR WRITING ■   **Pick one of the following characteristics that you've noted in an acquaintance. Then write an essay in which you define that characteristic, using your acquaintance as a basis for your definition.**

1. **sensitivity**
2. **sense of humor**
3. **assertiveness**
4. **charisma**
5. **class**

CITICORP N. A.

■ *The Bureaucrat*

At one time or another, almost everyone has run afoul of bureaucratic bungling and red tape. Why do such difficulties occur so often? In the selection below, the anonymous author defines "bureaucrat" and clears up the mystery for us.

Bureaucracy is a state of mind. True, every bureaucrat needs an organization, a milieu—to choose another useful word from the French—but it is the bureaucrat who makes the milieu, not the other way around.

Most of us associate bureaucracy and all its attendant evils with large organizations, especially governments, and we are not surprised to see it getting worse. As the earth's population grows and computers multiply along with the people, burgeoning bureaucracy appears a natural consequence. What Thomas Carlyle, a hundred years ago, could dismiss contemptuously as "the Continental nuisance called 'Bureaucracy' " is now to become the fate of all humanity because there are so many of us.

Before resigning ourselves to the inevitable, however, we might pause to consider that one of the most pervasive bureaucracies the world has ever known was oppressing the population of the Nile Valley 5,000 years ago, when there were fewer people in the entire world than now live in North America. Add to this the thought that the same number of people can be organized into (*a*) an army, (*b*) a crowd or (*c*) a mob, and it is clear that something more must be involved than time and numbers.

What distinguishes each of the aforementioned groups is not how many people it contains, nor where they happen to congregate, but their purpose for being there. And so it is with the bureaucrat.

The true bureaucrat is any individual who has lost sight of the underlying purpose of the job at hand, whether in government, industry—or a bank. The purpose of a library, for example, is to facilitate the reading of books. Yet to a certain type of librarian, perfection consists of a well-stocked library with a place for every book—and every book in its place. The reader who insists on taking books home, leaving empty spaces on shelves, is this librarian's natural enemy.

It is a cast of mind invulnerable even to the vicissitudes of war. We see it in James Jones's novel *From Here to Eternity* where American soldiers under surprise attack by Japanese planes at the outbreak of World War II rush to the arsenal for weapons, only to find the door barred by a comrade-in-arms loudly proclaiming that he cannot pass out live ammunition without a written request signed by a commissioned officer.

One of these custodians forgot the purpose of a library, the other, the purpose of an army. Both illustrate how, in institutionalized endeavors, means have a way of displacing the ends they are originally designed to serve. In fact, it is one of the bureaucrat's distinguishing features that, for him or for her, the means *become* the ends.

The struggle to prevent this subtle subversion is—or should be—a continual challenge to every policy maker in any organization, public or private. Bureaucrats love any policy and can be counted on to enforce it faithfully, as in, "I'm sorry, but that's the policy here." Unfortunately, they don't understand what a policy is.

A policy is a standard solution to a constantly recurring problem, not an inviolable law. As a weapon in the hands of literal-minded people, however, a "firm policy" can be as deadly as a repeating rifle. When matters finally become intolerable, the harassed administrator will usually "change the policy." Of

1 another. It is of course much easier to mouth the words, "I'm sorry, but that's the policy here" than it is to make individual adjustments for specific circumstances. "The Bureaucrat" should make for interesting reading.

TEACHING STRATEGIES

1. Ask the class to explain the statement in paragraph 1 that "it is the bureaucrat who makes the milieu, not the other way around" and why this statement is positioned at the outset.
2. You might discuss the parallelism, and even the alliteration, in paragraph 10.
3. Have students explain the meaning and significance of the following statements: Paragraph 13: ". . . one who, having forgotten his purpose, redoubles his efforts." Paragraph 14: "We has met the enemy, and they is us."
4. Ask what is accomplished by beginning and ending the essay with the assertion that "Bureaucracy is a state of mind." The answer of course requires an understanding of the entire essay.

CLASSROOM ACITVITY

Divide the class into small groups and ask them to identify and describe examples of bureaucrats. They might start with college bureaucrats they have encountered. The group discussions could culminate in reports that are presented to the entire class and serve as the springboard for a writing assignment.

course, this never helps because the problem was not the policy in the first place, but the manner of its application.

10   Every college student seeking entry into a course for which he lacks the exact prerequisite, every shopper trying to return a gift without receipt of purchase, every bank customer seeking to correct an error in an account is in danger of discovering that the rules imagined by Joseph Heller are in service wherever rote is more revered than reason.

11   The application of binary logic to human affairs through electronic computers has done nothing to retard the spread of *Catch 22* into the wider world. And thus the thought occurs that modern bureaucracy does, after all, present some problems new to history. Nothing lends itself so readily to "a standard solution to a constantly recurring problem" as a computer.

12   In the best of all possible worlds we might look forward to the day when computers handle all standard solutions, freeing human brains to concentrate on the singular and the exceptional. In the real world, it does not always work out that way—as anyone knows who has ever become trapped in a two-way correspondence with a computer and appealed in vain for human intervention.

13   A favorite student protest sign of the sixties read, "I am a Human Being. Do not fold, spindle or mutilate." What they objected to is real, only the fault is not in our computers, but in ourselves. It lies in our human propensity to let means become ends, and all too often to resemble Santayana's description of a fanatic; one who, having forgotten his purpose, redoubles his efforts.

14   We can denounce the bureaucrats and condemn their works, but they will not go away. They have been with us since the dawn of history, and if they seem to be getting worse, it is because *we* are getting worse. For, in the words of the comic strip *Pogo*: "We has met the enemy, and they is us."

15   Bureaucracy is a state of mind, and the best way to fight it—whether you work for government, industry, a private foundation or a bank—is not to be a bureaucrat. Or at least try not to.

DISCUSSION QUESTIONS ■

1. Where does the essential definition of *bureaucrat* appear? The essential definition of *policy*?

2. What methods of writing are used to develop paragraphs 3, 5, and 6?

3. What seems to be the purpose of this essay? Refer to the text to explain your answer.

4. To what audience is it addressed? Again, when answering cite appropriate examples.

SUGGESTION FOR WRITING ■   Write a definition of a corporate raider or a politician. Aim your essay at a specific audience and develop it with several strategies of writing.

Argument

EDWARD I. KOCH

■ *Death and Justice*

Edward Koch (born 1924) is a native of New York, a veteran of World War II, and a graduate of New York University, where he earned a law degree in 1948. For some two decades after graduation, he practiced law in New York City, during which time he began playing an active role in Democratic Party politics. In 1966, he became a district leader and three years later was elected to the city council. Between 1969 and 1977, he served in the U.S. House of Representatives, where he became known for his strong liberal stance on social issues. In 1977, he waged a successful campaign for mayor of New York, pledging to cut crime and reduce wasteful spending. He held the mayor's office until 1990. While mayor, Koch authored two books: Mayor *(1984), an examination of his city's politics, and* Politics *(1985), which records his years as a political fledgling. The following essay, which critiques the views of those opposed to capital punishment, reflects Koch's long-term commitment to crime fighting.*

Last December a man named Robert Lee Willie, who had been convicted of raping and murdering an 18-year-old woman, was executed in the Louisiana state prison. In a statement issued several minutes before his death, Mr. Willie said: "Killing people is wrong. . . . It makes no difference whether it's citizens, countries, or governments. Killing is wrong." Two weeks later in South Carolina, an admitted killer named Joseph Carl Shaw was put to death for murdering two teenagers. In an appeal to the governor for clemency, Mr. Shaw wrote: "Killing is wrong when I did it. Killing is wrong when you do it. I hope you have the courage and moral strength to stop the killing."

It is a curiosity of modern life that we find ourselves being lectured on morality by cold-blooded killers. Mr. Willie previously had been convicted of aggravated rape, aggravated kidnapping, and the murders of a Louisiana deputy and a man from Missouri. Mr. Shaw committed another murder a week before the two for which he was executed, and admitted mutilating the body of the 14-year-old girl he killed. I can't help wondering what prompted these murderers to speak out against killing as they entered the death-house door. Did their new-

1   Introduction: paragraphs 1 and 2   Examples

2   Provides background

found reverence for life stem from the realization that they were about to lose their own?

Body: paragraphs 3–14
Proposition of fact   3

Development by example

Life is indeed precious, and I believe the death penalty helps to affirm this fact. Had the death penalty been a real possibility in the minds of these murderers, they might well have stayed their hand. They might have shown moral awareness before their victims died, and not after. Consider the tragic death of Rosa Velez, who happened to be home when a man named Luis Vera burglarized her apartment in Brooklyn. "Yeah, I shot her," Vera admitted. "She knew me, and I knew I wouldn't go to the chair."

Author's qualifications   4

During my 22 years in public service, I have heard the pros and cons of capital punishment expressed with special intensity. As a district leader, councilman, congressman, and mayor, I have represented constituencies generally thought of as liberal. Because I support the death penalty for heinous crimes of murder, I have sometimes been the subject of emotional and outraged attacks by voters who find my position reprehensible or worse. I have listened to their ideas. I have weighed their objections carefully. I still support the death penalty. The reasons I maintained my position can be best understood by examining the arguments most frequently heard in opposition.

First refutation: rejects
emotional appeal   5

1. *The death penalty is "barbaric."* Sometimes opponents of capital punishment horrify with tales of lingering death on the gallows, of faulty electric chairs, or of agony in the gas chamber. Partly in response to such protests, several states such as North Carolina and Texas switched to execution by lethal injection. The condemned person is put to death painlessly, without ropes, voltage, bullets, or gas. Did this answer the objections of death penalty opponents? Of course not. On June 22, 1984, The *New York Times* published an editorial that sarcastically attacked the new "hygienic" method of death by injection, and stated that "execution can never be made humane through science." So it's not the method that really troubles opponents. It's the death itself they consider barbaric.

Concedes point   6
Rational appeal: analogy

Ethical appeal: concedes
point

Admittedly, capital punishment is not a pleasant topic. However, one does not have to like the death penalty in order to support it any more than one must like radical surgery, radiation, or chemotherapy in order to find necessary these attempts at curing cancer. Ultimately we may learn how to cure cancer with a simple pill. Unfortunately, that day has not yet arrived. Today we are faced with the choice of letting the cancer spread or trying to cure it with the methods available, methods that one day will almost certainly be considered barbaric. But to give up and do nothing would be far more barbaric and would certainly delay the discovery of an eventual cure. The analogy between cancer and murder is imperfect, because murder is not the "disease" we are trying to cure. The disease is injustice. We may not like the death penalty, but it must be available to punish crimes of cold-blooded murder, cases in which any other form of punishment would be inadequate and, therefore, unjust. If we create a society in which injustice is not tolerated, incidents of murder—the most flagrant form of injustice—will diminish.

Second refutation   7

2. *No other major democracy uses the death penalty.* No other major democracy—in fact, few other countries of any description—are plagued by a murder rate such as that in the United States. Fewer and fewer Americans can

remember the days when unlocked doors were the norm and murder was a rare and terrible offense. In America the murder rate climbed 122 percent between 1963 and 1980. During that same period, the murder rate in New York City increased by almost 400 percent, and the statistics are even worse in many other cities. A study at M.I.T. showed that based on 1970 homicide rates a person who lived in a large American city ran a greater risk of being murdered than an American soldier in World War II ran of being killed in combat. It is not surprising that the laws of each country differ according to differing conditions and traditions. If other countries had our murder problem, the cry for capital punishment would be just as loud as it is here. And I daresay that any other major democracy where 75 percent of the people supported the death penalty would soon enact it into law.

	Evidence: statistics

3. *An innocent person might be executed by mistake.* Consider the work of Adam Bedau, one of the most implacable foes of capital punishment in this country. According to Mr. Bedau, it is "false sentimentality to argue that the death penalty should be abolished because of the abstract possibility that an innocent person might be executed." He cites a study of the 7,000 executions in this country from 1893 to 1971, and concludes that the record fails to show that such cases occur. The main point, however, is this. If government functioned only when the possibility of error didn't exist, government wouldn't function at all. Human life deserves special protection, and one of the best ways to guarantee that protection is to assure that convicted murderers do not kill again. Only the death penalty can accomplish this end. In a recent case in New Jersey, a man named Richard Biegenwald was freed from prison after serving 18 years for murder; since his release he has been convicted of committing four murders. A prisoner named Lemuel Smith, who, while serving four life sentences for murder (plus two life sentences for kidnapping and robbery) in New York's Green Haven Prison, lured a woman corrections officer into the chaplain's office and strangled her. He then mutilated and dismembered her body. An additional life sentence for Smith is meaningless. Because New York has no death penalty statute, Smith has effectively been given a license to kill.

8   Third refutation

Evidence: statistics

Established truths

Development by examples

Emotional appeal

But the problem of multiple murder is not confined to the nation's penitentiaries. In 1981, 91 police officers were killed in the line of duty in this country. Seven percent of those arrested in the cases that have been solved had a previous arrest for murder. In New York City in 1976 and 1977, 85 persons arrested for homicide had a previous arrest for murder. Six of these individuals had two previous arrests for murder, and one had four previous murder arrests. During those two years the New York police were arresting for murder persons with a previous arrest for murder on the average of one every 8.5 days. This is not surprising when we learn that in 1975, for example, the median time served in Massachusetts for homicide was less than two-and-a half years. In 1976 a study sponsored by the Twentieth Century Fund found that the average time served in the United States for first-degree murder is ten years. The median time served may be considerably lower.

9   Evidence: statistics

4. *Capital punishment cheapens the value of human life.* On the contrary, it can be easily demonstrated that the death penalty strengthens the value of human life. If the penalty for rape were lowered, clearly it would signal a lessened

10   Fourth refutation

Rational appeal: analogy

regard for the victims' suffering, humiliation, and personal integrity. It would cheapen their horrible experience, and expose them to an increased danger of recurrence. When we lower the penalty for murder, it signals a lessened regard for the value of the victim's life. Some critics of capital punishment, such as columnist Jimmy Breslin, have suggested that a life sentence is actually a harsher penalty for murder than death. This is sophistic nonsense. A few killers may decide not to appeal a death sentence, but the overwhelming majority make every effort to stay alive. It is by exacting the highest penalty for the taking of human life that we affirm the highest value of human life.

Fifth refutation 11	*5. The death penalty is applied in a discriminatory manner.* This factor no longer seems to be the problem it once was. The appeals process for a condemned prisoner is lengthy and painstaking. Every effort is made to see that the verdict and sentence were fairly arrived at. However, assertions of discrimination are not an argument for ending the death penalty but for extending it. It is not justice to exclude everyone from the penalty of the law if a few are found to be so favored. Justice requires that the law be applied equally to all.

Sixth refutation   12

Evidence: authoritative opinion

6. Thou shalt not kill. The Bible is our greatest source of moral inspiration. Opponents of the death penalty frequently cite the sixth of the Ten Commandments in an attempt to prove that capital punishment is divinely proscribed. In the original Hebrew, however, the Sixth Commandment reads, "Thou Shalt Not Commit Murder," and the Torah specifies capital punishment for a variety of offenses. The biblical viewpoint has been upheld by philosophers throughout history. The greatest thinkers of the 19th century—Kant, Locke, Hobbes, Rousseau, Montesquieu, and Mill—agreed that natural law properly authorizes the sovereign to take life in order to vindicate justice. Only Jeremy Bentham was ambivalent. Washington, Jefferson, and Franklin endorsed it. Abraham Lincoln authorized executions for deserters in wartime. Alexis de Tocqueville, who expressed profound respect for American institutions, believed that the death penalty was indispensable to the support of social order. The United States Constitution, widely admired as one of the seminal achievements in the history of humanity, condemns cruel and inhuman punishment, but does not condemn capital punishment.

Seventh refutation   13

7. The death penalty is state-sanctioned murder. This is the defense with which Messrs. Willie and Shaw hoped to soften the resolve of those who sentenced them to death. By saying in effect, "You're no better than I am," the murderer seeks to bring his accusers down to his own level. It is also a popular argument among opponents of capital punishment, but a transparently false one. Simply put, the state has rights that the private individual does not. In a democracy, those rights are given to the state by the electorate. The execution of a lawfully condemned killer is no more an act of murder than is legal imprisonment an act of kidnapping. If an individual forces a neighbor to pay him money under threat of punishment, it's called extortion. If the state does it, it's called taxation. Rights and responsibilities surrendered by the individual are what give the state its power to govern. This contract is the foundation of civilization itself.

Rational appeal: analogy

14   Everyone wants his or her rights, and will defend them jealously. Not everyone, however, wants responsibilities, especially the painful responsibilities that come with law enforcement. Twenty-one years ago a woman named Kitty

Genovese was assaulted and murdered on a street in New York. Dozens of neighbors heard her cries for help but did nothing to assist her. They didn't even call the police. In such a climate the criminal understandably grows bolder. In the presence of moral cowardice, he lectures us on our supposed failings and tries to equate his crimes with our quest for justice.

The death of anyone—even a convicted killer—diminishes us all. But we are diminished even more by a justice system that fails to function. It is an illusion to let ourselves believe that doing away with capital punishment removes the murderer's deed from our conscience. The rights of society are paramount. When we protect guilty lives, we give up innocent lives in exchange. When opponents of capital punishment say to the state: "I will not let you kill in my name," they are also saying to murderers: "You can kill in your *own* name as long as I have an excuse for not getting involved."

It is hard to imagine anything worse than being murdered while neighbors do nothing. But something worse exists. When those same neighbors shrink back from justly punishing the murderer, the victim dies twice.

	Development by example

15 · Conclusion: paragraphs 15 and 16 · Ethical appeal · Rational appeal: deduction

16 · Emotional appeal

DISCUSSION QUESTIONS ■

1. Why do you think Koch ends paragraph 2 with a question rather than a direct statement of his opinion?

2. Why does Koch tell us in paragraph 8 that Bedau is "one of the most implacable foes of capital punishment in this country"?

3. Why do you think Koch devotes most of his essay to refuting opposition arguments?

SUGGESTION FOR WRITING ■   Write an essay that argues against capital punishment and that refutes Koch's evidence. If you agree with Koch, select another controversial issue (perhaps a particular solution to the waste disposal or street crime problem), take a position, and argue for it.

ANDREW KUPFER

■ *What to Do About Drugs*

Andrew Kupfer holds a Bachelor of Arts degree in anthropology from Brandeis University and advanced degrees in regional and urban planning from the London School of Economics and Cambridge University. He worked as a planner for the New York City Department of Housing Preservation and Development and as a copyeditor for the American Institute of Physics. In 1982, he began working for Fortune *as a reporter. Since 1988, he has been an associate editor for that magazine. In our selection, Kupfer offers his suggestions for coping with one of our most pressing social problems.*

DISCUSSION QUESTIONS

1. Koch allows readers to answer the question for themselves (although his opinion is obvious). He does this because only the two murderers and their confidants knew the real motivation behind their statements and because he (Koch) wants to establish an acceptable ethical image. Boldly stating that the two murderers were merely trying to "save their skin" would be counterproductive to this image.

2. It is significant that an implacable opponent of capital punishment concedes that the innocent victim argument is not effective. Had Bedau been neutral or in favor of capital punishment, his quotation would have carried much less weight.

3. In order to be effective, a topic of popular controversy such as capital punishment should refute some key arguments on the other side. Because the opposing views are so well known to many readers, Koch probably decided he could best address these views by centering his argument on them.

1
    Drugs are dangerous. Even users agree on that. Yet the U.S. seems to be getting nowhere in its war against them. In frustration, large numbers of Americans, including academics, members of Congress, and some big city mayors, are talking about waving a white flag. Legalize the stuff, some of them say, and be done with it. Let multinational companies take the business—and the profits—away from criminals. Stop the gunfights, the car bombs, the street crime, the bribes. Drug barons can sell their fleets of airplanes and go back to stealing cars, or whatever they were doing when all this started.

2
    The idea is tantalizing, but simplistic. It addresses only one aspect of drug use—the prevailing criminality—without raising the question of how people can be persuaded not to use drugs in the first place. Moreover, legalization would have different effects on the markets for different drugs. At best it is not a solution but a trade-off: lower crime, perhaps, in return for the risk of greater drug use, addiction, and health costs.

3
    Still, as Ronald Reagan used to say about the economy when he was running for President in 1980, what we're doing now isn't working. America needs a radical rethinking of its stance toward drugs. There might even be a place for legalization as part—but only part—of a carefully crafted policy that seeks to create a legal market for marijuana separate from that for heroin, cocaine, and its cheaper derivative crack. The money and police time freed up by legalizing pot could help pay for a more effective crackdown on hard drugs plus more programs for rehabilitation of addicts.

4
    Legalization of all drugs is a last-stand position based not on the notion that hard drugs are good for people, but on the widespread perception that the government has thrown all its resources into the struggle and failed. That perception is flawed. Despite the tough rhetoric, the war on drugs has been less than total. The Administration's most recent policy is Zero Tolerance, which is supposed to mean just that. The smallest pinch of drugs found in a million-dollar yacht would be enough to justify seizure. No holds barred, nobody gets off. The reality is different. Yachts were seized, then given back. Punishment of offenders is wildly inconsistent. A Florida court in May convicted Carlos Lehder, a handsome pilot who looks as if he stepped out of a television thriller. He faces a prison sentence of life plus 150 years for smuggling cocaine into the U.S. About the same time, a judge in Manhattan put on probation a woman convicted of attempting to sell 174 vials of crack. As long as street sellers go free, Carlos Lehder's colleagues in the Colombian cartel can keep on producing and shipping cocaine to the U.S.

5
    Nor can it be said that society is uniformly tough on drug users. When traces of drugs were found in the body of a railroad engineer, killed when he rammed into the rear of a standing train last spring in New York, his union resisted the understandable call for mandatory drug testing. Job seekers in other kinds of work aren't so keen on testing either.

6
    Probably Americans have no stomach for pushing drug law enforcement anywhere near the max. In Malaysia, after all, drug trafficking is punished by hanging. The task is to develop a policy in line with American concepts of civil liberties and within the limits of U.S. resources.

A first step is to decide that a drug-free society should not be the goal of policy. The thinking behind Zero Tolerance, says Dr. David F. Musto, professor of psychiatry at Yale, "is part of a typically American ideal about the perfectibility of man." Total success is unattainable and policymakers who try to achieve it will overlook intermediate measures that may do a better job of helping people kick the habit or keep from developing one in the first place.

One of those steps could be the unthinkable: legalization of marijuana. Since the early 1970s aging flower children have pushed for legal pot on grounds of—as they would put it—common sense. They argue that the drug is nonaddictive, widely used, and probably no worse a health hazard than alcohol. This "Why not?" approach never got anywhere, because it was easily countered with "Why?" Who needed another social problem no worse than alcohol? Now some surprising data from the Netherlands suggest that there might be a more compelling reason to legalize marijuana.

Pot has already been decriminalized in some U.S. states, though not completely legalized. Possessing small amounts of marijuana is punishable only by a small fine in New York, Ohio, California, Oregon, and seven other states; it could result in prison elsewhere. In places where the harsher laws remain on the books, police often put a low priority on making arrests for small transactions involving marijuana and hashish, because of limits on the number of cops, courtrooms, and jail cells. The result is de facto decriminalization in much of the country at the local level. Still, the Drug Enforcement Administration (DEA) continues to watch out for marijuana use and U.S. Customs officers might confiscate your car if they catch you bringing in some joints from Mexico. Drug enforcement agents still spend a lot of time and money chasing down foreign suppliers.

The importance of a legal market for marijuana is that it could help steer young people away from hard drugs by breaking the connection between marijuana smokers and drug pushers. The chief agent in the descent of people into hard drugs is the pusher. In the inner cities especially, pushers are walking drugstores, selling marijuana and hashish, barbiturates, stimulants, cocaine, and heroin. The first sample is usually free. Data from the National Institute of Drug Abuse show that, aside from alcohol, marijuana is the first drug most young people try. It they are buying pot on the street, as most of them must, then they will be exposed to the rest of the pharmacopeia.

The Netherlands provides a fascinating example of how creating a separate market for marijuana and hashish can help cut heroin use. As hard drugs washed across the world in the late 1960s and early 1970s, many young people in the Netherlands became addicted. A dozen years ago, in an attempt to reverse the trend, the government tripled the jail term for trafficking in hard drugs. At the same time officials declared that they would not prosecute anyone found with less than 30 grams of marijuana and hashish, though laws against the drugs remained on the books.

Since then small amounts have been sold openly by operators of coffeehouses in Amsterdam, usually under the watchful eye of the police. "Because we want separation of markets," says ministry of justice drug policy adviser M. A. A.

van Capelle, "we're interested in keeping a small market in soft drugs so people will know where to get it." Police don't look too closely into where the coffee-houses get their supplies, but if proprietors start mixing in hard drugs or sell amounts of pot deemed excessive, the place is shut down. The result is that a youngster curious about pot can buy it and use it in a safe place. He won't be arrested and he won't be exposed to pushers of hard drugs.

13   The Dutch worried at first that their new policy would cause a surge in marijuana use. In fact, according to the government, consumption has fallen. This decline may reflect the growing disaffection with drugs characteristic of the post-Flower Power era, but it is no less noteworthy that it occurred in a period of more open availability. The real payoff, though, is that use of heroin, the hard drug of choice in the Netherlands, has fallen too, particularly among young people. In 1981, 14% of heroin addicts were under 22; today the figure is 4.8%.

14   Critics of legalization will argue that the United States is not the Netherlands. Indeed not. The U.S. is a more heterogeneous society, with no institution quite comparable to the friendly Dutch coffeehouse. Americans might not be as comfortable relying on the discretion of local cops in the enforcement of—or in winking at—marijuana laws. Another approach here could be to legalize marijuana outright and make liquor stores the point of sale. The age restriction could be the same as for alcohol. The government could tax pot, with the revenue used to finance hard-drug treatment programs. If pot were taxed like cigarettes, it would generate an estimated $11 billion a year. Some $1.2 billion in state and federal money is now spent annually on drug treatment.

15   Legal pot would likely be a home-grown U.S. industry, removing it still further from the criminal elements in the international drug trade. American-grown marijuana now satisfies 25% of domestic demand, up from 9% when Reagan took office. The U.S. Drug Enforcement Administration believes that the U.S. will be the world's largest producer by the early 1990s, and soon after that a net exporter. Marijuana is already the largest cash crop in California.

16   Doctors still differ about the damage marijuana smoking inflicts, though they are beginning to agree that prolonged regular use may be risky, particularly to short-term memory and the lungs (marijuana contains tar, like cigarettes). As does alcohol, marijuana impairs perception, coordination, and memory. Long-term effects on the brain and the lungs are not yet known. The heart works harder, increasing blood pressure, a risk to people with hypertension. THC, the active ingredient, lowers the concentration of reproductive hormones in the bloodstream. But occasional use is unlikely to cause lasting health problems, and most people tend to use marijuana for only a short period of their lives.

17   A larger concern is whether more people would use marijuana if sanctions were removed. No one knows for sure. The ranks of drinkers grew by only about 10% after Prohibition ended. A recent survey of high school seniors across the nation by the University of Michigan shows that while fewer are smoking marijuana, the vast majority (85%) find it readily available. Those who don't probably haven't been looking.

18   The case against legalizing hard drugs is twofold. First and foremost, the possibility of an explosion of addiction is too grave a risk regardless of any supposed benefits. Second, many of those benefits are illusory. One of the

arguments for legalization is that the price would drop dramatically with the elimination of the huge criminal-risk premium, and addicts would no longer have to steal to support their habits. Dr. Mitchell S. Rosenthal, president of Phoenix House, a New York-based drug rehabilitation center, disputes that. For many addicts, he points out, crime is the way they earn money for all their needs, not just for drugs; because they are addicts they are unsuited to ordinary occupations. "If you give somebody free drugs you don't turn him into a responsible employee, husband, or father," says Rosenthal. "A large number of drug addicts have serious underlying problems."

Some advocates of legalization point to the British system of the 1950s,   19
when heroin was available to addicts by prescription. The number of addicts remained stable for many years, and almost all were known to doctors. The aim was to wean addicts from the drug, but if doctors could not, they gave small doses that prevented withdrawal without producing a high. That ended with the worldwide drug boom of the 1970s. With drugs flooding into the country illegally, doctors could no longer control an addict's habit. Addicts will go for a kick if they can find one. Unable to get enough heroin from doctors, they turned to the illegal market. The prescription system died out.

Even if a separate, legal market for marijuana were successful in slowing   20
the growth of hard-drug users, the U.S. would still have to contend with those already hooked. That means continued, even increased, pressure on heroin and cocaine dealers, but with a more balanced effort than the U.S. has been pursuing. The emphasis has been on stopping drugs in the source countries. The huge profits of drug producers have worked against that approach. The drug barons are so rich they have managed to bribe high officials and sometimes whole governments. "In the long run the real answer to the drug problem is not interdiction," says Robert Stutman, special agent in charge of the Drug Enforcement Administration office in New York. "Even using the military won't make a major difference." Peter Reuter, a senior economist at the Rand Corp., points out that since prices are so high, a drug dealer can still make big money even if lawmen seize most of a shipment.

But there are some steps the U.S. can take. International cooperation may   21
be the most promising. Countries where drugs are produced once took the view that drug use was an American problem. Now that they are discovering that the number of addicts within their borders is growing, they have become more willing to explore joint action against drug producers and dealers.

At home, the U.S. needs a unified, coordinated policy that extends from   22
federal drug enforcement officers down to local judges and cops. Agents from the DEA and the FBI conducted separate undercover investigations into laundering of Colombian drug money. Both operations hit pay dirt, but did there have to be two?

More enforcement dollars should be pushed down to the street. New York   23
City officials claim to have had great luck with Operation Pressure Point, which focused police manpower on the streets of the Lower East Side. Says Sterling Johnson Jr., special narcotics prosecutor for the city: "Pressure Point was a tremendous success in taking the community back, literally, from the drug dealers." Mark Kleiman, a lecturer on criminal justice at Harvard University's

24

25

26

27

28

Kennedy School of Government, says that if police are active in the streets, they can increase the time a drug user must spend to find dope. "If you are a heavy user and the probability of not connecting is great," says Kleiman, "that becomes a strong argument for getting into a treatment program."

If an addict looks for a program, however, he had better be able to get in. In New York City, New Haven, and Portland, Oregon, the waiting list for treatment can be several months long. Not every addict would avail himself of help even with limitless facilities, but it is unconscionable that people must be turned away when billions are being spent on interdiction that at most raises the street price of drugs by a few dollars. When a drug user is ready to go for help, he should be able to do so without a long wait. "One of the differences between drug users and us is time scale," says David Turner, director of the Standing Conference on Drug Abuse, based in London. "We want things immediately, but we can cope with delay. An addict is used to taking heroin and getting immediate relief. It's not surprising that if he is told he can have an appointment in four weeks, he will probably forget about it."

The best solution to the drug problem is societal change. That takes a long time. A good start is instilling an understanding of the potential hazards of drug use at an early age. Signs are that the numerous school programs across the country are beginning to work. The University of Michigan survey shows drug use among high school seniors down 13.6% since 1982. (The survey excludes teenagers who have dropped out, however, the biggest group of crack users.)

The role that education can play is apparent in Massachusetts, which has developed a range of curricula for kindergarten to the 12th grade. "The program is really one part hard facts about drug education and three parts comprehensive health education," says Marianne Lee, deputy director of the Massachusetts Governor's Alliance Against Drugs. "A fourth of all children live in a home where there is a substance-abuse problem. We teach kids how to deal with that, and how to keep their self-esteem intact." Since 1984 the number of high school students who have tried illicit drugs has dropped 11%, vs. a national decline of 7%. The downside is that alcohol use remains high in Massachusetts; 61% of students said they had used it at least once in the 30 days before the survey.

Is the Just Say No campaign helping? "It's not enough to tell kids to say no," says Lee. "We have to give them a reason to say no." Perhaps the phrase has had to bear more weight than it was meant to. Originally coined as a slogan for very young children, it was latched onto as a motto by drug treatment programs of all types. More sophisticated kids are not impressed by it.

Some educators worry that legalizing marijuana while continuing a tough stance toward hard drugs might send a confusing message. But American society transmits many conflicting signals about addictive substances. For example, while the Surgeon General rails against smoking, Congress continues to subsidize tobacco growing. A policy of compromise could give an outlet to people who wish to experiment with soft drugs and their small intoxications, deglamorizing those drugs while vilifying those that are deadly. That just might help break the spiral of criminality and violence without throwing open the doors of chemical invention to those who may not be able to resist.

DISCUSSION QUESTIONS ▪

1. With the essay as a whole in mind, point out the significance of the following sentence in paragraph 1: "In frustration, large numbers of Americans, including academics, members of Congress, and some big city mayors, are talking about waving a white flag."

2. What is Kupfer's proposition and where is it located? Is it one of fact, action, or value?

3. According to Kupfer, how would a separate legal market for marijuana help in the fight against hard drugs—heroin, cocaine, and crack?

4. Point out several places where Kupfer uses authoritative opinion as evidence.

5. Where does he refute, that is, counter the arguments of, opposing positions?

6. Consider the essay as a whole and then comment on the significance of the following sentence in paragraph 28: "A policy of compromise could give an outlet to people who wish to experiment with soft drugs and their small intoxications, deglamorizing those drugs while vilifying those that are deadly."

7. Kupfer's views on legalizing all drugs differ markedly from those of Hamill in the following essay (pages 507–518). Read Hamill's essay and then evaluate their differing attitudes.

SUGGESTION FOR WRITING ▪ Write an essay favoring (or opposing) the death penalty for certain crimes but not others. Support your argument with well-chosen authoritative opinions.

PETE HAMILL

▪ *Facing up to Drugs: Is Legalization the Solution?*

Pete Hamill (born 1935) is a native of Brooklyn, New York, and attended Pratt Institute and Mexico City College. Following jobs as a sheet-metal worker and advertising designer, he turned to journalism, becoming a reporter for the New York Post *in 1960. Since then, he has written and reported for a great many periodicals, including among others the* Saturday Evening Post, New York Daily News, Village Voice, Cosmopolitan, Playboy, *and* Reader's Digest. *He is the author of an array of novels and screenplays and has authored the scripts for several recordings with music. In the selection we present, Hamill recommends a controversial way of dealing with the problem of drugs.*

Hard drugs are now the scariest fact of New York life. They have spread genuine fear among ordinary citizens. They have stained every neighborhood in

1

4. Kupfer cites authoritative opinion in paragraphs 7, 12, 18, 20, 23, 24, 26, and 27.
5. Kupfer refutes the argument for legalization of *all* drugs in paragraphs 2, 4–6, and 18–19.
6. This sentence summarizes Kupfer's main argument: provide a separate market for marijuana by legalizing it and at the same time put increased pressure on heroin and cocaine dealers as part of a balanced campaign against hard drugs. Since no one can forecast precisely the effects of legalized marijuana, Kupfer says that this action "could" prove beneficial. Students should be cautioned against making unjustified claims.
7. Reading these paired essays exposes students to the differing viewpoints in an argument, teaches them to weigh both sides before forming their own opinion, and allows you to generate a class debate which, considering the topic, should be a spirited one.

PERSPECTIVE

A few years ago, public opinion was overwhelmingly against the legalization of drugs as a way of dealing with the problems they cause. As the drug situation has worsened, however, legalization has gained more advocates, Hamill among them. Students should note that Hamill recommends legalization only on a 10-year trial basis. If the results don't prove satisfactory, the present system could be reinstated. Hamill's plan, then, represents a variation upon the usual pro-legalization stance and, like Kupfer's, illustrates that multiple options are often possible.

TEACHING STRATEGIES

1. Teaching strategies 1–3 and 5 that accompany the preceding essay by Kupfer could also apply to this essay.
2. Ask students to explain why the opening paragraph is effective. Possible answers include the arresting statement in the first sentence and the parallelism that helps set up the argument for legalization.
3. Ask students to examine Hamill's use of colons in paragraphs 7, 12, 14, 15, 34, 40, and 52 and then formulate some guidelines for the proper use of colons.
4. Although his essay is grounded on rational appeal, Hamill also uses emotional and ethical appeals to strengthen his argument. Ask students to identify these appeals and comment on their effectiveness.

CLASSROOM ACTIVITIES

1. Divide the class into small groups and have students brainstorm to determine what educational steps would be most effective in combatting drug use. Their conclusions could be presented as reports to the entire class.
2. These same groups might explore and present reports on such options as mandatory, random (and this of course is the key word) drug tests and other possibilities not dealt with at length by Kupfer or Hamill. Any or all of these reports could serve as the basis for a writing assignment.

2

every borough, respecting no boundaries of class or color or geography. They have destroyed marriages, corrupted cops and banks, diminished productivity, fed the wild spiral of rents and condominium prices, overwhelmed the public hospitals, and filled the prisons to bursting.

The price of the drug scourge increases by the day. Hard drugs have injured thousands of families, some named Zaccaro and Kennedy, many others less well known. They have ruined uncountable numbers of careers and distorted others. Last year, when Dwight Gooden was sent off to the Smithers clinic, hard drugs almost certainly cost the Mets a championship. Gooden's friend, the brilliant pitcher Floyd Youmans of the Montreal Expos, learned no lesson from this; he was recently suspended indefinitely after once more failing a drug test. But Gooden and Youmans are not isolated cases, young men ensnared by the lifestyle of the poor neighborhoods of Tampa. Hard drugs have damaged the lives of pitcher Steve Howe, prizefighter Aaron Pryor, and football players Mercury Morris, Hollywood Henderson, and Don Reese, to mention only a few. Many other talented Americans, with no excuses to make about poverty or environment, have been hurt by hard drugs. And they cost Len Bias, Janis Joplin, Jimi Hendrix, Jim Morrison, and John Belushi their lives.

3

These terrible examples seem to make no difference; for the druggies, there are no cautionary tales. All over New York today, thousands of people are playing with drugs as if nothing will happen to *them*. And in this dense and dangerous city, such a taste for folly usually results in corpses.

4

New York, of course, is not unique. With the drug plague spreading all over the United States, the Feds now estimate that the country's cocaine-user population is now at 5.8-million. These new druggies include prep-school students, bankers, policemen, railroad workers, pilots, factory hands, stockbrokers, journalists, and—with the arrival of crack—vast numbers of the urban poor. According to the National Institute on Drug Abuse, the average age of first-time drug-users in the United States is now thirteen.

5

The drug trade is one of the most successful of all multinational capitalist enterprises, brilliantly functioning on the ancient rules of supply and demand. The demand is insatiable, the supply apparently limitless. In a business estimated by the president's South Florida Task Force to gross more than $100 billion a year, there are fortunes, large and small, to be made. And the art of the drug deal always contains the gun. As the authority of the old mob faded in the seventies (with the breakup of the Istanbul–Marseilles–New York pipeline), new bad guys moved in: Cubans and Colombians first; then, as the cocaine business flourished, Bolivians and Dominicans. Israeli hoodlums out of Brighton Beach took a big hunk of the heroin trade. And 30 to 40 Jamaican "posses" began operating in the United States, starting with marijuana and hashish, then moving hard into the cocaine trade. The Shower Posse works out of the Bronx, the Spangler Posse in Brooklyn, the Dunkirk Boys in Harlem. Experts say the posses killed about 350 people last year, and the number could be much higher (more than 200 homicides here last year involved Jamaicans). Now the word on the street is that the Pakistanis are moving into town, with an endless supply of heroin from home.

6

But the advent of crack has led to the true decentralization of the drug trade. The old days of iron control by the Gambino or Bonanno families are clearly over. Small groups of violent entrepreneurs now run the trade in individual housing projects, on specific streets, in the vicinity of valued high schools. Men have been killed in disputes over control of a single street corner. Such drug gangs as the Vigilantes in Harlem, the Wild Bunch in Bed-Stuy, and the Valley Boys in the northeast Bronx are young and deadly. And unless something is done, they are here to stay.

They all have guns, including automatic weapons, and they have a gift for 7 slaughter that makes some people nostalgic for the old Mafia. Nearly every morning, the newspapers carry fresh bulletins from the drug wars, full of multiple homicides and the killing of women and children. The old hoodlums were sinister bums who often killed one another, but they had some respect for the innocence of children. Not this set. The first indication that the rules of the game had changed dawned on us in 1982. In February of that year, on the Grand Central Parkway, the eighteen-month-old daughter and the four-month-old son of a Colombian drug-dealer were destroyed by shotgun blasts and automatic weapons, after their parents had been blown away. One Dominican dealer was forced to watch the disembowelment of his wife before being shotgunned to death. In Jackson Heights, according to New York *Newsday*, the favored method of execution is now the "Colombian necktie": The throat is cut and the tongue pulled through the slit to hang down upon the chest. The drug gangs are not misunderstood little boys. Their violence is at once specific and general: When they get rid of a suspected informer, they send chilling lessons to many others. Yet most of us read about their mayhem as if it were taking place in some barbarous and distant country and not the city that also contains the Metropolitan Museum.

It isn't as if these people are simply breaking the law; in some places, the 8 law doesn't even exist. Whole neighborhoods in Brooklyn and Queens have been abandoned to the rule of the men with the Uzis, the MAC-10s, and the 9-mm. pistols. When police officer Edward Byrne was stationed outside the South Jamaica home of a witness in a drug case, the bad guys just walked up and killed him. When police officer George Scheu started crusading last year against drug-dealers in his Flushing neighborhood, he was shot down and killed outside his home. These actions remind us of the criminal anarchy in Colombia, where scores of police officers, judges, and public officials (including the minister of justice) have been assassinated by the drug caudillos. The new drug gangs enforce their power with violence, demonstrating that they can successfully murder witnesses and cops who might get in the way. When the first prosecutor is killed, there may be outrage in New York, but there will be no surprise.

Officers of the law are not the only casualties. Every weekend, discos erupt 9 in gunfire as drug gangs fight over money or women or the ambiguous intentions of a smile. Every other week, innocent bystanders are shot down, provided a day of tabloid mourning, swiftly forgotten.

These killers are servicing a huge number of New Yorkers. The population 10 of the stupefied can no longer be accurately counted. It is estimated that New York heroin addicts number about 200,000, or ten full-strength army divisions. But nobody knows how many people are using cocaine or crack. Some cops say it is more than a million. This might be hyperbole, the result of what some perceive to be anti-drug hysteria. But nobody who lives in New York can deny the daily evidence of the drug plague.

11   You see blurred-out young men panhandling for crack money from Columbus Avenue to Wall Street. Every night, wide-eyed, gold-bedecked teenage crackheads do 75 miles an hour on the Henry Hudson Parkway, racing one another in BMWs. In the age of AIDS, schoolgirls are hooking on street corners. Thousands of other young New Yorkers, whacked on drugs, are now incapable of holding jobs or acquiring the basic skills that might make a decent life possible. They amble around the ghettos. They fill the welfare hotels. They mill about the Port Authority bus terminal. They careen through subway cars, sometimes whipping out knives or pistols. The eyes of the heroin-users are glazed, their bodies filthy. The shooters among them often share "works," knowing that dirty needles can give them AIDS; they choose to risk an agonizing death in order to get high. The crackheads are wilder—eyes pinwheeling, speed-rapping away, or practicing various menacing styles. Smack or crack: They'd rather do either than go to a ball game, love someone, raise a child, listen to music, read a book, or master a difficult craft.

12   All of us are paying for this sick and disastrous binge. Crime in New York, after tailing off for a few years, has risen drastically. The reason is simple: Most junkies don't work. To feed their habits, addicts must either deal or steal. A Justice Department study released last winter showed that 79 percent of men arrested in New York for serious crimes tested positive for recent use of illegal drugs, 63 percent for cocaine. In 1977, there were 505 cops in this city's Narcotics Division; today, there are nearly 1,200. They made 35,774 drug-related arrests last year and estimate that 40 percent of the city's murders (there were 1,672 in 1987) were drug-related. In the first three months of this year, murder was up 10 percent in the city; car theft, 18.2 percent; assault, 9.4 percent; larceny, 5 percent; robbery, 4 percent. New Yorkers must come up with billions of tax dollars to pay for the police work involved, along with the cost of the druggies' hospital treatment, the operation of various clinics, and welfare payments to those who are so blitzed they can't support themselves.

13   With the pervasive use of hard drugs, and the enormous profits involved, it is no surprise that policemen all over the country have been dirtied, most sickeningly in Miami. But there is evidence that the corruption goes beyond cases of underpaid street cops looking the other way for their kids' tuition. A few years ago, a veteran agent became the first FBI man to plead guilty to cocaine-trafficking. Assistant U.S. Attorney Daniel N. Perlmutter, a rising star in Rudolph Giuliani's office, went to jail for stealing cocaine and heroin from a safe where evidence was stored.

14   No wonder Jesse Jackson was able to make drugs a major part of this year's presidential campaign. No wonder a *New York Times*/CBS News poll in March showed that Americans were far more concerned with drug-trafficking than with Central America, arms control, terrorism, or the West Bank. Americans have learned one big thing in the past few years: There has been a war on drugs, all right, and we have lost. Nobody knows this better than New Yorkers.

15   The ancient question is posed: What is to be done? The drug culture is now so pervasive, the drug trade so huge, powerful, and complex, that there are no

simple answers. But the attack on the problem must deal with the leading actors in this squalid drama: dealers and users. That is, any true war on drugs must grapple with the problems of supply and demand.

SUPPLY

It is one of the more delicious ironies of the Cold War era that the bulk of the cocaine and heroin supply comes from countries that used to be called part of the free world. While trillions have been spent on national security, the security of ordinary citizens has been destroyed by countries that are on our side. The cocaine cartel is headquartered in Medellín, Colombia. Most coca leaves are produced in Bolivia and Peru, where they are turned into coca paste for processing in Colombia. Most heroin is coming from Pakistan, Thailand, Turkey, and Mexico. The Colombians and Mexicans also produce much of the marijuana crop that is grown outside the United States.

16

The big supply-side coke-dealers control processing and distribution, leaving the grungy details of retailing to thousands of Americans. Many Caribbean islands are crucial to distribution, as was Panama until the indictment of Noriega. Mexico also is used as a transshipment point for huge supplies of cocaine and heroin that it does not produce. In all these countries, the governments themselves have been corrupted by the trade. The government of Colombia has virtually surrendered to the violence of the drug barons, while the governments of Panama and Bolivia are flat-out drug rings. Some Caribbean nations—the Bahamas in particular—have been accused of the same partnership with traffickers. The civilian government of Haiti was recently overthrown by the military in a dispute over the drug trade. In Mexico, the corruption is low-level in many places but is said to involve higher-ups in various state governments. In Thailand and Pakistan, drug-traffickers ply their trade with little interference from their governments; Thailand is more worried about Vietnam than about 110th Street, and Pakistan is making too much money off the war in Afghanistan to care about junkies in the United States.

17

Frustrated Americans have demanded that something drastic be done about the drug traffic. And over the past few years, the following measures have been advocated:

18

1. *War*. This is one of the most frequently voiced demands, what Maxwell Smart would have called the old let's-go-in-and-bomb-the-bejesus-out-of-them plan. Massachusetts senator John Kerry and Los Angeles police chief Daryl Gates are among those who have suggested military action. After all, if the United States is truly the most powerful nation on earth, why can't it *go to the source*?

From 1839 to 1842, the British actually did fight a war in China over drugs. But in the case of the Opium War, the British were the drug-pushers. They went ashore in China and killed a lot of Chinese in the name of their holy cause (opium was produced in British India, sold in China), the equivalent of Colombia's attacking the United States for the right to sell cocaine.

19

But a United States war against the drug-producing countries would be a forbiddingly expensive enterprise. You can't do it with one or two Grenada-style public-relations spectacles. And a war against one country—say, Colombia—would have no effect; the bad guys would just move next door. To use military

20

force effectively to stop the production of poppies and coca leaves, the United States would have to attack all of the offending countries *at the same time*.

21 But it is hard to imagine a simultaneous declaration of war against Panama, Colombia, Peru, Bolivia, Mexico, Turkey, Thailand, and Pakistan, with a smaller expedition against the Bahamas. We have had some comical adventurers in the National Security Council lately, but none *that* comical. There are 80 million people in Mexico alone, with rugged, mountainous terrain through the center of the country and dense jungles in the southern regions. Bolivia is twice the size of France and also mountainous. In Pakistan, American troops would face all the guns the CIA has been supplying to the anti-Communist Afghans, many of whom have been ripped off by Pakistani gangsters. Another war in Southeast Asia (to cut off the Thai supply) would be no fun, but it would carry its own ironies, since much of the current mass stupefaction in America can be traced to the Vietnam era.

22 The logistics of Drug War One would be staggering; planes, ships, and rockets would be sent on their way to three continents. In every country from Turkey to Thailand, an American invasion would unite most of the local population on nationalist grounds. (We had a mild sample of that recently in the wholly owned CIA subsidiary of Honduras when the arrest of a drug-dealer by U.S. agents led to the burning down of one of the embassy buildings, along with several nights of anti-U.S. rioting.) Various international agreements would get in the way (the Organization of American States is unlikely to authorize a mass invasion of its own most important member states). U.S. casualties in such a worldwide operation would be very heavy as local armies and nationalist guerrilla bands descended upon the invaders, prepared to die, as they say, for their country. In the event that the Americans won all of these simultaneous wars, they would then have to occupy those countries for a generation if they truly hoped to wipe out the sources of drugs. The cost of a dozen huge garrisons would finish off the already precarious U.S. economy.

23 *2. Economic pressure.* On paper, this sounds like a more rational means of eradicating drugs. The United States (and the other leading industrial countries) would cut off credits, foreign aid, and all legitimate trade with the drug-producing countries. Presumably, the governments of those countries would then realize swiftly that they must get rid of the drug barons and would dispatch their own soldiers to wipe them out. While wielding the economic Big Stick, the United States would hold out the carrots of crop replacement, expanded foreign aid, guaranteed purchase of legitimate crops. (Bolivia, for example, went heavily into coca-leaf production in the seventies after its cotton industry collapsed with the fall of worldwide cotton prices. This followed the sharp decline of its tin industry.) The idea would be to create as much domestic pain as possible, so the local governments would get out of the drug racket—or crush it.

24 Unfortunately, the recent fiasco in Panama showed us on a small scale that this probably wouldn't work. Again, nationalism would be a major factor (in Panama, most people blamed the U.S. for their plight, not Noriega). And in using economic sanctions, the U.S. could not make distinctions among drug-dealers; Washington would have to be as tough on NATO ally Turkey as it is on Bolivia, as ferocious against Thailand and Pakistan as against Colombia and Mexico.

But U.S. companies also need most of these countries as markets. Economic sanctions work both ways; all American goods would be stopped at other nations' borders, thus closing plants all over our own country. Mexico would stop paying its multi-billion-dollar debt to U.S. banks, which would then collapse—perhaps pulling the entire country into a major depression.   25

3. *Moral persuasion.* Don't even bother.   26

4. *The sealing of the borders.* Again, this would cost uncountable billions. We have a 5,426-mile undefended border with Canada. It was crossed without problem by Prohibition rumrunners, vaulted for decades by Mafia drug-peddlers, and is easily traversed these days by the cocaine-runners. The 1,942-mile border with Mexico is a sieve. In spite of tough immigration laws, several million illegal aliens are expected to cross it this year; well-financed drug-runners with their fleets of small aircraft and trucks are unlikely to be stopped.   27

Enlisting the Armed Forces as border guards almost certainly would only complicate matters—as the Israelis have learned on the West Bank, soldiers are not policemen. Chasing druggies back home to Mexico or Canada (in "hot pursuit") could lead to an international incident every other day. The first time a private plane flown by some orthodontist with a defective radio was shot down over Toronto, the plan would be abandoned.   28

America's miles of coastline are guarded by an underfinanced, undermanned Coast Guard. Florida alone has 580 miles of coast, and there are more than 120,000 pleasure boats registered in southern Florida. Smugglers have become very sophisticated about penetrating our feeble defenses. The South Florida Task Force—headed by Vice-President George Bush and supported by the Drug Enforcement Administration, the FBI, the Customs Service, the U.S. Army (which supplied Cobra helicopters), the Bureau of Alcohol, Tobacco & Firearms, the Internal Revenue Service, the Coast Guard, the U.S. Navy (whose warships gave the Coast Guard support), the U.S. Border Patrol, the U.S. Marshals, and the Treasury Department—has been a colossal flop. After more than six years of this effort, there are more drugs on the streets than ever before, and their lower prices (down from $47,000 a kilo for cocaine six years ago to about $12,000 now) indicate that all those well-photographed record-setting busts haven't stopped the flow.   29

The reason is simple. The demand and the profits are enormous. So it's no surprise that when the government concentrates its efforts in one spot (as it did in southern Florida), the druggies simply go elsewhere: to the Florida panhandle, the bayous of Louisiana, the shores of Mississippi. Many even follow the old rumrunner trails, dropping anchor off Montauk and using small boats to make runs against the unguarded shores of Long Island. One unexpected consequence of the patchwork War on Drugs has been the spread of the trade to places that once were free of it. Brilliant.   30

5. *Draconian measures, including the death penalty.* Mayor Koch and others have called for the death penalty for big-time drug-dealers. The problem is that most of them don't live here. For every Carlos Lehder, convicted recently after a long trial in Florida, there are thousands of others whose immunity is guaranteed by use of violence.   31

But if the death penalty is to be employed to solve the drug problem, why   32 should it be limited to the few foreign wholesalers who are extradited and tried here? To be fair, you would have to attack every participant in the production and distribution systems. That is, you would have to do more than fry a few thousand pushers; you would have to execute every crooked cop, every corrupt banker who launders drug money, every politician who is on the take. You would also have to lock up all members of the CIA involved in the *contra* drug-running scheme (persuasively described in Leslie Cockburn's *Out of Control*) and strap them into the electric chair, along with their bosses and whoever in the White House collaborated in these operations. The death penalty for drug-dealing is a slogan, not a solution. Even if exceptions were made for ideological zealots, the state would have to kill several hundred thousand people. And the drugs would continue to flow.

DEMAND

33   One night a year ago, I had dinner with a Mexican diplomat and asked him about the drug problem in Mexico. He said, "You have to understand something: If thousands of North American yuppies suddenly decided tomorrow to get high by shoving bananas up their noses—and they were willing to pay $10 a banana—Mexico would bloom in bananas."

34   His point was a simple one: The drug problem in the United States is one of demand, not of production. Poor countries are like poor people—in order to survive, they will sell whatever the market demands. In our time, in this country and this city, the market demands hard drugs.

35   There have been a variety of suggestions about dealing with the insatiable appetite that Americans have developed for cocaine and heroin.

36   1. *Willpower*. This is the Nancy Reagan plan, beautifully described by a recent beauty contestant as "Just Say Don't." It is primarily directed at teenagers, imploring them to resist the peer pressure that could lead to using drugs. A few weeks ago, I asked some New York street kids about this program. They just laughed and laughed.

37   2. *Education.* This is getting better. In the past, the country paid a heavy price for lies told in the name of education (marijuana will lead to heroin, etc.). Television has been playing a more responsible role lately, with a variety of series and programs about the cost and consequences of drugs (*48 Hours on Crack Street*; the two Peter Jennings specials on ABC). If this effort is sustained, we may begin to see a slow, steady decline in drug use (the way cigarette-smoking began to wane after the truth was told about its connection to lung cancer and heart disease). The great risk is that education about drugs will merely provoke curiosity and lead to wider use. Kids always think they are immortal.

38   3. *Treatment*. I visited a drug-treatment center in Suffern a few weeks ago. The facilities were secure, the 28-day program tough, the staff dedicated. There were exactly 28 beds for junkies. There are 250,000 smack addicts in New York State alone. Around the state, there are about 5,000 beds available to treat heroin addicts. Obviously, not everyone who wants treatment can get it. Those who have summoned all the desiccated vestiges of their pride and hope in order to enter a treatment program should be able to do so. But this, too, will cost many billions if all the country's addicts are to be handled by such programs.

4. *More Draconian measures*. This would follow examples set in China, Singapore, and a few other places. It would attack both dealer and user, supply and demand. All would be subject to heavy prison sentences (or the electric chair, if the death-penalty advocates had their way). The user would be considered as guilty as the seller.

39

Again, those good old Draconian measures make better rhetoric than reality. In New York, the Rockefeller drug law was one such measure. Put into effect in 1973, this was the "nation's toughest" drug legislation: For possession of two ounces of heroin, the minimum sentence was 15 to 25 years in prison; the maximum was life. A repeat conviction for possessing any stimulant or hallucinogen "with intent to sell" sent a felon to jail for one to eight and a half, again with a maximum of life. Probation, alternate sentences, and plea bargaining were forbidden. Yes, a lot of bad guys did go to jail, and by 1975, 91 percent of convicted drug felons were serving maximum prison sentences.

40

But these measures also helped cause the current crisis. The courts were soon jammed with accused drug felons demanding jury trials. The spending of many additional millions on judges and new courtrooms didn't ease the problem. And it was also now worth killing cops to avoid doing life in Attica. The old mob *did* respond to the new laws. Many of them got out of the smack racket (with the usual exceptions), but that only opened the way for the Cubans and Colombians. Judges began releasing first offenders and low-level dealers for the simple reason that there was no room in our prisons: They were already packed with druggies. And as cops became more cynical about the justice system, corruption became more possible.

41

New Yorkers are already the most heavily taxed Americans. It's unlikely that they would agree to billions of dollars in additional taxes to pay for another 30 prisons or an additional 500 judges to deal with all the users and pushers in the state. Nor would anybody be happy paying even more for welfare to handle the women and children left behind by the imprisoned druggies.

42

WHAT IS TO BE DONE?

After watching the results of the plague since heroin first came to Brooklyn in the early fifties, after visiting the courtrooms and the morgues, after wandering New York's neighborhoods to see for myself, and after consuming much of the literature on drugs, I've reluctantly come to a terrible conclusion: The only solution is the complete legalization of these drugs.

43

I did not originate this idea, of course. In the past year, the mayors of Baltimore, Washington, and Minneapolis have urged that legalization be looked into. Various shapers of public opinion, including such conservatives as William F. Buckley Jr. and Milton Friedman, have done the same. Many have cited articles in such publications as *The Economist, Foreign Policy*, and the British medical journal *The Lancet*, all suggesting that the only solution is legalization.

44

Legalization doesn't mean endorsement. Cigarettes, liquor, and prescription drugs such as Valium are now legal, though neither government nor society endorses their use. Any citizen can now endanger his health with cigarettes (and 300,000 people die each year from smoking-related illnesses). Or make a mess of his life with whiskey (alcohol abuse costs us more than $100 billion a year). Or

45

take too many Valiums and die. These drugs, however, have become respectable over the years. State banquets are often marked by the drinking of toasts, in which the drug called liquor is offered in honor of the distinguished visitor. Business, politics, and love affairs are often conducted with the lubricant of alcohol. I have no patience anymore for drunks, and I can't abide the company of cokeheads and junkies. But every sensible citizen must recognize that the current system under which some drugs are legal and others are not is hypocritical.

46   I think a ten-year experiment with legalization is worth the risk. If it doesn't accomplish its goals, legislators could always go back to the present disastrous system. And we might learn that we can live without hypocrisy.

47   The strongest argument for legalization is economic. We simply don't have the money to deal with eliminating supply or demand. Too many Americans want this stuff, and we are again falling into the trap created by Prohibition: We try to keep people from buying things they want, we cite moral reasons as our motives, and we create a criminal organization that will poison all of our lives for decades. The old mob was the child of Prohibition. A new mob, infinitely more ruthless, is certain to come out of the present crisis. That can be prevented by eliminating the illegal profits that fund and expand the power of the drug gangs.

48   How would legalization work? A few possibilities:

1. Marijuana—not a hard drug, of course, but described as one in the debate—could be the first to be legalized. About 20 million Americans smoke grass on a regular basis and about 400,000 are arrested every year for possession. Mark Kleiman, former director of policy analysis for the Criminal Division of the Justice Department, estimates that legalizing the sale of marijuana would save about $500 million in law-enforcement costs and produce about $7 billion in revenues. Those numbers alone should settle this part of the argument.

49   Pot could be sold openly in licensed liquor stores all over the country (legalization must be national; if it were limited to New York, every pothead, cokehead, and junkie in the country would soon arrive here). All laws now applicable to selling liquor (used legally by 100 million Americans) would apply to marijuana. Citizens would be arrested for driving under the influence. The weed could not be sold to minors. Advertising would be restricted. All taxes—including those on domestic farmers and importers—would be applied to drug treatment, education, and research for the duration of the ten-year experiment.

50   2. Heroin could be legalized a year later, dispensed through a network of neighborhood health stations and drugstores. While the old British system of registering addicts was in effect, the number of those receiving daily maintenance doses was low (about 500 in London). In the late sixties, the system was changed. The number of dispensing doctors was reduced nationwide to a few hundred (from thousands), and new registered addicts were required to enter methadone programs. The number of addicts soared. Obviously, the old system was better.

51   After legalization, this vile drug would be banned from commercial sale. The price would be very low (25 cents a dose), perhaps even free. All current addicts would have to register within six months of the passage of the enabling legislation. They would be supplied with identity cards resembling driver's licenses, showing their faces. They would also be given the opportunity to go drug-

free through a greatly expanded system of treatment centers (funded by the marijuana tax and import fees). Their records would be kept confidential, but they would have to register.

Presumably, this would accomplish two things: (1) take the profits out of heroin sales and (2) contain the present addict population. Most junkies support their habits by dealing; they create new addicts to have more customers. There would be no economic point to creating new junkies. The street junkie also would gain relief from the degrading process of making his day's connection. He would stop stealing from old ladies, his family, and strangers. He would no longer have to risk AIDS infection by sharing works.

52

The mechanics would be difficult; some junkies need five or six doses a day, and if you hand them the supply all at once, they are likely to sell some of it to others. The cost of six separate needles a day for 200,000 junkies would be very high. New junkies would be a different problem. Certainly, there would be a continuing, if diminished, supply of young addicts, for a variety of reasons. Some would get heroin from family members who are junkies, the way young alcoholics have been known to raid the family liquor cabinet. There will always be sick old junkies ready to corrupt the young and others who may want to spread their personal misery to as many as possible. But new junkies would be able to enter the system only by telling the authorities how they got turned on. And this would be a point where one of those good old Draconian measures would be useful. Part of the law could mandate life sentences for anyone who created a new junkie.

53

3. Cocaine could be legalized soon after heroin and sold in its conventional forms through liquor stores. The same regulations that govern the sale and use of liquor and marijuana would apply. The drug barons of the world could then go legitimate. The drug-user would have a regulated supply of cocaine that was not cut with Ajax or speed. He would pay a variety of prices depending on quality, as the drinker does for various wines, liquors, and champagnes. Even the crack-users, at the bottom of the social scale of coke-users, would be able to buy cocaine legally, thus putting the hoodlums out of business. If the customers wanted to go home, then, and cook up some crack in the microwave (all they would need is cocaine hydrochloride, baking soda, and water or ammonia), they could do so. If they then sold it to kids, they would end up doing life.

54

I say all of this with enormous reluctance. I hate the idea of living in a country that is drowning in drugs. I know that if drugs were freely available, some of the most damaged people in society could fall into degradation, as many of the poor have across the years in countries where alcohol is legal. There would be casualties everywhere, and the big-city ghettos might suffer terribly (although the assumption that blacks and Hispanics automatically would fall into addiction faster than others is a kind of racism). I know that it would be strange to travel around the world and be an automatic drug suspect, my luggage searched, my body frisked, a citizen of the drug country. Alas, while researching this article, I realized that I live in that country now.

55

There are good and decent arguments against legalization that go beyond the minor problems of embarrassment and humiliation. The most obvious is that the number of addicts might increase dramatically as legalization and easy access

56

57

58

59

60

61

DISCUSSION QUESTIONS

1. The proposition, one of action and favoring the complete legalization of drugs, is stated in paragraph 43. Hamill delays offering it because he proposes such an extreme solution. He feels it necessary to first show the wide-ranging dimensions of the drug problem and that other approaches to it won't work. Students should note the effective use of parallelism in the proposition sentence: "After watching . . . after visiting . . . after wandering . . . after consuming. . . ." Hamill establishes his qualifications for writing and makes clear that his position is a considered one.

2. Paragraph 15 is a transition paragraph. The first 14 paragraphs detail the dimensions of the drug problem; paragraph 15 raises, and in general terms answers, the question of how to cope with it; and the remaining paragraphs explore these answers in detail. Students should understand that longer essays often require transition paragraphs.

3. Hamill uses statistics in the following paragraphs: 5, 10, 12, 27, 29; 38, 40, 42, 45, 48, 50, and 56. Paragraph 44 cites a number of authoritative opinions, all of which favor legalization. Paragraphs 33, 36, 38, and 43 use personal experience.

4. Hamill refutes proposed supply solutions in paragraphs 18–32; he refutes proposed demand solutions in paragraphs 35–42. These refutations lead him to his proposal for legalization in paragraph 43. In addition, paragraph 45 opens with a refutation of sorts. By saying "Legalization doesn't mean endorsement," Hamill anticipates and answers a likely objection to his proposal.

tempted millions of citizens to experiment. History suggests that this is likely to happen, at least for a while. One study shows that the number of drinkers in this country increased by more than 60 percent after the end of Prohibition, returning to the level reached before the noble experiment. Forty years after the British drug-dealers won the Opium War, the number of opium addicts in China had risen to 90 million. In laboratory experiments with cocaine, animals keep taking larger and larger amounts of the drug, until they die. Dr. Frank H. Gawin, director of stimulant abuse, treatment, and research at Yale University, said recently, "I would be terrified to live in a cocaine-legalized society."

Another objection is that nobody knows whether legalization would work—and if it drastically increased the number of addicts over a ten-year period, reversing the process might be impossible. So I'm not suggesting that legalization would transform this violent city into Pericles' Athens. But all of us know that the present system doesn't work. And if the tax revenues from sales of legal drugs could fund real treatment programs, if we treated drug addiction the way we treat alcoholism (as a health problem instead of a crime problem), if education more powerfully stressed that all drug abuse is the pastime of idiots, an experiment with legalization might be worth the attendant risks.

Some of those risks could be covered by specific proposals in the new laws. Congress could insist, for example, that all law-enforcement money freed by legalization be used to attack the deeper problems of poverty, housing, family disintegration, and illiteracy, which make life in the ghettos so hopeless and drugs so tempting. With any luck, we then might see the number of drug-users decline as more citizens realized drugs' heavy costs and as the young realized that it isn't very hip to make yourself stupid. Certainly, as the huge illicit profits vanished, the level of urban violence would be swiftly reduced.

The police who have been diverted to the drug wars could be employed against more terrible crimes. The strain on the courts and prisons would ease, leading to a criminal-justice system that guarantees more thoughtful prosecutions, fairer trials, and certain punishment for malefactors.

Legalization wouldn't be a license to go wild. Drug use would continue to be regulated, perhaps in a tougher way, with heavy penalties for doctors, nurses, pilots, train engineers, and others who have heavy social responsibilities. The Armed Forces could continue to forbid the use of drugs. Employers could insist that they don't want drug-users working for them any more than they want drunks. There would be sad and tragic examples of people fallen into the gutter, as there have always been with alcohol. A few hustlers would work the margins of the legal-drug business, trying to avoid taxes and duties. But we would rid ourselves of a lot of hypocrisy. We would be forced to face some truths about ourselves, deprived at last of the comforting figures of those foreign ogres who are supposed to be corrupting all these poor innocent Americans.

Perhaps, along the way, we might even discover why so many millions of Americans insist on spending their days and nights in a state of self-induced mental impairment. Perhaps. For now, we just have to discover a way to get home alive.

DISCUSSION QUESTIONS ■

1. Hamill does not state his proposition at the beginning of his argument. What is his proposition and where is it located? Is it one of fact, action, or value? Why do you think he delayed offering it?

2. Think of the essay as a whole and then indicate what function paragraph 15 serves.

3. Hamill uses statistics, authoritative opinion, and personal experience as evidence. Point out examples of each.

4. Where does Hamill refute—that is, point out shortcomings in, opposing positions? What do these refutations accomplish?

5. Hamill concedes, in paragraphs 55–57, that there are some "good and decent arguments against legalization." Do you think that this acknowledgment weakens his argument? Explain.

6. Paragraphs 7, 30, and 61 contain intentional sentence fragments. Identify them and explain why they are effective.

7. Do you agree with the complete legalization favored by Hamill, the limited legalization favored by Kupfer (pages 502–506), or a position not advocated by either? Defend your answer.

SUGGESTION FOR WRITING ■ **Write an argument favoring (or opposing) the legalization of casino gambling or alcohol sales to eighteen-year-olds. Develop your essay with appropriate statistics, authoritative opinions, and personal experience.**

MARTIN LUTHER KING, JR.

■ *I Have a Dream*

Martin Luther King, Jr. (1929–1968) has earned lasting fame for his part in the civil rights struggles of the 1950s and 1960s. Born in Atlanta, Georgia, he was ordained a Baptist minister in his father's church in 1947. A year later, he graduated from Morehouse College, then went on to take a Bachelor of Divinity degree at Crozier Theological Seminary (1951) and a Ph.D. in philosophy at Boston University (1954), after which he accepted a pastorate in Montgomery, Alabama. King's involvement with civil rights grew when he organized and led a boycott that succeeded in desegregating Montgomery's bus system. In 1957, he founded and became the first president of the

5. It is probably necessary for Hamill to concede these points. Most informed people are aware of them. But students should note that he counters these concessions in paragraph 57: "The present system doesn't work" and "an experiment with legalization might be worth the attendant risks." Generally speaking, it doesn't weaken an argument to acknowledge that the opposition has some merit. Whether Hamill's concessions are major must be decided by each individual.

6. The fragments are as follows: Paragraph 7: "Not this set." Paragraph 30: "Brilliant." Paragraph 61: "Perhaps." These fragments help Hamill make his points with added punch, and they also help vary the pace of the writing. Have students substitute complete sentences for the fragments and then notice the different effects.

7. This question, which of course has no precise answer, should spark a stimulating class discussion. You might use the discussion as the basis for a writing assignment.

PERSPECTIVE

King's speech is a masterful example of emotional and ethical argument. Drawing upon the full resources of formal diction, he exhorts his followers to persist in the peaceful pursuit of equality, holding forth the vision of a transfigured nation, purged of racism and basking in brotherhood. In our discussion of the emotional appeal (pages 166–167), we stress its power to "win the heart and the help" of its audience. In this connection, you might point out that King's speech was instrumental in the passage of the Civil Rights Act of 1964 and the Voting Rights Act of 1965, which together have helped transform the status of America's blacks.

Reader

1. You might reinforce the circumstances, explained in the biographical note on King, that prompted this speech. Many students will probably not be old enough to recall it.
2. Ask the class to identify and discuss the effectiveness of some of King's allusions. Responses could be tied to a discussion of audience and what assumptions King makes about his listeners.
3. Ask students why King links his dream to the broader concept of the American dream.
4. In paragraph 9 King mentions a number of injustices suffered by blacks. Discuss how the situation has changed today. Also discuss whether whites, native Americans, Mexican-Americans, senior citizens, teenagers, or the handicapped are victims of injustice. Views on contemporary discrimination might lead to an argument essay on how to cope with it.
5. Throughout his campaign for civil rights, King consistently rejected the use of violence. Are there any situations where violence is justified? A discussion of this question might also lead to an argument essay.

DISCUSSION QUESTIONS (p. 522)

1. The speech was delivered as the capstone of a march to commemorate Lincoln's signing of the Emancipation Proclamation 100 years before, so it is only fitting that King begin as he does. Moreover, by mentioning Lincoln and the Emancipation Proclamation, King draws attention to the hopes that blacks experienced a century before and that are paralleled by those stirring in the blacks of his day, while reminding his listeners that the original hopes still haven't been realized.
2. King's proposition is implied. It might be stated as follows: Today, black Americans do not enjoy the rights guaranteed by the Declaration of Independence and Constitution, but if they persevere in the nonviolent

Southern Christian Leadership Conference and assumed a leading role in the civil rights movement. King advocated a policy of nonviolent protest based on the beliefs of Thoreau and Gandhi and never veered from it despite many acts of violence directed at him. The success of King's crusade helped bring about the passage of the Civil Rights Act of 1964 and the Voting Rights Act of 1965 and won him the Nobel Peace Prize in 1964. King was assassinated on April 4, 1968, in Memphis. Since then, his birthday, January 15, has been made a national holiday. The speech "I Have a Dream" was delivered August 28, 1963, at the Lincoln Memorial in Washington, D.C., before a crowd of 200,000 people who had gathered to commemorate the centennial of the Emancipation Proclamation and to demonstrate for pending civil rights legislation. It stands as one of the most eloquent pleas ever made for racial justice.

1   I am happy to join with you today in what will go down in history as the greatest demonstration for freedom in the history of our nation.

2   Five score years ago, a great American, in whose symbolic shadow we stand today, signed the Emancipation Proclamation. This momentous decree came as a great beacon light of hope to millions of Negro slaves who had been seared in the flames of withering injustice. It came as a joyous daybreak to end the long night of their captivity.

3   But one hundred years later, the Negro still is not free; one hundred years later, the life of the Negro is still sadly crippled by the manacles of segregation and the chains of discrimination; one hundred years later, the Negro lives on a lonely island of poverty in the midst of a vast ocean of material prosperity; one hundred years later, the Negro is still languishing in the corners of American society and finds himself in exile in his own land.

4   So we've come here today to dramatize a shameful condition. In a sense we've come to our nation's capital to cash a check. When the architects of our republic wrote the magnificent words of the Constitution and the Declaration of Independence, they were signing a promissory note to which every American was to fall heir. This note was the promise that all men, yes, black men as well as white men, would be guaranteed the unalienable rights of life, liberty, and the pursuit of happiness.

5   It is obvious today that America has defaulted on this promissory note in so far as her citizens of color are concerned. Instead of honoring this sacred obligation, America has given the Negro people a bad check; a check which has come back marked "insufficient funds." But we refuse to believe that the bank of justice is bankrupt. We refuse to believe that there are insufficient funds in the great vaults of opportunity of this nation. And so we've come to cash this check, a check that will give us upon demand the riches of freedom and the security of justice.

6   We have also come to this hallowed spot to remind America of the fierce urgency of now. This is no time to engage in the luxury of cooling off or to take the tranquilizing drug of gradualism. Now is the time to make real the promises of democracy; now is the time to rise from the dark and desolate valley of segregation to the sunlit path of racial justice; now is the time to lift our nation from the quicksands of racial injustice to the solid rock of brotherhood; now is

the time to make justice a reality for all of God's children. It would be fatal for the nation to overlook the urgency of the moment. This sweltering summer of the Negro's legitimate discontent will not pass until there is an invigorating autumn of freedom and equality.

Nineteen sixty-three is not an end, but a beginning. And those who hope that the Negro needed to blow off steam and will now be content will have a rude awakening if the nation returns to business as usual. There will be neither rest nor tranquility in America until the Negro is granted his citizenship rights. The whirlwinds of revolt will continue to shake the foundations of our nation until the bright day of justice emerges.

But there is something that I must say to my people, who stand on the worn threshold which leads into the palace of justice. In the process of gaining our rightful place, we must not be guilty of wrongful deeds. Let us not seek to satisfy our thirst for freedom by drinking from the cup of bitterness and hatred. We must forever conduct our struggle on the high plain of dignity and discipline. We must not allow our creative protests to degenerate into physical violence. Again and again we must rise to the majestic heights of meeting physical force with soul force. The marvelous new militancy, which has engulfed the Negro community, must not lead us to a distrust of all white people. For many of our white brothers, as evidenced by their presence here today, have come to realize that their destiny is tied up with our destiny. And they have come to realize that their freedom is inextricably bound to our freedom. We cannot walk alone. And as we walk, we must make the pledge that we shall always march ahead. We cannot turn back.

There are those who are asking the devotees of Civil Rights, "When will you be satisfied?" We can never be satisfied as long as the Negro is the victim of the unspeakable horrors of police brutality; we can never be satisfied as long as our bodies, heavy with the fatigue of travel, cannot gain lodging in the motels of the highways and the hotels of the cities; we cannot be satisfied as long as the Negro's basic mobility is from a smaller ghetto to a larger one; we can never be satisfied as long as our children are stripped of their selfhood and robbed of their dignity by signs stating "For White Only"; we cannot be satisfied as long as the Negro in Mississippi cannot vote and a Negro in New York believes he has nothing for which to vote. No! No, we are not satisfied, and we will not be satisfied until "justice rolls down like waters and righteousness like a mighty stream."

I am not unmindful that some of you have come here out of great trials and tribulations. Some of you have come fresh from narrow jail cells. Some of you have come from areas where your quest for freedom left you battered by the storms of persecution and staggered by the winds of police brutality. You have been the veterans of creative suffering. Continue to work with the faith that unearned suffering is redemptive. Go back to Mississippi. Go back to Alabama. Go back to South Carolina. Go back to Georgia. Go back to Louisiana. Go back to the slums and ghettos of our Northern cities, knowing that somehow this situation can and will be changed. Let us not wallow in the valley of despair.

I say to you today, my friends, that even though we face the difficulties of today and tomorrow, I still have a dream. It is a dream deeply rooted in the American dream. I have a dream that one day this nation will rise up and live out the true meaning of its creed, "We hold these truths to be self-evident, that all

struggle for civil rights they can win these rights for themselves and their children.

3. King's immediate purpose is twofold: to inspire his followers to continue their struggle for racial justice and to prick the consciences of white Americans. To inspire his followers, he points out the rewards that they will reap if they avoid despair and continue to persevere. To appeal to white consciences, he notes that America has not lived up to the ideal expressed in the Declaration of Independence and the Constitution (paragraph 4) and points out some of the abuses and burdens that blacks must put up with (paragraphs 9 and 10). By doing all these things King hopes to accomplish a third, less immediate purpose: to win congressional and presidential support for the civil rights legislation then being considered.

4. King's primary audience is his followers in the civil rights movement. In addition he hopes to reach white Americans, many of whom were indifferent or hostile toward his aims.

5. King's speech has four main parts. In paragraphs 3–7 he reminds his listeners of the bleak situation in which blacks find themselves and of the need for change. In paragraphs 8–10 he exhorts them to take heart and continue their struggle for justice without succumbing to bitterness and hatred. In paragraphs 11 through the first part of paragraph 16, he lays out his hopes for the future, and in the remainder of the speech he foresees victory.

6. King's speech is a masterful example of emotional and ethical appeal. Emotion is evident in every part of the speech, but perhaps most strongly in paragraph 9, which points out the injustices still suffered by blacks, and in paragraphs 16–19, which set out King's dreams for the future. In calling for racial justice, King emerges as a deeply ethical individual, an impression that is enhanced by his rejection of physical violence (paragraph 8) and his religious allusions (paragraphs 6, 15, 16, and 18).

7. King relies heavily on metaphors and repetition to accomplish his purpose. Metaphors abound throughout the speech. Brief examples include "beacon light of hope" and "flames of withering injustice" (paragraph 2); "Manacles of segregation," "chains of discrimination," and "vast oceans of material prosperity" (paragraph 3); "sweltering summer . . . discontent," and "invigorating autumn of freedom" (paragraph 6); "bright day of justice" (paragraph 7); "palace of justice" and "cup of bitterness and hatred" (paragraph 8); "Storms of persecution," "winds of police brutality," and "valley of despair" (paragraph 10); "table of brotherhood," "heat of injustice, sweltering with the heat of oppression," and "oasis of freedom and justice" (paragraph 11); and "mountain of despair," "stone of hope," and "beautiful symphony of brotherhood" (paragraph 16). Paragraphs 4 and 5 constitute an extended metaphor or analogy that likens the rights guaranteed by the Constitution and Bill of Rights to a promissory note drawn on a bank. This extended metaphor includes two short metaphors: "bank of justice" and "vaults of opportunity." Repetition is likewise prominently featured in much of the speech. In paragraph 3 we have "one hundred years later," in paragraph 6 *"Now* is the time," in paragraph 9 "We can never be satisfied" and variations thereon, and in paragraph 10 "Go back." This technique reaches its climax with the powerful and moving repetition of "I have a dream" (paragraphs 11–15) and "Let freedom ring" (paragraphs 17 and 18). Other stylistic devices include balanced sentences "from the dark and desolate valley of segregation to the sunlit path of racial justice" and "from the quicksands of racial injustice to the solid rock of

men are created equal." I have a dream that one day on the red hills of Georgia, sons of former slaves and the sons of former slave owners will be able to sit down together at the table of brotherhood. I have a dream that one day even the state of Mississippi, a state sweltering with the heat of injustice, sweltering with the heat of oppression, will be transformed into an oasis of freedom and justice. I have a dream that my four little children will one day live in a nation where they will not be judged by the color of their skin, but by the content of their character.

12   I HAVE A DREAM TODAY!

13   I have a dream that one day down in Alabama—with its vicious racists, with its Governor having his lips dripping with the words of interposition and nullification—one day right there in Alabama, little black boys and black girls will be able to join hands with little white boys and white girls as sisters and brothers.

14   I HAVE A DREAM TODAY!

15   I have a dream that one day every valley shall be exalted, every hill and mountain shall be made low. The rough places will be plain and the crooked places will be made straight, "and the glory of the Lord shall be revealed, and all flesh shall see it together."

16   This is our hope. This is the faith that I go back to the South with. With this faith we will be able to hew out of the mountain of despair, a stone of hope. With this faith we will be able to transform the jangling discords of our nation into a beautiful symphony of brotherhood. With this faith we will be able to work together, to pray together, to struggle together, to go to jail together, to stand up for freedom together, knowing that we will be free one day. And this will be the day. This will be the day when all of God's children will be able to sing with new meaning, "My country 'tis of thee, sweet land of liberty, of thee I sing. Land where my fathers died, land of the pilgrim's pride, from every mountain side, let freedom ring." And if America is to be a great nation, this must become true.

17   So let freedom ring from the prodigious hilltops of New Hampshire; let freedom ring from the mighty mountains of New York; let freedom ring from the heightening Alleghenies of Pennsylvania; let freedom ring from the snowcapped Rockies of Colorado; let freedom ring from the curvaceous slopes of California. But not only that. Let freedom ring from Stone Mountain of Georgia; let freedom ring from Lookout Mountain of Tennessee; let freedom ring from every hill and mole hill of Mississippi. "From every mountainside, let freedom ring."

18   And when this happens, and when we allow freedom to ring, when we let it ring from every village and every hamlet, from every state and every city, we will be able to speed up that day when all of God's children, black men and white men, Jews and Gentiles, Protestants and Catholics, will be able to join hands and sing in the words of the old Negro spiritual: "Free at last. Free at last. Thank God Almighty, we are free at last."

DISCUSSION QUESTIONS ▪

1. Why do you think King begins with a reference to Lincoln?

2. Does this speech have a stated or an implied proposition? What is the proposition?

3. What does King hope to accomplish by the speech? How does he go about achieving his aim(s)?

4. What is the audience for the speech?

5. How does King organize his speech? How does this organization advance his purpose?

6. Which type(s) of argumentative appeal does King use? Cite appropriate parts of the speech.

7. What kinds of stylistic devices does King use? Where do they occur? How do they increase the effectiveness of the speech?

SUGGESTION FOR WRITING ■   **Write an essay calling for some major social or political change. For example, you might recommend that the country enact national health insurance, institute a peacetime draft, ban smoking in all public places, amend the Constitution to ban or legalize abortions, or establish federally funded day-care centers for working mothers.**

WILLIAM GEIST

■ *Home Sick*

William Geist, a native of Urbana, Illinois, holds an M.A. in journalism from the University of Missouri. Following his graduation in 1972, he worked as a reporter, and later as suburban editor, for the Chicago Tribune. *In 1980, he became a reporter for the* New York Times's *metropolitan desk; then, in 1987, he joined CBS News, where he does feature reports and sports segments for the program "Sunday Morning." In 1988, he began writing the "Fun City" feature for* New York *magazine, from which our selection comes. In it, he offers some wry observations about working at home rather than at the employer's office.*

Writing this should be a snap, now that I'm working at Home.   1

Working At Home is the Trend of The Future, combining new Enlightened   2
Employee Relations with the latest Galloping Technological Advances allowing
Millions of Americans to enjoy The Best of Both Worlds and Just Stay Home.

Not all of us, yet. You can't stay home and make *molten steel* on the stove.   3
It would play hell with the countertops. You'd never get away with it in my house.
Nor can an autoworker stay home and make cars on an assembly line—unless he
has a good-sized ranch home.

But, hell, leave all that stuff to the Japanese and the Koreans. We'll be at   4
home, if you need us, in The Home Office, processing, trading, investing,
consulting, and writing—using personal computers, home copiers, home fax
machines, answering machines, and microwave ovens (popcorn).

Work has always been a chore. Getting there has been worse. By the time   5
we get to work, we suffer from combat fatigue. The New Age worker telecom-

mutes from his electronic cottage. It takes but nanoseconds and requires no subway tokens or embarrassing galoshes.

6   I Work At Home as often as I can. A touch of self-discipline is all that's required.

7   With the more than two hours a day I save by not commuting, I have time to read the paper thoroughly and to watch Geraldo and Regis Philbin, making *me* a better-informed employee.

8   I get to take my daughter to school. Spending some time with the kids makes me a *happier* employee.

9   My commute? Just up a flight of steps to The Home Office in the attic, where I have my computer, my printer, and a modem—my lifeline to the office.

10   Why, it almost doesn't matter that I have no idea how to *use* the modem—all I have to do is print out my piece and take it two blocks away to a store that has a fax machine that can speed things anywhere in the world in a matter of seconds (with great accuracy, too, when you punch in the right receiver number).

11   Federal Express delivers things to my home faster than interoffice mail delivers down the hall. It (and UPS) delivers my neighbors' things, too, since I'm here to sign for them while they're at work in outmoded conventional-office-building situations.

12   Working At Home means there is someone here to field important phone calls that might otherwise go unanswered. "Hello. Jersey Brickface? No, I don't think we need any polyvinyl-brick-like sheet goods for the front of our home today, thanks."

13   I'm also here to answer the door: "Oh, hi, Carol. No, Jody's not home. She's at the office until about seven. Then how about me(!) as a fourth for bridge tomorrow at Martha Neal's?" The audacity! I'm at home, so how busy can I be? Is that it?

14   Working At Home means wearing comfortable leisurewear if I feel like it—although I found that not getting out of my pajamas makes it pretty tough to buckle down. Watch out for lapses in personal hygiene. Occasionally, laundering that plaid flannel shirt can be essential to maintaining a modicum of self-esteem, basic to mental health.

15   That was my wife calling to ask if I'd mind taking a moment out from my workday to put a couple loads of dirty laundry in the washer—since she's At The Office.

16   Time for lunch. No more of that hopping over to the Four Seasons for power lunches, which strain the pocketbook and hack away at productivity. You feel good about that as you dine on Skippy and Welch's on Wonder. Who's hungry anyway? When you Work At Home, the refrigerator is your constant companion.

17   I take a moment out to catch *The Young and the Restless* and "As" *(As the World Turns)*.

18   Sometimes, my daughter comes home for lunch. It's better now that the kids are in school. My daughter answered the phone "Goo-goo, gaa-gaa" when Lee Iacocca's office called back about my request for an interview. His office seemed reluctant to grant it, and sitting there in my bathrobe, with my daughter drooling on my keyboard, I caved in: "You're right. I should never have asked. Mr. Iacocca shouldn't lower himself."

DISCUSSION QUESTIONS

1.   Geist appears to make a case for working at home, the "Trend of The Future." But his real argument is just the reverse because of the assorted distractions

Jersey Brickface is on the line again, apparently thinking my imitation-brickface needs might have changed since this morning. "No!" I snap. "But would you like to chat?" You can start to get a little lonely, Working At Home.   19

On the way back to the attic, I pass my bedroom, and since I always feel a little woozy after lunch, I take time out from my workday to lie down for a moment and rest my eyes, recharging the old batteries to make me an even *more* productive employee later in the afternoon.   20

I put the clothes in the dryer (maybe I should start taking in ironing, too!), then I'm off to pick up my daughter at school. I like to get there a little early to chat with the other mothers. "We're going to a designer-outlet sale tomorrow," one of them says to me. "I think they have a men's department. Why don't you come along?"   21

"Love to," I say. "Can't. Bridge at Martha Neal's."   22

I drive my daughter to gymnastics, my son to basketball practice, pick up daughter at gym, take her to violin, pick up son, take to friend's house, pick up daughter, bring home, rotate tires, pick up son, bring home.   23

Seven P.M. I go up to The Home Office in the attic with my nine-year-old daughter. I bang my head on the slanted ceiling. (Aiiee!) My daughter shuts off the computer, explaining, "There wasn't anything on the screen."   24

"Shut up," I reply.   25

Wife calls, saying she's running a bit late and asking if I'd start cooking dinner. She has a taste for braised shoulder of lamb with glazed asparagus.   26

DISCUSSION QUESTIONS ■

1. What does Geist appear to be arguing? What is he really arguing?

2. At what point in the essay do you begin to suspect Geist's actual intent?

3. Particularly in his first six paragraphs Geist capitalizes certain phrases that would normally be written in lowercase letters. Suggest why. How do you explain the infrequent use of such phrases in the remainder of the essay?

4. Note the listings of things to do in paragraphs 4 and 23. Consider the essay as a whole and then point out how these two listings balance each other.

5. Why is the last sentence a fitting end for the argument?

6. Discuss the effectiveness of the essay's title.

SUGGESTION FOR WRITING ■   Write an essay arguing against any trend, activity, or development that appears to offer numerous advantages. Possibilities might include ocean dumping of garbage, credit consolidation loans, or the ten-hour-per-day four-day work week.

which prevent any work accomplishments. Thus this essay is an example of ironic argument.

2. The first 10 paragraphs generally sing the praises of working at home. But in paragraphs 11–13 the distractions, and Geist's actual intent, start to surface. Paragraph 11: "since I'm here"; paragraph 12: "there is someone here"; paragraph 13: "I'm also here." These three consecutive references signal the alert reader.

3. These phrases appear to represent "New Age" (paragraph 5) advancements that herald changes in the way we work. Therefore Geist capitalizes them to emphasize their supposed importance. As Geist becomes disenchanted with them, however, he uses them infrequently in the latter part of his essay.

4. Paragraph 4 lists apparent accomplishments and the means of achieving them at home. Paragraph 23 lists some distractions that thwart these accomplishments. Thus these two paragraphs point up the difference between Geist's apparent and actual intent.

5. The items his wife wants require considerable preparation time and thus represent yet another distraction that inhibits work at home.

6. The title is highly effective. It simultaneously suggests his desire to return home to work and his fill of the distractions he encounters.

Re the suggestion for writing accompanying this essay; note that we do *not* suggest that students attempt an ironic argument. We feel that such an assignment is too ambitious for most of them.

Although all three essays in this
section combine several writing
strategies, two are fundamentally arguments, and one is fundamentally illustration. Both argument essays are grounded in
logic, one relying on statistics to
help make its case and the other
on both statistics and authoritative opinions. The third essay
uses several brief examples rather than a single extended one.
One essay uses formal–informal
diction, one uses technical diction, and one is written informally.

Mixing the Writing Strategies

As we noted on page 183, most essays mix various writing strategies for assorted purposes. This section features three examples. Marginal notations on the Commoner essay point out the interplay of several strategies, and the discussion questions following the Klass and Williams essays direct your attention to the strategies these writers use.

BARRY COMMONER

Title indicates causes

■ *Why We Have Failed*

Barry Commoner (born 1917) is one of our best-known writers on environmental matters. Born in New York, he earned his undergraduate degree at Columbia University (1937) and graduate degrees at Harvard University (1938 and 1941). Following graduation, Commoner embarked on an academic career that has led him to the directorship of the Center for the Biology of Natural Systems at New York's Queens College. He is a member of numerous professional organizations and has held executive positions with a number of them. In addition, he has served on the editorial boards of numerous publications. His books include Science and Survival *(1966),* The Closing Circle: Nature, Man, and Technology *(1971),* The Poverty of Power *(1976), and* The Politics of Energy *(1979). He has edited several volumes on energy as well as written hundreds of journal articles. In our example, from the journal published by the environmental group Greenpeace, he criticizes our way of handling environmental problems and proposes a radically different approach.*

Introduction: narrative

1   In 1970, in response to growing concern, the U.S. Congress began a massive effort to undo the pollution damage of the preceding decades. In short order, legislators in Washington passed the National Environmental Protection Act (NEPA) and created the Environmental Protection Agency (EPA) to administer it. These two events are the cornerstone of what is indisputably the world's most vigorous pollution control effort, a model for other nations and a template for dozens of laws and amendments passed since. Now, nearly 20 years later, it is

time to ask an important and perhaps embarrassing question: how far have we progressed toward the goal of restoring the quality of the environment?

The answer is indeed humbling. Apart from a few notable exceptions, environmental quality has improved only slightly, and in some cases worsened. Since 1975, emissions of sulfur dioxide and carbon monoxide are down by about 19 percent, but nitrogen oxides are up about 4 percent. Overall improvement in major pollutants amounts to only about 15 to 20 percent, and the rate of improvement has actually slowed considerably.

2	Body: paragraphs 2–21
	Effects: paragraphs 2 and 3

There are several notable and heartening exceptions. Pollution levels of a few chemicals—DDT and PCBs in wildlife and people, mercury in the fish of the Great Lakes, strontium 90 in the food chain and phosphate pollution in some local rivers—have been reduced by 70 percent or more. Levels of airborne lead have declined more than 90 percent since 1975.

3

The successes explain what works and what does not. Every success on the very short list of significant environmental quality improvements reflects the same remedial action: production of the pollutant has been stopped. DDT and PCB levels have dropped because their production and use have been banned. Mercury is much less prevalent because it is no longer used to manufacture chlorine. Lead has been taken out of gasoline. And strontium has decayed to low levels because the United States and the Soviet Union had the good sense to stop the atmospheric nuclear bomb tests that produced it.

4	Argument by illustrations

The lesson is plain: pollution prevention works; pollution control does not. Only where production technology has been changed to eliminate the pollutant has the environment been substantially improved. Where it remains unchanged, where an attempt is made to trap the pollutant in an appended control device— the automobile's catalytic converter or the power plant's scrubber— environmental improvement is modest or nil. When a pollutant is attacked at the point of origin, it can be eliminated. But once it is produced, it is too late.

5	Argument by comparison
	Illustrations

Most of our environmental problems are the inevitable result of the sweeping technological changes that transformed the U.S. economic system after World War II: the large, high-powered cars; the shift from fuel-efficient railroads to gas-guzzling trucks and cars; the substitution of fertilizers for manure and crop rotation and of toxic synthetic pesticides for ladybugs and birds.

6	Cause: paragraphs 6 and 7
	Illustrations

By 1970, it was clear that these technological changes were the root cause of environmental pollution. But the environmental laws now in place do not address the technological origin of pollutants. I remember the incredulity in Senator Edmund Muskie's voice during NEPA hearings when he asked me whether I was really testifying that the technology that generated postwar economic progress was also the cause of pollution. I was.

7

Because environmental legislation ignored the origin of the assault on environmental quality, it has dealt only with its subsequent problems—in effect defining the disease as a collection of symptoms. As a result, all environmental legislation mandates only palliative measures. The notion of preventing pollution—the only measure that really works—has yet to be given any administrative force.

8	Cause and effect

The goal established by the Clean Air Act in 1970 could have been met if the EPA had confronted the auto industry with a demand for fundamental changes in engine design, changes that were practical and possible. And had

9	Argument by illustrations: paragraphs 9 and 10

American farmers been required to reduce the high rate of nitrogen fertilization, nitrate water pollution would now be falling instead of increasing.

10   If the railroads and mass transit were expanded, if the electric power system were decentralized and increasingly based on cogenerators and solar sources, if American homes were weatherized, fuel consumption and air pollution would be sharply reduced. If brewers were forbidden to put plastic nooses on six-packs of beer, if supermarkets were not allowed to wrap polyvinyl chloride film around everything in sight, if McDonalds restaurants could rediscover the paper plate, if the use of plastics was cut back to those things considered worth the social costs (say artificial hearts or video tape), then we could push back the petrochemical industry's toxic invasion of the biosphere.

Effect	11

Of course, all this is easier said than done. I am fully aware that what I am proposing is no small thing. It means that sweeping changes in the major systems of production—agriculture, industry, power production and transportation—would be undertaken for a social purpose: environmental improvement. This represents social (as contrasted with private) governance of the means of production—an idea that is so foreign to what passes for our national ideology that even to mention it violates a deep-seated taboo.

Comparison

Effect	12

The major consequence of this powerful taboo is the failure to reach the goals in environmental quality that motivated the legislation of the 1970s.

Process: paragraphs 13 and 14	13

In the absence of a prevention policy, the EPA adopted a convoluted pollution control process. First, the EPA must estimate the degree of harm represented by different levels of the numerous environmental pollutants. Next, some "acceptable" level of harm is chosen (for example, a cancer risk of one in a million) and emission and/or ambient concentration standards that can presumably achieve that risk level are established.

Illustration

14   Polluters are then expected to respond by introducing control measures (such as automobile exhaust catalysts or power plant stack scrubbers) that will bring emissions to the required levels. If the regulation survives the inevitable challenges from industry (and in recent years from the administration itself), the polluters will invest in the appropriate control systems. Catalysts are attached to cars, and scrubbers to the power plants and trash-burning incinerators. If all goes well—and it frequently does not—at least some areas of the country and some production facilities are then in compliance with the regulation.

Illustrations

Effect	15

The net result is that an "acceptable" pollution level is frozen in place. Industry, having invested heavily in equipment designed to reach just the required level, is unlikely to invest in further improvements.

Comparison	16

Clearly, this process is the opposite of the preventive approach to public health. It strives not for the continuous improvement of environmental health, but for the social acceptance of some, hopefully low, risk to health. By contrast, the preventive approach aims at progressively reducing the risk to health. It does not mandate some socially convenient stopping point. The medical professions, after all, did not decide that the smallpox prevention program could stop when the risk reached one in a million. They kept on, and the disease has now been wiped out worldwide.

Analogy

17   How do you decide when to stop, where to set the standard for acceptable pollution? The current fashion is to submit the question to a risk/benefit analysis. Since the pollutants' ultimate effect can often be assessed by the number of lives

lost, the risk/benefit analysis requires that a value be placed on human life. Such reckoning often bases that value on lifelong earning power, so that a poor person's life is worth less than a rich person's. So, on the risk/benefit scale, the poor can be exposed to more pollution than the rich. In fact, this is what is happening in the United States: the burden of an environmental risk—say the siting of a municipal incinerator or a hazardous waste landfill—falls disproportionally on poor people, who lack the political and financial clout to deter the risk.

In this way, risk/benefit analysis—a seemingly straightforward numerical computation—conceals a profound, unresolved moral question: should poor people be subjected to a more severe environmental burden than rich people, simply because they lack the resources to evade it? Since in practice the risk/benefit equation masquerades as science, it relieves society of the duty to confront this question. One result of failing to adopt the preventive approach is that the regulatory agencies have been driven into positions that seriously diminish the force of social morality.

The fate of Alar, the pesticide used to enhance the marketability of apples, provides a recent instructive example of what prevention means. Like many other petrochemical products, Alar poses a health risk. It has been proven to induce cancer in test animals. As in many other such cases, a debate has flourished over the extent of the hazard to people, especially children, and over what standards should be applied to limit exposure to "acceptable" levels.

In June, Alar broke out of the pattern when the manufacturer, Uniroyal, decided that regardless of the toxicological uncertainties, Alar would be taken off the market. They acted simply because parents were unhappy about raising their children on apple juice that represented *any* threat to their health. Food after all, is supposed to be good for you.

This is a clear-cut example of the benefits of prevention, as opposed to control. Pollution prevention means identifying the source of the pollutant in the production process, eliminating it from that process and substituting a more environmentally benign method of production. This differentiates it from source reduction (reducing the amount of the pollutant produced, either through altering processes or simple housekeeping) and pollution control. Once a pollutant is eliminated, the elaborate system of risk assessment, standard setting and the inevitable debates and litigation become irrelevant.

Instituting the practice of prevention rather than control will require the courage to challenge the taboo against questioning the dominance of private interests over the public interest. But I suggest that we begin with an open public discussion of what has gone wrong, and why. That is the necessary first step on the road toward realizing the nation's unswerving goal—restoring the quality of the environment.

Comparison

Effect
Illustrations

18 Effects

19 Illustration: paragraphs 19 and 20

20

21 Argument
Definition

Comparison
Definition

Effects

22 Conclusion:
Effect

DISCUSSION QUESTIONS ■

1. For what audience does Commoner write? How do you know?
2. Discuss the effectiveness of the short sentence ("I was.") that ends paragraph 7.

DISCUSSION QUESTIONS

1. Commoner has directed this essay at an audience of educated, environmentally sophisticated people. As a result, he uses a technical level of diction that in-

cludes a high percentage of rather long and complex sentences and words, such as "template" (paragraph 1), "appended" (paragraph 5), "palliative" (paragraph 8), and "ambient" (paragraph 13), that might well send a general audience to a dictionary. His use of terms like "DDT" and "PCB" (paragraphs 3 and 4), "strontium 90" (paragraph 3), "cogenerators " (paragraph 10), and "risk/benefit analysis" (paragraphs 17 and 18) show the assumptions he makes about his audience's grasp of environmental matters.

2. This sentence draws attention to itself because its length contrasts markedly with that of the preceding sentences in the paragraph. As a result, the short sentence hits with impact and helps emphasize Commoner's point about technology causing pollution.

3. The parallelism gives the writing continuity, rhythm, and balance. In addition, the detailing of possibilities and their beneficial effects leads Commoner to his proposal (in paragraph 11) for social rather than private governance of the means of production.

4. This question should spark a lively class discussion.

PERSPECTIVE

This essay offers an excellent opportunity to explain jargon to your students and to differentiate it from deadwood and gobbledygook. You might point out that since jargon is the specialized vocabulary of a particular group, students should avoid it if possible in papers directed at other readers, and that when a term must be used, an explanation is required.

3. Why do you think Commoner uses the "If . . . , then . . . " pattern of expression in paragraph 10?

4. Do you agree with the approach that Commoner proposes in paragraph 11? Why or why not?

SUGGESTION FOR WRITING ■   **Write an essay showing why someone or some organization has succeeded at some endeavor. Select a situation you know well and then develop it with an appropriate mixture of writing strategies.**

PERRI KLASS

■   *She's Your Basic L.O.L. in N.A.D.*

Perri Klass (born 1958) has pursued dual careers as physician and writer. A native of Trinidad, she was brought to the United States by her parents, attended schools in New York and New Jersey, and in 1986 graduated from Harvard Medical School. Her fiction writings include one novel, Recombinations *(1985), a short-story collection,* I Am Having an Adventure *(1986), and numerous short stories in popular magazines. Her essays have appeared in a variety of newspapers and magazines, as well as in a collection entitled* A Not Entirely Benign Procedure *(1987). In our essay, Klass examines the gains and losses that result from understanding and using medical jargon.*

1   "Mrs. Tolstoy is your basic L.O.L. in N.A.D., admitted for a soft rule-out M.I.," the intern announces. I scribble that on my patient list. In other words Mrs. Tolstoy is a Little Old Lady in No Apparent Distress who is in the hospital to make sure she hasn't had a heart attack (rule out a myocardial infarction). And we think it's unlikely that she has had a heart attack (a *soft* rule-out).

2   If I learned nothing else during my first three months of working in the hospital as a medical student, I learned endless jargon and abbreviations. I started out in a state of primeval innocence, in which I didn't even know that "s̄ C.P., S.O.B., N/V" meant "without chest pain, shortness of breath, or nausea and vomiting." By the end I took the abbreviations so for granted that I would complain to my mother the English Professor, "And can you believe I had to put down *three* NG tubes last night?"

3   "You'll have to tell me what an NG tube is if you want me to sympathize properly," my mother said. NG, nasogastric—isn't it obvious?

4   I picked up not only the specific expressions but the patterns of speech and the grammatical conventions; for example, you never say that a patient's blood pressure fell or that his cardiac enzymes rose. Instead, the patient is always the subject of the verb: "He dropped his pressure." "He bumped his enzymes." This

sort of construction probably reflects the profound irritation of the intern when the nurses come in the middle of the night to say that Mr. Dickinson has disturbingly low blood pressure. "Oh, he's gonna hurt me bad tonight," the intern may say, inevitably angry at Mr. Dickinson for dropping his pressure and creating a problem.

When chemotherapy fails to cure Mrs. Bacon's cancer, what we say is, "Mrs. Bacon failed chemotherapy."   5

"Well, we've already had one hit today, and we're up next, but at least we've got mostly stable players on our team." This means that our team (group of doctors and medical students) has already gotten one new admission today, and it is our turn again, so we'll get whoever is next admitted in emergency, but at least most of the patients we already have are fairly stable, that is, unlikely to drop their pressures or in any other way get suddenly sicker and hurt us bad. Baseball metaphor is pervasive: A no-hitter is a night without any new admissions. A player is always a patient—a nitrate player is a patient on nitrates, a unit player is a patient in the intensive-care unit and so on, until you reach the terminal player.   6

It is interesting to consider what it means to be winning, or doing well, in this perennial baseball game. When the intern hangs up the phone and announces, "I got a hit," that is not cause for congratulations. The team is not scoring points; rather, it is getting hit, being bombarded with new patients. The object of the game from the point of view of the doctors, considering the players for whom they are already responsible, is to get as few new hits as possible.   7

These special languages contribute to a sense of closeness and professional spirit among people who are under a great deal of stress. As a medical student, it was exciting for me to discover that I'd finally cracked the code, that I could understand what doctors said and wrote and could use the same formulations myself. Some people seem to become enamored of the jargon for its own sake, perhaps because they are so deeply thrilled with the idea of medicine, with the idea of themselves as doctors.   8

I knew a medical student who was referred to by the interns on the team as Mr. Eponym because he was so infatuated with eponymous terminology, the more obscure the better. He never said "capillary pulsations" if he could say "Quincke's pulses." He would lovingly tell over the multinamed syndromes—Wolff-Parkinson-White, Lown-Ganong-Levine, Henoch-Schonlein—until the temptation to suggest Schleswig-Holstein or Stevenson-Kefauver or Baskin-Robbins became irresistible to his less reverent colleagues.   9

And there is the jargon that you don't ever want to hear yourself using. You know that your training is changing you, but there are certain changes you think would be going a little too far.   10

The resident was describing a man with devastating terminal pancreatic cancer. "Basically he's C.T.D.," the resident concluded. I reminded myself that I had resolved not to be shy about asking when I didn't understand things. "C.T.D.?" I asked timidly.   11

The resident smirked at me. "Circling The Drain."   12

The images are vivid and terrible. "What happened to Mrs. Melville?"   13

"Oh, she boxed last night." To box is to die, of course.   14

Then there are the more pompous locutions that can make the beginning medical student nervous about the effects of medical training. A friend of mine   15 was told by his resident, "A pregnant woman with sickle-cell represents a failure of genetic counseling."

16   Mr. Eponym, who tried hard to talk like the doctors, once explained to me, "An infant is basically a brainstem preparation." A brainstem preparation, as used in neurological research, is an animal whose higher brain functions have been destroyed so that only the most primitive reflexes remain, like the sucking reflex, the startle reflex and the rooting reflex.

17   The more extreme forms aside, one most important function of medical jargon is to help doctors maintain some distance from their patients. By reformulating a patient's pain and problems into a language that the patient doesn't even speak, I suppose we are in some sense taking those pains and problems under our jurisdiction and also reducing their emotional impact. This linguistic separation between doctors and patients allows conversations to go on at the bedside that are unintelligible to the patient. "Naturally, we're worried about adeno-C.A.," the intern can say to the medical student, and lung cancer need never be mentioned.

18   I learned a new language this past summer. At times it thrills me to hear myself using it. It enables me to understand my colleagues, to communicate effectively in the hospital. Yet I am uncomfortably aware that I will never again notice the peculiarities and even atrocities of medical language as keenly as I did this summer. There may be specific expressions I manage to avoid, but even as I remark them, promising myself I will never use them, I find that this language is becoming my professional speech. It no longer sounds strange in my ears—or coming from my mouth. And I am afraid that as with any new language, to use it properly you must absorb not only the vocabulary but also the structure, the logic, the attitudes. At first you may notice these new alien assumptions every time you put together a sentence, but with time and increased fluency you stop being aware of them at all. And as you lose that awareness, for better or for worse, you move closer and closer to being a doctor instead of just talking like one.

DISCUSSION QUESTIONS ■

1. Klass develops her essay by using one primary writing strategy and several secondary ones. Identify her primary strategy and point out where she uses it.

2. Where does she use definition? Cause and/or effect? Narration? Analogy?

3. How does Klass use contrast when she evaluates medical jargon?

4. Klass tells us in paragraph 17 that the use of jargon to describe medical conditions helps in "reducing their emotional impact." Explain what she means.

5. Point out why the last sentence in paragraph 18 is an appropriate ending for the essay.

SUGGESTION FOR WRITING ■   **Write an essay that clarifies the jargon used in some profession or that used by fitness fanatics, social climbers, dieters, or some other people with shared values. Use several writing strategies to make your point.**

DISCUSSION QUESTIONS

1. Klass develops her essay primarily by a substantial number of illustrations of medical jargon and abbreviations. These examples are found in the title as well as in paragraphs 1–7, 9, 11–12, and 14–17.
2. Definition: paragraphs 1–4, 6, 7, 12, 14, 16, 17; cause and/or effect: paragraphs 2–4, 8–15, 17, and 18; narration: paragraph 9; analogy: in paragraphs 6 and 7, Klass develops a type of analogy between a baseball team and a hospital team.
3. Klass draws a contrast between the desirable and undesirable uses of medical jargon. Such jargon establishes an effective means of communication between medical professionals, contributes to "closeness and professional spirit" (paragraph 8), helps doctors "maintain some distance from their patients" (paragraph 17), and enables Klass to feel that she's "cracked the code" (paragraph 8). On the other hand, "C.T.D." (paragraphs 11 and 12), "boxed" (paragraph 14), the sickle-cell reference (paragraph 15), and Mr. Eponym's uses (paragraph 9) leave something to be desired.
4. Jargon helps establish some distance and thus diminishes the doctor's emotional involvement with the patient.
5. Klass reflects on the new language she learned during her first three months working as a medical student in the hospital. In addition, "for better or for worse" sums up the contrasting feelings discussed in answer 3.

MONCI JO WILLIAMS

■ *Is Workfare the Answer?*

A Philadelphian by birth, Monci Jo Williams holds a degree in writing from Carnegie-Mellon University. Following graduation, she became an advertising copywriter and wrote campaigns for a variety of clients, including the Public Broadcasting Corporation, Alcoa, and Stouffer's. She joined the staff of Fortune *in 1981 as a reporter-researcher, and in 1984 she was named an associate editor. In our selection, she examines the effectiveness of workfare as a means of helping welfare recipients to become self-sufficient.*

1   In the compassion-packed Sixties and Seventies, welfare became a right, checks became grants, and social workers turned into "human services technicians." But now the buzzword in the welfare bureaucracy is workfare—the array of programs that make people work or accept training in return for checks. With the federal and state governments looking to cut the $31 billion they are expected to spend on welfare programs this year, welfare reform is nearing the top of the national agenda. Five years of trial have turned up problems in workfare. But it is still a good idea—and can be made better.

2   To many people workfare means requiring welfare recipients to work for welfare payments in government-assigned jobs. In reality it is much more elaborate. Most states give welfare recipients a choice: Look for a job, go to school, or attend job-hunting classes in return for checks. This flexibility has led many administrators to prefer the term "welfare employment."

3   Though workfare programs are still experimental, they are widespread. Like welfare, they are administered by states and counties. Thirty-nine states run workfare programs for recipients of Aid to Families With Dependent Children (AFDC), the $9-billion-a-year federal program for poor single parents, overwhelmingly mothers. In most states, food stamp recipients must also hunt for jobs, and the federal government, which provides the stamps, will require all 50 states to set up education and training programs for food stamp beneficiaries by next spring. . . .

4   So far workfare programs do appear to save the government money and help welfare recipients find jobs. But most AFDC workfare programs involve only a small part of states' welfare caseloads. Full-scale programs will be more complicated and expensive. It is also too soon to tell whether workfare program alumni who find jobs will keep them.

5   The Manpower Demonstration Research Corp., a New York-based independent non-profit organization that evaluates poverty and employment programs, is studying welfare employment in 11 states. It has found that the states can reduce spending by propelling welfare recipients into the work force. The MDRC's studies compare the employment rates—the percent of people who find jobs—for workfare program graduates with those of a control group of welfare recipients. Results: Employment rates for workfare graduates were three to eight percentage points higher than for other welfare recipients. In addition, by finding jobs workfare alumni increased their incomes—in one group by 36% over the control

---

PERSPECTIVE

Some three decades ago, when the concept of workfare first surfaced, it encountered widespread hostility, and the few communities that adopted workfare programs soon dropped them. Today, workfare is receiving serious consideration not only because it promises to cut welfare costs but also because of its benefits to those who participate. Similar shifts in thinking about matters of public concern are of course a fact of life, and letting students know that shifts do happen often encourages them to be less dogmatic in their thinking.

TEACHING STRATEGIES

1. To illustrate that public attitudes about important matters often change, refer students to the paired essays proposing solutions to the drug problem (pages 502–518) and point out that just a few years ago hardly anyone would have seriously considered legalizing drugs.

2. Although we present this essay to illustrate the mixture of writing strategies, it is basically an argument. If you've already covered that strategy, you could have students locate the writer's proposition and identify it as one of fact, action, or value as well as determine the kinds of evidence used and their effectiveness.

3. Ask students to identify the audience Williams has in mind and to characterize her level of diction. Encourage them to support their answers by referring to the text.

4. While she clearly favors workfare, Williams notes several possible problems with the program. Ask students to identify these problems.

CLASSROOM ACTIVITIES

1. Divide the class into small groups; then have them discuss the advantages and disadvantages of workfare and present their conclusions in reports to the entire class. The reports could lead to a writing assignment.

2. Ask students to bring in articles exploring one or more of the topics mentioned in the suggestion for writing. Divide the class into small groups, give each an article, and ask students to identify the writing strategies employed. A class discussion of the findings helps students see how prevalent the mixture of strategies is.

6   group's. Eighteen months after the studies began, the MDRC found that about a third of the workfare group were employed.

7   When the MDRC weighed the costs of running workfare programs against the savings in AFDC outlays, it found that most states came out ahead. The reductions in AFDC outlays ranged from almost none in Maryland to 11% in Arkansas; in most cases they were 5% to 8%. These calculations do not include the drop in payroll costs when welfare recipients are assigned to useful public work, a common practice. Says Judith M. Gueron, president of MDRC: "Workfare is not a shortcut to balancing the budget. But the savings can be significant."

If workfare's achievements seem modest, consider the difficulties. Research in 1983 by professors Mary Jo Bane and David T. Ellwood of Harvard University concluded that about half the women on welfare were unmarried mothers, high school dropouts, or others without recent work experience. They may be the daughters and granddaughters of women who spent much of their lives on welfare. They may not know anyone who has held a steady job. They may be housewives whose lives are turned topsy-turvy by divorce. Bane and Ellwood found that these women tend to stay on welfare the longest—an average of eight years—and account for most government welfare spending. The world of work is alien to many of them; they have little reason to believe they can compete for jobs, and they are paralyzed by fright.

8   A good example is Julie A. Williams, 32, of Little Rock, Arkansas. She dropped out of high school at 16 and has two daughters and an unemployed husband. Although she received a high school equivalency certificate in 1972, she has been on and off the welfare rolls for years. She was, she says, "a hopeless case. I got drunk by day. I just didn't give a damn." She received $370 a month in food stamps and AFDC benefits and sold her blood at the North Little Rock Plasma Center to help make ends meet. She had not worked for four years when, in 1985, she registered for Arkansas's workfare program in order to continue receiving benefits.

9   After being trained as a phlebotomist, Williams got a job in May at the North Little Rock Plasma Center—now she draws donors' blood. The starting pay was about $400 a month, but Williams has already received a $234 raise. "I get up at 4:30 A.M., catch the bus at 5:40 and am in here by 6:50," she says. She believes she is setting a better example for her daughters than she did as a welfare mother. "My children love it. They say, 'I want to do that when I grow up.'" Getting off welfare also improved Williams's relationship with her mother. "We hadn't spoken in 15 years because she thought I'd be a tramp all my life," she says. "Now we're talking. I have never felt so well about myself."

10   Arkansas's programs and others suggest that workfare works best when participants can choose what they will do in return for their checks. Welfare recipients, like most people, want to feel some control over their lives. They participate more willingly when given a choice than when, as Norma Hill, a welfare mother from San Diego, puts it, government agencies are "pulling your strings." Many choose education, and as a practical matter they need a high school diploma or other training before looking for jobs.

11   Most workfare programs require AFDC recipients whose youngest child is 6 or older to participate, paying them additional stipends for child care and transportation. Women who do not go back to school start off job hunting; many

states' welfare offices provide phones and Yellow Pages to help locate potential employers. Thelma McDaris, 24, recently spend a week calling from a welfare office in San Diego; now she calls from home. She has not found a job but lauds the program, which she says gave her self-confidence—"and it comes over on the phone."

Poor states such as Arkansas and West Virginia cannot afford to give job hunters much help, but in richer states the search phases of workfare programs are quite elaborate. Some offer one- or two-week job-hunting workshops that teach welfare recipients how to fill out applications, write résumés, and answer such questions as, "Why have you been out of work so long?" A recommended answer: "I was married and taking care of my family and my home." In San Diego and elsewhere, students in job-search workshops hone their interview skills by watching themselves in mock interviews on videotape.   12

Often a state puts job-hunting welfare recipients into the job club, a sort of therapy group in which peers offer motivation and moral support. In San Diego when a job club member tells the group she has found employment, the group leader, a social worker, rings a cowbell.   13

Some job club members find that a little hokey. But for Barbara Norris, 44, a mother of five who went on welfare after her husband of eight years walked out, the ringing of the bell signified a giant achievement. Until she took a short-term workfare assignment as a junior clerk in the county welfare office, Norris had never been anything other than a housewife. The welfare office was impressed with her performance and gave her a permanent job, and the three-month-old memory of that ringing cowbell still brings tears to her eyes. "It meant," says Norris, "that I did it. *I did it.*"   14

Norris' workfare job in the county welfare office is typical. These jobs are not menial or make-work: Welfare mothers toil as file clerks and receptionists in community outreach centers; as teachers' assistants in government-funded day-care centers and schools for the mentally retarded; as billing clerks in public hospitals. Participants continue to receive welfare checks but are not paid. In states that offer AFDC for couples, many workfare jobs go to men, who work as mechanics or maintenance men in housing projects and state parks. A few states go further. In Chicago the Illinois Department of Public Aid and a local nonprofit organization recently collaborated to launch a window shade and screen manufacturing company staffed by welfare mothers, who can eventually earn equity in the for-profit enterprise.   15

Massachusetts welfare administrators believe their employment program, ET Choices (ET stands for employment and training), may be one of the most successful in the country, though it is not really a workfare program. Reason: It does not require welfare recipients to accept training or take workfare jobs but merely offers them training as word processors, electronic technicians, medical secretaries, and more. The state contracts with private training organizations and the local employment office to rustle up real jobs for ET graduates. That has not been too hard, since Massachusetts has experienced a high-tech miniboom in recent years, and unemployment is only 3.9%, vs. 6.8% nationally.   16

Since ET's inauguration in October 1983, 30,000 graduates have found jobs, and state officials hope to nearly double the figure by 1988. Dorothy Hayman, for example, is a mother who was on and off welfare for many years   17

18   before enrolling in ET and being trained as a surgical technician. She now works full time at Beth Israel Hospital in Boston.

18   The Massachusetts Department of Public Welfare estimates that by getting welfare mothers off the dole it will reduce federal and state expenditures for AFDC benefits by $188 million, outlays for food stamps by $31 million, and spending on Medicaid by $24 million between 1983 and 1988. It also believes that the graduates who go to work will add $43 million to state and federal coffers in income and sales taxes. Massachusetts spent $71 million on ET during its first two years but figures it racked up gross savings of $223 million during that time.

19   Though the figures seem impressive, they are more than a trifle inflated. Massachusetts has not compared the ET graduates with a control group and is claiming savings from thousands of employed welfare recipients who probably would have found jobs anyway. The numbers that state officials like to toss around also tend to distort the program's success, since only 31% of welfare recipients participated in ET. But the income levels of ET graduates really are impressive. Those who found full-time jobs during the first half of the year received an average annual starting salary of $12,000 vs. an average annual AFDC grant of about $5,000.

20   Canny bureaucratic incentives help push up the starting salaries. Until recently the welfare department paid the employment department a bounty of $1,100 for each job it found for a welfare recipient, plus a $100 bonus if the job paid $5 per hour or more. Now it has upped the ante: It will fork over the $1,100 only for jobs that pay $5 an hour or more and only if the person is still on the job after 30 days.

21   Why is the Massachusetts welfare department in the bounty business? Because a welfare recipient might turn down a minimum-wage job or soon give it up. Since states may augment federal funds for AFDC benefits, choosing welfare over a low-paying job may be a rational economic decision. In California, one of the most generous states, Norma Hill could net $533 a month for a minimum-wage job, but as a mother of three she can collect at least $860 a month in AFDC benefits and food stamps and perhaps bolster that with a federal housing subsidy.

22   Massachusetts officials estimate that when administrative, training, and bounty costs are taken into account, it spends an average of $3,800 to place ET graduates in jobs. Charles M. Atkins, the state welfare commissioner, says these placement costs will probably increase. Like most workfare programs, ET has placed the most easily employable in jobs first. The test of ET and other programs will be whether they can put long-term welfare recipients, who account for most government welfare spending, into jobs at a reasonable cost. . . .

23   Congress should give states a few more years to continue the workfare experiments and should come up with the money to let them. The states have been sloppy and inconsistent in their attempts to measure workfare programs' performance; Congress should set data standards so it can compare results in different states to determine which workfare programs work best. Until then it is hard to be sure of much about workfare, except that it's an idea worth pursuing.

DISCUSSION QUESTIONS ■

1. What primary writing strategy does Williams use to develop her essay? At what point are you first aware of this intention?

2. Where does Williams use illustration? Cause and/or effect? Classification? Comparison? Definition? Narration?

3. How does she answer the question posed in her title? Refer to the essay when answering.

4. Comment on the effectiveness of the quotations cited in paragraphs 8, 9, 10, 11, and 14.

5. Why does Williams object to the Massachusetts statistics cited in paragraph 18?

SUGGESTION FOR WRITING ■ Write an essay that addresses and answers a controversial question. Possibilities: should we implement sobriety check-lanes? Pay college athletes? Negotiate with terrorists? Use several writing strategies to formulate your answer.

DISCUSSION QUESTIONS

1. This is primarily an argument essay. The proposition at the end of the opening paragraph first signals Williams' intention.

2. Illustration: paragraphs 8, 9, 11, 14, 17, 21; cause and/or effect: paragraphs 5, 6, 9, 10–22; classification: paragraphs 7, 15; comparison: paragraphs 1–3, 5, 6, 9, 10, 12, 19–22; definition: paragraphs 1–3, 5, 16; narration: paragraphs 8, 9.

3. Williams argues in favor of workfare (as opposed to welfare) but notes that the jury is still out on some aspects of the program. Paragraphs 4–6 point out that workfare saves money, and paragraphs 8, 9, 14, and the end of paragraph 19 illustrate the benefits of the system at work. The proposition indicates the need for improving the system, and paragraphs 3, 4, 22, and 23 suggest the need for more evidence before a verdict can be reached.

4. These quotations enhance the argument for workfare and help make the writing vivid.

5. The ET graduates are not compared with a group of nongraduates, many welfare recipients would have found jobs without ET, and only 31% of welfare recipients participated in ET. Thus the figures are characterized as "inflated" and "distorted" (paragraph 19). Students should learn to avoid this type of misuse.

Handbook

Sentence Elements

Learning the parts of English sentences won't in itself improve your writing, but it will equip you to handle errors at the sentence level. Before you can identify and correct unwarranted shifts from past to present time, for example, you need to know about verbs and their tenses. Similarly, recognizing and correcting pronoun case errors requires a knowledge of what pronouns are and how they are used. In this section we first cover subjects and predicates, then complements, appositives, and the parts of speech, and finally phrases and clauses.

SUBJECTS AND PREDICATES

The subject of a sentence tells who or what it is about. A *simple subject* consists of a noun (that is, a naming word) or a noun substitute. A *complete subject* consists of a simple subject plus any words that limit or describe it.

The predicate tells something about the subject and completes the thought of the sentence. A *simple predicate* consists of one or more verbs (words that show action or existence); a *complete predicate* includes any associated words also. In the following examples the simple subjects are underlined once and the simple predicates twice. The subjects and predicates are separated with slash marks.

William / laughed.

Mary / has moved.

Sarah / painted the kitchen.

The student over there in the corner / is majoring in art.

A sentence can have a compound subject (two or more separate subjects), a compound predicate (two or more separate predicates), or both.

The elephants and their trainer / bowed to the audience and left the ring.

Sentences that ask questions don't follow the usual simple subject–simple predicate order. Instead, the order may be reversed; or if the simple predicate consists of two verbs, the simple subject may come between them.

When is / your / theme due? (Simple subject follows simple predicate.)

Has / Joan / walked her pygmy goat yet? (Simple subject comes between verbs.)

sent

EXERCISE ■ **Place a slash mark between the complete subject and the complete predicate; then underline the simple subject once and the verb(s) twice. If a subject comes between two verbs, set it off with two slash marks.**

1. The new recruits were exhausted by the strenuous exercise.
2. My favorite color is red.
3. Myron and his sister shouted and laughed at the good news.
4. Where are the minutes of last month's meeting?
5. The cruisers and destroyers wheeled and fired their guns.
6. This new sports car has won several awards for its design.
7. The glowering bouncer stood menacingly near the door.
8. A small statue sat on the mantel.
9. Have you heard about Doug's accident?
10. A good slogan can contribute to the success of a new product.

COMPLEMENTS

A complement is a word or word group that forms part of the predicate and helps complete the meaning of the sentence. Complements fall into four categories: direct objects, indirect objects, subject complements, and object complements.

A *direct object* names whatever receives, or results from, the action of a verb.

The millwright repaired the *lathe*. (Direct object receives action of verb *repaired*.)

Hilary painted a *picture*. (Direct object results from action of verb *painted*.)

They took *coffee* and *sandwiches* to the picnic. (Direct objects receive action of verb *took*.)

As the last sentence shows, a sentence may have a compound direct object—two or more separate direct objects.

An *indirect object* identifies someone or something that receives whatever is named by the direct object.

Doris lent *me* her calculator. (Indirect object *me* receives *calculator*, the direct object.)

Will and Al bought their *boat* new sails. (Indirect object *boat* receives *sails*, the direct object.)

An indirect object can be converted to a prepositional phrase that begins with *to* or *for* and follows the direct object.

Doris lent her calculator *to me.*

Will and Al bought new sails *for their boat.*

A *subject complement* follows a linking verb—one that indicates existence rather than action. It renames or describes the subject.

sent

Desmond is a *carpenter.* (Complement *carpenter* renames subject *Desmond.*)

The lights are too *bright* for Percy. (Complement *bright* describes subject *lights.*)

An *object complement* follows a direct object and renames or describes it.

The council named Donna *treasurer.* (Object complement *treasurer* renames direct object *Donna.*)

The audience thought the play *silly.* (Object complement *silly* describes direct object *play.*)

APPOSITIVES

An appositive is a noun or word group serving as a noun that follows another noun or noun substitute and expands its meaning. Appositives may be restrictive or nonrestrictive. Restrictive appositives distinguish whatever they modify from other items in the same class. They are written without commas.

My sister *Heidi* is a professional golfer. (Appositive *Heidi* distinguishes her from other sisters.)

I have just read a book by the novelist *Henry James.* (Appositive *Henry James* distinguishes him from other novelists.)

Nonrestrictive appositives provide more information about whatever they modify. This sort of appositive is set off by a pair of commas except at the end of a sentence; then it is preceded by a single comma.

Nicolai Karpov, *the Rusitarian Consul,* was interviewed on TV last week. (Appositive names *Karpov's* occupation.)

Todd plans to major in paleontology, *the study of fossils.* (Appositive defines *paleontology.*)

EXERCISE ■   **Identify each italicized item as a direct object (DO), an indirect object (IO), a subject complement (SC), an object complement (OC), or an appositive (AP).**

1. The players called their coach *incompetent.*
2. The small boy kicked the *can* along the sidewalk.
3. Lisa sent *Dick* a Valentine.

4. Nancy was a *nurse* for ten years.
5. Bernice Alcott, *my old chemistry teacher,* now works for Monsanto.
6. Brian's co-workers thought him a *workaholic.*
7. Mary is a *buyer* for Macy's department store.
8. The bellhop carried Michelle's *luggage* toward the elevator.
9. Miguel's mother made *him* a sandwich.
10. My brother *Tom* spends every weekend in New York.

PARTS OF SPEECH

Traditional English grammar classifies words into eight parts of speech: *nouns, pronouns, verbs, adjectives, adverbs, prepositions, conjunctions,* and *interjections.* This section discusses these categories as well as verbals, phrases, and clauses, which also serve as parts of speech.

Nouns

Nouns name persons, places, things, conditions, ideas, or qualities. Some nouns, called *proper nouns,* identify one-of-a-kind items like the following:

France
Pacific Ocean
George Washington
Pulitzer Prize
Spirit of St. Louis
Declaration of Independence

Christmas
North Dakota
Mona Lisa
World Series
Wyandotte Corporation
Miami–Dade Junior College

Mount Everest, on the border of *Tibet* and *Nepal,* was named for *Sir George Everest,* an Englishman.

Common nouns name general classes or categories of items and include abstract, concrete, and collective nouns.

Abstract Nouns. An abstract noun names a condition, idea, or quality—something we can't see, feel, or otherwise experience with our five senses.

arrogance   harmony   sickness
envy   liberalism   understanding
fear   love

His *desire* to win caused him to cheat.

Mary felt great *loyalty* to her family.

Concrete Nouns.   A concrete noun identifies something that we can experience with one or more of our senses.

man	desk	pillow	needle
bicycle	lemon	airplane	pan
building	piston	carton	smoke

The *air* was thin at the *peak* of the *mountain*.

The *hammer* had a broken *handle*.

Collective Nouns.   A collective noun is singular in form but stands for a group or collection of items.

assembly	committee	crowd	group	tribe
class	convoy	family	herd	troop

The *jury* filed into the courtroom to announce its verdict.

The *flock* of geese settled onto the lake.

EXERCISE ■   Identify the nouns in the following sentences.

1. My roommates play loud music every evening.
2. Isabel lives in Phoenix, Arizona.
3. You showed great strength and courage when disaster struck.
4. The Kiwanis Club places great stress on service to the community.
5. Mr. Fowler assigned the class twenty chemistry problems.
6. The driver collected tickets as the passengers boarded the bus.
7. For twenty years, the Christian Democrats have held power in this country.
8. Ben Franklin proved that lightning is a form of electricity.
9. A car was parked in the alley behind the building.
10. My grandmother rides a bicycle to work every day.

Pronouns

Pronouns, which take the place of nouns in sentences, help you avoid the awkward repetition of nouns.

If Brad doesn't like the *book,* take *it* back to the library.

There are eight categories of pronouns: *personal, relative, interrogative, demonstrative, reflexive, intensive, indefinite,* and *reciprocal.*

Personal Pronouns.   Personal pronouns refer to one or more clearly identified persons, places, or things.

CLASSROOM ACTIVITY

Have students list as many nouns as possible, perhaps allowing them to refer to textbooks, then determine which are abstract and which are concrete. For example, use the nouns "arrogance" and "smoke," pointing out that while we can see only the symptoms of arrogance, we can clearly see smoke itself.

CLASSROOM ACTIVITY

Have students identify activities that a class can do as a group. For example, a class might make an average test score, produce a book with chapters written by individual students, and so on.

EXERCISE ANSWERS

1. roommates, music, evening
2. Isabel, Phoenix, Arizona
3. strength, courage, disaster
4. Kiwanis Club, stress, service, community
5. Mr. Fowler, class, problems
6. driver, tickets, passengers, bus
7. years, Christian Democrats, power, country
8. Ben Franklin, lightning, form, electricity
9. car, alley, building
10. grandmother, bicycle, work, day

TEACHING STRATEGY

To help students appreciate the importance of pronouns, have them substitute the appropriate pronouns in the following passage:

The roommate John has a serious problem with John's girlfriend. John is terrified of meeting the girlfriend's fami-

Subjective	Objective	Possessive
I	me	my, mine
you	you	your, yours
he	him	his
she	her	her, hers
it	it	its
we	us	our, ours
you	you	your, yours
they	them	their, theirs

Subjective pronouns serve as the subjects of sentences or clauses; objective pronouns serve as direct and indirect objects; and possessive pronouns show possession or ownership. *My, your, our,* and *their* always precede nouns and thus function as possessive adjectives. *His* and *its* may or may not precede nouns.

He bought a sport shirt. (pronoun as subject)

Donald saw *them.* (pronoun as direct object)

Simon lent *her* ten dollars. (pronoun as indirect object)

That car is *theirs.* (pronoun showing ownership)

Relative Pronouns.   A relative pronoun relates a subordinate clause—a word group that has a subject and a predicate but does not express a complete idea—to and antecedent in the main part of its sentence. The relative pronouns include the following:

who	whose	what	whoever	whichever
whom	which	that	whomever	whatever

Who in its various forms refers to people, *which* to things, and *that* to either people or things.

Mary Beth Cartwright, *who* was arrested last week for fraud, was Evansville's "Model Citizen" two years ago. (The antecedent of *who* is *Mary Beth Cartwright.*)

He took the typewriter, *which* needed cleaning, to the repair shop. (The antecedent of *which* is *typewriter.*)

David Bullock is someone *whom* we should definitely hire. (The antecedent of *whom* is *someone.*)

Montreal is a city *that* I've always wanted to visit. (The antecedent of *that* is *city.*)

Which typically introduces nonrestrictive clauses, that is, clauses that provide more information about whatever they modify (see page 543).

The palace, *which* was in bad condition a century ago, is finally going to be restored. (Clause adds information about palace.)

---

ly. The family members apparently don't approve of John. John's roommate tried to cheer John up by reassuring John that the girlfriend loves John, and that is what matters. John's roommate suspects that John didn't believe John's roommate. John finally went and had a terrible time. In the end, though, John and John's roommate had to laugh about the whole event. (Hint: the roommate is the writer of the passage.)

Corrected Version

My roommate John has a serious problem with his girlfriend. He is terrified of meeting her family. They apparently don't approve of him. I tried to cheer him up by reassuring him that his girlfriend loves him, and that is what matters. I suspect that he doesn't believe me. He finally went and had a terrible time. In the end, though, he and I had to laugh about the whole event.

PERSPECTIVE

Relative pronouns help writers formulate more complex sentences. You might introduce relative clauses through sentence-combining exercises.

CLASSROOM ACTIVITY

Have students combine the following sentences using relative pronouns:

1. He owns the Toyota Camry. The Toyota Camry has a broken headlight.
2. George Bush was once the director of the CIA. George Bush is now President.
3. The streets are peppered with potholes. The streets will be paved this spring.

That is typically used in other situations, especially to introduce restrictive clauses: those that distinguish the things they modify from others in the same class (see page 543).

> The used car *that* I bought last week at Honest Bill's has already broken down twice. (Clause distinguishes writer's used car from others.)

Interrogative Pronouns. Interrogative pronouns introduce questions. All of the relative pronouns except *that* also function as interrogative pronouns.

who	which	whoever	whichever
whom	what	whomever	whatever
whose			

> *What* is the matter?
>
> *Who* asked you?
>
> *Whatever* do you mean?

When *what* and *which* are followed by nouns, they act as adjectives, not pronouns.

> *Which* movie should we see?

Demonstrative Pronouns. As their name suggests, demonstrative pronouns point things out. There are four such pronouns.

this	these
that	those

This and its plural *these* identify recent or nearby things:

> *This* is the play to see.
>
> *These* are the times that try men's souls.

That and its plural *those* identify less recent or more distant things:

> *That* is Mary's house across the road.
>
> *Those* were very good peaches you had for sale last week.

Reflexive and Intensive Pronouns. A reflexive pronoun reverses the action of a verb, making the doer and the receiver of the action the same. An intensive pronoun lends emphasis to a noun or pronoun. The two sets of pronouns are identical.

myself	herself	ourselves
yourself	itself	yourselves
himself	oneself	themselves

pro

4. The word-processing program works very well. I purchased the word-processing program last year.
5. *Buddenbrooks* is a novel. I have always wanted to read *Buddenbrooks*.

Combinations

1. He owns the Toyota Camry that has a broken headlight.
2. George Bush, who was once the director of the CIA, is now President.
3. The streets that are peppered with potholes will be paved this spring. OR The streets, which are peppered with potholes, will be paved this spring.
4. The word-processing program that I purchased last year works very well.
5. *Buddenbrooks* is a novel that I have always wanted to read.

My father cut *himself* while shaving. (reflexive pronoun)

The President *himself* has asked me to undertake this mission. (intensive pronoun)

Don't substitute a reflexive pronoun for a personal pronoun.

Faulty	Jill and *myself* are going to a movie.
Revision	Jill and *I* are going to a movie.

Faulty	Give the tickets to John and *myself.*
Revision	Give the tickets to John and *me.*

Sometimes you'll hear people say things like "He made it *hisself,*" "They're only fooling *theirself,*" or "They bought *theirselves* sodas." Such forms are non-standard. Say "himself" and "themselves" instead.

Indefinite Pronouns.   The pronouns in this group refer to unidentified persons, places, or things. The group includes the following:

anybody	everything	one
anyone	nobody	somebody
anything	no one	someone
everybody	nothing	something
everyone		

These words consistently act as pronouns. Other words may function either as indefinite pronouns or as adjectives:

all	any	most	few	much
another	each	either	many	neither

Here are some examples:

Everyone is welcome. (indefinite pronoun)

Many are called, but *few* are chosen. (indefinite pronouns)

Many men but only a *few* women attend the Air Force Academy. (adjectives)

Reciprocal Pronouns.   The two reciprocal pronouns show an interchange of action between two or more parties. *Each other* is used when two parties interact, *one another* when three or more do.

Pam and Patty accidentally gave *each other* the same thing for Christmas. (two persons)

The members of the football team joyfully embraced *one another* after their victory. (more than two persons)

EXERCISE ■   Identify each pronoun in the following sentences and indicate its type.

1. He blames himself for his poor test score.
2. If you act friendly toward whoever comes along, you will find life much more pleasant.
3. This is the best-equipped auditorium for the demonstration she is planning.
4. You yourself must bear the responsibility for the accident.
5. What are they planning to do next summer?
6. Which of you would like to talk to me next?
7. If we help one another, we will finish the job soon.
8. Of the two plans, yours is more feasible than hers.
9. These are times that anyone would find trying.
10. Everyone who wishes to take the tour can sign up for it tomorrow.

Verbs

A verb indicates action or existence: what something is, was, or will be. Verbs fall into three classes: *action verbs, linking verbs,* and *helping verbs.*

Action Verbs.   As its name suggests, an action verb expresses action. Some action verbs are transitive, others intransitive. A *transitive* verb has a direct object which receives or results from the action and rounds out the meaning of the sentence.

> The photographer *took* the picture.

Without the direct object, this sentence would not express a complete thought. In contrast, an *intransitive* verb requires no direct object to complete the meaning of the sentence.

> Lee Ann *gasped* loudly.

> Little Tommy Tucker *sings* for his supper.

Many action verbs can play both transitive or intransitive roles, depending on the sentences they are used in.

> Kari *rode* her bicycle into town. (transitive verb)

> Karl *rode* in the front seat of the car. (intransitive verb)

Linking Verbs.   A linking verb shows existence—what something is, was, or will be—rather than action. Linking verbs are intransitive and tie their subjects to subject complements. Some subject complements are nouns or noun substitutes that rename their subjects. Others are adjectives that describe their subjects.

vbs

Ms. Davis *is* our new director. (Complement *director* renames subject *Ms. Davis*.)

The soup *was* lukewarm. (Complement *lukewarm* describes subject *soup*.)

The most common linking verbs are forms of the verb *to be* (*is, are, am, was, were, been*). Some other verbs that may function as linking verbs are *seem, become, appear, remain, feel, look, smell, sound,* and *taste*.

Helping Verbs. Helping verbs accompany action or linking verbs, allowing them to express with great precision matters such as possibility, obligation, and time. Common helping verbs include the following:

has	been	had (to)
have	do	shall
had	does	will
am	did	going (to)
is	used (to)	about (to)
are	may	would
was	might	should
were	must	ought (to)
be	have (to)	can
being	has (to)	could

I *shall ask* him. (helping verb *shall* with action verb *ask*)

The driver *was being lifted* onto a stretcher. (helping verbs *was* and *being* with action verb *lifted*)

You *have been* good. (helping verb *have* with linking verb *been*)

The patient *will feel* better soon. (helping verb *will* with linking verb *feel*)

We *might go* to Corvallis next weekend. (helping verb *might* with action verb *go*)

Helping verbs usually appear next to the main verbs, but they don't have to:

Ellen *will* undoubtedly *resign*.

Combinations of two or more verbs are called verb phrases.

EXERCISE ■ Identify each verb in the following sentences and indicate its type.

1. Electra and Ismene have been arguing all afternoon.
2. Frank must be tired after his long journey.
3. I am still working at Barrett's clothing store.
4. If you will jog a mile a day, you will soon be in much better physical condition.
5. Please talk slowly when you make your speech.
6. Will you please hand those shoes to me?

7. At the time of the accident, I had been driving for twelve hours.
8. Have you read this new best-seller?
9. The car handled beautifully, but its brakes were defective.
10. These chairs and tables were made at the time of Louis XV.

Principal Parts.   Verbs change in form to show time (tense) distinctions. For every action verb, tenses are built from three principal parts: *present, past,* and *past participle.* The present is the principal part you would look up in the dictionary (*win, skip, go,* and so on). If the subject of a verb is a singular pronoun (*he, she, it*) or a singular noun, add an *s* or *es* to the dictionary form (*wins, skips, goes*). Most verbs have identical past and past participles.

7. had been (helping), driving (action)
8. have (helping), read (action)
9. handled (action), were (linking)
10. were (helping), made (action)

	Present	*Past*	*Past Participle*
I, you, we, they	talk	talked	talked
He, she, it, Henry	talks	talked	talked
I, you, we, they	stand	stood	stood
He, she, it, the decision	stands	stood	stood

Of the remaining verbs, all three principal parts are identical.

	Present	*Past*	*Past Participle*
I, you, we, they	swim	swam	swum
He, she, it, the boy	swims	swam	swum
I, you, we, they	bite	bit	bitten
He, she, it, the dog	bites	bit	bitten

With a few verbs, the past and past participles are identical to the dictionary form.

	Present	*Past*	*Past Participle*
I, you, we, they	set	set	set
He, she, it	sets	set	set

If you're uncertain about the principal parts of a verbal, check your dictionary.

Tense.   English has six basic tenses: present, past, future, present perfect, past perfect, future perfect. They are formed from the principal parts of action and linking verbs, either alone or combined with helping verbs.

The *present tense* is formed from the present principal part of the main verb. It shows present condition and general or habitual action, indicates permanent truths, tells about past events in the historical present, and sometimes denotes action at some definite future time.

PERSPECTIVE

Some students have trouble using the past tense in a sustained manner. Others have trouble with the irregular past tense or the future tense, and few are comfortable using the perfect tenses. Because these problems are so common, it is important that they be properly addressed.

Helen *looks* beautiful in her new gown. (present condition)

John *works* on the eighteenth floor. (general action)

vbs

I *brush* my teeth each morning. (habitual action)

The sun *rises* in the East. (permanent truth)

On November 11, 1918, the guns *fall* silent, and World War I *comes* to an end. (historical present)

Monday, I *begin* my new job. (future action)

The *past tense* is based on the past principal part of the verb. The past tense shows that a condition existed or an action was completed in the past. The verb tense leaves the time indefinite, but surrounding words may specify it.

Paul *was* angry with his noisy neighbors. (past condition, time indefinite)

Sandy *received* a long letter yesterday. (past action, time specified by *yesterday*)

The *future tense* combines *shall* or *will* and the present principal part of the main verb. It indicates that a condition will exist or an action will take place in the future.

You *will feel* better after a good night's sleep. (future condition)

I *shall attend* the concert next week. (future action)

The *present perfect* tense is formed with *has* or *have* and the past participle of the main verb. It shows that a past condition or action, or its effect, continues until the present time.

The players *have been* irritable since they lost the homecoming game. (Condition continues until present)

Juanita *has driven* a United Parcel Service truck for five years. (Action continues until present.)

William *has repaired* the snow blower. (Effect of action continues until present, although the action itself was completed in the past.)

The *past perfect* tense combines *had* and the past participle of the main verb. It refers to a past condition or action that was completed before another past condition or action.

He *had been* in the army two years when the war ended. (Past perfect condition occurred first.)

Vivian moved into the house that she *had built* the summer before. (Past perfect action occurred first.)

The *future perfect* tense is formed from the verbs *shall have* or *will have* plus the past participle of the main verb. It shows that a condition or an action

TEACHING STRATEGIES

1. With certain assignments, you might specify a particular tense. For example, assign the past tense for a narrative and the present tense for a description. To familiarize students with using the future tense, ask them to write a short paper explaining their plans for the next ten years.
2. Inexperienced writers may need additional help in order to stay in the past tense. After students write a narrative, have them read their papers aloud, checking for verbs and testing to be sure each is in the past tense. You could provide students with a list of irregular verbs to help ensure that they use the right past-tense forms.

TEACHING STRATEGY

Some students don't use the present perfect tense when it is appropriate. To solve this problem, pose questions that should be answered in the present perfect tense, such as the following: How long have you been in this class? How long has this text been in print? How many years have you lived in this state? From what point have you been interested in your career choice?

TEACHING STRATEGY

The past perfect tense, like the present perfect, can be taught by having students convert questions into answers that use this tense, such as the following: How many times had Gary missed work before he was fired? How many home runs had Lou Gehrig hit before he retired from baseball? What other states had Mary lived in when she moved to Connecticut? How long had he been sick before he died?

will have been completed at some time in the future. Surrounding words specify time.

> Our sales manager *will have been* with the company ten years next July. (Condition will end.)

> By the end of this year, I *shall have written* the great American novel. (Action will be completed.)

Each of these basic tenses has a *progressive tense* that indicates action in progress. The progressive tense always includes some form of the verb *to be* followed by a present participle, a verb that ends in *-ing*.

Present progressive	I *am running.*
Past progressive	I *was running.*
Future progressive	I *shall be running.*
Present perfect progressive	I *have been running.*
Past perfect progressive	I *had been running.*
Future perfect progressive	I *shall have been running.*

Voice. Transitive verbs have two voices: active and passive. A verb is in the *active voice* when the subject carries out the action named by the verb.

> Barry *planned* a picnic. (Subject *Barry* performs action.)

A verb is in the *passive voice* when the subject receives the action. The performer may be identified in an accompanying phrase or go unmentioned.

> A picnic *was planned* by Barry. (The phrase *by Barry* identifies the performer.)

> The picnic *was canceled.* (The performer goes unmentioned.)

A passive construction always uses a form of *to be* and the past participle of an action verb. Like other constructions, the passive may show past, present, or future time.

> Amy *is paid* handsomely for her investment advice. (present tense)

> I *was warned* by a sound truck that a tornado was nearby. (past tense)

> I *will be sent* to Ghana soon by the Peace Corps. (future tense)

> I *have been awarded* a sizable research grant. (present perfect tense)

> The city *had been shelled* heavily before the infantry moved in. (past perfect tense)

> By the end of this month, the site for our second factory *will have been chosen.* (future perfect tense)

To convert a sentence from the passive to the active voice, make the performer the subject, the original subject the direct object, and drop the form of *to be.*

---

vbs

TEACHING STRATEGY

If you have students write a narrative, ask them to check it for sentences where they have used the present perfect or past perfect. Ask them to read the sentences aloud or write them on the board, so the class can discuss whether each use was appropriate.

PERSPECTIVE

Students are far too inclined to use the passive voice. Sometimes they do it to imitate what they believe to be the academic style of writing. At other times, they want to avoid specifying a subject or repeating the same sentence construction. Encourage students to use the active voice more often and to try other ways of varying sentence structure.

TEACHING STRATEGY

Have students check their writing for sentences that use the passive voice, determine which are effective, and if necessary, recast the sentences in the active voice.

CLASSROOM ACTIVITY

Have students rewrite the following passage, using the active voice, and then compare the effectiveness of the two versions.

All grade reports should be carefully reviewed by the instructor before they are turned in to the records office. Any errors should be corrected and initialed. When a grade is not recorded, an F will be assigned automatically to the student. Grade changes will not be processed by this office for the first three weeks of the new term.

vbs

The treaty *was signed* by the general. (passive)

The general *signed* the treaty. (active)

Technical and scientific writing commonly use the passive voice to explain processes since its flat, impersonal tone adds an air of scientific objectivity and authority. Other kinds of writing, however, avoid the passive voice except when it is desirable to conceal the doer of the action or when the action is more significant than the actor. See pages 226–227 for more information on usage.

EXERCISE ■   **Identify each verb in the following sentences, indicate its tense, and note any use of the passive voice.**

1. Alan is changing his clothes for dinner.
2. I will oversee the construction of the building.
3. I shall have finished the report by Friday.
4. The instructions have been followed by Todd.
5. Jennifer kept her first car for twelve years.
6. The President was informed of the incident two hours after it took place.
7. Twenty minutes after he began the crossword puzzle, Terry finished it.
8. I have seriously considered two majors: sociology and political science.
9. These shrubs will be pruned tomorrow.
10. Sally leaves for London on Saturday.
11. He is constantly humiliated by his supposed friends.
12. Prudence shouted angrily at the fighting children.

Mood.   The mood of a verb shows whether the writer regards a statement as a

1. fact
2. command or request
3. wish, possibility, condition contrary to fact, or the like.

English has three moods: the indicative, imperative, and subjunctive.

A sentence in the *indicative mood* states a real or supposed fact or asks a question.

Nancy *graduates* from high school tomorrow.

We *lived* in Oakmont when Rachel was born.

He *had been* a sailor during the war.

Has Joe *asked* anyone to the prom yet?

Most verbs are used in the indicative mood.

A sentence in the *imperative mood* delivers a command or makes a request.

Leave the room immediately! (command)

Please *turn* the phonograph down. (request)

The subject of a sentence in the imperative mood is always *you*. Although ordinarily unstated, the subject sometimes appears in the sentence.

You leave the room immediately!

The *subjunctive mood* is used

1. in *if, as if,* and *as though* clauses to express a possibility or an action or condition contrary to fact
2. in *that* clauses expressing orders, demands, requests, resolutions, proposals, or motions
3. with modal auxiliaries to express wishes, probability, possibility, permission, requirements, recommendations, suggestions, and conditions contrary to fact.

To express a present or future wish, possibility, condition or action in an *if, as if,* or *as though* clause, use *were* with any personal pronoun or noun serving as the subject of the clause.

If only Stan *were* less gullible! (present wish contrary to fact)

Even if Kay *were* to explain, Mary wouldn't believe her. (future possibility)

Arthur is behaving as if he *were* a millionaire. (present condition contrary to fact)

To express a wish, possibility, or condition contrary to past facts, use *had been* or *had* plus the past participle of an action verb.

If the engine *had been lubricated*, the bearing wouldn't have burned out. (past condition contrary to fact)

Alice looked as if she *had lost* her best friend. (condition expressed in clause occurs before action of verb *looked*)

When writing *that* clauses expressing orders, demands, requests, resolutions, proposals, or motions, use *be* or the present plural form of an action verb.

I move that they *be* rewarded for their bravery.

The group proposed that Margaret *go* to the scene of the accident and *inspect* it personally.

In other *that* clauses, use the appropriate indicative form of the verb.

I know that they *were* rewarded for their bravery.

The group believed that Margaret *had gone* to the scene of the accident and *inspected* it personally.

The modal auxiliaries include the helping verbs *can, could, may, might, must, shall, will, would, should,* and *ought to.* The examples below illustrate the meanings they can express.

1. Wishes (*could, would*)

   I wish I *could* shimmy like my sister Kate.

   The Republicans wish the Democrats *would* go away and vice versa.

2. Probability (*should*)

   Because I've studied diligently, I *should* do better on my next chemistry test.

3. Possibility (*may, might, can, could*)

   High interest rates *could* cause our housing industry to collapse.

   I *might* stay up to watch the eclipse of the moon tonight.

4. Permission (*can, may*)

   The public *can* use these tennis courts every afternoon.

   You *may* leave as soon as you've finished filing these folders.

5. Requirements (*must*)

   The landlord has raised our rent again; we *must* find another apartment.

6. Recommendations, suggestions (*should, ought to*)

   Randy *should* see a doctor about his chest pains.

   The nuclear powers *ought to* reduce their stockpiles of atomic weapons.

7. Conditions contrary to fact (*could*)

   If only I *could* live my life over!

EXERCISE ■ **For each of the following sentences, identify the mood as indicative (IND), imperative (IMP), or subjunctive (SUB).**

1. Have a good time at the party.
2. They demanded that the secretary be removed for failing to keep adequate records of the meetings.
3. Senator Conwell will seek reelection next year.
4. Can you believe that Mr. Scrooge has raised Bob Cratchet's wages?
5. Don't you dare to make this foolish mistake again.
6. I'd put a statue of myself on every street corner if I were running the world.
7. Everybody should visit our nation's capital and tour its public buildings.
8. Someday the earth may establish colonies on Mars.
9. The American public has lost its infatuation with the automobile.
10. Unless attendance drops off drastically, this movie should make more money than any other.

EXERCISE ANSWERS

1. IMP	6. SUB
2. SUB	7. SUB
3. IND	8. SUB
4. IND	9. IND
5. IMP	10. SUB

Adjectives

An adjective *modifies* a noun or pronoun by describing it, limiting it, or otherwise making its meaning more exact.

The *brass* candlestick stood next to the *fragile* vase. (*Brass* modifies *candlestick*, and *fragile* modifies *vase.*)

The cat is *long-haired* and *sleek*. (*Long-haired* and *sleek* modify *cat.*)

There are three general categories of adjectives: limiting, descriptive, and proper.

PERSPECTIVE

Some students avoid adjectives as though such descriptive additions might infect their writing. Others write essays that are soggy with adjectives. In discussing adjectives, you might have students assess their own use of them.

Limiting Adjectives.   A limiting adjective identifies or points out the noun or pronoun it modifies. It may indicate number or quantity. Several categories of pronouns can serve as limiting adjectives, as can numbers and nouns.

Whose briefcase is on the table? (interrogative adjective)

The couple *whose* car was stolen called the police. (relative adjective)

This restaurant has the best reputation for gourmet food. (demonstrative adjective)

Some people have no social tact at all. (indefinite adjective)

Sally swerved *her* car suddenly to avoid an oncoming truck. (possessive adjective)

Three people entered the lecture hall late. (number as adjective)

The *schoolgirl* look is fashionable this year. (noun as adjective)

TEACHING STRATEGIES

1. Have students review several essays in the Reader to determine where adjectives have been used and to what effect. Be sure the review is not confined to narration and description essays; students need to realize that adjectives play an important role in all writing, not just "literary" essays.

2. Have students review one of their own drafts to determine where they need adjectives to help limit their nouns and where they have used adjectives to excess.

Descriptive Adjectives.   A descriptive adjective names a quality, characteristic, or condition of a noun or pronoun. Two or more of these adjectives, members of the largest category of adjectives, may modify the same noun or pronoun.

The *yellow* submarine belongs to the Beatles.

He applied *clear* lacquer to the table top.

The *slim, sophisticated* model glided onto the runway.

The child wore a *thick, green, quilted* jacket.

CLASSROOM ACTIVITY

Have students identify adjectives that might help limit and qualify a long list of nouns. Discuss the different effects the use of these adjectives would have. You might note that adjectives help answer the question, "What kind of ____?" Sample nouns: dog, man, house, woman, student, child, boy, car, tire, tree, star, restaurant, potatoes, and so on.

Proper Adjectives.   A proper adjective is derived from a proper noun and is always capitalized.

Harwell is a *Shakespearean* actor.

Articles as Adjectives.   Articles appear immediately before nouns and can therefore be considered adjectives. There are three articles in English: *a, an,* and *the. The* points to a specific item, *a* and *an* do not. *A* precedes words beginning with consonant sounds; *an* precedes words with vowel sounds, making pronunciation easier.

The right word at *the* right moment can save a friendship. (Definite articles suggest there is one right word and one right moment.)

A right word can save *a* friendship. (Indefinite articles suggest there may be several right words and friendships.)

I think I'd like *an* apple with my lunch. (No particular apple is specified.)

Sometimes the definite article refers to a class of items.

The tiger is fast becoming an endangered species.

Context shows whether such a sentence refers to particular items or entire classes.

TEACHING STRATEGY
To reinforce the material on comparisons, try combining it with the section on comparison errors on pages 591–592.

Comparison with Adjectives. Adjectives may be used to show comparison. When two things are compared, shorter adjectives usually add *-er* and longer adjectives add *more*. When three or more things are compared, shorter adjectives usually add *-est* and longer ones add *most*.

John is *taller* than Pete. (short adjective comparing two things)

Sandra seems *more* cheerful than Jill today. (long adjective comparing two things)

John is the *tallest* of the three brothers. (short adjective comparing three things)

Sandra is the *most* cheerful girl in the class. (longer adjective comparing more than three things)

Some adjectives, like the examples below, have irregular forms for comparisons.

Good—better—best

bad—worse—worst

Don't use the *-est* form of the shorter adjective for comparing just two things.

Faulty   This is the *smallest* of the two castles.

Instead, use the *-er* form.

Revision   This is the *smaller* of the two castles.

Position of Adjectives. Most adjectives come immediately before the words they modify. In a few set expressions (for example, heir *apparent*), the adjective immediately follows the word it modifies. Similarly, adjective pairs sometimes appear in a follow-up position for added emphasis (The rapids, *swift* and *dangerous,* soon capsized the raft). Sometimes adjectives also serve as subject complements and follow their subjects (The puppy was *friendly*).

EXERCISE ■   **Identify the adjectives in the following sentences.**

1. We had three weeks of vacation.
2. A tall, cool drink is very welcome on a hot day.
3. Because of bad weather, only ten people attended the meeting.
4. The short, slight jockey wore a yellow outfit in the race.
5. The pretty girl sat quietly, her golden hair blowing in the breeze.
6. The Chinese ambassador speaks beautiful English.
7. An apple a day keeps the doctor away.
8. Lilacs may be purple, white, or pink.
9. The sharp rocks on the beach bruised my bare feet.
10. Sue Ellen was tired after her difficult day in school.

Adverbs

An adverb modifies a verb, an adjective, another adverb, or a whole sentence. Adverbs generally answer questions such as "how?" "when?" "where?" "how often?" and "to what extent?"

The floodwaters receded *very* slowly. (Adverb modifies adverb and answers the question "how?")

My sister will visit me *tomorrow*. (Adverb modifies verb and answers the question "when?")

The coach walked *away* from the bench. (Adverb modifies verb and answers the question "where?")

The tire is *too* worn to be safe. (Adverb modifies adjective and answers the question "how much?")

The teller is *frequently* late for work. (Adverb modifies adjective and answers the question "how often?")

Unfortunately, the game was canceled because of rain. (The adverb modifies the whole sentence but does not answer any question.)

Formation of Adverbs.   Most adverbs are formed by adding *-ly* to adjectives.

The wind is *restless*. (*Restless* is an adjective modifying *wind*.)

He walked *restlessly* around the room. (*Restlessly* is an adverb modifying *walked*.)

Many common adverbs, however, (*almost, never, quite, soon, then, there* and *too*) lack *-ly* endings.

I *soon* realized that pleasing my boss was impossible.

This move is *too* gruesome for my taste.

Furthermore, some words such as *better, early, late, hard, little, near, only, straight,* and *wrong* do double duty either as adjectives or adverbs.

We must have taken a *wrong* turn. (*Wrong* is an adjective modifying the noun *turn*.)

Where did I go *wrong*? (*Wrong* is an adverb modifying the verb *go*.)

Comparison with Adverbs.   Like adjectives, adverbs can show comparison. When two things are compared, shorter adverbs add *more*. When three or more things are compared, *most* is used.

Harold works *more* efficiently than Don. (adverb comparing two people)

Of all the people in the shop, Harold works the *most* efficiently. (adverb comparing more than three people)

Some adverbs, like some adjectives, use irregular forms for comparisons:

well—better—best

much—more—most

Position of Adverbs.   Adverbs are more movable than any other part of speech. Usually, adverbs that modify adjectives and other adverbs appear next to them to avoid confusion.

Her *especially* fine tact makes her a welcome guest at any party. (Adverb *especially* modifies adjective *fine*.)

The novel was *very* badly written. (Adverb *very* modifies adverb *badly*.)

Adverbs that modify verbs, however, can often be shifted around in their sentences without causing changes in meaning.

Quickly, he slipped through the doorway.

He slipped *quickly* through the doorway.

He slipped through the doorway *quickly*.

EXERCISE ■   **Identify the adverbs in the following sentences.**

EXERCISE ANSWERS
1. tirelessly, upstream
2. very
3. now
4. more, quickly

1. Sue paddled her canoe tirelessly upstream.
2. Curt thought the graduation address was very inspiring.
3. Nothing can save the troops now.
4. The deer flashed by more quickly than the hunter had thought possible.

5. Pam yawned sleepily and soon went to sleep.
6. This restaurant is too expensive for us.
7. The service station attendant told us that our turnoff was ten miles south.
8. They divided the pizza evenly and ate it quickly.
9. Actually, I thought the movie was very dull.
10. I felt quite energetic yesterday, but now I am totally exhausted.

5. sleepily, soon
6. too
7. south
8. evenly, quickly
9. actually, very
10. quite, yesterday, now, totally

PERSPECTIVE

Few things give foreign students more difficulty in learning our language than prepositions. Only after years of speaking English can they use them with any confidence. Fortunately, most native speakers have an intuitive sense of how to use prepositions.

CLASSROOM ACTIVITIES

1. To help students see the importance of prepositions, have them identify the difference in meaning between the following pairs:
   The bird flew to the rooftop. The bird flew toward the rooftop.
   The couple walked on the beach. The couple walked onto the beach.
   James pushed his way through the crowd. James pushed his way into the crowd.
   Besides taking the final, you will have to write a paper. Instead of taking the final, you will have to write a paper.
2. Students can often develop sentences by using prepositional phrases. You might want to refer them to the unit on prepositional phrases, page 564.

Prepositions

A preposition links its object—a noun or noun substitute—to some other word in the sentence and shows a relationship between them. The relationship is often one of location, time, means, or reason or purpose. The word group containing the preposition and its object makes up a prepositional phrase.

The new insulation *in* the attic keeps my house much warmer now. (Preposition *in* links object *attic* to *insulation* and shows location.)

We have postponed the meeting *until* tomorrow. (Preposition *until* links object *tomorrow* to *postponed* and shows time.)

The tourists traveled *by* automobile. (Preposition *by* links object *automobile* to *traveled* and shows means.)

Warren swims *for* exercise. (Preposition *for* links object *exercise* to *swims* and shows reason or purpose.)

The following list includes the most common prepositions, some of which consist of two or more words.

above	beside	in	out of
after	between	instead of	over
against	by	into	since
along with	by reason of	like	through
among	contrary to	near	to
at	during	next to	toward
because of	except	of	under
before	for	on	with
below	from	onto	without

Many of these combine to form additional prepositions: *except for, in front of, by way of, on top of,* and the like.

Certain prepositions sometimes occur in close association with certain verbs, forming verb units with altered meanings. When this happens, we call the prepositions verb particles. Here is an example.

The instructor let Jeff make *up* the test.

Note the great difference between the meaning of the foregoing sentence and "The instructor let Jeff make the test."

EXERCISE ■   Identify the prepositions and their objects in the following sentences.

1. The nun sang softly as she walked through the chapel.
2. Aunt Sharon will probably visit us at the end of September.
3. With a rattle, Carrie amused the fussing baby.
4. The judge sentenced the arsonist to prison for ten years.
5. The architect chose Italian marble for the walls of the lobby.
6. Because of the epidemic of flu, several schools in this town have closed for the week.
7. Over the river and through the woods to Grandmother's house we go.
8. Admittance to this sale is by special invitation only.
9. Nelson has been busy with household tasks this morning.
10. For exercise, Harriet jogs five miles each day.

Conjunctions

Conjunctions serve as connectors, linking parts of sentences or whole sentences. These connectors fall into three groups: coordinating conjunctions, subordinating conjunctions, and conjunctive adverbs.

Coordinating Conjunctions.   Coordinating conjunctions connect terms of equal grammatical importance: words, word groups, and simple sentences. These conjunctions can occur singly (*and, but, or, nor, for, yet, so*) or in pairs called correlative conjunctions (*either–or, neither–nor, both–and,* and *not only–but also*). The elements that follow correlative conjunctions must be parallel; that is, have the same grammatical form.

Tom *and* his cousin are opening a video arcade. (Coordinating conjunction connects nouns.)

Shall I serve the tea in the living room *or* on the veranda? (Coordinating conjunction connects phrases.)

I am going to Europe this summer, *but* Marjorie is staying home. (Coordinating conjunction connects simple sentences.)

Amy *not only* teaches English *but also* writes novels. (Correlative conjunctions connect parallel predicates.)

You can study nursing *either* at Ferris State University *or* at DeWitt College. (Correlative conjunctions connect parallel phrases.)

Friendship is *both* pleasure *and* pain. (Correlative conjunctions connect parallel nouns.)

Subordinating Conjunctions.   Like relative pronouns, subordinating conjunctions introduce subordinate clauses, relating them to independent clauses, which can stand alone as complete sentences. Examples of subordinating conjunctions include *because, as if, even though, since, so that, whereas,* and *whenever* (see page 569 for a more complete list).

(see page 569 for a more complete list)

con

> I enjoyed the TV program *because* it was so well acted. (Conjunction connects *because it was so well acted* to rest of sentence.)

> *Whenever* you're ready, we can begin dinner. (Conjunction connects *whenever you're ready* to rest of sentence.)

Conjunctive Adverbs.   These connectors resemble both conjunctions and adverbs. Like conjunctions, they serve as linking devices between elements of equal rank. Like adverbs, they function as modifiers, showing such things as similarity, contrast, result or effect, addition, emphasis, time, and example. The following list groups the most common conjunctive adverbs according to function.

> *Similarity:* likewise, similarly
> *Contrast:* however, nevertheless, on the contrary, on the other hand, otherwise
> *Result or effect:* accordingly, as a result, consequently, hence, therefore, thus
> *Addition:* also, furthermore, in addition, in the first place, moreover
> *Emphasis or clarity:* in fact, in other words, indeed, that is
> *Time:* afterwards, later, meanwhile, subsequently
> *Example:* for example, for instance, to illustrate

> The job will require you to travel a great deal; *however,* the salary is excellent.

> Sean cares nothing for clothes; *in fact,* all of his socks have holes in their toes.

An interjection is an exclamatory word used to gain attention or to express strong feeling. It has no grammatical connection to the rest of the sentence. An interjection is followed by an exclamation point or a comma.

> *Hey!* Watch how you're driving! (strong interjection)

> *Oh,* is the party over already? (mild interjection)

EXERCISE ■   Identify the coordinating conjunctions (CC), subordinating conjunctions (SC), conjunctive adverbs (CA), and interjections (I) in the following sentences.

1. The fish we ordered finally arrived; however, it was stone cold.
2. Marianne walked away from the panhandler, but he kept following her.
3. Can you talk to me now, or are you too busy?
4. Wow! Did you see that slam dunk?
5. Mark and Terry attended the dance even though both felt under the weather.
6. Glen had both strawberry ice cream and chocolate cake for dessert.
7. Because we have classes at the same hour, let's drive to school together.

CLASSROOM ACTIVITY

Have students combine the following sets of sentences with the appropriate subordinating conjunctions:

The USSR has moved to a more democratic form of government. The United States has had to change its foreign policy.

They turn down the heat on the weekends. The university can save on fuel bills.

He had studied for two days. He did poorly on the chemistry final.

EXERCISE ANSWERS:

1. however (CA)
2. but (CC)
3. or (CC)
4. Wow (I)
5. and (CC), even though (SC)
6. both, and (CC)
7. Because (SC)
8. Golly (I)
9. in fact (CA)
10. not only, but also (CC)
11. Because (SC)
12. as a result (CA)

8. Golly, it's a relief to be home again.
9. I don't want the job; in fact, I've refused it once already.
10. Gina is not only attractive but also intelligent.
11. Because I forgot to punch the time clock, I lost several hours' pay.
12. Andrea misread the instructions for carrying out the experiment; as a result, she had to repeat it.

PHRASES AND CLAUSES

Phrases

A phrase is a group of words that lacks a subject and a predicate and serves as a single part of speech. This section discusses four basic kinds of phrases: *prepositional phrases, participial phrases, gerund phrases,* and *infinitive phrases.* The last three are based on participles, gerunds, and infinitives, verb forms known as verbals. A fifth type of phrase, the verb phrase, consists of sets of two or more verbs (*has fixed, had been sick, will have been selected,* and the like).

Prepositional Phrases.   A prepositional phrase consists of a preposition, one or more objects, and any associated words. These phrases serve as adjectives or adverbs.

The picture *over the mantel* was my mother's. (prepositional phrase as adjective)

He bought ice skates *for himself.* (prepositional phrase as adverb modifying verb)

The toddler was afraid *of the dog.* (prepositional phrase as adverb modifying adjective)

Our visitors arrived late *in the day.* (prepositional phrase as adverb modifying another adverb)

Frequently, prepositional phrases occur in series. Sometimes they form chains in which each phrase modifies the object of the preceding phrase. At other times some or all of the phrases may modify the verb or verb phrase.

John works *in a clothing store / on Main Street / during the summer.*

Here the first and third phrases serve as adverbs modifying the verb *works* and answering the questions "where?" and "when?" while the second phrase serves as an adjective modifying *store.*

On occasion, especially in questions, a preposition may be separated from its object, making the phrase difficult to find.

This is the book *that* I've been looking *for.*

What are you shouting *about?*

Participial Phrases.   A participial phrase consists of a participle plus associated words. Participles are verb forms that, when used in participial phrases, function as adjectives or adverbs. A present participle ends in *-ing* and indicates an action currently being carried out. A past participle ends in *-ed, -en, -e, -n, -d,* or *-t* and indicates some past action.

> The chef *preparing dinner* trained in France. (present participial phrase as adjective)

> The background, *sketched in lightly*, accented the features of the woman in the painting. (past participial phrase as adjective)

> She left the room *whistling a jolly melody.*

A perfect participial phrase consists of *having* or *having been* plus a past participle and any associated words. Like a past participial phrase, it indicates a past action.

> *Having alerted the townspeople about the tornado,* the sound truck returned to the city garage. (perfect participial phrase)

> *Having been alerted to the tornado,* the townspeople sought shelter in their basements. (perfect participial phrase)

Some participial phrases that modify persons or things distinguish them from others in the same class. These phrases are written without commas. Other phrases provide more information about the persons or things they modify and are set off with commas.

> The man *fixing my car* is a master mechanic. (Phrase distinguishes man fixing car from others.)

> Mr. Welsh, *fatigued by the tennis game,* rested in the shade. (Phrase provides more information about Mr. Welsh.)

Gerund Phrases.   A gerund phrase consists of a gerund and the words associated with it. Like present participles, gerunds are verb forms that end in *-ing.* Unlike participles, though, they function as nouns rather than as adjectives or adverbs.

> Kathyrn's hobby is *collecting stamps.* (gerund phrase as subject complement)

> Kathryn's hobby, *collecting stamps,* has made her many friends. (gerund phrase as appositive)

> He devoted every spare moment to *overhauling the car.* (gerund phrase as object of preposition)

Infinitive Phrases.   An infinitive phrase consists of the present principal part of a verb preceded by *to (to fix, to eat),* together with any accompanying words. These phrases serve as adjectives, adverbs, and nouns.

phr

This looks like a good place *to plant the shrub*. (infinitive phrase as adjective)

Lenore worked *to earn money for college*. (infinitive phrase as adverb)

My goal is *to have my own business some day*. (infinitive phrase as noun)

Gerunds can often be substituted for infinitives and vice versa.

To repair this fender will cost two hundred dollars. (infinitive phrase as subject)

Repairing this fender will cost two hundred dollars. (gerund phrase as subject)

At times the *to* in an infinitive may be omitted following verbs such as *make, dare, let,* and *help.*

Kristin didn't dare *(to) move* a muscle.

The psychiatrist helped me *(to) overcome* my fear of flying.

Verbals Not in Phrases.   Participles, gerunds, and infinitives can function as nouns, adjectives, or adverbs, even when they are not parts of phrases.

That *sunbathing* woman is a well-known model. (participle)

Dancing is fine exercise. (gerund)

The children want *to play*. (infinitive as noun)

If you're looking for a job, Sally is the person *to see*. (infinitive as adjective)

I'm prepared *to resign*. (infinitive as adverb)

EXERCISE ■   Identify the italicized phrases as prepositional, participial, gerund, or infinitive and tell whether each is used as a noun, an adjective, or an adverb.

1. *Annoyed by Sam's remarks,* Darcie closed her magazine and left the room.
2. Next summer the Whittakers plan *to buy a lakeside cottage.*
3. *Losing this game* will eliminate us from the playoffs.
4. The coffee will be ready *in about five minutes.*
5. Louis flipped *through the report* until he found the "Results" section.
6. The bluff *overlooking the rapids* is called Lover's Leap.
7. *Parched by the heat,* Roseann quickly downed two glasses of lemonade.
8. The Jeffersons are quite pleased *with their new car.*
9. Amy went to the library *to study her biology lesson.*
10. The refrigerant *used to cool our food* was ordinary ice.
11. *Burdened by mountainous debts and ill health,* Mr. Goodman shot himself.
12. My favorite sport is *fishing for salmon.*
13. This is the best spot *for our flower garden.*
14. The host shouted loudly *to get the guests' attention.*
15. *To do well in college* has been my goal ever since I set foot on campus.

Clauses

A clause is a word group that includes a subject and a predicate. An *independent clause,* sometimes called a main clause, expresses a complete thought and can function as a simple sentence. A *subordinate clause,* or dependent clause, cannot stand by itself. Subordinate clauses may serve as nouns, adjectives, or adverbs.

Noun Clauses. A noun clause can serve in any of the ways that ordinary nouns can.

> *What the neighbor told John* proved to be incorrect. (noun clause as subject)
>
> The woman asked *when the bus left for Spokane.* (noun clause as direct object)
>
> I'll give a reward to *whoever returns my billfold.* (noun clause as object of preposition *to*)

Noun clauses normally begin with one of the following words:

Relative Pronouns		Subordinating Conjunctions
who	whoever	when
whom	whomever	why
whose	that	where
what	whatever	how
which	whichever	whether

The relative pronoun *that* is sometimes omitted from the beginning of a clause that acts as a direct object.

> Dr. Kant thinks (*that*) *he knows everything.*

If a clause is serving as a noun, you can replace it with the word *something* or *someone,* and the sentence will still make sense.

> Dr. Kant thinks *something.*

If the clause is serving as an adjective or an adverb, making the substitution turns the sentence into nonsense.

> The person *who wins the lottery* will receive two million dollars.
>
> The person *someone* will receive two million dollars.

Adjective Clauses. Like ordinary adjectives, adjective clauses modify nouns and noun substitutes.

> Give me one reason *why you feel the way you do.* (Adjective clause modifies noun.)
>
> I'll hire anyone *that Dr. Stone recommends.* (Adjective clause modifies pronoun.)

Generally, adjective clauses begin with one of the following words:

Relative Pronouns	*Subordinating Conjunctions*
who	when
whom	where
whose	why
what	after
which	before
that	

Sometimes the word that introduces the clause can be omitted.

> The chair *(that) we ordered last month* has just arrived. (pronoun *that* omitted but understood)

> The man *(whom) we were talking to* is a movie producer. (pronoun *whom* omitted but understood)

Sometimes, too, a preposition comes ahead of the introductory pronoun.

> The grace *with which Nelson danced* made the onlookers envious.

An adjective clause may be restrictive and distinguish whatever it modifies from others in the same class, or it may be nonrestrictive and provide more information about whatever it modifies.

> Flora wiped up the cereal *that the baby had spilled.* (restrictive clause)

> Harriet Thomas, *who was born in Alaska,* now lives in Hawaii. (nonrestrictive clause)

As these examples show, restrictive clauses are not set off with commas, but nonrestrictive clauses are.

Adverb Clauses.   These clauses modify verbs, adjectives, adverbs, and sentences, answering the same questions that ordinary adverbs do.

> You may go *whenever you wish*. (Adverb clause modifies verb.)

> Sandra looked paler *than I had ever seen her look before.* (Adverb clause modifies adjective.)

> Darryl shouted loudly *so that the rescue party could hear him.* (Adverb clause modifies adverb.)

> *Unless everyone cooperates,* this plan will never succeed. (Adverb clause modifies whole sentence.)

The word or word group that introduces an adverb clause is always a subordinating conjunction. Here are the most common of these conjunctions, grouped according to the questions they answer.

When? after, as, as soon as, before, since, until, when, whenever, while
Where? where, wherever
How? as if, as though
Why? as, because, now that, since, so that
Under what conditions? although, if, once, provided that, though, unless
To what extent? than

Occasionally in an adverb clause, the omission of one or more words won't hurt its meaning. Such a construction is called an *elliptical clause.*

While (he was) making a sandwich, Garth hummed softly. (*he was* omitted but understood)

Unlike noun and adjective clauses, adverb clauses can often be moved about in their sentences.

Garth hummed softly *while (he was) making a sandwich.*

EXERCISE ■ Identify the italicized clauses as noun, adjective, or adverb.

1. *That he was no friend* became apparent when he started gossiping about me.
2. We will leave *whenever everybody is ready.*
3. Anyone *who has ever heard him speak* recognizes his power to sway crowds.
4. *If the taxi doesn't arrive soon,* we will miss our flight.
5. The used car *Sam bought last week* has already broken down.
6. I don't know *what you're talking about.*
7. The committee will give *whoever has the best costume* two tickets to the theater.
8. I had to work last weekend *because I couldn't finish the job on schedule.*
9. We have found a lake *where the fishing is excellent.*
10. Sandra had an accident *while driving to Spokane.*
11. I hope *Barry solves his financial problems soon.*
12. The producer *with whom he signed a contract* proved dishonest.

EXERCISE ANSWERS

1. noun
2. adverb
3. adjective
4. adverb
5. adjective
6. noun
7. noun
8. adverb
9. adjective
10. adverb
11. noun
12. adjective

PERSPECTIVE
Students commit sentence errors for a variety of reasons. Some, despite knowing the rules, simply make mistakes. Others have a poor grasp of the rules or misconstrue a particular one. Still others write as their community speaks, sometimes contrary to standard written grammar. Some students im-

frag

prove markedly when told they'll lose points for grammatical errors; others improve when you make them proofread their drafts several times. Still others need a review of the rules. Depending upon your students and personal preference, you can handle errors as they occur in student papers or set aside ten minutes of a class period to review a type of error.

PERSPECTIVE
Usually sentence fragments result because students place periods where they pause, or where they signal phrase and clause breaks. As a result, many fragments are nothing more than isolated phrases and clauses.

TEACHING STRATEGIES
1. Students sometimes have problems proofreading for sentence fragments because they unconsciously leap across the period to read the complete sentence. You might show them how to check any suspicious sentence by reading it aloud and seeing whether it is complete. Be careful what you say. If you tell students they should check for the presence of a subject and a verb, they might mistake subordinate clauses for sentences.

Editing to Correct Sentence Errors

Accepted usage improves the smoothness of your prose, makes your writing easier to understand, and demonstrates that you are a careful communicator. These assets, in turn, increase the likelihood that the reader will accept your ideas.

When you've finished revising the first draft of a piece of writing, edit it with a critic's eye to ensure that your English is standard. Circle sentences or parts of them that are faulty or suspect. Then check your circled items against this section of the handbook, which deals with the most common errors in college writing.

SENTENCE FRAGMENTS

A sentence fragment is a group of words that fails to qualify as a sentence but is capitalized and punctuated as if it were a sentence. To be a sentence, a word group must (1) have a subject and a verb and (2) make sense by itself. The first of the following examples has a subject and a verb; the second does not. Neither makes sense by itself.

> If you want to remain.
> His answer to the question.

Methods of Revision. Eliminating a sentence fragment is not hard. Careful reading often shows that the fragment goes with the sentence that comes just before or just after it. And sometimes two successive fragments can be joined. Note how we've corrected the fragments (italicized) in the following pairs.

Faulty	*Having been warned about the storm.* We decided to stay home.
Revision	Having been warned about the storm, we decided to stay home.
Faulty	*After eating.* The dog took a nap.
Revision	After eating, the dog took a nap.
Faulty	Sally went to work. *Although she felt sick.*
Revision	Sally went to work although she felt sick.
Faulty	Dave bought a new suit. *Over at Bentley's.*
Revision	Dave bought a new suit over at Bentley's.

Faulty	*That bronze clock on the mantel. Once belonged to my grandmother.*
Revision	That bronze clock on the mantel once belonged to my grandmother.

Joining a fragment to a sentence or to another fragment works only if the problem is simply one of mispunctuation. If the fragment stems from an improperly developed thought, revise the thought into correct sentence form.

Punctuating Your Corrections.   When you join a fragment to the following sentence, you need not place a comma between the two unless the fragment has six or more words or if omitting a comma might cause a misreading. When joining a fragment to the preceding sentence, omit a comma unless there is a distinct pause between the two items. The preceding examples illustrate these points.

Intentional Fragments.   Fragments are commonly used in conversation and the writing that reproduces it. Professional writers also use fragments to gain special emphasis or create special effects. Pages 228–229 discuss these applications.

frag

CONNECTED DISCOURSE EXERCISE ■   Identify and correct the sentence fragments in the following letter.

```
Dear Phone Company:

Recently I received a phone bill for over $500. While I do

use the phone fairly extensively. Most of the calls I make

are local ones. In this case, many of the calls on my bill

were to other countries. Including a phone call to New

Delhi, India. I can hardly be held responsible for these

calls. Especially since I don't know anyone who lives

overseas. Since the only long-distance call I made was to

Kalamazoo, Michigan. I have deducted the charges for all

the other long-distance calls from my bill and am sending

you the balance. In order to prevent this type of error

from happening again. Would you please have a

representative determine why these charges appeared on my

bill?

                    Sincerely,

                    Desperate
```

2. Sometimes students recognize a sentence fragment only when you make them see how it leaves them waiting for the other shoe to drop. Present them with a series of fragments such as the following and ask whether they are satisfied or believe more is needed: The people who live next door. Since I have to read a paper at the conference next week. Although many of you wrote fairly good papers. Since this is a college class. During the last week of September.

EXERCISE ■   Twelve main clauses paired with fragments are shown below. In each case identify the sentence and the fragment and then eliminate the fragment.

1. After a short wait. I was summoned into the interviewer's office.
2. Chris ate three sandwiches and drank six root beers. While he watched the game.
3. Because the workers are fast and efficient. They receive large bonuses every year.
4. If my parents will lend me the money. I'll go to Florida during the Easter break.
5. Jack told Anne. That he was moving to another state in one month.
6. I'd like you to meet Dr. Gorbichou. Our chief chemist.
7. I crashed into a tree. To avoid hitting the car ahead of me.
8. Jill bought a dress. Where I did.
9. To make more accurate engineering drawings. Mary Jane sharpened her pencil frequently.
10. Suzette bought a stuffed bear. For her daughter's bed.
11. Frustrated by his lack of progress. Delbert abandoned his project.
12. Muddy and wet after a two-mile walk through sodden fields. Phil was eager for hot coffee and a shower.

RUN-ON SENTENCES AND COMMA SPLICES

A run-on, or fused, sentence occurs when one sentence runs into another without anything to mark their junction. A comma splice occurs when only a comma marks the junction. These errors lead your readers to think that you are hasty or careless. Here are several examples.

Run-on sentence	Laura failed to set her alarm she was late for work.
Comma splice	Violets are blooming now, my lawn is covered with them.
Run-on sentence	Rick refused to attend the movie he said he hated horror shows.
Comma splice	Perry watched the road carefully, he still missed his turn.
Run-on sentence	Janet worked on her term paper her friend studied for a calculus test.
Comma splice	Janet worked on her term paper, her friend studied for a calculus test.

Testing for Errors.   To check out a possible comma splice or fused sentence, read what precedes and follows the comma or suspected junction and see whether the two parts can stand alone as sentences. If *both parts* can stand alone, there is an error. Otherwise, there is not.

> Darryl is a real troublemaker, someday he'll find himself in serious difficulty.

Examination of the parts preceding and following the comma shows that each is a complete sentence:

> Darryl is a real troublemaker.
> Someday he'll find himself in serious difficulty.

The writer has therefore committed a comma splice that needs correction.

Methods of Revision.   You can correct run-on sentences and comma splices in several ways.

1. Create two separate sentences.

   Revision   Violets are blooming now. My lawn is covered with them.

   Revision   Rick refused to attend the movie. He said he hated horror shows.

2. Join the sentences with a semicolon.

   Revision   Violets are blooming now; my yard is covered with them.

   Revision   Rick refused to attend the movie; he said he hated horror shows.

3. Join the sentences with a comma and a coordinating conjunction (*and, but, or, nor, for, yet, so*).

   Revision   Laura failed to set her alarm, *so* she was late for work.

   Revision   Perry watched the road carefully, *but* he still missed his turn.

4. Join the sentences with a semicolon and a conjunctive adverb (see page 563).

   Revision   Laura failed to set her alarm; *consequently*, she was late for work.

   Revision   Violets are blooming now; *in fact*, my yard is covered with them.

5. Introduce one of the sentences with a subordinating conjunction (see pages 562–563).

   Revision   *Because* Laura failed to set her alarm, she was late for work.

   Revision   Janet worked on her term paper *while* her friend studied for a calculus test.

As our examples show, you can often correct an error in several ways.

students sometimes omit implicit subordinating or coordinating conjunctions.

TEACHING STRATEGY

Have students review their own writing to identify where and why they produce comma splices and run-ons. Because many students think that a pronoun and its antecedent cannot appear in separate sentences, stress that they can.

ro cs

EXERCISE ANSWER

Dear Desperate:

We are sorry to hear that you are having difficulty paying your bill; it is, however, your responsibility. Unfortunately we have no way to prevent you from making overseas calls; you have to curb your own tendency to reach out and touch your friends. Following your instructions, we are sending a technician to remove your phone. Please be home this Friday morning, for he will arrive then. Even though we will remove your phone,

ro cs

you are still responsible for the unpaid portion of your bill. It is your financial obligation. We would dislike referring this matter to a collection agency since it could ruin your credit rating.

Sincerely,

Your friendly phone representative

EXERCISE ANSWERS

1. C.
2. CS. Stress often leads to heart attacks; everyone. . . . (Stress often leads to heart attacks. Everyone. . . .)
3. CS. Paul left the room. He . . . . (Paul left the room; he . . . . /Paul left the room because. . . .)
4. RO. Here's Jackie. She'll . . . . (Here's Jackie; she'll. . . .)
5. CS. The exercises looked easy. Nevertheless. . . . (The exercises looked easy; nevertheless. . . .)
6. CS. John was certain he had locked his house door, but when. . . .
7. C.
8. C.
9. CS. We are not accepting job applications now. Try again. . . . (We are not accepting job applications now; try again. . . . /We are not accepting job applications now, but try again. . . .)

CONNECTED DISCOURSE EXERCISE ■ Identify and correct the comma splices and run-on sentences in the following letter.

Dear Desperate:

We are sorry to hear that you are having difficulty paying your bill, it is, however, your responsibility. Unfortunately we have no way to prevent you from making overseas calls, you have to curb your own tendency to reach out and touch your friends. Following your instructions, we are sending a technician to remove your phone. Please be home this Friday morning he will arrive then. Even though we will remove your phone, you are still responsible for the unpaid portion of your bill, it is your financial obligation. We would dislike referring this matter to a collection agency, it could ruin your credit rating.

Sincerely,

Your friendly phone representative

EXERCISE ■ Indicate whether each item is correct (C), is a run-on sentence (RO), or contains a comma splice (CS) and then correct the faulty items.

1. I like your sport coat; perhaps I'll buy one like it for myself.
2. Stress often leads to heart attacks, everyone should know how to combat it.
3. Paul left the room, he was tired of being harassed.
4. Here's Jackie she'll tell us where Father and Mother went.
5. The exercises looked easy, nevertheless, they proved very difficult to do.
6. John was certain he had locked his house door, when he arrived home again he found it unlocked.
7. We were all wide awake, so we took sleeping pills before going to bed.
8. The battle was savagely fought; consequently, there were many casualties.
9. We are not accepting job applications now, try again in another two months.
10. Chieu spent just two days in Chicago she can hardly be said to know the city well.

SUBJECT–VERB AGREEMENT

A verb should agree in number with its subject. Singular verbs should have singular subjects, and plural verbs should have plural subjects.

Correct My *boss is* a grouch. (singular subject and verb)

Correct The *apartments have* two bedrooms. (plural subject and verb)

Ordinarily, matching subjects and verbs causes no problems. The following special situations, however, can create difficulties.

Subject and Verb Separated by a Word Group. Sometimes a word group that includes one or more nouns comes between the subject and the verb. When this happens, match the verb with its subject, not a noun in the word group.

Correct Our *basket* of sandwiches *is* missing.

Correct Several *books* required for my paper *are* not in the library.

Correct *Mr. Schmidt*, along with his daughters, *runs* a furniture store.

Correct The old *bus*, crammed with passengers, *was* unable to reach the top of the hill.

Two Singular Subjects. Most singular subjects joined by *and* take a plural verb.

The *couch* and *chair were* upholstered in blue velvet.

Sentences like the one above almost never cause problems. With subjects like *restoring cars* and *racing motorcycles*, however, singular verbs are often mistakenly used.

Faulty *Restoring cars* and *racing motorcycles consumes* most of Frank's time.

Revision *Restoring cars* and *racing motorcycles consume* most of Frank's time.

When *each* or *every* precedes the subjects, use a *singular* verb in place of a plural.

Correct Every *book* and *magazine was* badly water-stained.

Singular subjects joined by *or, either–or,* or *neither–nor* also take singular

Correct A *pear* or an *apple is* a nice afternoon snack.

Correct Neither *rain* nor *snow slows* our letter carrier.

One Singular and One Plural Subject. When one singular subject and one plural subject are joined by *or, either–or,* or *neither–nor,* match the verb with the closer of the two.

Correct   Neither *John* nor his *parents were* at home.

Correct   Neither his *parents* nor *John was* at home.

As these examples show, the sentences are usually smoother when the plural subject follows the singular.

Collective Nouns as Subjects. Collective nouns (*assembly, class, committee, family, herd, majority, tribe,* and the like) are singular in form but stand for groups or collections of people or things. Ordinarily, collective nouns are considered to be singular and therefore take singular verbs.

Correct   The *class is* writing a test.

Correct   The *herd was* clustered around the water hole.

Sometimes, though, a collective noun refers to the separate individuals making up the grouping, and then it requires a plural verb.

Correct   The *jury are* in dispute about the verdict.

Sentences in Which the Verb Comes Ahead of the Subject. Sentences that begin with words such as *here, there, how, what,* and *where* fall into this category. With such sentences, the verb must agree with the subject that follows it.

Correct   Here *is* my *house.*

Correct   Where *are* my *shoes?*

Correct   There *is* just one *way* to solve this problem.

Correct   There *go* my *chances* for a promotion.

CONNECTED DISCOURSE EXERCISE ■ Identify and correct the subject–verb agreement errors in the following letter.

```
Regional Accounts Manager:

One of your area phone representatives have seriously

misread a letter I submitted with my bill. I refused to

pay for long-distance overseas calls since neither I nor

my roommate know anyone who live overseas. Instead of

deducting the calls from my bill, she sent someone to
```

sv agr

remove my phone. Now my phone, along with many of my valuable possessions, have been removed. Unfortunately the technician, whom I allowed into my apartment only after carefully checking his credentials, were a thief. He locked me in a closet and cleared out the apartment. I have called the police, but I also expect the phone company to reimburse me for my losses. There is only two choices. Either the stolen items or a check covering the loss need to be sent to me immediately. Otherwise I am afraid I will be forced to sue. A jury are sure to rule in my favor. In addition, I expect to find that those overseas calls has been deducted from my bill.

                    Sincerely,

                    Desperately Desperate

phone, along with many of my valuable possessions, has been removed. Unfortunately the technician, whom I allowed into my apartment only after carefully checking his credentials, was a thief. He locked me in a closet and cleared out the apartment. I have called the police, but I also expect the phone company to reimburse me for my losses. There are only two choices. Either the stolen items or a check covering the loss needs to be sent to me immediately. Otherwise I am afraid I will be forced to sue. A jury is sure to

pa agr

rule in my favor. In addition, I expect to find that those overseas calls have been deducted from my bill.

Sincerely,

Desperately Desperate

EXERCISE ■ **Choose the correct verb form from the pair in parentheses.**

1. Either Sonia or Sophie (owns, own) this notebook.
2. The rules governing this contest (seem, seems) terribly complicated.
3. Jane's sister, together with her two cousins, (is, are) at the hockey game.
4. Either the puppy or the kittens (is, are) responsible for this terrible mess.
5. A line of black clouds (was, were) forming on the horizon.
6. Holding a full-time job and caring for a small child (leaves, leave) Penny with no time for recreation.
7. Every car and truck (is, are) slated to be overhauled this month.
8. Neither Kevin nor his brothers (plays, play) paddleball very well.
9. There (is, are) several possible solutions to this problem.
10. Each of my classes (requires, require) me to do a great deal of homework.
11. The committee (has, have) agreed to my proposal for a research project.
12. (Has, Have) either of your children been immunized against polio?

EXERCISE ANSWERS

1. owns
2. seem
3. is
4. are
5. was
6. leave
7. is
8. play
9. are
10. requires
11. has
12. Has

PRONOUN-ANTECEDENT AGREEMENT

The antecedent of a pronoun is the noun or pronoun to which it refers. Just as subjects should agree with their verbs, pronouns should agree with their antecedents: singular antecedents require singular pronouns, and plural anteced-

PERSPECTIVE

English teachers often find themselves having to take a stand concerning changes in standard English. Today, partially in an attempt to avoid sexist language, the popular press has become less consistent in its treatment of pronoun–antecedent agreement, and it is not uncommon for "their" to be used with indefinite pronouns.

This usage may someday become standard; however, we do our students a disservice if we do not, at least initially, observe the established practice. You might show how to use the plural to avoid sexist language, referring to page 256.

referring to page 256.

pa agr

TEACHING STRATEGIES

1. Some students balk at the idea that "everybody" and other indefinite pronouns actually are singular. To set matters straight, ask everybody to raise his or her hand and then point out that one hand was raised per individual. Seeing indefinite pronouns as consisting of two words—"any one," "every body," and the like—also emphasizes that they are singular.
2. Because the rules and problem areas for pronoun–antecedent agreement are the same as those for subject–verb agreement, you might point out the similarities. This approach will help reinforce the material in both sections.
3. Although the rules for agreement are not difficult, students often have trouble proofreading their own papers. Since they are unaccustomed to going back and checking for agreement, their attention tends to push forward. To help them overcome this tendency, have them read their most recent draft, identify the pronouns, and then draw an arrow back to the antecedent to determine whether there is agreement. Now is also a good time to have students see whether they are using too many pronouns.

ents require plural pronouns. Ordinarily, you will have no trouble matching antecedents and pronouns. The situations below, however, can cause problems.

Indefinite Pronouns as Antecedents.   Indefinite pronouns include words like *each, either, neither, any, everybody, somebody,* and *nobody.* Whenever an indefinite pronoun is used as an antecedent, the pronoun that refers to it should be singular.

> *Faulty*   *Neither* of the actors had learned *their* lines.

> *Revision*   *Neither* of the actors had learned *his* lines.

When the gender of the antecedent is unknown, you may follow it with *his or her;* or if this results in awkwardness, rewrite the sentence in the plural.

> *Correct*   *Anyone* who has studied *his or her* assignments properly should do well on the test.

> *Correct*   *Those* who have studied *their* assignments should do well on the test.

Occasionally, a ridiculous result occurs when a singular pronoun refers to an indefinite pronoun that is obviously plural in meaning. When this happens, rewrite the sentence to eliminate the problem.

> *Faulty*   *Everybody* complained that the graduation ceremony had lasted too long, but I didn't believe *him.*

> *Revision*   Everybody complained that the graduation ceremony had lasted too long, but I didn't agree.

Two Singular Antecedents.   Two or more antecedents joined by *and* ordinarily call for a plural pronoun.

> *Correct*   Her briefcase and umbrella were missing from *their* usual place on the hall table.

When *each* or *every* precedes the antecedent, use a singular pronoun.

> *Correct*   Every college and university must do *its* best to provide adequate student counseling.

Singular antecedents joined by *or, either–or,* or *neither–nor* call for singular pronouns.

> *Correct*   Neither Carol nor Irene had paid *her* rent for the month.

Applying this rule can sometimes yield an awkward or foolish sentence. When this happens, rewrite the sentence to avoid the problem.

Faulty   Neither James nor Sally has finished *his or her* term project.

Revision   James and Sally have not finished *their* term projects.

Singular and Plural Antecedents.   If one singular and one plural antecedent are joined by *or, either–or,* or *neither–nor,* the pronoun agrees with the closer one.

Correct   Either Terrence James or the Parkinsons will let us use *their* lawn mower.

Correct   Either the Parkinsons or Terrence James will let us use *his* lawn mower.

Sentences of this sort are generally smoother when the plural subject follows the singular.

Collective Nouns as Antecedents.   When a collective noun is considered a single unit, the pronoun that refers to it should be singular.

The *troop* of scouts made *its* way slowly through the woods.

When the collective noun refers to the separate individuals in the group, use a plural pronoun.

Correct   The staff lost *their* jobs when the factory closed.

pa agr

CONNECTED DISCOURSE EXERCISE ■   Identify and correct the pronoun–antecedent agreement errors in the following letter.

Dear Desperately Desperate:

We were sorry to hear about the theft from your apartment. Apparently a gang of con artists recently had their base of operations in your community. It posed as repair technicians and presented false credentials to anyone expecting their phone to be repaired. Someone also must have intercepted your mail and written their own response since we have no record of any previous letter from you. Clearly neither the representative you mentioned nor the phony phone technician could have held their position with our company. Every one of our technicians must

EXERCISE ANSWER

Dear Desperately Desperate:

We were sorry to hear about the theft from your apartment. Apparently a gang of con artists recently had its base of operations in your community. They posed as repair technicians and presented false credentials to customers expecting their phones to be repaired. Someone also must have intercepted your mail and written his or her own response since we have no record of any previous letter from you. Clearly neither the representative you mentioned nor the phony phone technician could have held a position with our company.

Our technicians must provide us with their fingerprints and take periodic lie detector tests. Further, our representatives will not answer correspondence since it is not a part of their job description. For these reasons, we do not believe we are responsible for your losses. However, a review of our records does show that you owe $500; we have included a copy of the bill in case you have misplaced the original.

Sincerely,

Accounts Manager

provide us with their fingerprints and take periodic lie detector tests. Further, none of our representatives will answer correspondence since it is not a part of their job description. For these reasons, we do not believe we are responsible for your losses. However, a review of our records does show that you owe $500; we have included a copy of the bill in case you have misplaced the original.

Sincerely,

Accounts Manager

---

pa agr

EXERCISE ANSWERS

1. himself
2. its
3. his or her
4. its
5. their
6. their
7. his or her
8. him
9. their
10. his

EXERCISE ■   Choose the right pronoun from the pair in parentheses.

1. Anyone who believes ballet is for sissies should try it for (himself, themselves).
2. Each bus and taxi must have (its, their) engine overhauled twice a year.
3. Everyone planning to attend the reunion should have (his or her, their) hotel reservations by July 15.
4. After flying for many days, the flock reached (its, their) destination in Canada.
5. Vernon and Harry made (his, their) way slowly through the packed room.
6. I understand that neither Joan nor the Benson sisters made (her, their) tuition payments on time.
7. Nobody should leave a hotel room without locking (his or her, their) door.
8. If someone wants to commit suicide badly enough, no one can stop (him, them).
9. The jury filed into the courtroom and took (its, their) seats.
10. Either the Meursaults or Pierre Chardonnay will let us use (his, their) house for the wine-tasting party.

AVOIDING FAULTY PRONOUN REFERENCE

Any pronoun except an indefinite pronoun should refer to just one noun or noun substitute—its antecedent. Reference problems result when the pronoun has two or more antecedents, a hidden antecedent, or no antecedent. These errors can cause mixups in meaning as well as ridiculous sentences.

TEACHING STRATEGY

This section can easily be combined with the section on pronoun–antecedent agreement. As students check their drafts for pronoun agreement, they might also determine whether the pronouns have appropriate and clear antecedents.

More Than One Antecedent.   The following sentences lack clarity because their pronouns have two possible antecedents rather than just one.

Faulty   Take the screens off the windows and wash *them*.

Faulty   Harry told Will that he was putting on weight.

The reader can't tell whether the screens or the windows should be washed or who is putting on weight.

Sometimes we see a sentence like this one:

Faulty   If the boys don't eat all the Popsicles, put *them* in the freezer.

In this case, we know it's the Popsicles that should be stored, but the use of *them* creates an amusing sentence.

Correct these faults by replacing the pronoun with a noun or by rephrasing the sentence.

Revision   Wash the windows after you have taken off the screens.

Revision   Take off the screens so that you can wash the windows.

Revision   Harry told Will, "I am (you are) putting on weight."

Revision   Put any uneaten Popsicles in the freezer.

pr ref

Hidden Antecedent.   An antecedent is hidden if it takes the form of an adjective rather than a noun.

Faulty   The movie theater is closed today, so we can't see *one*.

Faulty   As I passed the tiger's cage, *it* lunged at me.

To correct this fault, replace the pronoun with the noun used as an adjective or switch the positions of the pronoun and the noun and make any needed changes in their forms.

Revision   The theater is closed today, so we can't see a movie.

Revision   As I passed its cage, the tiger lunged at me.

No Antecedent.   A no-antecedent sentence lacks any noun to which the pronoun can refer. Sentences of this sort occur frequently in everyday conversation but should be avoided in formal writing. The examples below illustrate this error.

Faulty   The lecture was boring, but *they* took notes anyway.

Faulty   On the news program, *it* told about a new crisis in the Persian Gulf.

To set matters right, substitute a suitable noun for the pronoun or reword the sentence.

Revision   The lecture was boring, but the students took notes anyway.

Revision   The news program told about a new crisis in the Persian Gulf.

Sometimes a *this, that, it,* or *which* will refer to a whole idea rather than a single noun. This usage is acceptable provided the writer's meaning is obvious, as in this example.

Correct   The instructor spoke very softly, *which* meant we had difficulty hearing him.

Problems occur, however, when the reader can't figure out which of two or more ideas the pronoun refers to.

Faulty   Ginny called Sally two hours after the agreed-upon time and postponed their shopping trip one day. *This* irritated Sally very much.

What caused Sally to be irritated—the late call, the postponement of the trip, or both? Again, rewording or adding a clarifying word will correct the problem.

Revision   Ginny called Sally two hours after the agreed-upon time and postponed their shopping trip one day. This *tardiness* irritated Sally very much.

Revision   Ginny called Sally two hours after the agreed-upon time and postponed their shopping trip one day. Ginny's *change of plans* irritated Sally very much.

The first of these examples illustrates the addition of a clarifying word; the second illustrates rewriting.

pr ref

CONNECTED DISCOURSE EXERCISE ■   **Identify and correct any faulty pronoun references in the following memorandum.**

TO: Director of Food Services, Groan University

FROM: Vice-President of College Services

DATE: February 19, 19--

SUBJECT: Student Complaints about Cafeteria

Complaints about food quality and cafeteria hours are common but easily resolved. They can be extended by simply installing vending machines. It might not make for a nutritious meal, but it certainly will undercut some of the dissatisfaction. Of course, no matter how good the food, they will complain. Still, you can partially defuse those complaints by having students list their major

concerns and then meet them. Of course, you can always

increase student satisfaction by purchasing a soft ice

cream machine and offering it for dessert.

EXERCISE ■   Indicate whether each sentence is correct (C) or contains a faulty pronoun reference (F) and then correct any faulty sentences.

1. Remove the clothes from the trunks and give them to the Salvation Army.
2. I'm not married and don't plan on it for another two years.
3. Mary asked Cheryl whether she danced well.
4. In the humanities department, they offer several courses in popular culture.
5. I am experienced in turfgrass management and irrigation procedures, which qualifies me for your summer job.
6. Eaton had lived among cannibals, and it led him to reject the belief that savages are noble.
7. When the children had finished playing with the bicycles, we chained them to a tree for the night.
8. As I walked toward the dog's pen, it started barking.
9. They say that the Atlas Company will hire 150 more people soon.
10. Sue told Barbara that she was getting gray hair.
11. The store was crowded with customers because it was holding a sale.
12. My father made me turn down my radio and clean my room, which annoyed me greatly.

AVOIDING UNWARRANTED SHIFTS IN PERSON

Pronouns can be in the first person, second person, or third person. *First-person* pronouns identify people who are talking or writing about themselves, *second-person* pronouns identify people being addressed directly, and *third-person* pronouns identify persons or things that are being written or spoken about. The following table sorts pronouns according to person.

First Person	Second Person	Third Person
I	you	he
me	your	she
my	yours	it
mine	yourself	his
we	yourselves	hers

EXERCISE ANSWERS

1. F. Remove the clothes from the trunks; then give the clothes (trunks) to the Salvation Army. (Give the trunks to the Salvation Army after removing the clothes from them.)
2. F. I'm not married and don't plan on marrying for another two years.
3. F. Mary asked Cheryl, "Do I dance well?" (Mary asked Cheryl, "Do you dance well?")
4. F. The humanities department offers several courses in popular culture.
5. F. I am experienced in turfgrass management and irri-

shft

gation procedures, which together qualify me for your summer job. (I am experienced in turfgrass management and irrigation procedures, the first of which.../I am experienced in turfgrass management and irrigation procedures, the second of which....)
6. F. Eaton had lived among cannibals, and his experience led him to reject the belief that savages are noble.
7. F. After the children had finished playing with them, we chained their bicycles to a tree for the night.
8. F. As I walked toward its pen, the dog started barking.
9. F. A spokesperson says that the Atlas Company will hire 150 more people soon.
10. F. Sue told Barbara, "You are getting gray hair." (Sue told Barbara, "I am getting gray hair.")
11. C.
12. F. My father made me turn down my radio and clean my room, both of which annoyed me greatly. (My father made me turn down my radio and clean my room. That job annoyed me greatly.)

PERSPECTIVE
When students shift paragraphs, they sometimes lose track of the form of address they are using and shift person as well. Shifts are especially likely when students are uncertain whether they will adopt a formal or informal tone.

TEACHING STRATEGY
As students review for pronoun–agreement errors, have them check for unwarranted shifts in person. These are especially likely to occur if students are not sure whether to use "one" or "you."

shft

First Person	*Second Person*	*Third Person*
us		its
our		one
ours		they
ourselves		their
		theirs
		indefinite pronouns

All nouns are in the third person. As you revise, be alert for unwarranted shifts from one person to another.

Faulty   I liked *my* British vacation better than *my* vacation in France and Italy because *you* didn't have language problems.

Revision   I liked *my* British vacation better than *my* vacation in France and Italy because *I* didn't have language problems.

Faulty   Holidays are important to *everyone*. They boost *your* spirits and provide a break from *our* daily routine.

Revision   Holidays are important to *everyone*. They boost *one's* spirits and provide a break from *one's* daily routine.

Faulty   The taller the *golfer,* the more club speed *you will* have with a normally paced swing.

Revision   The taller the *golfer,* the more club speed *he* or *she* will have with a normally paced swing.

As these examples show, the shift can occur within a single sentence or when the writer moves from one sentence to another.

All shifts in person, however, are not unwarranted. Read the following correct sentence:

Correct   *I* want *you* to deliver these flowers to Ms. Willoughby by 3 o'clock. *She* needs them for a party.

Here the speaker identifies himself or herself (I) while speaking directly to a listener (you) about someone else (she). In this case, shifts are needed to get the message across.

EXERCISE ANSWER
Good health is clearly important to you. But it is your responsibility to ensure your own good health. You can start with simple exercises. We would like to provide you with a low-impact aerobics video tape for only $9. We guarantee that the more out of shape you are, the quicker you will notice the benefits. The way your body feels affects the quality of your life. Let our tape help you to a better life.

CONNECTED DISCOURSE EXERCISE ■   **Identify and correct the unwarranted shifts in person in the following paragraph.**

Good health is clearly important to everyone. But it is one's responsibility to ensure one's own good health. You can start with simple exercises. We would like to provide you with a low-impact aerobics video tape for only $9. We guarantee that the more out of shape the customer, the

quicker you will notice the benefits. The way our bodies

feel affects the quality of our lives. Let our tape help

you to a better life.

EXERCISE ■   Indicate whether the sentence is correct (C) or contains an unwarranted shift in person (S). Correct faulty sentences.

1. Would you ask Julio to bring his guitar to my party?
2. Those people who plan to attend the potluck should bring a dish to pass and your own dishes and silverware.
3. Why should I enlist in the armed forces when a person can get a better paying civilian job?
4. Our neighborhood is very friendly; you are always being invited to get-togethers.
5. Once we have taken a position on some issue, it is difficult for people to alter their attitudes.
6. Whenever we worked late, the company provided employees with a free meal.
7. Anyone wanting to exercise your option to purchase stock must do so within three months.
8. Millions of people celebrate Mother's Day by giving gifts to our mothers.
9. We think this hotel is outstanding; it offers you spacious rooms and friendly service for a low price.
10. Unless you have an aptitude for mathematics, nobody can successfully complete an engineering program.

USING THE RIGHT PRONOUN CASE

Case means the changes in form that a personal pronoun (see pages 545–546) undergoes to show its function in a sentence. English has three cases: the *subjective,* the *nonsubjective* (objective), and the *possessive.* The following chart shows the different forms.

Subjective Form	Nonsubjective Form	Possessive Form
I	me	my, mine
he	him	his
she	her	her, hers
we	us	our, ours
you	you	your, yours
they	them	their, theirs
who	whom	whose

will soon disappear. Still, until this change is definitively established, it is not difficult for students to learn this distinction. After all, whom could it hurt?

TEACHING STRATEGY

To counteract the effects of faulty rules, have students repeat the correct form until it seems less odd.

case

CLASSROOM ACTIVITY

One effective way to teach the distinction between *who* and *whom* is through sentence-combining exercises that force students to make a choice, such as the following:

That man stole my jacket. The man is heading toward us.

I am studying chemistry with the professor. The professor won a Nobel Prize.

Miss Jenkins is a dean. Very few people know Miss Jenkins.

Dick Pulaski enjoys the company of students. Students like to discuss ideas.

Combinations

The man who stole my jacket is heading toward us.

The professor with whom I am studying chemistry won a Nobel Prize.

Miss Jenkins is a dean whom very few people know.

Dick Pulaski enjoys the company of students who like to discuss ideas.

The subjective case is used for subjects and subject complements, the nonsubjective for direct objects, indirect objects, and objects of prepositions. The possessive case shows ownership and is also used with gerunds.

The following pointers will help you select the proper pronoun as you revise.

We and Us Preceding Nouns. Nouns that serve as subjects take the pronoun *we*. Other nouns take the pronoun *us*.

Correct   *We* tourists will fly home tomorrow. (*We* accompanies the subject.)

Correct   The guide showed *us* tourists through the cathedral. (*Us* accompanies a nonsubject.)

If you can't decide which pronoun is right, mentally omit the noun and read the sentence to yourself, first with one pronoun and then with the other. Your ear will indicate the correct form.

My mother made (we, us) children vanilla pudding for dessert.

Omitting *children* shows immediately that *us* is the right choice.

Correct   My mother made *us* children vanilla pudding for dessert.

Pronouns Paired with Nouns. When such a combination serves as the subject of a sentence or accompanies the subject, use the subject form of the pronoun. When the combination plays a nonsubject role, use the nonsubject form of the pronoun.

Correct   Arlene and *I* plan to join the Peace Corps. (*I* is part of the compound subject.)

Correct   Two people, Mary and *I*, will represent our school at the meeting. (*I* is part of a compound element accompanying the subject.)

Correct   The superintendent told Kevin and *him* that they would be promoted soon. (*Him* is part of a compound nonsubject.)

Correct   The project was difficult for Jeffrey and *him* to complete. (*Him* is part of a compound nonsubject.)

Again, mentally omitting the noun from the combination will tell you which pronoun is correct.

Who and Whom in Dependent Clauses. Use *who* for the subjects of dependent clauses; otherwise use *whom*.

Correct   The Mallarys prefer friends *who are interested in the theater*. (*Who* is the subject of the clause.)

Correct   Barton is a man *whom very few people like.* (*Whom* is not the subject of the clause.)

A simple test will help you decide between *who* and *whom.* First, mentally isolate the dependent clause. Next, block out the pronoun in question and then insert *he* (or *she*) and *him* (or *her*) at the appropriate spot in the remaining part of the clause. If *he* (or *she*) sounds better, *who* is right. If *him* (or *her*) sounds better, *whom* is right. Let's use this test on the sentence below.

The woman *who(m) Scott is dating* works as a mechanical engineer.
Scott is dating (she, her.)

Clearly *her* is correct; therefore, *whom* is the proper form.

Correct   The woman *whom Scott is dating* works as a mechanical engineer.

Pronouns as Subject Complements.   In formal writing, pronouns that serve as subject complements (see page 543) always take the subject form.

Correct   It is *I.*

Correct   It was *she* who bought the old Parker mansion.

This rule, however, is often ignored in informal writing.

It's *her.*

That's *him* standing over by the door.

Comparisons Using than or as . . . as.   Comparisons of this kind often make no direct statement about the second item of comparison. When the second naming word is a pronoun, you may have trouble choosing the right one.

Harriet is less outgoing than (*they, them*).

My parents' divorce saddened my sister as much as (*I, me*).

Not to worry. Expand the sentence by mentally supplying the missing material. Then try the sentence with each pronoun and see which sounds right.

Harriet is less outgoing than (*they, them*) are.

My parents' divorce saddened my sister as much as it did (*I, me*).

Obviously *they* is the right choice for the first sentence, and *me* is the right choice for the second one.

Correct   Harriet is less outgoing than *they* are.

Correct   My parents' divorce saddened my sister as much as it did *me.*

case

Pronouns Preceding Gerunds.   Use the possessive form of a pronoun that precedes a gerund (see page 565).

> I dislike *their* leaving without saying goodbye.

> Ted can't understand *her* quitting such a good job.

This usage emphasizes the action named by the gerund instead of the person or persons performing it. Thus, in the above sentences, the possessive form of the pronoun signals that it's the *leaving* you dislike and the *quitting* that Ted can't understand. The persons involved are secondary.

When the pronoun precedes a participle (see page 565), it should be in the nonsubject case. The emphasis is then on the actor rather than the action.

> Jennifer caught *them* listening to records instead of studying.

case

In this example, Jennifer caught the listeners, not the listening.

If you have trouble deciding between the nonsubject and possessive forms of a pronoun, ask yourself whether you want to emphasize the action or the actor; then proceed accordingly.

CONNECTED DISCOURSE EXERCISE ■   **Identify and correct the pronoun case errors in the following paragraph.**

EXERCISE ANSWER

Between my brother and me, we are always able to pull at least five good-sized trout a day from the creek behind our house. We rural trout fishermen just seem to have the knack. Of course, those city fishermen who insist on employing artificial flies won't appreciate our methods even if they can't do as well as we do. We just let our bait, usually a juicy worm, float downstream to the waiting trout. Of course, my brother won't let the fishing interfere with his sleeping. In fact, it was he that developed the idea of looping the line around his toe so that he would wake up when a trout took the bait. Others have told my brother and me that this method is dangerous, but neither of us has lost a toe yet. Of course, the people whom we invite to dinner don't complain about our methods, and they seem to enjoy the fish.

Between my brother and I, we are always able to pull at least five good-sized trout a day from the creek behind our house. Us rural trout fishermen just seem to have the knack. Of course, those city fishermen whom insist on employing artificial flies won't appreciate our methods even if they can't do as well as us. We just let our bait, usually a juicy worm, float downstream to the waiting trout. Of course, my brother won't let the fishing interfere with him sleeping. In fact, it was him that developed the idea of looping the line around his toe so that he would wake up when a trout took the bait. Others have told my brother and I that this method is dangerous, but neither of us has lost a toe yet. Of course, the people who we invite to dinner don't complain about our methods, and they seem to enjoy the fish.

EXERCISE ■   Choose the right form of the pronoun for each of the following sentences.

1. Bob, Joe, and (I, me) plan to attend the Willie Nelson concert in Omaha.
2. The strong American dollar is hurting (we, us) farmers by reducing the overseas markets for our crops.
3. John is a better student than (I, me).
4. (We, us) Democrats stand a good chance of capturing the state house this year.
5. Sandra is the only person (who, whom) I think has the right background for this job.
6. The boss recommended two people, Clarissa and (I, me), for raises.
7. Two people in the class, Roberta and (I, me), were born outside the United States.
8. I don't know (who, whom) to blame for this mistake.
9. The police officer told Debra and (I, me) that we were trespassing and would have to leave.
10. The travel agent said that (we, us) fellows would enjoy Montreal.
11. Ben's advisor approved of (his, him) changing his major.
12. I am not as enthusiastic a skier as (they, them).

time

CONSISTENCY IN SHOWING TIME

Inconsistencies occur when a writer shifts from the past tense to the present or vice versa without a corresponding shift in the time of the events being described. The following paragraph contains an uncalled-for shift from the present tense to the past.

As *The Most Dangerous Game* opens, Sanger Rainsford, a famous hunter and author, and his old friend Whitney are standing on the deck of a yacht and discussing a mysterious island as the ship passes near it. Then, after everyone else has gone to bed, Rainsford manages to fall overboard. He swims to the island and ends up at a chateau owned by General Zaroff, a refugee from the Communist takeover in Russia. Zaroff, bored with hunting animals, has turned to hunting humans on his desert island. Inevitably, Rainsford is turned out into the jungle to be hunted down. There were [shift to past tense] actually four hunts over a three-day period, and at the end of the last one, Rainsford jumped into the sea, swam across a cove to the chateau, and killed Zaroff in the general's own bedroom. Afterward he sleeps [shift back to present tense] and decides "he had never slept in a better bed."

The sentence with the unwarranted shift in tense should read as follows:

There are actually four hunts over a three-day period, and at the end of the last one, Rainsford jumps into the sea, swims across a cove to the chateau, and kills Zaroff in the general's own bedroom.

The time shift in the quotation part of the final sentence is justified because the sleeping has occurred before Rainsford's thoughts about it.

PERSPECTIVE

Writers of course legitimately shift tenses to reflect changes in time. Student problems arise chiefly because events can be presented from more than one temporal perspective. A narrative of a past event could be presented in either the past or the present tense. For instance, the sample paragraph in the text uses the present to describe an event that is clearly past. Students can easily shift focus without knowing it. When proofreading at the sentence level, they overlook the changes in tense. Furthermore, some students forget to put tense endings on some or all of their verbs.

TEACHING STRATEGIES

1. Ask students to review their narratives and check the tenses of their verbs. When they see a shift from past to present, or even to future, have them determine whether the shift is appropriate.

2. Have students review one or more of the narratives in the Reader to determine if, when, and why the authors shift time.

mis
adj/adv

CONNECTED DISCOURSE EXERCISE ■ Identify and correct any inconsistencies in showing time in the following passage.

There is no better time to go swimming than at night. The summer after I had graduated from high school, I worked for a landscaping company. After a sweaty day mowing lawns and digging up gardens, all of us who worked there would jump into the back of Dick's old pick-up and rattle out to Woods Lake. It is just dark as we arrive. The moon is beautiful, reflected in that black mirror set in a frame of hills. We stumble down a small, sandy hill to the beach, where we strip off our dusty jeans and sweaty shirts before plunging into the cool reflection of stars.

EXERCISE ■ Indicate whether each sentence is correct (C) or contains an unwarranted shift in tense. Then correct the faulty sentences.

1. I am working as a gardener this summer and liked the work very much.
2. Once the sirens sounded, people start heading for air-raid shelters.
3. The buses start running at 6 A.M. and continued operating until 10 P.M.
4. Before the game started, the audience stood and sang the national anthem.
5. While the instructor lectured, the students take notes.
6. As I turned slightly to the right, I see the hazy outline of a tall building.
7. After he had rested awhile, he resumed his hike.
8. Lois laid her cards face up on the table, then swept the pot toward her.
9. When Miranda starts to play, everyone gathered around the piano.
10. Arthur waved goodbye to his friends, starts his car, and left on his vacation.

AVOIDING MISUSE OF ADJECTIVES AND ADVERBS

Beginning writers often use adjectives when they should use adverbs and also confuse the comparative and superlative forms of these parts of speech when making comparisons.

Misusing Adjectives for Adverbs. Although most adjectives can be misused as adverbs, the following seven, listed with the corresponding adverbs, cause the most difficulty.

Adjectives	Adverbs
awful	awfully
bad	badly
considerable	considerably
good	well
most	almost
real	really
sure	surely

The following sentences show typical errors.

Faulty   Bryan did *good* in his first golf lesson. (*good* mistakenly used to modify verb *did*)

Faulty   *Most* every graduate from our auto service program receives several job offers. (*Most* mistakenly used to modify adjective *every*)

Faulty   The speech was delivered *real* well. (*real* mistakenly used to modify adverb *well*)

Because adverbs modify verbs, adjectives, and other adverbs (see pages 559–560), and adjectives modify nouns and noun substitutes (see pages 557–558), the above sentences clearly require adverbs.

Revision   Bryan did *well* in his first golf lesson.

Revision   *Almost* every graduate from our auto service program receives several job offers.

Revision   The speech was delivered *really* well.

If you can't decide whether a sentence requires an adjective or an adverb, determine the part of speech of the word being modified and proceed accordingly.

Confusing the Comparative and Superlative Forms in Comparisons. The comparative form of adjectives and adverbs is used to compare two things, the superlative form to compare three or more things. Adjectives with fewer than three syllables generally add *-er* to make the comparative form and *-est* to make the superlative form (tall, tall*er*, tall*est*). Adjectives with three or more syllables generally add *more* to make the comparative and *most* to make the superlative (enchanting, *more* enchanting, *most* enchanting), as do most adverbs of two or more syllables (loudly, *more* loudly, *most* loudly).

When making comparisons, beginning writers sometimes mistakenly use double comparatives or double superlatives.

Faulty   Harry is *more taller* than James. (double comparative)

Faulty   The Chrysler Building has the *most splendidest* lobby I've ever seen. (double superlative)

The correct versions read as follows:

> *Revision*   Harry is *taller* than James.
>
> *Revision*   The Chrysler Building has the *most splendid* lobby I've ever seen.

In addition, writers may erroneously use the superlative form, rather than the comparative form, to compare two things.

> *Faulty*   Barry is the *richest* of the two brothers.
>
> *Faulty*   Jeremy is the *most talented* of those two singers.

Here are the sentences correctly written.

> *Revision*   Barry is the *richer* of the two brothers.
>
> *Revision*   Jeremy is the *more talented* of those two singers.

Reserve the superlative form for comparing three or more items.

> *Correct*   Barry is the *richest* of the three brothers.
>
> *Correct*   Jeremy is the *most talented* of those four singers.

mis adj/adv

CONNECTED DISCOURSE EXERCISE ■   Identify and correct the adjective—adverb errors in the following paragraph.

This year our football team is outstanding. Spike Jones, our quarterback, has been playing real good this past season. Stan Blunder, the most talented of our two ends, hasn't dropped a pass all season. The team can most always count on Stan to catch the crucial first-down pass. Of course, the team wouldn't be where it is today without John Schoolyard's good coaching. He has made this team much more better than it was even a year ago. Only the kicking team has done bad this season. Of course, with this most wonderfulest offense, they haven't gotten much practice. The good news is, then, that we can sure expect to watch some terrific college football for years to come.

EXERCISE ANSWER

This year our football team is outstanding. Spike Jones, our quarterback, has been playing really well this past season. Stan Blunder, the more talented of our two ends, hasn't dropped a pass all season. The team can almost always count on Stan to catch the crucial first-down pass. Of course, the team wouldn't be where it is today without John Schoolyard's good coaching. He has made this team much better than it was even a year ago. Only the kicking team has done badly this season. Of course, with this wonderful offense, they haven't gotten much practice. The good news is, then, that we can surely expect to watch some terrific college football for years to come.

EXERCISE ■   For each of the following sentences, choose the proper word from the pair in parentheses.

1. If I do this job (good, well), the boss will promote me.
2. Nell is a (more gentler, gentler) horse than Dobbin.
3. The Grand Canyon is the (most awesome, most awesomest) sight I've ever seen.
4. Betty lost (most, almost) everything she owned in the fire.
5. By now, you (surely, sure) realize that you made a serious mistake when you changed majors.
6. This is the (better, best) of the two plans for rerouting Oakport's traffic.
7. You behaved (bad, badly) at the party and should apologize to the hostess.
8. I'm (awful, awfully) depressed today; the gloomy weather must be responsible.
9. The art critic looked (careful, carefully) at the supposed Picasso painting.
10. Antigua is the (most, more) exciting of the three vacation spots.

mm

AVOIDING MISPLACED MODIFIERS

A misplaced modifier is a word or word group that is improperly separated from the word it modifies. When separation of this type occurs, the sentence often sounds awkward, ridiculous, or confusing.

Usually, you can correct this error by moving the modifier next to the word it is intended to modify. Occasionally, you'll also need to alter some of the phrasing.

PERSPECTIVE

Don't be surprised if students actually produce more misplaced and dangling modifiers after you teach these units. In part, this happens because stressing modifiers can stimulate students to use more of them. When errors do increase, direct students to restructure their sentences so that their modifiers are more effective.

Faulty	There is a bicycle in the basement *with chrome fenders.* (The basement appears to have chrome fenders.)
Faulty	David received a phone call from his uncle *that infuriated him.* (The uncle appears to have infuriated David.)
Revision	There is a bicycle *with chrome fenders* in the basement.
Revision	David received an *infuriating* phone call from his uncle. (Note the change in wording.)

In shifting the modifier, don't inadvertently create another faulty sentence.

Faulty	Fritz bought a magazine with an article about Michael Jackson *at the corner newsstand.* (The article appears to tell about Jackson's visit to the corner newsstand.)
Faulty	Fritz bought a magazine *at the corner newsstand* with an article about Michael Jackson. (The corner newsstand appears to have an article about Jackson.)
Revision	*At the corner newsstand,* Fritz bought a magazine with an article about Michael Jackson.

EXERCISE ANSWERS

1. MM. Driving on the highway, Jane was ticketed for a broken taillight.
2. MM. After class, the principal told the teacher to stop by his office. (The principal told the teacher to stop by his office after class.)
3. MM. At the pet shop, Mercedes bought a mynah bird that could talk.
4. MM. Last week, we heard that he had suffered a heart attack. (We heard that he had suffered a heart attack last week.)

dm

5. MM. I drove the car that needed an overhaul to the repair shop.
6. C.
7. MM. Geologists found a coal deposit of great value on Uncle George's abandoned farm.
8. MM. Cedric showed the steak that was too tough to eat to the waitress.
9. MM. At the local dog pound, Eleanor found a collie that could do tricks.
10. MM. Swollen by heavy rains, the river overflowed its banks and swept away dozens of houses.

As you revise, watch also for *squinting modifiers*—that is, modifiers positioned so that the reader doesn't know whether they are supposed to modify what comes ahead of them or what follows them.

Faulty   The man who was rowing the boat *frantically* waved toward the onlookers on the beach.

Is the man rowing frantically or waving frantically?

Correct this kind of error by repositioning the modifier so that the ambiguity disappears.

Revision   The man who was *frantically* rowing the boat waved toward the onlookers on the beach.

Revision   The man who was rowing the boat waved *frantically* toward the onlookers on the beach.

EXERCISE ■   **Indicate whether each sentence is correct (C) or contains a misplaced modifier (MM). Correct faulty sentences.**

1. Jane was ticketed for driving on the highway with a broken taillight.
2. The principal told the teacher after class to stop by his office.
3. Mercedes bought a mynah bird at the pet shop that could talk.
4. We heard last week he had suffered a heart attack.
5. I drove the car to the repair shop that needed an overhaul.
6. The computer error was discovered by the bank before the account was overdrawn.
7. Geologists found a coal deposit on Uncle George's abandoned farm of great value.
8. Cedric showed the steak to the waitress that was too tough to eat.
9. Eleanor found a collie that could do tricks at the local dog pound.
10. The river overflowed its banks and swept away dozens of houses swollen by heavy rains.

AVOIDING DANGLING MODIFIERS

A dangling modifier is a phrase or clause that lacks clear connection to the word or words it is intended to modify. As a result, sentences are inaccurate, often comical. Typically, the modifier leads off the sentence, although it can also come at the end.

Sometimes the error occurs because the sentence fails to specify who or what is modified. At other times, the separation is too great between the modifier and what it modifies.

Faulty   *Walking in the meadow,* wildflowers surrounded us. (The wildflowers appear to be walking in the meadow.)

Faulty   Dinner was served *after saying grace.* (The dinner appears to have said grace.)

Faulty   *Fatigued by the violent exercise,* the cool shower was very relaxing. (The cool shower appears to have been fatigued.)

The first of these sentences is faulty because the modifier is positioned too far away from *us.* The other two are faulty because they do not identify who said grace or found the shower relaxing.

You can correct dangling modifiers in two basic ways. First, leave the modifier unchanged and rewrite the main part of the sentence so that it begins with the term actually modified. Second, rewrite the modifier so that it has its own subject and verb, thereby eliminating the inaccuracy.

Revision   *Walking in the meadow,* we were surrounded by wildflowers. (The main part of the sentence has been rewritten.)

Revision   *As we walked in the meadow,* wildflowers surrounded us. (The modifier has been rewritten.)

Revision   Dinner was served *after we had said grace.* (The modifier has been rewritten.)

Revision   *Fatigued by the violent exercise,* Ted found the cool shower very relaxing. (The main part of the sentence has been rewritten.)

Revision   *Because Ted was fatigued by the violent exercise,* the cool shower was very relaxing. (The modifier has been rewritten.)

Ordinarily, either part of the sentence can be rewritten, but sometimes only one part can.

dm

EXERCISE ■ Indicate whether each sentence is correct (C) or contains a dangling modifier (DM). Correct faulty sentences.

1. After typing for two hours, a cup of coffee refreshed me.
2. At the age of sixteen, my father bought me a car.
3. While picking cherries, a bee stung me.
4. Lying in the hot sun, I got a severe sunburn.
5. Our car broke down while on a trip to Georgia.
6. In order to install this part, you will need a special tool.
7. The engine must be shut off before putting gasoline in the car's tank.
8. By making use of anecdotes and examples, Professor Yamashita's students find her lectures easy to understand.
9. Because the road was slick with ice, Vernon couldn't make it to the top of the steep hill.
10. As a child, Halloween was one of my favorite days.

EXERCISE ANSWERS
1. DM. After I had typed for two hours, a cup of coffee refreshed me. (After typing for two hours, I was refreshed by a cup of coffee.)
2. DM. When I was sixteen, my father bought me a car. (At the age of sixteen, I received a car from my father.)
3. DM. While I was picking cherries, a bee stung me. (While picking cherries, I was stung by a bee.)
4. C.
5. DM. Our car broke down while we were on a trip to Georgia.
6. C.
7. DM. The engine must be shut off before gasoline is put in the car's tank. (You must shut the engine off before putting gasoline in the car's tank.)
8. DM. Because Professor Yamashita makes use of anecdotes and examples, her students find her lectures easy to understand.
9. C.
10. DM. When I was a child, Halloween was one of my favorite days.

AVOIDING NONPARALLELISM

TEACHING STRATEGY

Because student writers rarely use parallelism, you might have them complete the following sentences: I enjoy _____ , _____ , and _____ . My room is not only _____ but also _____ . The instructor warned the class about _____ , _____ , and _____ . A good education requires _____ and _____ . That sound was either a(n) _____ or a(n) _____ .

II

Nonparallelism results when equivalent ideas follow different grammatical forms. One common kind of nonparallelism occurs with words or word groups in pairs or in a series.

Faulty   Althea enjoys *jogging, to bike,* and *to swim.*

Faulty   The superintendent praised the workers *for their productivity* and *because they had an excellent safety record.*

Faulty   The banner was *old, faded,* and *it had a rip.*

Note how rewriting the sentences in parallel form improves their smoothness.

Revision   Althea enjoys *jogging, biking,* and *swimming.*

Revision   The superintendent praised the workers for *their productivity* and *their excellent safety record.*

Revision   The banner was *old, faded,* and *ripped.*

Nonparallelism also occurs when correlative conjunctions (*either . . . or, neither . . . nor, both . . . and,* and *not only . . . but also*) are followed by unlike elements.

Faulty   That sound *either <u>was a thunderclap</u> or <u>an explosion</u>.*

Faulty   The basement was *not only <u>poorly lighted</u> but also <u>it had a foul smell</u>.*

Ordinarily, repositioning one of the correlative conjunctions will solve the problem. Sometimes, however, one of the grammatical elements must be rewritten.

Revision   That sound was *either <u>a thunderclap</u> or <u>an explosion</u>.* (*Either* has been repositioned.)

Revision   The basement was *not only <u>poorly lighted</u> but also <u>foul smelling</u>.* (The element following *but also* has been rewritten.)

EXERCISE ANSWERS

1. NP. Despite having a week's preparation time, Jethroe could recite neither the Pledge of Allegiance nor the Preamble to the Constitution.
2. C.
3. NP. The tryouts involved not only acting but also singing.
4. NP. Playing cards is more boring than playing baseball.
5. NP. This winter I want to vacation either in Florida or in Bermuda.

EXERCISE ■   Indicate whether each sentence is correct (C) or nonparallel (NP). Correct faulty sentences.

1. Despite having a week's preparation time, Jethroe could neither recite the Pledge of Allegiance nor the Preamble to the Constitution.
2. The room was large, sunny, and pleasant.
3. The tryouts involved not only acting, but there was singing also.
4. Playing cards is more boring than to play baseball.
5. This winter I want either to vacation in Florida or in Bermuda.

6. Annette hates math, history, and to draw.
7. Keith is neither a good dancer nor an interesting conversationalist.
8. As the midnight countdown began, corks popped, champagne spurted, and cheers filled the air.
9. Danielle has many virtues, including reliability, kindness, and she is honest.
10. Next term Sandy will be taking beginning math and work in the library.

6. NP. Annette hates math, history, and drawing.
7. C.
8. C.
9. NP. Danielle has many virtues, including reliability, kindness, and honesty.
10. NP. Next term Sandy will be taking beginning math and working in the library. (Next term Sandy will take beginning math and work in the library.)

AVOIDING FAULTY COMPARISONS

comp

A faulty comparison results if you (1) mention one of the items being compared but not the other, (2) omit words needed to clarify the relationship, or (3) compare different sorts of items. Advertisers often offend in the first way.

Faulty   Irish tape has better adhesion.

With what other tape is Irish tape being compared? Scotch tape? All other transparent tape? Mentioning the second term of a comparison eliminates reader guesswork.

Revision   Irish tape has better adhesion than any other transparent tape.

Two clarifying words, *other* and *else*, are frequently omitted from comparisons, creating illogical sentences.

Faulty   Sergeant McNabb has made more arrests than any officer in his precinct.

Faulty   Stretch French is taller than anyone on his basketball team.

The first sentence is illogical because McNabb is one of the officers in his precinct and therefore cannot be more conscientious than any officer in the precinct. Similarly, because French is a member of his basketball team, he can't be taller than anyone on his team. Adding *other* to the first sentence and *else* to the second corrects matters.

Revision   Sergeant McNabb has made more arrests than any *other* officer in his precinct.

Revision   Stretch French is taller than anyone *else* on his basketball team.

Comparing unlike items is perhaps the most common kind of comparison error. Here are two examples.

Faulty   The cities in California are larger than North Dakota.

Faulty   The cover of this book is much more durable than the other book.

The first sentence compares the cities of California with a state while the second compares the cover of a book with a whole book. Correction consists of rewriting the sentence so that it compares like items.

> *Revision*   The cities in California are larger than *those in* North Dakota.

> *Revision*   The cover of this book is much more durable than *that of* the other book.

CONNECTED DISCOURSE EXERCISE ■   Identify and correct the misplaced modifiers, dangling modifiers, nonparallelism, and faulty comparisons in the following memorandum.

TO: All Residency Hall Advisors in Knuckles Hall

FROM: John Knells, Residency Hall Director

DATE: March 13, 19--

SUBJECT: Noise in Residence Hall

Recently I received a report from a student that deeply disturbed me. Apparently, after quiet hours students still have visitors in their rooms, are playing their stereos loudly, and are even staging boxing matches in the halls. The student who wrote me desperately tries to study. However, he is often forced to leave his room disturbed by the noise. He was not the only one to complain. You should know that we have had more complaints about Knuckles Hall than any dorm on campus. Since discussing this problem with you at the last staff meeting, things haven't seemed to get any better. The rules are not only poorly enforced but also they are completely ignored. Your job performance is worse than the students. If you don't improve immediately, I will be forced to dismiss you.

EXERCISE ■   Indicate whether the sentence is correct (C) or contains a faulty comparison (FC). Correct any faulty comparison.

1. Compared with Harry, Chad is a much less efficient worker.
2. Unlike my brother's house, I have a fireplace in mine.
3. Tests conducted on Steelgrip glue show that its bonding strength is much greater.
4. That novel was better than anything I've read.
5. The duties of a firefighter are just as hazardous as a police officer.
6. I found it hard to surf in Florida because the waves in the Gulf of Mexico weren't as big as the Pacific Ocean.
7. The relationship between Brett and Bryant is not as good as most brothers.
8. Our house is larger than any house on our block.
9. The English Department has more members than any other department on this campus.
10. The trees on the far riverbank are different from this riverbank.

EXERCISE ANSWERS

1. C.
2. FC. Unlike my brother's house, mine has a fireplace.
3. FC. Tests conducted on Steelgrip glue show that its bonding strength is much greater than that of Holdfast glue.
4. FC. That novel was better than anything else I've read.
5. FC. The duties of a firefighter are just as hazardous as those (the duties) of a police officer.

comp

6. FC. I found it hard to surf in Florida because the waves in the Gulf of Mexico weren't as big as those (the waves) in the Pacific Ocean.
7. FC. The relationship between Brett and Bryant is not as good as that (the relationship) between most brothers.
8. FC. Our house is larger than any other house on our block.
9. C.
10. FC. The trees on the far riverbank are different from those (the trees) on this riverbank.

Editing to Correct Faulty Punctuation and Mechanics

PERSPECTIVE

Although students have been told to use their speech patterns as clues to correct punctuation, this advice often creates more trouble than it is worth, as speech patterns can vary. Punctuation is best viewed as related to the structure of our language; it helps us make sense of the written word.

PERSPECTIVE

It is common for students to confuse plurals and possessives. Often, students who have not been using possessives will, after studying possessive apostrophes, overcompensate by placing an apostrophe next to every "s" that concludes a word.

TEACHING STRATEGY

Introduce possessives in direct contrast to plurals so that students will have to determine whether an apostrophe is actually needed. Try using the following sentence pairs:

The managers are meeting in the next room. The managers' reorganization plan will take effect next week.

All the workers' lockers were moved. All the workers checked their paychecks.

The teachers' lounge is being redecorated. The teachers insisted upon the redecoration.

Punctuation marks indicate relationships among different sentence elements. As a result, these marks help clarify the meaning of written material. Similarly, a knowledge of mechanics—capitalization, abbreviations, numbers, and italics—helps you avoid distracting inconsistencies.

This part of the handbook covers the fundamentals of punctuation and mechanics. Review it carefully when you edit your final draft.

APOSTROPHES

Apostrophes (') show possession, mark contractions, and indicate plurals that are singled out for special attention.

Possession.   Possessive apostrophes usually show ownership. (*Mary's cat*). Sometimes, though, they identify the works of creative people (*Hemingway's novels*) or indicate an extent of time or distance (*one hour's time, one mile's distance*).

Possessive apostrophes are used with nouns and with pronouns like *someone, no one, everybody, each other,* and *one another.* The possessive form is easily recognized because it can be converted to a prepositional phrase beginning with *of.*

The collar of the dog

The whistle of the wind

The intention of the corporation

The birthday of Scott

To show possession with pronouns, singular nouns, and plural nouns that do not end in an *s,* add an apostrophe followed by an *s.*

Someone's car is blocking our drive. (possessive of pronoun *someone*)

The *manager's* reorganization plan will take effect next week. (possessive of singular noun *manager*)

600

The *women's* lounge is being redecorated. (possessive of plural noun *women*)

The *boss's* orders must be obeyed. (possessive of singular noun *boss*)

With singular nouns that end in *s,* the possessive is sometimes formed by merely adding an apostrophe at the end (James' helmet). The preferred usage, however, is *'s* (James's helmet) unless the addition of the *s* would make it awkward to pronounce the word.

Moses's followers entered the Promised Land. (awkward pronunciation of *Moses's*)

Moses' followers entered the Promised Land. (nonawkward pronunciation of *Moses'*)

Plural nouns ending in *s* form the possessive by adding only an apostrophe at the end.

All the *ladies'* coats are on sale today. (possessive of plural noun *ladies*)

The *workers'* lockers were moved. (possessive of plural noun *workers*)

To show joint ownership by two or more persons, use the possessive form for the last-named person only. To show individual ownership, use the possessive form for each person's name.

Ronald and *Joan's* boat badly needed overhauling. (joint ownership)

Laura's and *Alice's* term projects are almost completed. (individual ownership)

Hyphenated nouns form the possessive by adding *'s* to the last word.

My *mother-in-law's* house is next to mine.

Never use an apostrophe with the possessive pronouns *his, hers, whose, its, ours, yours, theirs.*

This desk is *his;* the other one is *hers.* (no apostrophes needed)

Contractions.   Contractions of words or numbers omit one or more letters or numerals. An apostrophe shows exactly where the omission occurs.

Wasn't that a disappointing concert? (contraction of *was not*)

Around here, people still talk about the blizzard of *'79.* (contraction of 1979)

Don't confuse the contraction *it's,* meaning *it is* or *it has*, with the possessive pronoun *its,* which should never have an apostrophe. If you're puzzled by an *its* that you've written, try this test. Expand the *its* to *it is* or *it has* and see whether the sentence still makes sense. If it does, the *its* is a contraction and needs the apostrophe. If the result is nonsense, the *its* is a possessive pronoun and does not get an apostrophe. Here are some examples.

Its awfully muggy today.

Its been an exciting trip.

Every dog has *its* day.

The first example makes sense when the *its* is expanded to *it is*.

It is awfully muggy today.

The second also makes sense when the *its* is expanded to *it has*.

It has been an exciting trip.

Both of these sentences therefore require apostrophes.

It's awfully muggy today.

It's been an exciting trip.

The last sentence, however, turns into nonsense when the *its* is expanded.

Every dog has *it is* day.

Every dog has *it has* day.

In this case, the *its* is a possessive pronoun and requires no apostrophe.

Every dog has *its* day.

Plurals. To improve clarity, the plurals of letters, numbers, symbols, and words being singled out for special attention are written with apostrophes.

Mind your *p's* and *q's*. (plurals of letters)

Your *5's* and *6's* are hard to tell apart. (plurals of numbers)

The formula was sprinkled with *Π's* and *Σ's*. (plurals of symbols)

Don't use so many *however's* and *therefore's* in your writing. (plurals of words)

Apostrophes are often used to form the plurals of abbreviations.

How many *rpm's* does this shaft turn at? (plural of abbreviation for revolutions per minute)

When no danger of confusion exists, an *s* alone will suffice.

During the late *1960s*, many university students demanded changes in academic life.

CONNECTED DISCOURSE EXERCISE ■ Supply, delete, or relocate apostrophes as necessary in the following memorandum.

TO: The Records Office Staff

FROM: The Assistant Registrar

DATE: January 27, 19--

SUBJECT: Faulty Student Transcripts

Recently, we have had too many student complaints' about handwritten transcripts. Apparently its hard to tell the Bs and Ds apart. One staff members' handwriting is totally illegible. This staffs carelessness is unacceptable. Someones even gone so far as to write grade change's in pencil, which allows students to make changes. This cant continue. In a short time, John and Marys student assistants will be typing the past transcripts into our new computer system. Once grades are entered, the computers ability to generate grade reports will solve this problem. Until that time, lets make an effort to produce clear and professional-looking transcripts.

EXERCISE ■ Supply apostrophes where necessary to correct the following sentences.

1. The automobile accident happened in front of Tom and Margarets house.
2. Too many *ands* weaken a persons writing.
3. Dan mowed two neighbors lawns and weeded one neighbors garden.
4. When everyones going on a trip, somebodys got to take responsibility for the arrangements.
5. Lets leave the gifts in the childrens room.
6. Kens embarrassment was due to his borrowing his teachers pen and losing its cap.
7. How many *ts* are in your history teachers name?
8. Its clear that this book is on its way to becoming a best-seller.
9. For Petes sake, havent you heard the news about Julie?
10. Eloises costume outshone all her companions costumes.

COMMAS

Since commas (,) occur more frequently than any other mark of punctuation, it's vital that you learn to use them correctly. When you do, your sentence structure is clearer, and your reader grasps your meaning without having to reread.

Commas separate or set off independent clauses, items in a series, coordinate adjectives, introductory elements, places and dates, nonrestrictive expressions, and parenthetical expressions.

Independent Clauses. When you link two independent clauses with a coordinating conjunction (*and, but, or, nor, for, yet,* or *so*), put a comma in front of the conjunction.

> Arthur is majoring in engineering, *but* he has decided to work for a clothing store following graduation.

> The water looked inviting, *so* Darlene decided to go for a swim.

Don't confuse a sentence that has a compound predicate (see page 541) with a sentence that consists of two independent clauses.

> Tom watered the garden and mowed the lawn. (single sentence with compound predicate)

> Tom watered the garden, *and* Betty mowed the lawn. (sentence with two independent clauses)

Here's a simple test. Read what follows the comma. Unless that part can stand alone as a sentence, don't use a comma.

Items in a Series. A series consists of three or more words, phrases, or clauses following on one another's heels. Whenever you write a series, separate its items with commas.

> *Sarah, Paul,* and *Mary* are earning A's in advanced algebra. (words in a series)

> Nancy strode *across the parking lot, through the revolving door,* and *into the elevator.* (phrases in a series)

> The stockholders' report said *that the company had enjoyed record profits during the last year, that it had expanded its work force by 20 percent,* and *that it would soon start marketing several new products.* (clauses in a series)

Coordinate Adjectives. Use commas to separate coordinate adjectives—those that modify the same noun or noun substitute and can be reversed without altering the meaning of the sentence.

> Andrea proved to be an efficient, cooperative employee.
>
> Andrea proved to be a cooperative, efficient employee.

When reversing the word order wrecks the meaning of the sentence, the adjectives are not coordinate and should be written without a comma.

> Many new brands of video cassette recorders have come on the market lately.

Reversing the adjectives *many* and *new* would turn this sentence into nonsense. Therefore, no comma should be used.

Introductory Elements. Use commas to separate introductory elements—words, phrases, and clauses—from the rest of the sentence. When an introductory element is short and the sentence will not be misread, you can omit the comma.

Correct	After bathing, Jack felt refreshed.
Correct	Soon I will be changing jobs.
Correct	Soon, I will be changing jobs.
Correct	When Sarah smiles her ears wiggle.
Correct	When Sarah smiles, her ears wiggle.

The first example needs a comma; otherwise, the reader might become temporarily confused.

> After bathing Jack. . . .

Always use commas after introductory elements of six or more words.

Correct	Whenever I hear the opening measure of Beethoven's *Fifth Symphony,* I get goose bumps.

Places and Dates. Places include mailing addresses and geographical locations. The following sentences show where commas are used.

> Sherry Delaney lives at 651 Daniel Street, Memphis, Tennessee 38118.
>
> I shall go to Calais, France, next week.
>
> Morristown, Oklahoma, is my birthplace.

TEACHING STRATEGY

Have students test for coordinate adjectives by mentally inserting an "and" between the pair in question. If the meaning does not change, the adjectives are coordinate, and a comma is required.

TEACHING STRATEGIES

1. Sometimes students suspect that a sentence has an introductory element, but they don't know for sure. When this happens, have them reposition the suspected element at the end of the sentence. If it is indeed an introductory element, the meaning of the sentence will not be materially altered. Note that the preceding sentence passes this test.

2. Students sometimes mistake complete subjects for introductory phrases: Studying late at night, isn't always the best strategy. (incorrect) Studying late at night isn't always the best strategy. (correct) In most cases, the "move" test will usually reveal the error. "Isn't always the best strategy, studying late at night" just doesn't make sense, even to an undiscriminating eye.

TEACHING STRATEGY

Because students often fail to put needed commas after names of places and dates, ask them to proofread with this oversight in mind.

Note that commas appear after the street designation and the names of cities, countries, and states, except when the name of the state is followed by a zip code. Dates are punctuated as shown in the following example.

On Sunday, June 9, 1985, Elaine received a degree in environmental science.

Here, commas follow the day of the week, the day of the month, and the year. With dates that include only the month and the year, commas are optional.

Correct   In July 1979 James visited Scotland for the first time.

Correct   In July, 1979, James visited Scotland for the first time.

Nonrestrictive Expressions.   A nonrestrictive expression supplies added information about whatever it modifies. This information, however, does not affect the basic meaning of the sentence. The two sentences below include nonrestrictive expressions.

Senator Conwell, *the senior senator from this state,* faces a tough campaign for reelection.

My dog, *frightened by the thunder,* hid under my bed while the storm raged.

If we delete the phrase *the senior senator from this state* from the first sentence, we still know that Senator Conwell faces a tough reelection battle. Likewise, if we delete *frightened by the thunder* from the second sentence, we still know that the dog hid during the storm.

Restrictive expressions, which are written *without commas,* distinguish whatever they modify from other persons, places, or things in the same category. Unlike nonrestrictive expressions, they are almost always essential sentence elements. Omitting a restrictive expression alters the meaning of the sentence, and the result is often nonsense.

Any person *caught stealing from this store* will be prosecuted.

Dropping the italicized part of this sentence leaves us with the absurd statement that any person, not just those caught stealing, faces prosecution.

Parenthetical Expressions.   A parenthetical expression is a word or a word group that links one sentence to another or adds information or emphasis to the sentence in which it appears. Parenthetical expressions include the following:

Clarifying phrases
Names and titles of people being addressed directly
Abbreviations of degree titles and of *junior* and *senior* following people's names
Echo questions

"Not" phrases
Adjectives that come after, rather than before, the words they modify

The examples that follow show the uses of commas.

All of Joe's spare time seems to center around reading. Kevin, *on the other hand,* enjoys a variety of activities. (phrase linking two sentences together)

Myra Hobbes, *our representative in Seattle,* is being transferred to Spokane next month. (clarifying phrase)

I think, *Jill,* that you'd make a wonderful teacher. (name of person addressed directly)

Tell me, *Captain,* when the cruise ship is scheduled to sail. (title of person addressed directly)

Harley Kendall, *Ph.D.,* will be this year's commencement speaker. (degree title following name)

Peter Bradley, *Jr.,* has just taken over his father's plumbing business. (personal abbreviation following name)

Alvin realizes, *doesn't he,* that he stands almost no chance of being accepted at West Point? (echo question)

Mathematics, *not home economics,* was Tammy's favorite high school subject. ("not" phrase)

The road, *muddy and rutted,* proved impassable. (adjectives following word they modify)

CONNECTED DISCOURSE EXERCISE ■   Add or delete commas as necessary in the following letter.

Dear Loy Norrix Knight:

While we know you will be busy this summer we hope you will take time to join us for the 20-year reunion of the graduating class of 1970. The reunion will include a cocktail hour a buffet dinner and a dance. For your entertainment we are going to bring in a professional band and a band starring some of your good, old high school chums. John Mcleary who is now a well-known professional nightclub performer will serve as the emcee. Do you remember him hosting our senior-year assemblies?

EXERCISE ANSWER

Dear Loy Norrix Knight:

While we know you will be busy this summer, we hope you will take the time to join us for the 20-year reunion of the graduating class of 1970. The reunion will include a cocktail hour, a buffet dinner, and a dance. For your entertainment we are going to bring in a professional band and a band starring some of your good old high school chums. John McLeary, who is now a well-known professional nightclub performer, will serve as the emcee. Do you remember him hosting our senior-year assemblies?

Yes, many of your former, hardworking teachers will be at the reunion. You can thank them for the difference they made in your life, or you can tell them what you've thought of them all these years. This reunion will also be your opportunity to catch up on the lives of your former friends, find out what that old flame now looks like, and brag a little about your own successes. And if you are really lucky, you might even be able to sneak a dance with your high school prom partner.

We hope you will make plans to join us here at the Kalamazoo Hilton on July 28, 1990, at 7 p.m. Wear your best 1970s style clothes. Remember, revisiting the past can be fun.

Sincerely,

The Reunion Committee

EXERCISE ANSWERS

1. The solenoid valve is faulty, so we'll have to replace it.
2. His suit, which he had tailor-made in England, cost him over seven hundred dollars.
3. The rewards of hard work include financial security, peace of mind, and self-respect.

4. Annette Dorian, 341 Plainfield Avenue, Augsburg, Maine, has won the Pulitzer Prize for literature.
5. After eating, the lion licked his paws and rested.
6. Norton Hillburg, my closest friend in college, now works for the State Department.
7. Pete is a dedicated, skillful fisherman.
8. You realize, don't you, that you must write an A final to pass this course?
9. When I have graduated from college, I plan to spend a summer in Europe.
10. On Saturday, June 4, 1975, a train derailment near my hometown took six lives.

Yes many of your former, hardworking teachers will be at the reunion. You can thank them for the difference they made in your life or you can tell them what you've thought of them all these years. This reunion will also be your opportunity to catch up on the lives of your former friends find out what that old flame now looks like and brag a little about your own successes. And if you are really lucky you might even be able to sneak a dance with your high school prom partner.

We hope you will make plans, to join us here at the Kalamazoo Hilton, on July 28 1990 at 7 p.m. Wear your best 1970's style clothes. Remember revisiting the past, can be fun.

Sincerely,

The Reunion Committee

EXERCISE ▓ Supply commas as necessary to correct the following sentences.

1. The solenoid valve is faulty so we'll have to replace it.
2. His suit which he had tailor-made in England cost him over seven hundred dollars.
3. The rewards of hard work include financial security peace of mind and self-respect.
4. Annette Dorian 341 Plainfield Avenue Augsburg Maine has won the Pulitzer Prize for literature.
5. After eating the lion licked his paws and rested.
6. Norton Hillburg my closest friend in college now works for the State Department.
7. Pete is a dedicated skillful fisherman.
8. You realize don't you that you must write an *A* final to pass this course?
9. When I have graduated from college I plan to spend a summer in Europe.
10. On Saturday June 4 1975 a train derailment near my home town took six lives.

SEMICOLONS

The main use of the semicolon (;) is to separate independent clauses, which may or may not be connected with a conjunctive adverb (see page 563). Other uses include separating

two or more series of items
items containing commas in a single series
independent clauses that contain commas and are connected with a coordinating conjunction.

Independent Clauses. The examples that follow show the use of semicolons to separate independent clauses.

The fabric in this dress is terrible; its designer must have been asleep at the swatch. (no conjunctive adverb)

Steve refused to write a term paper; *therefore*, he failed the course. (conjunctive adverb *therefore* joining independent clauses)

Conjunctive adverbs can occur within, rather than between, independent clauses. When they do, set them off with commas.

Marsha felt very confident. Jane, *on the other hand*, was nervous and uncertain. (conjunctive adverb within independent clause)

To determine whether a pair of commas or a semicolon and comma are required, read what comes before and after the conjunctive adverb. Unless both sets of words can stand alone as sentences, use commas.

Two or More Series of Items. With sentences that have two or more series of items, writers often separate the series with semicolons in order to lessen the chances of misreading.

My duties as secretary include typing letters, memos, and purchase orders; sorting, opening, and delivering mail; and making plane and hotel reservations for traveling executives.

The semicolons provide greater clarity than commas would.

Comma-Containing Items Within a Series. When commas accompany one or more of the items in a series, it's often better to separate the items with semicolons instead of commas.

The meal included veal, which was cooked to perfection; asparagus, my favorite vegetable; and brown rice, prepared with a touch of curry.

Once again, semicolons provide greater clarity than additional commas.

Handbook

about a power failure. Just imagine a power failure in such heat. Fans would come to a standstill. Refrigerators would turn into stinking coffins for rotten food. Worst of all, no air conditioning would be available anywhere. The hospitals would be jammed to overflowing with victims of heat prostration.

Dear Student:

Our college, as you are well aware, has been going through a number of changes; and these developments, both in the registration system and the curriculum, will continue next year. In the end these improvements will only benefit you, but we know that many of you have been anxious about the exact nature of the changes. To answer your questions, we have arranged an open forum with Linda Peters, president of the college; Drake Stevens, the registrar; and Jerry Mash, vice-president of academic affairs. The meeting will be held in Johnston Hall, 2 p.m., March 23. Please come

;

with your questions; this is your opportunity to put your fears to rest.

Sincerely,

John X. Pelle

Dean of Students

Independent Clauses with Commas and a Coordinating Conjunction. Ordinarily, a comma is used to separate independent clauses joined by a coordinating conjunction. When one or more of the clauses have commas, however, a semicolon provides clearer separation.

The long, black limousine pulled up to the curb; and Jerry, shaking with excitement, watched the President alight from it.

The semicolon makes it easier to see the two main clauses.

CONNECTED DISCOURSE EXERCISE ■   Add and delete semicolons as appropriate in the following letter. You may have to substitute semicolons for commas.

Dear Student:

Our college, as you are well aware, has been going through a number of changes, and these developments, both in the registration system and the curriculum, will continue next year. In the end these improvements will only benefit you; but we know that many of you have been anxious about the exact nature of the changes. To answer your questions, we have arranged an open forum with Linda Peters, president of the college, Drake Stevens, the registrar, and Jerry Mash, vice-president of academic affairs. The meeting will be held in Johnston Hall; 2 p.m.; March 23. Please come with your questions, this is your opportunity to put your fears to rest.

Sincerely,

John X. Pelle
Dean of Students

1. I don't want the job; as a matter of fact, I'll turn it down if it's offered to me.
2. Worthington plays golf, tennis, and handball; collects china, Tiffany lamps, and art prints; and attends plays, concerts, and operas.

EXERCISE ■   Supply semicolons wherever they are necessary or desirable in the following sentences. You may have to substitute semicolons for commas. If a sentence is correct, write C.

1. I don't want the job, as a matter of fact, I'll turn it down if it's offered to me.
2. Worthington plays golf, tennis, and handball, collects china, Tiffany lamps, and art prints, and attends plays, concerts, and operas.

3. Victoria wanted a house that was large, well-constructed, and in an established neighborhood, and finally, after many months of looking, she found one that suited her perfectly.

4. The ship, battered by the furious storm, finally made port, and the sailors, exhausted by their dangerous ordeal, received permission to spend the weekend ashore.

5. The heat in this office is unbearable; therefore, I think I'll take the afternoon off.

6. So far I've been a very unlucky investor; all my stocks are now worth less than I paid for them.

7. Remove yourself from my presence posthaste, in other words, get lost immediately.

8. It's OK for you to be here, I crashed this party myself.

9. Mildred forgot to put a stamp on the letter, as a result, the Post Office returned it to her.

10. The photograph showed Donald McAndrews, president of the college, Barth James, the registrar, and Amelia Conklin, dean of women.

PERIODS, QUESTION MARKS, AND EXCLAMATION POINTS

Since periods, question marks, and exclamation points signal the ends of sentences, they are sometimes called *end marks*. In addition, periods and question marks function in several other ways.

Periods.   Periods (.) end sentences that state facts or opinions, give instructions, make requests that are not in the form of questions, and ask indirect questions—those that have been rephrased in the form of a statement.

Linda works as a hotel manager. (Sentence states fact.)

Dean Harris is a competent administrator. (Sentence states opinion.)

Clean off your lab bench before you leave. (Sentence gives instruction.)

Please move away from the door. (Sentence makes request.)

I wonder whether Ruthie will be at the theater tonight. (Sentence asks indirect question.)

Periods also follow common abbreviations as well as a person's initials.

Mr.	Sr.	P.M.
Mrs.	B.C.	a.s.a.p.
Ms.	A.D.	St.
Dr.	A.M.	Corp.

Mark Valentini, Jr., has consented to head the new commission on traffic safety.

Answer column (right):

3. Victoria wanted a house that was large, well-constructed, and in an established neighborhood; and finally, after many months of looking, she found one that suited her perfectly.

4. The ship, battered by the furious storm, finally made port; and the sailors, exhausted by their dangerous ordeal, received permission to spend the weekend ashore.

5. C.

6. C.

7. Remove yourself from my presence posthaste; in other words, get lost immediately.

8. It's OK for you to be here; I crashed this party myself.

9. Mildred forgot to put a stamp on the letter; as a result, the Post Office returned it to her.

10. The photograph showed Donald McAndrews, president of the college; Barth James, the registrar; and Amelia Conklin, dean of women.

PERSPECTIVE

In some ways, you have been teaching end marks throughout this Handbook. Whether you are helping students to identify sentences or to avoid comma splices, you need to refer to end marks. Although most college instructors would like to take these marks for granted, many students have problems with them. Inexperienced writers sometimes fail to use them. Why? Mina Shaughnessy has suggested that these writers see the period as ending a thought, something they don't like to do since it seems so hard for them to get started again. Furthermore, students usually don't construct sentences one at a time. Halfway through one sentence, they are already thinking of the next. As a result, they may link everything together with commas.

. ? !

Writers today often omit periods after abbreviations for the names of organizations or government agencies, as the following examples show.

ABC	FBI	IRS
ACLU	FHA	NAM
AFL-CIO	GM	USAF

An up-to-date college dictionary will indicate whether a certain abbreviation should be written without periods.

Periods also precede decimal fractions and separate numerals standing for dollars and cents.

0.81 percent	$5.29
3.79 percent	$0.88

Question Marks. A question mark (?) ends a whole or a partial sentence that asks a direct question (one that repeats the exact words of the person who asked it).

Do you know how to operate this movie projector? (whole sentence asking a direct question)

Has Cinderella scrubbed the floor? Swept the hearth? Washed the dishes? (sentence and sentence parts asking direct questions)

Dr. Baker—wasn't she your boss once?—has just received a promotion to sales manager. (interrupting element asking a direct question)

The minister inquired, "Don't you take this woman to be your lawful wedded wife?" (quotation asking a direct question)

A question mark in parentheses may be used to indicate uncertainty about some piece of information.

Winfield reached America in 1721 (?) and spent the rest of his life in Philadelphia.

Exclamation Points. Exclamation points (!) are used to express strong emotion or especially forceful commands.

Darcy! I never expected to see you again!

Sam! Turn that radio down immediately!

Help! Save me!

Use exclamation points sparingly; otherwise, they will quickly lose their force.

CONNECTED DISCOURSE EXERCISE ■ **Add, change, or remove end marks as necessary in the following passage.**

It was horrifying, the mob of screaming fans

grabbed Jack Slitherhips as he left the concert hall.

Soon all I could see were his arms reaching for help. But

it never came. Why do fans act this way. I am left
wondering whether they love or hate their idols? They
tore the clothes off Slitherips, they tore out patches
of his hair, someone even snatched his false teeth. Is
this any way to treat a fading rock star. Jack is now in
the hospital in a complete body cast; when I finally got
to see him, he mumbled that he was giving up show
business, he plans to settle down on a small farm. Who can
blame him?

or hate their idols. They tore the clothes off Slitherhips. They tore out patches of his hair. Someone even snatched his false teeth. Is this any way to treat a fading rock star? Jack is now in the hospital in a complete body cast. When I finally got to see him, he mumbled that he was giving up show business to settle down on a small farm. Who can blame him!

You might have students try several different methods of punctuating this passage, including some changes in sentence structure, to see the stylistic effect.

EXERCISE ■   Supply periods, question marks, or exclamation points wherever they are necessary. If a sentence is correct, write C.

1. Porterhouse steak costs $395 a pound this week.
2. What would you like for Christmas.
3. My brother asked me whether I wanted to go fishing.
4. Where would you like me to set this sack of groceries.
5. Please don't touch the exhibits.
6. For heaven's sake, stop making that darn noise.
7. Washington Square—it was once a burial ground for paupers—is a popular park in New York's Greenwich Village.
8. The play starts at 8 PM sharp, and latecomers will not be admitted until the end of the first act.
9. Last year the inflation rate was 350 percent, a very low figure indeed.
10. When you are in London, will you see Buckingham Palace Visit the Tower of London Shop at Harrod's department store.

EXERCISE ANSWERS

1. Porterhouse steak costs $3.95 a pound this week.
2. What would you like for Christmas?
3. C.
4. Where would you like me to set this sack of groceries?
5. C.

6. For heaven's sake, stop making that darn noise!
7. C.
8. The play starts at 8 P.M. sharp, and latecomers will not be admitted until the end of the first act.
9. Last year the inflation rate was 3.50 percent, a very low figure indeed.
10. When you are in London, will you see Buckingham Palace? Visit the Tower of London? Shop at Harrod's department store?

PERSPECTIVE

These punctuation marks allow students to experiment with new sentence structures. When you teach this section, encourage such experimentation.

COLONS, DASHES, PARENTHESES, AND BRACKETS

Colons, dashes, parentheses, and brackets separate and enclose, thereby clarifying relationships among the various parts of a sentence.

Colons.   Colons (:) introduce appositives, formal lists, and explanations following materials that could stand alone as a complete sentence.

His aim in life is grandiose: to corner the market in wheat. (appositive)

Three students have been selected to attend the conference: Lucille Perkins, Dan Blakely, and Frank Napolis. (list)

Three factors account for the financial problems of most farmers: (1) high interest rates, (2) falling land values, and (3) the strong dollar, which makes it difficult to sell crops abroad. (explanation)

The first of the following sentences is incorrect because the words preceding the colon can't stand alone as a sentence.

Faulty   The tools needed for this job include: a hacksaw, a file, and a drill.

Revision   The tools needed for this job include a hacksaw, a file, and a drill.

Colons are frequently used to introduce formal quotations that extend beyond a single sentence.

The speaker stepped to the lectern and said: "I am here to ask for your assistance. Today several African nations face a food crisis because drought has ruined their harvests. Unless we provide help quickly, thousands of people will die of starvation."

In such situations, the material preceding the quotation need not be a complete sentence.

Colons also separate hours from minutes (8:20 AM), salutations of business letters from the body of the letters (Dear Ms. Stanley:), titles of publications from subtitles (*The Careful Writer: A Guide to English Usage*), numbers indicating ratios (a 3:2:2 ratio), and chapter from verse in Biblical references (Luke 6:20–49).

Dashes.   Like colons, dashes (—) set off appositives, lists, and explanations but are used in less formal writing. A dash emphasizes the material it sets off.

Only one candidate showed up at the political rally—Jerry Manders. (appositive)

The closet held only three garments—an out-at-the-elbows sportscoat, a pair of blue jeans, and a tattered shirt. (list)

I know what little Billy's problem is—a soiled diaper. (explanation)

Dashes set off material that interrupts the flow of thought within a sentence.

Her new car—didn't she get it just three months ago?—has broken down twice.

Similarly, dashes are used to mark an interrupted segment of dialogue.

"I'd like to live in England when I retire."

"In England? But what will your wife—?"

"My wife likes the idea and can hardly wait for us to make the move."

Dashes set off parenthetical elements containing commas, and a dash can set off comments that follow a list.

> The comedian—short, fat, and squeaky-voiced—soon had everyone roaring with laughter. (parenthetical element with commas)

> A brag, a blow, a tank of air—that's what Senator Conwell is. (comment following a list)

Type a dash as two unspaced hyphens and leave no space between it and the words on either side of it.

Parentheses.   Parentheses ( ) are used to enclose numbers or letters that designate the items in a formal list and to set off incidental material within sentences. Except in the kind of list shown in the first example below, a comma does not usually precede a parenthesis.

> Each paper should contain (1) an introduction, (2) several paragraphs developing the thesis statement, and (3) a conclusion.

> Some occupations (computer programming, for example) may be overcrowded in ten years.

If the material in parentheses appears within a sentence, don't use a capital letter or period, even if the material is itself a complete sentence.

> The use of industrial robots (one cannot foresee their consequences) worries some people today.

If the material in parentheses is written as a separate sentence, however, then punctuate it as you would a separate sentence.

> Paula's angry outburst surprised everyone. (She had seemed such a placid person.)

If the material in parentheses comes at the end of a sentence, put the final punctuation after the closing parenthesis.

> This company was founded by Willard Manley (1876–1951).

In contrast to dashes, parentheses deemphasize the material they enclose.

Brackets.   In quoted material, brackets [ ] enclose words or phrases that have been added to make the message clearer. They are also used with the word *sic* (Latin for "thus") to point out errors in quoted material.

Combinations

They offer only one thing for breakfast—cold oatmeal.
It frequently takes students five years—wasn't it supposed to take four?—to earn a college diploma.
The movie star—beautiful, charming, and witty—had the politicians completely captivated.
He certainly made a spectacle of himself—blowing her kisses, waving his handkerchief, and yelling out her name.

PERSPECTIVE

Students are often confused about when to use parentheses, when commas, and when dashes. In some cases, the difference is really a matter of style; however, these punctuation marks do produce different effects. While commas tend to incorporate the set-off material into the sentence, parentheses tend to exclude it. Dashes, if anything, tend to draw attention to the material.

CLASSROOM ACTIVITY

Have students compare the following sets of punctuation to determine the different effects that they produce:

It frequently takes a college student five years, instead of four, to earn a diploma. It frequently takes a college student five years (instead of four) to earn a diploma. It frequently takes a college student five years—instead of four—to earn a diploma.

Mitch Data, our computer programmer, has trouble with basic math. Mitch Data (our computer programmer) has trouble with basic math. Mitch Data—our computer programmer—has trouble with basic math.

"This particular company [Zorn Enterprises, Inc.] pioneered in the safe disposal of toxic wastes," the report noted. (The bracketed name is added to the original.)

"[Carl Sagan's] expertise in science has made him a popular figure on the lecture circuit," his friend stated. (The bracketed name replaces *his* in the original.)

"The principle [sic] cause of lung cancer is cigarette smoking," the article declared. (The word *principal* is misspelled "principle" in the original.)

To call attention to an error, follow it immediately with the bracketed *sic*. The reader will then know that the blame rests with the original writer, not with you.

CONNECTED DISCOURSE EXERCISE ■   Supply any necessary or appropriate colons, dashes, parentheses, and brackets in the following letter.

Wayout Auto Company

We at Oldfield Sales a subsidiary of Jip, Inc., have had a serious problem with the cars we ordered from your company for leasing to our customers who will probably never return to us again. Two major parts fell off while the cars were sitting in the customers' driveways the exhaust system and the transmission. If this had happened while they were driving thank goodness it didn't, our customers could have been killed. Just imagine what that especially once it got into the newspapers would have done to our business. We must hold you to your claim that "while our cars are the cheapest sic on the market, we garnishee sic every car we sell." We expect immediate reimbursement for all the cars we purchased from you plus one million dollars to cover the damage to our reputation. A menace, a rip-off, a bad business deal, that's what your cars are. If you don't issue a formal recall for all your vehicles by 530 p.m., Friday, July 23,

EXERCISE ANSWER

There is more than one way to punctuate this passage.

Wayout Auto Company:

We at Oldfield Sales (a subsidiary of Jip, Inc.) have had a serious problem with the cars we ordered from your company for leasing to our customers--who will probably never return to us again. Two major parts fell off while cars were sitting in customers' driveways: the exhaust system and the transmission. If this had happened while they were driving (thank goodness it didn't), our customers could have been killed. Just imagine what that--especially once it got into the newspapers--would have done to our business. We must hold you to your claim that "while our cars are the cheepest [sic] on the market,

[ ]

we garnishee [sic] every car we sell." We expect immediate reimbursement for all the cars we purchased from you plus one million dollars to cover the damage to our reputation. A menace, a rip-off, a bad business deal--that's what your cars are. If you don't issue a formal recall for all your vehicles by 5:30 p.m., Friday, July 23, we will be forced to forward this matter to the federal government.

Sincerely,

Ken Swindelle
Service Manager

```
we will be forced to forward this matter to the federal

government.

                    Sincerely,


                    Ken Swindelle
                    Service Manager
```

EXERCISE ■ Supply colons, dashes, parentheses, and brackets wherever they are necessary.

1. The fire was reported at 235 AM.
2. Four pieces of equipment are required for downhill skiing 1 skis, 2 boots, 3 bindings, and 4 ski poles.
3. Lucy told Santa she wanted two things for Christmas a doll and a picture book.
4. The results of van Groot's investigation see Chapter 4 support earlier findings concerning the harmful effects of cocaine.
5. All that week Andreas had his mind on just one thing hitting the mountain trails for a weekend of backpacking.
6. The newspaper story noted that "Any rock star who captures the public's attention can expect to recieve sic several thousand fan letters each week."
7. The havoc wreaked by the hurricane two thousand people killed and five thousand buildings destroyed or damaged led the President to declare the city a disaster area.
8. To begin the experiment, combine water and glycerin in a 31 ratio.
9. Love, good health, an adequate income, a pleasant home what sensible person would trade them for wealth alone?
10. Remember this rule smoking is prohibited in the respiratory care unit.
11. Three corporals Nimms, Kravitz, and Steiner have been promoted to sergeant.
12. "His Senator William Proxmire's crusade against waste in the federal government has occupied him for many years," the columnist noted.

QUOTATION MARKS

Quotation marks (" ") set off direct quotations, titles of short pieces of writing, subdivisions of books, and expressions singled out for special attention.

Direct Quotations.   A direct quotation repeats a speaker's or writer's exact words.

EXERCISE ANSWERS

1. The fire was reported at 2:35 A.M.
2. Four pieces of equipment are required for downhill skiing: (1) skis, (2) boots, (3) bindings, and (4) ski poles.
3. Lucy told Santa she wanted two things for Christmas—a doll and a picture book. (Too informal for a colon)
4. The results of van Groot's investigation (see Chapter 4) support earlier findings concerning the harmful effects of cocaine.
5. All that week Andreas had his mind on just one thing—hitting the mountain trails for a weekend of backpacking. (Too informal for a colon)
6. The newspaper story noted that "Any rock star who captures the public's attention can expect to recieve [sic] several thousand fan letters each week."
7. The havoc wreaked by the hurricane—two thousand people killed and five thousand buildings destroyed or damaged—led the President to declare the city a disaster area.
8. To begin the experiment, combine water and glycerin in a 3:1 ratio.

9. Love, good health, an adequate income, a pleasant home—what sensible person would trade them for wealth alone?
10. Remember this rule: smoking is prohibited in the respiratory care unit.
11. Three corporals—Nimms, Kravitz, and Steiner—have been promoted to sergeant.
12. "His [Senator William Proxmire's] crusade against waste in the federal government has occupied him for many years," the columnist noted.

"Tell me about the movie," said Debbie. "If you liked it, I may go myself."

The placement director said, "The recruiter for Procter and Gamble will be on campus next Thursday to interview students for marketing jobs." (spoken comment)

"The U.S. trade deficit is expected to reach record levels this year," *The Wall Street Journal* noted. (written comment)

Jackie said the party was "a total flop."

As these sentences show, a comma or period that follows a direct quotation goes inside the quotation marks. When a quotation is a sentence fragment, the comma preceding it is omitted.

When an expression like "he said" interrupts a quoted sentence, use commas to set off the expression. When the expression comes between two complete quoted sentences, use a period after the expression and capitalize the first word of the second sentence.

"Hop in," said Jim. "I'll give you a ride to school."

"Thank you," replied Kelly, opening the car door and sliding into the front seat.

"I can't remember," said Jim, "when we've had a worse winter."

Titles of Short Works and Subdivisions of Books.   These short works include magazine articles, essays, short stories, chapters of books, one-act plays, short poems, songs, and television and radio programs.

The article was titled "The Real Conservatism." (article)

Last night I read John Cheever's "The Enormous Radio," "Torch Song," and "The Swimmer." (short stories)

Many John Denver fans consider "Take Me Home, Country Roads" to be his greatest piece of music. (song)

Here, as with direct quotations, a comma or period that follows a title goes outside the quotation marks.

Expressions Singled Out for Special Attention.   Writers who wish to call the reader's attention to a word or symbol sometimes put it within quotation marks.

The algebraic formula included a "π," a "θ," and a "Δ."

"Bonnets" and "lifts" are British terms for car hoods and elevators.

More frequently, however, these expressions are printed in italics (page 630).

Again, any commas and periods that follow expressions set off by quotation marks go inside the marks.

Quotation Marks Within Quotation Marks. When a direct quotation or the title of a shorter work appears within a direct quotation, use single quotation marks (' ').

> "I heard the boss telling the foreman, 'Everyone will receive a Christmas bonus,' John said."
>
> The instructor told the class, "For tomorrow, read Ernest Hemingway's 'The Killers.' "

Note that the period comes ahead of both the single and the double quotation marks.

Positioning of Semicolons, Colons, and Question Marks. Position semicolons and colons that come at the end of quoted material after, not before, the quotation marks.

> Marcia calls Francine "that greasy grind"; however, I think Marcia is simply jealous of Francine's abilities.
>
> There are two reasons why I like "Dallas": the plot is interesting, and the acting is good.

When a question mark accompanies a quotation, put it outside the quotation marks if the whole sentence rather than the quotation asks the question.

> Why did Cedric suddenly shout, "This party is a big bore"?

Put the question mark inside the quotation marks if the quotation, but not the whole sentence, asks a question or if the quotation asks one question and the whole sentence asks another.

> Marie asked, "What college is your brother planning to attend?" (The quoted material, not the whole sentence, asks the question.)
>
> Whatever possessed him to ask, "What is the most shameful thing you ever did?" (The whole sentence and the quoted material ask separate questions.)

CONNECTED DISCOURSE EXERCISE ■ Use quotation marks correctly in the following paragraph.

Mr. Silver recently lectured our class on Stephen Crane's The Bride Comes to Yellow Sky. One thing we shouldn't forget, Mr. Silver insisted, is that the town is deliberately named Yellow Sky. What is the significance of Crane's choice of the words Yellow Sky? Mr. Silver pointed out a number of possible associations,

EXERCISE ANSWER

Mr. Silver recently lectured our class on Stephen Crane's "The Bride Comes to Yellow Sky." "One thing we shouldn't forget," Mr. Silver insisted, "is that the town is deliberately named Yellow Sky." What is the significance of Crane's choice of the words "Yellow Sky"? Mr. Silver pointed out a number of possible associations, including coward-ice, the setting sun, the open expanse of the West, freedom, the sand in the concluding passage. "The story," Mr. Silver stated, "is drenched in color words." "For example," he pointed out, "in the first three paragraphs alone Crane mentions 'vast flats of green grass,' 'brick-colored hands,' 'new black clothes,' and 'a dress of blue cashmere.' "

EXERCISE ANSWERS

1. Elizabeth called the following "my favorite flowers": roses, peonies, and carnations.
2. What poem has the lines "And malt does more than Milton can/To justify God's ways to man"?
3. I have strong objections to such jargon expressions as "sibling rivalry," "meaningful relationships," and "parenting."
4. "Orlando," said the boss, "I'd like you to step into my office for a moment."
5. Hand me the dictionary; I want to look up "macerate."
6. What made the instructor say, "Whoever told you that you should major in chemistry?"
7. Herbert told his friends, "I care little for TV"; nevertheless, he owns two expensive sets.
8. Patrick said the party had been "one super bash."

9. Larry asked Sally, "Would you like to have dinner with me tonight?"
10. "This weather is terrible," sighed John. "I think I'll stay inside all day."
11. "Quit saying 'you know' so many times," the instructor told the student.
12. The word "fractious," according to *Webster's New World Dictionary*, means "hard to manage, unruly, rebellious."

PERSPECTIVE

While the rules for hyphenation might seem fairly simple, it takes practice to learn when to hyphenate. This is especially true of compound nouns, which are subject to historical change.

including cowardice, the setting sun, the open expanse of the West, freedom, the sand in the concluding passage. The story, Mr. Silver stated, is drenched in color words. For example, he pointed out, in the first three paragraphs alone Crane mentions vast flats of green grass, brick-colored hands, new black clothes, and a dress of blue cashmere.

EXERCISE ■ **Supply properly positioned quotation marks wherever they are necessary.**

1. Elizabeth called the following my favorite flowers: roses, peonies, and carnations.
2. What poem has the lines, And malt does more than Milton can/To justify God's ways to man?
3. I have strong objections to such jargon expressions as sibling rivalry, meaningful relationships, and parenting.
4. Orlando, said the boss, I'd like you to step into my office for a moment.
5. Hand me the dictionary; I want to look up macerate.
6. What made the instructor say, Whoever told you that you should major in chemistry?
7. Herbert told his friends, I care little for TV; nevertheless, he owns two expensive sets.
8. Patrick said the party had been one super bash.
9. Larry asked Sally, Would you like to have dinner with me tonight?
10. This weather is terrible, sighed John. I think I'll stay inside all day.
11. Quit saying you know so many times, the instructor told the student.
12. The word fractious, according to *Webster's New World Dictionary*, means hard to manage, unruly, rebellious.

HYPHENS

Hyphens(-) are used to join compound adjectives and nouns, compound numbers and word–number combinations, and certain prefixes and suffixes to the words with which they appear. In addition, hyphens help prevent misreadings and awkward combinations of letters or syllables.

Compound Adjectives and Nouns. Hyphens are often used to join separate words that function as single adjectives and come before nouns. Typical examples follow.

Howard is a very *self-contained* person.

The *greenish-yellow* cloud of chlorine gas drifted toward the village.

Betty's *devil-may-care* attitude will land her in trouble someday.

When the first word of the compound is an adverb ending in *-ly* or when the compound adjective follows the noun it modifies, no hyphen is used.

The *badly* burned crash victim was rushed to the hospital.

The color of the chlorine gas was *greenish yellow*.

When two or more compound adjectives modify the same last term, the sentence will flow more smoothly if that term appears just once, after the last item in the series. The hyphens accompanying the earlier items in the series are kept, however.

Many seventeenth-, eighteenth-, and nineteenth-century costumes are on display in this museum.

Hyphenated nouns include such expressions as the following:

secretary-treasurer   good-for-nothing
sister-in-law   man-about-town

Here is a sentence with hyphenated nouns.

Denton is *editor-in-chief* of the largest newspaper in this state.

Compound Numbers and Word—Number Combinations.   Hyphens are used to separate two-word numbers from twenty-one to ninety-nine and fractions that have been written out.

Marcy has worked *twenty-one* years for this company.

One-fourth of my income goes for rent.

Similarly, hyphens are used to separate numerals from units of measurement that follow them.

This chemical is shipped in *50-gallon* drums.

Prefixes and Suffixes.   A prefix is a word or set of letters that precedes a word and alters its meaning. A suffix is similar but comes at the end of the word. Although most prefixes are not hyphenated, the prefixes *self-* and *all-* do get hyphens, as does the suffix *-elect* and the prefix *ex-* when it accompanies a noun.

This stove has a *self-cleaning* oven.

Let Claire Voyant, the *all-knowing* soothsayer, read your future in her crystal ball.

Encourage students to check a dictionary when they are unsure whether a hyphen is needed. Don't expect students to become adept at using hyphens overnight.

Ethel is the *chairperson-elect* of the club.

Several *ex-teachers* work in this department.

A prefix used before a capitalized term is always hyphenated.

The *ex-FBI* agent gave an interesting talk on the operations of that agency.

Preventing Misreadings and Awkward Combinations of Letters and Syllables.

Hyphens help prevent misreadings of certain words and also break up awkward combinations of letters and syllables between certain prefixes and suffixes and their core words.

The doctor *re-treated* the wound with a new antibiotic. (The hyphen prevents the misreading *retreated*.)

The company plans to *de-emphasize* sales of agricultural chemicals. (The hyphen prevents the awkward repetition of the letter *e* in *deemphasize*.)

Between Syllables.

Whenever you have to split a word between two lines, place a hyphen at the end of the first line to show the division. The word is always broken, and the hyphen inserted, between syllables. (Any good dictionary shows the syllable divisions of each word it includes.) Never divide a one-syllable word or leave two letters to be placed on the second line, even if those two letters constitute a syllable.

EXERCISE ■ **Supply hyphens wherever they are necessary. If the sentence is correct, write C.**

1. The signal had a deep, belllike tone.
2. The hostess said there would be a ten to twenty minute wait before we could be seated for dinner.
3. About three fourths of the students who begin our electrical engineering program complete it.
4. Silvano Columbo is the presidentelect of our fraternity.
5. The antidemocratic measures of the new regime soon led to its overthrow.
6. The canary yellow walls of the room provided a sharp contrast to the dark green of the curtains.
7. I plan to take a 60 day cruise to the Far East this summer.
8. At the age of twenty nine, I became a father for the first time.
9. The upholsterer recovered the Victorian sofa in sky blue plush.
10. Many selfemployed people make no financial preparations for their retirement.
11. Mr. Perez is an exstockbroker.
12. Langley has always been a ne'er do well.

CAPITALIZATION

Capitalize the first word in any sentence, the pronoun *I*, proper nouns and adjectives, titles used with—or in place of—names, and the significant words in literary and artistic titles.

Proper Nouns. A proper noun names one particular person, group of persons, place, or thing. Such nouns include names of the following:

Persons
Organizations
Racial, political, and religious groups
Countries, states, cities, and streets
Companies and buildings
Geographical locations and features
Days, months, and holidays
Trademarks
Languages
Ships and aircraft
Names of academic degrees and the abbreviations for them
Sacred writings and pronouns standing for God and Jesus
Titles used in place of names

The sentences below show the capitalization of proper nouns.

Sigmund works for the *National Psychoanalytical Institute*, an organization which has done much to advance the science of psychiatry.

How much does this roll of *Saran Wrap* cost?

Gwen Greene moved to *Paris, France,* when her father became the consul there.

On *Friday, October* 13, 1989, *George Bush* visited our city.

Larry has a *Master of Arts* degree, and his sister has a *Ph.D.*

My father works for the *Ford Motor Company,* but I work for *Chrysler.*

Do not capitalize words like *institute, college, company, or avenue* unless they form part of a proper name. Likewise, do not capitalize the names of non-language courses unless they start a sentence or are accompanied by a course number.

I have a 95 average in *English* 112 but only a 73 average in sociology.

Do you plan to attend *Drew College* or some other college?

Proper Adjectives. Adjectives created from proper nouns are called proper adjectives. Like the nouns themselves, they should be capitalized.

cap

Lolita Martinez, our class valedictorian, is of *Mexican* ancestry. (*Mexican* is derived from the proper noun *Mexico.*)

Abbreviations.   As a general rule, capitalize abbreviations only if the words they stand for are capitalized.

Milton DeWitt works for the *IRS*. (*IRS* is capitalized because "Internal Revenue Service" would be.)

The flask holds 1,500 *cc* of liquid. (The abbreviation *cc* is not capitalized because "cubic centimeters" would not be.)

A few abbreviations are capitalized even though all or some of the words they stand for aren't. Examples include TV (television) and VCR (video cassette recorder). Others are shown on page 626.

Personal titles.   Capitalize a personal title if it precedes a name or is used in place of a name. Otherwise, do not capitalize.

The division is under the command of *General* Arnold Schafer.

Tell me, *Doctor,* do I need an operation?

The *dean* of our Engineering Division is Dr. Alma Haskins.

Many writers capitalize titles of high rank when they are used in place of names.

The *President* will sign this bill tomorrow.

The *president* will sign this bill tomorrow.

Either usage is acceptable.

Titles of Literary and Artistic Works.   When citing the title of publications, pieces of writing, movies, television programs, paintings, sculptures, and the like, capitalize the first and last words and all other words except *a, an, the,* coordinating conjunctions, and one-syllable prepositions.

Last week I played *Gone with the Wind* on my VCR and read Christopher Isherwood's *Goodbye to Berlin*. (The preposition *with*, the article *the*, and the preposition *to* are not capitalized.)

John is reading a book called *The Movies of Abbott and Costello*. (The preposition *of* and the coordinating conjunction *and* are not capitalized.)

My favorite TV show is "Murder, She Wrote." (All the words in the title are capitalized.)

cap

Note that the titles of literary and artistic works are italicized and that the titles of TV programs are set off by quotation marks.

EXERCISE ■ Identify any word or abbreviation that should be capitalized in the following sentences.

1. Jennifer works for the federal housing administration (fha).
2. Let's ask professor Jablonski about this problem.
3. It looks as if the dispute between clarkson university and the nea will have to go to arbitration.
4. The edwardian period of english history (1901–1910) takes its name from king Edward VII, the son of queen Victoria.
5. Tell me, senator, how you'd go about cutting the federal deficit.
6. What is the price of this swingline stapler?
7. When I took english 321, I did my term paper on robert browning's poem *the ring and the book.*
8. The article "japanese and american industry: a comparison" appeared in *the wall street journal.*
9. The present governor of our state is governor helen markus.
10. The brandt corporation has just announced a two-for-one stock split.

ABBREVIATIONS

Items that are abbreviated include certain personal titles, names of organizations and agencies, Latin terms, and scientific and technical terms.

Personal Titles. Abbreviate *Mister, Doctor,* and similar titles when they come just ahead of a name, and *Junior, Senior,* and degree titles when they follow names.

Will *Mr.* Harry Babbitt please come to the front desk?

Arthur Compton, *Sr.,* is a well-known historian; his son, Arthur Compton, *Jr.,* is a television producer.

This article on marital discord was written by Irma Quarles, *Ph.D.*

Names of Organizations and Agencies. Many organizations and agencies are known primarily by their initials rather than their full names. Several examples follow.

AAA	FBI	NBC
CARE	FHA	NATO
CIA	IBM	UNESCO

EXERCISE ANSWERS

1. Jennifer works for the Federal Housing Administration (FHA).
2. Let's ask Professor Jablonski about this problem.
3. It looks as if the dispute between Clarkson University and the NEA will have to go to arbitration.
4. The Edwardian period of English history (1901–1910) takes its name from King Edward VII, the son of Queen Victoria.
5. Tell me, Senator, how you'd go about cutting the federal deficit.
6. What is the price of this Swingline stapler?
7. When I took English 321, I did my term paper on Robert Browning's poem *The Ring and the Book.*
8. The article "Japanese and American Industry: A Comparison" appeared in the *Wall Street Journal.*
9. The present governor of our state is Governor Helen Markus.
10. The Brandt Corporation has just announced a two-for-one stock split.

Latin Terms. Certain Latin terms are always abbreviated; others are abbreviated when used with dates or times.

> e.g. (*exempli gratia:* for example)
> i.e. (*id est:* that is)
> etc. (*et cetera:* and [the] others)
> vs. (*versus:* against)
> A.D. (*anno Domini*: in the year of our Lord)
> A.M. or a.m. (*ante meridiem*: before noon)
> P.M. or p.m. (*post meridiem*: after noon)

The play starts at 8 *P.M.*

Many writers (*e.g.,* Dylan Thomas and Truman Capote) have had serious problems with alcohol.

For consistency with A.D., the term "before Christ" is abbreviated as B.C.

Scientific and Technical Terms. For brevity's sake, scientists and technicians abbreviate terms of measurement that repeatedly occur. Terms that the reader would not know are written out the first time they are used, and they are accompanied by their abbreviation in parentheses. Unfamiliar organizations and agencies that are mentioned repeatedly are handled in like manner.

The viscosity of the fluid measured 15 centistokes (cks) at room temperature.

Common practice calls for writing such abbreviations without periods unless they duplicate the spelling of some word.

Standard dictionaries list common abbreviations. When you don't recognize one, look it up. Use abbreviations sparingly in essays. If you're unsure about what is appropriate, don't abbreviate.

EXERCISE ■ **Supply abbreviations wherever they are necessary or are customarily used.**

1. The train is scheduled to pull out at 2:35 *post meridiem*.
2. If you'll remove your shirt, Mister Franklin, I'll check your heart and lungs.
3. The Central Intelligence Agency and the Federal Bureau of Investigation will be getting larger budgets during the next fiscal year.
4. The experiment requires a 500-milliliter flask.
5. My stock in International Business Machines has jumped nine points in the last two days.
6. Doctor Pierre Coeur, Junior, will do the heart transplant.
7. Water freezes at 32° Fahrenheit and 0° Celsius.
8. The Food and Drug Administration is expected to approve a new artificial sweetener soon.
9. Jeremy didn't realize that *exempli gratia* means "for example."
10. The book is coauthored by Sally Westfall, Master of Science, and Amy Gonson, Doctor of Philosophy.

EXERCISE ANSWERS

1. The train in scheduled to pull out at 2:35 P.M.
2. If you'll remove your shirt, Mr. Franklin, I'll check your heart and lungs.

3. The CIA and the FBI will be getting larger budgets during the next fiscal year.
4. The experiment requires a 500-ml flask.
5. My stock in IBM has jumped nine points in the last two days.
6. Dr. Pierre Coeur, Jr., will do the heart transplant.
7. Water freezes at 32°F and 0° C.
8. The FDA is expected to approve a new artificial sweetener soon.
9. Jeremy didn't realize that *e.g.* means "for example."
10. The book is coauthored by Sally Westfall, M.S., and Amy Gonson, Ph.D.

NUMBERS

Some instructors ask their students to use figures for numbers larger than ninety-nine and to spell out smaller numbers.

Boise is *100* miles from here.

Boise is *ninety-nine* miles from here.

Other instructors prefer that students switch to figures beginning with the number ten.

My son will be *nine* years old on his next birthday.

My son will be *10* years old on his next birthday.

With either practice, the following exceptions apply.

Numbers in a Series.   Write all numbers in a series the same way regardless of their size.

Gatsby has *64* suits, *110* shirts, and *214* ties.

In just one hour the emergency room personnel handled *two* stabbings, *five* shootings, and *sixteen* fractures.

We have *150* salespeople, *51* engineers, and *7* laboratory technicians.

Dates.   Use figures for dates that include the year.

February 14, 1985 (not February 14th, 1985)

When the date includes the day but not the year, you may use figures or spell out the number.

June 9
June ninth
the ninth of June

Page Numbers and Addresses.   Use figures for page numbers and street numbers in addresses.

Check the graph on page *415*.

I live at *111* Cornelia Street, and my office is at *620* Fifth Avenue.

num

Numbers Beginning Sentences. Spell out any number that begins a sentence. If this requires three or more words, rephrase the sentence so that the number comes after the opening and numerals can be used.

The year *1980* was a good one for this wine.

Sixty thousand fans jammed the stadium.

An army of *265,000* troops assaulted the city. (If this number began the sentence, five words—an excessive number—would be needed to write it out.)

Decimals, Percentages, Times. Use figures for decimals and percentages as well as for expressions of time that are accompanied by A.M. or P.M.

The shaft is *0.37*-inch in diameter.

Last year the value of my house jumped *25* percent.

The plane leaves here at *9:50* A.M. and reaches New Orleans at *2:30* P.M.

One Number Following Another. When one number comes immediately after another, spell out the first number, if smaller than 100, and use numerals for the second one. If the first number is larger than 100, use numerals for it and spell out the second one.

We ordered *six 30*-gallon drums of solvent for the project.

The supplier shipped us *600 thirty*-gallon drums by mistake.

As noted earlier, this rule does not apply to dates that include the year.

num

EXERCISE ■ **Identify any miswriting of numbers in the following sentences and rewrite these numbers correctly.**

1. During the last two years, Frank has worked 8 months as a checkout clerk in a supermarket, 5 months as a busboy, and six months as a plumber's helper.
2. The *Small Publishers' Directory*, page seventeen, lists the address of the Phoenix Publishing Company as two hundred twenty-three Fuego Street, Phoenix, Arizona.
3. On June twenty-nine, 1971, I began work for the General Tool and Die Company.
4. The movie begins at eight P.M. on channel 13.
5. For tomorrow, do the exercise on page nineteen of your text.
6. My newest IRA account is earning eight and one half percent interest.
7. On November eleven, 1918, at eleven A.M., the guns fell silent, and World War I came to an end.
8. The outer wall should have a thickness of seventy-five hundredths inch.
9. 500 of our employees face indefinite layoffs within the next month.
10. Nineteen eighty-five did not go at all well for me.

ITALICS

Italics are used for the titles of longer publications, the names of vehicles and vessels, foreign words and phrases, and expressions singled out for special attention. When writing or typing papers, use underlining to represent italics.

Titles of Longer Publications and Artistic Works.   These items may include the following:

books	record albums	long musical works and poems
magazines	paintings	plays
newspapers	movies	sculptures

As noted on page 618, quotation marks are used for the titles of articles, short stories, short poems, one-act plays, and other brief pieces of writing.

Last night I finished F. Scott Fitzgerald's *The Great Gatsby* and read two articles in *The New Yorker.* (book, magazine)

Michelangelo's *David* is surely one of the world's greatest sculptures. (sculpture)

The *Detroit Free Press* had praise for the revival of Tennessee Williams's play *The Glass Menagerie.* (newspaper, play)

Stephen Vincent Benét's poem *John Brown's Body* won a Pulitzer Prize in 1929. (book-length poem)

Do not use italics when naming the Bible or its parts.

Joanna's favorite book of the Bible is the Book of Ecclesiastes, part of the Old Testament.

Names of Vehicles and Vessels.   Names of particular airplanes, ships, trains, and spacecraft are italicized.

The plane in which Charles Lindbergh flew over the Atlantic Ocean was named *The Spirit of St. Louis.*

Foreign Expressions.   Use italics to identify foreign words and phrases that have not yet made their way into the English language.

The writer has a terribly pessimistic *weltanschauung.* (philosophy of life)

This season, long skirts are the *dernier cri.* (the latest thing)

ital

When such expressions become completely assimilated, the italics are dropped. Most dictionaries use an asterisk (*), a dagger (†), or other symbol to identify expressions that need italicizing.

Expressions Singled Out for Special Attention.   These include words, letters, numerals, and symbols.

The Greek letter *pi* is written II.

I can't tell whether this letter is meant to be an *a* or an *o* or this number a *7* or a *9*.

In England, the word *lorry* means truck.

As noted on page 618, quotation marks sometimes replace italics for this purpose.

CONNECTED DISCOURSE EXERCISE ■ **Use hyphens, capitalization, abbreviations, numbers, and italics properly in the following passage.**

Because I can speak russian fluently, I was recruited by the central intelligence agency while still at Boston college. I suspected that it was professor Hogsbottom, a Political Science teacher, who had suggested that they consider me. After all, he had been a General during World War Two and still had connections with the intelligence community. It turned out that my brother in law was responsible; he was an ex FBI agent. Soon I was an american spy located, of all places, in England. Who would suspect that we had to spy on the english? For 3 years I posed as a british aristocrat who was a general bon vivant and man about town. I went by the alias of Mister Henry Higgins, Junior. Everyone, of course, wanted to know if I had seen My Fair Lady. Personally I thought the whole thing was a monty python style joke until I found a position in the british secret service. Who could have believed the british kept so many secrets from their american allies? For twenty one years

ital

EXERCISE ANSWER

Because I can speak Russian fluently, I was recruited by the CIA while still at Boston College. I suspected that it was Professor Hogsbottom, a political science teacher, who had suggested that they consider me. After all, he had been a general during World War II and still had connections with the intelligence community. It turned out that my brother-in-law was responsible; he was an ex-FBI agent. Soon I was an American spy located, of all places, in England. Who would suspect that we had to spy on the English? For three years I posed as a British aristocrat who

I spied on the british without anyone suspecting that I was an all american boy. I did find out recently, however, that because of my fluent russian they had suspected me of being a russian spy and had been feeding me false information all along.

EXERCISE ■   **Supply italics wherever they are necessary.**

1. His carpe diem philosophy led him to make no financial provision for his future.
2. I subscribe to two publications: the Chicago Tribune and Business Week.
3. When John leaves London for Venice, he'll travel on a famous train, the Orient Express.
4. Yesterday, Althea bought a copy of Miro's painting Fishes.
5. The column As I See Things is the most popular feature of this newspaper.
6. Is this letter supposed to be a q or a g?
7. Tonight, I plan to play a tape of High Noon, my favorite Gary Cooper movie.
8. In a sudden coup d'etat, the army seized control of Gorgistan and ousted the president.
9. When you're at the library, will you please check out a copy of Pride and Prejudice for me?
10. The ship Tropic Seafarer offers several different Caribbean cruises each winter.

was a general *bon vivant* and man-about-town. I went by the alias of Mr. Henry Higgins, Jr. Everyone, of course, wanted to know if I had seen *My Fair Lady.* Personally I thought the whole thing was a Monty-Python-style joke until I found a position in the British secret service. Who could have believed the British kept so many secrets from their American allies? For twenty-one years I spied on the British without anyone suspecting that I was an all-American boy. I did find out recently, however, that because of my fluent Russian they had suspected me of being a Russian spy and had been feeding me false information all along.

EXERCISE ANSWERS

1. His *carpe diem* philosophy led him to make no financial provision for his future.
2. I subscribe to two publications: the *Chicago Tribune* and *Business Week.*
3. When John leaves London for Venice, he'll travel on a famous train, the *Orient Express.*
4. Yesterday, Althea bought a copy of Miro's painting *Fishes.*
5. The column *As I See Things* is the most popular feature of this newspaper.

ital

6. Is this letter supposed to be a *q* or a *g*?
7. Tonight, I plan to play a tape of *High Noon*, my favorite Gary Cooper movie.
8. In a sudden *coup d'etat*, the army seized control of Gorgistan and ousted the president.
9. When you're at the library, will you please check out a copy of *Pride and Prejudice* for me?
10. The ship *Tropic Seafarer* offers several different Caribbean cruises each winter.

1. Some students rarely commit spelling errors, while others misspell the most common words. It is essential to teach weaker spellers how they can improve. One way to help them is to make them responsible for their misspelled words, for example, by deducting points for errors. To regain the lost points, a student should have to turn in a sheet listing each misspelled word, its correct spelling, the likely reason for the misspelling, and some kind of mnemonic device to help him or her remember the correct spelling. The student should also be held responsible for spelling the word correctly in the future.

2. It is helpful to observe the pattern of a weak speller's errors. Once you begin to grasp the pattern, you can be more effective in helping. Here are some common kinds of errors: (a) Errors of haste. Dropped letters or strange letter substitutions are often the mark of a writer in such a hurry that proofreading has been haphazard. In this case, the best cure is simply to insist on better proofreading. (b) Confusion resulting from the unpredictability of the sound–letter relationship. Some students have learned phonics too well and attempt to spell words as they sound. When they do, the same letter group may be represented differently in the same paper. For example, the words "though," "through," and "tough" may be written as "tho," "throo," and "tuff." In such cases, students need to be familiarized with the morphological features of English so that they can understand the "meaningful" regularities among words. (c) Misspellings resulting from poor pronunciation. Students

"Dear Mom, Wud you belive I lost my job at the offise today? I gess sumwun thair doesnt like me."

From *Recess Time*, The Best Cartoons from *The Kappan*, edited by Kristin Herzog, 1983.

Spelling

"Why the big deal about accurate spelling?"
"Does it really make that much difference if I have an *i* and an *e* turned around or if I omit a letter when spelling a word?"

Students frequently question the importance of proper spelling. Perhaps the answer is suggested by the following sentence, taken from a student essay:

I spent over seven hours *studing* one day last week.

The omission of a *y* in *studing* changes the person from one who is studious to one who is a dreamer. Not only does inaccurate spelling smack of carelessness, but also it sometimes drastically alters meaning.

sp

Although there is no sure-fire way of becoming a good speller, you can minimize the difficulties by learning basic spelling rules, applying helpful spelling tips, and memorizing the proper spelling of troublesome words.

SPELLING RULES

The following four rules should ease spelling pains.

Rule 1.   If a word has the double vowels[1] *ie* or *ei* and the combination has a long *e* sound (as in *me*), use *ie* except after *c*. If the combination has an *a* sound, use *ei*.

ie (*as long* e)	ei *after* c	ei *as* a
achieve	deceive	freight
belief	receive	neighbor
grieve	receipt	reign
piece	perceive	weigh

The main exceptions to this rule include *either, financier, leisure, neither, seize, species,* and *weird.*

Rule 2.   If a one-syllable word (example: *sin*) ends in a single consonant preceded by a single vowel, double the consonant before adding a suffix (see page 621) that starts with a vowel. Apply the same rule with a word of two or more syllables (example: *admit*) if the final syllable is accented and ends with a single consonant preceded by a vowel.

Words with Single Syllables	*Words with Two or More Syllables*
rig — rigged	admit — admittance
sin — sinned	control — controller
stop — stopping	equip — equipped

If the accent does not fall on the last syllable, do not double the final consonant.

audit — audited	chatter — chattered
counsel — counselor	simmer — simmering

Rule 3.   If a word ends in *y* preceded by a single consonant, change the *y* to an *i* unless you are adding the suffix *-ing.*

y *changed to* i	y *retained*
beauty — beautiful	busy — busying
busy — business	defy — defying
easy — easily	dry — drying
vary — various	vary — varying

---

[1]The vowels are *a, e, i, o,* and *u*. The consonants are the remaining letters of the alphabet.

who say "bafroom" may not hear the "th" in "bathroom." If you see errors of this sort, help students by teaching them the right pronunciation. (d) Confusion of homophones. Some students consistently confuse words like "know" and "no." When this is the source of the misspelling, bring the homophones to the student's attention. (e) Difficulty in seeing the structure of words. Some students blur syllables or even omit some. As a result, "parallel" becomes "parall." Such students must first learn how to sound out the word, then how to break it into its syllables. (f) Poor visual memory. Some students are poor readers and have little visual memory. Have such students copy the correctly spelled word in different colored ink, break it into its key parts, and compare the copy to the original. Some students even benefit from writing a word in the air with their hands while they say it.

3.   Mina Shaughnessy's book *Errors and Expectations* has such important suggestions about approaching extremely weak spellers that they are worth repeating here. (a) "Assume at the outset that the misspellings of young adults can be brought under control" (175). (b) "Begin by teaching the student to observe himself as a speller" (175). (c) "Before attempting to work on individual errors, make certain the student understands certain terms and operations" (177). (d) "If possible start to work on misspellings that can be controlled by the application of rules" (177). (e) "Develop an awareness of the main discrepancies between the student's pronunciation of words and the models of pronunciation upon which the spelling system is

sp

based" (179). (f) "Develop an awareness of the ways in which pronunciation helps the speller" (179). (g) "Develop the student's ability to discriminate among graphemic options" (181). (h) "Teach the use of the dictionary" (185).

4. The term "dyslexia" should be reserved for a very specific neurological condition that causes students to have problems processing what they hear and see. Usually a student with dyslexia will show pronounced reversals of letters or even confuse letters like *d*'s and *b*'s. Some students will wrongly identify themselves as dyslexic to explain their spelling problems. When a student seems to have excessive problems mastering spelling and you suspect a learning difficulty, refer him or her to your school's testing service or office of student developmental services. Even students with mild dyslexia can be helped. A student's learning disability should not be a call to surrender but rather a challenge to be overcome.

Rule 4.   If a word ends in a silent *e*, the *e* is usually dropped when a suffix starting with a vowel is added.

blue — bluish   fame — famous
dense — density   grieve — grievous

In a few cases, the *e* is retained to avoid pronunciation difficulties or confusion with other words.

dye — dyeing (not dying)   singe — singeing (not singing)
shoe — shoeing (not shoing)

The *e* is also retained when it is preceded by a soft *c* sound (pronounced like the letter *s*) or a soft *g* sound (pronounced like the letter *j*) and the suffix being added starts with an *a* or an *o*.

peace — peaceable   courage — courageous
change — changeable   manage — manageable

HELPFUL SPELLING TIPS

Here are some tips that can further improve your spelling.

1. Examine each problem word carefully, especially prefixes (*au*dience, *au*dible), suffixes (superintend*ent*, descend*ant*), and double consonants (sate*ll*ite, roo*mm*ate, and co*ll*apsible).
2. Sound out each syllable carefully, noting its pronunciation. Words like *height*, *governor*, and *candidate* are often misspelled because of improper pronunciation.
3. Make a list of your problem words and review them periodically. Concentrate on each syllable and any unusual features (arctic, ambig*uous*).
4. Use any crutches that will help: there is *gain* in *bargain*; to *breakfast* is to *break a fast*; a disease causes *dis-ease*).
5. When you copy anything from the blackboard or a textbook, copy it carefully. Writing a word correctly helps you to spell it correctly the next time.
6. Buy a good collegiate dictionary and look up the words you don't know how to spell. (See pages 236–238 for more information on dictionaries.)

LIST OF TROUBLESOME WORDS

sp

Students frequently misspell the words in the following list. Study these words carefully until the correct spelling becomes automatic. Then have a friend read them to you while you write them down. Tag the ones you misspell and whenever you revise a paper check especially for these words.

abbreviate
absence
absorb
absorption
absurd
academy
accelerate
accept
access
accessible
accident
accidentally
accommodate
accomplish
accumulate
accustom
achieve
achievement
acknowledge
acknowledgment
acquaintance
acquire
acquit
acquitted
address
advice
advise
aerial
aggravate
aggravated
aggression
aggressive
aging
alcohol
allege
alleviate
alley(s)
allot
allotted
allowed
all right
already
although
altogether
always
amateur

ambiguous
among
analysis (analyses)
analyze
anonymous
anxiety
apartment
apparent
appearance
appreciate
appropriate
architecture
arctic
argue
arguing
argument
arithmetic
ascent
assassin
assent
assistance
assistant
athlete
athletics
attempt
attendance
average
bachelor
balance
balloon
barbarous
barbiturate
beautiful
beggar
believe
beneficial
benefit
benefited
biscuit
boundary
bourgeois
breathe
Britain
bulletin
bureau
bureaucracy

business
cafeteria
calendar
camouflage
campaign
candidate
carburetor
carriage
carrying
casual
category
causal
ceiling
cellar
cemetery
changeable
changing
characteristic
chauffeur
chief
colloquial
colonel
column
commission
commit
commitment
committed
committee
committing
comparatively
competent
competition
concede
conceive
condemn
condescend
confident
connoisseur
conqueror
conscience
conscientious
conscious
consistency
consistent
conspicuous
contemptible

continuous
controversy
convenience
convenient
coolly
cooperate
corollary
corps
corpse
correlate
counterfeit
courteous
criticism
criticize
cruelty
curiosity
curriculum
dealt
deceit
deceive
decent
decision
defendant
defense
definite
definitely
dependent
descent
describe
description
desert
desirable
despair
desperate
dessert
develop
development
difference
dilemma
disappear
disastrous
discernible
disciple
discipline
discussion
disease

sp

sp

dissatisfied	forward	knowledge	occur
dissipate	friend	knowledgeable	occurred
dominant	fulfill	laboratory	occurrence
drunkenness	gaiety	legitimate	occurring
echoes	gases	leisure	official
ecstasy	gauge	library	omission
efficiency	genius	license	omit
efficient	genuine	lightning	omitted
eighth	government	loneliness	omitting
eligible	grammar	loose	opinion
eliminate	guarantee	lose	opponent
embarrass	guard	magnificent	opportunity
emphasis	handkerchief	maintain	optimistic
employee	harass	maintenance	original
engineer	height	maneuver	outrageous
enthusiastic	heroes	manual	pamphlet
environment	hindrance	marriage	parallel
equal	hygiene	mathematics	paralysis
equip	hypocrisy	mattress	parliament
equipment	hysterical	meant	particularly
equipped	illiterate	medicine	pastime
equivalent	illogical	medieval	patent
especially	illusion	mediocre	peaceable
exaggerate	immediate	melancholy	perceive
exceed	implement	miniature	perfectible
excellent	impromptu	minute	perform
except	inadequate	miscellaneous	permanent
excerpt	incident	mischievous	permissible
excess	incidentally	misspell	perseverance
excitement	independent	modifies	persuade
exercise	indict	modify	physical
existence	indispensable	modifying	physician
experience	individual	moral	picnic
extraordinary	inevitable	morale	picnicked
extremely	infinitely	mortgage	playwright
fallacy	ingenious	mosquitoes	pleasant
familiar	ingenuous	muscle	pleasurable
fascinate	innocent	mysterious	politician
fascist	intelligent	necessary	possess
February	interest	neither	possession
fiery	interfere	nevertheless	possible
finally	irresistible	niece	potatoes
financier	irresponsible	noticeable	practice
foreign	jeopardy	obedience	precede
foreword	judgment	occasion	precedent
forfeit	judicial	occasionally	precious

predominant	reminiscence	statistics	twelfth
preference	reminiscent	steely	typical
preferred	rendezvous	strategy	tyrannical
prejudice	repellent	studying	tyranny
preparation	repentance	subtle	unanimous
privilege	repetition	subtlety	unconscious
probably	representative	subtly	undoubtedly
procedure	resemblance	succeed	unmistakable
proceed	resistance	success	unnecessary
professor	restaurant	successful	until
prominent	rhetoric	succinct	unwieldy
pronounce	rhyme	suffrage	urban
pronunciation	rhythm	superintendent	urbane
propaganda	roommate	supersede	usage
propagate	sacrifice	suppose	useful
propeller	sacrilege	suppress	using
prophecy	sacrilegious	surprise	usual
prophesy	safety	syllable	usually
prostate	salary	symmetry	vacancy
prostrate	sandwich	sympathize	vacillate
protein	scarcely	synonym	vacuum
psychiatry	scene	synonymous	valuable
psychology	scenic	tangible	vegetable
pursue	schedule	tariff	vengeance
pursuit	science	technical	victorious
quantity	secretary	technique	village
questionnaire	seize	temperament	villain
quiet	sensible	temperature	waive
quite	separate	temporary	warrant
quiz	sergeant	tenant	warring
quizzes	severely	tendency	weather
realize	siege	thorough	Wednesday
receipt	similar	thought	weird
receive	simultaneous	through	whether
recipe	sincerely	traffic	whole
recognizable	skeptical	trafficking	wholly
recommend	skiing	tragedy	wield
refer	skillful	tranquillity	wintry
reference	skis	transcendent	wiry
referring	society	transcendental	worshiped or
reign	sophomore	transfer	worshipped
relevant	source	transferred	wreak
relieve	specifically	transferring	wreck
religious	specimen	translate	writing
remembrance	sponsor	tries	written
reminisce	spontaneous	truly	yield

sp

Glossary of Word Usage

The English language has many words and expressions that confuse writers and thereby lessen the precision and effectiveness of their writing. These troublesome items include the following:

Word pairs that sound alike or almost alike but are spelled differently and have different meanings

Word pairs that do not sound alike but still are often confused

Words or phrases that are unacceptable in formal writing

The following glossary identifies the most common of these troublemakers. Familiarize yourself with its contents. Then consult it as you revise your writing if you have even the slightest doubt about the proper use of a word, phrase, or expression.

a, an   Use *a* with words beginning with a consonant sound (even if the first written letter is a vowel); use *an* with words beginning with a vowel or a vowel sound.

a brush, *a* student, *a* wheel, *a* risky situation, *a* once-in-a-lifetime opportunity

an architect, *an* apple, *an* unworthy participant, *an* interesting proposal, *an* honest politician

accept, except   *Accept* is a verb meaning "to receive" or "to approve." *Except* is used as a verb or a preposition. As a verb, *except* means "to take out, exclude, or omit." As a preposition, it means "excluding," "other than," or "but not."

She *accepted* the bouquet of flowers.

Linda *excepted* Sally from the list of guests. (verb)

All of Linda's friends *except* Sally came to the party. (preposition)

access, excess   *Access* is a noun meaning "means or right to enter, approach, or use." In the computer field it is a verb meaning "gain entrance to." *Excess* is an adjective meaning "too much; more than needed; lack of moderation."

I have *access* to a summer cottage this weekend.

The code permits users to *access* the computer.

The airline booked an *excess* number of passengers on that flight.

adapt, adopt   To *adapt* is "to adjust," often by modification. To *adopt* is to "take as one's own."

He *adapted* to the higher elevations of the Rocky Mountains.

She *adopted* the new doctrine expounded by the prophet.

adverse, averse   *Adverse* is an adjective meaning "unfavorable." *Averse* is an adjective meaning "disinclined" or "feeling distaste for."

> *Adverse* circumstances caused the ceremony to be postponed.

> Martha was *averse* to naming all the guilty children.

advice, advise   *Advice* is a noun meaning "a recommendation about how to deal with a situation or problem." *Advise* is a verb meaning "to recommend or warn."

> The young man followed his sister's *advice*.

> Mr. Smith *advised* John to buy 10,000 shares of the stock.

affect, effect   Although both words may function as nouns and verbs, usually *affect* is a verb and *effect* is a noun. The verb *affect* means "to influence, cause a change in, or arouse the emotions of." The noun *affect* is a technical term in psychology and refers to feeling. The noun *effect* means "result or outcome." The verb *effect* means "to bring about or achieve."

> His speech *affected* me greatly. (verb)

> The *effect* of the announcement was felt immediately. (noun)

> The doctor was soon able to *effect* a cure. (verb)

aggravate   *Aggravate* is a verb meaning "to intensify or make worse" an existing situation. The use of *aggravate* to mean "annoy" or "anger" is colloquial.

> *Colloquial*   Susan's behavior at the dance really *aggravated* me.

> *Standard English*   Marcy's interference only *aggravated* the conflict between Bill and Nadine.

ain't   This nonstandard term for *isn't* or *aren't* is unacceptable in college writing.

all ready, already   *All ready* means "completely prepared" or "everyone is ready." *Already* means "previously, even now, even then."

> The scouts are *all ready* for the camp out.

> When we arrived we found he had *already* gone.

> The report is *already* a week overdue.

all right, alright   *Alright* is a nonstandard spelling of *all right* and is not acceptable in college writing.

all together, altogether   *All together* means "all in one place." *Altogether* is an adverb meaning "completely, entirely."

> The family was *all together* at the wedding.
> Mr. Doe is *altogether* at fault for writing the letter.

usage

Kolln, M. "Closing the Books on Alchemy." *College Composition and Communication* 32 (1981): 139–51. Argues that we should still teach grammar to ensure a shared vocabulary and conceptual framework.

Kroll, B. and J. Schafer. "Error Analysis and the Teaching of Composition." *College Composition and Communication* 29 (1978): 242–48. Explains how we can effectively observe the pattern in student errors, determine the source of those errors, and then provide the most effective instruction.

Pooley, R. C. *The Teaching of English Usage*. 2nd ed. Urbana, IL: NCTE, 1974. It is important to recognize that there is a history to the public attitude about usage errors. Pooley reviews public attitudes about usage from the 1700s to the present and analyzes typical usage problems.

Shaughnessy, M. P. *Errors and Expectations: A Guide for the Teacher of Basic Writing*. New York: Oxford UP, 1977. If there is any one work that today's writing teacher must read, this is it. Shaughnessy provides a careful analysis of the reasons weaker students have problems with grammar, punctuation, spelling, and vocabulary and offers very specific, carefully considered, and tested teaching methods.

Summey, G., Jr. *American Punctuation*. New York: Ronald, 1949. Provides both a brief history of punctuation and a trenchant discussion of all the conventions of punctuation.

allusion, delusion, illusion An *allusion* is an indirect reference. A *delusion* is a mistaken belief, often part of a psychological condition. An *illusion* is a deceptive appearance presented to the sight or created by the imagination.

> In his sermon, the minister made many *allusions* to the New Testament.

> He suffers from the *delusion* that he is a millionaire.

> They wore makeup to give the *illusion* of beauty.

a lot, alot *Alot* is an erroneous spelling of the two words *a lot*. The phrase *a lot* is usually colloquial; in formal writing replace it with "many."

already See *all ready, already*.

alright See *all right, alright*.

alternately, alternatively *Alternately* means "occurring by turns, one after the other." *Alternatively* means "providing a choice between two items."

> The U.S. flag has seven red and six white stripes, arranged *alternately*.

> Highway 44 offers the most direct route to Junction City. *Alternatively*, Highway 88 is much more scenic.

altogether See *all together, altogether*.

among, between Use *between* when referring to two things and *among* when referring to more than two.

> He divided the candy *between* Allan and Stephanie.

> He divided the candy *among* the five children.

amoral, immoral *Amoral* means "outside or beyond the moral order or code." *Immoral* simply means "not moral."

> The movie, which takes no clear position on the behavior it depicts, seems curiously *amoral*.

> Murder is an *immoral* act.

amount, number *Amount* refers to total quantities, things in bulk, or weight. *Number* refers to countable things. Never use *amount* when referring to people.

> Cassandra inherited a large *amount* of money.

> Cassandra now has a large *number* of friends.

an, a See *a, an*.

and/or Although often used in commercial and legal documents, this combination should be avoided in other writing.

angry, mad *Mad* means "insane," although it is often used colloquially to mean "annoyed" or "angry." To be precise, use *mad* only to mean insane.

> *Colloquial* I was *mad* at Debbie.

> *Standard*
> *English* I was *angry* with Debbie.

any, any other   Do not use *any* when you mean *any other*. Using *any* in the following example would mean that Theresa is more qualified than herself.

> Theresa is more qualified than *any other* candidate.

anyone, any one   *Anyone* means "any person." *Any one* means "any single person or thing."

> I can whip *anyone* in this room.

> I saw three movies last week but didn't like *any one* of them.

appraise, apprise   *Appraise* means "to determine the value of something." *Apprise* means "to notify" or "to tell."

> The jeweler *appraised* the gold brooch at $1,500.

> Having been *apprised* of the situation, the family priest was able to reconcile the parents and the children.

apt, liable, likely   Both *apt* and *liable* express a tendency or inclination. *Liable* suggests something unpleasant or likely to result in legal action. It should be used only when the event may have unpleasant consequences.

> We are *liable* to miss the train.

> My lawyer said that I was *liable* for the damage my car had caused.

If the probable consequences are not unpleasant, *apt* is the better word.

> I am *apt* to buy books if we go to the shopping center.

Likely merely implies strong probability.

> Sandra is *likely* to pass this course without any difficulty.

around   *Around* is colloquial use for "approximately" or "about."

Colloquial	She arrived *around* 10:00 P.M.
	The blouse cost *around* $15.
Standard English	She arrived at *approximately* 10:00 P.M.
	The blouse cost *about* $15.

as   *As* is frequently used as a weak substitute for *because, since, when,* and *while.*

Weak	She ran out of the house *as* it was on fire.
Better	She ran out of the house *because* it was on fire.

As should not be used in place of *whether* or *that.*

Nonstandard	I don't know *as* I like her.
Standard English	I don't know *that* I like her.
	I don't know *whether* I like her.

as, like   *As* may be used as a conjunction that introduces an adverb clause, but *like* should not be used this way.

Unacceptable	*Like* my father always said, "You can fool some of the people all of the time."
Standard English	*As* my father always said, "You can fool some of the people all of the time."

Like may, however, be used as a preposition.

In times *like* this, it's hard not to despair.

Any woman *like* Sally can expect a successful career in business.

assure, ensure, insure   To *assure* is "to make safe from risk, to guarantee" or "to convince." *Ensure* and *insure* can be variant spellings meaning "to make certain." *Insure*, however, is now generally associated with the business of insurance.

The counselor tried to *assure* the students that they had made a wise choice.

The captain *assured* them that they would be rescued.

The father, wanting to *ensure* his son's college education, applied for a federally *insured* loan.

averse   See *adverse, averse*.

awful, awfully   In everyday speech, *awful* is used to describe things disagreeable or objectionable: "an *awful* movie," "an *awful* character." *Awfully* is used colloquially as an intensifier: "*awfully* nice," "*awfully* bad." Unless they are used to mean "solemnly impressive," however, both words should be avoided in formal writing.

The *awful* majesty of the cathedral silenced the chattering tourists.

awhile, a while   *A while*, consisting of the noun *while* and the article *a*, means "a period of time." *Awhile* is an adverb meaning "for a short time."

Dinner will be served in *a while*.

Sit *awhile* and tell me the latest gossip.

bad, badly   *Bad* is an adjective. *Badly* is an adverb. *Badly* is colloquial when used to mean "very much."

Unacceptable	She feels *badly* about her mistake. Tom behaved *bad* at the circus. I want a new car *badly*.
Standard English	She feels *bad* about her mistake. (predicate adjective) Tom behaved *badly* at the circus. (adverb) I want a new car *very much*.

being as, being that   When used as substitutes for *because* or *since*, these expressions are nonstandard.

Nonstandard	*Being that* I was the first in line, I was able to purchase choice tickets.

*Standard
English*   *Because* I was first in line, I was able to purchase choice tickets.

beside, besides   Both words are prepositions, but they have different meanings. *Beside* means "at the side of," and *besides* means "in addition to."

Sheila and Bill sat *beside* the trailer to eat their lunch.

Besides Harvey, Seymour is coming to dinner.

between   See *among, between.*

breath, breathe   *Breath* is a noun and *breathe* is its verb counterpart.

Nicole stepped outside the stuffy cabin for a *breath* of fresh air.

The cabin was so stuffy that Nicole could hardly *breathe.*

broke   *Broke,* when used to mean "without money," is colloquial.

Colloquial   Because Shelley was *broke,* she had to miss the movie.

*Standard
English*   Because Shelley *had no money,* she had to miss the movie.

can, may   *Can* refers both to permission and to the ability to do something, while *may* refers to permission only.

I think I *can* pass the exam on Friday. (ability)

My mother says I *can* go to the movies. (permission)

May I take the test next Monday? (permission)

When used to denote permission, *can* lends a less formal air to writing than does *may.*

cannot, can not   The use of *cannot* is preferred unless the writer wishes to italicize the *not* for emphasis.

You *cannot* expect a raise this year.

No, you can *not* expect a raise this year.

can't hardly   This nonstandard form for *cannot, can't,* or *can hardly* is unacceptable in college writing.

can't help but   In college writing, this colloquial phrase should be revised to the simpler *I can't help* or *I cannot help.*

Colloquial   I *can't help but* wish that I were going to the concert.

*Standard
English*   I *can't help* wishing that I were going to the concert.

capital, capitol   *Capital* means "a city that serves as a seat of government." *Capitol* means "a building in which a state legislature meets" or "the building in which Congress meets."

usage

Dover is the *capital* of Delaware.

The *capitol* in Dover is popular with visitors.

censor, censure   To *censor* is "to judge"—literature, movies, letters, and the like—and to decide what material is unfit to be read or seen. To *censure* is "to judge harshly" or "find fault with."

The warden *censored* all the prisoners' mail.

The judge *censured* Clyde's criminal behavior.

childish, childlike   Both of these terms mean "like a child." *Childish*, however, has a negative connotation.

He is fifty-two years old, but he behaves in a *childish* manner.

Jon's face has a *childlike* quality that everyone likes immediately.

cite, sight, site   *Cite* means "to mention or quote as an example," *sight* means "to see" or "a view," and *site* means "a location."

Cheryl *cited* Abraham Lincoln's Emancipation Proclamation in her talk.

He was able to *sight* the enemy destroyers through the periscope.

The building *site* is a woody area south of town.

climactic, climatic   *Climactic* is an adjective that means "of, being, or relating to a climax." *Climatic* is an adjective meaning "of or relating to a climate."

Riding the roller coaster was the *climactic* event of Alice's day.

The *climatic* features of Arizona are desirable to many people.

complement, compliment   Both words can act as nouns or verbs. As a noun, *complement* means "something that completes or makes up the whole." As a verb, it means "to complete or perfect." As a noun, *compliment* means "a flattering or praising remark." As a verb, it means "to flatter or praise."

A *complement* of navy personnel boarded the foreign freighter. (noun)

This fruit will *complement* the meal nicely. (verb)

Scott paid Sara Jane a lovely *compliment* at the time of her graduation. (noun)

Mother *complimented* me for cleaning my room. (verb)

conscience, conscious   *Conscience* refers to the sense of moral right or wrong. *Conscious* refers to the awareness of one's feelings or thoughts.

Edgar's *conscience* forced him to return the money.

Basil was not *conscious* of his angry feelings.

Do not confuse *conscious* with *aware*; although these words are similar in meaning, one is *conscious* of feelings or actions but *aware* of events.

contemptible, contemptuous   *Contemptible* means "deserving of contempt." *Contemptuous* means "displaying contempt."

Peter's drunkenness is *contemptible*.

Mary is *contemptuous* of Peter's drunkenness.

continual, continuous   *Continual* means "frequently or regularly repeated." *Continuous* means "uninterrupted."

> The telephone's *continual* ringing made the morning a nightmare.

> His wound caused him *continuous* pain for a week.

could have, could of   *Could of* is an unacceptable substitute for *could have* because a preposition cannot substitute for a verb.

> *Nonstandard*   I *could of* gone with my parents to Portugal.

> *Standard*
> *English*   I *could have* gone with my parents to Portugal.

council, counsel   A *council* is a group of people that governs or advises. *Counsel* can be used as both a noun and a verb. The noun means "advice," and the verb means "to advise."

> The city *council* meets on the second Tuesday of every month.

> The lawyer's *counsel* was sound. (noun)

> The psychologist *counsels* many abused children. (verb)

couple   *Couple* denotes two things and should not be used to refer to more than that number.

criteria, criterion   *Criterion* is always singular, *criteria* always plural.

> The primary *criterion* for performing this job is manual dexterity.

> Manual dexterity is but one of many *criteria* on which you will be judged.

cute   *Cute*, an overused colloquialism, should be avoided; it has too many connotations to be used precisely in writing.

data   *Data* is the plural of *datum*. Today, however, it is usually used with a singular verb.

> *Acceptable*   These *data* are incorrect.

> *Acceptable*   This *data* is incorrect.

definite, very definite   Since *definite* means "precise" or "unmistakable," *very definite* is repetitive. One really cannot be more definite than *definite*.

delusion   See *allusion, delusion, illusion*.

desert, deserts, dessert   *Desert* is land that is arid. With the accent on the last syllable, it is a verb meaning "to abandon." *Deserts* means "that which is deserved." *Dessert* is food served after dinner.

> The Sonoran *desert* is full of plant life.

usage

You'll get your just *deserts* if you *desert* me now.

They had cheesecake for *dessert* every Thursday night.

device, devise   *Device* is a noun meaning "a mechanical contrivance, gadget, or tool." *Devise* is a verb meaning "to plan or invent."

This new *device* gives us better gas mileage.

We must *devise* a new approach to our problem.

different from, different than   *Different from* is preferred over *different than.*

His ideas on marriage were *different from* those of his wife.

Different than is accepted, however, when a clause follows and the *from* construction would be wordy.

Acceptable   Susan looks *different than* she did last summer.

Wordy   Susan looks *different from* the way she looked last summer.

discreet, discrete   To be *discreet* means to be "prudent, tactful, or careful of one's actions." *Discrete* means "distinct or separate."

Jack was always *discreet* when he talked to his grandparents.

When two atoms of hydrogen combine with one atom of oxygen, they are no longer *discrete* entities.

disinterested, uninterested   A person who is *disinterested* is impartial or unbiased. A person who is *uninterested* is indifferent or not interested.

We need a *disinterested* judge to settle the dispute.

Joe is completely *uninterested* in sports.

don't   This contraction for *do not* should never be used with singular subjects such as *he*, *she*, or *it*. Instead, use *doesn't*, the contraction for *does not*, with singular subjects.

Nonstandard   *Don't* he know how to spell?
She *don't* think of anyone except herself.
That mistake *don't* help your image.

Standard English   *Doesn't* he know how to spell?
She *doesn't* think of anyone except herself.
That mistake *doesn't* help your image.

due to   *Due to* has always been acceptable following a linking verb.

Her success was *due to* hard work.

Purists, however, object to *due to* when it is used in other situations, especially in introductory phrases.

Due to the many requests we have had, not everyone who wishes tickets will receive them.

In such cases, it's best to recast the sentence.

Because we have had so many requests, not everyone who wishes tickets will receive them.

effect   See *affect, effect.*

e.g.   This abbreviation, from the Latin *exempli gratia,* means "for example." Avoid using it except in comments in parentheses and in footnotes.

elicit, illicit   *Elicit* is a verb that means "to draw forth." *Illicit* is an adjective meaning "not permitted."

>   A good professor can always *elicit* responses from students.

>   He was engaged in many types of *illicit* activities.

emigrate, immigrate   When people *emigrate,* they move out of a country. When people *immigrate,* they move into a country.

>   The family *emigrated* from Poland.

>   Many Russians *immigrated* to America.

eminent, imminent   *Eminent* means "prominent," whereas *imminent* means "about to happen."

>   Niels Bohr was an *eminent* physicist.

>   Our instruments show that an earthquake is *imminent.*

ensure   See *assure, ensure, insure.*

enthused, enthusiastic   *Enthused* is a colloquial word and should not be used in place of *enthusiastic.*

>   *Colloquial*   John was *enthused* about the prospects for jobs in his hometown.

>   *Standard*
>   *English*   John was *enthusiastic* about the prospects for jobs in his hometown.

especially, specially   The term *especially* means "particularly, notably." *Specially* means "for a specific purpose."

>   He is an *especially* talented pianist.

>   He was *specially* chosen to represent his group.

et al.   This expression, from the Latin *et alii,* means "and others," referring to people. Ordinarily, the abbreviation should be used only in footnotes and bibliographic entries.

etc.   This abbreviation, from the Latin *et cetera,* means "and other things" and is used in reference to objects rather than people. It should be avoided except in comments in parentheses or in footnotes. It should never be preceded by *and.*

everyone, every one   *Everyone* means "every person." *Every one* means "every particular person or thing."

>   *Everyone* who wants to go to the ball game should let me know today.
>   If you carefully check *every one* of your paragraphs, you can improve your writing.

usage

except See *accept, except.*

excess See *access, excess.*

explicit, implicit *Explicit* means "clearly expressed" or "straightforward." *Implicit* means "implied" or "understood without direct statement."

You must state your needs *explicitly* if you want them fulfilled.

When I took on the project, I made an *implicit* commitment to see it through.

extant, extent *Extant* is an adjective meaning "still existing." *Extent* is a noun meaning "scope, size, range, limit."

The dodo bird is no longer *extant.*

From Nevada to Colorado is the *extent* of my travels.

farther, further The traditional distinction is that *farther* refers to physical distance and *further* to distance in time. *Further* is now generally accepted in either context. Only *further* should be used to mean "additional."

In the race for the Muscular Dystrophy Association, Janet ran *farther* than Cindy.

If you think *further* on the matter, I am certain we can reach an agreement.

Let me make one *further* point.

fewer, less *Fewer* refers to countable items. *Less* refers to quantity or degree.

Mrs. Smith has *fewer* dogs than cats.

There is *less* money in Joan's checking account than in Stanley's.

Jack was *less* ambitious in his later years.

Never use *less* to refer to people.

Nonstandard *Less* people were there than I expected.

Standard *Fewer* people were there than I expected.

flaunt, flout To *flaunt* is "to display in a showy way." To *flout* is "to express contempt" or "to show scorn."

Jay *flaunted* his handsome physique before all his friends.

Jerrold *flouted* the convention of dressing for dinner by arriving in tennis shoes.

formally, formerly *Formally* means "according to established forms, conventions, and rules; ceremoniously." *Formerly* means "in the past."

The ambassador *formally* greeted his dinner guests.

Formerly, smallpox was one of our most serious diseases.

funny *Funny* refers to something that is amusing. It should not be used to mean "odd" or "unusual" in college writing.

Colloquial I felt *funny* visiting my old fourth-grade classroom.

Standard
English   I felt *odd* visiting my old fourth-grade classroom.

further   See *farther, further.*

get   *Get,* in any of its many colloquial senses, should not be used in writing.

Colloquial   Her way of looking at a man really *gets* me.
I'll *get* him if it's the last thing I do.

Standard
English   Beth will *get* at least a *B* in this course.

good and   Replace this colloquial phrase with *very.*

Colloquial   She is *good and* tired of the cafeteria food.

Standard
English   She is *very* tired of the cafeteria food.

good, well   Do not mistakenly use *good* as an adverb when an adjective is required.

Unacceptable   John did *good* on his first test.

Standard   John is making *good* progress on his report.
English   John is a *good* student.

Well can be used as an adjective meaning "in good health." Otherwise it should always be used as an adverb.

Last week I had a bad cold, but now I am *well.* (adjective)

John did *well* on his first test. (adverb)

got, gotten   Both are acceptable past-participle forms of the verb *to get.*

had ought, hadn't ought   Both are incorrect in formal writing. The correct forms are *ought* and *ought not.*

I *ought* to start studying.

You *ought not* to cut class again.

hanged, hung   People may be *hanged.* Objects may be *hung.*

The prisoner was *hanged* at noon.

Mavis *hung* the picture in the dining room.

hisself, theirself, theirselves   These are nonstandard forms of *himself* and *themselves.*

hopefully   *Hopefully* means "in a hopeful manner." In informal speaking, it is used to mean "it is hoped" or "I hope," but this usage is not correct in formal writing. (Compare this with *carefully,* which means "in a careful manner"; no one uses *carefully* to mean "it is cared.")

Colloquial   *Hopefully*, it will not rain during the class picnic.

Standard
English   *Hopefully* I bought a lottery ticket.

hung   See *hanged, hung.*

i.e.   This abbreviation, meaning "that is," comes from the Latin *id est.* Avoid using it except in comments in parentheses or footnotes.

if, whether   *If* is used to introduce adverb clauses, where it means "assuming that."

If I finish my report on time, I'll attend the concert with you.

If and *whether* are often used interchangeably to introduce noun clauses that follow verbs such as *ask, say, doubt, know,* and *wonder.*

In formal writing, however, *whether* is preferred.

Less Desirable   I don't know *if* we'll be able to see the North Star tonight.

More Desirable   I don't know *whether* we'll be able to see the North Star tonight.

illicit   See *elicit, illicit.*

illusion   See *allusion, delusion, illusion.*

immigrate   See *emigrate, immigrate.*

imminent   See *eminent, imminent.*

immoral   See *amoral, immoral.*

implicit   See *explicit, implicit.*

imply, infer   To *imply* is "to indicate indirectly or give implication." To *infer* is "to conclude from facts, evidence, or indirect suggestions."

Jack *implied* that he wanted a divorce.

Doris *inferred* that Jack wanted a divorce.

incidence, incidents   *Incidents* are separate, countable experiences. *Incidence* refers to the rate at which something occurs.

Two *incidents* during childhood led to her reclusiveness.

The *incidence* of cancer in Japan is less than in the United States.

incredible, incredulous   *Incredible* means "fantastic, unbelievable." *Incredulous* means "skeptical, disbelieving."

That she could run so fast seemed *incredible.*

Why is Bill wearing that *incredulous* look?

infer   See *imply, infer.*

ingenious, ingenuous *Ingenious* means "clever and inventive." *Ingenuous* means "unsophisticated and innocent."

> Sue presented an *ingenious* solution to our problem.

> Mary's *ingenuous* comments amused everyone in the room.

in regards to This is an incorrect use of *in regard to*.

insure See *assure, ensure, insure*.

inter-, intra- *Inter-* means "between or among." *Intra-* means "within."

> From Chicago to Milwaukee is an *interstate* drive of approximately ninety miles.

> From San Francisco to Los Angeles is an *intrastate* drive of about 400 miles.

in terms of Avoid this vague, overused expression.

Vague	*In terms of* the price he is asking, I would not recommend purchasing Tom's car.
Preferred	*Because* of the price he is asking, I would not recommend purchasing Tom's car.

irregardless This nonstandard form of *regardless* includes the repetitive elements of *ir* and *less*, both of which mean "without."

is when, is where *Is when* properly refers only to time.

> April *is when* our lilac bush blooms.

Is where properly refers only to place.

> Athens *is where* I met him.

The following sentences are *faulty* because muckraking is not a place, and an abscess is not a time.

> Muckraking *is where* someone investigates corporate or governmental abuses of power.

> An abscess *is when* some spot in body tissue fills with pus.

These sentences should be rephrased to eliminate the faulty assertion.

> Muckraking is the investigation of corporate or governmental abuses of power.

> An abscess occurs when some spot in body tissue fills with pus.

its, it's, its' *Its* is a possessive pronoun. *It's* is a contraction of *it is* or *it has*.

> The gold chair was ruined, for someone had torn *its* seat.

> *It's* all I have to offer. (It is all I have to offer.)

> *It's* been a difficult day. (It has been a difficult day.)

There is no correct use for *its'*.

usage

kind of, sort of   In college writing, these are unacceptable substitutes for *somewhat*, *rather*, or *slightly*.

Colloquial	She is *sort of* angry.
	I am *kind of* glad she went away.
Standard	She is *somewhat* angry.
English	I am *rather* glad she went away.

When *kind* and *sort* refer to a type, use them with singular nouns and verbs. With their plural forms, *kinds* and *sorts*, use plural nouns and verbs.

Unacceptable	These *kind* of exams are difficult.
Standard	This *kind* of exam is difficult.
English	These *kinds* of exams are difficult.

In such constructions, be certain that *kind of* or *sort of* is essential to your meaning. Otherwise, these phrases are unnecessary.

later, latter   *Later* refers to time; *latter* points out the second of two items. If more than two items are listed, use *last* to refer to the final one.

He arrived at the party *later* than he was expected.

Although Professors Stein and Patterson both lectured during the course, only the *latter* graded the final exam.

Of my three cats, Sheba, Tiger, and Spot, only the *last* still needs the vaccination.

lay, lie   *Lie* means "to recline" or "to remain in a particular position." It never takes a direct object. *Lay* means "to place" and always takes a direct object. These verbs are often confused, in part because the past tense of *lie* is *lay*. (The past tense of *lay* is *laid*.)

If I *lie* here a minute, I shall feel better.

Lay the book on the table, please.

As I *lay* asleep, a robber entered my apartment and stole my stereo.

He *laid* a hand on her shoulder.

leave, let   *Leave* means "to depart," and *let* means "to allow." Never use *leave* when *let* is meant.

Nonstandard	*Leave* him figure it out alone.
Standard *English*	*Let* him figure it out alone.

lend, loan   Traditionally, *loan* has been classed as a noun and *lend* as a verb. Today, the use of *loan* as a verb is so commonplace that it is accepted as colloquial English.

Standard *English*	I have applied for a *loan* so that I can buy a car. (noun)
	Please *lend* me your class notes. (verb)
Colloquial	Please *loan* me your class notes. (verb)

less   See *fewer, less.*

let   See *leave, let.*

liable   See *apt, liable, likely.*

lie   See *lay, lie.*

like   See *as, like.*

likely   See *apt, liable, likely.*

literally   The word *literally* means "restricted to the exact, stated meaning." In formal writing, use *literally* only with factual statements.

> *Colloquial*   It was 65°, but I was *literally* freezing.
>
> *Standard English*   It was 65°, but I was *very* cold.

loan   See *lend, loan.*

loose, loosen, lose   *Loose* can be used as both a verb and an adjective. As a verb, it means "untie or unfasten"; as an adjective, it means "unattached, unrestrained, not confined." *Loosen* is a verb meaning "undo or ease." *Lose* can be used only as a verb meaning "mislay, fail to win, unable to maintain."

> He *loosed* the restraints on the tiger. (verb)
>
> One should wear *loose* clothing when bowling. (adjective)
>
> When will Mrs. Brady *loosen* her control over young Tom?
>
> You would *lose* your nose if it were not attached to your face.

lots, lots of   *Lots* and *lots of* colloquially mean "many, much, a large amount, or a great amount." Avoid these expressions in college writing.

> *Colloquial*   I've spent *lots of* money in my life.
>
> *Standard English*   I have spent *much* money in my life.

mad   See *angry, mad.*

many, much   *Many* is used when referring to a certain quantity; *much* is used when referring to an indefinite amount or to abstract concepts.

> There are *many* students in the biology class.
>
> How did Betty learn so *much* in so little time?

may   See *can, may.*

may be, maybe   *May be* is always used as a verb phrase. *Maybe* is an adverb meaning "perhaps."

> I *may be* chairman of the board by next June.
>
> *Maybe* we will see Jim at home.

medium, media   *Medium* is the singular form of this word; *media* is the plural.

Television is the *medium* I use most to get the news.

The *media* have given extensive coverage to the brain transplant story.

much   See *many, much.*

myself   *Myself* is an intensive and a reflexive pronoun; it cannot substitute for a personal pronoun such as *I* or *me.*

Unacceptable   Four other students and *myself* founded the club.

Standard
English   Four other students and *I* founded the club.

nice   Do not use this word to mean "pleasing, enjoyable, attractive."

not hardly   This is a nonstandard variation of *hardly* and is inappropriate in college writing.

number   See *amount, number.*

of between, of from, off of   Eliminate the unnecessary *of* from these colloquial phrases.

Colloquial   There was a crowd *of between* three and four thousand people at the contest.
Get *off of* my property!

Standard   The crowd at the contest numbered *between* three and four thousand
English   people.
Get *off* my property!

on account of   This is a nonstandard substitute for *because.*

Nonstandard   The team was unable to practice *on account of* everyone was still upset over Tuesday's loss.

Standard   The team was unable to practice *because* everyone was still upset
English   over Tuesday's loss.

passed, past   *Passed* is a verb designating movement that has taken place. *Past* is a noun or an adjective designating a former time.

The parade *passed* the reviewing stand at 10:30 A.M.

In the *past*, few people were concerned about the environmental effects of pesticides.

This *past* summer, I visited the Soviet Union.

patience, patients   *Patience* means "the ability to wait or endure without complaining." *Patients* are "people being treated by physicians or dentists."

Thad's *patience* was exhausted by the slow service in the restaurant.

Following the tornado, doctors in the emergency room treated over sixty *patients*.

persecute, prosecute   *Persecute* means "to harass persistently because of race, religion, or belief." *Prosecute* means "to bring legal suit against."

> Ethnic groups are often *persecuted*.

> The company will *prosecute* anyone caught stealing.

personal, personnel   *Personal* is an adjective meaning "private, individual." *Personnel* are the people working in an organization.

> Religious preference is a *personal* matter that you do not have to reveal during a job interview.

> The *personnel* of the sanitation department will not be involved in the city workers' strike.

plenty   When used as an adverb, *plenty* should be replaced by *very*.

> *Colloquial*   That geology exam was *plenty* hard.

> *Standard*
> *English*   That geology exam was *very* hard.

precede, proceed   *Precede* means "to go before or ahead of." *Proceed* means "to go on" or "to go forward."

> The ritual of sharpening his pencils always *preceded* doing his homework.

> The guide then said, "If you will *proceed*, I will show you the paintings by da Vinci."

predominant, predominate   *Predominant* is an adjective meaning "chief, main, most frequent." *Predominate* is a verb meaning "to have authority over others."

> The *predominant* European influence on South American culture was Spanish.

> In America, the will of the people should *predominate*.

presently   *Presently* means "soon" rather than "at the present time." *Currently* is preferred for the second meaning.

> I will be there *presently*.

> *Currently*, I am otherwise engaged.

principal, principle   *Principal*, which means "chief," "most important," or "the amount of money on which interest is computed," is used as both a noun and an adjective. *Principle* is used only as a noun and means "truths, beliefs, or rules generally dealing with moral conduct."

> The *principal* suspect in the case was arrested last Friday by the police.

> The *principal* of Lewiston High School is Alison Cooperstein.

> At this interest rate, your *principal* will double in ten years.

> His *principles* are unconventional.

proceed   See *precede, proceed*.

prosecute   See *persecute, prosecute*.

usage

quiet, quite   *Quiet* is an adjective meaning "silent, motionless, calm." *Quite* is an adverb meaning "entirely, to a considerable extent or degree."

> The class grew *quiet* when the teacher walked in.

> He is *quite* wrong.

> The movie was *quite* good.

raise, rise   *Raise* is a transitive verb and therefore requires a direct object. *Rise*, its intransitive counterpart, takes no direct object.

> We plan to *raise* horses on our new farm.

> The temperature is expected to *rise* to 75°F tomorrow.

Raise can also be a noun meaning "an increase in pay."

> Tammy received a 25 percent *raise* last week.

real, really   *Real* is an adjective; *really* is an adverb.

> She had *real* plants decorating the bedroom.

When used as an adverb, *real* is a colloquialism and should be replaced with *really*.

> *Colloquial*   We had a *real* good time at the party.

> *Standard*
> *English*   We had a *really* good time at the party.

reason is because, reason is that   The *reason is because* is colloquial and unacceptable in formal writing; the *reason is that* is the preferred usage.

> *Colloquial*   The *reason is because* I love her.

> *Standard*
> *English*   The *reason is that* I love her.

respectfully, respectively   *Respectfully* means "with respect." *Respectively* indicates that the items in one series are related to those in a second series in the order given.

> Joseph should treat his parents *respectfully*.

> Tom, Anna, and Susan were assigned *Bleak House*, *Great Expectations*, and *Dombey and Son*, *respectively*, for their reports.

rise   See *raise, rise*.

sensual, sensuous   *Sensual* refers to bodily or sexual sensations. *Sensuous* refers to impressions experienced through the five senses.

> Singles bars offered *sensual* pleasures without emotional commitments.

> The Tivoli Garden provides many *sensuous* delights for visitors.

set, sit   Generally, *set* means "to place" and takes a direct object. *Sit* means "to be seated" and does not take a direct object.

Alice *set* her glass on the mantel.

May I *sit* in this chair?

When it refers to the sun, however, *set* is used without a direct object.

As the sun *set*, we turned homeward.

shall, will   *Shall* is used in first-person (see page 583) questions and in specialized forms of writing such as military orders and laws. Otherwise, *will* is used.

Shall we go to the movies tonight?

The company *shall* fall into formation at precisely twelve noon.

No family home *shall* be assessed at more than 50 percent of its actual value.

should have, should of   *Should of* is an unacceptable substitute for *should have* because a preposition cannot substitute for a verb.

Nonstandard   I *should of* gone to the lake.

Standard
English   I *should have* gone to the lake.

[sic]   This Latin word, always enclosed in brackets, follows quoted errors in grammar, spelling, or information. Inclusion of [sic] indicates that the error appeared in the original, which is being quoted exactly.

sight   See *cite, sight, site*.

sit   See *set, sit*.

site   See *cite, sight, site*.

so   *So* is an acceptable coordinating conjunction but tends to add an informal effect to writing and should therefore be used sparingly. For example, "Tom said he was divorcing me, *so* I began to cry" would be more effective if restated as follows: "When Tom said he was divorcing me, I began to cry." Do not use *so* as a substitute for *extremely* or *very* except with adverb clauses beginning with *that*.

Colloquial   You are *so* careless in what you say.
                 The discussion was *so* informative that I took many notes.

Standard   You are *very* careless in what you say.
English   The discussion was *extremely* informative.

some   *Some* is colloquial and unacceptable in writing when used as an intensifier (We had *some* time of it!) or an adverb (He'll probably pout *some* after you leave).

sometime, some time, sometimes   *Sometime* means "at a future unspecified time," *some time* means "a span of time," and *sometimes* means "occasionally."

We should get together *sometime* and play bridge.

The weather has been hot for *some time.*

Sometimes I go to dinner with Ethel.

sort of See *kind of, sort of.*

specially See *especially, specially.*

stationary, stationery *Stationary* means "not moving" or "fixed." *Stationery* means "paper for writing letters."

The circular part in the center must remain *stationary,* or the machine will not function.

Sue always writes on scented *stationery.*

such, such . . . that The use of *such* when it means "very" or "extremely" is unacceptable unless it is followed by a *that* clause completing the thought.

Colloquial They were *such* good cookies.

Standard English They were *such* good cookies *that* I asked Steve for his recipe.

suppose to, supposed to *Suppose to* is the nonstandard form of *supposed to.* In speech, it is difficult to hear the final *d* on *supposed,* and one may say *suppose to* without being detected; however, the written form is always *supposed to.*

sure, surely *Sure* is colloquial for the adverb *surely.*

Colloquial You *sure* know how to make good coffee, Mrs. Olsen.

Standard English You *surely* know how to make good coffee, Mrs. Olsen.

Although *surely* is correct, it may sound too formal and insincere. Therefore, *certainly* is often a better word to use.

take and, try and Avoid these expressions. Simply eliminate them from the sentence or substitute *try to* for *try and.*

Unacceptable If you *take and* cover the tomato plants, they probably won't freeze.
I think you should *try and* settle your differences.

Standard English If you cover the tomato plants, they probably won't freeze.
I think you should *try to* settle your differences.

than, then *Than* is used to make comparisons; *then* means "at that time, in that case."

Jill is taller *than* her brother.

First we will eat, and *then* we will discuss business.

that, which These two words have the same meaning. *That* may refer both to things and groups of people; *which,* only to things. When referring to things, *that* is generally used with clauses that distinguish the things they modify from others in the same class (restrictive clauses). *Which* is generally used with clauses that add information about the things they modify (nonrestrictive clauses).

> Any book *that* she likes is certain to be trashy. (restrictive clause)

> The Winthrop Building, *which* cost two million dollars to construct, could not now be duplicated for ten times that much. (nonrestrictive clause)

See page 606 of the Handbook for a more complete explanation of restrictive and nonrestrictive expressions.

their, there, they're   These three separate words are often confused because they sound alike. *Their* is the possessive form of *they*. *There* is an expletive that appears at the beginning of a sentence and introduces the real subject, or it is an adverb meaning "in or at that place, at that point." *They're* is a contraction of *they are*.

> It is *their* basketball.

> *There* are many reasons why I cannot come.

> Put the sofa down *there*.

> *They're* going to be here soon.

theirself, theirselves   See *hisself, theirself, theirselves*.

then   See *than, then*.

there   See *their, there, they're*.

thorough, through   *Thorough* means "careful, complete, exact, painstaking." *Through* means "in one side and out the other, from end to end, from start to finish, over the whole extent of, finished."

> Brenda has done a *thorough* job.

> Let's run *through* the plan again.

thusly   *Thusly* is a nonstandard form of *thus*.

to, too, two   *To* is a preposition meaning "as far as, toward, until, onto." *Too* is an adverb meaning "excessively" or "also." *Two* is a number.

> I'm going *to* the store.

> Are you going *too?*

> This car is *too* expensive for me.

> There are *two* characters in the play.

toward, towards   Both forms are correct. *Toward* generally is used in the United States and *towards* in England.

try and   See *take and, try and*.

two   See *to, too, two*.

uninterested   See *disinterested, uninterested*.

unique *Unique* means "without an equal" or "extremely unusual" and thus should not be modified by an adverb such as *very*.

use to, used to *Use to* is the nonstandard form of *used to*. In speech it is difficult to hear the *d* on *used*, and one may say *use to* without being detected; however, the written form is always *used to*.

used to could This phrase is nonstandard for *used to be able to*.

> *Nonstandard* I *used to could* run ten miles.
>
> *Standard*
> *English*   I *used to be able to* run ten miles.

very definite See *definite, very definite*.

wander, wonder *Wander* is a verb meaning "to move about without a plan or set destination." *Wonder* is a noun meaning "something causing surprise, admiration, or awe" or a verb meaning "to be curious about."

> Some people like to *wander* through shopping malls for recreation.
>
> That child is a *wonder* at mathematics.
>
> I *wonder* whether I have received an *A* on that test.

way, ways *Ways* may be used to refer to two or more means or methods but not to time or distance.

> *Unacceptable* Timbuktu is a long *ways* from the United States.
>
> *Standard*   There are two *ways* of thinking about that issue.
> *English*   Timbuktu is a long *way* from the United States.

well See *good, well*.

were, where *Were* is the past form of the verb *to be* and is used with *we, you,* and *they*. *Where* is an adverb or a pronoun meaning "in, at, to, from a particular place or situation" or "which or what place."

> I'm sorry that you *were* ill yesterday.
>
> Mr. Morris will show you *where* to register.

where . . . at, to *At* and *to* are unnecessary after *where*.

> *Wordy*   *Where* are you taking the car *to?*
>   *Where* does she live *at?*
>
> *Standard*   *Where* are you taking the car?
> *English*   *Where* does she live?

whether See *if, whether*.

which See *that, which*.

vho, whom   In formal writing, *who* should be used only as a subject in clauses and sentences and *whom* only as an object.

Unacceptable	*Who* are you taking to dinner on Friday?
	I know *who* the boss will promote.
	John is the candidate *whom* I think will be elected.
Standard	*Whom* are you taking to dinner on Friday?
English	I know *whom* the boss will promote.
	John is the candidate *who* I think will be elected.

See pages 586–587 of the Handbook for a fuller discussion of *who* and *whom*.

who's, whose   *Who's* is a contraction of *who is* or *who has,* and *whose* is the possessive form of *who.*

Who's coming to see us tonight?

I would like to know *who's* been dumping trash in my yard.

Whose book is that?

will   See *shall, will.*

wise   Do not randomly add *wise* to the ends of nouns. Such word coinings are ineffective.

Ineffective	Personality*wise*, Sheila is ideal for the job.
Standard	
English	Sheila has an *ideal personality* for the job.

without   See *unless, without.*

wonder   See *wander, wonder.*

would have, would of   *Would of* is an unacceptable substitute for *would have.* A preposition cannot substitute for a verb.

Nonstandard	I *would of* enjoyed seeing the Picasso exhibit.
Standard	
English	I *would have* enjoyed seeing the Picasso exhibit.

would have been, had been   When *would* occurs in the main part of a sentence, use *had been* (not *would have been*) in an "if" clause.

Nonstandard	If the engine *would have been* lubricated, the bearing *would not* have burned out.
Standard	If the engine *had been* lubricated, the bearing *would not* have
English	burned out.

your, you're   *Your* is a possessive form of *you; you're* is a contraction of *you are.*

Where is *your* history book?

Tell me when *you're* ready to leave.

Glossary of Grammatical Terms

This glossary provides a convenient checklist of the grammatical terms used in the Handbook and elsewhere in this text. For a more detailed discussion of each entry, consult the page reference in the parentheses following the entry.

abstract noun   The name of something we can't experience with our five senses. (page 544)

action verb   Expresses action carried out by or upon the subject of a sentence or a clause. (page 549)

active voice   The form of a verb used when the subject of the sentence performs the action. (page 553)

adjective   A word that modifies a noun or a pronoun by describing it, limiting it, or otherwise making its meaning more exact. (pages 557–558)

adjective clause   A subordinate clause that functions as an adjective. (pages 567–568)

adverb   A word that modifies a verb, an adjective, another adverb, or a whole sentence and generally answers questions such as "how?" "when?" "where?" "how often?" and "to what extent?" (pages 559–560)

adverb clause   A subordinate clause that functions as an adverb. (pages 568–569)

antecedent   A word or word group to which a pronoun refers. (pages 577–578)

appositive   A noun or word group serving as a noun and expanding the meaning of a preceding noun or noun substitute. (page 543)

article   The words *a*, *an*, and *the*, which modify nouns and can therefore be considered adjectives. (pages 557–558)

case   The form of a pronoun that shows whether it is serving as, or accompanying, the subject or some other part of the sentence or is showing possession. (pages 585–589)

clause   A word group that includes a subject and a predicate. It may or may not express a complete thought. (pages 567–569)

collective noun   Singular in form but stands for a group or collection of items. (page 545)

comma splice   The error of using only a comma to join two sentences. (pages 572–574)

complement   A word or word group that forms part of the predicate and helps complete the thought of the sentence. (pages 542–543)

concrete noun   Identifies something we can experience with one or more of our five senses. (page 545)

conjunction   A connecting word or word group that links parts of sentences or whole sentences. (pages 562–563)

conjunctive adverb   A word or phrase that links elements of equal grammatical rank and shows some relationship–for example, similarity, contrast, or result— between them. (page 563)

coordinating conjunction   A word that links terms of equal grammatical importance–words, word groups, and simple sentences. (page 562)

dangling modifier   A word group that lacks clear connection to what it is intended to modify, either because the sentence does not specify what is modified or because the separation between the modifier and what is modified is too great. (pages 594–595)

demonstrative pronoun   A pronoun that points out things. (page 547)

dependent clause   See *subordinate clause*. (page 567)

descriptive adjective   An adjective that names a quality, characteristic, or condition of a noun or pronoun. (page 557)

direct object   A noun or noun substitute that names whatever receives, or results from, the action of a verb. (page 542)

faulty comparison   A fault that occurs when a writer or speaker fails to mention one of the items being compared, omits words needed to clarify the relationship between the items, or compares different sorts of items. (pages 597–599)

first-person   The form of a pronoun that indicates the writer or speaker is talking about himself or herself. (page 583)

future perfect tense   Shows that a continuing action or a condition will have been completed at some time in the future. (pages 552–553)

future tense   Indicates that an action will occur or a condition will exist in the future. (page 552)

gerund   A verb form ending in *-ing* and serving as a noun. (page 565)

gerund phrase   A phrase that consists of a gerund plus associated words. Like a gerund, it serves as a noun. (page 565)

helping verb   Accompanies an action or linking verb, giving it a high degree of precision in expressing matters such as time, possibility, and obligation. (page 550)

hidden antecedent   Takes the form of an adjective rather than a noun. (page 581)

imperative mood   The form of a verb indicating that the sentence is delivering a command or making a request. (pages 554–555)

terms

indefinite pronoun   Refers to an unidentified person, place, or thing. (page 548)

independent clause   Expresses a complete thought and can function as a simple sentence. (page 567)

indicative mood   The form of a verb that asks a question or indicates that the writer regards the statement as a fact. (page 554)

indirect object   A noun or noun substitute identifying someone or something that receives whatever is named by the direct object. (page 542)

infinitive   The word *to* plus the base form of a verb (*to hit, to swim*). Infinitives serve as nouns, adjectives, and adverbs. (pages 565–566)

infinitive phrase   An infinitive plus associated words. Like an infinitive, it can serve as a noun, an adjective, or an adverb. (pages 565–566)

intensive pronoun   Lends emphasis to a noun or pronoun. (pages 547–548)

interjection   A word used to gain attention or to express strong feeling. (page 563)

interrogative pronoun   Introduces a question. (page 547)

intransitive verb   An action verb that has no direct object. (page 549)

limiting adjective   Identifies or points out the noun it modifies. (page 557)

linking verb   Shows existence—what someone or something is, was, or will be—rather than action. (pages 549–550)

main clause   See *independent clause*. (page 567)

misplaced modifier   A word group that is improperly separated from the word it modifies. (pages 593–594)

modal auxiliary   A helping verb that is used to express a wish, probability, possibility, requirement, recommendation, suggestion, or condition contrary to fact. (page 556)

mood   The form of a verb that indicates whether the writer regards a statement as a fact; a command or request; or a wish, possibility, condition contrary to fact, or the like. (pages 554–556)

nonparallelism   A fault that results from the use of different grammatical forms to express equivalent ideas. (pages 596–597)

noun   A word that names a person, place, thing, condition, idea, or quality. (pages 544–545)

noun clause   A subordinate clause that functions as a noun. (page 567)

object complement   A noun or an adjective that follows a direct object and renames or describes it. (page 543)

participle   A verb that is used to form the perfect (pages 552–553) and progressive (page 553) tenses and that can serve as an adjective. (page 565)

terms

participial phrase   A participle plus associated words. Like a participle, it serves as an adjective or occasionally an adverb. (page 565)

passive voice   The form of transitive, active verb indicating that the subject of the sentence is acted upon. (pages 553–554)

past perfect tense   Indictes that a past action was completed or a past condition ended before or after another past action or condition. (page 552)

past tense   Shows that an action was completed or a condition existed in the past. (page 552)

person   The form of a pronoun that reveals whether the speaker or writer is referring to himself or herself, addressing someone directly, or referring to one or more other persons. (pages 583–585)

personal pronoun   Refers to one or more clearly identified persons, places, and things. (pages 545–546)

phrase   A group of words that lacks a subject and a predicate and that serves as a single part of speech. (pages 564–566)

predicate   The part of a sentence that tells something about the subject and completes the thought of the sentence. (page 541)

preposition   A word that links its object, a noun or noun substitute, to some other word in the sentence and shows a relationship between them. (page 561)

prepositional phrase   A preposition with one or more objects and associated words, serving as an adjective or an adverb. (page 564)

present perfect tense   Shows that a past action or condition, or its effects, continues until the present. (page 552)

present tense   Denotes present condition, present action, permanent truths, and sometimes action at some definite future time. (pages 551–552)

progressive tense   Shows action in progress. There is a progressive tense for each of the six basic tenses. (page 553)

pronoun   A word that takes the place of a noun in a sentence. (pages 545–548)

proper noun   A noun identifying a one-of-a-kind item. (page 544)

reciprocal pronoun   Establishes an interchange of action between two or more parties. (page 548)

reflexive pronoun   Reverses the action of a verb, making the doer and receiver of the action the same. (pages 547–548)

relative pronoun   Relates a subordinate clause to the main part of its sentence. (pages 546–547)

run-on sentence   Two (or more) sentences that are run together with nothing to mark their junction. (pages 572–574)

second-person   The form of a pronoun indicating that the writer or speaker is addressing someone directly. (page 583)

terms

sentence fragment   A group of words that fails to qualify as a sentence but is capitalized and punctuated like one. (pages 570–572)

subject   The part of a sentence that tells who or what the sentence is about. (page 541)

subject complement   A noun or an adjective, together with any accompanying words, that follows a linking verb and renames or describes the subject. (page 543)

subjunctive mood   The form of a verb indicating that the sentence is expressing a wish, possibility, condition contrary to fact, or the like. (pages 555–556)

subordinate clause   Does not express a complete thought and cannot stand alone. (page 567)

subordinating conjunction   A word that links a subordinate clause to an independent clause (simple sentence). (pages 562–563)

tense   The form of a verb that indicates the time of an action. (pages 551–553)

third-person   The form of a pronoun revealing that the writer or speaker is referring to someone else rather than writing about himself or herself or addressing someone directly. (page 583)

transitive verb   An action verb having a direct object that receives or results from the action. (page 549)

verb   A word that shows action or existence–what something is, was, or will be. (pages 549–556)

voice   The form of a verb that indicates whether the subject of the sentence performs or receives the action. (pages 553–554)

terms

Author-Title Index

Subject Index

ACKNOWLEDGMENTS *(continued from p. iv)*

Carl Becker, *Freedom and Responsibility in the American Way of Life* (N.Y.: Vintage-Knopf, 1945).

Eric Berne, "Can People Be Judged by Their Appearance?" From *A Layman's Guide to Psychiatry and Psychoanalysis*. Copyright © 1947, 1957, 1968 by Eric Berne. Reprinted by permission of Simon & Schuster, Inc.

Bruno Bettelheim, "Joey: A 'Mechanical Boy,'" *Scientific American* March 1959, p. 122.

Ray Allen Billington, "The Frontier Disappears," *The American Story*, ed. Earl Schenck Miers (Great Neck, N.Y.: Channel, 1956).

"The Brink of a Disaster," *America*, March 31, 1979, p. 247.

Suzanne Britt, "That Lean and Hungry Look," *Newsweek*, Oct. 9, 1977. Reprinted by permission of the author.

Claude Brown, *Manchild in the Promised Land* (N.Y.: Macmillan, 1965), p. 304.

James L. Buckley, "Three Cheers for the Snail Darter," *National Review*, September 14, 1979, pp. 1144–45.

"The Bureaucrat," Citicorp. Reprinted by permission. All rights reserved.

Gladys Hasty Carroll, *Sing Out the Glory* (Boston: Little Brown, and Co., 1958).

Rachel Carson, *Silent Spring*, (Boston: Houghton Mifflin, 1962).

Bruce Catton, "Grant and Lee: A Study in Contrasts," From *The American Story*, ed. Earl Schenck Miers. Reprinted by permission of U.S. Capital Historical Society.

John Ciardi, "What is Happiness?" in *Manner of Speaking* (New Brunswick, N.J.: Rutgers University Press, 1972).

Robert Claiborne, "Future Schlock," *The Nation*, January 25, 1971, p. 117.

Cecil Clutton and John Stanford, *The Vintage Motor-car* (N.Y.: Charles Scribner's Sons, 1955), p. 135.

Judith Coburn, "Dolores Huerta: La Pasionaria of the Farm Workers," *Ms.*, Nov. 1976, pp. 12–13.

Barry Commoner, "Why We Have Failed," from *Greenpeace*, Sept.–Oct., 1989 (all rights reserved).

Joseph Conrad, *Lord Jim* (N.Y.: Holt, Rinehart and Winston, 1957), p. 13.

"Controlling Phobias Through Behavior Modification," *USA Today*, August 1978.

Harry Crews, "Why I Live Where I Live." Copyright © 1980 by Harry Crews. Reprinted by permission of John Hawkins & Associates, Inc.

Kelly Davis, "Health and High Voltage: 765 KV Lines," *Sierra*, July–August 1978.

Vine Deloria, Jr., "Custer Died for Your Sins," *Playboy*, Aug. 1969.

Lester del Ray, *The Mysterious Sky* (N.Y.: Chilton Book Company, 1964).

Magda Denes, In *Necessity and Sorrow: Life and Death in an Abortion Hospital* (N.Y.: Basic Books, 1976), p. xiv.

Robert Dick-Read, *Sanamu: Adventures in Search of African Art* (N.Y.: E.P. Dutton, 1964), pp. 228–29.

Joan Didion, "On Self-Respect," in *Slouching Toward Bethlehem* (N.Y.: Farrar, Straus and Giroux, 1968), pp. 143–44.

Annie Dillard, "A Total Eclipse" from *Teaching a Stone to Talk* by Annie Dillard. Copyright © 1982 by Annie Dillard. Reprinted by permission of Harper & Row, Publishers, Inc.

Leo Durocher, *Nice Guys Finish Last* (N.Y.: Simon & Schuster, 1975), p. 54.

Wayne Dyer, *What Do You Really Want for Your Children?* (New York: William Morrow, Inc., 1985).

Loren Eiseley, "The Judgment of the Birds," in *The Immense Journey* (N.Y.: Random House, 1956), pp. 174–75.

Loren Eiseley, *The Unexpected Universe* (N.Y.: Harcourt Brace Jovanovich, 1969), p. 88.

Marian Engle, review of *The Goddess and Other Women*, by Joyce Carol Oates, *New York Times Book Review*, Nov. 24, 1974, p. 7.

Howard Ensign Evans, *Life on a Little-Known Planet* (N.Y.: E.P. Dutton, 1968), pp. 107–8.

Henry Fairlie, "A Victim Fights Back," *The Washington Post*, April 30, 1978.

David Finkelstein, "When the Snow Thaws," *The New Yorker*, Sept. 10, 1979, p. 127.

James F. Fixx, "What Running Can't Do For You," *Newsweek*, Dec. 18, 1978, p. 21. Copyright © 1978, Newsweek, Inc.

"Formlessness," From *Roget's International Thesaurus* by Robert L. Chapman. Copyright © 1977 by Harper & Row, Publishers, Inc. Reprinted by permission of the publisher.

E. M. Forster, "My Wood" slightly abridged from *Abinger Harvest* by E. M. Forster, Copyright 1936 and renewed 1964 by Edward Morgan Forster, reprinted by permission of Harcourt Brace Jovanovich, Inc.

Bruce Friedman, "Eating Alone in Restaurants." From *The Lonely Guy's Guide to Life*. Copyright © 1979 by McGraw-Hill, Inc.

Otto Friedrich, "There are 00 Trees in Russia," *Harper's Magazine*, Oct. 1964.

Kathleen Fury, "It's Only a Paper World," *Working Woman*, August 1986. Reprinted by permission.

Gustave A. Garotti, "How to Fight the Drug War," *Atlantic Monthly*, July, 1989.

William Geist, "Home Sick." Copyright © 1989 News America Publishing, Inc. All rights reserved. Reprinted by permission of *New York* magazine.

William Golding, "Thinking As a Hobby." Reprinted by permission of Curtis Brown, Ltd. Copyright © 1961 by William Golding.

Ellen Goodman, "The Company Man." From *At Large*. Copyright © 1981 by The Washington Post Company. Reprinted by permission of Summit Books, a division of Simon & Schuster, Inc.

Amy Gross, "The Appeal of the Androgynous Man." *Mademoiselle*. Copyright © 1976 by The Condé Nast Publications, Inc. Reprinted by permission of Amy Gross.

Pete Hamill, "Facing Up to Drugs: Is Legalization the Answer?" Copyright © 1988, News America Publishing, Inc. All rights reserved. Reprinted by permission of *New York* magazine.

L. D. Hamilton, "Antibodies and Antigens," *The New Book of Knowledge* 1967, I, 317.

S. I. Hayakawa, *Language in Thought and Action*, 3rd ed. (N.Y.: Harcourt Brace Jovanovich, 1972), p. 50.

John Hersey, *Hiroshima* (N.Y.: Modern Library, 1946), p. 4.

Nancy K. Hill, "Scaling the Heights: The Teacher as Mountaineer," *The Chronicle of Higher Education*, June 16, 1980, p. 48.

Thomas Henry Huxley, "A Liberal Education and Where to Find It," *Macmillan's Magazine*, March 17, 1868.

Dina Ingber, "Computer Addicts," *Science Digest*, July 1981.

Washington Irving, "The Spectre Bridegroom," in *Selected Writings of Washington Irving*, ed. Saxe Commins (N.Y.: Modern Library, 1945), p. 53.

Bruce Jackson, "Who Goes to Prison: Caste and Careerism in Crime," *Atlantic Monthly*, Jan. 1966, p. 52.

Robert Jastrow, *Until the Sun Dies* (N.Y.: Norton, 1977).

Samuel Johnson, "Preface to the Plays of William Shakespeare," in *Johnson on Shakespeare*, ed. Arthur Sherbo (New Haven: Yale University Press, 1968), p. 74.

Vernon E. Jordan Jr., "The New Negativism," *Newsweek*, Aug. 14, 1978, p. 13. Copyright © 1978, Newsweek, Inc.

Doris Kearns, "Who Was Lyndon Baines Johnson?", from *Lyndon Johnson and the American Dream* (N.Y.: Harper & Row, 1976).

Helen Keller, "Three Days to See," *Atlantic Monthly*, Jan. 1933, p. 35.

John F. Kennedy, "Inaugural Address," Washington, D.C. Jan. 20, 1961.

Walter Kiechel III, "How to Give a Speech, From *Fortune*, June 8, 1987. Reprinted by permission.

Martin Luther King, Jr., "I Have a Dream." Reprinted by permission of Joan Daves. Copyright © 1963 by Martin Luther King, Jr.

Martin Luther King, Jr., extracts from "Letter from Birmingham Jail," in *Why We Can't Wait* by Martin Luther King, Jr. Copyright © 1963, 1964 by Martin Luther King, Jr. Reprinted by permission of Harper & Row, Publishers, Inc.

Martin Luther King, Jr., "Pilgrimage to Nonviolence," in *Stride Toward Freedom* (N.Y.: Harper & Row, 1958), p. 84.

Perri Klass, "She's Your Basic L.O.L. in N.A.D." Reprinted by permission of the Putnam Publishing Group from *A Not Entirely Benign Procedure* by Perri Klass. Copyright © 1987 by Perri Klass. This essay originally appeared in the October 4, 1984, *New York Times*.

Marilyn Kluger, "A Time of Plenty," *Gourmet*, Nov. 1976, p. 22.

Edward I. Koch, "Death and Justice." Published by permission of *The New Republic*.

Andrew Kupfer, "What to Do about Drugs," from *Fortune*, June 20, 1988. Reprinted by permission.

Kenneth Labich, "The Scandal of Killer Trucks," *Fortune*, March 30, 1987.

Pär Lagerkvist, "Father and I," from *The Marriage Feast* (N.Y.: Hill & Wang, 1954). © 1954 by Albert Bonniers Vörlag.

Laurie Lee, "Charm." From *I Can't Stay Long*. Copyright © 1976 by Laurie Lee. Reprinted by permission of Andre Deutsch, Ltd.

Sinclair Lewis, *Babbitt*, Harcourt, Brace and World, 1922.

Robert Lipsyte, *Sports World* (N.Y.: Quadrangle Books, 1975), p. ix.

John Lovesey, "A Myth is as Good as a Mile," *Sports Illustrated*, Nov. 9, 1964.

Marilyn Machlowitz, "Workaholism: What's Wrong with Being Married to Your Work?", *Working Woman*, May 1978, p. 51.

Malcolm X, *The Autobiography of Malcolm X* (N.Y.: Ballantine Books, 1964), p. 171.

Marshall Mandell, "Are You Allergic to Your House?", *Prevention*, Sept. 1979, p. 101.

Marya Mannes, "Wasteland," in *More in Anger* (Philadelphia: J.B. Lippincott, 1958), p. 40.

Margaret Mead, "New Superstitions for Old," from *A Way of Seeing* by Margaret Mead and Rhoda Metraux. Copyright © 1966 by Margaret Mead and Rhoda Metraux.

L. David Mech, "Where Can the Wolves Survive?", *National Geographic*, Oct. 1977, p. 536.

H. L. Mencken, "The Libido for the Ugly," Copyright 1927 by Alfred A. Knopf, Inc., and renewed 1955 by H. L. Mencken. Reprinted from *A Mencken Chrestomathy*, edited and annotated by H. L. Mencken, by permission of the publisher.

Thomas H. Middleton, "The Magic Power of Words," *Saturday Review*, Dec. 11, 1976, p. 90.

Don Ethan Miller, "A State of Grace: Understanding the Martial Arts," *Atlantic Monthly*, Sept. 1980. Copyright © 1980 by Don Ethan Miller.

Jessica Mitford, "Behind the Undertaker's Door." From *The American Way of Death*. Copyright © 1963, 1978 by Jessica Mitford. Reprinted by permission of Simon & Schuster, Inc.

Lance Morrow, "Waiting As a Way of Life," *Time*, July 23, 1984. Copyright © 1984 Time, Inc. Reprinted by permission.

George Orwell, excerpt from "Shooting an Elephant," in *Shooting an Elephant and Other Essays*, copyright 1950 by Sonia Brownell Orwell; renewed 1978 by Sonia Pitt-Rivers. Reprinted by permission of Harcourt Brace Jovanovich, Inc., and Martin Secker & Warburg Ltd.

Jo Goodwin Parker, "What is Poverty?" in George Henderson, *America's Other Children: Public Schools Outside Suburbia* (University of Oklahoma Press, 1971).

Nancy Perry, "Saving the Schools: How Business Can Help," from *Fortune*. Nov. 7, 1988.

Alexander Petrunkevitch, from "The Spider and the Wasp," *Scientific American*, August, 1952. Copyright © 1952 by Scientific American, Inc. All rights reserved.

J. Winston Porter, "We'll Trash *U.S.A. Today* too." from *U.S.A. Today*, July 11, 1988. All rights reserved.

Lord Richie-Calder, "The Doctor's Dilemma," *The Center Magazine*, Sept/Oct. 1971.

Edwin Arlington Robinson, "The Miller's Wife," *The Three Taverns*, Charles Scribner's Sons, 1920.

Edwin Arlington Robinson, "Richard Cory," *The Children of the Night*, Charles Scribner's Sons, 1897.

Philip Ross, "The Boy and the Bank Officer." From *New York*, March 13, 1979. Reprinted by permission of Roberta Pryor, Inc. Copyright © 1979 by Philip Ross.

Kathy Roth, "How to Adopt a Stray." Reprinted from *The Cat Catalog: The Ultimate Cat Book*, ed. by Judy Fireman. © 1976 Workman Publishing Company, New York. Reprinted by permission of the publisher.

Bertrand Russell, *The ABC of Relativity* (London: Allen and Unwin, 1965), pp. 46–47.

Bertrand Russell, "Respect for Law," *San Francisco Review*, Winter, 1958, pp. 63–65. Reprinted by permission of June Oppen Degnan.

John Ryor, "Save Our Schools," *Today's Education: Journal of the National Education Association*, Sept./Oct. 1978. Used by permission.

Laurence Shames, "The Sweet Smell of Success Isn't All That Sweet." Copyright © 1986 by The New York Times Company. Reprinted by permission.

Gideon Sjöberg, "The Origin and Development of Cities," *Scientific American*, Sept. 1965, p. 55.

Bernard Sloan, "Old Folks at Home," *Newsweek*, Feb 12, 1979. Reprinted by permission of Alexandria Hatcher Agency.

Elliott L. Smith and Andrew W. Hart, *The Short Story: A Contemporary Looking Glass* (N.Y.: Random House, 1981).

C. P. Snow in *the Two Cultures, A Second Look* (Cambridge University Press, 1964), pp. 17–18.

Joyce Susskind, "Surprises in a Woman's Life," *Vogue*, Feb. 1979, p. 252.

Barry Tarshis, "Islands of Tennis: Where to Vacation in the Southeast," *Tennis*, April 1977.

Alex Taylor III, "Why Women Managers Are Bailing Out." From *Fortune*, August 18, 1986. Reprinted by permission.

Deems Taylor, "The Monster" in *Of Men and Music* (N.Y.: Simon & Schuster, 1965).

James Alexander Thom, "The Perfect Picture." Reprinted with permission from the August 1976 *Reader's Digest*. Copyright © 1976 by The Reader's Digest Ass'n, Inc.

Lewis Thomas, "The Technology of Medicine." From *The Lives of a Cell* by Lewis Thomas. Copyright © 1971 by the Massachusetts Medical Society. Reprinted by permission of Viking Penguin. a division of Penguin Books, USA.

James Thurber, "Courtship Through the Ages." Copyright © 1942 by James Thurber. Copyright © 1970 by Helen W. Thurber and Rosemary A. Thurber. From *My World and Welcome To It*, published by Harcourt Brace Jovanovich.

James Thurber, "University Days." Copyright 1933, 1961 by James Thurber. From *My Life and Hard Times*, published by Harper & Row.

Carll Tucker, "Fear of Dearth." © 1979 *Saturday Review* Magazine. Reprinted by permission.

James Tuite, "The Sounds of the City." Copyright © 1966/69/82/84 by The New York Times Company. Reprinted by permission.

Mark Twain, "Innocence and Experience: Two Views of the River," *Life on the Mississippi*, 1883.

Mark Twain, "Corn-Pone Opinions," *Europe and Elsewhere*, 1923.

Marjorie Waters, "Coming Home." Copyright © 1982 by Marjorie Waters. Originally published in the *Bedford Reader* (Bedford Books of St. Martin's Press, 1982). Reprinted by permission of the author.

Eudora Welty. "A Visit of Charity," from *A Curtain of Green and Other Stories* (N.Y.: Harcourt, 1941, 1969).

E. B. White, "Once More to the Lake." From *Essays of E. B. White*. Copyright 1941, by E. B. White. Copyright renewed 1969 by E. B. White. Reprinted by permission of Harper & Row, Publishers, Inc.

Stephen White, "The New Sophistication: Defining the Terms," *Esquire*, July, 1961, p. 42.

Monci Jo Williams, "Is Workfare the Answer?" From *Fortune*, October 27, 1986. Reprinted by permission.

Tom Wolfe, *The Pump House Gang* (N.Y.: World Journal Tribune, 1966), p. 293.

Orville Wyss and Curtis Eklund, *Microorganisms and Man* (New York: John Wiley and Sons, 1971), pp. 232–33.

John V. Young, "When the Full Moon Shines Its Magic over Monument Valley," *New York Times*, March 16, 1969. Section 10, p. 1. Copyright © 1969/1982/1984 by the New York Times Company. Reprinted by permission.

David Zimmerman, "Are Test-Tube Babies the Answer for the Childless?", *Woman's Day*, May 1979, p. 26.

EDITING SYMBOLS

Symbol	Problem	Page
ab	improper abbreviation	625-626
agr pa	faulty agreement of pronoun and antecedent	580-582
agr sv	faulty agreement of subject and verb	575-576
∨ *or apos*	missing or misused apostrophe	600-602
awk	awkward phrasing	
bib	faulty bibliographic form	324-331
cap	capital letter needed	623-625
case	wrong case	585-588
cl	cliché	254-255
∧ *or com*	missing or misused comma	604-607
cs	comma splice	572-573
comp	faulty comparison	597-598
dm	dangling modifier	594-595
⬭ *or ellip*	missing or misused ellipsis	317-318
frag	sentence fragment	570-571
ital	missing or misused italics	629-630
lc	lowercase (small) letter needed	623-625
ll or lev	wrong level of usage	239-243
log	faulty logic	
mm	misplaced modifier	593-594
num	use numerals	627-628

Symbol	Problem	Page
usu	nonstandard usage	
¶	new paragraph needed	
no ¶	new paragraph not needed	
⊙	period needed	611-612
‖ *or para*	nonparallelism	596
? *or ques*	missing or misused question mark	612
" / " *or quot*	missing or misused quotation marks	617-619
ref	unclear reference of pronoun to antecedent	580-582
ro	run-on sentence	572-573
; *or sem*	missing or misused semicolon	609-610
sp	spelling error	632-637
shift p	shift in person	583-584
shift t	shift in tense	589-590
sq	squinting modifier	594
t or tense	wrong tense	551-553
trans	poor transition	
vb	wrong verb form	
wdy	wordiness	253-254
ww	wrong word	
ℒ	delete (omit)	
∧	material omitted	
⊘	meaning unclear or word illegible	